Instructor's Resource Manual

to accompany

Uba/Huang

Psychology

Theresa J. Martin, PhD
Eastern Washington University

An Imprint of Addison Wesley Longman, Inc.

New York • Reading, Massachusetts • Menlo Park, California • Harlow, England
Don Mills, Ontario • Sydney • Mexico City • Madrid • Amsterdam

Instructor's Resource Manual
to accompany
Uba/Huang
Psychology

Copyright © 1999 by Addison Wesley Longman, Inc.

All rights reserved. No part of this book may be reproduced, stored in a retrieval system, or transmitted in any form or by any means electronic, mechanical, photocopying, recording, or otherwise, without the prior permission of the publisher.

Please visit our website at http://longman.awl.com

ISBN: 0-321-40152-2

12345678910 - VG - 02010099

Table of Contents

The Instructor's Resource Manual: Key Elements		v
Introduction to the *Longman Mind Matters* CD		viii
Audio-Visual Support		xii
Teaching the Introductory Course		xvii
The Syllabus		xxxi
Writing Assignments in the Introductory Class		xxxvii
On Teaching Sensitive Issues in the College Classroom		xl
Chapter 1	Introduction: What is Psychology?	1
Chapter 2	Biopsychology: The Biological Bases of Behavior	65
Chapter 3	Sensation and Perception	117
Chapter 4	Consciousness	181
Chapter 5	Learning	217
Chapter 6	Memory	275
Chapter 7	Cognition and Intelligence	319
Chapter 8	Development from Birth through Childhood	375
Chapter 9	Development from Adolescence through Old Age	427
Chapter 10	Communication	471
Chapter 11	Motivation and Emotion	519
Chapter 12	Personality and Testing	565
Chapter 13	Stress, Coping, and Health	609
Chapter 14	Psychological Disorders	649
Chapter 15	Therapy	703
Chapter 16	Social Psychology	751
Statistics Appendix		801

The Instructor's Resource Manual: Key Elements

Preface

Much has been written elsewhere about teaching the introductory psychology course, and a growing set of literature addresses specifically the inclusion of multicultural and gender issues in psychology courses. My primary intention in this preface is to provide you with some additional resources for expanding your pedagogy in these areas. Two additional resources have been included as well: major excerpts from Barbara Brown's Instructor's Manual to accompany Wade/Tavris *Psychology* (5th ed.; Longman Publishers) with some included observations/comments that I have made. Ms. Brown has touched on a number of topics and issues for the development of the introductory psychology course that I think you will find helpful. Second, I have provided a summary of a sensitive article written by Lisa Whitten (originally presented in the journal *Transformations* and reprinted in S. Schneiderís instructor's course planner for Halonen/Santrock, *Psychology: Contexts of Behavior* (2nd ed.)) covering the topic of managing students' reactions to sensitive topics in the classroom setting.

Other Supplements (Please see the text preface for detailed listings of media ancillaries.)

Test Bank: Written by Martha Ellis of Collin County Community College, this in-depth supplement provides 75 multiple-choice, 10 short answer, and 2-3 essay questions per chapter. Many questions emphasize the multicultural perspective and all questions are referenced by text topic, page number and skill type (conceptual, application, and factual). The test bank is also available in a computerized format.

Study Guide: Written by Robert Pellegrini of San Jose State University, this valuable study tool provides students with content mastery objectives, an outline overview of key terms and concepts, self-generated questions, completion questions, self-quizzes with answer keys for each chapter, teaching-to-learn exercises, critical thinking and integrative thinking questions, and "Bringing Psychology to Life" exercises.

General Resources for College Teaching and Teaching Introductory Psychology

You might find reading from the following resources to be particularly helpful in course development, particularly if you haven't taught introductory psychology before (or recently).

Brewer, C. (Ed.) Teaching of Psychology (journal). American Psychological Association.

Benjamin, L. & Lowman, K. (1981). Activities handbook for the teaching of psychology. Washington DC: American Psychological Association.

Brookfield, S. (1990). The skillful teacher: On technique, trust and responsiveness in the classroom. San Francisco: Jossey-Bass.

Erikson, B., & Strommer, D. (1991). Teaching college freshman. San Francisco: Jossey-Bass.

Halonen, J. (1995). The critical thinking companion for Introductory Psychology. New York: Worth Publishers.

Makosky, V., Whittemore, L., & Rogers, A. (Eds.), Activities handbook for the teaching of psychology (Vol. 2). Washington, DC: American Psychological Association.

Makosky, V., Sileo, C., Whittemore, L., & Skutley, M. (1995). Activities handbook for the teaching of psychology (Vol. 3). Washington DC: American Psychological Association.

McKeachie, W. (1986). Teaching psychology: Research and experience. In The G. Stanley Hall Lecture Series (Vol. 6). Washington, DC: American Psychological Association.

McKeachie, W. (1986). Teaching tips: A guidebook for the beginning college teacher (8th ed.). Lexington, MA: Heath.

Stanovich, K. (1986). How to think straight about psychology. Glenview, IL: Scott, Foresman.

Sternberg, R. (Ed.) (1997). Teaching introductory psychology: Survival tips from the experts. Washington, DC: American Psychological Association.

Resources for Teaching with a Multicultural/Gender Emphasis

The following resources may be useful in expanding your multicultural and gender issues knowledge bases. Some of these listings discuss more generally multicultural and nonsexist education.

Aguirre, A. & Baker, D. (Eds.) (1995). Sources: Notable Selections in Race and Ethnicity. Guilford, CN: Dushkin Publ.

Berry, J., Poortinga, Y., Segall, M., & Dasen, P. (Eds.) (1992). Cross-cultural psychology: Research and applications. London: Methuen.

Bohan, J. (Ed.) (1992). Re-placing women in psychology: Readings toward a more inclusive history (2nd ed.). Dubuque, IA: Kendall/Hunt.

Brislin, R. (Ed.) (1990). Applied cross-cultural psychology. Newbury Park, CA: Sage.

Bronstein, P., & Quina, K. (Eds.). (1988). Teaching a psychology of people: Resources for gender and sociocultural awareness. Washington, DC: American Psychological Association.

Burlew, K., Banks, W., McAdoo, H. & Azibo, D (Eds.) (1992). African-American psychology. Thousands Oaks, CA: Sage.

Espin, O. (1995). On knowing you are the unknown: Women of color constructing psychology. In Adleman, J. & Enguidanos, G. (Eds.) Racism in the Lives of Women: Testimony, Theory, and Guides to Antiracist Practice. New York: Haworth Press.

Espin, O. & Gawelek, M. (1992). Women's Diversity: Ethnicity, Race, Class, and Gender in Theories of Feminist Psychology. in Brown, L. & Ballou, M. (Eds.) Personality and Psychopathology: Feminist Reappraisals. New York: Guilford Press.

Fox, R. (1996). Bisexuality in Perspective: A Review of Theory and Research In Firestein, B. A. (Ed.) Bisexuality: The Psychology and Politics of an Invisible Minority. Thousand Oaks, CA: Sage Publ.

Goodchilds, J. (Ed.) (1991). Psychological perspectives on human diversity in America. Washington, DC: American Psychological Association.

Greene, B. (1996). Lesbian and Gay Sexual Orientations: Implications for Clinical Training, Practice, and Research In Greene, B., and Herek, G. M. (Eds.) Lesbian and Gay Psychology: Theory, Research, and Clinical Applications. Thousand Oaks, CA: Sage Publ.

Jones, J. (1998). Cultural psychology of African Americans. Boulder, CO: Westview Press.

Lonner, W., & Malpass, R. (Eds.) (1994). Psychology and culture. Boston: Allyn & Bacon.

Matsumoto, D. (1994). People: Psychology from a cultural perspective. Pacific Grove, CA: Brooks/Cole.

Padilla, A. (Ed.) (1994). Hispanic psychology: Critical issues in theory and research. Thousand Oaks, CA: Sage.

Pusch, M. (Ed.) (1979). Multicultural education: A cross-cultural training approach. ME: Intercultural Press.

Segall, M., Dasen, P., Berry, J., & Poortinga, Y. (Eds.) (1990). Human behavior in global perspective: An introduction to cross-cultural psychology. New York: Pergamon Press.

Singelis, T. (1998). Teaching about culture, ethnicity, & diversity: Exercises and planned activities. Thousand Oaks, CA: Sage.

Trickett, E., Watts, R., & Birman, D. (Eds.) (1994). Human diversity: Perspectives on people in context. San Francisco: Jossey-Bass.

INTRODUCTION TO THE LONGMAN MIND MATTERS CD

The CD is designed to work as a supplement to virtually any introductory psychology textbook. It includes chapters devoted to history, methods, biopsychology, learning, memory, sensation, and perception. Each chapter, in turn, contains a series of self-contained modules that cover "core" psychological concepts (e.g., selective attention, signal detection theory, classical conditioning, and natural selection) through a combination of text, graphics, humor, and activities. The point was not to create an exhaustive reference tool about psychology, but rather to present and integrate concepts in ways that invite readers to explore the "science of the mind." Rather than rewarding memorization, the CD is designed to nurture exploration and integration.

WHAT KINDS OF ACTIVITIES ARE ON THE CD?

The CD includes a variety of activities ranging from movies and interactive animations to full-blown simulations and interactive explorations. Every chapter includes interactive quizzes, rapid reviews, movies and sounds. But every chapter also includes a more ambitious set of activities that allow students to experience abstract principles and theories concretely. Because we think this is the most exciting and novel aspect of the **Longman Mind Matters** CD we've provided thumbnail descriptions of six of these to give you a feel for what they are like. More complete descriptions of the activities available for the Sensation chapter are available in that portion of this instructor's manual. A separate instructor's manual containing similar information for each chapter of this CD-ROM is available separately.

- **Signal Detection:** This interaction is designed to get students to see that perceptual discriminations are judgments that are influenced by both the actual stimulus information present and the person's decision criteria (their "willingness" to say that they detect something). Students will be presented with a detection task (e.g., seeing a true blip on a simulated "noisy" radar screen) with a stimulus that varies in its detectability. On some trials the students will be encouraged to be especially vigilant because a failure to detect the event could be disastrous (e.g., they are looking for incoming missiles, or planes in the landing pattern). On other trials they are told that they may relax and be less vigilant. After multiple trials, students will see a table for each condition that will show their "score" in terms of hits, correct rejections, false alarms, and misses. In conjunction with relevant narration, what students should see from these tables is that the differing instructions influenced primarily their willingness to say that an event happened (i.e., overall accuracy remains constant, but the ratio of false alarms and misses changes.)

- **Natural Selection:** In this activity, Darwin's concept of natural selection is introduced via a simulation. In the simulation, students see a gaggle of simulated creatures milling about randomly on the edge of a cliff, with some periodically falling off the cliff. The students can control the height of the cliff (i.e., the selection pressure) and

the time frame (i.e., present, near future, and distant future). The primary goal of the simulation
is to help students to see that selection is not an "intelligent" or anthropomorphic process. The simulation should help students to see that natural selection pressures can vary and thus produce effects on behavior to varying degrees. It should also help them see how adaptation occurs over generations rather than within a single generation.

- **Universality of Emotions:** In this activity, emotion is viewed from an adaptive perspective. The core concept that is presented is the notion that we have and express certain "feelings" because it is instinctive to do so. As a demonstration of the universality of several core emotions, students can play a drag and drop matching game in which they look at pictures of people expressing different emotions (from Paul Ekman's research) and match the pictures with the right emotion label.

- **The Navigable Brain:** In this activity, students can explore the functions of various parts of the brain. When students click on a particular part of the brain, they hear a brief explanation of the primary function of that area accompanied by an animation. The goal of this activity is to help students to remember both the location and primary functions of the major structures in the brain.

- **Brain Structure and Function Game:** This "drag and drop" activity requires students to match brain structures with their respective functions. Icons representing various functions (e.g., "relaying sensory data") have to be matched correctly to the corresponding structure in the brain (e.g., the thalamus). This activity should help reinforce the ideas of specialization and localization of function in the brain.

- **Color and Motion Afterimage:** These activities use color and motion afterimages to introduce students to the idea that visual information is processed both in the visual cortex and in the retina. The activities begin with brief explanations of the processes (i.e., receptor depletion and opponent processes) that are involved in the production of color and motion afterimage effects. The students are then given 20 seconds to adapt to either a color or motion afterimage stimulus. Following the adaptation phase, this stimulus is replaced by a colorless screen (in the case of color afterimage), and the students should experience an afterimage effect. (Be advised, however, that motion afterimages are extremely transient, lasting for perhaps a second or two.)

HOW CAN THE LONGMAN MIND MATTERS CD BE USED?

The modular nature of the CD allows it to be used in a variety of ways.

- Because each concept is presented in a self-contained manner, you can use it to whet your students' appetites for topics you haven't covered yet. You could, for example, ask your class to go through the entire Sensation unit on the disk before you cover sensation in class. The activities are designed to stimulate their interest in the topic.

- Similarly, the modular nature of the CD means that your students can use it as a review tool. In keeping with this use, each chapter includes quizzes and rapid reviews. In addition, the level of writing is intended to provide summaries of the important points.

- You can also use the disk in your lectures. The navigation of the disk allows you to access individual activities and use them in your lectures. The annotated guide contains suggestions for activities that are particularly well suited to this use (e.g., afterimages).

- The CD can also be used in a laboratory setting. Here students can be asked to keep notes about their experiences with the various activities, and these notes can become the basis for class discussions, term papers, or multi-media assignments. Each chapter also includes a quiz, with an option to print the results. These quizzes can be used to mark your students' progress as they work their way through the disk.

CAN I TEST STUDENTS ON THE MATERIAL COVERED IN THE CD?

Yes. As noted above, each chapter has an interactive quiz with printable results. In addition, this guide contains additional quizzes that you can use to assess your students' progress. The quizzes on the CD are also contained in a separate section in each relevant chapter of the Wade/Tavris *Invitation to Psychology* Test Bank.

HOW TECHNOLOGICALLY LITERATE MUST MY STUDENTS BE TO USE THE LONGMAN MIND MATTERS CD?

Minimally. The CD is designed to be easy to use and easy to navigate. The navigation and activities are all "point and click."

HOW TECHNOLOGICALLY LITERATE MUST I BE TO USE THE CD?

If you use the CD in your lectures, you will need to know how to connect your computer to a data projector of some sort. Otherwise, you don't need to know much about the technology to use the CD.

Chapter-Specific Materials
For each chapter the following supplemental material suggestions are included in this Instructor's Manual:

Chapter Overview
- Learning Objectives: a summary of the objectives listed at the beginning of each chapter by Uba & Huang
- Chapter Outline: a point-by-point outline overview of the chapter

Additional Lecture Ideas
- Lecture Topics: additional lecture topics pulled from a broad array of literature with a specific focus on gender and multicultural issues.
- Additional Readings: a listing of potential resources for additional materials to include in your lecture format

In-Class Activities and Demonstrations
- Activities and Demonstrations: descriptions of activities and demonstrations to include in class with particular emphasis on gender and multicultural topics
- Sources for Additional Activities: a listing of potential resources for additional demonstrations and in-class projects/activities to complement topics covered in class
- Journey II Software: an overview of the computer activities and simulations provided in the Journey II software package.

World Wide Web
- URL addresses of sites containing information and/or activities related to chapter topics

Audio-Visual Support
- Films/Videos: listings of available videos and films relevant to chapter content. Other films and videos may be found through these locators:
    Educational Film/Video Locator (Vol. 1 & 2) (4th Ed.) (1991). New York: Bowker.
    Film and Video Finder (Vol. I-III) (1987). Albuquerque, NM: National Information Center for Education Media.
    PBS Video Catalog. Alexandria, VA: PBS.

Cited Film Distributors in Instructor's Manual:

ABC ABC News 1330 Avenue of the Americas New York, NY 10019 1-800-913-3434	AEF American Educational Films 132 Lasky Drive P.O. Box 5001 Beverly Hills, CA 90212
AIMS AIMS Media 9710 DeSoto Avenue Chatsworth, CA 91311-4409 1-800-367-2467	AIT Agency for Instructional Television Box A 1111 West 17th Street Bloomington, IN 47402
Ambrose Ambrose Video Publishing Executive Distributors of Time Life Video 381 Park Ave. S. Suite 1601 New York, NY 10016	American Psychological Association American Psych. Association Order Department P.O. Box 2710 Hyattsville, MD 20794-0710 1-800-374-2721
Annenberg Annenberg/CPB Collection 901 E St. NW Washington, DC 20004	BARR Barr Films 12801 Schabarum Ave. P.O. Box 7878 Irwindale, CA 91706-7878 1-800-234-7878
BENM Benchmark Films, Inc. 145 Scarborough Road Briarcliff Manor, NY 10510	Brooks Brooks/Cole reps.

California Newsreel
149 Ninth Street
Suite 420
San Francisco, CA 94103
1-415-621-6196

CBS
Columbia Broadcasting System
1830 Avenue of the Americas
New York, NY 10019

CF
Campus Film Distributors Corp.
24 Depot Square
Tuckahoe, NY 10707

Concept Media
Concept Media
P.O. Box 19542
Irvine, CA 92714

CRM
CRM Films
2215 Faraday Avenue, Suite A
Carlsbad, CA 92008

DOCA/Document
Document Associates, Inc.
211 East 43 Street
New York, NY 10017

EMC UC or UC/EMC
Univ. of California Ext. Media Ctr
2000 Center Street
4th Floor
Berkeley, CA 94707
1-510-643-8683

Cambridge
Cambridge Documentary Films
P.O. Box 385
Cambridge, MA 02139
1-617-354-3677

CHUH
Churchill Films
12210 Nebraska Avenue
Los Angeles, CA 90025

Comap
Comap
Suite 210
57 Bedford Street
Lexington, MA 02173

CORT
Coronet
Division of Simon & Schuster Comm.
108 Wilmot Road
Deerfield, IL 60015
1-800-621-2131

CUAV
Cornell University Audio-Visual Resource Catalog
8 Research Park
Cornell University
Ithaca, NY 14850

EBEC
Encyclopedia Britannica Educational Corporation
425 N. Michigan Avenue
Chicago, IL 60611
1-800-554-9862

Encinitas
Encinitas Ctr. for Family and Personal Dev.
P.O. Box 231533
Encinitas, CA 92023-1533
1-619-436-7031

Fanlight or FANL
Fanlight Productions
47 Halifax Street
Boston, MA 02130
1-617-524-0980

FI
Films, Inc.
Public Media, Inc.
5547 Ravenswood Avenue
Chicago, IL 60640
1-800-323-4222

FIN
Focus International
14 Oregon Drive
Huntington Station, NY 11746
1-800-843-0305

HBJ or HARBJ or
HARCOURT
Harcourt Brace Jovanovich
College Division
7555 Caldwell Avenue
Chicago, IL 60648

IFB
International Film Bureau, Inc.
3325 S. Michigan Ave.
Chicago, IL 60604-4382
1-312-427-4545

IU
Indiana University AV Ctr
Bloomington, IN 47401-5901
1-800-552-8620

Light-Saraf
Light-Saraf Films
131 Concord Street
San Francisco, CA 94112
1-415-469-0139

FFHS
Film for the Humanities and Sciences
Box 2053
Princeton, NJ 08543-2053
1-800-257-5126

Filmakers
Filmakers Library
124 East 40th Street
New York, NY 10016
1-212-808-4980

FML
Filmmaker's Library, Inc.
133 E. 58th Street
Suite 703a
New York, NY 10022
1-212-355-6545

HARR
HarperCollins Publishers, Inc.
10 East 53rd Street
New York, NY 10022
1-212-207-7000

Insight Media
Insight Media
121 W. 85th Street
New York, NY 10024-4401

LCA
Learning Corporation of America
4640 Lankashim Blvd.
Suite 600
North Hollywood, CA 91602

McGraw-Hill or MCGH
CRM Films
2215 Faraday Avenue, Suite A
Carlsbad, CA 92008

Menninger
Menninger Clinic
Box 829
Topeka, KS 66601-0829
1-913-273-7500

MOTO
Motorola Teleprograms
Division of Simon and Schuster Communications
108 Wilmot Road
Deerfield, IL 60015
1-800-621-2131

MTI
MTI Teleprograms
Simon & Schuster Comm.
108 Wilmot Road
Deerfield, IL 60015
1-800-621-2131

MTP
Modern Talking Picture Service, Inc.
5000 Park Street, N.
St. Petersburg, FL. 33709-2200
1-800-243-6877

National Film Board
National Film Board of Canada
350 N. Pennsylvania Ave.
P.O. Box 7600
Wilkes-Barre, PA 18773-7600

NDF or New Day
New Day Film Library
22D Hollywood Avenue
Ho-Ho-Kus, NJ 07423
1-201-652-6590

NET
National Ed. Television, Inc.
WNET
Indiana University
Bloomington, IN 47401

OASIS
O.A.S.I.S.
15 Willoughby St.
Brighton, MA 02135
1-617-782-7769

PBS
PBS Video
1320 Braddock Place
Alexandria, VA 22314-1698
1-800-424-7963

PERED
Perennial Education, Inc.
930 Pitner Avenue
Evanston, IL 60202
1-312-328-7600

PHENIX
Phoenix/BFA Films and Video, Inc.
470 Park Avenue South
New York, NY 10016

POLY
Polymorph Films, Inc.
118 South Street
Boston, MA 02111

Prentice-Hall
Prentice-Hall, Inc.
Route 9W
Englewood Cliffs, NJ 07632

PSU
Pennsylvania State University
Audio-Visual Services
Special Services Building
University Park, PA 16802

Psychological Films
Psychological Films Dist Ctr
110 N. Wheeler
Orange, CA 92669

Quest
Quest Productions, Inc.
2600 10th Street
Berkeley, CA 94710

Research or REPR
Research Press
Box 3177
Dept. R
Champaign, IL 61821
1-217-352-3273

SP
Southerby Productions
5000 E. Anaheim Street
Long Beach, CA 90804

UM
University of Minnesota
University Film & Video
1313 Fifth Street SE
Suite 108
Minneapolis, MN 55414
1-800-847-8251

Wellness
Wellness Reproductions, Inc.
23945 Mercantile Road #2
Beechwood, OH 44122-5924
1-800-669-9208

WMM
Women Make Movies, Inc.
462 Broadway
5th Floor
New York, NY 10013

Pyramid or PYR
Pyramid Film and Video
P.O. Box 1048
Santa Monica, CA 90406

Redshoes
Redshoes Production
P.O. Box 1793
Des Moines, IA 50306
1-515-243-7116

RMI
RMI Media Productions, Inc.
2807 West 47th Street
Shawnee Mission, KS 66205
1-800-745-5480

Time/Life or TLF
see Amrose Video

Veritas
Veritas Programming
343 Seventh Avenue
New York, NY 10001

Wiley
John Wiley and Sons, Inc.
Media Guild
118 South Acacia
Box 881
Solana Beach, CA 92075
1-619-755-9191

Zimbardo
Phil Zimbardo
P.O. Box 2996
Stanford, CA 94309-2996

- **Psychology Encyclopedia Laserdisc IV**: listings of still images and video segments included on this laserdisc.

Handout and Transparency Masters
- transparency and handout masters for activities listed in the Activities and Demonstrations section of the Instructor's Manual.

Excerpts and modifications of B. Brown's Teaching the Introductory Course
by
Barbara L. Brown
Instructor's Resource Manual to accompany
Wade/Tavris *Psychology* (5th ed.); Longman Publishing

Unique Challenges of Teaching the Introductory Psychology Course

The size of introductory psychology classes varies considerably from one institution to another. Enrollment in a typical introductory class may range from 25 students to 500 students. Even in the smaller psychology classes, there is typically more diversity in the student population than will be found in other psychology courses. Introductory psychology courses are typically taken by both psychology majors and by non-majors. Introductory psychology courses are often elected by students in their first term of college. Some of these student will not have the academic skills to make it through the course, let alone to make it to more advanced psychology courses; other students will possess excellent academic skills. Some students will have taken an introductory psychology course in high school or at another college; for others this will be their first experience with a psychology course. Students taking introductory psychology courses typically have diverse racial and ethnic backgrounds. Your class may also include students with a variety of disabilities, including vision and hearing problems, attention deficit hyperactivity disorder, and various learning disabilities; you may be asked to make special accommodations for these students. Introductory psychology classes may also attract students with a variety of psychological problems.

There is also considerable diversity among instructors in introductory psychology courses. Some have years of experience in teaching such courses; others will be teaching introductory psychology for the first time. Some instructors are full-time teachers, others have other full-time jobs and teach psychology part-time. Some instructors have clinical background; others have research backgrounds. Instructors vary widely in their goals for students taking this course; some see introductory psychology as an opportunity to enhance their personal growth; others see it as an opportunity for students to sharpen critical thinking skills; still others see it as an opportunity to teach students about the scientific aspects of psychology.

The factors that make the teaching of introductory psychology so challenging also create opportunities for teaching the introductory psychology course to be a richly rewarding experience. As a teacher in an introductory psychology course you have an opportunity to make a difference with students who are typically near the beginning of their academic careers. If you succeed in finding ways to communicate psychology to your students, you may encourage students who have had little academic success prior to taking your course. You may stimulate an interest in psychology as a career in others. You may learn from students who bring differing viewpoints and experiences into your classroom. Whether you come from a clinical or research background, there will be plenty of ways to incorporate your own experience and expertise into the material you teach in this course. And, even at institutions that standardize the overall content of the introductory psychology course, with a little creativity you will almost certainly find ways to emphasize your own personal goals for your students in your teaching of the course.

There are Many Ways to Communicate Psychology to Students

The key to effective delivery of the message is variation. Although lecturing continues to be the most common teaching method, it is most effective in small doses, particularly if you are not an outstanding performer. Other methods include discussions, demonstrations, films and other audio-visual resources, group projects, experiments, and written or oral exercises.

Lectures:

1. The key to an effective lecture is organization. Your goal is not just to present the material, but to present it in a clear manner that will make the material understandable to the students in your class. Pay careful attention to the hierarchical organization of your material, and to ways that each concept relates to other concepts you will cover.

2. Begin your lecture with attention-capturing material. You might orient the lecture around some thought-provoking introductory question or theme.

3. Preview and summarize the content of your lecture. An outline of your lecture written on the board or projected on a screen will help students follow the logic of your presentation.

4. Use the blackboard to emphasize important concepts, to put information in visual form when possible, and to provide the spelling for names and unfamiliar terms.

5. Use concrete examples to illustrate the many unfamiliar concepts introduced in the course. Lots of examples! (Note from TJM: I have found that one should also consider the shared cultural meanings of examples....some examples make sense only if the student can relate to them from previous personal experiences. International students may not have the same context of understandings as do acculturated students.)

6. To maintain students' attention, vary the pitch and loudness of your voice, use gestures and facial expression, and move. Review your lecture notes thoroughly before class so you will not be glued to the lectern.

7. Use the lecture to amplify and enrich the material in the text, to illustrate difficult concepts, to relate psychology to personal experience, or to motivate and stimulate

students. Avoid trying to duplicate the text; too much information can overwhelm students and result in little or no retention. (Note from TJM: additional lecture topics such as those reviewed in this Instructor's Manual may be used to "push beyond" or extend the text presentation.)

Discussion:
Discussion has limited value in introductory courses for several reasons. Classes are frequently too large for its effective use; extroverts in the front rows may carry on a lively dialogue while their peers at the rear call up their favorite daydreams. Also, discussion can result in a "pooling of ignorance" because students may not have read the assigned material in the text and may lack the background necessary to contribute to a meaningful discussion.

1. If you plan to have a point discussed, make your intention clear to the students by saying, "Let's talk about how you feel when you've been punished: when your parents criticize you or you get a ticket for a traffic violation," or "What do you think influences our self-esteem? How do we form our opinions about ourselves?"

2. Plan topics for discussion around experiences students have had, a film that has been shown, or a situation that you have described.

3. Pause after introducing the topic or asking the question to give students time to consider a response.

4. Tactfully summarize or repeat aloud the point made by a student if the point was poorly expressed or if the student did not speak loudly enough to be heard by class members.

5. Be receptive to students' contributions to the discussion and reinforce them for participating even if what they say is erroneous or irrelevant. Never call attention to a stupid comment. In class discussions, your goal is to praise effort as well as content.

6. Divide the class into small groups for discussion. Prepare explicit directions for them, and require each group to make a report to you or to the class. One way to encourage productivity in small groups is to give students blank transparencies and appropriate markers and to instruct them to outline a topic or write down key words and concepts to present to the class.

Demonstrations:
Demonstrations can be a very effective addition to the classroom experience, but preparation is the key to their success. If equipment or props are required, they should be assembled, set up, and tested before class. If something goes wrong, it is better to abandon or postpone the demonstration than to fiddle with the equipment or send a student for a missing ingredient. Remember that competent people are more lovable if they make an occasional blunder, particularly if they handle the situation with humor.

Relate the demonstration to everyday experiences. For example, if you demonstrate how an additive mixture of red and green produces yellow, suggest that students look at their color-television screen with a magnifying glass.

Films and Videos:

Films and videos are an effective and enjoyable way of communicating psychological concepts to students. With films, videocassettes, slides, and audiocassettes, you can personally introduce your students to B.F. Skinner, put your students in the teacher's role in Milgram's Yale laboratory, and ask your students to testify as an eyewitness to a robbery. Pictures can save you a thousand words. And research tells us that students are more likely to remember those pictures than your words.

You can be more effective in achieving the objectives in your introductory psychology lectures with a few well-chosen and well-placed audiovisual presentations. Films lend credibility to research and theorists discussed in the text and in your lectures because student "see it with their own eyes." Your lectures can focus on the underlying principles discovered in the research, since students are able to visualize the experimental settings and procedures.

Media in the classroom has gradually become a respected teaching tool to support and enhance, rather than replace, lectures. Rapid-paced, brief films and videos are often used, as well as other innovations, such as interactive films and self-produced videos.

Here are some reasons psychology professors use media presentations:

To provide an unforgettable picture of an important concept
To generate an emotional response from students
To present students with an overview of a large body of work
To show students a new perspective on a familiar topic
To simulate an in-class demonstration
To introduce students to interesting and famous "guest speakers"
To present both sides of the great debates in psychology

Advantages of media presentations to students. From the students' perspective, audiovisual presentations:

Provide a change of pace from the daily routine of listening to professors.
Enliven the text material. "I actually saw the monkey run to the terry-cloth monkey when the loud toy was placed in the cage. It's amazing because the monkey was being fed by the wire monkey!"
Invite participation, allowing the students to "discover" the concepts.

Experience is the best teacher, and some media presentations create a sense of film-audience interaction.

Capture the students' attention. Students must pay attention before they can learn, and a lively, emotion-provoking film primes students to listen to your conclusions on the topic.

Selecting the best film or video. Media presentations are beneficial whenever they move the class toward the achievement of your objectives for the course. But the pedagogical usefulness of such presentations depends on your selection of the best material for your class, and on your integration of that material into your class.

As you preview media presentations for possible use in your class, consider the following criteria:

Parsimony: Does the film make the important points in a relatively short time? Films that take up the entire class period are likely to be less effective than shorter films because you need some class time to prepare the students before the film, and to review the material after the film. With longer films, show only those sections that are most relevant to the topic of your lecture, even though that means starting a film in the middle, or stopping a film before it's finished.

Logic: If the film structurally clear so students can easily recognize the key points? The film can be logical by following either deductive logic (i.e., discussion of the principles followed by numerous examples) or inductive logic (i.e., lots of examples leading to a summary of the underlying ideas or principles).

Credibility: Do experts explain their own theories? Does the evidence support the conclusion?

Accuracy: Does the film or video convey information that is scientifically accurate?

Effective examples: Does the film or video use effective examples? Are examples realistic (i.e., do they portray recognizable situations or situations with which students can relate?)? Are examples meaningful in that they illustrate key principles? Are the examples lively, colorful, and/or dramatic? Do they tell a story in such a way that students can put themselves into the situation? Do examples generate an emotional reaction from the audience (laughter, anxiety, or sadness)?

Using media in the classroom. Once you've selected the film or video, consider the best placement of the presentation within the context of your lecture. If you have access to the film or video for a limited time and the material is out of sequence with your course, don't show it. Ideally, from the students' perspective there should be no separation of ideas between your lecture and those set forth in the presentation by your "visiting expert." When only part of a film fits with your objectives and time frame, show just that segment. Students benefit most from media presentations if they know where to focus their attention. Rather than having their interest driven by the color or music, provide advance organizers to direct the students' attention to the significant points. You can organize the presentation by providing a lecture outline for them to complete during the film, or by giving them a few questions before the film that they will need to be able to answer at the end of the film. It is also helpful to define and spell words used in the film that are new to students. Students can more fully focus on the film's content if they're not worried that they missed "that weird word."

In order to communicate to your class that the media presentation is a meaningful and legitimate activity, remain with your class during the film and appear to take notes. Even though you may be writing a letter, students are likely to infer that you're creating a few quiz questions based on the film, which is probably a good idea as a way to further support the idea that media presentations are as important as the lecture. (Note from TJM: I have found this to be effective generally only if I actually do create some questions concerning the films for tests...otherwise, students will see through this "note-taking" pretty quickly.) Also, remaining with the class is preferred in case you need to deal with any equipment problems. Immediately after the presentation, follow up on the film by responding to students' questions and by reviewing the pre-film outline or questions.

(Another note from TJM: Immediate follow-up appears crucial to tying the content of the film directly to your topic of the day, especially to clarifying for students the points you saw for those who didn't quite catch the relevance of the film. Don't assume students "get the point", even with the aid of a handout, of the video. If the film contains issues that students may need to think about for a bit of time, urge them to do so and then remember to return to the topic at the beginning of the next class session.)

A few final words of advice:

Make sure you know how to operate the audio visual equipment.
Sources for appropriate films, slides, or videocassettes include your college or university's library, distributors' catalogues, the film and video lists within this manual, and your colleagues' recommendations.

Order the media presentation about a month before you intend to show it in class. Schedule the material to arrive a few days early so you can preview it and prepare questions, lecture outlines, and handouts. These few days also allow you time to prepare a back-up presentation in the event that the material doesn't arrive as scheduled.

On the day of the media presentation, double-check the equipment before class. Run the film or videocassette past the leader so the action of the presentation begins immediately.

During the film, remain with the class to legitimize the activity, to deal with any equipment malfunctions, and to stop the film if you decide to only show part of a lengthy presentation.

Slides and Transparencies:

Slides and transparencies project an image large enough to be seen by the entire class. Transparencies have the extra advantage of being able to be used in a lighted room. A big picture of an eyeball, an illusion, the brain, or a Rorschach inkblot is worth a thousand words.

1. Learn how to make your own transparencies; it's easy. You can write directly on the masters if you wish or you can photocopy an illustration and transfer it to a transparency master using a photocopying machine.
2. If you are preparing your own transparencies, be sure to use font sizes and images that are large enough to be seen clearly by students in the back of your classroom. Typically, this will mean that you cannot put very much information on one slide or transparency.
3. If you use slides, be sure you load them in the order you want to present them and that they are correctly positioned to show the sky at the top and the cars on the right side of the road (TJM: assuming you're showing traffic in this country of course!) Again, it is important to test your props.
4. Additional points from TJM: If you deliver lecture notes or visual images via computer-generated presentation packages (such as Power Point for example), many of the points Brown makes about lecture notes and overhead transparencies are combined. I regularly use presentation packages for delivery of my lectures and visual images and have found some of the following points important to keep in mind:

Select font sizes and styles carefully. Test a few and then stand in the back of the room to make sure they can be easily read!

Watch out for the colors you use for text and backgrounds! Test out effective color combinations for the material you're presenting; try a sample of what you intend to use on the equipment you have available in the room in which you teach.

Be judicious in the use of the glitzy aspects of some presentation packages. Words or phrases that "fly in" or magically appear on screen can certainly add drama to your presentation but sometimes distract from the point you're attempting to make.

Watch out for overly busy displays! Wild graphics and colors may capture attention...at the same time they can distract and bewilder.

If you have a graphics arts department or radio/TV department at your university, consult them about making effective graphic presentations. (I observed professional educational television producer/directors for some pointers in how they developed their computer-generated graphics for live and recorded television productions.)

Be aware of copyright issues that may affect your use of photos or other graphics that you scan for use in presentation packages.

Follow Brown's basic suggestions concerning decisions of meaningful and effective material to add to your presentation. Images that aren't explained or tied to the content of the presentation don't clarify...they confuse.

Conduct a trial run of the equipment and your presentation package. Murphy's law seems to apply! Always have a back-up plan just in case the equipment fails. Many presentation packages allow you to print your presentation screens--you may need to make overhead transparencies of your presentation to use if you can't get your equipment going...even if you've used that equipment countless times before! Technology is great but it can sure foul you up if you don't second guess potential problems.

All in all, I have found that students enjoy materials presented with these technologies...if you have the chance, explore their use in your classroom situation. You come off looking like a techno-wizard and your computer-literate students may appreciate your up-to-date presentational skills!

Experiments, Group Projects, and Class Exercises:

Specific suggestions for in-class experiments, projects, and exercises are provided in each chapter of this Instructor's Manual. The following are general pieces of advice:

1. Be prepared before class. Have all the material you will need assembled and think through the procedure before class (Note from TJM: Do a trial run of the activity on yourself to practice instructions, uncover points about you are not clear, & consider good places where the exercise make sense in the context of the materials you're covering in class.)
2. Use class members or others to assist if the class is large or if there are more chores to be done than you can do rapidly alone.
3. Minimize the length and number of intervals when students have nothing to do.

Quizzes and examinations:

Students and instructors tend to think of quizzes and examinations strictly as a means of evaluation. However, they can also serve as an important learning tool. If nothing else, knowledge of upcoming quizzes and examinations provides students with an important incentive to keep up with (or catch up with) their reading and study. In addition, quizzes and exams may provide students with feedback if they have not adequately understood a particular concept. Frequent quizzes may provide students with an "early warning" system that their study methods are not effective, that they are emphasizing the wrong points in their study, or that they are misconstruing crucial concepts.

There are several ways you can maximize the value of quizzes and exams as learning tools. Some instructors use a system where students are quizzed on material before it is covered in class, with the goal of encouraging students to read the chapter before class so they will be prepared for class and will feel more comfortable in asking questions. To decrease the anxiety factor, ask students only fairly straightforward questions that anyone who has read the text should be able to answer. Allow students to bring a one page "cheat sheet" with them to the quiz, on which they may write anything they think will help them on the quiz.

Other instructors, myself included, allow students to bring some form of "cheat sheet" to exams. If you decide to do this, be sure to specify the allowable size of the cheat sheet and whether it can be written on one side only or on both sides. I allow students to bring a 3x5 index card, written on both sides, to exams. This legitimate "cheat sheet" has two advantages: first, students have to do some form of studying to prepare their cheat sheet, and they will probably learn a lot from the exercise of having to decide what material is important enough to go on their cheat sheet; second, having the cheat sheet decreases exam anxiety for many students. Even with the cheat sheet, students are not likely to have all the information they need written down on the cheat sheet, particularly if you ask a good number of questions requiring thought and analysis. (Note from TJM: I include short answer questions on my exams and provide my students with a 3-4 short answer question pool 3-4 days prior to the exam. Students know the question to be selected for the test is in that pool and they have time to develop answers to the entire pool. I have found that students have less anxiety to short answer questions and spend some time thinking about potential responses if they have the general pool ahead of time.)

Another way to encourage use of exams as a learning tool is to provide an opportunity for students to identify and correct their own mistakes on an exam. I first heard about this idea at a presentation at one of the Annual Institutes on the Teaching of Psychology (presentation by Russell Veitch, Bowling Green State University, "Using intraterm examinations to promote learning.") and have since modified it to fit my own teaching situation. The basic procedure is as follows. My exams consist of 50 multiple choice items. Students have 1 1/2 hours or 2 hours for the exam period. Students enter their answers on an machine scoreable answer sheet. During the first hour, students answer the questions using their own minds and memories or with the aid of a "cheat sheet" as described above. At the end of one hour, or when all students have completed the exam, whichever comes first, I collect all of the exams and answer sheets, and take a brief break to grade the answer sheets. By marking the appropriate box on the answer sheet, I can get the scoring machine to mark how many answers each student got right, without indicating exactly which items each student got wrong. I then return each students' answer sheet and exam. Students may use the last 1/2 hour or hour to try to identify and correct their own mistakes. I allow students to use notes and textbooks for this part. At the end of the period, I again collect all of the exams and answer sheets and regrade the answer sheets, this time marking the "regrade" box on the answer key. The scoring machine now marks answers that are still incorrect, and prints the second score in a "regrade" box below the original score. (I have found it necessary, however, to promise students that if their regrade score is lower than their original score, I will give them their original score. Otherwise, most of my students take the attitude that they would rather "quit while they're ahead.") According to Veitch's original presentation, students who were allowed to use the regrade procedure during the term made higher scores on a cumulative final exam (no regrade was allowed on this exam) at the end of the term than students using a more conventional test procedure during the term. While I have not replicated his outcome studies, this procedure has worked beautifully in my classes and students love it!

Key Instructional Decisions
Will I assign readings from publications other than the text?

Some instructors prefer to select a limited number of chapters from the text and to assign other readings related to the chosen chapters. Although this provides more in-depth coverage of some areas, it neglects other areas of psychology completely. As the areas covered in the course are reduced, the course becomes less and less the broad survey it is intended to be.

The more common practice in introductory psychology classes is to assign all or most of the chapters in the text and little or no outside reading. Because of their familiarity with the material covered in the introductory course, instructors may underestimate the difficulty of the text for students. Students who do well in the introductory course study, rather than just read, the text.

If you do want to assign some additional readings, be sure that your campus library can supply enough copies of the assigned material.

Will I require written assignments?

Your decision concerning writing assignments is likely to be influenced by the size of your class and the amount of assistance you can expect for reading papers. Writing experience is an important element in education and if you have the time and resources, you should include some written work in your requirements. You might consider assigning several short papers rather than a traditional term paper. If you do decide to assign written work, you may want to read the material in this section of the resource manual on *Writing Assignment in the Introductory Course*.

How many tests will I give?

Given the scope of the material in introductory psychology, frequent tests are generally recommended. However, tests do take class time, and if you think of tests as purely a means of evaluation, you may feel that frequent testing takes too much class time. Keep in mind that tests are a powerful pedagogical tool because they inspire students to study and provide feedback on the effectiveness of their efforts.

Marvels of modern technology, like the TestGen EQ Computerized Testing System, have made test construction relatively easy for the instructor. It is user-friendly because it is menu-driven and has readily available help screens. You choose the items from the test bank and it will number them, scramble them, print them, and provide you with an answer key, or keys if you use more than one order of items. You can also edit test questions and add your own.

What kind of tests will I give?

Multiple-choice tests are the standard evaluative method in introductory psychology. Martha Ellis' test bank to accompany Psychology (Uba & Huang) contains many questions that emphasize the multicultural perspective and assess conceptual, application, and factual skills. If you prefer to give essay tests or like to include short answer or essay questions with objective items, you will find an ample supply of both in the test bank.

What will my tests cover?

Tests in introductory classes cover primarily the text. Inform students in the syllabus that tests will also cover assignments done outside of class as well as anything that occurs in class, including lectures, films, demonstrations, and experiments. The strategy here is to encourage students to attend class regularly. If they see that all the test questions are from the text, they are likely to decide that class attendance is a waste of time.

How long should my tests be?

Most student can read and answer a multiple choice question in less than a minute, so if your class lasts 50 minutes, the test can have 50 items. If your class period is longer than 50 minutes, give a longer test. Reliability increases with test length. It is not a good idea to try to have other activities on test days.

What will I do about students who miss tests?

There is no ideal solution to this problem. One must is that you have a policy you can live with and enforce, and that students be informed of it in the syllabus. Another helpful generalization is to do whatever you can to discourage students from missing tests. One way to do this is to require verification of illness or other legitimate reasons for absence on test days.

One option that poses problems is to let students take the test later. If you don't have another test on the material, the class will have to wait until all the make-ups are done before they get feedback. Even if you do have another test you can use, you may find yourself proctoring individual students at times that are more convenient for them than for you.

A second option that applies if you give several tests during the term is to let all students drop their lowest score. This is an attractive option because students who miss a test can use the missed test as their lowest score. One caution in this situation is that you should not let the final test score be the one that is dropped, especially if you give a final that covers only the material since the last test. If you let students drop the score on the final test, those who are satisfied with their scores on earlier tests may consider the class finished for them several weeks before the end of the term.

Another caution is that if the means for the tests vary considerably, and if you grade on a curve, then dropping the lowest score penalizes students who did better than usual on the more difficult tests. For example, if the means of the tests are quite different, it is possible that a student's lowest raw score can be her highest standard score. This problem can be resolved by recording and using standard scores or by adding a constant to test scores to equalize the means.

Still another option is to assign a score for the missing test based on the student's performance on the remainder of the tests. Substituting the lowest test score for the missing score discourages students from missing tests, but it penalizes students who miss a test for legitimate reasons. Using the average of the other test scores seems fair, but students who are good strategists will figure out that it is better to be sick than to take a test for which they haven't prepared.

How can I prevent cheating on tests?

This is something we don't like to think or talk about, but cheating in the classroom is a reality and you should do what you can to prevent it. Students who don't cheat become justifiably upset if they perceive that you are not doing your best to prevent cheating. Here are some methods of cheating and some preventative measures:

1. Copying from an unsuspecting neighbor. Use TestGen EQ Computerized Testing System to construct two or more forms of your test. Each form should include the same items, but in a different scrambled order.
2. Collaborating with a friend by exchanging test papers. Use vigilant proctoring, and watch for students to exchange papers.
3. Getting a copy of the test before it is given. Keep tests in a securely locked cabinet or file drawer. Be sure stencils or discarded pages are not left in a wastebasket that is accessible to students.
4. Failure to hand in the test and answer sheet and claiming absence on the day of the test. Have students sign an attendance sheet as they enter the classroom.
5. Getting someone else to take the test. Most campuses that have classes large enough for this to be a problem issue identification cards with pictures. Have students bring their card to class and show it as they hand in their test.
6. Surreptitious use of notes (not a very effect method of cheating on multiple-choice test in introductory psychology). Have students put all books and papers under their seats and have them leave them there until they are ready to hand in their papers and leave. You may choose to allow students to bring to an exam one page of notebook paper with anything they want written on it. This legitimate pony has value in that preparing it is a type of study activity, and because clutching their pony tends to reduce anxiety for students who panic on test day. It is a good idea to have a proctor help you on test days even if your class is not very large. You may need to confer with students who have questions or return to your office to get more pencils. It is good to have another pair of eyes available.

How will I provide feedback to students after tests?

The longer students have to wait for correct answers, the less interested they become in checking their work. Provide immediate feedback if you can. For example, you can have students record their answers on both the test and the answer sheet. They hand in the answer sheet and keep the test, scoring it themselves from a key or keys you post immediately after the test. TestGen EQ Computerized Testing System makes it possible for you to provide feedback that includes both correct answers and page references from the text. Instructors who want to reuse their tests can collect the students' answer sheets and review the questions with the class before collecting the tests.

How can I avoid hassles about test items?

First, choose and write items carefully, being sure that you agree that the keyed answer is the best answer. Then make your key carefully. Examine the printout of scores before posting it, checking items marked right by less than half the class for ambiguity or incorrect keying. If you make a mistake in your choice of items or on the key, correct it graciously. Do not spend class time arguing about test items. If necessary, have students submit their case in writing if they feel that their choice for an item is better than the keyed answer.

Another way to avoid hassles about multiple choice test items is to allow students to write explanations of answers to questions that they perceive to be tricky or ambiguous on their answer sheets. (This can be done even on machine gradeable answer sheets, as long as students write in an area that will not interfere with machine grading.) Students are instructed to write the number of the item, an explanation of what they know about the item, and why they picked the answer they did. If their explanation indicates that they really did have adequate understanding of the material in question, and that they were just hampered by the wording of the question, they get full credit for the question. Such explanations should be written before the answer sheet is turned in, not after it has been graded. Comments such as "Question 38 is ambiguous" receive no credit because they reveal nothing about the student's understanding of the material. A more detailed explanation of this procedure can be obtained from the original source:

Dodd, D. K. & Leal, L. (1988). Answer justification: Removing the trick from multiple-choice questions. Teaching of Psychology, 15, 37-38.

Should I use numbers or letters to grade students' work?
Any assigned activity that is to contribute to students' grades should be assigned a numerical score so an unambiguous point system can be used for assigning final grades. Some students have difficulty understanding that an A on a minor assignment is not weighted as heavily as a D on the final exam. Using numerical grades may be helpful as long as students are aware of the relative weighting of each assignment. Alternatively, you may use a point system, where each assignment is worth a certain number of points. Minor assignment are worth fewer points than major assignments. Keep in mind that a fairly large total number of points increases the range of final totals for your class and makes the cutoff between letter grades appear reasonable.

How do I keep track of student grades?

You can , of course, record student grades in an old-fashioned gradebook. The biggest disadvantage of this method is that you may find yourself with quite a lot of calculating to do at the end of the term. If you keep grades in a gradebook, it is a good ideas to photocopy your gradesheets periodically and to put the photocopies in a safe place, in case your gradebook is lost or stolen.

Many instructors record grades on their computers. This offers the great advantage of automating the calculation of grades. Instructors who keep their computerized gradebooks up to date are able to offer concerned students instant calculations of their grades throughout the term. Grading programs are widely available from commercial sources as well as through shareware. If you are comfortable using spreadsheet programs such as Excel or Lotus, however, these are excellent for recording and calculating grades. In general, multipurpose spreadsheet programs will offer more flexibility and larger capacity for grade recording and calculation than will dedicated grading programs. If you keep your grades on a computer, be sure to print out hard copies periodically and to make back-up copies of your grades so that you will not lose everything in case of hardware or software problems.

How will I assign final grades?

There are two traditional methods for assigning grades: the criterion-based system and the normative-based or on-the-curve system.

In criterion-based grading, criteria are published in the syllabus. For example, if a student gets 92% to 100% of the maximum number of points, the student can be assured of an A. This method is preferred by the majority of instructors because it is easy for students to understand and accommodates variability in performance of different classes. It has the potential disadvantage of obligating you to give more high grades than you may have expected.

In a normative-based grading, it is predetermined that you will, for example, give an A to the top 10% of the students, a B to students in the next 20%, and so forth. This method has the advantage of not requiring you to commit yourself to absolute criteria, but it has the disadvantage of causing some students to be uncertain about where they stand during the term. Also, normative-based grading assumes that your class is a random sample of students who take introductory psychology at your school and does not take into account that some classes as a whole are better than others. Identical student performance could earn an A in one class and a B in another when the normative-based system is used.

Should I provide an opportunity for students to get course credit for work that is not a class requirement?

If you fail to state a firm policy on extra-credit work in the syllabus, you will be visited by failing students during the closing weeks of the term. They would like to write a paper, or do something to raise their grade. In general, a no-extra-credit policy is best, for students who are failing the required work would be better off spending their time on it rather than writing a paper which will detract from the time and energy they can devote to the existing assignments. If there are to be opportunities for extra-credit, they should be available to all the students, not just to those who come to your office with sad stories. For your best students, extra-credit work is likely to be perceived as required, and you may find that they are more likely to take advantage of opportunities to earn points that students who need them more. Extra-credit work may increase your work load. The bookkeeping for volunteer work or research participation can be a headache, and rewritten or replaced papers means more papers to read and grade. However, this should not deter you if you can provide extra-credit work that is truly a beneficial experience for students.

<u>What kind of extra-credit opportunities could I provide?</u>
   One extra-credit option that is a learning experience for students and a service to the community is volunteer work in places such as sheltered workshops, child-care centers, nursing homes, and shelters for the homeless. If you can arrange this type of activity, be sure to set a limit on the amount of credit that can be earned.
   Introductory students are frequently an important source of human subjects for research. If research participation is not a requirement at your school, you might consider using it as an extra-credit option.
   If you assign several short papers during the term, you could allow students to rewrite or replace a paper that has received a low score. Rewriting a poor paper and incorporating your comments and corrections into the revised paper can be especially beneficial for students who need help with writing skills.

Preparing Your Course
   Preparation to teach introductory psychology should begin months before the first day of class, and you should expect to devote considerable time to the task, particularly if you have not taught the course before.

1. Read the text. Make notes concerning points you want to emphasize, or concepts you think will be especially difficult for students. Look through the Instructor's Resource Manual to choose ideas or material that you may want to use in class. Familiarize yourself with the resources that are available to students.
2. Make a tentative schedule, recording on a large calendar what you expect to do or cover in each class meeting during the term along with reading assignments and due dates for projects or written work. Use a pencil, since you are likely to revise your plan a number of times.
3. Choose films and videos that you think would be appropriate for your class. Reserve films that are available on your own campus and order those that are to come from other sources.
4. If you assign readings from material in the library, have the relevant publications put on reserve.
5. If you have Teaching Assistants, meet with them as soon as possible so they can contribute to your planning. Have in mind a job description so they will know what assistance you expect during the term.
6. If you plan to invite guest lecturers, confirm these arrangements early. Make an alternative plan in case of last-minute changes. Post a reminder for yourself to send your guests instructions concerning parking and where to meet you before class.
7. Check the resources of your department for equipment you might want to use in a demonstration or a standardized test you might want to administer.
8. Check facilities and procedures for printing tests and other material. Find out about facilities and procedures for machine-scoring tests.
9. Make the decisions discussed in the Key Instructional Decisions section of this introduction.
10. After you have finalized your class schedule and made the relevant decisions, prepare a syllabus.

11. Plan the first few class meetings in some detail.

The First Class

Research in social psychology supports the idea that first impressions are important. Based on first impressions, we classify people into social schemas or stereotypes; after that our impression of those people is typically distorted to some extent by the schema or stereotype we have applied to that person. This tendency applies inside our classrooms as well as outside our classrooms. If you appear disorganized or disagreeable at your first class meeting, you students are likely to continue to see you that way for the rest of the term. Therefore, it is important to think about the impressions you want to convey at that first class. Typically, disorganization is not one of them. I recommend that you be extraordinarily well-organized for your first class. Make sure you are well rested. Groom yourself and dress in a way that conveys the message you want to convey. Students will overlook a multitude of sins in the middle of the term if you have conveyed a positive impression during the first class. Typically, the syllabus is given out during the first class, and basic details of grading are gone over. It is important to go over some of this information with students so that they know what they are committing to and so they have an opportunity to ask questions. However, I recommend that you do not spend the entire class period gong over the syllabus. Both you and the students would probably die of boredom. In order to insure that students actually do read the syllabus, you may wish to attach a syllabus quiz to the back of the syllabus, and ask students to read the syllabus and answer the questions on their own time. When they turn the syllabus quiz in, you can score it and give them some appropriate form of credit.

Remember, the theme here is that the first class sets the tone for things to come. Try to make sure that your first class emphasizes the key themes that you want to emphasize in the course. Two of the themes I like to emphasize in my course are active learning and the notion that psychology is empirical. Accordingly, I devote a considerable portion of my first class to a series of memory demonstrations, which allow students to participate actively while learning the material. In addition, use of these memory demonstrations very clearly illustrates ways that psychologists can use empirical methods to study subjects such as memory.

Try not to let students out early from your first class. Running a full class allows student to get a full sample of what you and this class are about. In addition, conducting a full length class on the first day indicates that you are approaching the teaching of introductory psychology with both seriousness and enthusiasm; hopefully students will be more likely to adopt that same attitude.

The Syllabus

The class syllabus informs students of the objectives and requirements for the course and explains your policies and procedures. Time spent preparing your syllabus will be rewarded by avoiding problems during the term and facilitating a comfortable relationship with students. Preferences concerning the comprehensiveness of syllabi vary widely among introductory instructors. Some are only a page or two and others are much longer. The following list of elements in a syllabus are divided into essentials and options. (TJM: a sample of a syllabus I use for Uba & Huang follows this section).

Syllabus Essentials:
- General information
- Name of the text and study guide
- Other supplies needed for the course
- Goals and/or objectives
- Course requirements
- Class schedule
- Reading assignments
- Dates of tests
- Due dates for papers and/or activities
- Testing format and procedures
- Class policies: attendance, missed tests, grading, extra-credit work, dropping the class

Syllabus Options:
- Expanded class calendar
- Lecture topics, films, activities
- Detailed description of testing procedure
- Autobiographical information about yourself
- Where to get help
- Effective study habits and efficient use of study time
- Guidelines and topics for papers
- Learning objectives for each chapter
- Discussion of section meetings and activities

General Psychology
Psyc 100-02

M - F, 10 am
Martin 158

Instructor:	Dr. Theresa J. Martin
Office:	151G Martin Hall
Office Hours:	11 am - 12:00 pm - Mon. through Fri. and appointments by arrangement
Phone:	111-2222

Teaching Asst:	T. Assist
Office:	Graduate Student Study Carrels
Office Hours:	Mon., 11 am-12 pm; Thurs., 11:30 am-1 pm

Course Goals

Psychology is an extremely diverse discipline devoted to the scientific study of the various ways in which individuals think, feel, and behave. The primary goal of all

introductory psychology courses is to explore the subject matter of the discipline. Over the course of this quarter, we will
explore the major topical areas that psychologists investigate. You will become familiar with the vocabulary and concepts of the field and with some of the research findings upon which our knowledge of human thought and behavior is based.

Another goal of this class is to emphasize the development of critical thinking skills and to prepare you to be a cautious and analytical consumer of information that proclaims to be scientific or be based on research.

I also hope that you will derive some personal benefits from the class; that at the end of the quarter you will have increased your understanding and acceptance of yourself and others; and that you will gain something from this class that will enrich your personal relationships and add to your success in your chosen occupations.

Classroom Dynamics and Conduct

The course is designed around a number of instructional techniques including lectures, small group exercises, demonstrations, guest speakers, and films. I invite, encourage, implore your active participation--this is our class (not just mine). I will call upon you for comments and answers to in-class questions. Be prepared to participate. At the same time, be considerate of the opinions and knowledge expressed by your classmates and special guests to the class--don't dominate the class with your input, put others down by your comments or behavior, etc. Also, please be aware that your participation in in-class demonstrations may be requested; however, like any research participant, you have the right to decline participation and can withdraw your participation at any point in a demonstration. You will be told something about the activity before you participate and the purpose of the demonstration will be explained at its conclusion.

A word on general conduct in the classroom -- this is a large room and your private conversations with peers sitting next to you will definitely distract and disturb others. Please show respect for others by not talking over the classroom activity. If you have questions or missed something I said, ask to have the material repeated. If you disrupt the class, I will ask you to leave the room.

Special comments: Let me say at the onset that I feel saddened that I have to include the following comments in a syllabus, but several unfortunate events over last year have made it abundantly clear to me that I need to "lay it on the line" from Day One. Be aware that the university policy and procedures on student conduct and cheating will be implemented as necessary. In particular, although you are free to work on take home assignments/labs and, of course, study with other students from the class, I expect that the answers on all assignments and examinations represent your unique effort and knowledge. Therefore, I should not see "carbon copy" responses on assignments. If I do, the assignment will be graded as failing (i.e., zero points). Moreover, anyone cheating on examinations will receive at least a failing grade on that test. In repeated cases, a more severe penalty, such as failing the course, may occur.

Special comment is also required concerning computer use. At probably the midpoint of the quarter, we will begin using the department computer lab to complete laboratory assignments. Some assignments may involve Internet use and university ethical guidelines for computer use will be followed. Basically, that involves using the computer and printers only for class-related work and some restrictions on types of files accessed via the Internet. You are personally responsible for your conduct on the computer.

Text

The course text will serve as our primary information source (be aware that additional information not found in the text is also covered in class). The text for the course is Laura Uba and Karen Huang's *Psychology*. I do reserve the right to make changes to the reading schedule if needed
but ALL changes will be announced in class.

Reading assignments/Exam & lab schedule

Week 1 (Sept. 21 to Sept. 24)   -- Introduction & Chapter 1
*** Exam 1 is on Sept. 28 ***   (Introduction: What is Psychology?)
(exam 1 covers only the Introduction & Chapter 1)

Week 2 (Sept. 28 to Oct. 1)   -- Chapter 2
*** Exam 2 is on Oct. 5 ***   (Biopsychology: The biological bases of behavior)
(exam 2 covers only Chapter 2)

Week 3 (Oct. 5 to Oct. 8)   -- Chapter 4
*** Exam 3 is on Oct. 12 ***   (Consciousness)
(exam 3 covers Chapter 7 only)

Week 4 (Oct. 12 to Oct. 16)   -- Chapter 5
*** Lab 1 review & signup is on Oct. 16 ***   (Learning)
due date for Lab 1: Oct. 26

Week 5 (Oct. 19 to Oct. 22)   -- Chapter 6
*** Lab 2 review & signup is on Oct. 22 ***   (Memory)
due date for Lab 2: Nov. 2

Makeup Test date: Oct. 23 (for Exams 1, 2, & 3 and Quizzes 1 & 2)

Week 6 (Oct. 26 to Oct. 29)   -- Chapters 8 & 9
*** Lab 3 review & signup is on Oct. 29 ***   (Dev. Psychology)
due date for Lab 3: Nov. 9

Week 7 (Nov. 2 to Nov. 5)   -- Chapter 13
*** Lab 4 review & signup is on Nov. 5 ***   (Stress, Coping, & Health)
due date for Lab 4: Nov. 16

Week 8 (Nov. 9 to Nov. 12)   -- Chapter 12
*** Lab 5 review is on Nov. 12 ***   (Personality & Testing)
due date for Lab 5: Nov. 23

Weeks 9 & 10 (Nov. 16 to Nov. 24)   -- Chapters 14 & 15
*** Exam 4 is on Nov. 25 ***   (Psychological Disorders & Therapy)
(exam 4 covers only Chapts. 15 & 16)

Week 11 (Nov. 30 to Dec. 4)   -- Chapter 16
*** Exam 5 is on Dec. 4 ***   (Social Psychology)
(exam 5 covers Chapter 18 only)

Makeup Test date: Finals Week (for Exams 4 & 5 and Quizzes 3, 4, 5, & 6)

Evaluation

      Exams (250 pts. total): Five multiple-choice/short-answer exams will be administered during the quarter (see readings schedule for designated exam Fridays). These exams cover lecture and text material for the segment listed on the readings list and are worth 50 points each. NOTE: 10 POINTS WILL BE TAKEN OFF ALL LATE EXAMS UNLESS DOCTOR'S EXCUSE (OR OTHER VALID EXCUSE). I will set aside in-class time to review information concerning the exam on the class day prior to each major exam. I will also be happy to meet with you to cover questions during office hours.

      Quizzes (120 pts. total): There will be 6 quizzes held during the quarter. These quizzes are given on weeks when there is not a major exam and will cover reading materials for that week only. They will consist of 5 multiple choice questions. Each quiz will be worth 20 points. No makeups of these quizzes will be given without medical OR otherwise valid excuses.

      Labs (300 pts. total): There will be a total of six graded laboratory units consisting of a variety of activities including computerized mini-experiments, observational opportunities, etc. These labs will be introduced/reviewed on designated Fridays and completed outside regular class time. All work is expected to be done on an individual basis (i.e., no "group" papers) and are worth 50 points each. NOTE: 10 POINTS WILL BE TAKEN OFF ALL LATE LABS UNLESS DOCTOR'S EXCUSE (OR OTHER VALID EXCUSE).

      Classroom Participation/Attendance (55 pts. total): Participation points will be awarded for your presence in the classroom. On 11 different randomly selected occasions throughout the quarter, I will collect in-class exercise sheets and use those as indicators of attendance.

Extra Credit (30 pts. possible): You may earn extra credit points through participation in department experiments (as they become available), by bringing in clippings from magazines or newspaper that illustrate examples of the theories we'll be talking about, by writing brief summaries of TV shows or movies with a psychological theme, by writing about personal experiences that are relevant to topics discussed in the text or class, or by writing brief summaries of journal articles or books you've read concerning psychology (some examples will be shown in class or handed out by your instructor). Additionally, extra credit questions will periodically appear on exams. You will earn at least 1 extra credit point per item/event and you can earn up to 30 extra credit points. I will bring extra credit forms with me to class on a weekly basis (generally on Fridays).

Grading
(Total of 725 points possible)
The following distribution will be used for final grades.

GRADE		POINTS NEEDED	GRADE		POINTS NEEDED
4.0	(95%)	688	2.4	(79%)	573
3.9	(94%)	681	2.3	(78%)	566
3.8	(93%)	674	2.2	(77%)	558
3.7	(92%)	667	2.1	(76%)	551
3.6	(91%)	660	2.0	(75%)	544
3.5	(90%)	653	1.9	(74%)	537
3.4	(89%)	645	1.8	(73%)	529
3.3	(88%)	638	1.7	(72%)	522
3.2	(87%)	631	1.6	(71%)	515
3.1	(86%)	624	1.5	(70%)	508
3.0	(85%)	616	1.4	(69%)	500
2.9	(84%)	609	1.3	(68%)	493
2.8	(83%)	602	1.2	(67%)	486
2.7	(82%)	595	1.1	(66%)	479
2.6	(81%)	588	1.0	(65%)	471
2.5	(80%)	580	0.0	(< 65%)	< 471

Writing Assignments in the Introductory Class

As student writing skills have deteriorated, educators have become increasingly reluctant to include writing assignments as a course requirement. If this deterioration is to be reversed, it seems apparent that instructors in disciplines other than English must assume some of the responsibility for providing writing experiences for students. The method of assigning a few short papers on specific topics is generally better than assigning a single, lengthy paper on a topic outside of the scope of the textbook. Keep in mind your goals for these assignments: to give students another opportunity to sharpen their writing skills, to foster the development of critical thinking, and to provide them with assignments that have direct impact on their comprehension of the text content.

Criteria for Writing Assignments:

1. The assignments should be related to the objectives of the course. They should do such things as increase insight into psychological concepts, develop critical thinking skills, stimulate personal growth, or develop appreciation of psychology as an empirical science.
2. The requirements of each assignment should be clearly worded. Instructions should give detailed information on how the paper is to be prepared. The topics of papers should be described in such a way that the possibility of misinterpretation is minimized. You may need to give a step-by-step plan for a paper, or enumerate the points you expect to be covered.
3. State a specific purpose or audience for the paper. The instructor is the traditional audience for students' papers, and since you know so much, students tend to expect that they can omit important information or comprehensive explanations. An example of a specific purpose would be to encourage a friend to see a behavior therapist about a particular phobia. The targeted audience could be students who have not taken introductory psychology, the readers of Parents Magazine, or a person who has written to Dear Abby about a psychological problem.
4. Inform students about the criteria you will use to evaluate their papers.

(Note from TJM: I use a scoring rubric such as follows for one-page papers on a chapter from the textbook and actually give students a copy of the rubric so they know ahead of time the basis for grades I will assign on the paper.)

Scoring Rubric: Scoring for contents and each objective will be performed according to the following scoring rubric:

a. Contents:
    5 - 6 pts. = summary statement given; all major points/concepts highlighted.
    3 - 4 pts. = all major points/concepts highlighted.
    1 - 2 pts. = some major points/concepts highlighted; some errors might be noted.
    0 pts. = major inaccuracies in information highlighted.

b. Objective 1: reviewing important research issue and results

7 - 8 pts. = student is able to accurately identify major key results, assumptions and logic in the research issue.
5 - 6 pts. = student is able to accurately identify some of the key results, assumptions and logic in the research issue.
3 - 4 pts. = student reviews some of the results, assumptions and logic in the research issue but may have some inaccuracies.
1 - 2 pts. = student may review some results but supplements those with views based on self-interest or preconceptions (i.e., non-empirical data).
0 pt. = no evidence that this objective has been addressed.

c. Objective 2: alternative perspectives
7 - 8 pts. = student provides an accurate analysis and evaluation of major alternative points of view.
5 - 6 pts. = student offers some analysis and evaluation of obvious alternative points of view.
3 - 4 pts. = student superficially evaluates obvious alternative points of view or thoroughly presents only 1 perspective.
1 - 2 pts. = student ignores obvious alternative points of view and/or makes significant errors in the perspectives presented.
0 pt. = no evidence that this objective has been addressed.

d. Objective 3: drawing conclusions
7 - 8 pts. = based on information from Obj. 1 and Obj. 2, student is able to develop warranted, non-biased, empirically-based conclusions.
5 - 6 pts. = based on information from Obj. 1 and Obj. 2, student is able to develop warranted, non-biased conclusions.
3 - 4 pts. = student develops some unwarranted conclusions (based on information from Obj. 1 and 2) but attempts to draw the conclusion logically.
1 - 2 pts. = student argues/develops conclusions using fallacious or irrelevant information and makes unwarranted claims based largely on personal opinion.
0 pt. = no evidence that this objective has been addressed.

Topics for and Discussing Requirements for Student Papers
Student papers may include a number of topics ranging from student's reactions to chapter readings, examining personal experiences in light of topics discussed in class, reports on scholarly psychology journal articles, or reports of student research projects you assign to the class. Again, the selection of topics should meet with your goals and objectives for the course. To help students understand the requirements and your expectations for their writing assignments, provide a handout with the following:
1. General discussion of written assignments: In this section of the handout, tell students such things as how many papers are required, how long each paper is to be, how topics are to be selected, and whether or not papers that receive a low score can be rewritten. Student should not be allowed to write more than one paper related to a chapter. State clearly when papers are due. You should collect the papers throughout the

term to prevent students from handing in all their papers at once, for instance on the last day of the term. (Note from TJM: many writing instructors urge a
write-rewrite method to help students learn writing skills by reading your reactions to an initial draft, which they can then correct and return to you. A more lengthily process but one that frequently helps students to improve writing based on feedback and practice with writing.)
2. Specific guidelines for preparation of papers: In this section tell students such things as: use 8 1/2 x 11 paper, write on one side only, put the title, assignment number and their name at the top of the first page, don't put pages in plastic covers or the paper in a binder, type using double-spacing and one-inch margins. It is a good idea to discuss plagiarism with students and to indicate how students should handle quoted material (Note from TJM: the APA Publications Manual may serve as a discipline specific resource concerning these issues.)
3. Evaluation criteria: the three traditional criteria for evaluation of papers are content or ideas, organization, and mechanics. You may want to assign weights to each of these criteria. For example, if the maximum number of points for a paper is 25, you might assign 12 for content, 8 for organization, and 5 for mechanics.
4. Topics: Provide a chapter-by-chapter list of the topics or questions from which students can choose. Having this list at the beginning of the term gives students a chance to make tentative choices of topics that interest them.

Evaluation of Student Writing

There are two extremes to be avoided in evaluating papers: one is overgrading and the other is putting a grade on the paper with no marks or comment to justify your evaluation. Both extremes tend to discourage students; a paper without any marks doesn't teach students how to improve their performance, and a paper filled with comments is likely to overwhelm and discourage students.

To avoid both extremes you might devise an evaluation plan that is relatively easy to use and to communicate to students. One author suggested drawing a straight line under ideas or other aspects of a paper that you particularly like, and to draw a wavy line under passages that are poorly written or confusing. This system can be extended by developing a code to indicate the reason for a wavy line, for example, G for poor grammar, U for unsupported generalization, I for irrelevance, and E for erroneous information or conclusion.

Critical thinking is an aspect of student writing that you may want to emphasize in evaluating papers. Wade & Tavris (1998) discuss the following guidelines for critical thinking in their introductory text:

Ask questions; be willing to wonder.
Define the problem.
Examine the evidence.
Analyze assumptions and biases.
Avoid emotional reasoning: If I feel this way, it must be true.
Don't oversimplify.
Consider other interpretations.
Tolerate uncertainty.

You are likely to find that some of these guidelines are violated rather frequently in student writing.

Further Thoughts on Student Writing

Having students write short papers during the term has been suggested. If you do this, consider having students read outstanding papers to the class. This give recognition to the writer and provides a model of good writing for other students.

A psychological diary provides writing experience and alerts students to applications of psychological concepts. In writing the diary, students describe everyday events related to what they are learning in class, for example: a student hears a commercial for a cold remedy on TV, and wonders about the basis for the claim that the product is twice as effective as remedy X; or a student notes that her father trots out all his dissonance-reducing strategies whenever something goes wrong with the lemon he bought.

Some instructors have students write a paragraph in class expressing their opinion on an issue, evaluating a film, or describing a film. It is probably best not to grade these mini-papers, but it may encourage attendance if students are rewarded with a few points for participation.

Many students find writing distasteful, but they are aware of their deficiency in written communication, and are apprehensive about the implications of the problem for future employment. There may be nothing you can do for your students that will benefit them as much as writing assignments.
(Additional notes from TJM: If your university has a writer's center, become familiar with it. Send students who have particular difficulty in writing in that direction. Attend writing-in-the-curriculum workshops if your university holds them. Provide students with example papers to help as a framework--sometimes I write my own example of a writing assignment, although I notice that more insecure students will attempt to merely mimic my paper....at least they're writing though.)

On teaching sensitive issues in the college classroom..........

Several years ago, at the end of what I thought had been a successful one-day workshop on inclusion of gender issues in the psychology curriculum, one undergraduate student leapt to his feet during the closing evaluation period and shouted "I'm sick of all this male-bashing!!!" I was totally bewildered.....the room fell into an astonished, awkward silence...how had this young man participated in an 8-hour workshop that was based in exploration of almost mundane empirical data and objective, balanced theory discussions and yet experienced such an obviously emotionally-charged, personal reaction? How was it that after similar presentations some students had offered that gender issues were "old hat"? Why were some students grumbling about having to satisfy our university's new requirement for taking a diversity credit for graduation as simply another tacked on requirement? At the same time, well-educated colleagues have referred to gender and multicultural issues as dead, superficial, and politically correct agendas being forced into the college curriculum. In stating the obvious, both students and faculty are likely to have very mixed reactions, ranging from benign apathy to overt hostility toward inclusive courses and textbooks. Paradoxically, racism and sexism continue to influence, restrict, and damage the lives of countless numbers of people in our country. For academics in psychology, some issues to consider include the extent to which our disciplinary theory, research, and practice reflects a psychology of humanity as opposed to a psychology of the select.

Lisa Whitten has suggested that, since one of the few requirements for earning a college degree is that a student must enroll in classes, this is often the ideal opportunity to have an impact on students regarding their racial attitudes, knowledge, and beliefs, and it must not be missed (pg. 182). For faculty to engage in multicultural and gender inclusive instruction, she suggests that faculty must be aware of their own racial and cultural (and gender) prejudices, and be prepared for the variety of student reactions to the presentation of this type of material. She includes the following as possible student reactions: ethnocentricity and lack of empathy, denial of the problem/flight into health, defensiveness, frustration and anger, acting-out behavior, apathy/silence, despair, a positive sense of affirmation and empathy.

Whitten offers some effective strategies for presenting racial, cultural, and gender issues in class:

...   creating clear ground rules for discussion: creating a safe environment for discussion is crucial and rules for discussion can be established and modeled by the instructor. I have found that incorporating students' suggestions in developing ground rules facilitates ownership of the classroom experience and actually encourages more participation in discussion. Frequently suggestions include not interrupting, not dominating conversation, using respectful language, using each other's names in discussion, using "I" statements. Whitten also suggests (and I agree) that instructors may also wish to model their own process (i.e., struggles and thoughts) regarding the topics to demonstrate to students critical thinking modes of addressing diversity.

...   recognizing individual and cultural differences: students will vary in their levels of ethnic/racial identity and Whitten urges that these differences should be kept in mind when preparing instructional materials. Additionally, cultural differences regarding classroom conduct, expression of ideas, and interpersonal interactions should be kept in mind.

...   facilitating inclusion and cohesion in the classroom: course materials should be oriented to include worldviews representing various cultures. Additionally, discussions focusing on similarities and differences across cultures may contribute to students' feelings of being valued and recognized within the class.

...   encouraging broad participation: in discussions, some students are more practiced or feel more confident in offering their reactions or opinions. Whitten urges faculty to encourage, incorporate, and support the responses of less-vocal students. One technique I have used to encourage more extensive participation is to ask each student to write down 1-2 reactions to a question, and then either ask each student in turn what they've written, or call on a representative sample of students, varying who gets called upon across the quarter. I also make sure to thank students for their observations, especially when their observation involves expressing a sensitive or perhaps unpopular perspective.

...   facilitating a classroom atmosphere rather than group therapy atmosphere: Whitten cautions that faculty should avoid interpreting students' comments or behaviors and instead should remember to facilitate discussions through active listening such as paraphrasing and mirroring so that students might feel they have been heard and acknowledged.

... encouraging objectivity: especially if students' comments are volatile or contain overgeneralizations, faculty can manage the discussion by encouraging a critical thinking focus, having students rephrase their original statements, using humor to diffuse the situation, or mirroring feelings being expressed. Use of relevant, local examples of topics may make concepts feel more important and immediate.

... recognizing and managing diversity in academic preparedness: faculty must remember the various levels of academic preparation and learning styles for students in the introductory psychology course. To that end, visual/auditory/tactile experiences, out-of-class review sessions, group study, linking lesser-prepared students with better-prepared students may be included in your pedagogy.

... infusing diversity topics across the curriculum: here Whitten urges faculty to discuss diversity across the quarter, not during sections where it seems to be more easily applied.

... using collaborative learning strategies: small group exercises, presentations, and written assignments encourage students to work together.

(Note: many of the exercises/activities provided in this manual are oriented toward small group work and discussion).

... sharing experiences with faculty: Whitten suggests that group discussions with colleagues to share ideas, concerns for classroom activity and management, discuss audio/visual materials, develop resources can be helpful. At my university I developed a Introductory Psychology interest group among the faculty who teach the course and we have discussed the goals and objectives for the course, pedagogy, materials, etc. Moreover, frequent discussions and meetings with those faculty currently assigned the course keep us in touch with the day-to-day problems arising in our courses on an on-going basis. Additionally, I frequently discuss issues of inclusion with a group of faculty at our university who are actively involved in developing inclusive course curricula. They have been a marvelous support group and sounding board.

In the 9 years since leaving graduate school, I admit my personal experiences with developing a more inclusive introductory psychology course have been both painful and exhilarating, but have certainly pushed me into exploring a broader set of intellectual and practical pedagogical issues than those to which I was exposed during my graduate school experience. As a result, I approach instruction with enthusiasm and the full realization that we have a distance to go in the discipline before we'll see a transformed discipline of psychology. Textbooks such as Uba and Huang move us in that direction. I applaud their effort.

Acknowledgements

This has been for Hayward...
flesh of my flesh, bone of my bone.....I will always love you

CHAPTER 1

INTRODUCTION: WHAT IS PSYCHOLOGY?

Chapter Overview
    Learning Objectives
    Chapter Outline

Additional Lecture Ideas
    Lecture Topics
    Additional Readings

In-Class Activities and Demonstrations
    Activities and Demonstrations
    Sources for Additional Activities
    Journey II Software

World Wide Web

Audio-Visual Support

Handout and Transparency Masters

Chapter Overview

Learning Objectives

After studying this chapter, you should be able to do the following:

1. Define psychology and its main goals.

2. Describe the seven major perspectives in psychology.

3. Identify several areas of study in psychology.

4. Explain the scientific method.

5. Describe four data-gathering strategies used by psychologists.

6. Explain how to interpret psychological research

Chapter Outline

INTRODUCTION: WHAT IS PSYCHOLOGY?

I. What is Psychology? Goals and History
  A. Defining Psychology
    1. The study of behavior (observable actions), including mental processes (thinking, remembering, feeling)
  B. Goals of Psychology
    1. Describe
    2. Explain
    3. Predict
    4. Alter or control
  C. Historical Foundations of Psychology
    1. The emphasis on rational analysis and observation
    2. Wundt: first laboratory & introspection
    3. Titchener: structuralism
    4. James: functionalism
    5. Contributions by women and minority psychologists

II. Modern Psychology: Alternative Perspectives and Uses
  A. Psychological Perspectives
    1. Psychodynamic Perspectives
      a. <u>Leaders</u>: Freud
      b. <u>Underlying assumptions/concepts</u>: the role of the unconscious; intrapsychic forces/conflict
    2. Learning Perspectives (Behaviorism & Social Learning)
      a. <u>Leaders</u>: Pavlov, Watson, Thorndike, Skinner, Bandura
      b. <u>Underlying assumptions/concepts</u>: the S-R approach; de-emphasis on mental processes; cross-species applications; the S-O-R approach & the influence of cognition
    3. Cognitive Perspectives
      a. <u>Underlying assumptions</u>: focus on thinking processes; information-processing models
    4. Humanistic Perspectives
      a. <u>Leaders</u>: Maslow, Rogers
      b. <u>Underlying assumptions/concepts</u>: the role of choice; potentiality
    5. Biopsychological Perspectives
      a. <u>Underlying assumptions</u>: studying how brain, chemicals, biology, genetics affect behavior
    6. Cultural Perspectives
      a. <u>Underlying assumptions/concepts</u>: behavior is a consequence of culture; cross-cultural & multicultural approaches

7. Gender Perspectives
    a. <u>Underlying assumptions/concepts</u>: sex v. gender; gender differences

B. Areas of Study in Psychology
1. Example sub-disciplines in Psychology
   a. Biopsychology
   b. Developmental Psychology
   c. Clinical Psychology
   d. Social Psychology

C. Careers in Psychology
1. Example careers for Psychologists
   a. Sport Psychology
   b. Forensic Psychology
   c. Environmental Psychology
   d. Industrial/Organizational Psychology
   e. Counseling/Clinical Psychology
   f. School Psychology

III. Research Methods in Psychology
A. Introduction
1. Basic v. applied research

B. The Scientific Method: Combining Analysis and Evidence
1. Scientific Method
   a. <u>Concepts</u>: theory, hypothesis, data
   b. dependable, accurate procedural standards
2. Study design
   a. <u>Concepts</u>: controlled observation; eliminating extraneous, confounding variables
3. Beyond the Study Subjects
   a. <u>Concepts</u>: population, sample, subjects/participants/respondents; representative samples; (unbiased) random samples; generalizability of findings
4. Producing Consistent, Accurate Information
   a. <u>Concepts</u>: replication; operational definitions; reliability; validity

C. Types of Studies: Alternative Methods
1. Surveys
   a. description
   b. examples
   c. advantages
   d. disadvantages
   e. <u>concepts</u>: correlations (negative, positive)
2. Field Studies (Naturalistic Observation)
   a. description
   b. examples

        c. advantages
        d. disadvantages
3. Case Studies (Case Histories)
        a. description
        b. examples
        c. advantages
        d. disadvantages
4. Experimental Studies
        a. description
        b. <u>concepts</u>: independent variables, dependent variables, experimental group, control group, random assignment, matching, placebo, single-blind experiment, double-blind experiment
        c. advantages
        d. disadvantages

C. Ethical Issues in Psychological Research
1. Minimizing exposure to physical/psychological risks
2. Use of Institutional Review Boards
3. The use of deception & debriefing sessions
4. Informing participants about unpleasant consequences
5. Freedom to withdraw from research
6. Confidentiality
7. Informed consent
8. Use of animal participants

IV. Interpreting Psychological Research: Alternative Meanings
A. The Final Step: analysis of results
B. Looking at the Group, Remembering the Individual
1. The Search for Group Differences
    a. the role of journals
    b. statistical v. meaningful differences
    c. difference v. similarity
2. Remembering the Individual
    a. individual differences & within-group variability
    b. knowing the "exception to the finding"

C. More than One Way to Interpret Data
1. The search for plausible alternative explanations: viewing results through different theoretical lenses
2. The effects of historical, social, economic, and cultural factors on the meaning given to findings

D. A Critical Thinking Approach
1. rational analysis based on evidence; avoiding rejecting conclusions because they don't match personal feelings
2. ethnocentrism
3. embracing uncertainty and alternative explanations
4. oversimplification
5. ignoring evidence

Additional Lecture Topics

1. <u>Meet the Faculty: A Poster Session on Local Research</u>
Early in the term, arrange a 1-day poster session (a la WPA, MPA, EPA, etc.) to introduce your students to the current research interests and activities of faculty in your department. Ahead of time invite the faculty in your department to prepare or use last year's posters that they may have presented at conferences for concurrent presentations held during class time. Those faculty who would rather present information concerning their unique course offerings could develop posters including syllabi, example activities, etc. For an activity, students (much as we do during conferences) would be expected to tour the poster location, talk with faculty members, obtain information that coincides with the research/theory sections of Chapter 1 and report on their "findings" concerning 2-3 faculty members.

2. <u>Founders: Up Close and Personal</u>
Make the theorists you describe in the theory section of the chapter come alive through photos and personalized information concerning their life histories. Most personality and history of psychology textbooks include life and times overviews for major theorists that give students an eye into the contemporary influences and personal events that often tended to influence eminent theorists in our discipline.

Some suggested sources for biographical information:

Fancher, R. (1979). <u>Pioneers of Psychology</u>. New York: Norton.

Feist, J. (1994). <u>Theories of Personality</u> (3rd Ed.). Madison: Brown & Benchmark.

O'Connell, A. & Russo, N. (Eds.) (1983). <u>Models of achievement: Reflections of eminent women in psychology</u>. New York: Columbia University Press.

O'Connell, A. & Russo, N. (Eds.) (1988). <u>Models of achievement: Reflections of eminent women in psychology (Vol. II)</u>. Hillsdale, NJ: Lawrence Erlbaum.

Schultz, D. & Schultz, S. (1992). <u>A History of Modern Psychology</u> (5th Ed.). Fort Worth: Harcourt Brace.

Thorne, B. & Henley, T. (1997). <u>Connections in the History and Systems of Psychology</u>. Boston: Houghton Mifflin.

3. <u>Research participant selection and its effect on theory</u>
In 1986, David Sears wrote on the impact of psychologists' use of college sophomores tested in academic settings (mainly the laboratory) using academic-like dependent measures. In his article, he argues that participants in this age range are likely to present some age-dependent characteristics that are exaggerated due to the laboratory environment. As a result, conclusions drawn from research may reflect unique qualities in participants, setting, and the interaction between the two. Although Sears speaks more specifically to the impact of these issues in

Social Psychology, many of his points could provide ripe discussion issues for the General/Introductory Psychology student. I frequently review this article for students, listing the various ways he sees the college student in the laboratory as unusual. One particularly interesting conclusion that I discuss is his assertion that the "....use of relatively well-educated subjects, selected for their superior cognitive skills, along with research sites, procedures, and tasks that promote dispassionate, academic-like information-processing, should help produce empirical evidence that portrays humans as dominated by cognitive processes....", a point that interfaces in an interesting way with the current rise in the cognitive perspective in psychology. Finally, I review the recommendations toward cautious interpretation of findings and a broader sample of participants. This is generally a real thinking article for students to digest.

    Source:

        Sears, D. (1986). College sophomores in the laboratory: Influences of a narrow data base on Social Psychology's view of human nature. Journal of Personal and Social Psychology, 51(3), 515-530.

4. Models for Transforming Psychology

Adopting a feminist perspective regarding the place of women in the curriculum, McIntosh (1983) identified five interactive phases through which scholarship in a discipline would progress to arrive, eventually, at full inclusion. Jane Torrey has written an interesting application of this model in her 1987 paper, "Phases of Feminist Re-Vision in the Psychology of Personality". Consider incorporating parts of her critical arguments after students have read the section concerning the role of women and people of color in psychology.

    Sources:

        McIntosh, P. (1983). Interactive phases of curricular re-vision: A feminist perspective. Working paper no. 124. Wellesley, MA: Wellesley College Center for Research on Women.

        Torrey, J. (1987) Phases of feminist re-vision in the Psychology of Personality. Teaching of Psychology, 14(3), 155-160.

5. The Cultural Context in Research Methods

Moghaddam, F., Taylor, D., & Wright, S. (1993) provide a very interesting perspective on the cultural context in which research is conducted. In Chapter 2 of their book, Social Psychology in Cross-Cultural Perspective, they review the use of culture as a subject variable in research as well as the cultural understandings that influence researcher and participant alike during the research process. Through the re-examination of some classic studies in Social Psychology, the authors point out some differences we might expect to observe when methodologies are transported across cultural settings. Discussion of this chapter exposes students to some of the intricacies involved in creating experiment scripts, as well as to issues involving shared meaning of language, the need for stimulus equivalence and back translation in survey, field study, and laboratory environments.

Source:
> Moghaddam, F., Taylor, D., & Wright, S. (1993). <u>Social Psychology in Cross-Cultural Perspective</u>. New York: Freeman.

6. <u>Ethical Guidelines for Psychologists</u>

As an expansion of the discussion concerning research methodologies, include a more in-depth presentation of the <u>Ethical Principles of Psychologists and Code of Conduct</u> (1992). In particular, cover Standards 6.06 (Planning Research) to 6.20 (Care and Use of Animals in Research). Consider also reviewing components of an informed consent form, perhaps from a previous research study conducted in your department. I also review forms used in the IRB proposal.

Source:
> American Psychological Association (1992). Ethical Principles of Psychologists and Code of Conduct. <u>American Psychologist</u>, <u>47</u>(12), 1597-1611.

7. How to read a psychological journal article.

Many students arrive at the General Psychology classroom with little prior experience in reading scientific journals generally or psychological journals in particular. If part of the expectation for the class involves reading and reporting on findings in journal articles in class or in papers, giving some pointers on how to read a psychological journal article would probably be helpful. Select a brief journal article and cover in some detail the APA format for the seven parts of most typical psychology articles. Consider covering some of the following issues:

Title & author:

What is the psychological phenomenon this article is addressing? (If you're doing a paper, the title of an article might be what first captures your eye and leads you to look more closely at whether it fits with your paper topic.)

Who wrote it? (Once you become familiar with an area of research, seeing a name that you recognize may tell you a bit about what to expect in the article.)

Abstract:

What is this article about; how did they do the work; what did they find? (The abstract provides a concise overview of the entire article and thus may help you determine if you want to read the whole thing.)

Introduction:

What is the question being addressed in this paper; how does the current study or paper address that problem? What are the specific hypotheses or predictions being tested in this research? (The introduction established the rationale for doing the current study or writing an in-depth paper. Previous research is reviewed, with general findings and/or shortcomings pointed out. Generally, interesting questions that remained after that research or reasons to believe that some other issues need to be addressed are stated as the bases for doing the current work.)

Method:

Who were participants in the study; what materials or apparati were used; what were the specific procedures used to conduct the study; what experimental design was used? (This section describes in detail how the study was conducted.)

Results:

What types of analyses were conducted to address the predictions; what were the findings for each prediction? (Descriptive and inferential statistics are used to describe the data obtained from the study. Tables and graphs may be used to summarize findings. Expected and unexpected results as well as the results from exploratory or additional analyses are presented.)

Discussion:
> *What conclusions does the author draw from the results? Are there limitations to the study? What further research might be suggested?* (The author(s) tie together the results with their original predictions and generally interpret their study through the context of gaps in earlier research literature. They explore problematic issues that emerged in the process of conducting and analyzing their study and look to theoretical or methodological questions that need to be addressed in future research.)

References:
> *What work has been referenced in the current article? Do I want to go find some of these articles for my own paper?* (The reference section tells us what journals to access for additional or more detailed information.)

Dissecting an article in this manner not only produces some immediate benefits for students in the Introductory Psychology class but also tends to interface well with the reading and writing requirements that most students will experience across the curriculum.

Source:
> Elmes, D., Kantowitz, B., & Roediger, H. (1985). <u>Research Methods in Psychology</u>. St. Paul: West Publ.

8. <u>So...thinking about being a psych major</u>?

If your university is anything like mine, the Introductory Psychology course is the first formal exposure to our discipline for many students. Moreover, most students tend to be in their first 2 years of college-level work and are, therefore, still considering what careers to pursue. Although the text gives students some ideas about possible career options, a bit more detail can be presented in the class. One source book, written by Betsy Morgan and Ann Korschgen, covers a number of FAQs such as "Should I be a psychology major?", "Will I get a job?", "What kinds of jobs are available?", "Will I make any money?", "How do I do a job search?", "Do I want to go to graduate school?", etc. I like to prepare a handout covering some of the major FAQs and interface that will the job market and application processes for local graduate programs (such as our own) early on in the quarter. Although the coverage doesn't need to occupy an entire lecture period, it provides potential majors or minors with some information and practical tips about where to go and of whom to ask questions.

Source:
> Morgan, B., & Korschgen, A. (1998). <u>Majoring in Psych? Career Options for Psychology Undergraduates</u>. Boston: Allyn and Bacon.

Suggestions for Additional Readings

Aguirre, A. & Baker, D. (Eds.) (1995). <u>Sources: Notable Selections in Race and Ethnicity.</u> Guilford, CN: Dushkin Publ.

Albert, R. D. (1988). The place of culture in modern psychology in Bronstein, P., & Quina, K. (Eds.) <u>Teaching the psychology of people: Readings for gender and sociocultural awareness.</u> Washington, DC: American Psychological Association.

Asch, A. (1988). Disability: Its place in the psychology curriculum in Bronstein, P., & Quina, K. (Eds.) <u>Teaching the psychology of people: Readings for gender and sociocultural awareness.</u> Washington, DC: American Psychological Association.

Bennett, S. (1994). The American Indian: A psychological overview. in Malpass, R. & Lonner, W. (Eds.) <u>Psychology and Culture.</u> Boston: Allyn and Bacon.

Bohan, J. S. (Ed.). (1992). <u>Re-Placing Women in Psychology: Readings toward a more inclusive history.</u> Dubuque, IA: Kendall/Hunt Publ.

Bronstein, P., & Paludi, M. (1988). The Introductory Psychology Course From a Broader Human Perspective in Bronstein, P., & Quina, K. (Eds.) <u>Teaching the psychology of people: Readings for gender and sociocultural awareness.</u> Washington, DC: American Psychological Association.

Bronstein, P., & Quina, K. (Eds.) <u>Teaching the psychology of people: Readings for gender and sociocultural awareness.</u> Washington, DC: American Psychological Association.

Espin, O. (1995). On knowing you are the unknown: Women of color constructing psychology. in Adleman, J. & Enguidanos, G. (Eds.) <u>Racism in the Lives of Women: Testimony, Theory, and Guides to Antiracist Practice.</u> New York: Haworth Press.

Espin, O. & Gawelek, M. (1992). Women's Diversity: Ethnicity, Race, Class, and Gender in Theories of Feminist Psychology. in Brown, L. & Ballou, M. (Eds.) <u>Personality and Psychopathology: Feminist Reappraisals.</u> New York: Guilford Press.

Fox, R. (1996). Bisexuality in Perspective: A Review of Theory and Research in Firestein, B. A. (Ed.) <u>Bisexuality: The Psychology and Politics of an Invisible Minority.</u> Thousand Oaks, CA: Sage Publ.

Greene, B. (1996). Lesbian and Gay Sexual Orientations: Implications for Clinical Training, Practice, and Research in Greene, B., and Herek, G. M. (Eds.) <u>Lesbian and Gay Psychology: Theory, Research, and Clinical Applications.</u> Thousand Oaks, CA: Sage Publ.

Guthrie, R. J. (1976). <u>Even the rat was white: A historical view of psychology.</u> New York: Harper and Row.

Jones, J. (1994). The African American: A duality dilemma? in Malpass, R. & Lonner, W. (Eds.) <u>Psychology and Culture.</u> Boston: Allyn and Bacon.

Jones, R. L. (1980). <u>Black Psychology</u> (2nd Edition). New York: Harper & Row

Keith-Spiegel, P., & Koocher, G. P. (1985). <u>Ethics in psychology:</u>

Professional standards and cases. New York: Random House.

Korn, J. H. (1988). Students' roles, rights, and responsibilities as research participants. Teaching of Psychology, 15, 74-78.

Lee. D. & Hall, C. (1994). Being Asian in North America. in Malpass, R. & Lonner, W. (Eds.) Psychology and Culture. Boston: Allyn and Bacon

Marin, G. (1994). The experience of being a Hispanic in the United States. in Malpass, R. & Lonner, W. (Eds.) Psychology and Culture. Boston: Allyn and Bacon.

May, V. M. (1988). Even the rat was white and male: Teaching the psychology of black women in Bronstein, P., & Quina, K. (Eds.) Teaching the psychology of people: Readings for gender and sociocultural awareness. Washington, DC: American Psychological Association.

McIntosh, P. (1988). White privilege and male privilege: A personal account of coming to see correspondence through work in Women's Studies (Working Paper, No. 189). Wellesley, MA: Center for Research on Women, Wellesley College.

O'Connell, A. & Russo, N. (Eds.) (1980). Eminent women in psychology: Models of achievement [special issue]. Psychology of Women Quarterly, 5(1).

O'Connell, A. & Russo, N. (Eds.) (1983). Models of achievement: Reflections of eminent women in psychology. New York: Columbia University Press.

O'Connell, A. & Russo, N. (Eds.) (1988). Models of achievement: Reflections of eminent women in psychology (Vol. II).Hillsdale, NJ: Lawrence Erlbaum.

O'Connell, A. & Russo, N. (1990). Women in psychology: A bio-bibliographic sourcebook. New York: Greenwood.

Padilla, A. (Ed.). (1995). Hispanic Psychology: Critical Issues in Theory and Research. Thousand Oaks, CA: Sage Publ.

Paludi, M. (1998). The Psychology of Women. Upper Saddle River, NJ: Prentice Hall.

Pettijohn, T. (Ed.) (1994). Sources: Notable Selections in Psychology. Guilford, CN: Dushkin Publ.

Quina, K., & Kulberg, J. M. (1988). The History of Psychology Course in Bronstein, P., & Quina, K. (Eds.) Teaching the psychology of people: Readings for gender and sociocultural awareness. Washington, DC: American Psychological Association.

Reed, J. G., & Baxter, P. M. (1992). Library Use: A handbook for psychology. Washington, D.C: American Psychological Association.

Sinha, D. (1996). Chapter 2: Cross-Cultural Psychology : The Asian Scenario in Pandy, J., Sinha, D., and Bhawuk, D. (Eds.) Asian Contributions to Cross-Cultural Psychology. Thousand Oaks, CA: Sage Publ.

Stanovich, K. E. (1988). How to think straight about psychology (2nd Ed.). Glenview, IL: Scott, Foresman

Vasquez, M. J., and Baron, A. (1988). The Psychology of the Chicano Experience: A Sample Course Structure in Bronstein, P., & Quina, K. (Eds.)

Teaching the psychology of people: Readings for gender and sociocultural awareness. Washington, DC: American Psychological Association.

Yee, A., Fairchild, H., Weizmann, F., & Wyatt, G. (1993). Addressing Psychology's Problems with Race. American Psychologist, 48 (11), 1132-1140.

In-Class Activities and Demonstrations

Activities and Demonstrations

1. Psychology and You - Have students complete Handout # 1.1: Psychology and You as a first day activity. Questions provided on the handout will expose students to differences in definitions about psychology (how does it relate to other disciplines in terms of theory/methodology, what are considered "appropriate" topics for study within the discipline), how they perceive that the discipline has affected them either directly or indirectly, and their personal goals for studying psychology (to satisfy a credit requirement, to explore whether psychology might be their career choice).

2. You and culture: Have students read Box 1.1: Alternative Perspectives--Can't I Just Be An "American"? and then complete Handout # 1.2: You and culture. After completing the handout, have students review their responses in small groups. Allow enough time for each member of the small group to discuss his or her answers and then cover the questions as a class and look for any trends in experiences.

3. TRAIL Blazing: Using Transparency Masters 1.1 - 1.5, review with students the Checking Your TRAIL sections in the chapter. Have students work in small groups to answer the questions and then review with the class at large to tie the text reading to activity in class.

4. Reaching Critical Mass: Using Transparency Masters 1.6 - 1.10, review with students the Critical Thinking sections in the chapter. Have students work in small groups to answer the questions and then review with the class at large to tie the text reading to activity in class.

5. Finding Diversity in Psychology Textbooks: In a review of introductory textbooks, Hogben & Waterman (1997) noted that some changes are occurring in the level of diversity demonstrated in current as opposed to older textbooks in psychology. However, some ethnic groups still tend to be under-represented. Perhaps in conjunction with the suggested lecture addition concerning the transforming of psychology, have students look for evidence of increased diversification in an analysis of the photographs used in Introductory Psychology textbooks. Using Handout #1.3: Diversity in Introductory Psychology textbooks, divide students into small groups and have them compare the photographs in 2 chapters out of an older textbook with the photographs in similar chapters out of the Uba & Huang textbook. (Most libraries carry copies of older versions of texts and many faculty have collections of texts from which one could develop the pool of texts to be used for this exercise). After students have compared the texts, compile the data and review it in class.

Source: Hogben, M., and Waterman, C. (1997). Are all of your students represented in their textbooks? A content analysis of coverage of diversity issues in Introductory Psychology textbooks. <u>Teaching of Psychology</u>, 24(2), 95-100.

Finding Psychologists in Your Community: Using <u>Handout # 1.4: Psychologists in Our Community</u>, have students work in pairs or small groups to discover different types of psychologists currently working in the community. As an out-of-class activity to be discussed later in class, have students call private practice offices, assessment centers, student counseling services, local hospitals, mental health facilities, universities/colleges, etc. and inquire as to the numbers of psychologists on staff, their educational backgrounds, and their duties. Students might also ask questions concerning how many clients or consumers are seen each year to assess the impact of the presence of psychologists on the community and whether student volunteers are welcomed (if so, what could a student volunteer do there?). Finally, after the class has had an opportunity to share their findings, have each group consider the availability and impact of psychological services available in your community. Are gender and multi-cultural issues sufficiently addressed?

Research Methods and Errors: Have students complete <u>Handout #1.5: Research Methods and Errors</u>. For each of the six examples of research methods provided, students are to identify the type of methodology, any potential problem with how the method was applied or conducted, and a possible correction for that problem.

> *Answers*:
> **Example 1:**
> <u>Method</u>: survey
> <u>Problem</u>: nonrepresentative sample of respondents (only those who happen to stick around prior to Thanksgiving holiday)
> <u>Correction</u>: administer individual evaluations immediately after each film
> **Example 2:**
> <u>Method</u>: Telephone survey
> <u>Problem</u>: nonrepresentative sample (only those students with phones, only from the 3 biggest schools -- rather than a distributed sampling across schools of different sizes, only those students who happen to be home on the day the survey was conducted); possibility of students feeling coerced due to superintendent asking them to participate; parental informed consent doesn't appear to have been obtained
> <u>Correction</u>: Ethics issues would need to be addressed (obtain

parental consent); have someone other than superintendent conduct the survey (e.g., student council representatives), conduct the survey across a broader sample of students to include those with/without telephones, those from different kinds of schools

Example 3:
Method: Naturalistic Observation
Problem: can't determine the causes of different social behaviors due to experimenter's lack of control over the situations (different types of music, different types of beverages for example)
Correction: Quasi-experiments where the experimenter stages dances and controls for music/beverages

Example 4:
Method: Case study
Problem: low generalizability
Correction: conduct interviews with children from across a variety of child-rearing experiences

Example 5:
Method: Correlational study
Problem: implying causation from a correlational study
Correction: rewrite the conclusions drawn by the tabloid author to be consistent with implications of a correlational study or conduct an experiment to varying weight and study the effects of that change on IQ

Example 6:
Method: Experiment
Problem: temperatures of beverages are confounded with type of beverage
Correction: offer students in the latte group iced lattes or offer students caffeinated and decaffeinated lattes

Critical Thinking and Media Reports of Research

Randolph Smith expresses a sentiment that resonates with the experience of many Introductory Psychology students when he says that "Many students who enroll in psychology courses are convinced that they already know something about psychology because they have read about psychology in the popular press--the newspapers and magazines found in supermarkets and bookstores." Students, like many readers of the popular press, tend to rely on these distillations of research and theory to quickly learn about our discipline due to lack of time, energy, or the expertise and ability to conduct such research on their own. However, due to the summary nature of these reviews, information needed to critically evaluate the research is not given and sometimes the conclusions drawn about a piece of research are exaggerated or blatantly incorrect. Providing your students with two examples of inappropriate interpretations of research by popular media might highlight the need for in-depth critical thinking.

Example 1: Patricia Connor-Greene has developed an exercise contrasting a *USA Today* report on Simon LeVay's work on brain differences between heterosexual and homosexual men with LeVay's original article reported in *Science*. She has students read both articles and note ways in which the former article leads the reader to form inaccurate impressions of the purpose and findings discussed in the latter. For your class, place both articles on reserve and, using **Handout Master # 6: LeVay vs. *USA Today***, have students compare and contrast the two articles out side of class time. Review and discuss both articles in an in-class discussion period.

Example 2: For a somewhat less controversial example, consider Smith's example of differences between *The Star*'s report of Dr. Catherine Fichten's work on the accuracy and usefulness of horoscopes and her original work, reported in *The Journal of Psychology*. The Star misreported Dr. Fichten as finding that daily and monthly horoscope forecasts had validity (i.e., were really true). Again, place both articles on reserve, and using **Handout Master # 7: Fichten vs. *The Star***, have students compare and contrast the two articles for use in an in-class discussion.

Sources:

Connor-Greene, P. (1993). From the Laboratory to the Headlines: Teaching critical evaluation of press reports of research. Teaching of Psychology, 20(3), 167-169.

Fichten, C. S., & Sunerton, B. (1983). Popular horoscopes and the "Barnum" effect. The Journal of Psychology, 114, 123-134.

Horoscopes really true, says psychologists. (1983, October 11). The Star, p. 32.

LeVay, S. (1991). A difference in hypothalamic structure between heterosexual and homosexual men. Science, 253, 1034-1037.

Snider, M. (1991, August 30). Gay men show cell distinction. USA Today, p. 1D.

Smith, R. (1995). Psychology and the popular press. Challenging your preconceptions: Thinking Critically about psychology. Pacific Grove: Brooks/Cole

<u>Blocking your observer bias</u>

This exercise is an adaptation of one reported by Miriam Goldstein and her colleagues in Teaching of Psychology. To demonstrate the impact of observer bias, Goldstein et al. (1994) had student "experimenters" observe a classmate attempting to complete a series of three mirror-tracing tasks after supposedly drinking alcohol. The experimenters were to rate the classmate, who was a trained confederate and whose performance was previously practiced so as to be consistent across all trials, on how the alcohol had affected his/her speech and performance on the tasks. All observer-experimenters witnessed the "alcohol consumption" during staged "drink-mixing" phases prior to each performance trial. Results across two classes indicated that, indeed, experimenters rated increasing effects of alcohol in their confederate participants. Moreover, they acknowledged after the deception concerning the alcohol consumption had been revealed, that their judgments concerning the performance tasks were influenced by their "knowledge" that the classmate had consumed alcohol and their expectations about the effects of alcohol.

In this modification of Goldstein et al.'s exercise, subjects will put together small building block toys after supposedly drinking caffeinated beverages (soda) to test the hypothesis that consuming some of the super-caffeinated beverages currently on the market improves performance. In fact, in this exercise, the confederate subjects will be drinking decaffeinated soda.

Prior to the exercise, assign your class into small groups and select one
- student who is willing to act as the experimental subject. Meet with all "subjects" a day or so before the demonstration and have them practice putting together small building-block toys (the small packaged groups that create a single person, animal, or piece of machinery) until they are able to all do so easily within a specified time frame (2-3 minutes or so). Also provide them with a specified script for comments to make during their "performance" trials and discuss with the entire subject group how they should behave to develop some consistency across "subjects". For example, they might start off expressing a lack of confidence in themselves ("Wow...this is harder than I thought it would be") and then become increasingly satisfied with their work ("Now I'm catching on"). To increase student participation in the activity, you can have the "subject" group generate 3 slightly different versions of the script that all "subjects" will need to memorize and use on their 3 performance trials during the exercise. Needless to say, your subject confederates need to remember not to reveal themselves to their classmates until the debriefing phase of the exercise.
- Before beginning the exercise, you will need to set up a "caffeine station" in the classroom where you place your containers of soda, drinking glasses, etc. Of course, you'll also need to switch the contents of what appears to be some kind of super-caffeinated soda (e.g., *Jolt*) with decaffeinated soda some time prior to class.
- Begin the exercise by reviewing with the entire class the hypothesis you are testing in your experiment and the procedures to be used...very simply that 3 performance trials are to be conducted in each group and that prior to each performance trial, the "subject" is to consume one glass of super-caffeinated beverage. Observer/experimenters are to rate the subject on each of the 3 performance trials on physical

skillfulness of performance, cognitive focus while performing the task, and the creative quality of their performance product. Spend some time with the class discussing the operational definitions for each dimension. After this discussion, groups should be ready to begin the exercise using **Handout # 8: In-Class Experiment** to record their data. Compile the class data after all groups are finished to determine if improvements in the DVs occur across performance trials.

- At this point, debrief the class on the true purpose for the exercise--to explore observer bias. I suggest using progressive debriefing: start by asking general questions about their experience with the exercise, then asking if they had any problems; if they wondered if something unusual was going on; finally, if they had any blatant suspicions about the study. Reveal at this point that the "subject" was a confederate, that all "subjects" drank decaffeinated beverages, and that the real purpose of the experiment was to demonstrate the observer/experimenter's prior expectations concerning the effects of caffeine might be revealed in the trends found in the data. Revisit the data trends to determine if this were the case. This is also a good point to consider that observer bias can be controlled in experimental settings via double blind studies. Have students generate corrections to any problems in their methodology.

Sources for Additional Activities
Books:

Benjamin, L. & Lowman, K. (1981). Activities Handbook for the Teaching of Psychology. Washington DC: American Psychological Association.

Halonen, Jane 1995). Chapter 1: Introduction to Psychology in The Critical Thinking Companion For Introductory Psychology (Worth Publ.).

Gardiner, H. (1998). Adventures in Cyberspace: A Cross-Cultural Scavenger Hunt. in Singelis, T. (Ed.) Teaching about culture, ethnicity, & diversity: Exercises and Planned Activities. Thousand Oaks, CA: Sage Publ.

Makosky, V. et al. (Eds.) (1995). Activities Handbook for the Teaching of Psychology (Vol. III). Washington DC: American Psychological Association.

McCormick, T. (1994). Creating the Nonsexist Classroom: A multicultural Approach. New York: Teachers College Press.

Journey II Software:
By clicking on the Library Icon, you'll find several "books" relevant to this introductory chapter:

Graduate Schools: invites the student to consider questions concerning whether to go to graduate school, career opportunities without going to graduate school, types of graduate degrees, guidelines for applying to graduate school, and what it's like in graduate school

History: a timeline that juxtapositions developments in psychology with other familiar historical events

Careers: defines psychology, what psychologists do professionally, opportunities for minorities and areas of study concentration

Glossary: general terms in psychology

Two other books are available under the Library icon: References (particular to texts other than Uba/Huang) and Conferences (which contains an outdated listing of national conferences in psychology)

World Wide Web: Check out the following WWW sites for information and activities relevant to this section of the text!

Addison Wesley Longman's Website -- **http://longman.awl.com/**
- PsychZone link -- **http://longman.awl.com/**
- American Psychological Association -- **http://www.apa.org/**
- American Psychological Society -- **http://psych.hanover.edu/psych/APS/aps.html**
- Psych Web -- **http://www.gasou.edu/psychweb/psychweb.htm**
- Specialties/graduate schools/careers in Psychology -- **http://www.gasou.edu/psychweb/tipsheet/specialt.htm**
or
http://www1.rider.edu/~suler/gradschl.html

Psychology Jumping Stand -- **http://www.indiana.edu:80/~iuepsyc/PsycJump.html**

The Psychology Place -- **http://www.psychplace.com**
- Research in Psychology -- **http://psych.hanover.edu/APS/exponnet.html**
or
http://www.indiana.edu/~gasser/experiments.html
or
http://www.york.ac.uk/depts/psych/web/etc/whatispsych.html

History of Psychology -- **http:/www.cwu.edu/~warren/today.html**
- Academic Psychology departments around the world -- **http://psy.ucsd.edu:80/otherpsy.html**

Audio-Visual Support
Films/Videos:

History and Theory in Psychology
Discovering Psychology: Past, Present, and Promise (Annenberg/CPB Project, 1990, 30 minutes)
Candid Camera in Introductory Psychology (McGraw-Hill College Division, 1992, 60 minutes)
The Great Ideas of Psychology (Insight Media, 1997, 48 lectures @ 45 minutes each)
What is Psychology? (Insight Media, 1990, 30 minutes)
Landmarks in Psychology (Insight Media, 1980, 50 minutes)
The Mind: The Search for Mind (PBS, 1988, 60 minutes)

Careers in Psychology
Career Encounters in Psychology (American Psychological Association, 30 minutes)
Careers in Psychology--Your Options are Open (American Psychological Association, 9 minutes)

Research Methodology
Discovering Psychology: Understanding Research. (Annenberg/CPB Project, 1990, 30 minutes)
Research Methods for the Social Sciences. (Insight Media, 1995, 33 minutes)
The Way of Science (Films for the Humanities & Science, 1998, 58 minutes)
Whazzat? (EBEC, 1975, 9 minutes)
Methodology: The Psychologist and the Experiment (CRM, 1973, 31 minutes)

Psychology Encyclopedia Laserdisc IV:
Movies
Historical overview   (3 min. 22 sec.)   Side 1, Frames 00884-07241

Still Images
Hypothesis testing [UN]   Frame 53417 Side 1
Variable types [UN]   53418   all
Correlations [1/3] [2.1]   53419   all
Correlations [2/3] [2.1]   53420   all
Correlations [3/3] [2.1]   53421   all
Correlation and causation [1/4] [2.2]   53422   all
Correlation and causation [2/4] [2.2]   53423   all
Correlation and causation [3/4] [2.2]   53424   all
Correlation and causation [4/4] [2.2]   53425   all
Smoking and driving hypothesis testing [1/3] [2.3]   53426   all
Smoking and driving hypothesis testing [2/3] [2.3]   53427   all
Smoking and driving hypothesis testing [3/3] [2.3]   53428   all
Mean and variances [1/3] [2.4]   53429   all
Mean and variances [2/3] [2.4]   53430   all
Mean and variances [3/3] [2.4]   53431   all

Handout 1.1: Psychology and You

How do you define the term psychology?

How has Psychology influenced your life (you or others around you)?

In your opinion, what types of questions should psychologists seek to address?

What is *your* goal in learning about Psychology?

Handout 1.2: You and culture

In your opinion, what does it mean to be an "American"?

Describe briefly your cultural/ethnic background.

Describe briefly the community and cultural/ethnic environment(s) in which you grew up.

How did living in a particular culture or ethnic group affect you? (i.e., your understanding of appropriate/inappropriate ways of behaving, thinking, feeling)

In what ways did you learn about your culture or ethnic group?

In your opinion, what is the role that the study of culture/ethnicity should take in psychology?

Handout Master 1.3: Diversity in Introductory Psychology textbooks

Diversity in Introductory Psychology textbooks

Instructions: This exercise is designed to explore Introductory Psychology textbooks for evidence of diversity represented in visual images. The members of your group are to select an older edition textbook for comparison with your current textbook for the course. To conduct your investigative comparison, select two similar chapters out of each textbook and review the photographs involving people presented in those chapters. Note any differences in numbers of males vs. females, numbers of peoples of various ethnicities, approximate ages of people presented, and the presence of any stereotypes in terms of activities or interactions. Prepare a brief summary of your findings for each book and then an overall summary comparison between the books.

Textbook # 1:
Title: _____   Authors: _____
Year of Publication: _____   _____

Chapter # 1 Title: _____
Number of Pictures reviewed: _____
Males vs. Females: _____
Ethnicities presented: _____
_____
Ages of persons in pictures: _____
Stereotypes noted: _____
_____
_____

Chapter # 2 Title: _____
Number of Pictures reviewed: _____
Males vs. Females: _____
Ethnicities presented: _____
_____
Ages of persons in pictures: _____
Stereotypes noted: _____
_____
_____

Summary :
_____
_____
_____
_____
_____
_____

Class Textbook:
Title: _____ Authors: _____
Year of Publication: _____ _____

Chapter # 1 Title: _____
Number of Pictures reviewed: _____
Males vs. Females: _____
Ethnicities presented: _____
_____
Ages of persons in pictures: _____
Stereotypes noted: _____
_____
_____

Chapter # 2 Title: _____
Number of Pictures reviewed: _____
Males vs. Females: _____
Ethnicities presented: _____
_____
Ages of persons in pictures: _____
Stereotypes noted: _____
_____
_____

Summary :
_____
_____
_____
_____
_____

OVERALL SUMMARY OF FINDINGS:
_____
_____
_____
_____
_____
_____
_____
_____
_____
_____

Handout Master 1.4: Psychologists in Our Community

Psychologists in Our Community

Agency contacted: _____

Number of psychologists employed: _____

Type(s) of educational backgrounds:

_____
_____
_____
_____
_____

Duties performed:

_____
_____
_____
_____
_____
_____

Number of clients/consumers served:

_____

Are gender and multi-cultural issues specifically addressed in this setting? How?

_____
_____
_____

Student Volunteers welcomed? Duties?

_____
_____
_____
_____

After hearing what you and your classmates report, write a brief summary of your findings. Are there any obvious needs for psychological services within your community not currently being addressed? If so, what are they?

_____
_____
_____
_____
_____
_____

Handout Master 1.5: Research Methods and Errors

Research Methods and Errors

INSTRUCTIONS: For each of the following examples of research, identify the methodology, a problem in how the method was applied or conducted, and one possible correction for the problem.

1. Dr. Berrara, the professor of an Introductory Psychology class, is interested in his students' reactions to various films shown in class. The day before Thanksgiving break, a notoriously low attendance day, he administers a brief series of questions to those students in attendance.

2. A school district administrator from a large urban center decides to assess the level of bullying experienced by junior high school students. She randomly selects 10 students from each of the 3 biggest junior high schools in her district and asks as many of them as she can a series of questions via a telephone call immediately after school one day.

3. Dr. Ling decides to observe college students' social behavior at local dances. She sends her research team to dances held throughout the school year. When she reviews her team's notes she notices a wide variety of observed behaviors but also notices differences in types of bands that played at the events. Moreover, some dance organizers provided alcoholic beverages whereas others did not.

4. To study language acquisition in children, Dr. Young selects a sample of 12 children who have been raised under conditions of extreme deprivation (i.e., they had little to no contact with people other than few isolated moments with a parent). He interviews each child extensively and, as a result, develops a general theory concerning how children learn speech.

5. In a recent newsstand tabloid, research was reported concerning the relationship between the size of a person's posterior and his or her I.Q. More specifically, high IQ scores were linked to increased posterior size . The tabloid author implied that a person's physical size was the cause of IQ fluctuations.

6. To determine the impact of caffeine on alertness in class, Dr. Bean conducts an in-class experiment. She randomly assigns the class into 2 groups: one which receives 2 double tall (12 oz.) lattes prior to class and the other which drinks 2 glasses of ice water (12 oz. each) before class. At the end of her experiment, the caffeine group recalls more information from the class.

Handout Master 1.6: LeVay vs. *USA Today*

LeVay Article:
Underline: Purpose of Study:

Underline: Methods Used to Test Hypotheses:

Underline: Conclusions drawn:

Underline: Cautions or Limitations to the Study:

USA Today **Article**:
Underline: Stated Purpose of LeVay's Study:

Underline: Description of Methods Used in LeVay's Study:

Underline: Conclusions drawn about LeVay's Study:

Obvious Omissions or Incorrect Interpretations Noted:
_____
_____
_____
_____

Handout Master 1.7: Fichten vs. *The Star*

Fichten Article:
Purpose of Study:

Methods Used to Test Hypotheses:

Conclusions drawn:

Cautions or Limitations to the Study:

Star **Article**:
Stated Purpose of Fichten's Study:

Description of Methods Used in Fichten's Study:

Conclusions drawn about Fichten's Study:

Obvious Omissions or Incorrect Interpretations Noted:
_____
_____
_____
_____

Handout Master 1.8: In-Class Experiment

Name: _____
Group Number: _____

In-Class Experiment: Super-Charged Performance!!

Hypothesis: _____
_____
_____
_____

Dependent Variables:
Physical skillfulness of performance:
    fluidity: subject performs task without excessive fumbling with blocks
    purposeful movements: subjects moves from one portion of the construction to the next in goal directed manner
Cognitive focus: subject remains focused on task (i.e., not easily distracted)
Creative quality of product: subject completes complicated version of construction vs. simplest version possible

Performance Trial 1:

Fluidity:	1 Low	2	3	4	5	6	7 High
Purposeful movements:	1 Low	2	3	4	5	6	7 High
Cognitive focus:	1 Low	2	3	4	5	6	7 High
Creative quality:	1 Low	2	3	4	5	6	7 High

Performance Trial 2:

Fluidity:	1 Low	2	3	4	5	6	7 High
Purposeful movements:	1 Low	2	3	4	5	6	7 High
Cognitive focus:	1 Low	2	3	4	5	6	7 High
Creative quality:	1	2	3	4	5	6	7

	Low						High

Performance Trial 3:

Fluidity:	1	2	3	4	5	6	7
	Low						High

Purposeful movements:	1	2	3	4	5	6	7
	Low						High

Cognitive focus:	1	2	3	4	5	6	7
	Low						High

Creative quality:	1	2	3	4	5	6	7
	Low						High

Average Scores Across Trials For the Group:

Trial 1:
Fluidity: _____
Purposeful movements: _____
Cognitive focus: _____
Creative quality: _____
Total: _____

Trial 2:
Fluidity: _____
Purposeful movements: _____
Cognitive focus: _____
Creative quality: _____
Total: _____

Trial 3:
Fluidity: _____
Purposeful movements: _____
Cognitive focus: _____
Creative quality: _____
Total: _____

Conclusions for your group: _____
_____
_____
_____
_____

Overall conclusions: _____
_____
_____
_____
_____

Transparency Master 1.1: Checking Your TRAIL 1.1

Psychology is the study of _____, including _____ and _____.

You want to use psychology to teach your dormitory roommate to lock the door when leaving your room. Which goal of psychology are you seeking?

The first psychology laboratory was established by Wundt in:
- A. ancient Greece
- B. the 1700s
- C. the 1800s
- D. the 1900s

Identify which of these approaches to psychology are related to structuralism and which are related to functionalism.
- A. explaining behavior in terms of what people consciously report
- B. looking for the reasons for behavior by observing the behavior in context
- C. analyzing a response by breaking it into parts

Transparency Master 1.2: Checking Your TRAIL 1.2

Name the seven principal perspectives in psychology.

Identify which school of thought is exemplified in the following statements:
 A. Just look at the behavior; don't bother with the stuff you can't see.
 B. Examine nerve cells and chemical messengers to find out about the origins of behaviors.
 C. Look at the choices people make to understand why they behave as they do.
 D. Behavior results from the processing of information.

Which of the following statements is true?
 A. Culture refers only to observable behaviors, not mental processes.
 B. Shared ways of interacting and interpreting behavior are part of what "culture" means.
 C. Multicultural research compares people in different countries.
 D. "Ethnic group is just another way of saying "race."

A _____ psychologist might work with engineers on designing the driver control switches on an automobile.
 A. clinical
 B. industrial/organizational
 C. forensic
 D. counseling

Transparency Master 1.3: Checking Your TRAIL 1.3

Basic or **applied** research? Studying ways to treat drug dependency effectively is an example of _____ research; studying how a drug affects brain chemistry in a rat is an example of _____ research.

Describe theory, hypothesis, and data as components of the scientific method.

The scientific method is based on which of the following four choices:
- A. beliefs and rational analysis
- B. rational analysis and data
- C. assumptions and rational analysis
- D. assumptions and claims

Which one of the following statements is true?
- A. sample is larger than its population.
- B. When scientists repeatedly find the same results, the results must be valid.
- C. The set of reference books carrying summaries of psychological studies is the *Psychological Abstracts*.
- D. Most participants in psychology studies have been members of racial minorities.

Transparency Master 1.4: Checking Your TRAIL 1.4

True or False: Psychologists can get different types of information by gathering data in different scientific ways, providing alternative perspectives on behavior.

In a study, a subject's responses are the
- A. independent variable
- B. extraneous variable
- C. confounding variable
- D. dependent variable

Fill in this chart of methods of psychological study:

Name of Method	How Data are Gathered
1.	
2.	

Studies that can show causes of behaviors or attitudes.

You want to examine whether insecurity causes jealousy. Which type of study would be best for you to use?
- A. survey
- B. naturalistic observation
- C. case study
- D. experiment

Transparency Master 1.5: Checking Your TRAIL 1.5

Which one of the following statements is true?
- A. statistically significant difference must be large.
- B. Even when differences are found between groups, the groups must be more different than they are alike.
- C. When differences are statistically significant, researchers believe that the differences probably reflect real differences rather than coincidence.
- D. Psychologists can usually predict with certainty how an individual will behave in a given situation.

True or False: A researcher's interpretation of his or her findings is always correct.

Critical thinking:
- A. involves rational analysis based on evidence.
- B. means finding fault in studies and interpretations of results.
- C. involves rational analysis based on personal values.
- D. is the same as remembering what researchers have found.

Identify six aspects of critical thinking.

Transparency Master 1.6: Critical Thinking 1.1

Sometimes people dismiss psychological research as invalid when it conflicts with common sense and their own impressions of people. What assumptions are they making about their own sampling and common sense?

Transparency Master 1.7: Critical Thinking 1.2

A local news show tells viewers to call a 1-900 phone number at 95 cents a minute to register whether they agree or disagree with a particular position on Issue A. Identify three biases introduced by obtaining a sample in this way.

Transparency Master 1.8: Critical Thinking 1.3

Suppose you want to know why some young people join gangs and others do not. Which of the four research methods would give you the most detailed view of why someone joins a gang? Which would give you a sense of the multiple reasons people join gangs?

Transparency Master 1.9: Critical Thinking 1.4

People often incorrectly assume that if two groups are "different," one of the groups must be inferior to the other. Give two examples of differences that do not indicate inferiority.

Transparency Master 1.10: Critical Thinking 1.5

The LaPiere (1934) study described in the text has been referred to as a classic study of the differences between attitudes and behaviors. One alternative explanation is that the European American traveling with the Chinese couple was viewed as their "keeper."

Provide two additional explanation for these findings on the Chinese couple and the European American man.

Mind Matters CD-ROM Faculty Guide

HISTORY AND METHODS

I. Introduction
    A. The Big Questions
        A1. ★The Mystery of the Human Mind
        A2. ★Studying Human Nature
        A3. ★What Is This?

II. Psychology's Roots
    A. Structuralism: The Mind Is a Molecule
    B. Functionalism: The Mind Is a Tool
    C. Psychoanalysis: The Mind Is an Iceberg
    D. Behaviorism: Psychology Loses Its Mind
    E. Gestalt Psychology: The Mind Is More Than Meets the Eye
    F. Humanism: The Mind Has Potential
    G. Schools of Psychology: Recess
        G1. ★Pop-Up: Schools of Psychology Matching Game
        G2. ★Pop-Up: All-Star Psychologists

III. Recent Trends in Psychology
    A. Cognitive Psychology
    B. Biopsychology
        B1. ★Depression Among the Amish
    C. Psychology's Careers and Branches
        C1. ★Branches of Psychology
    Rapid Review 1

IV. The Science of Psychology
    A. Common Sense vs. Scientific Psychology
        A1. ★Pop-Up: Predicting the Results of Psychological Research
    B. The Scientific Method
    C. Having an Attitude
        C1. ★Pop-Up: Evidence and Psychic Abilities
        C2. ★What is Psychology?
    Rapid Review 2
    D. Collecting Evidence in Psychology
        D1. ★A Case Study in Schizophrenia
        D2. ★Pop-Up: Interactive Correlation
        D3. ★The Milgram Obedience Experiment
        D4. ★The Lewin Leadership Study
        D5. ★Pop-Up: A Methodological Decision Tree
    Rapid Review 3

Quick Quiz

HISTORY AND METHODS
Annotated Outline

I. Introduction

The history and methods unit begins by introducing psychology as a discipline concerned with explaining both ordinary and extraordinary behavior and mental activity.

A. The Big Questions

The introduction to psychology continues with three questions that frame the enormity of the task that confronts psychologists: What is the nature of the brain and its relationship to behavior? How can we use psychology to understand the very best and the very worst of human behavior? How do we come to know the world around us?

A1. ★The Mystery of the Human Mind

This is the first of three video clips that are intended to drive home the framing questions. In this clip, students see a brief narrated history of psychology beginning with pre-scientific approaches to understanding human behavior.

The Mystery of the Human Mind

Type of Activity: Movie

Learning Objective: Introduce students to the history of psychology.

Faculty Note: This is not intended as a detailed history, but more as a quick overview to stimulate thinking about the long history and diverse perspectives embodied in modern psychology.

Additional Resources:

Classics in the History of Psychology—This web site contains works of many classic psychologists including Watson, Pavlov, Freud, Titchner, Wundt, James, and many others. http://www.yorku.ca/dept/psych/classics/topic.htm

Major Events in the History of Psychology—This site contains an outline of the history of psychology. http://www.netaxs.com/people/aca3/lpm-hist.htm

The Letters of William James—Published by his son, these volumes contain many of the letters that William James wrote to friends, colleagues, and university officials. http://www.theatlantic.com/issues/96may/nitrous/jamii.htm

Timetable of significant events in Psychology—As advertised, this site contains a good

outline of the history of psychology.
http://paradigm.soci.brocku.ca/~lward/TIME/TIME_PSY.HTML

Today in the History of Psychology—This site allows you to enter a date and see what happened in psychology on that date.
http://www.cwu.edu/~warren/calendar/datepick.html

A2. ★Studying Human Nature

This video clip contains footage from the Los Angeles Riots. Examples of aggression and self-sacrifice are included in the clips.

> **Studying Human Nature**
>
> **Type of Activity:** Movie
>
> **Learning Objective:** Encourage students to think about how we might begin to explain the diversity of human behavior.
>
> **Faculty Note:** Extreme circumstances reveal interesting facets of human behavior. In this video clip, students can see footage from the L.A. riots. These riots revealed the power of social situations to foster antisocial behavior, and yet at the same time they contained numerous instances of individual altruism and prosocial behavior. It may be useful to point out here that while observation of abnormal behavior or the behavior of individuals in abnormal situations may prove valuable, many psychologists are also interested in "normal" behavior and the more typical situations in which people find themselves.
>
> The same point can be made about other areas, such as studies of perception. Research on both normal perceptual processes and unusual perceptual processes (e.g., illusions, hallucinations, etc.) contribute to our overall understanding.

A3. ★What Is This?

This video contains a visual illusion. It is included to help students see that much of our everyday life is not nearly as obvious as it first appears.

> **What is This?**
>
> **Type of Activity:** Movie
>
> **Learning Objective:** Encourage students to think about the role that context and situations play in shaping psychological experiences.
>
> **Faculty Note:** The goal of this clip is to help students see that perception, and, more generally, psychological experience are relative. The video shows what appears to be a light "hopping" across the screen. But when another light is added as a reference point, it creates a very different perception as the light now appears to rotate across the screen.
>
> This same video clip could be shown during discussions of the Gestalt perspective as it demonstrates the organizing principles we impose on perception.

II. Psychology's Roots

A. Structuralism: The Mind Is a Molecule

In this section, Structuralism, with its emphasis on finding the basic elements of conscious experience and reliance upon introspection is highlighted.

B. Functionalism: The Mind Is a Tool

Functionalism is introduced as a uniquely American school of psychology. Unlike structuralists, functionalists like William James argued that it is not possible to study the mind and behavior without understanding the functions that they serve.

C. Psychoanalysis: The Mind Is an Iceberg

Described as one of the great upheavals in human thought, the psychoanalytic perspective challenged the notion that behavior is primarily under the control of conscious thought. Instead, Freud argued that the unconscious is the driving force behind many of our behaviors.

D. Behaviorism: Psychology Loses Its Mind

In 1913, John Watson mounted an assault on what he perceived as the unscientific mysticism and mentalism of psychology. He and his fellow behaviorists argued that psychology should be concerned with the study of observable behaviors and the environments in which they occur.

E. Gestalt Psychology: The Mind Is More Than Meets the Eye

Unlike the behaviorist, Gestalt psychologists continued to argue for the need to study consciousness. In studies of illusions and perceptual constancies, they believed that they saw evidence of a mind that actively organizes and structures perception. In their terms, the perception is greater than the sum or its sensory parts.

F. Humanism: The Mind Has Potential

Sometimes called the Third Force in psychology, humanistic psychology emerged in response to the pessimistic views of human nature embodied in psychoanalysis and behaviorism. Humanistic psychologists emphasized the freedom of individuals to make choices and change their lives for the better.

G. Schools of Psychology: Recess

In this section, students can learn more about many of the leading figures in psychology and review their knowledge of the schools of psychology.

G1. ★Pop-Up: Schools of Psychology Matching Game

Although sharing the goal of establishing a viable science of psychology, the first psychologists
were often divided by arguments about the proper methods and subject matter of the field. In this game, students try to match some of the early theorists to the theories they advocated.

Schools of Psychology Matching Game

Type of Activity: Interactive Animation

Learning Objective: Reinforce students' mastery of the schools of psychology.

Faculty Note: In this activity, students can test their knowledge of the different schools of thought by matching the schools with their perspectives.

G2. ★Pop-Up: All-Star Psychologists

In this pop-up, students can take a somewhat whimsical tour of the contributions of many leading figures in the field.

All-Star Psychologists

Type of Activity: Interactive illustration

Learning Objective: Introduce students to a broad range of historically important figures in psychology.

Faculty Note: In this activity, students can explore the contributions of notable psychologists by clicking on their images. The information here is accurate, although it is presented in a whimsical manner. The visual and humorous associations supplied in this exercise can help to make the instructor's lesson materials more memorable.

III. Recent Trends in Psychology

A. Cognitive Psychology

By the mid-1950's, many psychologists had come to the conclusion that the behaviorists' approach was inadequate. Using the computer as a metaphor, cognitive psychologists began studying the ways that the mind interprets, processes, and stores information. Cognitive psychology embraces "mentalism" and it is currently one of the most influential paradigms in psychology.

B. Biopsychology

The other major trend in recent years has been an expanded interest in the evolutionary, physiological, and biochemical influences on behavior. This interest has been stimulated by our increasing knowledge of neurotransmitters, the development of more sophisticated procedures for measuring the structures and functions of the brain, and the emergence of evolutionary-based theories that are open to testing and refutation.

B1. ★Depression Among the Amish

In this video clip, students can see a summary account of one attempt to trace the inheritance of mood disorders.

Depression Among the Amish

Activity Type: Movie

Learning Objective: Introduce the notion that biology influences human behavior.

Faculty Note: In this video, students learn about one attempt to find a genetic cause for a mood disorder. Although many psychologists are convinced that a predisposition towards these disorders may be inherited, more recent attempts to identify the precise location of a specific "depression gene" have been unsuccessful. This subsequent failure to find a specific gene provides an opportunity to talk about the promise and limitations of the biopsychological approach to understanding behavior.

The instructor may want to return to this in other sections of the course as well, such as in a discussion of the medical model of psychological disorders. One question to ask students might be: If a disorder can be inherited, exactly **what** is passed on—a neurotransmitter imbalance? a structural flaw in the brain? hormonal differences?

It might be pointed out that some disorders have a more obvious genetic component (e.g., schizophrenia, certain forms of dementia, bipolar disorder, etc.) while others appear to be much less influenced by genetic predispositions.

Another potentially relevant topic would be the possible genetic contributions to personality traits. If predispositions toward emotional problems can be inherited, why not predispositions towards introversion, extraversion, or friendliness?

Additional Resources:

NAMI—this site, maintained by the National Alliance for the Mentally Ill, contains an update on the search for genetic links to bipolar disorder.

http://laami.nami.org/disorder/disordg.htm

C. Psychology's Careers and Branches

Modern psychology is a broad field. A 1993 survey of the nearly 120,000 members of the American Psychological Association found them working in 236 different specialty areas.

C1. ★Branches of Psychology

In this activity, students can explore a variety of specialties in psychology.

Careers in Psychology

Type of Activity: Interactive Illustration

Learning Objective: Allow students to explore the specialties and sub-disciplines of psychology.

Faculty Note: This "family tree" of psychological specialties should help convince students that the field of psychology accommodates a great variety of interests, and that almost all facets of human behavior are fair game for inquiries by psychologists.

Of course, even this relatively large "tree" does not cover all specialties, or the forms that they may take in other disciplines such as economics, decision sciences, political science, criminology, business, etc.

Additional Resources:

The American Psychological Association web site can be found at http://www.apa.org
The American Psychological Society web site can be found at
http://www.psychologicalscience.org

C2. ★What Is Psychology?
As diverse as psychology is, two threads link its various branches. The first is the idea that psychologists are concerned with the scientific study of human behavior. The second is the understanding that the various branches of psychology share a common history. The video presented here illustrates some of the diverse elements of psychology.

What is Psychology?

Activity Type: Movie

> **Learning Objective:** Portray the diversity of subject matter and research methods among modern psychologists.
>
> **Faculty Note:** This video provides a quick montage of segments showing different types of psychological inquiries, such as those conducted in clinical and laboratory settings. It is not intended to be a comprehensive review of methodology. However, it may be instructive to have students guess what questions the psychologists in the segments are investigating.

Rapid Review 1

IV. THE SCIENCE OF PSYCHOLOGY

The remainder of this unit is designed to introduce students to the principles and methods of scientific psychology.

A. Common Sense vs. Scientific Psychology

Psychology is often accused of being nothing more than common sense. In this section, the shortcomings of common sense are highlighted and psychology is distinguished from common sense on the basis of psychology's commitment to the principles of science.

A1. ★Pop-Up: Predicting the Results of Psychological Research

This section introduces an activity that allows students to test the accuracy of their common sense predictions. For most students, their common sense predictions will be poor predictors of their actual behavior.

> **Predicting the Results of Psychological Research**
>
> **Type of Activity:** Simulation
>
> **Learning Objective:** Encourage students to think critically about the differences between "common sense" views of behavior and psychological accounts of behavior.
>
> **Faculty Note:** In the activity, students see the solutions to several anagrams (i.e., scrambled words) and are asked to predict how long it would have taken them to solve the anagrams had they not seen the solutions. Because of hindsight bias (i.e., the answers seem obvious once known) most students will underestimate the amount of time it takes to solve these anagrams. They are then given a chance to actually complete several anagrams and their actual times are measured. The point that the activity makes is that we are often in the position of having known what happens when we try to understand psychological phenomena. The challenge to scientific psychology is to predict processes in advance.

> Sometimes, after being told of the conclusions reached by researchers, students respond that they had known them all along, or as if the outcomes were predictable. This exercise might be part of an antidote to this sort of hindsight bias. In line with this, it may be useful to remind your students of this when discussing early classical conditioning research, such as Pavlov's conditioning of salivation in dogs or the Little Albert experiment conducted by John Watson. The results of these studies may appear obvious or predictable to modern observers, but represented radically unconventional ideas at the time they were first presented. On the flip side, a number of studies continue to be surprising including Milgram's work on obedience, Nisbett and Wilson's work on explaining our own behavior, and much of the cognitive dissonance literature.

B. The Scientific Method

In this section the scientific method is described as a process that involves observation, theory construction, hypothesis generation, and data collection. Darley and Latané's work on bystander intervention is then presented as a case study in how the scientific method unfolds.

C. Having an Attitude

Using the scientific method also involves adopting a certain set of attitudes. Scientists are skeptical, always on the lookout for alternative explanations for what they observe. Similarly, scientists seek parsimony. As Einstein put it, "Everything should be made as simple as possible, but not any simpler."

C1. ★Pop-Up: Evidence and Psychic Abilities

Using themselves as subjects, students can apply the scientific method to claims of paranormal activities.

Evidence of Psychic Abilities

Type of Activity: Simulation

Learning Objective: Learn to apply the scientific method to psychological questions.

Faculty Note: Students are given an opportunity to take part in a "test" of their precognitive or clairvoyant abilities using the stimuli from Zener cards (circle, square, star, cross, and wavy lines). After the student makes a series of attempts to predict which of the cards the computer will present, their frequency of "hits" can be compared to the number expected by chance alone. It should be noted that whenever a hypothesis is tested scientifically, we should have a clear idea what would constitute sufficient evidence to reject the null hypothesis.

It should also be made clear to the students that "evidence" for or against extraordinary claims (such as claims of psychic abilities) must be objective and quantifiable, and should be decided upon beforehand. Anecdotes are not enough.

If by chance a student scores enough "hits" to make it appear as if something extraordinary is happening, instructors might want to remind him or her that a critical task in science is the **replication** of interesting results to insure against accidents, and then suggest repeat attempts.

Additional Resources:

Perhaps the only published article in an APA journal to make claims in support of ESP is Daryl Bem's work in *Psychological Bulletin*. Bem, D. J., and Honorton, C. (1994). Does psi exist? Replicable evidence for an anomalous process of information transfer. Psychological Bulletin, 115, 4-18

Bem also has a web page that can be found at http://www.psych.cornell.edu/dbem/online_pubs.html. This page even has a non-specialist's guide to the article.

Rapid Review 2

D. Collecting Evidence in Psychology

The actual techniques employed by psychologists to collect evidence vary widely depending on the area of psychology and the question being asked. This section reviews basic concepts involved in data collection including: descriptive and experimental data; field and laboratory studies; case studies; surveys; naturalistic observations; correlations and experiments; and random assignment and random sampling. Where appropriate, pop-ups are used to reinforce the concepts.

D1. ★A Case Study in Schizophrenia

This video clip contains a case study interview with a woman suffering from schizophrenia.

A Case Study in Schizophrenia

Type of Activity: Movie

Learning Objective: See an example of the case study method in psychology.

Faculty Note: While this is only a highly abbreviated case study, it does emphasize the personal, individual nature of this approach, as well as the humanizing effect of focusing on the individual instead of the disorder.

> Pioneering personality theorist Gordon Allport made the point that while nomothetic research (the search for general laws and principles in large populations) is crucial in science, psychologists should never lose sight of the uniqueness and importance of the individual; they should also conduct idiographic inquiries (case studies).
>
> **Additional Resources:**
>
> Schizophrenia Resources-NAMI—This site, maintained by the National Alliance for the Mentally Ill, contains a list of schizophrenia resources and links.
> http://schizophrenia.nami.org/schizophrenia/schizophrenia.html

D2. ★Pop—Up: Interactive Correlation

In this activity, students can explore the correlational concepts of size, direction, and causality.

> **Interactive Correlation**
>
> **Type of Activity:** Exploration
>
> **Learning Objective:** Help students master concepts related to correlation.
>
> **Faculty Note:** . Some of the most interesting ideas in the field started out as statements about a relationship between two variables: Conformity correlates with group size, dreaming correlates with REM sleep, recall correlates with depth of processing, job performance correlates with achievement motivation, IQ test scores correlate with school performance, etc. The concept of a correlation between variables is critical to many areas of psychology.
>
> The most important limitation to emphasize is probably the fact that correlation does not always imply causation. Although ice cream sales are correlated with the number of drowning deaths on any given day, we can't necessarily assume that the ice cream is causing the drownings. A third variable, daily temperature, would seem to explain the connection between the two.
>
> **Additional Resources:**
>
> Guessing Correlations—This site allows students to play a game in which they guess correlations. http://www.stat.uiuc.edu/~stat100/java/guess/GCApplet.html

D3. ★The Milgram Obedience Experiment

This video contains archival footage of Stanley Milgram's famous "Obedience to Authority Experiment." In the study, Milgram attempted to determine if the close proximity of an authority figure (the independent variable) could cause even normal individuals to engage in acts of destructive obedience (the dependent variable). Prior to this study, almost no one anticipated the degree to which these subjects would commit harmful acts at the request of such an authority.

The Milgram Obedience Experiment

Type of Activity: Movie

Learning Objective: Help students see the power that experiments have to establish the causes of behavior, and to uncover surprising and counter-intuitive findings.

Faculty Note: In this study Milgram found that even average, mentally healthy persons will (apparently) inflict great pain on another subject at the command of an experimenter. The Milgram experiment can be used to stimulate discussion on a variety of topics:

Finding a way to study destructive obedience in the laboratory was an innovative approach to understanding this phenomenon. Some critics were initially concerned about the external validity of the study: However, subsequent research has shown that the results do generalize to other real-world settings.

Prior to the study, Milgram described his experiment to a variety of psychologists and laypersons and asked them to predict what the subjects would do. Almost nobody believed that "normal" individuals would follow harmful orders to that degree. In fact, more than 60 percent obeyed to the end.

D4. ★The Lewin Leadership Study

This video contains archival footage of Kurt Lewin's groundbreaking use of experimental methods to discover the consequences of different leadership styles. In this study, children were randomly assigned to different groups, each governed by a different type of leader. Since membership in the groups was randomly determined, any differences between the groups that emerged during the study could be attributed to the effects of the leaders.

The Lewin Leadership Study

Type of Activity: Movie

Learning Objective: Help students see that behavior as complicated as "democracy" can be studied scientifically.

Faculty Note: In this study, children were randomly assigned to different groups, each governed by a different type of leader. Since membership in the groups was randomly determined, any differences between the groups that emerged during the study could be attributed to the effects of the leaders.

> One element of this study that is worth noting is the subject matter. Lewin was insistent that the results of psychological research should help us with practical, real-world problems such as those of leadership and government.
>
> Another point worth noting is the importance of random assignment to the experiment. The different leadership styles could not be fairly compared if the subjects were allowed to volunteer for particular groups. Random assignment allows you to assume that the groups in the study start out the same.

D5. ★Pop-Up: A Methodological Decision Tree

Psychologists use a variety of research methods. Each method has its advantages and disadvantages. In this activity, students are encouraged to consider the proposition that violent TV programming leads to increased levels of aggression among children. They are then encourage to use a decision tree to explore a variety of methods that could be used to test the proposition.

> **A Methodological Decision Tree**
>
> **Type of Activity:** Exploration
>
> **Learning Objective:** Allow students to make decisions about what methodologies can be applied to a common research question and illustrate how the conclusions one can draw from a study depend upon the methods used.
>
> **Faculty Note:** It is often useful to pick a famous study in psychology (such as the Milgram obedience study, the Little Albert study, Shepard's mental rotation study, Ebbinghaus' study on memory retention, or the Phineas Gage case study), to see how the basic questions addressed in that study might have been explored using other methods.

Rapid Review 3

CHAPTER 2

BIOPSYCHOLOGY: THE BIOLOGICAL BASES OF BEHAVIOR

Chapter Overview
　　Learning Objectives
　　Chapter Outline

Additional Lecture Ideas
　　Lecture Topics
　　Additional Readings

In-Class Activities and Demonstrations
　　Activities and Demonstrations
　　Sources for Additional Activities
　　Journey II Software

World Wide Web

Audio-Visual Support

Handout and Transparency Masters

Chapter Overview

Learning Objectives

After studying this chapter, you should be able to do the following:

1. Describe how genes influence psychological characteristics.

2. Explain how nerves transmit information.

3. Describe the effects of several key neurotransmitters.

4. Describe the production and function of several key hormones.

5. Describe the organization and functions of the peripheral nervous system.

6. Identify the major parts of the brain and describe their functions.

7. Give examples of biological variations in the human brain.

Chapter Outline

Biopsychology: The Biological Bases of Behavior

I. Introduction
   A. How the body and psychological states interact
      1. The body affects psychological functions v. psychological states affect bodily functions
   B. Psychologists' interest in biological bases for behavior
      1. Genes
      2. Glands
      3. The nervous system

II. Genes: The Bases For Biological Characteristics
   A. How genetic information is transmitted
      1. unique combinations of DNA creates individual uniquenesses
      2. dominant v. recessive genes
   B. Genetic and environmental effects
      1. unique and interactive effects of genetics and environment
      2. activities/interests of behavioral geneticists
      3. methodology: the twin study
   C. Are some psychological characteristics inherited?
      1. studying how genes influence behavior: the manufacturing of proteins
      2. example: homosexuality

III. Nerves: An Avenue For Sending Information
   A. The role of glial cells
   B. Neuron
      1. Basic unit of the nervous system
      2. Parts of a neuron
         a. soma
         b. dendrites
         c. axon
         d. nerves
      3. Types of neurons
         a. sensory nerves
         b. motor nerves
         c. interneurons
   C. Nerve impulses
      1. Definition: series of electrical charges and chemical movements that transmit information
      2. Communication within neurons
         a. involved ions: sodium, potassium, chloride
         b. resting potential
         c. action potential

           d. all-or-none principle
           e. myelin sheath
           f. nodes of Ranvier
           g. inadequate myelination
        3. Communication between neurons
           a. synapses
           b. terminal button (knob)
           c. neurotransmitters
           d. synaptic vesicles
           e. pre- and postsynaptic membrane
           f. synaptic cleft
           g. receptor sites
           h. excitatory v. inhibitory neurotransmitters
           i. reuptake v. enzymatic degradation
           j. effects of toxic substances

IV. Chemicals: A Means of Sending Information
   A. Neurotransmitters
      1. 70 different neurotransmitters
      2. Dopamine (DA)
         a. <u>functions</u>: attention levels, integration of information, control of muscle movement
      3. Acetylcholine (Ach)
         a. <u>functions</u>: alertness, attention, memory & motivation
      4. Norepinephrine (NE)
         a. <u>functions</u>: memory, learning, regulation of moods
      5. GABA
         a. <u>functions</u>: precision of muscular coordination
      6. Serotonin
         a. <u>functions</u>: mood regulation, sleep
   B. Hormones
      1. Endocrine system
      2. Effects of hormones
         a. affect transmission of nerve impulses
         b. act relatively slowly
         c. regulates metabolism
         d. influence physical characteristics and behavior
      3. The gonads
         a. produce eggs & sperm
         b. trigger sex-linked characteristics
      4. Pituitary glands
         a. controls release of other hormones
         b. regulates physical growth
      5. Thyroid gland
         a. regulates metabolism/growth

6. Adrenal glands
   a. affect energy levels, moods, reactions to stress

V. The Nervous System: A Network of Information Routes
A. The peripheral nervous system
1. <u>Function</u>: carrying info from brain & spinal cord to rest of body and vice versa
2. Major sub-divisions
   a. somatic nervous system
      i. function: control of movement of skeletal muscles
   b. autonomic nervous system
      i. sympathetic branch: prepares body for action
      ii. parasympathetic branch: calms and conserves energy

B. The central nervous system
1. Composition: brain & spinal cord
2. The spinal cord
   a. composition
   b. role in reflexes
3. Technologies for studying the brain

VI. The Subcortical Brain: Basic Biological Functions
A. The brain stem
1. <u>functions</u>: fundamental, autonomic activities
2. <u>locations</u>: medulla, pons, midbrain

B. The cerebellum
1. <u>functions</u>: balance, posture, smooth movements

C. The reticular formation
1. <u>functions</u>: level of arousal, directing nerve impulses

D. The thalamus
1. <u>functions</u>: info relay, maintaining awareness

E. The hypothalamus
1. <u>functions</u>: regulation of fear, aggression, appetite, thirst, sexual behavior, internal body temperature, heart rate, blood pressure

F. The limbic system
1. <u>functions</u>: memory & emotions
2. <u>structures</u>: hippocampus, amygdala

VII. The Cerebral Cortex: The Site of Complex Thought
A. Cerebral hemispheres
1. two symmetrical hemispheres
2. lateralization of functions

B. Cortical lobes
1. The occipital lobe

                a. <u>functions</u>: processing visual information
        2. The parietal lobe
                a. <u>functions</u>: processing pain, touch, pressure, temperature
        3. The temporal lobe
                a. <u>functions</u>: processing sounds, smells, language
        4. The frontal lobe
                a. <u>functions</u>: personality characteristics, decision-making & problem solving, information integration
   C. Functional divisions of the cerebral cortex
        1. The sensory cortex
                a. <u>functions</u>: processing information from sense organs
                b. <u>areas</u>: visual cortex, auditory cortex, somatosensory cortex
        2. The motor cortex
                a. <u>functions</u>: regulates voluntary movement
        3. Association areas
                a. <u>functions</u>: combine information from different senses, integrate sensory/motor information
        4. The biological bases of learning
                a. learning = development of new neural connections
        5. The brain's plasticity
                a. flexibility in brain functioning between hemispheres
        6. The split brain
                a. demonstrates some limits of plasticity
                b. severing the corpus callosum

VIII. Variations in the Human Brain
   A. The left-handed and the right-handed
        1. differences in functions lateralized in the brain
        2. differences in hemispheric dominance
   B. Sexual perspectives on the brain
        1. sex differences in the brain
                a. differences in skills
                b. differences in lateralization
        2. cautions on interpreting sex differences

Additional Lecture Topics

Why do birds sing?

Kalat (1995) offers that biological psychologists are interested in trying to understand and explain behaviors from a biological basis and that they tend to rely on four primary types of biological explanation:

physiological: the study of activity based on cellular and chemical events within the body.

ontogenetic: how a brain structure or behavior develops beginning with genes and considering how those genes combine with the influences from the environment.

evolutionary: how a brain structure or behavior is related to the evolutionary history of some species.

functional: discusses why a brain structure or behavior evolved as it has.

In an interesting application of these biological perspectives, he addresses the question of why birds sing from each perspective. Specifically, from the physiological perspective, birdsong is dependent on two areas of a bird's brain: the caudal nucleus of the hyperstriatum ventrale and the robust nucleus of the archistriatum. These areas are absent in birds without song. Moreover, testosterone levels influence the size of these areas such that when testosterone levels drop, song is eliminated and song can be induced in females of song species through the injection of testosterone. Damage to these areas affect abilities to respond to song and produce song. The ontogenetic perspective considers the nature of bird song -- the what or content of song. For example, for males to develop song normal to their species, they must hear that song performed by other males of their species during sensitive periods of development to develop the appropriate "template" for what song should sound like. Through natural selection, according to the evolutionary perspective, each species adapts and evolves distinctive songs containing general features consistent with its ancestors but unique features dependent on its unique evolution or interface with the environment. What good does song do for a species? The functionalist argues that song serves to attract females during breeding season and deter competition from other males. Kalat relates this example of birdsong to the behavior of humans when he says "When people are asked why they play, laugh, have sexual relations, or take care of babies, they sometimes reply that they simply "like to" or "want to " do these things. Evolution presumably constructed us to "like" certain activities because those activities increase our chance of passing on our genes." (pg. 8) Additionally, he suggests that some properties of the brain force some activities (such as pupil constriction, reflexive responses, etc.) and in other cases, make behaviors possible but not necessary (e.g., aggression).

Source:

Kalat, J. W. (1995). Biological Psychology (5th Edition). Pacific Grove: Brooks/Cole

Are we born male or female?

Two interesting case studies highlight the relative importance of nature vs. nurture in controlling human behaviors; in these cases in particular the development of gender identity. Are we male or female because we are born that way or do we behave as males or females because we are raised that way? In a now classic case study, one of a pair of identical twin boys suffered extensive injury to his penis during circumcision in 1965 which eventually required that the infant have surgery to remove the remainder of his penis and testes and to create female external sexual structures. The gender reassignment was completed during her adolescent years with additional vaginal surgery and estrogen replacement therapy. During her childhood, the girl's parents dressed her as a girl and treated her as they thought a girl should be raised. Indeed, early reports suggested that the little girl had "perfectly normal" gender identity development (suggesting to many that gender identity is largely a socially constructed phenomenon) and was marked by her parents' reports that she "so feminine" and preferred many traditional feminine activities such as having her hair styled and imitating her mother's behaviors. Later reports taken during her adolescent years indicated that the girl was experiencing difficulty adjusting to her female role identity and was taunted by her classmates for her unfeminine appearance and behaviors prompting some to say that her estrogen levels merely needed adjustment. Nevertheless, support slipped for the argument that gender identity development was influenced largely by social learning.

A second example supported a different argument (Imperato-McGinley, 1976). In 1974, a group of male pseudohermaphrodites were discovered in the Dominican Republic. These genetic males were born with an enzyme deficiency that produced female external genitalia (and male internal sex organs & testes). When typical male testosterone production occurred during puberty, definite masculine changes began to occur: deepening of the voice, the clitoris grew into a penis, the testes descended into a scrotum. Erections and intercourse were possible. Of the 18 males who had been raised as girls, 17 changed to a male gender identity and an additional 16 of 18 "girls" changed to a male gender role either during or after puberty. Some researchers claimed that this study demonstrates that biological sex overrides learned gender if typical hormone production occurs during puberty.

Again the question of nature vs. nurture presents itself in unusual ways....

Source:

Diamond, M. (1982). Sexual identity: Monozygotic twins reared in discordant sex roles and a BBC follow-up. Archives Sexual Behavior, 11(2), 181-186.

Imperato-McGinley, J., and Pertson, R. Male Pseudohermaphroditism: The complexities of male phenotypic development. American Journal of Medicine, 61, 251-272.

Money, J. & Tucker, P. (1975). Sexual signatures: On being a man or woman. Boston: Little, Brown.

Diversity in Psychobiology

Villars (1988) incorporates race and gender in discussions of psychobiology in her courses and outlines some relevant readings and techniques for doing so in several topic areas.

Nature vs. Nurture: Villars cautions us to remember that this debate can become artificially dichotomized into an either/or problem. Although acknowledging that historically biological explanations of different-ness have been translated into deficiencies and has been used to justify racial and gender inequities, she urges stronger consideration that biological predispositions don't necessarily translate into behavior and simplistic reduction into either biological or psychological doesn't capture the interactive nature of these phenomena.

Methodology: assumptions of the objective nature of science don't rest in some innate aspect of science itself but rather are dependent on adopting a critical analysis of the background assumptions within a scientific community. Thus, critiques of the underlying cultural views and assumptions upon which research in some topic areas is based (such as the ideas concerning male dominance) are warranted.

Sociobiology: Numerous critiques of sociobiology are noted including those that find the theory to be ideological in nature, gender-biased, androcentric, and highly anthropomorphic in tone. Villars uses student exercises designed to reveal judgments embedded in supposedly factual statements in reading literature supporting sociobiological theory.

Sexuality: Villars suggests incorporating more information relevant to discussions of menstruation, premenstrual syndrome, menopause, pregnancy, contraceptive technologies, and hormones & homosexuality into the curriculum and recommends books such as The New Our Bodies, Ourselves as resource materials.

Sex differences in the brain: Using popular summaries of the endocrinology of sex differentiation, Villar critiques the tendency for these overviews or summaries to reflect and reinforce sexist stereotypes often in subtle ways through tone and emphasis of material and omission of other environmental and experiential factors that might influence sex differences.

Source:
Villars, T. A. (1988). Chapter 9: Psychobiology in Bronstein, P.A. & Quina, K. (Eds.) Teaching a Psychology of People: Resources for Gender and Sociocultural Awareness. Washington, DC: APA

Methods for studying the brain

Students are often fascinated (and sometimes horrified) by some of the methods used to study the brain. I generally reserve up to a whole lecture period to describe and demonstrate different techniques. Kalat (1995) reserves an entire chapter for discussing methods of investigating how the brain controls our behavior and reviews the following:

<u>The stereotaxic instrument</u> -- procedure for use including locating skull landmarks, references to a stereotaxic atlas, & insertion of electrodes using reference distances listed in the atlas.

<u>Lesions & ablations</u> -- destroying or removing parts of the brain; the process and purpose of sham lesioning, histological techniques used to explore the structure of brain tissue, and problems of interpreting the results of lesion studies.

<u>Stimulation & recording from the brain</u> -- using electrodes to (1) stimulate areas of the brain to assess effects of that stimulation on behavior or (2) record brain activity from within the brain.

<u>Labeling brain activity</u> -- use autoradiography (to determine where labeled chemicals are located in the brain) or immuniohistochemistry (using dyed antibodies to locate receptors to certain neurotransmitter sites).

<u>Studies using the natural development of the brain</u> -- looking for differences in behavior between genetically-mutated animals and typically-developed animals, deliberately arresting brain development in animals via x-ray exposure or neurotoxins, or correlating on-going brain development with changes in behavior patterns.

<u>Studies of the structure of living human brains</u> -- using CAT scans, MRI, EEGs, PET scans, regional cerebral blood flow (rCBF) measures.

At the end of the lecture, I often ask students how I could discover the capabilities of some area "X" in the brain if I were interested in learning more about it. Often I get some creative (and pretty unethical) types of responses which provides an opportunity to review ethical considerations in research.

<u>Source:</u>
Kalat, J. W. (1995). <u>Biological Psychology (5th Edition).</u> Pacific Grove: Brooks/Cole

The mismeasure of woman and man

In 1981, Stephan Gould reviewed historical efforts by herditarians to classify and rank different races, socioeconomic classes, and sexes with respect to intelligence as little more than a reflection of social and political prejudices. In 1992, Carol Tavris expanded that argument from a feminist perspective when she explored the nature of sex differences literature from the viewpoint that "natural" differences between men and women also reflect society's biases and stereotypes. In her book, <u>The Mismeasure of Woman</u>, she examines "the stories behind the headlines and popular theories of sex differences, traveling the trail of the universal male, showing how the belief in male normalcy and female deficiency guides scientific inquiry, shapes its results, and determines which findings make the news and which findings we live by" (pg. 24).

Interestingly, in the section entitled *Brain: Dissecting the differences*, Tavris notes that on a number of occasions theories have been dramatically altered to stereotypes of greater male intellectual capability: equating women's "lesser intellectual capabilities" with smaller brain size (until differences in height and weight offset this finding) and with having larger parietal lobes than men (until it was reported that the parietal lobe might be the site of intellect). Now, she says, we chase the notion of left-right dichotomy, differences in lateralization, differences in size of corpus callosum and superiority of male functioning has been suggested for both the left and right hemispheres, depending on which skills were being viewed as valuable.

She offers as another example of bias Bleier's criticisms of Geschwind and Behan's sex difference studies which originally found no significant differences in a sample of 507 fetal brains, but later reported evidence of sex differences when rats were studied. Bleier wrote an extensive critique of the latter study, offered it to *Science*, was denied publication, offered more critiques of subsequently published reports of sex differences, was again denied publication. Other researchers have also argued that no gender differences are found in major performance dimensions such as verbal ability, mathematical performance, and spatial abilities. Thus the observation that sex difference often finds little difference between males and females, the overlap between men and women is larger, and there tends to be more variation within each than between them. She notes "Two decades ago, theorists postulated biological limitations that were keeping women out of men's work like medicine and bartending. When the external barriers to these professions fell, the speed with which women entered them was dizzying. Did everybody's brain change?" The question of the politics of publication and cultural values to support racism and sexism, albeit how subtle, continues to be asked. She ends with Bleier's statement "We are still mired in the naive hope that we can find something that we can *see* and *measure* and it will explain everything. It is silly science and it serves us badly."

Sources:
Gould, S. (1981). The mismeasure of man. New York: Norton
Tavris, C. (1992). The mismeasure of woman. New York: Simon

Personal accounts: When our bodies act against us.

In the book, *Psychology in Context: Voices and Perspectives*, several touching (and sometimes humorous) personal accounts provide a window on what life is like when persons and their families are affected by degenerative or intrusive disorders such as multiple sclerosis, Alzheimer's disease, Parkinson's disease, or epilepsy.

Nancy Mairs, author of *Carnal Acts*, talks about changes she experienced as multiple sclerosis progressively destroyed the myelin in her nervous system: her relationship with her cane, the leg brace that signaled the end of high heels, wearing trousers to cover the brace, how her three-wheeled scooter has rendered her invisible to many, the sexuality of the disabled, her struggles with fear, and her newly found sense of humor and fortitude in light of all these experiences.

Newton's Madness: Further Tales of Clinical Neurology is the account of Roberto d'Orta's life and decision to pursue experimental medication to curb the progression of Parkinson's disease. This article describes details of changes in physical capabilities, what it's like to feel like a "lizard in the eyes of the world", the hopes that patients place on the powerful effects of medications. Katherine Lipsitz' account of her denial of epilepsy may be one with which many of your students might identify....what it's like to struggle with the stigma associated with an illness when one is at college and struggling with perfectionism. Once accepting that change was in order, change she did...became an volunteer for the Epilepsy Society of New York City, improved how she treated her body, changed her relationships.

These accounts (and others that are presented in the book) help remind students that *people* are affected by changes in the brain...that the study of the biological basis of psychological experience is still rooted in humanity.

Source:
Sattler, D. N. & Shabatay, V. (Eds.) (1997). Psychology in context: Voices and perspectives. Boston: Houghton

Suggestions for Additional Readings

Villars, T. A. (1988). Chapter 9: Psychobiology in Bronstein, P.A. & Quina, K. (Eds.) Teaching a Psychology of People: Resources for Gender and Sociocultural Awareness. Washington, DC: APA

Bloom, F. E., & Lazerson, A. (1988). Brain, mind, and behavior (2nd ed.). New York: Freeman.

Carlson, N. R. (1988). Foundations of physiological psychology. Boston: Allyn and Bacon

Gazzaniga, M. S. (1985). The social brain: Discovering the Networks of the Mind. New York: Basic Books

Kramer, P. (1993). Listening to Prozac. New York: Viking

Laland, K. (1993). The mathematical modeling of human culture and its implications for psychology and the human sciences. British Journal of Psychology, 84, 145-169.

Levy, J. (1985). Right Brain, Left Brain: Fact or Fiction Psychology Today, May 1985

Sacks, O. (1985). The man who mistook his wife for a hat and other clinical tales. New York: Harper & Row

Sacks, O. (1995). An Anthropologist on Mars New York: Knopf

Springer, S. P. & Deutsch, G. (1994). Left brain, right brain. (4th ed.) New York: Freeman.

In-Class Activities and Demonstrations

TRAIL Blazing: Using Transparency Masters 2.1 - 2.6, review with students the "Checking Your TRAIL" sections in the chapter. Have students work in small groups to answer the questions and then review with the class as a whole to tie the text reading to activity in class.

Reaching Critical Mass: Using Transparency Masters 2.7 - 2.10, review with students the "Critical Thinking" sections in the chapter. Have students work in small groups to answer the questions and then review with the class as a whole to tie the text reading to activity in class.

Getting Down to IT: Using Transparency Masters 2.11 - 2.13, review the "Integrative Thinking" sections in the chapter with students. Have students work in small groups to answer the questions and then review with the class as a whole to tie the text reading to activity in class.

Neural Codes and Synaptic Transmission: Reardon, Durso, and Wilson (1994) describe two participatory exercises designed to get students actively engaged in illustrating the coding properties of neural stimulation and the role of neurotransmitters and psychoactive drugs in synaptic transmission.

    Exercise 1: Neural Coding: four simulations are described, all using one student (designated as the "receiving neuron") who receives "stimulation" when six other students (designated as "input" and holding flash cards with the letter E -- for excitation--) hold up their flash cards for designated time intervals. When the "receiving neuron" receives sufficient stimulation, it "fires" by writing "I fire" on the blackboard or overhead projector. Rates of firing of the receiving neuron are tallied after each simulation.

a. Basic Stimulation: Input neurons send their messages (i.e., flash their card) for 3 sec. at 5 sec. alternating intervals for 1-2 minutes. Each time the receiving neuron has received 3 E messages, he or she writes "I fire".

b. Excitation and Inhibition: A seventh input neuron is added with a flash card marked "I"--for inhibition. Input neurons flash their cards again as in the earlier simulation but this time the receiving neuron is to ignore one of the E cards that is present at the same time as the I card (thus the total rate of firing should be lower).

c. Temporal summation: Six E input messengers are used; five that flash their cards for 3 sec at 5 sec intervals and one that flashes his or her card for 3 sec at 3 sec intervals, resulting in a significant increase in firing of the receiving neuron.

d. Spatial summation of graded postsynaptic potentials: Input messengers are placed in different locations in the classroom with

4 messengers close to the front of the room and 2 in the rear of the room. All six messengers carry E flash cards but some of the messengers at the back of the room are likely not to be seen and thus be less likely to affect the firing of the neuron.

Exercise 2: Synaptic Transmission: Again, four simulations are described this time using a variation of musical chairs. To set up these simulations, two rows of four chairs each are arranged at the front of the room such that each row faces the other. One row is designated as the axon chairs (presynaptic neuron) and the other row, the receptor chairs (postsynaptic neuron).

a. Basic synaptic transmission: Four students sit in the axon chairs. When the presynaptic neuron "fires", the students cross the synaptic gap and sit in the receptor chairs (receptor sites). After sitting in the receptor chair, the students return to the axon chair (reuptake).

b. Mimicking a neurotransmitter: Four students (representing the neurotransmitter) occupy the axon chairs while an additional four students representing a drug that mimics the neurotransmitter stand behind the axon chair. When the neuron "fires", neurotransmitters and mimicking drug students both attempt to occupy the receptor chairs. If a neurotransmitter is successful at occupying the receptor chair, he or she must also return to the axon chair (via reuptake), leaving the receptor chair free to be occupied by the mimicking drug (to continue to stimulate the receptor site).

c. Occupying receptor sites: Four neurotransmitter students occupy the axon chairs while four receptor blocking students stand behind the receptor chairs. When the presynaptic neuron fires, both neurotransmitter and receptor blocking students attempt to sit in the receptor chair. Any neurotransmitter students who can't occupy a receptor chair must return to the axon chair before being released again.

d. Blocking reuptake: Four neurotransmitter students occupy the axon chairs and four reuptake blockers stand behind the axon chair. When the presynaptic neuron fires, the reuptake blockers sit in the axon chair thus forcing the neurotransmitter students to continually return to the receptor chairs.

Reardon and his colleagues report that both exercises produced exam performances on neural coding and synaptic transmission questions at least as effective as lecture alone.

Source:
Reardon, R., Durso, F., & Wilson, D. (1994). Neural Coding and Synaptic Transmission: Participation exercises for Introductory Psychology. Teaching of Psychology, 21(2), 96-98.

Split brain--a lateralization demonstration: This is a rather fun exercise, originally developed by Kemble (1987), that combines some concepts of lateralization of function with a review of experiment methodology. To conduct this exercise, you will need copies of **Handout Master # 2.1: Split brain--a lateralization demonstration**, enough wooden dowels and stopwatches so each group of students has one dowel and stopwatch, a list of words (for a rhyming task), and a list of 2-digit numbers (for an addition task). Students will be balancing the dowel on the right index finger and then the left index finger (or vice versa) without performing additional tasks and while performing competing tasks. Before the exercise, refresh students' memories for right/left hemisphere lateralization for mathematical reasoning and language and left vs. right motor control.
Basic hypothesis: Balancing the dowel on the right index finger should be more difficult when trying to engage in a language-related task whereas balancing the dowel on the left index finger should be more difficult when trying to engage in a mathematics-related task.
Procedure: Divide students into working groups, assigning one timekeeper in each group. After remaining students practice the dowel-balancing on each index finger, time their dowel-balancing for 5 trials each on right index finger without a task, right index finger while engaging in the language-task of producing rhyming words to the list of words read by a group member, left index finger without a task, and left index finger while engaging in an addition task for 2 2-digit numbers read by a group member. Each trial ends when the dowel falls off the finger. Compare time differences on non-task and task trials for each finger for the group and review data from the class as a whole.

Source:
Kemble, E. D. (1987). Cerebral lateralization. In Makosky et al. (Eds.) <u>Activities Handbook for the Teaching of Psychology</u>. Washington: APA.

Hairy-knuckles and bumps on our heads.....: Another light-hearted exercise that most students will probably find somewhat humorous based on Nesbit (1981). Nesbit designed his demonstration to illustrate biological heredity, self-fulfilling prophecy, stereotyping, and discrimination. Students were instructed to look at the back of their fingers with the explanation that hair on the section of finger closest to the knuckle results from a dominant gene, whereas hair on the middle section of the finger is the result of a rare recessive gene. Some students were likely to have this "middigital hair." These students were then asked to contact family members to determine if they too had evidence of middigital hair, and to make a list of positive and negative characteristics these relatives share. When students returned to class with their list of shared characteristics, a discussion was held concerning the meaning and consequences of having hairy middigits.

The concept of self-fulfilling prophecy was introduced when the consequences of having hairy middigits was discussed (Do we treat others who have a physical characteristic differently because we assume the physical trait is related in some way to some psychological trait?). This exercise can be extended to consider any number of physical differences such as the ability to roll one's tongue into a tube shape, having attached vs. unattached ear lobes. Conduct your class "survey" in a similar manner to Nesbit, looking for "connections" between these physical characteristics and trait differences. Discuss how these differences can lead to stereotypes about others and subsequent discrimination. Have the class consider to what extent relatively meaningless physical differences might translate into meaningful differences in treatment of others, how in the scientific process we may have exaggerated small differences in justification of differences of treatment. This exercise can act as an interesting tie-in to a discussion of phrenology as an early theory linking physiology and personality or the eugenics movement.

Source:
Nesbit, F. L. (1981). Biological bases of behavior and the self-fulfilling prophecy. in Makosky et al. (Eds.) Activities Handbook for the Teaching of Psychology (Vol. 3). Washington: APA

PhysioPursuit
Ackil has created a trivia-type board game using terms and concepts discussed by physiological psychologists. The game, available from Ackil, can be played as an in-class activity with teams receiving points for correct answers and extra points for explaining corrections to incorrect responses.

Source:
Ackil, J. E. (1986). PhysioPursuit: A trivia-type game for the classroom. Teaching of Psychology, 13, 91

Sources for Additional Activities
Books:
    Benjamin, L. & Lowman, K. (1981). Activities Handbook for the Teaching of Psychology. Washington DC: American Psychological Association.

    Diamond, M., Scheibel, A., & Elson, L. (1985). The human brain coloring book. New York: HarperCollins

    Halonen, J. (1995). Chapter 2: Neuroscience and Behavior in The Critical Thinking Companion For Introductory Psychology (Worth Publ.). (Exercises 2.1 - 2.3)

    Makosky, V. et al. (Eds.) (1995). Activities Handbook for the Teaching of Psychology (Vol. III). Washington DC: American Psychological Association.

    Slife, B. (1998). Taking sides: Clashing views on controversial psychological issues. Guilford: Dushkin (Issue 4: Is homosexuality genetically determined?)

Journey II Software:
The Physiology lab can be entered by clicking the icon on the Main Menu. There are some noteworthy errors in the program which make some parts of the lab very confusing.

Functional Anatomy: The student is presented with a case history of a person with intractable epilepsy and is then given the task of mapping and stimulating different areas of the "patient's" brain to advise a neurosurgeon on appropriate areas to consider removing via a surgical attempt to reduce the effects of epileptic seizures. The student is asked a series of questions concerning their observations and does a point & click drill on identifying parts of the brain. There are some errors in labels for different areas of the brain in the program.

Neuropsychology of Sex Differences: The student is presented with a series of 4 tasks including mental rotation of a 3-D object, listing all words beginning with "sh", finding a hidden figure, and calculation from a formula. Results are compared to general gender differences on each of the task.

Lateralization: A picture of 2 half-faces is presented as students are directed to stare at an X in the center of the screen. "Normal" people (i.e., people without a severed corpus callosum) would see 2 half-faces whereas those persons with split brain "see" something entirely different. A demonstration of what happens for the split brain patient is offered, but the results presented are not consistent with the literature and is very confusing....you might opt not to use this file.

World Wide Web: Check out the following WWW sites for information and activities relevant to this section of the text!

Addison Wesley Longman's Website -- **http://longman.awl.com/**
- . PsychZone link -- **http://longman.awl.com/**
- . Psych Web -- **http://www.gasou.edu/psychweb/psychweb.htm**

Self-Quizzes for Introductory Psychology --
http://www.gasou.edu/psychweb/selfquiz/selfquiz.htm

Psychology Jumping Stand --
http://www.indiana.edu:80/~iuepsyc/PsycJump.html

The Psychology Place --**http://www.psychplace.com**

Human Behavior and Evolution Society home page --
http://psych.lmu.edu.hbes.htm

Biological psychology -- **http://www.uwsp.edu/acad/psych/tbiopsy.htm**
Psychology and neuroscience -- **http://www.jhu.edu/~phil/relfold/psycho.html**
- . Sex differences in the brain --
http://fas.sfu.ca/css/gcs/scientists/Kimura/kimura.html

PET scans -- **http://students/gsm.uci.edu/~eakleine/bif/direct.htm**
- . Neuropsychology -- **http://www.premier.net/~cogito/neuropsyc.html**
- . Brain atlas -- **http://www.med.harvard.edu/AANLIB/home.html**
- . Research on the brain --
http://www-hbp.scripps.edu/
    or
http:// www.ornl.gov/TechResources/Human_Genome/home.html

Brain imaging -- **http://www.mni.mcgill.ca/**
- . Split brain -- **http://ezinfo.ucs.indiana.edu/~pietsh/split-brain.html**

Database on the Neurosciences -- **http://www.neuroguide.com/index4.html#live**

Neuropsychology Central --
http://www.premier.net/~cogito/neuropsy.html

Neural processes -- **http://psych.hanover.edu/Krantz/neurotut.html**
- . Resources on cognitive neuroscience --
http://www-cgi.cs.cmu.edu/afs/cs/project/cnbc/other/other-neuro.html

William Calvin's (neurophysiologist) home page --
http://weber.u.washington.edu/wcalvin/

Audio-Visual Support
Films/Videos:

Overviews
Birth of a Brain (CRM, 33 minutes)
The Brain, Mind, and Behavior Series (IU(FI), 60 minutes each)
> Program 1: *The Enlightened Machine*

The Hidden Universe: *The Brain, Parts 1 and 2* (IU(CRM), 49 minutes)
The Human Brain (Second Edition) (IU(EBEC), 1983, 24 minutes)
The Nervous System: Nerves at Work (FFHS, 26 minutes)
The Neuron Suite (PBS/Salubris Prod., 58 minutes)
Journey to the Centers of the Brain Series (FFHS, 58 minutes each)
> Program 1: *The Electric Ape*
> Program 2: *Through a Glass Darkly*
> Program 3: *Bubble, Bubble, Toil and Trouble*
> Program 4: *The Seven Ages of the Brain*
> Program 5: *The Mind's I*

Discovering Psychology (Annenberg/CPB Project, 30 minutes)
> Program 3: *The Behaving Brain*
> Program 4: *The Responsive Brain*

Brain and Nervous System: Your Information Superhighway (FFHS, 25 minutes)
The Development of the Human Brain (FFHS, 1998, 40 minutes)
The Brain (FFHS, 1998, 23 minutes)
The Brain: An Inside Look (FFHS, 1998, 20 minutes)
The Human Brain Series (FFHS, 1998, 21-35 minutes)
> Program 1: *Anatomy of the Human Brain*
> Program 2: *The Human Brain in Situ*

The Brain Series (FFHS, 1998, 58 minutes each)
> Program 1: *Inside Information: The Brain and How It Works*

Specific Brain Systems
The Autonomic Nervous System (IFB, 17 minutes)
Peripheral Nervous System (EMC UC, 19 minutes)

Neurotransmitter Activity
The Keys to Paradise, Parts 1 and 2 (TLF, 1979, 52 minutes)
Epilepsy: The Storm Within (FFHS, 27 minutes)

Split-Brain & Methods for Studying the Brain
The Brain, Mind, and Behavior Series (IU(FI), 1984, 60 minutes each)
> Program 6: *The Two Brains*

Discovering Psychology (Annenberg/CPB Project, 1990, 30 minutes)
> Program 5: *The Mind Hidden and Divided*

Left Brain, Right Brain, Parts 1 and 2 (IU(FML), 1979, 51 minutes)
Classic Experiments of Behavioral Neuropsychology (HARR, 1978, 22 minutes)
EEG: A Diagnostic Test (PSUPCR, 1980, 8 minutes)
The Enchanted Loom (FFHS, 1990, 26 minutes)
Marvels of the Mind (IU(NGS), 1980, 23 minutes)
Windows Into the Brain (obtain from: Office of Scientific Information, Room 14-105, 5600 Fishers Lane, Rockville, MD 20857, 9 minutes)
Within the Human Brain: A Dissection by Dr. Marion C. Diamond (EMC UC, 1991, 49 minutes)
Psychosurgery: Best Hope or False Hope? (FFHS, 1998, 52 minutes)
The Human Brain Series (FFHS, 1998, 21-35 minutes)
> Program 3: *Pathology Examples in the Human Brain*

Clinical Features of Myotonic Dystrophy and Huntington's Disease (FFHS, 24 minutes)
Advancements in Traumatic Brain Injury (FFHS, 19 minutes)
Biology and Behavior (MOTO, 22 minutes)

Psychology Encyclopedia Laserdisc IV:
Movies

Neural transmission: introduction	(21 sec.)	Side 1, Frames 12644-13259
Neural transmission: axon	(19 sec.)	Side 1, Frames 13260-13814
Neural transmission: action potential	(1 min. 21 sec.)	Side 1, Frames 13815-16279
Neural transmission: synapse	(1 min. 58 sec.)	Side 1, Frames 16180-19726
Neural transmission: effect of myelin sheathing	(34 sec.)	Side 1, Frames 19727-20753
Neural transmission: effect of cocaine	(1 min. 6 sec.)	Side 1, Frames 20754-22744
Brain: a 3-D model	(1 min. 22 sec.)	Side 1, Frames 22745-25515

Still Images

Hindbrain [UN]	Frame 53437	Side	all
Midbrain [UN]	53438		all
Forebrain [1/2] [UN]	53439		all
Forebrain [2/2] [UN]	53440		all
Central and peripheral nervous system [4.2]	53441		all
Autonomic nervous system [4.2]	53442		all
Nervous system organization [1/12] [4.3]	53443		all
Nervous system organization [2/12] [4.3]	53444		all
Nervous system organization [3/12] [4.3]	53445		all
Nervous system organization [4/12] [4.3]	53446		all
Nervous system organization [5/12] [4.3]	Frame 53447	Side	all
Nervous system organization [6/12] [4.3]	53448		all
Nervous system organization [7/12] [4.3]	53449		all
Nervous system organization [8/12] [4.3]	53450		all
Nervous system organization [9/12] [4.3]	53451		all
Nervous system organization [10/12] [4.3]	53452		all
Nervous system organization [11/12] [4.3]	53453		all
Nervous system organization [12/12] [4.3]	53454		all
Types of neurons [4.4]	53455		all
Neuron structure [4.5]	53456		all
Neurotransmitter crossing a synapse [1/3] [4.7]	53457		all
Neurotransmitter crossing a synapse [2/3] [4.7]	53458		all
Neurotransmitter crossing a synapse [3/3] [4.7]	53459		all
Brain activity in 3-D [4.10]	53460		all
Human brain anatomy [1/3] [4.11]	53461		all
Human brain anatomy [2/3] [4.11]	53462		all
Human brain anatomy [3/3] [4.11]	53463		all
Limbic system [4.12]	53464		all
Lobes of the cerebrum [4.13]	53465		all
Visual pathways [1/3] [4.15]	53466		all
Visual pathways [2/3] [4.15]	53467		all
Visual pathways [3/3] [4.15]	53468		all

Transparency Master 2.1: Checking Your TRAIL 2.1

<u>True</u> or <u>False</u>: The psychologists who focus on the combination of genetic and environmental influences on behavior are Freudian.

No two people, except _____, have the same set of genes.
- **A. mothers and fathers**
- **B. brothers and sisters**
- **C. identical siblings**
- **D. fraternal twins**

<u>True</u> or <u>False</u>: Most psychological characteristics appear to be the result of a pairing of dominant and recessive genes.

Which one of the following is true?
- **A. The idea that people belong to one of three races is based on a twentieth century classification.**
- **B. What we call "race" has little to do with genetic differences.**
- **C. There are far more genetic and biological differences than similarities across racial groups.**
- **D. The physical characteristics used to classify people into races account for about 15% of an individual's inherited characteristics.**

Transparency Master 2.2: Checking Your TRAIL 2.2

Name the three parts of a neuron and explain the functions of each part.

Which one of the following statements is true of a "fired" neuron?
- **A.** The more intense the stimulus, the more intense the action potential along the neuron.
- **B.** An action potential travels down the axon.
- **C.** It can be partially fired.
- **D.** It is no longer working.

What happens at a synapse?

Name and explain two processes by which the body stops neurotransmitters from continuing to send their messages?

Transparency Master 2.3: Checking Your TRAIL 2.3

Hearing a song reminds you of a special event or relationship. Which neurotransmitter is responsible?

Which one of these neurotransmitter is associated with feeling calm?
   A. GABA
   B. serotonin
   C. acetylcholine
   D. norepinephrine

Endocrine glands produce:
   A. DNA
   B. muscles
   C. gonads
   D. hormones

Which gland controls the release of hormones by other endocrine glands?
   A. adrenal gland
   B. thyroid gland
   C. pituitary gland
   D. gonad

Transparency Master 2.4: Checking Your TRAIL 2.4

Fill in the chart below:

Peripheral Nervous System

a. _____ nervous system   b. _____ nervous system

c. _____   d. _____

Movement of your voluntary muscles is controlled by which part of the peripheral nervous system?

If you witness an automobile accident, which part of your autonomic nervous system would become aroused? Identify it on the chart above.

The central nervous system is composed of two structures, the ____ ____ and _____.

90

Transparency Master 2.5: Checking Your TRAIL 2.5

What functions are performed by the brain stem?

What are the functions of the cerebellum?

What part of the brain might, if damaged, cause people to respond abnormally to emotional situations?
A. medulla
B. cerebellum
C. thalamus
D. limbic system

Which part of the brain determines which stimuli are most important?
A. pons
B. limbic system
C. reticular formation
D. thalamus

Transparency Master 2.6: Checking Your TRAIL 2.6

Identify the cortical lobes and describe the primary function of each lobe.

Mrs. S. was not aware of objects on her left side. Which functional section of her cortex was probably damaged?
- A. sensory cortex
- B. motor cortex
- C. association area
- D. the largest part of the cortex

Which functional section of the cerebral cortex is the largest?
- A. sensory cortex
- B. motor cortex
- C. association area
- D. somatosensory cortex

Based on what you know about lateralization, who is likely to experience greater loss of function following stroke damage on one cerebral hemisphere, a man or a woman? Why?

Transparency Master 2.7: Critical Thinking 2.1

Behavior geneticists study identical twins who have been adopted by different parents. Such twin studies have been criticized on the grounds that adopted twins are often placed in similar homes and some twins had contact with each other before testing took place (Adler, 1991). How could these factors, as well as fashion trends and shared socioeconomic status, have affected the similarities in the twins' behaviors?

Transparency Master 2.8: Critical Thinking 2.2

How would examining a damaged brain help scientists learn about the functions of different parts of the brain?

Transparency Master 2.9: Critical Thinking 2.3

Would you want to continue to live in the condition of that described for Ms. Cruzan? Why or why not? Use your knowledge of the brain and nervous system to support your opinion.

Transparency Master 2.10: Critical Thinking 2.4

Beethoven was able to compose music even after becoming profoundly deaf. In terms of association areas and plasticity, hypothesize how this achievement was possible.

Transparency Master 2.11: Integrative Thinking 2.1

How did the text discussion of the research on homosexuality reflect critical thinking, as described in the Introductory Chapter's Table 1.4.

Transparency Master 2.12: Integrative Thinking 2.2

Based on what you learned in the Introductory Chapter about types of psychological studies, was the study of H.M.'s memory an experiment, a case study, or a survey?

Transparency Master 2.13: Integrative Thinking 2.3

Suppose the experience of Phineas Gage were the only source of information that psychologists had about the frontal lobe. In light of what you learned in the Introductory Chapter about samples, why would psychologists then hesitate to draw conclusions about the functions of the frontal lobe?

Handout Master 2.1: Split Brain--A lateralization demonstration

Name: _____
Group Number: _____

Right Index Finger: No Task
    Trial 1: _____
    Trial 2: _____
    Trial 3: _____
    Trial 4: _____
    Trial 4: _____

average time : _____

Right Index Finger: Language Task
    Trial 1: _____
    Trial 2: _____
    Trial 3: _____
    Trial 4: _____
    Trial 4: _____

average time : _____   Difference: _____

Left Index Finger: No Task
    Trial 1: _____
    Trial 2: _____
    Trial 3: _____
    Trial 4: _____
    Trial 4: _____

average time : _____

Left Index Finger: Math Task
    Trial 1: _____
    Trial 2: _____
    Trial 3: _____
    Trial 4: _____
    Trial 4: _____

average time : _____   Difference: _____

Group Averages:
Right Index Finger: No Task   _____
Right Index Finger: Language Task   _____   Difference: _____
Left Index Finger: No Task   _____
Left Index Finger: Math Task   _____   Difference: _____

Conclusions:
_____
_____
_____
_____
_____
_____

Mind Matters CD-ROM Faculty Guide

BIOPSYCHOLOGY

I. Introduction to Biopsychology
    I1. ★Pop-Up: Bio-Fallacies

II. Evolution and Behavior
    A. Darwin's Theory of Evolution and Principle of Natural Selection
        A1. ★Pop-Up: A Profile of Charles Darwin
    B. Assumptions of Natural Selection
        B1. ★Pop-Up: Cyberlemmings: A Simulation of the Natural Selection Process
    C. Natural Selection and Behavior
        C1. ★Pop-Up: The Universality of Emotion
    D. The Evolution of Altruism and Dating
        D1. ★Pop-Up: Studying Mate Selection
    E. Natural Selection and Snake Phobia
    Rapid Review 1

III. Physiological Psychology: Neurons and the Endocrine System
    A. Neurons: The Building Blocks of the Nervous System
    B. The Structure of a Neuron
        B1. ★The Rollover Neuron
    C. Types of Neurons
    D. How Neurons Operate
    E. The Action Potential
    F. Crossing the Synapse
    G. At the Receiving Neuron
        G1. ★Pop-Up: An Exercise in Neural Communication
        G2. ★Pop-Up: The Navigable Neuron
    H. Neurotransmitters
        H1. ★Neurotransmitter Effects
        H2. ★Pop-Up: How Cocaine Works
    I. The Endocrine System
        I1. ★Elements of the Endocrine System
    Rapid Review 2

IV. Physiological Psychology: The Brain
    A. The Structure of the Nervous System
        A1. ★Pop-Up: The Classic Case of Phineas Gage
    B. The Hindbrain
        B1. ★Pop-Up: Brain Lateralization
    C. The Midbrain

D. The Forebrain
- D1. ★Pop-Up: The Interactive Brain
- D2. ★Pop-Up: The Brain Structure and Function Game

E. The Paradox of Plasticity
F. Biological Causality Revisited

Rapid Review 3

Quick Quiz

BIOPSYCHOLOGY
Annotated Outline

I. Introduction to Biopsychology

The Biopsychology unit begins with a distinction between proximal and distal causes. Proximal causes of a behavior are its immediate causes. When applied to biological explanations, proximal causes focus on the ways in which physiological changes shape the organism's behavior and psychological experience. Distal causes of behavior are its remote causes. When applied to biological explanations, distal causes focus on the ways in which the evolutionary heritage of the organism shapes behavior and psychological experience.

I1. ★Pop-Up: Bio-Fallacies

Through a combination of text and graphics, students are introduced to the nominal fallacy, the deterministic fallacy, naturalistic fallacy, and the false war between nature and nurture fallacy.

Bio-Fallacies

Activity Type: Illustrated Essay

Learning Objective: Encourage critical thinking about biological explanations of behavior.

Faculty Note: The **nominal fallacy** occurs when a phenomenon is simply renamed or labeled rather than understood. The **deterministic fallacy** occurs when someone concludes that genetics rigidly prescribe behavior. The **naturalistic fallacy** occurs when someone concludes that something is good because it occurs naturally. The **false war between nature and nurture** is a fallacy that involves pitting nature and nurture explanations against each other. Behavior is almost always influenced by an interaction between nature and nurture.

II. Evolution and Behavior

The notion that some behaviors may be explained by evolution is introduced by pointing out that people are much more likely to develop a fear of snakes, which annually kill approximately 15 U.S. citizens, than one of automobiles, which annually kill approximately 43,000 U.S. citizens.

A. Darwin's Theory of Evolution and Principle of Natural Selection

This section briefly introduces students to Darwin's notions of adaptation and natural selection.

A1. ★Pop-up: A Profile of Charles Darwin

This pop-up contains a brief biography of Darwin.

> **A Profile of Charles Darwin**
>
> **Type of Activity:** Illustrated Essay
>
> **Learning Objective:** Introduce students to Darwin and provide context for his theory of evolution by natural selection.
>
> **Faculty Note:** Darwin is, of course, remembered for his theory of evolution by natural selection. Most students probably know this from other classes. What students often don't know is what Darwin was like as a person. One of the goals of this pop-up is to humanize Darwin. He led a fascinating life. For example, his mother was the daughter of the founder of the Wedgwood china works. Similarly, Darwin was an unspectacular student while in college. And, although he spent five years traveling about the H.M.S. Beagle serving as the ship's naturalist after completing college, for the rest of his life he rarely traveled.
>
> **Additional Resources:** Darwin's *Voyage of the Beagle* and *The Origin of Species* can be found at http://www.literature.org/Works/Charles-Darwing/

B. Assumptions of Natural Selection

What separated Darwin's theory of evolution from other theories of adaptation was the principle of natural selection. This section presents four assumptions that are contained in natural selection. 1) Individual members of a species vary from one another. 2) Some characteristics are passed on genetically. 3) Some characteristics aid survival and reproduction. 4) For selection to take place, a characteristic must affect the rate of reproductive success.

B1. ★Pop-up: Cyberlemmings: A simulation of the Natural Selection Process

In this pop-up, students can explore the effects that varying selection pressure and time have on the rate of acrophobia in a mythical population of cyberlemmings.

> **Cyberlemmings: A simulation of the Natural Selection Process**
>
> **Type of Activity:** Simulation
>
> **Learning Objective:** Understand the concept of natural selection and how it influences evolution across generations.
>
> **Faculty Note:** The goal of this activity to help students understand how natural selection could shape a particular behavior: in this case, fear of heights. When students first observe the cyberlemmings, they see a gaggle of them milling about randomly near the edge of a cliff, with some periodically straying too close and falling over. Some of the cyberlemmings are somewhat acrophobic. They are labeled with a yellow streak down

their backs and they tend to stay farther from the edge. After observing the cyberlemmings, the students can then change the selection pressure by raising or lowering the height of the cliff and observe the effects that these changes have on subsequent generations of cyberlemmings. If selection pressure is low (i.e., if the cliff is low and therefore not lethal) the proportion of acrophobic lemmings will not change across generations. In contrast, if the selection pressure is high (i.e., if the cliff is tall and lethal) the proportion of acrophobic lemmings will tend to increase across generations. How quickly that increase occurs depends upon the magnitude of the selection pressure. The greater the selection pressure, the faster the change.

One of the main points of this simulation is to help students to see that evolution happens slowly, across thousands of generations. Students sometimes ask, for example, if recent inventions like the automobile have caused humans to evolve in ways that are different from our ancestors. From an evolutionary perspective, the clear answer is "not yet." The introduction of the automobile is far too recent to have affected the course of human evolution in any measurable way.

The computer simulation gets around the problem of the slow pace of evolution by looking at slices in time separated by thousands of generations. In real life, we can get around that problem by looking at organisms that have quick generations. For example, although we cannot observe evolution happening in real time with humans, a feature that makes it difficult to test evolutionary accounts of human behavior, we can see it happening among bacteria. The growing number of antibiotic resistant strains of bacteria provides strong support for Darwin's principle of natural selection.

Additional Resources:

Richard Dawkins, *The Blind Watchmaker*, provides an interesting tour of evolutionary principles.
If you are interested in other simulations of natural selection processes try the biology simulation page at http://biology.miningco.com/msub16.htm

C. Natural Selection and Behavior

This section continues with the idea that evolution not only shapes anatomy, it may also shape behavior.

C1. ★Pop-up: The Universality of Emotions

In this pop-up, students can try their hands at Ekman's emotion naming task. Ekman and Friesen (1975) found strong agreement across many cultures in the identification of fear, joy, anger, disgust, sadness, and surprise, suggesting that these "primary" emotions may have their basis in evolution.

> **The Universality of Emotions**
>
> **Type of Activity:** Exploration
>
> **Learning Objective:** Introduce students to the notion that some emotions are universal and possibly the product of evolution.
>
> **Faculty Note:** In this activity, the students' task it to match photos of people expressing a variety of emotions with the appropriate emotion label. The photos and labels that are used involve six "universal" emotions identified by Ekman (i.e., anger, fear, happiness, disgust, sadness, and surprise). Because these emotions are universal, students should have little difficulty matching them correctly. At the end of the activity, they can look at results from cross-cultural studies of emotions.
>
> A point that often comes up in the discussion of emotions is whether all emotions are similar across all cultures. Although there is good evidence that these six emotions hold true across vastly different cultures, the cross-cultural evidence for other "secondary" emotions (e.g., love or pride) is less compelling. Indeed, though not statistically significant, the cross-cultural data presented in this activity suggest that even among the primary emotions, cross-cultural agreement is lower for the negative emotions than for the positive emotions. This trend provides an opportunity to discuss the roles that culture plays in shaping both the experience and expression of emotions.
>
> **Additional Resources:**
>
> Emotion Laboratory Research—This site discusses ways to study emotions.
> http://www.psy.ulaval.ca/~arvid/R2e.html

D. The Evolution of Dating and Altruism

In this section, an evolutionary account of altruism is proposed. From the standpoint of evolution, altruism is only adaptive if it facilitates the transmission of the altruist's genes to the next generation. The principle of "kin selection" (i.e., the notion that we tend to help similar others) may provide one such mechanism of transmission.

D. ★Pop-up: Studying Mate Selection

In this pop-up, the characteristics that males and females look for in potential partners are explored from an evolutionary perspective. According to evolutionary theorists, differences emerge because of the different selection pressures that confront men and women. For men, the easiest way to maximize reproductive success would be to mate with as many fertile women as possible. In contrast, the route to reproductive success for women would be to ensure the survival of the relatively few offspring they can bear. The activity that is included in the pop-up asks students to guess the gender of the authors of a collection of personal ads that vary in their emphasis on status versus physical attractiveness.

Studying Mate Selection

Type of Activity: Exploration

Learning Objective: Introduce students to an evolutionary account of a complex human behavior. The goal is to help students to see the logic behind evolutionary-based explanations and to help them to think critically about the relationship between evolution and behavior.

Faculty Note: Evolutionary accounts of human behavior are often controversial. This is particularly true when the behavior in question is something as complex and mysterious as love. In this activity, students try to guess the gender of the authors of a series of personal ads. On
average, the ads written by males indicate an interest in finding a younger and physically attractive partner, while the ads written by females indicate an interest in finding an older, financially secure partner. Evolutionary psychologists argue that this difference has its origins in the different selection pressures that have confronted men and women. Because fertility varies as a function of age more among women than among men, for men the pressure has been to find fertile mates. According to this argument, because there is no clear indicator of fertility of humans, youth and beauty have become the proxies that signal fertility. In contrast, because the physical demands of birth fall disproportionately on women, evolutionary psychologists have argued that the pressure on women has been to find mates who can contribute to the protection of any offspring. In psychological terms, this translates to a preference for high-status, emotionally committed men.

In teaching evolutionary accounts of behavior, particularly when those accounts focus on gender differences, it is often worth reminding students of several things. First, although men and women do sometimes behave differently, we are far more similar than we are different. For example, although men may focus relatively more on physical features while women focus more on status and commitment, most men and women would prefer someone who is physically attractive and high in status. Second, students should keep the deterministic fallacy in mind. Even if evolution has shaped preferences, this does not mean that an individual is hostage to his or her evolutionary heritage. Third, students should also keep the naturalistic fallacy in mind. There is a tendency to assume that if something is the product of evolution, it is a good thing. Evolution and worth have nothing to do with each other.

Additional Resources:

One question that the mate selection research raises is "What is beauty?" A 1996 article by D. Singh pitted Waist to Hip Ratio (WHR) against overall weight to see how much each varies by time. Using archival data, Singh found that WHR, which is correlated with fertility, has stayed fairly constant across time and culture. In contrast weight, which is not correlated with fertility, varies considerably across time and culture. His web site can be found http://www.psy.utexas.edu/psy/FACULTY/Singh/Singh.html

E. Natural Selection and Snake Phobia

The evolution section ends where it began, with a consideration of the evolutionary account of snake phobia. In 1971, Seligman proposed that individuals who tended to avoid snakes might have had a greater chance of surviving and passing that tendency on to their offspring. Over many generations, the proportion of "phobic" individuals would have increased.

Rapid Review 1

III. Physiological Psychology

This section introduces the search for proximal causes of behavior, beginning with the nervous system.

A. Neurons: The Building Blocks of the Nervous System

In this section, neurons are introduced as cells that specialize in communication.

B. The Structure of a Neuron

This section divides neurons into three parts: the soma, which functions to keep the cell alive; the dendrites, which receive messages from nearby neurons; and the axon, which transmits information down the length of the neuron.

B1. ★The Rollover Neuron

In this interactive animation, students can explore the functions of various parts of the neuron.

The Rollover Neuron

Type of Activity: Interactive Illustration

Learning Objective: Learn and remember the major anatomical structures in a neuron including the dendrites, cell body, axon, and synapse.

Faculty Note: In this activity, students can explore the anatomy of a neuron by rolling their cursors over various structures in the neuron and seeing the names of the various structures pop up.

C. Types of Neurons

In this section, sensory neurons, motor neurons, and interneurons are all identified.

D. How Neurons Operate

All neurons are described as transmitting information in the same manner, by a combination of electrical and chemical processes. In this section, the resting state of the neuron is described.

E. The Action Potential

This section describes the changes that a neuron goes through as an action potential is generated.

F. Crossing the Synapse

This section describes the changes that occur when an action potential reaches the synapse between two neurons.

G. At the Receiving Neuron

This section describes the changes that occur at the receiving neuron (a.k.a., the post-synaptic neuron) as neurotransmitters bind at receptor cites.

G1. ★Pop-up: The Navigable Neuron

In this activity, students can explore the operation of neurons through a series of interactive animations and text.

The Navigable Neuron

Type of Activity: Exploration

Learning Objective: Discover the functions that various anatomical structures in a neuron perform.

Faculty Note: This activity is designed to reinforce and extend the rollover neuron animation that precedes it. In the rollover neuron animation, students are drilled on the names of the various parts of a neuron. In this activity, students can click on the various structures within a neuron and see animated descriptions of what a particular structures does.

Additional Resources: Neurosciences on the Internet—This site contains links to a variety or resources and also has a searchable database. http://www.neuroguide.com/

G2. ★Pop-up: An Exercise in Neural Communication

In this activity, students can explore the concept of the "graded potential" in greater detail by seeing what happens with various combinations of excitatory and inhibitory messages.

An Exercise in Neural Communication

Type of Activity: Exploration

Learning Objective: Understand excitation, inhibition, and the graded potential.

Faculty Note: While the navigable neuron helps students to explore an individual neuron, it does not capture the interaction between neurons. This activity is designed to help students see how neurons influence each other by allowing them to examine the conditions that lead an animated post-synaptic neuron to fire. In the activity, students will see a schematic of a neuron that includes the soma, dendrites, and axon hillock of a neuron. In addition, they will see an electrical gauge that measures the activity inside the neuron. The students' task in the activity is to experiment with different combinations of fast and slow excitatory and inhibitory inputs and observe the effect these inputs have on the post-synaptic neuron. Completing the activity should help students gain a better understanding of the graded potential and of the action potential threshold.

Additional Resources: A series of online neural tutorials can be found at http://psych.hanover.edu/Krantz/neurotut.html

H. Neurotransmitters

This section describes neurotransmitters and their functions.

H1. ★Neurotransmitter Effects

In this activity, students can explore the behavioral effects of various neurotransmitters.

Neurotransmitter Effects

Type of Activity: Interactive Illustration

Learning Objective: Learn and remember the physiological and psychological effects of selected neurotransmitters.

Faculty Note: In this activity, students can explore the behavioral effects of various neurotransmitters by clicking on the neurotransmitter and seeing a description of its behavioral and psychological effects.

Additional Resources: A gallery of animations depicting the actions of neurotransmitters at the synapse is available at
http://www.neuroguide.com/cajal_gallery.html

H2. ★Pop-up: How Cocaine Works

In this video, students can see an animation of the effects that cocaine has at the synapse. In large part, the feeling of intense pleasure that cocaine produces is due to cocaine's ability to block re-uptake of dopamine.

How Cocaine Works

Type of Activity: Movie

Learning Objective: Understand how neurotransmitters operate at the synapse and the effects that cocaine has on this process.

Faculty Note: This video clip contains an excellent animation of neurotransmitters crossing the synaptic cleft and binding on the post-synaptic neuron. The explanation about re-uptake and the effects that cocaine has on that process is engaging and frequently provokes questions. The video provides a good context for determining how well students understand the behavior of neurons and neurotransmitters.

Additional Resources: Another animation of cocaine blocking dopamine re-uptake can be found at http://www.neuroguide.com/newpump.html

I. The Endocrine System

In this section, the structure and function of the endocrine system is described.

I1. ★Elements of the Endocrine System

In this activity, students can explore the structure and functions of various parts of the endocrine system.

Elements of the Endocrine System

Type of Activity: Interactive Animation

Learning Objective: Learn and remember the functions of the major anatomical structures in the endocrine system.

> **Faculty Note:** In this activity, students can explore the structure of the endocrine system by rolling their cursors over various parts of the endocrine system and seeing their names and functions appear on screen.

Rapid Review 2

IV. Physiological Psychology: The Brain

In this section, the brain is discussed as a complex structure that is composed of a variety of specialized parts. The subsequent discussion of the functions of those parts is organized around the division between the central and peripheral nervous systems and the emergence of the hindbrain, midbrain, and forebrain.

A. The Structure of the Nervous System

In this section, the structure of the nervous system is described.

A1. ★Pop-up: The Classic Case of Phineas Gage

One of the first cases to provide insight into the relationships between the various structures of the brain and behavior was the case of Phineas Gage. The story of his injury and behavioral changes that followed are chronicled in this pop-up.

The Classic Case of Phineas Gage

Type of Activity: Illustrated Essay

Learning Objective: Introduce students to the notion that specific parts of the brain are involved in specific behaviors and psychological experiences.

Faculty Note: Phineas Gage was a construction foreman for the Rutland and Burlington Railroad in Vermont when he had an accident that resulted in an iron bar being blown through the front of his head. Although he survived the accident, his subsequent behavior and personality
were quite different. His case is historically important because it provides one of the first attempts to link brain damage to specific changes in behavior and personality.

Additional Resources: An entire web site devoted to Phineas Gage can be found at http://www.psych.unimelb.edu.au/phineas_gage.html

B. The Hindbrain

In this section, the functions of the various structures of that make up the hindbrain (i.e., the medulla, pons, and cerebellum) are discussed.

B1. ★Pop-up: Brain Lateralization

In this pop-up, the lateralized nature of the brain is discussed through a combination of text and graphics.

Brain Lateralization

Type of Activity: Illustrated Essay

Learning Objective: Understand the lateralized nature of the brain and where this does and does not make a difference.

Faculty Note: In this illustrated essay, the lateralized nature of the brain is discussed. The topics that are covered include hemispheric dominance, hemispheric specialization, and communication between the two hemispheres. As with evolutionary accounts of gender differences, one of the dangers inherent in any discussion of lateralization is that students will overestimate the differences between the two hemispheres. There is often the tendency among students and the general public to assume that some behaviors, like creativity or logical reasoning, reside exclusively in one hemisphere or the other. This pop-up ends with a caution against making such

> conclusions. Most human behaviors are complex and likely involve many different areas in each of the brain's hemispheres. Whatever caused Mozart's musical genius, for example, or Marie Curie's intellectual prowess was not likely to have been confined to one hemisphere.
>
> **Additional Resources:**
>
> Split-brain.html—This site gives some of the history of split-brain surgery. It contains information, drawings, and links to other sites. http://www.indiana.edu/~pietsch/split-brain.html

C. The Midbrain

In this section the functions of the midbrain and reticular activating system are described.

D. The Forebrain

In this section, the functions of the various structures that make up the forebrain are described. These structures include the two cerebral hemispheres, the various lobes of the cortex, and the corpus callosum.

D1. ★Pop-up: The Interactive Brain

In this activity, students can explore the operation of various parts of the brain through a series of interactive animations and text.

> **The Interactive Brain**
>
> **Type of Activity:** Exploration
>
> **Learning Objective:** Discover the functions that various anatomical structures in the brain perform.
>
> **Faculty Note:** In this activity, students can click on the various structures in the brain and see animated descriptions of what each particular structure does. The animations are designed to be memorable and are intended to convey the gist of each structure's function.
>
> **Additional Resources:**
> A variety of sites containing images and models of brains can be found at:
> The Whole Brain Atlas http://www.med.harvard.edu/AANLIB/home.html
> 3D MRI Rotation of the Human Head
> http://www.ncsa.uiuc.edu/SDG/DigitalGallery/MRI_HEAD.html

D2. ★Pop-up: The Brain Structure and Function Game

In this activity, students can test their knowledge of the functions and locations of various brain structures.

The Brain Structure and Function Game

Type of Activity: Interactive Reinforcement

Learning Objective: Test students' mastery of the anatomy of the brain.

Faculty Note: In this activity, students can test their knowledge of the brain by dragging the names and functions of various structures in the brain to the appropriate locations on a drawing of the brain.

E. The Paradox of Plasticity

In this section, students are introduced to the notion of plasticity. One of psychology's great paradoxes is the fact that, while it is true that various parts of the brain serve specific functions, it is also true that these functions can migrate to other parts of the brain when the structure that typically regulates the function is damaged. In extreme cases, children have had one entire hemisphere surgically removed and suffered minimal loss of function.

Faculty Note: A brief case history highlighting plasticity and the mysteries of the brain can be found at http://www.indiana.edu/~pietsch/Lorber.html

F. Biological Causality Revisited

This unit ends by encouraging students to think critically about the relationship between biology of causality. While it is true that biology shapes psychological experience, the plastic nature of the brain also means that psychological experience shapes biology. Change the brain and you will likely change someone's psychological experience. Change psychological experience and you will likely change the brain.

Rapid Review 3

Quick Quiz

CHAPTER 3

SENSATION & PERCEPTION

Chapter Overview
    Learning Objectives
    Chapter Outline

Additional Lecture Ideas
    Lecture Topics
    Additional Readings

In-Class Activities and Demonstrations
    Activities and Demonstrations
    Sources for Additional Activities
    Journey II Software

World Wide Web

Audio-Visual Support

Handout and Transparency Masters

Chapter Overview

Learning Objectives

After studying this chapter, you should be able to do the following:

1. Explain how each sense organ transforms physical stimuli into nerve impulses the brain can understand.

2. Describe how we perceive depth.

3. Recognize common perceptual tendencies.

4. Compare bottom-up and top-down perceptual processing.

5. Identify personal characteristics that affect our perceptions.

Chapter Outline

Sensation & Perception

I. Sensation: Detecting Our Surroundings
    A. Introductory Terms
        1. <u>Sensation</u>: detection of information about external/internal environments and transmission of that info to the brain
        2. <u>Transduction</u>: process of transforming physical energy into nerve impulses
        3. <u>Absolute threshold</u>: minimum level of stimulation needed for receptors to respond
        4. <u>Just noticeable difference (JND)</u>: smallest detectable difference between two stimuli that people can detect 50% of the time.
        5. <u>Weber's Law</u>: proportion of differences between stimuli
        6. <u>Sensory adaptation</u>: reduced sensory sensitivity and responsiveness following prolonged exposure to unchanging stimuli
        7. Responding to changing conditions
            a. <u>dark adaptation</u>: moving from light to dark
            b. <u>light adaptation</u>: moving from dark to light
        7. <u>Sensory deprivation</u>: extreme reduction of sensory stimulation
    B. Seeing: How the Eye Beholds
        1. Properties of light
            a. light waves
            b. wavelength: determines color
            c. amplitude: determines brightness
            d. visible spectrum: limitations on human vision
        2. Parts of the eye
            a. cornea: bends light
            b. iris: controls size of pupil
            c. pupil: adapts to amount of light present
            d. lens
                i. accommodation: changing the shape of the lens to bring objects into focus
            e. differences in vision
                i. myopia: near-sightedness
                ii. hyperopia: far-sightedness
                iii. presbyopia: far-sightedness due to age
        3. From light energy to information
            a. retina: site of conversion of light energy to nerve impulses
                i. photoreceptor cells: rods and cones
                ii. bipolar cells
                iii. ganglion cells
        4. From the eye to the brain
            a. <u>optic disc</u>: produces blind spot in vision

  b. <u>optic nerve</u>: connects eye to occipital lobe
  c. <u>occipital lobe</u>: contains nerve cells with specialized feature detectors for interpreting shape of objects
 5. Color variations
  a. <u>hue</u>: colors we experience
   i. brightness
   ii. saturation: purity of color
  b. cross-cultural differences treating colors as different
 6. Alternative perspectives on seeing color
  a. <u>trichromatic theory</u>: rods enable black-white vision; cones enable color vision via specific sensitivities to blue, green, or red.
  b. <u>opponent-process theory</u>: visual input processed as either blue/yellow, red/green, or black/white in an on/off process
  c. integration of trichromatic & opponent-process theories
  d. <u>color blindness</u>: result of genetic deficiency in presence or functioning of cones.

C. Hearing: What a Sound Signifies
 1. Sound waves
  a. <u>intensity of sound wave</u>: loudness of sound
  b. <u>frequency of sound wave</u>: pitch of sound
 2. From sound energy to the brain
  a. pinna: funnel sound waves
  b. external auditory canal
  c. eardrum
  d. middle ear
   i. hammer
   ii. anvil
   iii. stirrup
  e. inner ear
   i. oval window
   ii. cochlea
   iii. auditory hair cells: transform airwaves in to nerve impulses
  f. auditory nerve
  g. auditory cortex in temporal lobe
 3. Alternative perspectives on hearing pitch
  a. <u>place theory</u>: frequency of sound wave determines which hair cells bend most
  b. <u>frequency theory</u>: frequency of sound wave causes hair cells to vibrate at matching rate; rate of vibration is interpreted as pitch of sound
 4. Hearing impairments
  a. <u>conduction deafness</u>: damage to eardrum or middle ear
  b. <u>nerve deafness</u>: damage to hair cells or auditory nerve

D. Other Senses: Taste, Smell, Touch, & and Position

1. Taste
    a. <u>papillae</u>: contain taste buds & gustatory cells
    b. chemical molecules in foods activate different taste buds
    c. <u>four basic tastes</u>: sweetness, sourness, bitterness, and saltiness
    d. <u>flavor</u>: combination of taste and smell
    e. cultural differences in flavor preferences
    f. age differences in taste sensitivity
2. Smell (olfaction)
    a. <u>olfactory epithelium</u>: contains specialized olfactory cells
    b. <u>strength of odors</u>: more cells activated
    c. <u>olfactory nerves</u>: send impulses to temporal lobes and limbic system
    d. describe and remember smells holistically
    e. loss of sense of smell
        i. anosmia: complete loss of smell
        ii. specific anosmia: inability to smell certain odors
    f. individual and cross-cultural differences in sensitivity to smells
3. Skin sensations
    a. <u>skin</u>: largest sense organ; regulates internal temperature, holds body fluids & organs, protects us from environmental hazards
    b. <u>cutaneous sense</u>: sensations from the skin
        i. differences in skin sensitivities in different regions of body correspond with amount of somatosensory & parietal cortex involvement
    c. sensing pain
        i. <u>types:</u> sharp/quick v. dull/throbbing; result from involvement of different nerve fibers
        ii. <u>theories of pain</u>: gate control theory
        iii. acupuncture & pain relief
        iv. gender & cultural effects on interpretation and response to pain
4. Position senses
    a. <u>kinesthetic sense</u>: information about posture, balance, movements, and position of body parts
    b. <u>vestibular sense</u>: information about position of body gained from receptors in inner ear.

II. Perception: Interpreting Our Sensations
A. <u>Perception</u>: process of organizing, integrating, and giving meaning to sensory information
    1. <u>Role of Gestalt psychology</u>: "The whole is greater than the sum of its parts"
B. Depth Perception: Judging Distances
    1. <u>Depth perception</u>: the ability to recognize objects as three-dimensional and located at varying distances

2. <u>Monocular cues</u>: perceiving depth with one eye
    a. <u>relative size</u>: smaller items appear farther away
    b. <u>linear perspective</u>: converging parallel lines suggest distance
    c. <u>elevation</u>: higher an object appears in relation to horizon, more distance
    d. <u>texture & clarity</u>: blurred details suggest distance
    e. <u>overlap</u>: overlapped items appear farther away
    f. <u>shading</u>: shadows suggest depth, shape, and dimensionality
    g. <u>motion parallax</u>: when in motion, nearer items move more quickly than those farther away
3. <u>Binocular cues</u>: perceiving depth with both eyes
    a. <u>binocular disparity</u>: different views of same object contributes to dimensionality and depth
    b. <u>convergence</u>: as both eyes converge on an object (i.e., line of sight changes, calculation of distance occurs

C. Perceptual Tendencies: Organizing Interpretations
1. <u>Perception affected by</u>: stimulus item itself, sense organs, way we process info
2. <u>Schemata</u>: meaningful cognitive frameworks for organizing, interpreting information
3. Familiar, Simple, Normal
    a. assimilation: tendency to interpret stimuli in terms of what we already know
    b. simplicity: interpret stimuli according to the simplest interpretation
    c. constancy: inclination to interpret stimuli as remaining unchanged.
        i. color constancy
        ii. shape constancy
        iii. size constancy
4. <u>Figure-ground distinction</u>: tendency to perceive figure as standing out against a background, thus giving figure more importance
5. <u>Exaggerating differences among stimuli</u>: contrasts
6. Stimuli as part of a group
    a. <u>spatial proximity</u>: closeness suggests grouping
    b. <u>temporal proximity</u>: events close in time perceived as linked
    c. <u>similarity</u>: objects with similar features seen as a group
    d. <u>common fate</u>: objects moving in same direction at same speed perceived as linked
    e. <u>good form/closure</u>: stimulus perceived as closed and complete
        i. <u>phi phenomenon</u>: perception of motion when none exists
7. Perceptual context
    a. perception of stimuli (what is heard or seen) is determined also by context in which perceived
8. Bottom-up and top-down processing

              a. <u>bottom-up</u>: bits of sensory information combined into a recognizable pattern
              b. <u>top-down</u>: starting with previously held concepts and expectations that guide perception of current stimuli

III. **Psychosocial Perspectives on Perception**
   A. Are perceptions innate?
      1. evidence from case studies
   B. Experiences Affect Perception
      1. effects of learning demonstrated via animal studies
   C. Cultural Perspectives on Perception
      1. evidence of cross-cultural differences to common illusions
      2. <u>explanation</u>: carpentered world theory suggests that right angles produced by work of carpenters affects perception of illusions such as the Muller-Lyer illusion whereas peoples who live in different cultures without such angles are less likely to experience the illusion as confusing
   D. Personal Characteristics Affect Perception
      1. <u>Selective perception</u>: tendency to notice some stimuli and ignore others; a form of bottom-up processing
      2. <u>Expectations and beliefs affect perception</u>: a form of top-down processing; prior beliefs and what we expect to see affects what we see
         i. role in social perception
         ii. role in ESP, precognition, and telepathy

Additional Lecture Topics

Figure-ground: tokenism vs. invisibility

The figure-ground relationship in perception, as described in the textbook, can influence interpersonal interactions. Uba & Huang provide us with the example of an attractive female at a party standing out from the rest of the partygoers (i.e., she is the "figure" that stands out from the "ground") until her large boyfriend arrives to occupy the "figure" perspective. More generally speaking, women and people of color experience both phenomenon -- standing out and receding into an "invisible" background. For example, it has been noted that distinctive or novel stimuli receive more attention than do common or familiar stimuli. As a result, the one "token" woman or person of color in a group stands out perceptually speaking and will be noticed more (Hamilton, 1979). In an empirical study on the perceptions of a token woman or man, Taylor et al. (1978) had participants listen to a taped discussion supposedly occurring in a group of six people as they watched slides of the same group. Group content was manipulated such that one group consisted of 1 woman & 5 men, another with 3 women & 3 men, and the third with 5 women and 1 man. Study results showed that participants reacted most strongly to token persons; they were rated as has having talked more, made stronger impressions (both positive and negative) and were judged as more assertive. Being a "token" then suggests that a person will stand out more and be reacted toward more strongly. Consider employment situations where women and people of color are entering professions where their gender or ethnicity renders them a "token". If they are liked, all may be fine and well...they're really liked but if not, they may be responded to even more negatively than those around them. The implications of their greater noticeability as a "figure" in terms of job evaluation might have profound consequences.

What happens with the phenomenon of "invisibility"? The concept of invisibility has been discussed from a number of perspectives in the feminist critique of psychology and our culture at large. For example, in The Psychology of Women (Chapter 8), Margaret Matlin points out that women are relatively invisible in media presentations, in that men outnumber women in print photos, on television commercials (especially those for expensive items and during prime time viewing hours) and that African American women are even more invisible. What statements are advertisers making about who is expected or viewed as important when some people are present and others are not? Along a similar vein, in the film *The Color of Fear*, the men of color who were film participants reported experiences of being "looked through" as if they simply weren't present in lines at retail establishments. Thus, the concept of invisibility can be linked to the figure-ground distinction as a social example of a perceptually-based phenomenon.

Sources:

Hamilton, D. (1979). a cognitive-attributional analysis of stereotyping. In L. Berkowitz (Ed.), Advances in experimental social psychology (Vol 12). New York: Academic Press.

Matlin, M. (1993). The psychology of women (2nd ed). Fort Worth, TX: Harcourt.

Taylor, S. (1981). A categorization approach to stereotyping. In D. L. Hamilton (Ed.), Cognitive processes in stereotyping and intergroup behavior. Hillsdale, NJ: Erlbaum.

Cleanliness and culture

Fernea and Fernea (1998) note that, in American culture, "we are told we must smell sweet (or not at all) to remain socially acceptable." In other words, some body odors are culturally-endowed with positive meanings whereas other odors presumably carry negative meanings. This statement comes at the end of their article on cross-cultural practices regarding cleanliness and the perceptions or meanings given to cleanliness. They note that in many cultures, cleanliness of the body carries with it more than a statement of social acceptability; it is intricately connected to purity of the soul. As a result, a clean body ranks high among religious goals and becomes translated into many customary practices regarding sexual contact during menstruation, washing before and after meals and prior to prayer, showering rather than bathing, and maintaining clean clothing and living accommodations. Nevertheless, cleanliness is also regarded as a mark of social status. In Western societies, cleanliness has become justified by scientific theory (e.g., the germ theory of illness) and commercialized into a billion dollar industry. Being clean (and smelling clean), rather than emphasizing a connection to spiritual purity, represents some level of intellect and wealth.

Source:

Fernea, E. & Fernea, R. (1998). Cleanliness and culture. In Lonner, W., and Malpass, R. (Eds). Psychology and Culture. Boston: Allyn & Bacon.

When familiar meanings fail: First experiences in a different culture

Uba & Huang refer to "the familiar, simple, and normal" as bases for organizing and interpreting stimuli in our environment. Ernest Boesch's rendition of his "First Experiences in Thailand" incorporates similar themes as he describes his first days in a new environment. Two introductory statements articulate in a particularly illuminating way how meaning (or perception) strongly influences how we respond to an environment (our sensations) and what happens when those meanings no longer seem to apply: "All too often we think that, with some knowledge of the language or with a good interpreter, we can easily become acquainted with those quaint or colorful customs which we associate with an exotic culture and, thus, gain the impression of "knowing" it. I want, instead, to convey to the reader the fact that very often it is not the strikingly strange appearance, but deeper, less conspicuous meanings that are important for understanding other ways of life." (pg. 47)

For example, take his new experiences with the noises of the night found in the tropics. "None of these noises was known to me, none of them could be connected with the specific image of an animal, and it was even difficult to determine which noise came from the outside and which from the inside of the room.......So I confess that I passed an uneasy night, bedeviled by my imagination...." (p 47). The connection between sensation and meaning had become severed, disconnected to old sounds and interpretations. How did he have to respond? "I had met nature as an almost pure phenomenon, untainted by any knowledge precise enough to allow me to classify what I perceived, to identify the sounds and noises surrounding me." (pg. 48).

The sound of a gecko, he notes, would have had entirely different meaning to a local child, but to him the lack of context for understanding was frightening. "We only feel safe in a world which fits our expectations and patterns of explanation--therefore, we always will attempt to reduce new events to previous experience." (pg. 48). Through the process of assimilation, what is new becomes adjusted to be understood via what we already know. This process can be come a "trap" for the traveler who, relying on old meanings, fails to learn the new. An example? The Thai smile. Boesch notes that, in Western culture, a smile is comparatively rare. We smile when situations and interactions call for it. The Thai smile, he says, can mean or hide entirely different things: veiled hostility, insecurity, embarrassment, falseness, aggressive moods--all concealed with a smile as social lubricant to safeguard social relations. His valuable lesson: "Our reality is, as we might say, more than meets the eye; the ways in which we shape our space, our time or our social relations, are determined by many influences, often quite subtle to detect." (pg. 51).

Source:
Boesch, E. (1998). First experiences in Thailand. In Lonner, W., and Malpass, R. (Eds). Psychology and Culture. Boston: Allyn & Bacon.

Subliminal perception and persuasion
Conscious and unconscious perception are current topics in most Introductory Psychology texts and classrooms. Although students seem hardly astounded by the fact that they are affected by objects and events of which they are aware, finding out that they are being influenced by such stimuli when they are not aware of them is a bit more intriguing. The example of the "cocktail party phenomenon" makes intuitive sense to some students--that they must have been processing information to which they are not actively attending (i.e., the conversations around them) at some level in order to respond to their name from across the room. Empirical studies such as those by Bornstein et al. (1987) and Dagenbach et al. (1989), which demonstrate

preferences for faces and faster recognition for words based on prior exposure to subliminal primes introduce both methodology for studying and the limited impact of subliminal or unconscious perception and information processing. I find that students are even more interested in the possible implications of subliminally presented information on subsequent behavior...especially given that the consumer marketplace has offered promises of learning new skills and information (and even getting that elusive "someone" special to fall in love with us) through subliminal tapes (and some money to buy them).

Emphasizing critical thinking and evaluation of these claims, address the larger question of whether subliminal perception is the same as subliminal persuasion. Can subliminal messages prompt us to do things we have no control over? Are they that powerful? One early nonempirical report convinced some people. Movie audiences were exposed to subliminal messages to "eat popcorn" and "drink cola" and indeed food sales increased. Aside from the empirical studies mentioned earlier, some psychologists have found that subliminal messages may alleviate emotional distress (see Silverman & Weinberger, 1985). Although some limited effects have been demonstrated, the most telling criticisms come from empirical studies that knowledge of apparent subliminal messages produces placebo effects. For example, Greenwald and his colleagues (1991) had students listen to subliminal tapes designed to improve either memory or self-esteem, but labels on half the tapes were switched. Results indicated that improvements to memory or self-esteem were linked to the labels on the tapes as opposed to the subliminal content suggesting that motivation was the basis for these changes.

Does subliminal perception exist? Yes, but in a limited sense and it does not appear to be so powerful as to make people run out and purchase products because some elevator music contains a message to "Buy more". Empirical evidence and critical thinking suggests that consumers should probably save themselves $19.95 and focus on conscious efforts to change themselves.

Sources:
 Bornstein, R., Leone, D., & Galley, D. (1987). The generalizability of subliminal mere exposure effects: Influence of stimuli perceived without awareness on social behavior. Journal of Personality and Social Psychology, 53, 1070-1079.
 Dagenbach, D., Carr, T., Wilhelmsen, A. (1989). Task-induced strategies and near-threshold priming: Conscious influences on unconscious perception. Journal of Memory and Language, 28, 412-443.
 Greenwald, A., Spangenberg, E., Pratkanis, A., & Eskenazi, J. (1991). Double-blind tests of subliminal self-help audiotapes. Psychological Science, 2, 119-122.
 Silverman, L. & Weinberger, J. (1985). Mommy and I are one: Implications for psychotherapy. American Psychologst, 40, 1296-1308.

Pheromones and the sensuous nature of smell

New commercial products have been produced marketing the use of human pheromones as sexual attractants. Although the effects of similar chemicals have been demonstrated in sexual behavior for other animal species (e.g, the impact of pheromones on estrous cycles in mice; Bronson, 1974), the role of human pheromones in some kind of "chemistry of love" appears to play a minor role in complex human sexual response (Francoeur, 1991). One study has found that the menstrual cycles of women exposed to male underarm secretions become more regular suggesting that pheromones may have some effects on female hormones (Cutler et al., 1986). Human pheromones have also been implicated in observations that women living in close association develop synchronicity in menstrual cycles (McClintock, 1971). For example, two interesting studies found that the menstrual cycles of women exposed to the underarm secretions of a donor woman became synchronous with hers (Preti et al., 1986; Russell et al., 1980). More generally, an interesting array of studies have found that humans are able to detect clothing worn by themselves or family members on the basis of smell alone even informing us, it seems, about the gender of the wearer (e.g., Porter et al., 1986; Russel, 1976).

Source:

Ackerman, D. (1990). A natural history of the senses. New York: Random House.

Bronson, F. (1974). Pheromonal influences on reproductive activities in rodents. In M. C. Birch (Ed.), Pheromones. Amsterdam: North Holland

Cutler, W., Preti, G., Crier, A., Hugging, G., Garcia, C., & Lawless, H. (1986). Human axillary secretions influence women's menstrual cycles: The role of donor extract from men. Hormones and Behavior, 20, 463-473.

Francoeur, R. (Ed.) (1991). Becoming a sexual person (2nd ed.). New York: Macmillan

McClintock, M. (1971). Menstrual synchrony and suppression. Nature, 229, 244-245.

Porter, R., Balogh, R., Cernoch, J., & Franchi, C. (1986). Recognition of kin through characteristic body odors. Chemical Senses, 11, 389-395.

Russel, M. (1976). Human olfactory communication. Nature, 260, 520-522.

Russell, M., Switz, G., & Thompson, K. (1980). Olfactory influences on the human menstrual cycle. Pharmacology, Biochemistry, and Behavior, 13, 737-738.

Automatic and Controlled Processing: Racial Stereotyping and Top Down Processing of Events (Devine's work on cognitive processes underlying

stereotyping)
> Source:
> Devine, P. (1974). Pheromonal influences on reproductive activities in rodents. In M. C. Birch (Ed.), Pheromones. Amsterdam: North Holland

Suggestions for Additional Readings

Ackerman, D. (1990). A natural history of the senses. New York: Random House.

Agostini, F. (1988). Visual games. New York: Facts on File.

Engen, T. (1991). Odor sensation and memory. Westport, CT: Praeger

Fineman, M. (1981). The inquisitive eye. New York: Oxford.

Heller, M. & Schiff, W. (Eds.) (1991). The psychology of touch. Hillsdale, NJ: Erlbaum.

Hockenberry, J. (1997). Moving violations. In Sattler, D. N. & Shabatay, V. (Eds.) Psychology in context: Voices and perspectives. Boston: Houghton

Hubel, D. (1988). Eye, brain, and vision. New York: Scientific American Library.

Luria, A. (1968). The Mind of a Mnemonist: A little book about a vast memory. New York: Basic

Matlin, M. & Foley, H. (1992). Sensation and perception (3rd Ed.). Boston: Allyn & Bacon.

Sacks, O. (1997). To see and not see. In Sattler, D. N. & Shabatay, V. (Eds.) Psychology in context: Voices and perspectives. Boston: Houghton

Shephard, R. (1990). Mind sights. New York: Freeman.

Wright, D. (1997). Deafness: An autobiography. In Sattler, D. N. & Shabatay, V. (Eds.) Psychology in context: Voices and perspectives. Boston: Houghton

In-Class Activities and Demonstrations

TRAIL Blazing: Using Transparency Masters 3.1 - 3.4, review with students the "Checking Your TRAIL" sections in the chapter. Have students work in small groups to answer the questions and then review with the class as a whole to tie the text reading to activity in class.

Reaching Critical Mass: Using Transparency Masters 3.5 - 3.8, review with students the "Critical Thinking" sections in the chapter. Have students work in small groups to answer the questions and then review with the class as a whole to tie the text reading to activity in class.

Getting Down to IT: Using Transparency Masters 3.9 - 3.12, review the "Integrative Thinking" sections in the chapter with students. Have students work in small groups to answer the questions and then review with the class as a whole to tie the text reading to activity in class.

Classifying Differences in Colors: Although the physical properties of color appear to be universal, there is a great deal of variability in the number of terms in a given language used to describe color (Gourves-Hayward, 1998). After conducting an extensive study of 98 languages, Berlin and Kay (1969) found languages could be grouped into 22 groups using varying numbers of 11 basic color groups (including white, black, red, green, yellow, blue, brown, purple, pink, orange, and gray). Colors tend also to be linked with different associations cross-culturally. For example, colors in the Navaho color system are linked to objects and colors in ceremonial events (McNeill, 1972). To encourage discussion of the relationship between color terms in a language and the experience of the world around us, Gourves-Hayward (1998) suggests having individual members of small groups of students categorize a variety of color chips (obtained from paint store samples) with the 11 basic color groups. After the categorization phase, have students discuss their color group assignments with other groups and explore any differences in assignments and any differing bases for their decisions. The second step of the exercise involves reassigning the colors into the three color groups used by speakers of Gouro, a language spoken along the Ivory Coast. *Ti* (or black) consists of all very dark colors, all blues and greens; *Son* (or red) includes all warm colors, reds, oranges, yellows, and pinks excluding very dark or almost white shades; *Fou* (or white) includes all very pale colors. After this task, students again discuss their rationale for color assignments and any disagreements or difficulties in doing the reassignment. They are also encouraged to consider what difficulties speakers of other languages would having moving from their language system into English. Use **Handout Master # 3.1: Classifying Colors** to replicate her exercise.

Sources:
>Gourves-Hayward, A. (1998). Color my world. In Singelis, T. (Ed.). Teaching about culture, ethnicity, & diversity: Exercises and Planned Activities. Thousand Oaks, CA: Sage Publ.
>Berlin, B., & Kay, P. (1969). Basic color terms: Their universality and evolution. Berkeley: University of California Press
>McNeill, N. (1972). Colour and colour terminology. Journal of Linguistics, 8, 21-34.

Sensation and perception WordSearch: Have students complete **Handout Master # 3.2: Sensation & Perception WordSearch** using the relevant terms from Chapter 3 listed next to the puzzle. (Just for a fun tie-in to the book, you might also ask students if some kinds of word presentations were more difficult or easy than others to find and relate those observations to the chapter).

Detecting Odor: Giving name, meaning and memory to smells:
This exercise contains a combination of ideas related to the sense of smell. First, according to Cain (1981), people tend not to be particularly good at identifying even relatively common-place odors. Following Cain's suggestion and using **Handout Master # 3.3: Detecting odors**, place 10-12 common food items in covered, empty baby food jars and have students identify the contents by smell alone. Relatively low identification levels should be obtained. Next, Ackerman (1990) describes vivid childhood memories linked to the smell of eucalyptus. Indeed, she notes that retailers rely on similar associations when they spray used cars with "new car" scent and add food smells to air-conditioning systems to entice shoppers to visit restaurants. To extent Cain's basic exercise, ask students to (a) identify any specific memories associated with the odors they tested and (b) identify 3 odors for which they have particular strong memory associations.

>Sources:
>Ackerman, D. (1990). A natural history of the senses. New York: Random House.
>Cain, W. (1981). Educating your nose. Psychology Today, 7, 48-56.

Complex Perceptions
Bloomquist (1985) describes the use of puzzle pictures in demonstrations of sensation and perception. In a personalized variation of these visual stimuli, take black-and-white photographs of building, statues, familiar faces around your campus. After having the film developed, enlarge and lighten the pictures on a photocopier. Lastly, make an

overhead transparency of each photograph. When presenting the pictures to students, turn some overheads at 90, 180, or 270 degree angles and ask the students to identify the object in the picture. At first students are likely to be puzzled by what they see (i.e., trying to place some kind of organization on it). Based on the figure-ground distinction principle, elements of the picture are difficult to distinguish because both the figure and the ground appear made up of black & white blotches.

Source:

Bloomquist, D. (1985). Sensation and perception. In The G. Stanley Hall Lecture Series (Vol 5.). Washington, DC: APA

The Barnyard -- a demonstration of culture shock:

Distress and cognitive disorientation, referred to as culture shock, may occur when one moves to a new culture, away from familiar surroundings and customs. In such settings, it is not unusual to attempt to reestablish some sense of the familiar by seeking out others with which one has some kind of similarity (e.g., going to a familiar fast foot chain while traveling internationally). *The Barnyard* exercise was created by Thomas Connell and James Jacob to arouse in participants the complex feelings that occur when a person feels suddenly removed from familiar settings. The exercise involves organizing students into small groups of 5-12 members. Each group then decides on a barnyard animal sound to use for identification purposes. After all groups have decided on their group's sound, participants place blindfolds over their eyes. All students are mixed up together in the room with the assistance of the instructor and a group of "safety monitor" students. Once all the students have been thoroughly mixed (i.e., original group members are not all standing by each other), they are instructed to begin calling out their group's animal sound in an attempt to relocate other group members. Each group continues to make its animal sound until all group members have returned to the group. In the discussion that follows, ask students how it felt to be cut off from their surroundings by the blindfold and any feelings they discovered during the exercise (while wandering around and once reunited with the group). How does this experience relate to the sensation and perception chapter we've just studied?

Source:
Connell, T., & Jacob, J. (1998). The Barnyard. In Singelis, T. (Ed.). Teaching about culture, ethnicity, & diversity: Exercises and Planned Activities. Thousand Oaks, CA: Sage Publ.

Sources for Additional Activities
Books:

Benjamin, L. & Lowman, K. (1981). Activities Handbook for the Teaching of Psychology. Washington DC: American Psychological Association.

Halonen, Jane 1995). Chapter 4: Sensation and Perception in The Critical Thinking Companion For Introductory Psychology (Worth Publ.).

Makosky, V. et al. (Eds.) (1995). Activities Handbook for the Teaching of Psychology (Vol. III). Washington DC: American Psychological Association.

Smith, R. (1995). Challenging your preconceptions: Thinking critically about psychology. Pacific Grove, CA: Brooks/Cole (Chapter 5: Is what you see what you get?)

Journey II Software:
Enter the Perception lab by clicking on the icon in the Main Menu and discover 4 exercises pertaining to sensation and perception.

<u>Anatomy of the Eye</u>: This exercise contains a point-and-click quiz of different parts of the eye.

<u>Perception of Color</u>: After learning about rods and cones, students explore the trichromatic and opponent-process theories of color vision. Several examples of "seeing" opposing colors are demonstrated.

<u>Perception of Motion</u>: What produces the perception that the moon is moving when clouds move in front of it? Students are prompted to select an explanation for this everyday phenomenon from the concepts of real motion, induced motion, autokinetic movement, movement after effect, and apparent movement (stroboscopic movement) following demonstrations of each.

<u>Perception of Line Length</u>: Confronted with the Muller-Lyer illusion, students attempt to create equal length lines. The task is made more difficult by changing angle of arrows on the line and the horizontal/vertical orientation of the line. Causes for the illusion including incorrect comparison, eye movement, and misapplied constancy are discussed and applied in a cross-cultural example.

World Wide Web: Check out the following WWW sites for information and activities relevant to this section of the text!

Addison Wesley Longman's Website -- **http://longman.awl.com/**
- PsychZone link -- **http://longman.awl.com/**
- Psych Web -- **http://www.gasou.edu/psychweb/psychweb.htm**

Psychology Jumping Stand --
http://www.indiana.edu:80/~iuepsyc/PsycJump.html

The Psychology Place --**http://www.psychplace.com**
- Internet Psychology Laboratory --
http://kahuna.psyc.uiuc.edu/ipl/index.html
- Pheromones -- **http://www.csa.com/crw/pheromones.html**
- Self-Quizzes for Introductory Psychology --
http://www.gasou.edu/psychweb/selfquiz/selfquiz.htm
- Vision -- **http://vision.arc.nasa.gov/VisionScience/**
- Illusions -- **http://wwwlillusionworks.com/** or
http://aspen.uml.edu/~landrigad/ILLUSION.HTML
- Vision research -- **http://www.socsci.uci.edu/cogsci/vision.html**
- Auditory perception -- **http://www.music.mcgill.ca/auditory/Auditory.html**

Audio-Visual Support
  <u>Films/Videos</u>:
  Overview

Discovering Psychology: Sensation and Perception (Annenberg, 30 minutes)
The Sensory World (CRM, 33 minutes)
Sensation and Perception (Insight, 30 minutes)
Perception (CRM, 28 minutes)
Adventures in Perception (PHENIX, 21 minutes)
Behavior of Animals and Human Infants in Response to a Visual Cliff (PSUPCR, 15 minutes)
Brain Power (IU(LCA), 11 minutes)
The Mind's Eye (U.M., 50 minutes)
Perception: The Eye Within (IU(BARR), 12 minutes)
Senses and Perception:Links to the Outside World (UC(EMC), 18 minutes)

Hearing & Vision
Hearing Things (Filmakers, 55 minutes)
The Eye: An Inside Story (CORT, 10 minutes)
The Senses: Eyes and Ears (FFHS, 26 minutes)
Visual Illusions: Now You See It (PSU, 25 minutes)

Other Senses
The Knowing Nose (Filmakers, 46 minutes)
How Much Do You Smell? (FI, 50 minutes)
The Senses: Skin Deep (FFHS, 26 minutes)
The Skin as a Sense Organ (IFB, 12 minutes)
A Touch of Sensitivity (BBC, 50 minutes)

Pain
Patterns of Pain (Filmakers, 28 minutes)
The Mind: Pain and Healing (HARR, 24 minutes)
Migraine Headaches (FFHS, 21 minutes)

Case Studies in Sensation/Perception
The Man Who Mistook His Wife for a Hat (FFHS, 75 minutes)

Psychology Encyclopedia Laserdisc IV:

Movies

Motion afterimage	(1 min. 25 sec.)	Side 1, Frames 45469-48029
Transduction	(2 min. 3 sec.)	Side 1, Frames 25517-29191
Pitch Perception	(2 min. 39 sec.)	Side 1, Frames 29192-33949
Accommodation and convergence	(1 min. 4 sec.)	Side 1, Frames 33950-35868
Color mixing	(1 min. 44 sec.)	Side 1, Frames 35869-38979

Still Images

Proximity [1/2] [UN]	Frame 53476	Side	all
Proximity [2/2] [UN]	53477		all
Closure [UN]	53478		all
Similarity [1/2] [UN]	53479		all
Similarity [2/2] [UN]	53480		all
Continuity [UN]	53481		all
Muller-Lyer perceptual illusion [1/2] [UN]	53482		all
Muller-Lyer perceptual illusion [2/2] [UN]	53483		all
Perceptual illusion [1/2] [UN]		53484	all
Perceptual illusion [2/2] [UN]		53485	all
Visible spectrum of electromagnet energy [1/3] [6.1]		53486	all
Visible spectrum of electromagnet energy [2/3] [6.1]		53487	all
Visible spectrum of electromagnet energy [3/3] [6.1]		53488	all
Eye anatomy [1/3] [6.3]	53489		all
Eye anatomy [2/3] [6.3]	53490		all
Eye anatomy [3/3] [6.3]	53491		all
Retinal image [6.4]	53492		all
Retinal anatomy [1/4] [6.5]	53493		all
Retinal anatomy [2/4] [6.5]	53494		all
Retinal anatomy [3/4] [6.5]	53495		all
Retinal anatomy [4/4] [6.5]	53496		all
Blind spot [6.6]	53497		all
Negative afterimage [1/2] [6.7]	53498		all
Negative afterimage [2/2] [6.7]	53499		all
Figure and ground [6.9]	53500		all
Visual illusions [1/5] [6.11]	53501		all
Visual illusions [2/5] [6.11]	53502		all
Visual illusions [3/5] [6.11]	53503		all
Visual illusions [4/5] [6.11]	53504		all
Visual illusions [5/5] [6.11]	53505		all
Ear anatomy [1/3] [6.12]	53506		all
Ear anatomy [2/3] [6.12]	53507		all
Ear anatomy [3/3] [6.12]	53508		all
Taste receptors [6.13]	53509		all
Smell and taste [6.15]	53510		all
Olfactory receptor [1/3] [6.16]	53511		all
Olfactory receptor [2/3] [6.16]	53512		all
Olfactory receptor [3/3] [6.16]	53513		all
Visual cliff [6.17]	53514		all
Wechsler test [6.18]	53515		all
Color afterimage [1/2]		53904	all
Color afterimage [2/2]		53905	all
Color deficiency [1/5]	53906		all
Color deficiency [2/5]	53907		all
Color deficiency [3/5]	53908		all

Color deficiency [4/5]   53909   all
Color deficiency [5/5]   53910   all

Transparency Master 3.1: Checking Your TRAIL 3.1

Define sensation.

In vision, light waves enter the eyes by passing first through the ___(a)___, which bends lightwaves so that the image can be focused. The light then travels through the ___(b)___, the black part of the eye, which is actually an opening in the ___(c)___. That structure contains ___(d)___ that control the size of the ___(e)___ and therefore regulate the amount of light that enters the eyes. When light leaves the pupil, it reaches the ___(f)___, which change shape, bringing objects in focus. From there the light goes to the ___(g)___, which contains receptors that transform light into ___(h)___ impulses. The message is sent to the ___(i)___ lobe of the cerebral cortex.

While walking outside at night, are you mostly using cones or rods to guide your steps?

Which one of the following statements is FALSE?
    A. Rods enable us to see when light is dim.
    B. There are more rods than cones.
    C. The fovea contains only rods.
    D. Dark adaptation is a change from relying on cones to relying on rods.

Transparency Master 3.2: Checking Your TRAIL 3.2

In the movies, are lower-frequency pitches in the sound track associated with innocent or dangerous situations?

Which of the following is NOT an ossicle?
- **A. hammer**
- **B. saddle**
- **C. stirrup**
- **D. anvil**

Why do we perceive some odors as being stronger than others?

The vestibular sense relies on receptor cells
- **A. in the nose.**
- **B. in the inner ear.**
- **C. on the skin.**
- **D. throughout the body.**

Transparency Master 3.3: Checking Your TRAIL 3.3

What is the difference between sensation and perception?

True or False: Our perception that an object has particular characteristics simply reflects the characteristics of the object.

Which of the following are monocular cues of depth and distance?
- A. linear perspective
- B. overlap
- C. convergence
- D. elevation
- E. relative size
- F. texture gradient
- G. shading
- H. binocular disparity
- I. motion parallax

When stimuli have _____, they are perceived as complete and have good form.
- A. temporal proximity
- B. contrast tendencies
- C. a reversed figure-ground
- D. closure

Transparency Master 3.4: Checking Your TRAIL 3.4

Studies of the Muller-Lyer illusion have shown that:
   A. perceptual differences reflect racial differences.
   B. experiences affect what is perceived.
   C. every person perceives every stimulus in the same way.
   D. the carpentered-world theory is not true.

Name at least four personal characteristics that affect perception.

Selective perception:
   A. is the tendency to notice some stimuli and ignore others.
   B. means that we consciously choose to perceive whatever we wish.
   C. is always due to habituation.
   D. shows that perception is innate.

<u>**True**</u> or <u>**False**</u>: Based on what you have read about perception, if two people differ in their descriptions of the same event, one must be lying.

Transparency Master 3.5: Critical Thinking 3.1

Cameras work in a way that parallels the working of the eye. Based on what you know about the pupil, when does an automatically-focusing camera's aperture--its opening for light--stay open the longest? Why are some photographs overexposed or underexposed?

Transparency Master 3.6: Critical Thinking 3.2

In terms of the opponent-process theory, why does it make sense to have red and green traffic signals rather than blue and green?

Transparency Master 3.7: Critical Thinking 3.3

What are the cues to depth in figure 3.17 in your text?

Transparency Master 3.8: Critical Thinking 3.4

Think about gender or racial stereotypes. How might the tendencies to assimilate, exaggerate differences, group stimuli, and perceive the simple and familiar, contribute to the mistaken perception of "confirmation" of stereotypes?

Transparency Master 3.9: Integrative Thinking 3.1

Research indicates that people are able to identify relatives' clothes by smell because they repeatedly smelled those clothes (Porter et al., 1986). Based on what you learned in the Biopsychology Chapter about neural pathways, why would repeatedly smelling their clothes result in the ability to identify them?

Transparency Master 3.10: Integrative Thinking 3.2

Consider the example of Christina, the young woman described in the text (p. 106), who had difficulty standing, walking, and reaching for objects. Christina's problem was in the nerve connecting to her brain. Based on your understanding of the functions of the cerebral lobes from the Biopsychology Chapter, which of Christina's cerebral lobes was not receiving accurate information about the position of her hands?

Transparency Master 3.11: Integrative Thinking 3.3

In light of what you learned in the Introductory Chapter, why would structuralists like Wundt have difficulty explaining your perception of the Rouen Cathedral?

Transparency Master 3.12: Integrative Thinking 3.4

Consider the Buckhout (1980) research where 86% of callers who had watched a television clip of an assault misidentified the guilty party. In light of what you learned in the Introductory Chapter, in what ways was this sample biased?

Handout Master # 3.1: Classifying Differences in Colors

Name: _____

Part I: Classifying Color from an English language perspective
Instructions: Classify your paint chips according to the 11 color groups listed below.

White:

Black:

Red:

Green:

Yellow:

Blue:

Brown:

Purple:

Pink:

Orange:

Gray:

Part II: Classifying Color from a Gouro language perspective
Instructions: Classify your paint chips according to the 3 color groups listed below.

Ti:

Son:

Fou:

Sensation and perception WordSearch: Have students complete **Handout Master # 3.2: Sensation & Perception WordSearch** using the relevant terms from Chapter 3 listed next to the puzzle. (Just for a fun tie-in to the book, you might also ask students if some kinds of word presentations were more difficult or easy than others to find and relate those observations to the chapter). The solution to the puzzle is the concept, *acupuncture*.

Handout Master # 3.2: Sensation & Perception WordSearch

Chapter 3

```
C O N E S N O I T A T P A D A
M O N O C U L A R P I T C H Y
U G A T E C O N T R O L R C R
W C H Y R O T I D U A T T B O
A E O E C A L P R U R E A I T
R T T N R A N E H I T C R N C
Y S E A V T B S C A H A O O A
C A S P L E Z H D I L I H C F
N R L C W I R O N U T B O U L
A T E U K O M G B P C P S L O
T N W O M M N I E E E T O A S
S O O A O H T C S N M S I R T
N C T E S R D N S C I I O A
O I C O E E O A N F A E L E N
C A F V P R O X I M I T Y E G
```

Instructions: Complete the word search puzzle above by finding the following list of words from Chapter 3 and dictionary words. To solve the puzzle, use the letters that remain in the puzzle to create a term used in Chapter 3.

ACCOMMODATE	ADAPTATION	ANNE	RODS
ASSIMILATE	ATOP	AUDITORY	SIEG
BINOCULAR	BLAH	CHIN	SOHO
CONES	CONSTANCY	CONTRAST	VESTIBULAR
CONVERGENCE	COOK	EMILE	WARY
FOEHN	GATE CONTROL	GNATS	WEBER
HERTZ	LEAF	MONOCULAR	TOWELS
OLFACTORY	OPTIC	PERCEPTION	TRANSDUCTION
PITCH	PLACE	PROXIMITY	TRICHROMATIC

Puzzle solution: (Hints -- 11 letters: a sticky situation) __ __ __ __ __ __ __ __ __ __ __

Handout Master # 3.3: Detecting Odors

Name: _____

Part I: Detecting Odors

Instructions: Identify the common items in the numbered containers and listen any significant memories associated with that smell

Item 1: _____ Memory: _____
Item 2: _____ Memory: _____
Item 3: _____ Memory: _____
Item 4: _____ Memory: _____
Item 5: _____ Memory: _____
Item 6: _____ Memory: _____
Item 7: _____ Memory: _____
Item 8: _____ Memory: _____
Item 9: _____ Memory: _____
Item 10: _____ Memory: _____
Item 11: _____ Memory: _____
Item 12: _____ Memory: _____

Part II: Significant Memory and Emotional Associations Linked to Smells

Instructions: Think of 3 odors that you have very strong memory and emotional associations with some event (e.g., the cologne of an old boy/girlfriend, the smell of turkey at Thanksgiving). Describe those associations and how they might be affected by culture.

Smell 1:
_____
_____
_____
_____
_____

Smell 2:
_____
_____
_____
_____
_____

Smell 3:

Mind Matters CD-ROM Faculty Guide

SENSATION

I. Introduction to Sensation
    A. Sensation and Perception
    B. Bottom-Up and Top-Down Processing
        B1. ★ Pop-Up: Bottom-Up and Top-Down Processing
    C. How Many Senses Are There?
    Rapid Review 1

II. Sensory Transduction
    A. What Is Transduction?
    B. Transduction and Odor
    C. Transduction and Taste
    D. Transduction and Sound
        D1. ★ Pop-Up: Transduction in the Ear
        D2. ★ The Ear Structure and Function
    E. Sensory Thresholds and Psychophysics
        E1. ★ Pop-Up: Psychophysics and Thresholds
        E2. ★ Pop-Up: An Experiment in Thresholds
    Rapid Review 2

III. Sensory Coding
    A. What Is Sensory Coding?
    B. Coding and Odor
    C. Coding and Sound
        C1. ★ Pop-Up: Coding in the Ear
    D. Coding and Sight
        D1. ★ The Eye Structure and Function
    E. The Retina
    F. Electromagnetic Radiation
    G. Trichromatic Theory
        G1. ★ Pop-Up: Color Mixing
        G2. ★ Pop-Up: Defects in Color Perception
    H. Feature Detectors
        H1. ★ Pop-Up: A Nobel-Winning Study in Feature Detectors
    Rapid Review 3

IV. Sensory Adaptation
    A. The Challenge of Adaptation
    B. Adapting to the Dark

      B1. ★ Pop-Up: Exploring Intensity
  C. Color Afterimages
      C1. ★ Pop-Up: Creating Color Afterimages
  D. Motion Afterimages
      D1. ★ Pop-Up: Experiencing Motion Afterimages
  E. What Do We Learn From Afterimages?
      E1. ★ Pop-Up: In the Head or in the Eye?
Rapid Review 4

Quick Quiz

SENSATION
Annotated Outline

I. Introduction to Sensation

This unit begins with the distinction between sensation and perception.

A. Sensation and Perception

Sensation is defined as the raw experience of the stimulus. It occurs early in the sensation/perception cycle. Perception is defined as the final experience of an event or stimulus and the later steps the nervous system takes in interpreting that stimulus.

> **Faculty Note:** A classroom exercise that often helps with this distinction involves having students taste various items with and without the additional cues provided by smell. For example, under normal conditions 95% of the population can identify a single drop of coffee placed on the tongue. However, when smell is neutralized (e.g., when it is masked with a strong odor like camphor—the active ingredient in products like Vicks Vap-O-Rub or BenGay—only 3% of the population can correctly identify a drop of coffee (Mozell et al., 1969, Nasal chemoreception in flavor identification. Archives of Otolaryngology, 90, 367-373). This difference suggests that taste (i.e., the sensations provided by the sensory receptors on the tongue) is a sensation, while flavor is a perception that involves combining taste, smell, texture, and temperature.

B. Bottom-Up and Top-Down Processing

In bottom-up processing, our perceptions are formed mainly from the data supplied by our sense organs. Relatively little interpretation is used to understand the stimuli we have observed. In top-down processing, our past experience and expectations influence our perceptual experience.

B1. ★Pop-up: Bottom-Up and Top-Down Processing

This pop-up provides a closer look at the distinction between bottom-up and top-down processing.

> **Bottom-Up and Top-Down Processing**
>
> **Activity Type:** Illustrated Essay
>
> **Learning Objective:** Introduce/Reinforce the distinction between Bottom-up and Top-Down Processing
>
> **Faculty Note:** Because the distinction between bottom-up and top-down processing is

difficult for many students, this pop-up provides more details and examples of the difference and focuses on the interaction between the two processes.

C. How Many Senses Are There?

Students are reminded that psychologists study more than the traditional five senses. The senses identified on the disk also include equilibrium, kinesthesis, warmth, cold, and pain.

> **Faculty Note**: Our students often raise questions about ESP in the context of discussions of the senses. The Pop-Up "Evaluating Evidence--Psychic Abilities" from the History and Methods section of this CD-ROM may be useful in this context. There, students are encouraged to think critically about investigations of ESP and the evidence that would be required to demonstrate its existence.

Rapid Review 1

II. Sensory Transduction

The idea of transduction is introduced by asking the age-old question, "If a tree fell in the woods and no one was around to hear it, would it still make a sound?" The position taken here is that, psychologically speaking, the answer is "no."

A. What Is Transduction?

All sensory systems confront the problem of transduction, defined here as the processes by which the physical properties of the stimulus are converted into electro-chemical signals that the nervous system can interpret.

B. Transduction and Odor

Transduction of odor is covered in this section.

> **Faculty Note**: . Here, and later in the sensory coding and odor section, the popular "lock and key" model for olfaction is presented. According to this model, the shape of the molecule, determines which specific receptors are stimulated. The exact mechanisms of smell are still controversial and under intense investigation.

C. Transduction and Taste

Transduction of taste is covered in this section.

> **Faculty Note**: You may notice that the traditional "areas of taste" on the tongue are not presented in the graphics on the CD. Recent research suggests that specific tastes are not localized on particular parts of the tongue. In fact, taste receptors are not confined to the tongue. They are located throughout the mouth and throat (Bartoshuk, L. M., [1993]. Genetic and pathological taste variation: What can we learn from animal models and

human disease. In D. J. Chadwick, J. Marsh, & J. Good [Eds.], <u>The Molecular Basis of Smell and Taste Transduction</u> CIBA Foundation Symposia Series, No. 179, New York: Wylie.).

D. Transduction and Sound

Transduction of sound is covered in this section.

D1. ★Pop-up: Transduction and the Ear

The process of converting vibrations into neural messages is presented in the form of a narrated animation.

Transduction in the Ear

Type of Activity: Movie

Learning Objective: Understand the processes by which vibrations in the air are turned into neural signals.

Faculty Note: This animation provides a concrete visual presentation of the transduction in the ear. It covers transduction (i.e., getting the signal into the system), but not sensory coding. That is covered later in the CD under "Sensory Coding." If you decide to use these animations in your lecture, you may want to play the two movies sequentially.

D2. ★Ear Structure and Function

This activity allows students to explore the structures and functions of various parts of the ear.

Ear Structure and Function

Type of Activity: Interactive Reinforcement

Learning Objective: Learn and remember the functions of the major anatomical structures in the ear.

Faculty Note: In this activity, students can explore the anatomy of the ear by rolling their cursors over various structures in the ear and seeing their names and functions pop up. This information is later tested in the rapid review and a paper and pencil version of the activity is available in this guide.

Also, because this section is concerned with the transduction of sound, there is no discussion of the functions of the semicircular canals. However, these structures are labeled in the interaction, in case you want to discuss the transduction of acceleration and movement.

E. Sensory Thresholds and Psychophysics

Defines psychophysics as the study of the relationship between the physical properties of a stimulus and the psychological experience of that stimulus.

E1. ★Pop-up: Psychophysics and Thresholds

Focuses on the psychophysical exploration of sensory limits. Both absolute and difference thresholds are defined.

Psychophysics and Thresholds

Type of Activity: Illustrated Essay

Learning Objective: Understand the difference between absolute thresholds and difference thresholds.

Faculty Note: This pop-up concentrates on thresholds and should go well with the "experiment in thresholds" activity that follows.

E2. ★Pop-up: An Experiment in Thresholds

Introduces the notion of the j.n.d. (just noticeable difference) and the idea that our psychological experiences of the world are shaped by the world, but do not correspond to the world in a one-to-one fashion.

An Experiment in Thresholds

Type of Activity: Simulation

Learning Objective: Understand the orderly relationship between physical stimulation and psychological experiences.

Faculty Note: In this simulation, students are introduced to the notion of the j.n.d. (just noticeable difference) and to the idea that our psychological experiences of the world are shaped by the world, but do not correspond to the world in a one-to-one fashion. To that end, students are given an opportunity to drag "virtual candles" into a dark room and observe changes in the perceived illumination of the room. What they should discover as they do the activity is that the number of candles needed to produce a j.n.d. increases as the ambient light increases. One question that may come up is whether the effects they see on their screen are "real." In fact, this activity simulates a psychophysical experiment. Because of inconsistencies in calibration and video processing across different computers, it is not possible to do a "real" psychophysical experiment of this type. Though not covered explicitly in the text, this activity may serve as an engaging springboard for discussing the contributions of specific psychophysicists including Weber, Fechner, and Stephens.

Rapid Review 2

III. Sensory Coding

A. What Is Sensory Coding?

Sensory coding is defined as the process of registering the intensity of a stimulus and the translation of its qualities into specific neural codes that the brain can interpret.

B. Coding and Odor

The underlying mechanisms responsible for identifying particular odors and their intensities are presented.

C. Coding and Sound

Explores the relationship between the physical properties of sound waves (i.e., frequency and amplitude) and the psychological experience of sound (i.e., pitch and volume).

C1. ★Pop-up: Coding in the Ear

This pop-up contains a narrated animation in which the place/frequency theory of pitch perception is presented.

Coding in the Ear

Type of Activity: Movie

Learning Objective: Understand sensory coding, in general, and the place/frequency theory of pitch perception specifically.

Faculty Note: This pop-up contains a narrated animation in which the place/frequency theory of pitch perception is presented. On a technical note, you may want to point out to your students that the depiction of the wave in the cochlea is simplified. In reality, the waves in the cochlea are "standing waves" (i.e., they form a fairly static pattern on the membrane) rather than traveling waves.

Additional Resources: This site contains a multimedia presentation of selected topics in auditory perception. It provides an interesting overview and includes lots of resources. Much of the site is fairly technical http://www.music.mcgill.ca/auditory/history.html

D. Coding and Sight

The processes involved in sensory coding are explored in relatively greater detail for the visual system than they are for the other senses.

D1. ★Eye Structure and Function

This activity allows students to explore the structures and functions of various parts of the eye.

Eye Structure and Function

Type of Activity: Interactive Reinforcement

Learning Objective: Learn and remember the functions of the major anatomical structures in the eye.

Faculty Note: In this activity, students can explore the anatomy of the eye by rolling their cursors over the various structures of the eye and seeing their names and functions pop up. This information is later tested in the rapid review and a paper and pencil version of the activity is available in this guide.

E. The Retina

The structure and functions of the retina are reviewed.

F. Electromagnetic Radiation

The relationships between electromagnetic radiation and "visible" light for humans and selected other species are reviewed.

G. Trichromatic Theory

How we perceive different colors is addressed through the trichromatic theory of color perception.

G1. ★Pop-up: Color Mixing

In this activity, students can mix colors both additively and subtractively.

Color Mixing

Type of Activity: Exploration

Learning Objective: Understand the differences between additive and subtractive color mixing; know which one is most relevant to how they eye mixes colors.

Faculty Note: In our experience, additive color mixing is one of the single most difficult concepts to get students to understand. Perhaps it is because most of their experience comes from coloring with crayons, but no matter how many times we ask students in lecture what green and red add to make, they answer brown (i.e., the subtractive mix). Because additive mixing more closely resembles the working of the visual system, this activity is included to help make the difference between subtractive and additive mixing concrete. In the activity, students can experiment with different combinations of additive and subtractive mixes and see what the results are. The activity also contains a movie that summarizes the additive and subtractive processes that are involved in looking at a yellow object.

G2. ★Pop-up: Defects in Color Perception

This activity simulates the experience of various forms of "color blindness."

Defects in Color Perception

Type of Activity: Interactive Animation

Learning Objective: Explore four types of color deficiency.

Faculty Note: This pop-up allows students to simulate the experience of various forms of "color blindness." If a student has persistent problems in discriminating between the various portrayals of color deficiency, she may want to have her vision checked by a professional.

Additional Resources:

Color Deficiency Test Page – This site, accessible from either of the URLs listed, contains information about color deficiency and includes the pseudoisochromatic plates used in testing color perception. http://www.cactus.org/~kingman/CVDtest.html

On a related front, http://www.lava.net/~dewilson/web/color.html is a web site devoted to the applied side of color perception and color deficiencies. Specifically, the site deals with issues of web site design as they affect people with color deficiencies. The site provides an overview of color deficiencies, personal anecdotes, and recommended design strategies.

H. Feature Detectors

Visual coding occurs both at the retina, through rods and cones, and in the brain via specialized neurons called feature detectors.

H1. ★Pop-up: A Nobel-Winning Study in Feature Detectors

Reviews the Nobel Prize winning research of Hubel and Wiesel through a combination of interactive animations and text.

A Nobel-Winning Study in Feature Detectors

Type of Activity: Illustrated Essay

Learning Objective: Review the discovery and importance of feature detectors.

Faculty Note: In this pop-up, the Nobel Prize winning research of Hubel and Wiesel is reviewed through a combination of interactive animations and text.

Rapid Review 3

IV. Sensory Adaptation

A. The Challenge of Adaptation

Sensory adaptation is presented as a common principle affecting all sensory systems.

B. Adapting to the Dark

Reviews the processes that occur when the eye adapts to the dark.

B1. ★Pop-up: Exploring Intensity

Students can explore the processes of adaptation to brightness through a pair of interactive demonstrations.

Exploring Intensity

Type of Activity: Exploration

Learning Objective: Experience and understand the processes involved in sensory adaptation.

Faculty Note: In this activity, students explore the processes of adaptation to brightness through a pair of interactions. One interaction is done in color while the other is done in black and white. In each, students are asked to stare at the computer screen. While they stare at the screen, they see an image in which one side is blue (color version) or gray (black and white version) and the other side is black. After approximately 20 seconds (though it will probably seem longer), these images are replaced by a single uniformly colored image. However, because of adaptation, these images should briefly appear to be made up of two different shades of blue (color version) or gray (black and white version).

You may want to point out to your students that this activity has everything to do with brightness and little to do with color. In both the color and black and white versions, the adaptation is to the intensity of the stimulus, not to its hue.

C. Color Afterimages

This section introduces afterimages, generally, and explains color afterimages, specifically, in terms of opponent processes in the visual system.

C1. ★Pop-up: Creating Color Afterimages

Students can experience and explore afterimages by creating their own color combinations and seeing what happens when they adapt to them.

Creating Color Afterimages

Type of Activity: Exploration

Learning Objective: Understand how opponent processes and sensory adaptation contribute to the experience of afterimages.

Faculty Note: In this activity, students can create their own stimuli for creating color afterimages. A few of tips for this activity:

First, color afterimages tend to be robust. It is the rare student who does not experience color afterimage.

Second, if you have access to a digital projector, this activity works well as a lecture demonstration.

Third, color afterimages can also be used to demonstrate the constructed nature of depth perception (see the section on the Ponzo illusion on the CD). Specifically, if students adapt to the color afterimage stimulus, and then stare at a neutral wall, rather than at the computer screen, the afterimage should resize and appear much larger. This resizing happens because the retinal afterimage remains constant in size, but depth cues lead the brain to conclude that it has moved further away and must, therefore, be bigger.

D. Motion Afterimages

Motion afterimages are introduced and discussed in terms of opponent processes among feature detectors in the visual cortex.

D1. ★Pop-up: Experiencing Motion Afterimages

Students can experience and explore motion afterimages.

Experiencing Motion Afterimages

Type of Activity: Exploration

Learning Objective: Understand how opponent processes and feature detectors contribute to the experience of motion afterimages.

Faculty Note: In this activity, students are given an opportunity to stare at a rotating spiral image. This should lead to adaptation of inward feature detectors in the visual cortex. After approximately 20 seconds, the rotating spiral is replaced by a stationary drawing of an eye. However, because of the adaptation of the inward feature detectors, the eye should look like it is expanding (i.e., moving out). The accompanying text explains why this occurs.

One word of caution, unlike color afterimages, motion afterimages are fragile and happen very quickly. If your students don't experience the motion afterimage, they might want to try again, holding their heads as still as possible during the adaptation and test phases.

What Do We Learn From Afterimages?

In this section, the processes involved in color and motion afterimages are briefly reviewed.

E1. ★Pop-up: In the Head or in the Eye?

In this activity, students can compare color and motion afterimage effects and discover that color afterimages happen close to the retina, while the motion afterimages happen in the visual cortex.

In the Head or in the Eye?

Type of Activity: Exploration

Learning Objective: Experience and understand some of the differences between cortical and retinal processing.

Faculty Note: In this activity, students are encouraged to experiment further with color and motion afterimages. Specifically, the instructions for the activity ask them to try the adaptation activities again. This time, however, they are instructed to cover one eye during the adaptation phase of the activity and observe their experiences in the adapted and unadapted eyes. What the students should discover is that while color afterimages are experienced only in the adapted eye, motion afterimages can be experienced with either eye. The adaptation that occurs with color happens close to the retina, while the adaptation that occurs with motion happens in the visual cortex.

Rapid Review 4

Quick Quiz

PERCEPTION TABLE OF CONTENTS

I. INTRODUCTION TO PERCEPTION
    A. From Sensation to Perception
    B. Gestalt Psychology and Perceptual Laws
        B1. ★Perceiving Sound
        B2. ★Exploring Gestalt Principles

II. PERCEPTUAL CONSTANCY
        II1. ★Illustrations of Visual Constancy
        II2. ★Illustrations of Other Visual Constancies
    Rapid Review 1

III. PERCEPTIONS AS DECISIONS
    A. Signal Detection Theory
    B. Response Bias
    C. The Case of the USS Vincennes
    D. Detection and Decision
    E. Hits and Misses
    F. Types of Errors
        F1. ★Pop-Up: A Simulation of Signal Detection
    Rapid Review 2
    G. How Do We Perceive Depth?
        G1. ★Pop-Up: Types of Depth Cues
    H. How Do We Perceive Motion?
    I. Direct Perception of Motion
        I1. ★Perception of Motion Movie
    J. Constructed Perception of Motion
        J1. ★Pop-Up: Apparent Motion--The Phi Phenomenon
    Rapid Review 3

IV. PERCEPTUAL ILLUSIONS
    A. Bottom-Up Illusions
        A1. ★Pop-Up: The Twisted Cords Illusion
        A2. ★Pop-Up: The Hermann Grid Illusion
    B. Top-Down Illusions
        B1. ★Pop-Up: The Ponzo0 Illusion
        B2. ★Pop-Up: The Ambiguous Woman Illusion
        B3. ★Pop-Up: The Reversible Figure Illusion
    Rapid Review 4

Quick Quiz

PERCEPTION
- Annotated Outline

- I. INTRODUCTION TO PERCEPTION

- A. From Sensation to Perception

The metaphor of an artist is used to illustrate some of the differences between sensation and perception. Like an artist who uses the oils and canvas to create a painting that is more than the sum of its parts, perception relies upon the integration of many separate pieces of information.

> **Faculty Note:** One of the more ambitious projects on the web is a "web book" by Peter K. Kaiser. Entitled "The Joy of Visual Perception" this site/book combines hyperlinking and interactivity to present an overview of visual perception. It contains lots of graphics and examples, though the writing is fairly technical. http://www.yorku.ca/eye/

B. Gestalt Psychology and Perceptual Laws

The Gestalt perspective is introduced through two activities: an interactive sound clip and animations of selected Gestalt Principles.

B1. ★Perceiving Sound

Students can listen to an audio clip that contains two versions of the song "Twinkle, Twinkle, Little Star." Despite significant differences between the two versions, students will "hear" the same song because they will impose organization on the stimulus—the essence of the Gestalt position.

> - Perceiving Sound
> - Type of Activity: **Audio Demonstration**
> - Learning Objective: **Demonstrate that perception involves imposing order on the stimulus. Make concrete the Gestalt Dictum that maintains that the perceptual whole is greater than the sum of its parts.**
> - Faculty Note: **This audio clip contains two versions of the song "Twinkle, Twinkle, Little Star." Despite significant differences between the two versions (e.g., different pace and complexity), students will "hear" the same song. This effect highlights the fact that we often impose organization on the stimulus—the essence of the Gestalt position.**

- B2. ★Exploring Gestalt Principles

Animations are used to illustrate the gestalt principles of proximity, closure, similarity, and continuity.

> - Exploring Gestalt Principles
> - Activity Type: **Interactive Animation**
> - Learning Objective: **Understand basic Gestalt Principles.**

> •Faculty Note: **This activity includes animations that illustrate the gestalt principles of proximity, closure, similarity, and continuity.**
> •Additional Resources:
> •**One of the easiest ways to see Gestalt Principles in action is to look at how they emerge in art. An interesting web site that tackles this issue can be found at http://www.brad.ac.uk/acad/optom/SPTut/art/index.html**

- II. PERCEPTUAL CONSTANCY

Perceptual constancies are introduced to reinforce, again, the distinction between sensation and perception. Our sensory experiences frequently change (e.g., the light dims, the image on the retina gets smaller) but our perceptions often remain the same.

- II1. ★Illustrations of Visual Constancy

This pop-up allows students to explore color, size, and shape constancy through a series of animations.

> **Illustration of Visual Constancy**
>
> **Type of Activity:** Interactive Animation
>
> **Learning Objective:** Understand Shape Constancy.
>
> **Faculty Note:** The goal of this activity is to help students see how changes in the orientation of an object lead to dramatic changes in the shape of an image that is cast on the retina. Nevertheless, our perception of the object remains constant. To that end, the activity includes two animations that show a door opening and closing. One animation depicts the door in all its rendered glory. The other depicts the door in outline form as it would appear on the flat surface of the retina. As students play and pause the animations, they should get some idea about how the retinal shape of the image changes as the door's orientation varies.

- II2. ★Illustrations of Other Visual Constancy

In this section, students can continue to explore a variety of visual constancies.

> **Illustrations of Other Visual Constancies**
>
> **Type of Activity:** Interactive Animation
>
> **Learning Objective:** Understand shape, size, and color constancies and what they tell us about the constructed nature of perception.
>
> **Faculty Note:** We have found that students often lose sight of the critical points in illustrations like these. In all of these animations, the primary point is not that the stimulus doesn't change—it does. Instead, the point is that the general perception does not change. For example, when the illumination changes on the bananas contained in the color constancy animation, their appearance does change. But they would still be described as "yellow." Similarly, the image size of the cow in the size constancy animation does change as it is hurled into the distance. But the cow is not assumed to be getting smaller, just further away. It's perceived size is constant. (BTW, no cows were harmed in the making of this CD!)

Rapid Review 1

•III. PERCEPTIONS AS DECISIONS

In this section, perceptions are presented as decisions that depend both upon the stimulus and the response criteria of the perceiver. Specifically, signal detection theory, with its emphasis on detectability and response bias, is introduced.

A. Signal Detection Theory

Signal detection theory is introduced.

B. Response Bias

The notion that our responses depend, in part, upon our decision criteria is introduced.

C. The Case of the USS Vincennes

The 1988 downing of an Iranian jetliner is presented as a case study in signal detection theory.

D. Detection and Decision

Continuing the Vincennes example, this section emphasizes how the simple act of saying "I saw something" is not an automatic response, but rather the culmination of a decision process that depends upon more than the mere presence of a signal.

E. Hits and Misses

In this section, hits, misses, false alarms, and correct rejections are defined.

F. Types of Errors

This section focuses on the relationship between accuracy and response bias under conditions of marginal detectability.

- F1. ★Pop-up: A Simulation of Signal Detection

This activity allows students to participate in a signal detection task under two different decision criteria. After completing the two sets of judgments, the students see how they did and learn more about Type I and Type II errors.

A Simulation of Signal Detection

Type of Activity: Simulation

Learning Objective: Understand the key elements of signal detection theory including decision criteria, response bias, detectability, and Type I and Type II errors.

Faculty Note: In this activity, students are encouraged to imagine that they are radar operators on a military ship. Their task is to watch a radar screen and decide whether they "see" an enemy missile on each sweep of the radar. On the first set of eight trials, they are urged to be absolutely sure that they have seen an enemy missile before issuing an alarm. On the second set of eight trials, they are encouraged to sound the alarm if they think it is at all possible that they saw a missile. After completing the two sets of judgments, the students can see how they did. What students should discover from this activity is that their accuracy (i.e., the number of hits + correct rejections) was the same across the two kinds of judgment. What varies is the kind of errors they make. When urged to be cautious about sounding the alarm, students should frequently miss the missiles that were there (a.k.a., Type II error) but have few false alarms (a.k.a., Type I errors). In contrast, when instructed to sound the alarm at the slightest provocation, they should have relatively few misses and many false alarms.

To more dramatically illustrate the main points about response biases, students may also be encouraged to run through this exercise again. The second time through they can answer "Yes" to every question about the enemy missile, ultimately seeing the elimination of any dangerous "misses" but with the much greater cost in expensive false alarms. Conversely, answering "No" to all queries about the presence of the missiles will let all of them through their defenses (many misses), but no friendlies will be shot down (no false alarms). The trade-off in types of potential errors may be more vividly illustrated in this fashion.

Although the difficulty of the simulated radar detection task is intended to be identical with both sets of instructions, there may be a slight practice effect as students gain experience with the task. In other words, their total error rate may drop slightly during the second set of radar sweeps. The main point remains the same, however. The most significant change should be in the shift from misses to false alarms as the primary type of error made by the student.

You may want to continue discussion of the principles of signal detection theory in other (nonmilitary) contexts:

- When airport metal detectors are tuned to their maximum sensitivity in the aftermath of a publicized act of terrorism, the increased chance of correctly detecting a terrorist's weapon (a "hit") is accompanied by an irritating increase in the number of false alarms for watches, keys, and belt buckles.

- When scientists test hypotheses, the type of error that they are most concerned about is making a false claim of a significant finding when, in fact, the evidence doesn't support it. Responsible researchers should maintain a response bias that allows them to control any tendencies towards false alarms (Type I errors) while still having a reasonable chance of discovering something interesting. One of the reasons that inferential statistics are employed by scientists is to allow them to control these types of errors. (A classic example here is the case of the apparent discovery of "cold fusion" by chemists at the University of Utah. These researchers held press conferences claiming a dramatic and unexpected discovery of "nuclear fusion in a test tube" but in their enthusiasm had actually misinterpreted some ambiguous evidence in their experiments).

- Our judicial system is intended to balance various types of errors in making legal decisions. Jury members in a criminal trial are faced with what amounts to a signal detection task, making a decision about a defendant's guilt under conditions of uncertainty. Evidentiary rules (such as Miranda rights) are intended to produce a response bias that will minimize false alarms (convicting an innocent person), although critics sometimes bemoan the tradeoff in increased "misses" (guilty defendants set free on technicalities).

Rapid Review 2

G. How Do We Perceive Depth?

In this section, binocular and monocular depth cues are introduced as tools that perceivers use to construct a three dimensional perception from a two dimensional retinal image.

•G1. ★Pop-up: Types of Depth Cues

In this pop-up, students are encouraged to explore a variety of monocular and binocular depth cues.

> •Types of Depth Cues
> **Activity Type:** Interactive Animation
>
> **Learning Objective:** Understand binocular and monocular depth cues.
>
> **Faculty Note:** In this activity, students can click on the names of various depth cues and see how they are manifested in a photograph.

H. How Do We Perceive Motion?

This section raises the question of how we move from an erratic, constantly changing retinal image to a perception of smooth and continuous motion.

•I. Direct Perception of Motion
Direct perception theories argue that all of the information needed to perceive motion is contained in the stimulus itself. An animation depicting "optic flow" is used to illustrate this point.

> **Faculty Note:** In this CD-ROM (and in many textbooks) a great deal of attention is devoted to theories of motion perception that assume the individual is "constructing" an impression of movement based on inference and experience. A useful counterpoint is the direct perception theory of motion perception, originally articulated by Gibson, that assumes that it is a "bottom up" process that requires little in the way of inference or decisions on the part of the perceiver. Moving stimuli activate feature detectors in the brain, which directly responds to that pattern of stimulation by generating a subjective experience of movement. Recent discoveries of feature detectors intended to detect motion in particular directions, especially the "looming" movements of objects towards the perceiver, tend to lend credence to this model.

•I1. ★Perception of Motion Movie

This movie begins with a static image that appears to be of randomly placed dots on a gray background. Once the image is set in motion, it becomes clear that the movie is of a man climbing a stepladder. Presumably, this information becomes available directly from the moving stimulus, not through the addition of context or cues.

> **Perception of Motion Movie**
>
> **Type of Activity:** Movie
>
> **Learning Objective:** Encourage students to think critically about direct versus constructed theories of perception..
>
> **Faculty Note:** To further illustrate the direct perception perspective, students are first presented with a static image that appears to be of randomly placed dots on a gray background. It could be a picture of almost anything. Once the image is set in motion,

however, it becomes clear that the movie is of a man climbing a stepladder. The point of the movie is that all of the information becomes available directly from the moving stimulus, not through the addition of context or cues.

Additional Resources:

More information on the direct perception approach can be found at the International Society for Ecological Society web site at http://www.trincoll.edu/~psyc/isep.html

- J. Constructed Perception of Motion
- **Constructed theories of motion perception argue that we actively combine many sources of information to infer that a stimulus is moving.**
J1. ★Pop-up: Apparent Motion--The Phi Phenomenon

In this pop-up, students can examine the effects that various presentation rates have on the perception of motion via the phi phenomenon (a.k.a., stroboscopic motion).

Apparent Motion—The Phi Phenomenon

Type of Activity: Exploration

Learning Objective: Become familiar with the phi phenomenon and understand the implications it has for our understanding of motion perception.

Faculty Note: In this activity, students can explore the effects that various rates of presentation have on the phi phenomenon. The question of how the brain fuses the images together remains one of the great, unanswered questions in vision research.

Rapid Review 3

- IV. PERCEPTUAL ILLUSIONS

The final section of the perception unit focuses on illusions—instances in which the subjective experience of a stimulus does not match its objective characteristics.

Faculty Note: "Illusion galleries" are proliferating on the web. Two of the better galleries are http://www.illusionworks.com and http://valley.uml.edu/landrigan/illusion.html. The Illusion Works site, in particular, has very nice demonstrations and fairly accessible explanations.

- A. Bottom-Up Illusions
- **This section introduces bottom-up illusions. In bottom-up illusions, the illusions occur because of the ways in which our sensory systems are physiologically wired.**
- A1. ★Pop-up: The Twisted Cords Illusion

In this illusion, students can control the orientations of slanted lines that overwhelm the feature detectors in the visual cortex and cause the illusion to occur.

The Twisted Cords Illusion

Type of Activity: Exploration

Learning Objective: Understand feature detectors and the role that they play in the occurrence of the twisted cords illusion.

Faculty Note: In this activity, students can control the presence and orientation of angled lines that give rise to the twisted cords illusion. The illusion occurs because the many slanted lines comprising the "cords" over stimulate feature detectors that react specifically to lines of just that orientation. Presumably this stimulation overwhelms and distorts the perceived orientation of the larger vertical lines. Students can verify this explanation by exploring what happens as they change and remove the angled lines.

A2. ★Pop-up: The Hermann Grid Illusion

In this illusion, students can examine the effects of changing the size of the intersections in the Hermann Grid.

The Hermann Grid

Type of Activity: Exploration

Learning Objective: Demonstrate lateral inhibition.

Faculty Note: The Herman Grid illustrates the effects of lateral inhibition in the neural substrate of the eye. Receptors responding to the white intersections of the grid are relatively more inhibited by neighboring receptors (which are active due to the bright areas around the intersections). This creates "gray" splotches of lesser brightness at those intersections. In this activity, students can control the size of the intersections in the Hermann Grid and examine the subsequent changes in the experience of the illusion.

Additional Resources:

More information on the receptive fields of the retina and the principles of lateral inhibition which produce these effects can be found at: http://psych.hanover.edu/Krantz/receptive/index.html. In addition to general information about perception, this site contains an entire interactive tutorial devoted to the topic of receptive fields.

•B. Top-Down Illusions
Top-down illusions occur when our assumptions, preconceptions, and past experience

distort our interpretation of the objective properties of the stimulus.

- B1. ★Pop-up: The Ponzo Illusion

In this illusion, students can examine the effects that adding and removing depth cues have on the Ponzo Illusion (a.k.a. the "running monsters" illusion).

The Ponzo Illusion

Activity Type: Exploration

Learning Objective: Understand how depth cues contribute to the Ponzo Illusion.

Faculty Note: The Ponzo illusion occurs when one image subjectively appears larger than another, despite the fact that there is no objective difference in size. In this activity, students can control the presence of depth cues in the Ponzo illusion. When the depth cues are present (i.e., linear perspective, height in the scene), one image is perceived to be farther away than the other. Given that both images are the same size, the brain interprets the more distant image as larger. It is this inferential process that creates the illusory size differences.

The Ponzo Illusion can also be used as a starting point for a discussion of the moon illusion. Though multiple explanations for the moon illusion exist, depth cues clearly play a role. To demonstrate this role, you need an evening when the moon looks unusually large and a tube from a roll of paper towels. First look at the moon with the naked eye and then look at it through the tube. Because the tube blocks out the depth cues found on the horizon, the illusion should diminish.

- B2. ★Pop-up: The Ambiguous Woman Illusion

In this illusion, students can see various interpretations of an ambiguous figure highlighted.

The Ambiguous Woman Illusion

Activity Type: Demonstration

Learning Objective: Recognize the role that expectations and perceptual sets play in our interpretations of objects.

Faculty Note: This activity allows students to look at a version of the ambiguous young woman/old woman that has been around since the early 1900s. The original figure is from an advertising campaign. Students can look at the ambiguous figure or with the features that lead to each interpretation highlighted. The text focuses on the role that expectations play in determining how ambiguous stimuli are perceived.

•B3. ★Pop-up: The Reversible Figure Illusion

The face-vase illusion illustrates the Gestalt notions of "figure" and "ground," with students having control over what appears as figure or ground.

The Reversible Figure Illusion

Activity Type: Demonstration

Learning Objective: Explore the Gestalt notion of Figure/Ground.

Faculty Note: In this activity, students can see another classic stimulus from the perception literature. The face-vase illusion illustrates the Gestalt notions of "figure" and "ground." The student sees one element of the image (either the internal "vase" or the framing "faces") as the dominant figure, but not more than one simultaneously. It is possible for the perceiver to alternate between these varying impressions at will. The activity also allows students to see versions that accentuate the figure-ground reversals.

•Rapid Review 4
•Quick Quiz

CHAPTER 4

CONSCIOUSNESS

Chapter Overview
    Learning Objectives
    Chapter Outline

Additional Lecture Ideas
    Lecture Topics
    Additional Readings

In-Class Activities and Demonstrations
    Activities and Demonstrations
    Sources for Additional Activities
    Journey II Software

World Wide Web

Audio-Visual Support

Handout and Transparency Masters

Chapter Overview

Learning Objectives

After studying this chapter, you should be able to do the following:

1. Identify two biological mechanisms that affect our consciousness.

2. Describe evidence of multiple levels of consciousness.

3. Describe the effects of meditation and hypnosis.

4. Compare the effects of different types of consciousness-altering drugs.

5. Give possible reasons we sleep and dream.

6. Describe the characteristics of different stages of sleep and sleep disorders.

Chapter Outline

Consciousness

I. The Nature of Consciousness: Multiple Bases and Levels
   A. Characteristics of Consciousness
      1. Consciousness is a state, temporary condition.
      2. Consciousness has content (the sensations, thoughts, and feelings during a particular state.
      3. Impact of these characteristics: affect what we notice, think, feel, and do.
      4. Psychologists' interest in consciousness
   B. The Biological Roots of Consciousness
      1. Hormones and biological rhythms
         a. circadian rhythm
            i. impact on alertness
            ii. individual differences in circadian rhythm
            iii. effects of mismatch between occupation and circadian rhythm
            iv. effects of varying melatonin levels
      2. Neural connections and consciousness
         a. interplay between actual information from senses, personal experiences, and culture on consciousness
   C. Multiple Levels of Consciousness
      1. How do we know about the levels of consciousness?
         a. <u>types of evidence</u>: efforts to recall information, lucid dreaming, clinical observations
      2. A hidden and powerful unconscious?
         a. we have both conscious and unconscious knowledge that affects us
         b. <u>unconscious</u>: part of the mind that contains thoughts, motivations, and feelings about which we are unaware and which are not easily accessible
         c. <u>related examples</u>: deja vu and intuition
         d. the perspective of psychodynamic psychologists on the unconscious as the site of unacceptable desires and impulses
   D. Expanding Consciousness: Gaining Alternative Perspectives
      1. How might we expand the consciousness?
         a. psychodynamic insight
         b. becoming educated
         c. more conscious "space" when some behaviors become automatic
      2. Expanding the content of consciousness
         a. example of expanding consciousness by abandoning Western analytic tendencies

3. *Ki*, a cross-cultural perspective on consciousness
    a. *ki*, Japanese belief regarding "life force"

II. Altered States of Consciousness: Multiple Conditions
A. <u>Altered states of consciousness</u> = temporary mental states that are noticeably and qualitatively different from either wakeful alertness or sleep.
    1. produce changes in moods, perceptions, and actions
    2. <u>example methods</u>: fasting, prayer, religious ceremonies, drugs, exercise
B. Meditation: A Mellow Consciousness
    1. <u>methods</u>: focussed attention
    2. <u>effects</u>: calmness; increased creativity, perceptiveness, energy
    3. <u>criticism</u>: physical effects not measurably different than relaxed state although subjective reports suggest the experiences are different
C. Hypnosis: Increased Suggestibility
    1. <u>characteristics of hypnotic state</u>: increased suggestibility and focus
    2. <u>criticism</u>: physical effects not measurably different than relaxed state although subjective reports suggest the experiences are different
    3. <u>theories</u>: dissociation of consciousness v. weakening of normal control features in the brain
    4. becoming hypnotized
        a. typical process
        b. individual differences in susceptibility
    5. hypnotic suggestions
        a. distortion of memory
        b. effects of posthypnotic suggestion
    6. uses of hypnosis
        a. access unconscious thoughts, wishes, feelings, conflicts
        b. behavior change (e.g., smoking cessation)
        c. medical intervention (e.g., pain relief)
D. Drugged States: Chemically Changing Consciousness
    1. psychoactive drugs: chemicals that produce a psychological effect by influencing the nervous system.
        a. negative physical and social effects
        b. effects on neurotransmission
            i. increase/decrease amount of neurotransmitters
            ii. block normal receptor sites of neurotransmitters
            iii. prevent or accelerate reuptake of neurotransmitters
    2. Depressants
        a. act by inhibiting/slowing CNS
        b. <u>examples</u>: opiates, narcotics, barbiturates, alcohol
        c. effects of alcohol
            i. biological effects
        d. gender perspectives on alcohol consumption
            i. sex differences in metabolism

                    ii. social proscriptions for use of alcohol
            e. ethnic perspectives on alcohol consumption
                    i. cross-cultural differences in binge drinking
                    ii. cross-cultural differences and levels of within-group variability in drinking patterns
    3. Stimulants
        a. act by increasing/accelerating CNS
        b. <u>examples</u>: caffeine, nicotine, amphetamines, cocaine
        c. effects of different stimulants
    4. Hallucinogens
        a. <u>characteristics of use</u>: altered consciousness, thought processes, perceptions
        b. <u>examples</u>: PCP, LSD, marijuana, inhalants
        c. effects of different hallucinogens
    5. Drug tolerance and addiction
        a. <u>tolerance</u>: the body's habituation to a drug after repeated exposures to it, so increasing amounts of the drug are needed to produce the desired effect
        b. <u>psychological dependence</u>: when a person thinks a drug is needed to cope
        c. <u>addiction</u>: physical dependence on a drug
        d. <u>withdrawal</u>: unpleasant physical effects when a drug to which one is addicted is stopped
    6. Cultural perspectives on drug use
        a. natural v. synthetic forms of drugs
        b. group experiences with drugs
        c. ritual use of drugs
    7. Therapeutic uses of drugs
        a. <u>examples</u>: barbiturate use for psychological disorders; Prozac use for relaxation and pain relief; Valium use to reduce anxiety

III. Sleep: Its Multiple Stages and Contents
   A. Why we sleep
    1. <u>repair theory</u>: sleep to recover from physical, emotional, intellectual exertion
    2. to entrench and maintain synaptic connections
    3. <u>ecological (adaptive) theory</u>: sleep so we don't harm ourselves or waste energy
   B. The Stages of Sleep: Sequences in Our Sleeping Consciousness
    1. study of sleep: the sleep laboratory & the EEG
    2. stages of sleep
        a. stages 1 through 4
            i. brain waves patterns
            ii. physical effects
        b. REM sleep

                        i. rapid eye movement
                        ii. paradoxical sleep

            3. sleep cycles
                a. typical movement patterns through stages
                b. individual differences
                c. changes in patterns over the lifespan
    C. **Sleep Disorders: Problems of Our Sleeping State**
        1. insomnia
            a. definition: difficulty falling or staying asleep
            b. effects of sedatives
            c. recommendations
        2. narcolepsy
            a. hereditary sleep disorder characterized by sudden sleep attacks
        3. NREM sleep disorders
            a. somnambulism (sleep walking)
            b. enuresis (bed wetting)
            b. sleep apnea (stopping breathing)
            c. night terror
                i. a stage 4 sleep disorder
                ii. characteristics
    D. **Dreams: The Contents of Sleeping Consciousness**
        1. A neural perspective on why we dream
            a. <u>activation-synthesis theory of dreams</u>: dreams have no meaning but are brain's effort to understand and impose order on chaotic, incoherent, random neural signals arising in the brain
            b. <u>computer model of dreams</u>: dreams reflect efforts by brain to check and expand nerve connections in the brain
        2. A sensory perspective on what we dream
            a. dreams reflect sensory experience from the previous day
            b. supportive evidence
        3. A cognitive perspective on what we dream
            a. dreams provide a way of thinking about and solving one's problems
        4. A psychodynamic perspective on what we dream
            a. latent content of dreams reflect unconscious conflicts, desires, wishes, fears

Additional Lecture Topics

Sleep Deprivation

Students may be interested in a first hand account of what to is like to be a participant in a sleep experiment. Lydia Dotto describes her experience in a 2-day sleep deprivation study at the Defence and Civil Institute of Environmental Medicine in Toronto, Canada. Although she starts the experiment with enthusiasm, one day into it, she reports being anything but the happy camper. Irritable and fatigued by this point, she claims "Sleep is starting to ambush me." She finds resentment in the fact that the experimenter appears to not look sleep-deprived, she looks forward to a promised nap and suspected her computer somehow enjoys taunting her with the promise. She and a partner literally despair that they won't be able to make the entire experiment--an emotional and cognitive reaction the experimenters call "the first-night effect". The nap takes on psychological significance...if they can last until the nap, needing to fall asleep immediately so as to be able to sleep for as long as possible. Indeed, as it turns out, the study had to do with the effects of napping on performance and it appears that the 2-hour nap produced significant improvements in task performance as compared to pre-nap performance for up to 17 1/2 hours following it. Lydia was struck by the individual differences between herself and her lab partner, Julia. Having herself experienced the sensation of blanking out or "disappearing" as a result of her sleep deprivation, she was interested in Julia's experience of meandering thoughts and her inability to comprehend typical words printed on the computer screen. All in all, Ms. Dotto's account is very interesting and could inform students a bit about sleep researcher's methodologies and participants' subjective reactions to being in such a study.

Source:
Dotto, L. (1997). Asleep in the Fast Lane. In Sattler, D. N. & Shabatay, V. (Eds.) Psychology in context: Voices and perspectives. Boston: Houghton

Gender and Substance Abuse

Historically, women have engaged in fewer health impairing behaviors than have men. Some authors suggest that traditional gender roles encourage substance use in men and discourage it in women. As women entered the labor market in larger numbers and thus adopted more "male" roles, it was thought that their use of substances would eventually reach the level of that demonstrated by males. Although college women and men are similar in alcohol use (Sandmaier, 1980), that expectation has not been realized (Temple, 1987). With the exceptions of amphetamine and prescription drugs, men continue to use alcohol and other substances in greater amounts and frequency (Robbins & Clayton, 1989; Johnston, Bachman, and O'Malley, 1982). In women, frequency and volume of alcohol use increases with education (Parker et al., 1989) with some surveys reporting the highest levels of problematic use in women having difficulty finding jobs and women "stuck" in low-wage, dead-end jobs (Sandmaier, 1980). Women are more likely to consume alcohol in private or with their spouses, to be introduced to alcohol by males, and encouraged to drink by males (Andersen, 1993).

Unlike alcohol, women are more likely to use prescription and over-the-counter medications than are men--in fact, most women receiving drug treatment are being treated for tranquilizer, sedative, and barbiturate use. Women are also more likely to be prescribed these medications than are men. Cooperstock (1971) attributes this trend to social roles: women are more likely than men to report physical and emotional pain and physicians are more likely to see women as emotional. On the other hand, Fidell (1973) argues that women's complaints are realistic given the structured inequalities that make women's lives stressful. Some authors also call attention to the political and economic forces that may contribute to these prescription trends--in short, drug companies realize significant profit from drugs that are prescribed to and marketed to women (McKinley, 1978).

Gender role explanations for use patterns and reactions to individuals who are substance addicted have been offered. Andersen (1993) argues that substance use patterns reflect traditional cultural images of masculinity and femininity. The woman who becomes addicted to a substance however violates cultural expectations for substance use. For example, the woman with an addiction to heroin may be seen as "more deviant, more reprehensible, and less treatable than male addicts." (pg. 192). Women with alcoholism may be viewed as "hard" and more masculine. As a result, Andersen suggests that, while traditional gender roles insulate most women from substance use, they also result in significant stigmatization and barriers to treatment once a woman has become substance addicted.

Aside from the information available on substance use patterns, Matlin (1993) notes that research on addiction in women as compared to that on addiction in men is sparse. For example, Vannicelli & Nash (1984) reported that more than half of the 259 studies concerning alcoholism used all-male samples and only 6 studies had all-female samples. In the clinical arena, women constitute only 25 percent of individuals receiving treatment, perhaps due to a number of factors including greater indifference and less efforts of partners to encourage treatment (Leland, 1982), greater stigma concerning the addiction, and fewer resources for the woman addict.

Source:
Andersen, M. (1993). <u>Thinking about women: Sociological perspectives on sex and gender</u>. New York: Macmillan.
Matlin, M. (1993). <u>The psychology of women</u>. (pgs. 436-441). Fort Worth, TX: Harcourt Brace

Culture and Altered States of Consciousness

Colleen Ward, a scholar with extensive international experience, addresses psychology's reaction to and misunderstanding of nonWestern experiences of altered states of consciousness (ASCs). She notes that most introductory psychology textbooks are prone to reporting laboratory-based studies of phenomena such as sleep deprivation, hypnosis, dreaming, and meditation, and that other "exotic" ASCs (such as the hallucinations and trance and spirit possessions she considers in her article), are often ignored or viewed as pathological from Western standards. However, from other cultural perspectives, such events are relatively common and are meaningfully incorporated into cultural everyday life.

For example, hallucinations are reported across all cultures. However, she contends, "the experience of hallucination is a learned phenomenon with cultural values and social expectations providing the necessary cues for the ASC production and manifestation" and takes into consideration differences in hallucinations produced by mescaline ingestion as an illustration. Wallace (1959) reported that Anglo-Americans were likely to report lack of social inhibitions, extreme mood variations, idiosyncratic hallucinations, and an unsettling "split with reality" as a result of the drug, whereas Native-Americans were more likely to report religious ecstasy, hallucinations that were spiritual in nature, therapeutic benefits, and a sense of a "higher order" reality from their experience. The experiences themselves seemed influenced by cultural background. Moreover, the linkage between psychopathology and hallucination varies across cultures. Western psychiatry incorporates hallucinations as a defining characteristic of mental illness, whereas hallucinations are noticeably absent in other nonWestern culture definitions. Indeed, even when hallucinations are present in a person considered to be mentally ill, the hallucinations were not part of the basis for that diagnosis.

Ward differentiates active and receptive mental states, the former characterized by the typical state of focused attention and logical thought processes, whereas the latter is characterized by diffuse attention, unorthodox thinking, and the dominance of sensory experience. ASCs, she claims, are forms of this second category and <u>both</u> types of mental states should be considered adaptive and functional providing the means for psychological growth and development. Other important points included in her article:

> Culturally shared views of consciousness will pattern our experiences....in short our very potential for being able to experience various states of consciousness are culturally conditioned. She notes that the "repertoire of culturally patterned ASCs in Euro-American societies appears more limited and less ritualized than in many other cultures."

- NonWestern ASCs are typically public events imbued with meaning and social significance for both the individual experiencing them and the community at large.
- The cultural tradition expressed in experimental psychology emphasizes the laboratory setting and limits the phenomenon that can be studied in it.

- The Western definition of "normal" consciousness is limited, not shared cross culturally. Thus, the cross-cultural investigation of ASCs offers a unique opportunity to study them in the real world where such experiences have purpose and meaning.

Source:
Ward, C. (1994). Cultural and altered states of consciousness. In W. Lonner & Malpass, R. (Eds.), Psychology and culture. Boston: Allyn & Bacon.

Cultural variations in alcohol and drug use

Joseph Trimble raises some thought-provoking and interesting issues in this recent article concerning cultural variations in alcohol and drug use, and several points can enrich your discussion on drug use.

He notes that, historically, psychoactive drugs were used for religious and ceremonial purposes among the people indigenous to the Americas. Drugs were attributed with great power and the most powerful were reserved for use by the shaman and religious leaders. Otherwise, strict prohibitions for use were observed. In short, the drugs were imbued with meaning. In other cultural settings, drugs were incorporated into daily life experience as well as religious practice. The underlying purpose for drug use was, however, culturally significant and was not based on recreational or self-serving purposes and abuse appeared not to be an issue until the latter motivations entered the cultural picture.

When considering ethnic or cross-cultural differences and drug abuse, Trimble raises several cautionary points. First, he notes, we must carefully evaluate findings that suggest high concentrations of drug use in ethnic minorities in urban settings (or rural settings for some ethnic groups) from an understanding of the population distributions across the country. In other words, numbers of cases of substance abuse for a group may be artificially inflated by the fact that more people from that group live in a certain region. Second, media reports may bias our perceptions of who tends to use drugs through disproportionate numbers of stories or pictures of ethnic minorities arrested for drug-related crimes or drug problems in certain neighborhoods as opposed to others. Third, we need to remember that cultural groups establish the standards for drug use in addition to defining abuse. In cultures where use of a drug is considered part of everyday life, addiction is not considered to exist. Moreover, when different patterns of substance use are compartmentalized and labeled as favorable and unfavorable, the pattern given the negative label might be one group's means through which it might further stigmatize or suppress another group.

Source:
Trimble, J. (1994). Cultural variations in the use of alcohol and drugs. In W. Lonner & Malpass, R. (Eds.), Psychology and culture. Boston: Allyn &

Bacon.

Hypnosis on Trial

Smith (1995) notes that one of the benefits attributed to hypnosis is the recovery of lost memories or forgotten information. Some of your students may have read newspaper or magazine articles concerning recovered memories for sexual abuse and methods used to foster that recovery and wonder "why the controversy?"

Part of the skepticism surrounding these reports concerns the use of hypnosis as part of the recovery process. However, the phenomenon of hypnosis itself is subject to different interpretations. The neodissociation and social role theories provide different explanations for what is happening to the hypnotized individual. In particular, social role theory offers that the hypnotized person, in a state of heightened suggestibility and relaxation, is simply acting out a social role that is consistent with the social situation, whereas neodissociation theory offers that hypnosis produces a division in consciousness and posits the existence of a "hidden observer". Theoretical disagreements and difficulty in empirically testing some of these theoretical constructs contribute to some of the skepticism surrounding the use of hypnosis. Some people have difficulty accepting hypnosis as valid when its underlying process is difficult to articulate and test.

Despite these concerns, the use of hypnosis as a memory aid has been supported in law enforcement work. In 1967, Arons reported on a number of cases where hypnosis was used to aid in police investigations (although it is also interesting to note that Arons is regarded as being a leading pioneer in teaching hypnosis techniques to police investigators). In a critique of these findings, Smith (1983) found the use of hypnosis techniques with crime witnesses or victims to be problematic because (1) it is frequently impossible to objectively verify some of the "facts" remembered because of lack of cooperation from others and (2) there is generally no control group for comparison of the memory such as one would incorporate in a true experimental design.

Thus, efforts to determine if hypnosis can produce more accurate memory have moved to laboratory settings. For example, Cooper and London (1973) had participants read an article and then 2 weeks later take a test on the article. Participants answered the same questions twice, once hypnotized and once without being hypnotized. Using a countered-balanced design, they found that all participants demonstrated better memory on the second test--it did not matter if they were in the hypnotized-nonhypnotized or nonhypnotized-hypnotized group. In an application of this study's findings to the situation with the use of hypnosis with crime investigations, Smith (1983) noted that the typical practice during the police investigations was to ask the witness to recall the crime first, then hypnotize them and ask them to recount their observations a second time. The heightened recall under hypnosis observed using this procedure reveals nothing more than the order effect reported by Cooper and London, according to Smith. Additional studies have found that hypnotized participants demonstrated no better memory for realistic crime enactments (Putnam, 1979) and were more influenced by leading questions than were nonhypnotized participants (Smith, 1983). In a more recent study, Orne and Dinges (1989) reported that hypnotized participants were more likely to have stronger convictions about memories about which they had previously been relatively uncertain. Taken together, these studies fail to support the idea that hypnosis can contribute to recovery of memories.

Source:
Smith, R. (1995). Challenging your preconceptions: Thinking critically about psychology. (pgs. 49-57). Pacific Grove, CA: Brooks/Cole.

Suggestions for Additional Readings

Dement, W. (1992). The sleepwatchers. Stanford, CA: Stanford Alumni Association.

Farthing, G. (1992). The psychology of consciousness. Englewood Cliffs, NJ: Prentice Hall.

Glass, I. (Ed.) (1991). The international handbook of addiction behaviour. London: Tavistock/Routledge.

Kihlstrom, J. (1985). Hypnosis. Annual Review of Psychology, 36, 385-418.

Moorcroft, W. (1993). Sleep, dreaming, & sleep disorders: An introduction. (2nd ed.). Lanham, MD: University Press of America.

Ornstein, R. (1991). The evolution of consciousness: The origins of the way we think. Boston: Houghton Mifflin.

Segal, B. (1992). Ethnicity and drug taking behavior. In J. Trimble, Bolek, C., & Niemcryk, S. (Eds.), Ethnic and multicultural drug abuse: Perspectives on current research. Binghamton, NY: Harrington Park Press.

Siegel, R. (1977). Hallucinations. Scientific American, 237(4), 132-140.

Spanos, N., & Chaves, J. (1989). Hypnosis: The cognitive-behavioral perspective. Buffalo: Prometheus.

Trimble, J. (1998). Drug abuse prevention strategies among ethnic-minority populations. In R. Coombs, & Ziedonis, D. (Eds.), Handbook on drug abuse prevention. Englewood Cliffs, NJ: Prentice Hall.

Tucker, M. (1985). U.S. ethnic minorties and drug use: An assessment of the science and practice. International Journal of the Addictions, 20, 1021-1047.

Ward, C. (Ed.) (1989). Altered states of consciousness and mental health: A cross-cultural perspective. Thousand Oaks, CA: Sage

Zilbergeld, B., Edelstein, M., & Araoz, D. (1986). Hypnosis: Questions and answers. New York: Norton.

In-Class Activities and Demonstrations

TRAIL Blazing: Using Transparency Masters 4.1 - 4.5, review with students the "Checking Your TRAIL" sections in the chapter. Have students work in small groups to answer the questions and then review with the class as a whole to tie the text reading to activity in class.

Reaching Critical Mass: Using Transparency Masters 4.6 - 4.8, review with students the "Critical Thinking" sections in the chapter. Have students work in small groups to answer the questions and then review with the class as a whole to tie the text reading to activity in class.

Getting Down to IT: Using Transparency Masters 4.9 - 4.13, review the "Integrative Thinking" sections in the chapter with students. Have students work in small groups to answer the questions and then review with the class as a whole to tie the text reading to activity in class.

Do cultural stereotypes and gender roles appear in the content of dreams?: Heynick reports consistent gender differences in content of dreams. In particular, males are more likely to dream of being aggressive whereas women are likely to dream of being in danger, pursued, or victims of aggression. Males dream of travel, being naked in public places, explicit sex, or money. Women dream of indoor activities, emotions, and conversations with others. Using **Handout Master # 4.1**, have students record their dreams for 3 nights and assess them for similar trends. In reviewing students' data, discuss the extent to which their dream content reflects cultural expectations for women and men.

Source:
Heynick, F. (1993). Dream "mirror of the soul" reflects differences between cultures. Psychology International, 2, 1-3.

Problem solving during dreams:
In keeping with the cognitive perspective described by Uba & Huang, Dement suggests that problems can be solved while we are sleeping. In his now classic book, he describes several methods he used for studying creative problem solving that occur during dreaming. Using Handout Master # 4.2, have students test their creative problem solving capability while asleep. The handout contains two problems students may attempt to solve, one a logic brain teaser and the other an interpersonal dilemma. Have them read and think about possible solutions for each before going to sleep. After awaking the next day, they are to write down any dreams that occurred during the previous night and consider any possible relationships between the dream(s) and the problems. Dement found that, out of 500 students who engaged in these types of exercises, 87

had dreams that were either directly or indirectly related to the problem they had considered before falling asleep. In some rare instances, the logic problems were accurately solved in the dream. By the way, the correct solution for the logic brain teaser includes spelling out the names for the numbers and determining that the numbers are listed alphabetically.

Source:
Dement, W. (1978). <u>Some must watch while some must sleep</u>. New York: Norton

Gendered perceptions of alcoholism: As noted in the additional lecture topic concerning women and substance abuse, women tend to be more highly stigmatized by addiction than are men. Using **Handout Masters # 4.2a and #4.2b,** assess students' reactions to two different scenarios concerning a male vs. female diagnosed with alcoholism. Results consistent with the lecture topic would demonstrate more harsh judgments toward the female than the male. Discuss reasons why students have different reactions making sure to raise the issue of gender role violation. Note if male vs. female students respond more harshly toward John vs. Jane.

The power of suggestion: Before beginning the lecture on hypnosis, introduce the topic of suggestibility with some of the following exercises to highlight the idea that most people can be influenced by the suggestions of others.

Try feigning a few yawns during the beginning of class. Note how many students follow suit. Ask how many students either yawned or had to stifle a yawn.

- Instruct students to remove all items from their desk for an upcoming task. Most will respond to this direct instruction...why? Because it is part of the social role of being a good student.
- Remark that you think there must be "something" going around because you've been feeling like your nose is especially stuffy lately (and perhaps list a number of other rather vague symptoms). Ask if anyone else has noticed all the stuff in the air lately.
- Rub your arms and comment on how cold the room seems (after making sure the room is at a comfortable temperature). Note how many students follow suit.
- Pass around of jars containing only water but tell students that this is a test of olfactory accuity....each jar contains either vanilla or musk scent. Ask them to note which essence is in the jar they smell. Keep having them smell the jar until they are sure they smell something.

Note whether some students more quickly respond to your suggestions. Use these as demonstrations of individual differences to suggestibility.

Sources for Additional Activities
Books:
  Benjamin, L. & Lowman, K. (1981). <u>Activities Handbook for the Teaching of Psychology</u>. Washington DC: American Psychological Association.
  Halonen, J. (1995). Chapter 5: State of Consciousness. In <u>The Critical Thinking Companion For Introductory Psychology</u> (Worth Publ.).
  Makosky, V. et al. (Eds.) (1995). <u>Activities Handbook for the Teaching of Psychology</u> (Vol. III). Washington DC: American Psychological Association.

Journey II Software:
  Journey II contains 2 exercises relevant to the Consciousness chapter. Enter the Sleeping lab by clicking on the icon in the Main Menu.
- <u>Physiology of Sleep</u>: Many students can identify with the introductory question "When was the last time you stayed awake all night?" Four specific physiological measures that vary throughout the day (i.e., alertness, body temperature, growth hormone, and cortisol) are discussed and the student sees how these measures change over the course of a day for Sarah, a sleep lab participant.
- <u>Content of Dreams</u>: Do dreams come true? Students complete a 10 question survey and their responses are then compared with an in-depth description of those taken from a large sample of students. The common characteristics and unique gender characteristics regarding dream content are discussed. Suggestions for how to maintain a dream journal are provided.

World Wide Web: Check out the following WWW sites for information and activities relevant to this section of the text!
Addison Wesley Longman's Website -- **http://longman.awl.com/**
- PsychZone link -- **http://longman.awl.com/**
- Psych Web -- **http://www.gasou.edu/psychweb/psychweb.htm**

Psychology Jumping Stand --
http://www.indiana.edu:80/~iuepsyc/PsycJump.html
The Psychology Place --**http://www.psychplace.com**
- Dreams -- **http://www.iag.net/~hutchib/.dream/**
- Freud's *Interpretation of Dreams* --
http://www.gasou.edu/psychweb/books/interp/toc.htm
- Self-Quizzes for Introductory Psychology --
http://www.gasou.edu/psychweb/selfquiz/selfquiz.htm
- Sleep & Sleep Disorders -- **http://bisleep.medsch.ucla.edu/**

Psyche (Journal on Consciousness) -- **http://psyche.cs.monash.edu.au/**
- Substance use and abuse -- **http://orion.it.luc.edu/~pcrowe/375link.htm**

- National Clearinghouse for Alcohol and Drug Information --
  http://www.health.org/

Audio-Visual Support
Films/Videos:
(films noted with an * specifically address gender/multicultural issues)

Topic: Consciousness
The Mind vs. The Brain: Has Freud Slipped? (FFHS, 27 minutes)
Human Consciousness and Computers (FFHS, 28 minutes)
The Study of Attention (FFHS, 43 minutes)

Topic: Attentional Disruptions
The Diagnosis and Treatment of Attention Deficit Disorder in Children (FFHS, 27 minutes)
Coping with Attention Deficit Disorder: Taming the Turmoil (FFHS, 24 minutes)
Ritalin: Drug Treatment for Attention Deficit Disorder (FFHS 20 minutes)
The Treatment of Attention Deficit Disorder in Adults (FFHS, 27 minutes)

Topic: Sleep and Dreams
Discovering Psychology: The Mind Awake and Asleep (Annenberg, 30 minutes)
Sleep and Its Disorders (Insight, 60 minutes)
To Sleep...Perchance to Dream (NET, 30 minutes)
Sleep Alert (PBS, 30 minutes)
Dreams, Theater of the Night (FFHS, 27 minutes)
Dream Voyage (FFHS, 27 minutes)
The Secrets of Sleep (BBC, 52 minutes)
Sleep Disorders (FFHS, 28 minutes)
Sleeping Well (FFHS, 28 minutes)
Wake Up, America: A Sleep Alert (FFHS, 24 minutes)
Sleep: A Prerequisite for Health (FFHS, 18 minutes)

Topic: Body Rhythms
What Time Is Your Body? (Time/Life, 23 minutes)
Biological Clocks (FFHS, 28 minutes)
Biological Rhythms: Studies in Chronobiology (UI(EBEC) 22 minutes)
The Brain: The Animal Brain (PBS, 60 minutes)
Life's Clocks (AIMS, 27 minutes)
Fighting the Clock (FFHS, 24 minutes)
Chronobiology: The Times of Our Lives (FFHS, 58 minutes)

Topic: Substance Use
The Addicted Brain (FFHS, 26 minutes)
Cocaine Abuse: The End of the Line (AIMS, 25 minutes)
Cocaine and Human Physiology (AIMS, 20 minutes)

Cocaine Blues: The Myth and Reality of Cocaine (PYR, 30 minutes)
Drug Profiles (AIMS, 28 minutes)
An Easy Pill to Swallow (CRM, 28 minutes)
The Mind: Addiction (HARR, 60 minutes)
Pleasure Drugs: The Great American High, Parts 1 and 2 (FI, 51 minutes)
Altered States: A History of Drug Use in America (FFHS, 57 minutes)
- **The Substance in Question* (FFHS, 36 minutes)
- **Circle of Recovery: Healing the Wounds of Drugs and Alcohol* (FFHS, 60 minutes)
- **Walking Through the Fear: Women and Substance Abuse* (FFHS, 28 minutes)
- **Substance Abuse Among Latinos* (FFHS, 28 minutes)
- ** Calling the Shots* (Cambridge Documentary Films, 30 minutes)
- ** Women: Coming out of the shadows* (Fanlight, 27 minutes)

Animated Neuroscience and the Action of Nicotine, Cocaine, and Marijuana in the Brain (FFHS, 24 minutes)
Fetal Alcohol Syndrome and Other Drug Use During Pregnancy (FFHS, 19 minutes)
Driving Drunk: License to Kill? (FFHS, 52 minutes)
- **Here's to You, Sister: Women and Alcoholism* (FFHS, 24 minutes)

Inhalant Abuse: Breathing Easy (FFHS, 24 minutes)
Kids Under the Influence (FFHS, 58 minutes)
Teens and Alcoholism (FFHS, 18 minutes)
Running on Empty: Teens and Methamphetamines (FFHS, 27 minutes)
Heroin: The New High School High (FFHS, 45 minutes)
Alcohol and Tobacco: The Truth Series (FFHS, 30 minutes each)
   Program 1: *The Truth about Alcohol*
   Program 2: *The Truth about Tobacco*
Cigarettes: Who Profits, Who Dies? (FFHS, 49 minutes)
Behind the Smoke Screen: Facts About Tobacco Use (FFHS, 30 minutes)

Topic: Hypnosis
Discovering Psychology: The Mind Hidden and Divided (Annenberg, 30 minutes)
Hypnosis: Four BBC Documentaries Series (FI, 49-55 minutes)
  Program 1: *Hypnosis and Healing*
  Program 2: *Hypnosis: Can Your Mind Control Pain?*
  Program 3: *Hypnosis: Can Your Mind Control Your Body?*
  Program 4: *Hypnosis on Trial*
Captive Minds: Hypnosis and Beyond (Filmakers, 55 minutes)
Deeper into Hypnosis (Prentice-Hall, 27 minutes)

Psychology Encyclopedia Laserdisc IV:
Movies

Sleep and dreaming	(3 mins. 36 sec.)	Side 1, Frames 38980-45468

Still Images

Isolation and sleep length [5.1]	Frame	53469	Side	all
Mood change cycles [5.2]		53470		all
Brain-wave patterns during sleep [1/3] [5.3]		53471		all
Brain-wave patterns during sleep [2/3] [5.3]		53472		all
Brain-wave patterns during sleep [3/3] [5.3]		53473		all
Sleep rhythm changes [5.4]		53474		all
Cocaine's effect on the brain [5.5]		53475		all

Transparency Master 4.1: Checking Your TRAIL 4.1

True or False: Circadian rhythms affect people's alertness and ability to pay attention.

Which of the following statements is true?
- A. Melatonin levels are always at the same level.
- B. Melatonin levels have no effect on circadian rhythms.
- C. Melatonin levels appear to play a role in our abioity to use reason.
- D. Melatonin is released into the body when we are in a light environment and is no longer released when the retina is exposed to darkness.

Some people are aware that they are dreaming when they are dreaming. What does this phenomenon suggest about consciousness?

Intuition may be due to
- A. circadian rhythms
- B. unconscious knowledge and memory
- C. *deja vu*
- D. melatonin

Transparency Master 4.2: Checking Your TRAIL 4.2

How might meditating before attending a concert affect your experience of the event?

A person under hypnosis has a higher-than-normal willingness to sense, think, or behave in a way that has been
  A. pleaded.
  B. suggested.
  C. experienced.
  D. seen.

Explain hypnosis in terms of dissociation.

Hypnosis is used for all except one of the following purposes. For which of the following purposes in hypnosis NOT used?
  A. to relieve pain
  B. to relieve nausea
  C. to access unconscious thoughts, wishes, feelings, and conflicts
  D. to predict the future

Transparency Master 4.3: Checking Your TRAIL 4.3

Psychoactive drugs affect the nervous system, primarily by affecting _____ in the brain.
   A. myelin
   B. neurotransmitters
   C. membrane
   D. hormones

Describe three ways that psychoactive drugs affect neurotransmitters.

Put a *D* next to each depressant, an *S* next to each stimulant, and an *H* next to each hallucinogen.
   ___ alcohol   ___ LSD   ___ tranquilizers
   ___ caffeine   ___ nicotine   ___ barbiturates
   ___ cocaine   ___ PCP   ___ amphetamines

Valium is a
   A. stimulant
   B. amphetamine
   C. hallucinogen
   D. tranquilizer

Transparency Master 4.4: Checking Your TRAIL 4.4

According to the repair theory of sleep, sleep enables us to
- A. maintain synaptic connections.
- B. avoid harming ourselves during dark hours.
- C. conserve energy by not moving around at night.
- D. restore neurotransmitters used during the day.

Most dreams take place during which one period?
- A. Stage 2 sleep
- B. Stage 4 sleep
- C. REM sleep
- D. NREM sleep

During the first few hours of a full night's sleep, people spend more total time in _____ than in other stages.
- A. REM sleep
- B. Stages 1 and 2
- C. Stages 3 and 4
- D. paradoxical sleep

Which one of the following statements is true?
- A. The last REM period is shorter than the first REM period.
- B. The last REM period of the night lasts longer than the first REM period.
- C. Each REM period lasts about the same amount of time.
- D. REM periods last only an instant.

Transparency Master 4.5: Checking Your TRAIL 4.5

People tend to dream about ___ times per night.
    A. 0-1
    B. 2
    C. 4-5
    D. 10

People who temporarily stop breathing when they are asleep have
    A. insomnia
    B. pseudoinsomnia
    C. sleep apnea
    D. narcolepsy

Which of the following events occurs during REM sleep? (Choose all that apply.)
    A. somnambulism
    B. paradoxical sleep
    C. nightmares
    D. night terrors
    E. bed wetting
    F. vivid and story-like dreams
    G. sleep apnea

Suppose you have a dream in which you take a step and fall for a long time. There is nothing to hold onto as you fall. Interpret this dream using the concepts introduced in this chapter.

Transparency Master 4.6: Critical Thinking 4.1

How might a lack of sleep affect a person's ability to drive safely?

Transparency Master 4.7: Critical Thinking 4.2

The longest REM periods usually occur toward the end of a full night's sleep. What implication does the computer model have for cramming late into the night before a test and then waking up early to cram for exams?

Transparency Master 4.8: Critical Thinking 4.3

Explain a recent dream you had in terms of the various theories of the meaning of dreams.

Transparency Master 4.9: Integrative Thinking 4.1

Consider the experiment described on p.143 in your text. Based on what you read in the Biopsychology chapter, identify which cerebral hemisphere was probably dominating in those participants while they looked at the vase. Why did they have difficulty putting their feelings into words?

Transparency Master 4.10: Integrative Thinking 4.2

Consider the demonstration described on p.144 in your text concerning the Japanese concept of ki. In light of what you learned in the Introductory chapter about control and bias, why don't you want your friend to know your hypothesis before lifting you?

Based on your knowledge of reuptake and serotonin from the Biopsychology chapter, explain how Prozac works as an antidepressant.

Transparency Master 4.12: Integrative Thinking 4.4

In light of the Biopsychology chapter's discussion of tryptophan, why does milk help people fall asleep?

Transparency Master 4.13: Integrative Thinking 4.5

Some students have heard that if a person dreams of falling and, in the dream, actually hits the ground before waking up, the dreamer dies. In light of what you learned in the Introductory chapter about setting up experiments, could this idea be tested experimentally? What would be the experimental and control groups? What do you conclude about this rumor?

Handout Master # 4.1: Dream Content

Exercise #4.1: Dream Content
Instructions: Record the following information for three dreams. Consider the extent to which the content of your dreams reflect our cultural expectations for women and men.

Dream # 1:
The setting:
_____

People involved:
_____

Types of interaction between people in the dream:
_____

Activities engaged in during dream:
_____

Emotions:
_____

Outcome of the dream:
_____

Cultural expectations noted:
_____
_____
_____

Dream # 2:
The setting:
_____

People involved:
_____

Types of interaction between people in the dream:
_____

Activities engaged in during dream:
_____

Emotions:
_____

Outcome of the dream:
_____

Cultural expectations noted:

Dream # 3:
The setting:

People involved:

Types of interaction between people in the dream:

Activities engaged in during dream:

Emotions:

Outcome of the dream:

Cultural expectations noted:

Handout Master #4.2a: Gender and Substance Abuse

Exercise # 4.2: Substance Abuse

Instructions: Read the following scenario and answer the questions concerning John, the man described in the scenario.

John, a man in his mid-30s, is married with 3 young children. He runs a small electronics business. After going home from work each day, he drinks a six-pack of beer and has recently begun to top that off with 3 or 4 shots of hard liquor. Occasionally, he slips into his office during the day for a "nip" from a bottle he keeps hidden in his desk. Once a fairly attentive husband and father, he has begun doing less and less with his family and more arguments with his wife are occurring. Some bills are not getting paid. John says he does not have a problem and just needs to unwind from all the stress from his job.

Rate John on the following dimensions:

```
   1      2      3      4      5      6      7
Likeable                                  Unlikable

   1      2      3      4      5      6      7
Irresponsible                    Responsible

   1      2      3      4      5      6      7
Competent                        Incompetent

   1      2      3      4      5      6      7
Unintelligent                            Intelligent

   1      2      3      4      5      6      7
Appropriate                      Inappropriate
```

If you worked with John, would your reaction toward him be:
```
   1      2      3      4      5      6      7
Negative                                  Positive
```

How likely is it that John will overcome his problems?
```
   1      2      3      4      5      6      7
 Very                                      Very
Likely                                   Unlikely
```

Handout Master #4.2b: Gender and Substance Abuse

Exercise # 4.2: Substance Abuse

Instructions: Read the following scenario and answer the questions concerning Jane, the woman described in the scenario.

Jane, a woman in her mid-30s, is married with 3 young children. She runs a small electronics business. After going home from work each day, she drinks a six-pack of beer and has recently begun to top that off with 3 or 4 shots of hard liquor. Occasionally, she slips into her office during the day for a "nip" from a bottle she keeps hidden in her desk. Once a fairly attentive wife and mother, she has begun doing less and less with her family and more arguments with her husband are occurring. Some bills are not getting paid. Jane says she does not have a problem and just needs to unwind from all the stress from her job.

Rate Jane on the following dimensions:

```
    1     2     3     4     5     6     7
Likeable                              Unlikable

    1     2     3     4     5     6     7
Irresponsible                Responsible

    1     2     3     4     5     6     7
Competent                    Incompetent

    1     2     3     4     5     6     7
Unintelligent                         Intelligent

    1     2     3     4     5     6     7
Appropriate                  Inappropriate
```

If you worked with Jane, would your reaction toward her be:
```
    1     2     3     4     5     6     7
Negative                              Positive
```

How likely is it that Jane will overcome her problems?
```
    1     2     3     4     5     6     7
Very                                  Very
Likely                                Unlikely
```

CHAPTER 5

LEARNING

Chapter Overview
    Learning Objectives
    Chapter Outline

Additional Lecture Ideas
    Lecture Topics
    Additional Readings

In-Class Activities and Demonstrations
    Activities and Demonstrations
    Sources for Additional Activities
    Journey II Software

World Wide Web

Audio-Visual Support

Handout and Transparency Masters

Chapter Overview

Learning Objectives

After studying this chapter, you should be able to do the following:

1. Compare critical periods and sensitive periods.

2. Describe three ways we learn--classical conditioning, operant conditioning, and modeling.

3. Explain the significance of scripts.

4. Explain why males and females learn different behaviors.

5. Distinguish between individualist and collectivist cultures.

6. Identify which ethnic groups tend to be individualist and which tend to be collectivist.

Chapter Outline

Learning

I. Introduction
    A. Learning = the process by which experiences lead to relatively permanent changes in behavior and mental activities

II. Humans are Ready to Learn: A Biological Readiness
    A. Critical and Sensitive Periods for Learning
        1. critical period = limited window of time for learning some behaviors
        2. sensitive period = times when particular behavior can be learned easily but can still be learned at a later time albeit incompletely
        3. case study examples of humans and language acquisition
    B. The Importance of Learning for Human Survival
        1. human survival due largely to learning
        2. learning experiences related to development of neural connections

III. Conditioning: Learning by Forming Associations
    A. Classical Conditioning
        1. Pavlov's study with dogs & salivation
        2. classical condition
             a. an initially neutral stimulus becomes linked to another stimulus that naturally triggers a particular response so that eventually it also produces the response
        3. terms for classical conditioning
              a. unconditioned stimulus (UCS)
              b. unconditioned response (UCR)
              c. conditioned stimulus (CS)
              d. conditioned response (CR)
        4. behaviors commonly learned by classical conditioning
              a. examples: conditioned emotional responses such as fear, discomfort, taste aversions
        5. higher-order conditioning
              a. a process in which a neutral stimulus becomes linked with a CS that already triggers a CR resulting in the neutral stimulus triggering the CR
        6. generalization
              a. a process resulting in a stimulus similar to the original CS producing a behavior similar or identical to the CR
        7. discrimination
              a. a process resulting in responding to a distinct stimulus
        8. extinction and counterconditioning
              a. extinction: eliminating the linkage of a CS with a UCS so that the CS doe not produce the CR

b. counterconditioning: learning to associate a CS with a new response that competes with the CR, thereby weakening the connection between the CS and the CR

B. Operant Conditioning
1. definition: consequences of behavior determine whether that behavior is repeated
2. law of effect: behaviors followed by desirable outcomes are more likely to recur than behaviors without pleasant outcomes; behaviors followed by undesirable outcomes less likely to recur than behavior without such outcomes
3. reinforcement
    a. definition: any behavior/event that follows a behavior and increases the probability that the behavior will occur again
    b. positive reinforcement: presentation of a desired stimulus after a behavior thereby increasing the likelihood the behavior will occur again
    c. negative reinforcement: removal of a undesired stimulus by a behavior thereby increasing the likelihood the behavior will occur again
4. punishment
    a. definition: any behavior/event that follows a behavior and decreases the probability that the behavior will occur again
    b. positive punishment: presentation of an undesired stimulus after a behavior thereby decreasing the likelihood the behavior will occur again
    c. negative punishment: removal of a desired stimulus after a behavior thereby decreasing the likelihood the behavior will occur again
    d. side effects of punishment
    e. cultural differences in types of punishment
5. primary and secondary reinforcers
    a. primary reinforcers: objects/behaviors that satisfy basic biological needs
    b. secondary reinforcers: objects, symbols, or feelings that we learn to associate with positive experiences
6. schedules of reinforcement
    a. continuous reinforcement: reinforcing a behavior every time it occurs
    b. intermittent reinforcement: reinforcing a behavior on an intermittent basis
        i. fixed-ratio schedule: RFT after a fixed number of behaviors
        ii. fixed-interval schedule: RFT after a fixed time interval as elapsed
        iii. variable-ratio schedule: RFT after an average number of

                    behaviors has occurred
                iv. <u>variable-interval schedule</u>: RFT after an average time interval as elapsed
        c. effects of RFT schedules on learning and maintaining behaviors
    7. shaping
        a. reinforcing successive approximations of the desired behavior
    8. lack of reinforcement
        a. produces no behaviors
        b. get reinforcement through other means
        c. learned helplessness
    9. generalization
        a. when same behavior has been RFT in a similar situations
        b. similar behaviors have been RFT
    10. discrimination
        a. learning to distinguish which stimuli produce RFT/punishment
    11. extinction and counterconditioning
        a. extinction: positive consequences of behavior are removed
        b. spontaneous recovery: occasional reappearance of an extinguished behavior
        c. counterconditioning: when competing responses are RFT

C. Comparing Classical and Operant Conditioning
    1. Similarities
        a. processes of counterconditioning, generalization, discrimination, and extinction occur in both
    2. Differences
        a. what the term "learning" refers to
        b. differing emphases on what happens before or after the behavior of interest (i.e., where is the stimulus of interest)
        c. classical conditioning emphasizes innate drives; operant doesn't
        d. classical conditioning limited to physical/emotional responses; operant not as limited

D. Uses of Conditioning in Psychotherapy
    1. <u>behavior modification</u>: therapy using classical and operant conditioning principles
    2. <u>systematic desensitization</u>: form of counterconditioning based on classical conditioning involving an anxiety hierachy, learned relaxation, and pairing of relaxation state with a previously anxiety-provoking stimulus
    3. <u>flooding</u>: another form of counterconditioning which is less gradual than systematic desensitization in which person imagines being surrounded by the feared stimulus
    4. <u>token economy</u>: a behavior change system of RFT and punishments
    5. <u>biofeedback</u>: a learning theory based technique to altering biological functions such as heart rate, brain wave patterns, etc.

III. Modeling: Learning by Observation
A. Observational learning
1. learning theory based on observationing models and the reward/punishments for their behavior
2. to occur person must: pay attention to the model's behavior, remember the behavior, have the ability to imitate the behavior
3. <u>classic study</u>: Bandura's Bobo doll study with children
4. <u>vicarious classical conditioning</u>: learning emotional reactions via observation

B. Scripts
1. <u>definition</u>: knowledge of what happens in social relationships, the usual meaning of behaviors, and customary ways of relating to other people
2. <u>cultural scripts</u>: scripts that are learned and shared by members of a cultural group
3. <u>unshared scripts</u>: having different scripts for an event can lead to different interpretations and misunderstandings

C. Latent Learning and Insight Learning
1. latent learning: learning that occurs without apparent RFT and that is not manifested until the need arises
2. Kohler & insight learning: studied insights in chimps' problem solving strategies

IV. Gender, Culture, and Race: Influences on Learning
A. Gender Perspectives on What is Learned
1. social norms for conduct may be different depending on gender
B. Cultural Perspectives on What is Learned
1. collectivist v. individualist cultures may emphasize different goals in behavior and what is learned
C. Racial Perspectives on What is Learned
1. people in different racial groups may be reinforced for different behavior patterns
2. different scripts may be adopted in interaction with different racial groups
3. the combination of racial experience and socioeconomic status may affect what is learned

Additional Lecture Topics

Learning styles and culture

Generally speaking, the learning styles perspective has supported the argument that there are individual differences in ways in which people prefer to learn information. That is, some students learn best through experience and feelings-based approaches, others through the use of logic and rational evaluation (c.f., Kolb & McCarthy, 1980). One educational outgrowth of this perspective has been that classroom teachers, understanding that different students learn best using different approaches, should assess their students to better understand the different learning styles among their students and then teach materials using a variety of different exercises and techniques to provide relevant learning experiences across students.

Some academics have infused culture into the learning styles perspective. Guided by intuition and teachers' observations of learning patterns in different ethnic populations, the notion that persons from different cultures, as unique groups, possess different learning styles has proliferated. For example, Kleinfeld (1994) reported that, early in her career as an educator, she too was intrigued by the learning skills perspective and sought to incorporate that literature into her efforts to develop effective teaching approaches for working with native Alaskan students. Encouraged by the idea that the learning styles perspective offered a way in which she could utilize Alaskan students' intellectual strengths to their fullest advantage, she designed an educationally-based research project to test if Eskimo students did particularly well on visual and spatial tasks as compared to Caucasian students.

Her project idea was prompted by previous work by Berry (1966) in which he found that hunting and gathering groups (like the Eskimos) had high visual and spatial skills probably because, he surmised, these were the skills necessary to survive in an arctic environment and the child-rearing practices of parents in these cultural groups reinforced those kinds of survival skills. Moreover, her assumptions were reinforced by anecdotal reports concerning the extraordinary abilities of Eskimo peoples for recall of visual detail and anthropological studies indicating that the traditional means of teaching children in these cultures was through observation. Thus, Kleinfeld reasoned that teaching methods based largely on verbal skills (such as reading, class discussions, or lectures) would not be nearly so successful as those methods that capitalized on visual skills (such as using films, diagrams, or pictures).

However, in her repeated attempts to test this hypothesis, Kleinfeld found no support for the idea of cross-cultural learning style differences. Ultimately, she set aside her personal research efforts along these avenues, but continued to note that "teachers were still being urged to adapt their instruction to cultural differences in learning styles. But so far no one has been able to demonstrate with controlled research that teaching one cultural group in one way and another cultural group in an entirely different way had educational benefits." (pg. 155).

So what then does the learning styles perspective add to our understanding of culture and learning? Kleinfeld cautions that, just because teachers may discover experientially that students of a cultural group generally seem to fit particular learning molds, it does not warrant the global application of a particular teaching methodology in the classroom. Rather, teachers need to be reminded that different individuals learn in different ways. The learning style perspective is beneficial when it reminds teachers to add variety to their classroom teaching strategy. When considering the impact of culture on learning and learning styles, Kleinfeld points out, it is important for teachers to create learning situations or applications that are consistent with everyday life within communities and to develop their lesson plans from a culturally-informed perspective. In short, the manner in which people talk with one another, the extent of culturally-relevant background information or knowledge that is brought into the classroom situation, and the cultural importance placed on different experiences or topics all will affect the learning situation. When these issues are kept fresh in the teacher's awareness, the learning styles perspective adds to students' educational experiences. When applied globally, she worries, learning styles may result in dangerous racial stereotyping which unnecessarily limits children and restricts their learning opportunities.

Source:
Kleinfeld, J. (1994). Learning styles and culture. In
W. Lonner and Malpass, R. (Eds.), Psychology and culture. Boston: Allyn & Bacon.

Media aggression and observational learning

Does watching aggression on television or in the movies increase aggressive behavior? Widespread concern over the increasing amount of media violence has led researchers to look more empirically at the popular arguments, suggesting that the aggression displayed in the media acts as a powerful role model for subsequent aggressive behavior in its viewers. In short, do people tend to become aggressive via observational learning and imitation? Taylor, Peplau, and Sears (1997) have summarized research on the effects of aggression in media on those who observe it, and raise several pertinent points in their critical analysis of such research. Some relevant findings:

Comstock (1982) reports the trend of increasing amount and vividness of violence in theater films.

Sleek (1994) reports that the average child has seen more than 100,000 acts of violence including 8,000 murders on television before they leave elementary school.

The 1972 Surgeon General's Report concluded cautiously that there was an indication of a causal relation between viewing violence on TV and aggressive behavior only for those children who were predisposed toward aggression, and that the relationship operated only in some environmental contexts.

The 1982 National Institute of Mental Health report offered a stronger conclusion that there was consensus among the research community that TV violence does lead to aggressive behaviors in children and teens who watch it, and that the link was obvious.

From this, then, are we to conclude that a causal relationship between media violence and aggressive behavior is well-supported? Taylor and her colleagues suggest a more cautious interpretation and provide insightful critiques of laboratory experiments, correlational studies, and field experiments on the subject. (Indeed, the manner in which these authors engage in critical thinking and analysis of this topic serves as a valuable model for students...an example I use with General Psychology and advanced psychology students alike). Let's look in particular at what they say concerning laboratory studies. Taylor and her colleagues review 2 typical laboratory studies. Bandura (1961), in the now classic BoBo doll studies, found that children who had watched an adult beat up an inflatable doll and then receive a reward were more likely to imitate that aggressive behavior than were children who hadn't seen such behavior. Berkowitz (1974) found that angered college students who had watched a violent film clip were more likely to administer more and more intense shocks to an experimental confederate after he fails a learning task. In summary, laboratory experiments seem to find that observing aggression resulted in increased aggressive behavior, but are there issues with laboratory experiments and their methods that need to be taken into consideration in our analysis of this conclusion? Taylor et al. point out five:

One: The film clips used in laboratory experiments are usually brief and tend to be centered almost entirely around 1 violent episode. In real life, they note, shows with violence also have other topical themes (romance, other nonviolent activities). In other words, there are any number of behaviors which might be imitated from the real life show or movie.

Two: In the laboratory, the viewing focus is solely directed toward the film clip (that's the experiment participants' task) whereas in real life children often have various distractions going on around them while watching TV.

Three: In the laboratory, the potential for aggressive behavior is usually sanctioned in some way (i.e., the study participant is supposed to shock the confederate for failing in the shock-learning technique)--in other words, it is generally considered a form of prosocial aggression. In real life, we tend to be more concerned about anti-social aggressive acts such as murder or assault for which there is less general sanction.

Four: In the laboratory, the chance of retaliation from the victim seldom exists. In real life, that option is more generally present for a victim.

Five: Measurement of aggression in the laboratory tends to occur very shortly after exposure to the aggressive film. In some studies, the effects of watching an aggressive film appear to dissipate within a few minutes. In real life, most crimes do not appear immediately after having viewed an aggressive film.

Do these points suggest that the public should be less concerned about aggressive media? Taylor et al. suggest that "it seems fair to conclude that media violence is not a sufficient condition to produce aggressive behavior, nor is it a necessary one. Aggressive behavior is multiply determined, and media violence in and of itself is unlikely to provoke such behavior. However, from the evidence, we conclude that media violence can be a *contributing* factor to some aggressive acts in some individuals." (pg. 380). (note: emphasis on contributing factor is mine...not Taylor et al's. But also note that these authors offer a far more cautious relationship than the causal one put forward by NIMH in 1982).

Source:
Taylor, S., Peplau, L., & Sears, D. (1997). Social psychology. (9th ed.). Upper Saddle River, NJ: Prentice Hall.

Voices on the power of role models and observational learning.
Most students will probably have little difficulty identifying with the section in the textbook concerning observational learning and scripts (i.e., recalling important role models, articulating important scripts for appropriate conduct, etc.). It may be more difficult to image how scripts learned by other individuals, especially those persons who grew up in chaotic living environments, came into being. In her article, *Voices from the future*, Susan Goodwillie tunes in Manny's voice, a young man who grew up in the streetlife of Brooklyn. In a brief and sometimes brutally frank account (perhaps shocking for some students), Manny chronicles a life centered around violence in his home and on the streets, his use of drugs because they "somehow seemed to make it better", and rebellion against the school systems to which he had looked for opportunity and found none. Several examples of learning concepts are evident in this narrative: (1) the use of avoidance to stay clear of trouble on the street, (2) what happens when lack of follow-through on reward contingencies occurs such as when his step-father promised gifts for doing well in school and then failed to buy anything when Manny and his brother upheld their end of the requirement, (3) starting fights in school to get expelled because he didn't want to be in that school (an example of probably both positive and negative reinforcement), and (4) how getting beat up, robbed, and imprisoned helped him "realize" or learn what it had been like for the victims of his own behavior. With respect to his experiential learning Manny says "They say what goes around comes around and, I might say, it came around to me." (pg. 82). To survive, he buys and sells comics and lives a day-to-day existence ("I try to live day by day now. Buy my comics, read my comics, then sell them. If I die, at least I died reading my comics, you know, I did something I enjoy...."; pg. 82).

Continuing the dialogue of life on the streets, four teen reporters from *Children's Express* (one of whom had interviewed Manny) discuss their observations, several of which are relevant to observational learning. First, they note the living environment of their interviewees seldom provided encouragement to succeed...parents just didn't seem to care what was happening to their children. In addition, parents seemed to provide little in the way of being role models as a number of teens interviewed had parents who themselves were living strained lives, were in foster care situations, or were on the streets. Gangs became the family substitute. Secondly, violence was prevalent (as evidenced by metal detectors in schools) and was reinforced by media and the immediate reinforcement of getting things with which to survive. Third, media presentations of the "good life" were addressed as one basis for promoting violence. Fourth, these peer reporters voiced skepticism with developing more laws and putting people in jail as a means of curbing violence, citing that existing laws and legal practices haven't addressed these problems well. Rather, they suggest that a change in values including treating people with more kindness could go a long way to reversing such problems.

Written directly from the statements of teenagers, this article may serve as a basis for discussing some real world applications of observational learning in particular and learning theory concepts more generally.

Source:
Goodwillie, S. (1997). Voices from the future. In Sattler, D. N. & Shabatay, V. (Eds.) <u>Psychology in context: Voices and perspectives</u>. Boston: Houghton

Cultural images on television.

Consistent with the theme presented in additional lecture topic # 2, television as a socialization agent and source of information about how to act has been frequently discussed in many General Psychology textbooks. One interesting set of issues for students to consider is to what extent do television shows reflect larger social and political issues affecting the United States and, more specifically, how are people from different ethnic groups portrayed on television? Staples & Jones (1995) offer a pointed critique of the television industry for the images of African Americans presented on television since their first appearances in the 1940s. These authors note that, even as late as the 1980s, African Americans, although present in increasing numbers, were still portrayed stereotypically as athletes, criminals, servants, or entertainers, and rarely as "loving, sexual, sensitive, or cerebral people." Moreover, they argue, that during the 15,000 hours an average adolescent watches TV through high school, he or she would have seen "black people in a negatively, distorted light," and that "television serves no greater purpose than to create a false sense of superiority on the part of white people and a false sense of inferiority on the part of blacks." (pg. 326).

Although television was once heralded as having the potential to be the "great unifier", Staples & Jones offer that it has not lived up to that potential but, like any other product of a racist society, has been "trapped by the cultural, political, economic, and social ideology of that same society." (pg. 327). Early images, including shows such as the *Little Rascals*, *Amos 'n' Andy*, the *Jack Benny* show, the *Danny Thomas* show, and the *Trouble with Father* show, stereotypically presented African Americans as happy, carefree, musical, lazy and, if employed, the servants of Caucasians. Some early shows which did not necessarily conform to stereotypes, such as the *Nat King Cole* show, died from lack of commercial sponsors. During the 1960s and 70s, the increasing presence of African Americans only supported the illusion that they were making progress. The roles into which African American actors were cast, as spies, or as police officers, or in black situation comedies, served to legitimize espionage, call for respect for the law in a era of black militant activity, and trivialize the oppression of blacks, according to Staples & Jones. Some of your students are likely to bring up *The Bill Cosby Show* in a counter argument to the points raised by Staples & Jones and, in fact, they do address that show as a clear anomaly in television's portrayals of African Americans. More generally speaking, however, they contend that "television has not been kind to black America." And, indeed, television has historically been as unkind to people from other minority groups as well, with relatively few roles going to Latino or Asian actors and most roles being type cast in a negative light (e.g., as criminals).

What is the impact of such distorted images? Staples & Jones contend that prime time viewers get a very distorted view of the real world and that black children are likely to see that the people who are doing successful and interesting things in the world are white. Children also learn that many people are living in far better circumstances than are they and that, due to the high levels of unpunished crime and violence presented on TV, there are illegitimate means through which to obtain such affluence. In a review of Tony Brown's research, they also note that African Americans are more likely than Caucasians to: use TV as a source of news or product purchasing information, perceive TV as representative of real life, and African American children, in particular, learn about aggression and codes of social conduct through their viewing. They also suggest that African American males, many of whom are unemployed, make up most of the black viewing audience, and their TV viewing may contribute to the illiteracy rate found in that group.

Lest we forget, television is a business with significant sums of money at stake for the advertisers. Thus, advertising and television network executives are presented by Staples & Jones as "gatekeepers" who, once convinced that "whites will not accept blacks on television, or will accept them only in certain stereotyped situations" and supported by marketing or survey formulas that deduct points for introducing minority or controversial topics into the viewing arena, control a viewing content that glorifies white supremacy while at the same time demeans other ethnic groups. In conclusion, Staples & Jones caution "we should not be deluded into thinking the media operates that positively for whites. The entertainment complex is selling a fantasy for the mass public that obscures class inequalities in the economic substructure of American society. Most of the media reflects bourgeois values. Rarely are the lives of most working class Americans, white or black, reflected accurately in films or television. Instead, we are shown the lives, loves, and problems of the bourgeoisie and taught to identify with their lifestyles." (pg. 336).

Source:
Staples, R. & Jones, T. (1995). Culture, ideology, and black television images. In Aguirre, A. & Baker, D. (Eds.), Sources: Notable selections in race and ethnicity. Guilford, CN: Dushkin.

Suggestions for Additional Readings

Bandura, A. (1973). <u>Aggression: A social learning analysis</u>. Englewood Cliffs, NJ: Prentice-Hall.

Bandura, A. (1986). <u>Social foundations of thought</u>. Englewood Cliffs, NJ: Prentice-Hall.

Domjan, M. (1996). <u>Conditioning and learning</u>. Pacific Grove, CA: Brooks/Cole.

Logue, A. (1995). <u>Self-control</u>. Upper Saddle River, NJ: Prentice-Hall.

Malone, J. (1990). <u>Theories of learning: A historical approach</u>. Belmont, CA: Wadsworth.

Martin, G. & Pear, R. (1996). <u>Behavior modification: What it is and how to do it (5th ed.)</u>. Englewood Cliffs, NJ: Prentice-Hall.

Mazur, J. (1990). <u>Learning and behavior (2nd ed.)</u>. Englewood Cliffs, NJ: Prentice Hall.

National Institute of Mental Health. (1982). <u>Television and behavior: Ten years of scientific progress and implications for the eighties</u>. Rockville, MD: NIH.

Pryor, K. (1991). <u>Don't shoot the dog: How to improve yourself and others through behavioral training</u>. New York: Simon & Schuster.

Williams, R., & Long, J. (1991). <u>Manage your life</u> (4th ed.). Boston: Houghton Mifflin.

In-Class Activities and Demonstrations

TRAIL blazing: Using **Transparency Masters 5.1 - 5.5**, review with students the "Checking Your TRAIL" sections in the chapter. Have students work in small groups to answer the questions and then review with the class as a whole to tie the text reading to activity in class.

Reaching critical mass: Using **Transparency Masters 5.6 - 5.8**, review with students the "Critical Thinking" sections in the chapter. Have students work in small groups to answer the questions and then review with the class as a whole to tie the text reading to activity in class.

Getting down to IT: Using **Transparency Masters 5.9 - 5.14**, review the "Integrative Thinking" sections in the chapter with students. Have students work in small groups to answer the questions and then review with the class as a whole to tie the text reading to activity in class.

Learning emotional reactions through classical conditioning:
The following exercise is based on one developed by Bellezza et al. (1986) which demonstrates how emotional reactions can become linked to previously neutral stimuli via classical conditioning processes. To conduct the exercise have students first rate the 12 nonsense syllables provided on **Handout Master # 5.1** for pleasantness. During the classical conditioning acquisition trials, students pair each nonsense syllable with either a positive, negative, or neutral term. After several acquisition trials, have students re-rate the nonsense syllables. Results, if similar to Bellezza and colleagues, should show positive evaluations for the syllables linked with positive words, negative evaluations for the syllables linked with negative words, and no change for syllables linked with neutral words. Discuss how similar processes may occur during the formation of prejudice toward ethnic groups and point out that some researchers have found negative and positive reactions toward previously neutral nationalities in similar experiments (e.g., Staats & Staats, 1956).

Source:
Bellezza, F., Greenwald, A., & Banaji, M. (1986). Words high and low in pleasantness as rated by male and female college students. Behavior Research Methods, Instruments, & Computers, 18, 299-303.

Coming to terms with classical conditioning: Using **Handout Master # 5.2**, have students identify the UCS, CS, UCR, and CR for each example. They are also to identify whether the example represents acquisition, generalization, discrimination, extinction, or counterconditioning.

Your operantly conditioned behaviors: Using **Handout Master #5.3**, have students identify 1 adaptive and 1 maladaptive behavior that are part of their behavioral repertoire. To extend the exercise, students are asked to develop a behavior change plan for the maladaptive behavior using the principles of operant conditioning.

Coming to terms with operant conditioning: Using **Handout Master # 5.4**, have students identify whether each example represents positive reinforcement, negative reinforcement, positive punishment, or negative punishment. They are also to identify whether the example represents acquisition, generalization, discrimination, extinction, or counterconditioning.

What scripts have you learned?: In keeping with the discussions concerning the development of cultural scripts in the textbook and the role of television in relationship to aggression and racial stereotypes, have students watch 2 primetime television shows. Using **Handout Master # 5.5**, students are to describe cultural and gender scripts they observe in the shows.

Distributing rewards: Singelis & Brislin (1998) describe an exercise that focuses on some basic differences between individualistic vs. collectivistic cultures. One area they discuss is that people in individualistic cultures tend to think of output from group efforts as being the result of aggregated individual efforts. Any rewards given to a group, then, are divided according to each individual's effort such that greater effort results in greater reward, lesser effort in less reward (an equity perspective). In collectivistic cultures, rewards to a group are generally evenly distributed (an equality perspective). One exception appears to occur: when a group member is in clear need, collectivistic cultures are more likely to allocate more reward in that person's direction. The current exercise is a variation based on Singelis & Brislin's example. Have students read the scenario on **Handout Master # 5.6** and complete the questions concerning reward distribution. This may be an interesting exercise to do when discussing operant conditioning as it points out that rewards (or reinforcers) carry cultural meaning.

Sources:
Singelis, T., & Brislin, R. (1998). The distribution of rewards. In Singelis, T. (Ed.). Teaching about culture, ethnicity, & diversity: Exercises and Planned Activities. Thousand Oaks, CA: Sage Publ.

Sources for Additional Activities
Books:

Benjamin, L. & Lowman, K. (1981). <u>Activities Handbook for the Teaching of Psychology</u>. Washington DC: American Psychological Association.

Halonen, Jane 1995). Chapter 6: Learning. In <u>The Critical Thinking Companion For Introductory Psychology.</u> New York: Worth.

Makosky, V. et al. (Eds.) (1995). <u>Activities Handbook for the Teaching of Psychology</u> (Vol. III). Washington DC: American Psychological Association.

Journey II Software:

Journey II contains 2 exercises relevant to the Learning chapter. Enter the Learning lab by clicking on the icon in the Main Menu.

<u>Operant conditioning</u>: Students meet Harry, the white rat, in a Skinner (operant conditioning) box. They teach Harry to press the lever for food. Basic acquisition, discrimination, and chaining are incorporated into the exercise. Students also see the graphed results of Harry's lever pressing behavior under the interval schedules of reinforcement.

<u>Classical conditioning</u>: Students meet Rex, the friendly canine participant in Pavlov's physiology laboratory. After 5 conditioning trials, Rex learns to salivate after hearing a bell. Changes in salivation as a result of extinction, reconditioning, and generalization are presented. Classically conditioned aversions to foods and generalization of emotional responses to frightening objects are discussed as everyday examples of classical conditioning.

World Wide Web: Check out the following WWW sites for information and activities relevant to this section of the text!

Addison Wesley Longman's Website -- **http://longman.awl.com/**
- PsychZone link -- **http://longman.awl.com/**
- Psych Web -- **http://www.gasou.edu/psychweb/psychweb.htm**

Psychology Jumping Stand --
http://www.indiana.edu:80/~iuepsyc/PsycJump.html

The Psychology Place --**http://www.psychplace.com**

Self-Quizzes for Introductory Psychology --
http://www.gasou.edu/psychweb/selfquiz/selfquiz.htm

Behaviorism --
http://www.valdosta.peachnet.edu/~whuitt/psy702/behsys/behsys.html

Operant Conditioning --
http://www.biozentrum.uni-wuerzburg.de/genetics/behavior/learning/operant.html

Classical & operant conditioning --
http://www.indiana.edu/~iuepsyc/Ch_8/C8E1.html

Classical conditioning --
http://www.as.wvu.edu/~sbb/comm221/chapters/pavlov.htm

Reinforcement -- **http://spsp.clarion.edu/topss/tptn5031.htm**

- Behavior analysis -- **http://www.coedu.usf.edu/behavior/behavior.html**

Audio-Visual Support
Films/Videos:

Overview
Discovering Psychology: Learning (Annenberg, 30 minutes)
Learning (CRM, 30 minutes)
Learning (Insight, 30 minutes)
Learning and Behavior (CBS, 26 minutes)
Animal Behavior: The Mechanism of Imprinting (IU(CORT), 14 minutes)
Discovery of Animal Behavior: A Question of Learning (PSU, RI, 60 minutes)
Classical and Instrumental Conditioning (HARR, 20 minutes)
Classical and Operant Conditioning (FFHS, 56 minutes)
Further Approaches to Learning (FFHS, 57 minutes)
A Question of Learning (FI, 60 minutes)

Classical Conditioning
Pavlov: The Conditioned Reflex (FFHS, 25 minutes)
Pavlov's Experiment (CORT, 9 minutes)

Operant Conditioning
B.F. Skinner and Behavior Change (Research Press, 45 minutes)
The Power of Positive Reinforcement (CRM, 28 minutes)
A Conversation with B. F. Skinner (CRM, 23 minutes)
The Skinner Revolution (REPR, 23 minutes)
A World of Difference: B. F. Skinner and the Good Life, Parts 1 and 2 (Time/Life, 53 minutes)

Observational Learning
Observational Learning (MTI, 25 minutes)
- *Observational Learning* (HARR, 23 minutes)
Parents and Children (IU(REPR), 24 minutes)

Application
Token Economy: Behaviorism Applied (Insight, 23 minutes)
Behavior Therapy: An Introduction (MOTO, 29 minutes)
Helping Children Deal with Television (FI, 28 minutes)
To Alter Human Behavior...Without Mind Control (P.S.U., 21 minutes)
Learning Disabilities (FFHS, 19 minutes)

Psychology Encyclopedia Laserdisc IV:
Movies

Unconditioned response	(22 sec.)	Side 2, Frames 00885-01540
Neutral stimulus	(12 sec.)	Side 2, Frames 01541-01893
Conditioning	(20 sec.)	Side 2, Frames 01894-02494
Conditioned response	(29 sec.)	Side 2, Frames 02495-03375
Continuous reinforcement	(18 sec.)	Side 2, Frames 03376-03915
Fixed ratio schedule	(12 sec.)	Side 2, Frames 03376-03915
Variable ratio schedule	(19 sec.)	Side 2, Frames 04285-04847
Fixed interval schedule	(26 sec.)	Side 2, Frames 04848-05612
Variable interval schedule	(20 sec.)	Side 2, Frames 05613-06202
Skinner: operant conditioning of pigeon	(43 sec.)	Side 2, Frames 06203,07475

Still Images

Classical conditioning [1/2] [UN]	Frame 53516	Side all
Classical conditioning [2/2] [UN]	53517	all
Higher-order conditioning [1/3] [UN]	53518	all
Higher-order conditioning [2/3] [UN]	53519	all
Higher-order conditioning [3/3] [UN]	53520	all
Drug effects [UN]	53521	all
Conception of interaction [UN]	53522	all
Reciprocal determinism illustrated	53523	all
Pavlov's method modified	53524	all
Acquisition and extinction of salivary response [1/2] [7.2]	53525	all
Acquisition and extinction of salivary response [2/2] [7.2]	53526	all
Reinforcement in action [7.3]	53527	all
Skinner box [7.4]	53528	all
Latent learning [7.8]	53529	all

Transparency Master 5.1: Checking Your TRAIL 5.1

Learning is a process by which _____ lead to relatively permanent changes in behavior and mental processes.
    A.   critical periods
    B.   experiences
    C.   preparations
    D.   genes

Each species possesses biological and anatomical characteristics that make it _____ behaviors needed for survival of its species.
    A.   understand
    B.   ready to learn
    C.   sense
    D.   predict

Which one of the following statements is true?
    A.   Humans have critical periods rather than sensitive periods.
    B.   If a behavior is not learned during the sensitive period for that behavior, it will never be learned at all.
    C.   When we are born, trillions of neurons are not yet connected.
    D.   If immigrants learn English after the age of 12, they can usually lose their accents if they work hard enough.

True or False: Our experiences change the structure of our brains by affecting the connections formed among neurons.

Transparency Master 5.2: Checking Your TRAIL 5.2

Fill in the blanks with UCS, UCR, CS, or CR: In classical conditioning terms, the ___ is initially neutral and doesn't automatically evoke a response; the ___ naturally and automatically triggers a particular response without previous learning; the UCS triggers the ___; and, due to classical conditioning, the CS can cause the ___.

When a stimulus similar to the original _____ produces the _____, generalization has occurred.
  A. CS; CR
  B. CR; CS
  C. UCS; UCR
  D. UCS; CS

Draw a diagram showing the relationships among the UCS, UCR, CS, and CR. Then draw an *X* through the link that is lost in extinction.

In counterconditioning, a CS is associated with a new response that competes with the CR, thereby weakening the connection between
  A. the CS and the CR.
  B. the CS and the UCR.
  C. the UCS and the UCR.
  D. the UCR and the CR.

Transparency Master 5.3: Checking Your TRAIL 5.3

Identify whether the following are examples of positive or negative reinforcement.
Your date kisses you longer since you stopped smoking. The type of reinforcement you receive from your date for no longer having smoker's breath is _____.
Your pants used to be too tight. After dieting, you fit into those pants comfortably. What type of reinforcement have you received for dieting?

Unannounced sales are held at your favorite store at random times based on the manager's whims. What intermittent schedule of reinforcement is the store having?

A Korean immigrant is ridiculed by schoolmates for speaking English with an accent. Now that Korean doesn't talk to schoolmates much. Does this behavior reflect classical conditioning or operant conditioning?

A Texas cattle rancher wanted to teach his cattle to come in out of the rain without having to fetch them himself ("Calling all cows", 1995). Some of his cows followed other cows. The rancher put rainproof pagers on his "leader" cows and, although it took four months, he taught them to return to the barn for food when the pager beeped. Which technique did the rancher use: classical conditioning, shaping, or punishment?

Transparency Master 5.4: Checking Your TRAIL 5.4

Name three requirements for observational learning to occur.

True or False: Children tend to behave aggressively after witnessing aggressive behavior, whether or not the aggressive person was rewarded for that aggression.

What are scripts?

A young man goes to a nice restaurant with a date and is surprised to realize that he knows which fork is the salad fork. He was never specifically told which fork to use for salad, and he was never reinforced for picking the fork farthest from the plate for salad. What has occurred?
  A. spontaneous recovery
  B. learned helplessness
  C. latent learning
  D. insight learning

Transparency Master 5.5: Checking Your TRAIL 5.5

True or False: One reason that males and females differ in what they learn is that they are sometimes reinforced for behaviors that are consistent with different social norms.

Describe the differences between individualist and collectivist cultures.

Which of the following ethnic groups tend to be individualistic?
  A. African American
  B. Asian American
  C. European American
  D. Latin American

Why would individuals belonging to one ethnic group, race, or gender differ from other individual from the same ethnic group, race, or gender in what they learn?

Transparency Master 5.6: Critical Thinking 5.1

Drug programs that treat people in a hospital and then release them often fail because patients return to their former hangouts and drug-using friends. In terms of classical conditioning, why would people treated for a drug problem return to the locales where they used to take drugs and people who encouraged them to use drugs in the first place? How could operant conditioning explain their behavior?

Transparency Master 5.7: Critical Thinking 5.2

The Washington D.C. National Zoological Park had a polar bear who needed dental care (Pryor, 1981). Anesthetizing the bear was not practical, and no veterinary dentist wanted to work on the teeth of an unanesthetized bear. Park officials solved their problem by using shaping. How would you shape a bear so that it would let someone work on its teeth?

Transparency Master 5.8: Critical Thinking 5.3

Perhaps unintentionally, parents in the U.S. tend to touch, hold, and talk to female infants more than male infants (Golombok & Fivush, 1994; Power & Parke, 1982). Assume that being touched, held, and talked to are comforting to infants. In terms of modeling and scripts, how might this parental behavior affect whether females or males tend to touch and talk with people they wish to comfort?

Transparency Master 5.9: Integrative Thinking 5.1

Which one feature of the human brain--the brain stem, cerebellum, reticular formation, thalamus, hypothalamus, limbic system, or cerebral cortex, as described in the Biopsychology chapter--most strongly suggests that humans are biologically prepared to learn a great deal of information? Why does this feature suggest preparedness?

Transparency Master 5.10: Integrative Thinking 5.2

In terms of what you read in the Biopsychology chapter, which parts of the subcortex and autonomic nervous system and which cerebral hemisphere would you expect to be most involved in conditioned emotional responses? Why?

Transparency Master 5.11: Integrative Thinking 5.3

Consider the experiments described on p.191 of your text in which inescapable shocks were given to some rats but not others. Based on what you learned in the Introductory chapter, identify which rats were members of the experimental group and which were parts of the control group. What was the operational definition of learned helplessness?

Transparency Master 5.12: Integrative Thinking 5.4

With flooding techniques, people find that they can't sustain their initial levels of fear. How is this phenomenon related to habituation, described in the Consciousness chapter?

Transparency Master 5.13: Integrative Thinking 5.5

The Introductory chapter identified major areas of study and careers in psychology. Would you expect that Bandura's experiment described on pg. 198 of your text was conducted by an industrial/organizational psychologist, developmental psychologist, or biopsychologist? Why?

Transparency Master 5.14: Integrative Thinking 5.6

How might latent learning account for intuition and deja vu, described in the Consciousness chapter? How can the concept of multiple levels of consciousness help us to understand latent learning?

Handout Master # 5.1: Emotional reactions and classical conditioning

Exercise #5.1: Emotional reactions and Classical Conditioning

STEP 1: Rate the following list of 9 nonsense syllables on their pleasantness. Use a 1-7 scale where **1 = extremely pleasant** and **7 = extremely unpleasant**.

___ QWR	___ TXV	___ NKP
___ RTD	___ WNK	___ ZTW
___ NBK	___ QMT	___ WQB

STEP 2: For the next 10 minutes, study and repeat the following pairings between the nonsense syllables and some common words as many times as you can.

QWR - mucous	TXV - joy	NKP - fence
RTD - maggots	WNK - happy	ZTW - door
NBK - vomit	QMT - comfort	WQB - desk

STEP 3: Rate the nonsense syllables again using the 1-7 scale.

___ QWR	___ TXV	___ NKP
___ RTD	___ WNK	___ ZTW
___ NBK	___ QMT	___ WQB

STEP 4: Compare your ratings from Step 1 with those obtained in Step 3. The nonsense syllables in column 1 were paired with negative words, column 2 with positive words and column 3 neutral words.

__ - __ = __ QWR	__ - __ = __ TXV	__ - __ = __ NKP
__ - __ = __ RTD	__ - __ = __ WNK	__ - __ = __ ZTW
__ - __ = __ NBK	__ - __ = __ QMT	__ - __ = __ WQB
average change: ___	average change: ___	average change: ___

Considering what you know about classical conditioning, what would you predict should happen regarding changes in evaluations for the nonsense syllables?

_____

Did your data support that prediction? How?

_____
_____

Consider how similar processes may contribute to the development of prejudice toward ethnic groups:

Handout Master # 5.2: Classical Conditioning

Exercise #5.2: Coming to terms with classical conditioning

Instructions: For each of the following examples, identify the unconditioned stimulus (UCS), unconditioned response (UCR), conditioned stimulus (CS), and conditioned response (CR). Also identify the appropriate phenomenon or process that is occurring (acquisition, generalization, discrimination, extinction, or counterconditioning) but note that not all processes are described.

1. Jose recently got into a serious argument with his Caucasian lab partner, Tom, while they were preparing for a chemistry exam. During the argument, Tom made several threatening remarks about Jose's intelligence. Jose started sweating, his heart was pounding, and he got a "knot" in his stomach as a result of his anger. Now he finds that whenever he even thinks about Tom, the knot in his stomach returns. He does not have the same reaction to his other Caucasian classmates.
UCS: _____   Process: _____
UCR: _____
 CS: _____
 CR: _____

2. Jessica was "dumped" by her long-time boyfriend which made her very sad. When other men ask her out on dates she becomes tearful.
UCS: _____   Process: _____
UCR: _____
 CS: _____
 CR: _____

3. Kiko had a difficult first semester at school. Although she did well in some classes, she failed an important English Composition course. She becomes anxious whenever she thinks about that failing grade. This semester she has to retake the course and wants to do well. Each day before her Composition class she takes some time to practice a few relaxation exercises a counselor taught her. She also uses a few of these techniques during class when she starts feeling uncomfortable.
UCS: _____   Process: _____
UCR: _____
 CS: _____
 CR: _____

4. Jeremy has developed an enormous crush on LaToya. Every time he sees her, his heart starts racing and his palms start sweating. He always says "Hi" to her. LaToya does not respond. Eventually Jeremy no longer gets excited when he sees her.

UCS: _____   Process: _____
UCR: _____
 CS: _____
 CR: _____

Handout Master # 5.3: Operant Conditioning

Exercise #5.3: Your operantly conditioned behaviors

Instructions: Think for a moment about the many kinds of behaviors in which you engage on a fairly routine basis. You would probably consider some to be assets or adaptive behaviors, behaviors that work for you. And if you are being honest with yourself there are probably some behaviors that are excesses or maladaptive behaviors, behaviors that work against you. For this exercise, select one adaptive and one maladaptive behavior and pay special attention to it over the next three days watching for three times each day that it occurs. Note the antecedents that occur immediately before the behavior begins, the particulars of the behavior (what is it you did), and the consequences that followed it. For the maladaptive behavior, develop a behavior change strategy using what you have learned about operant conditioning principles.

Adaptive behavior: _____

DAY	Antecedent	Behavior	Consequence
One 1. 2. 3.			
Two 1. 2. 3.			
Three 1. 2. 3.			

What things do you notice about what maintains this behavior? _____

Can you think of ways to make this desirable behavior occur even more frequently?

Maladaptive behavior: _____

DAY	Antecedent	Behavior	Consequence
One 1. 2. 3.			
Two 1. 2. 3.			
Three 1. 2. 3.			

What things do you notice about what maintains this behavior? _____
_____

What is your behavior change strategy?: _____
_____
_____
_____

Handout Master # 5.4: Operant Conditioning

Exercise #5.4: Coming to terms with operant conditioning

Instructions: Identify whether each example represents positive reinforcement, negative reinforcement, positive punishment, or negative punishment. Also indicate whether the example represents acquisition, generalization, discrimination, extinction, or counterconditioning.

1. Frank receives an electrical shock every time he touches his stereo. Eventually Frank stops listening to his stereo and listens to his roommate's instead.

2. Amanda offers comments in her psychology class on a daily basis. Every time she raises her hand, Professor Huang calls on her. She has started making more comments in other classes as well.

3. Marguerite has started getting frequent headaches. She finds that when she exercises she is less likely to get a headache so she is exercising more and more.

4. Hiroko always bought her pop from the vending machine down the hall from her dorm room. Lately the machine has not been working right. It takes her money but doesn't give her any pop. She stops using it.

5. Chad is an 8-year-old elementary student who frequently teases other students during recess. His teacher has established a contingency with Chad that, if he teases anyone while playing, he will have to sit down for the remainder of the recess period. If he plays cooperatively, however, he earns extra activity time in art class.

6. Melinda's friends want her to go out partying instead of studying so much so they tease her frequently. Melinda ignores their comments until eventually their teasing stops.

7. Luis finds that every time he wears his special athletic socks he is the high scorer on the basketball court. He starts wearing only that pair of socks whenever he plays.

Handout Master # 5.5: Observational Learning and Television

Exercise #5.5: What scripts have you learned?

Instructions: Watch 2 primetime television shows. In keeping with your textbook's discussion of cultural scripts, describe 2 scripts you see being presented in each show. In particular, do the interactions between men and women and between people of different cultures say something to viewers about ways in which people are to behave?

Show #1: _____
Main characters: _____
_____

Observed scripts: _____
_____
_____
_____
_____
_____
_____
_____
_____

Are the scripts you observed fair or accurate representations of men? women? people from your or other ethnic groups? Explain your answer.
_____
_____
_____
_____
_____
_____
_____
_____

Show #2: _____
Main characters: _____
_____

Observed scripts: _____
_____
_____
_____
_____
_____
_____
_____

Are the scripts you observed fair or accurate representations of men? women? people from your or other ethnic groups? Explain your answer.

_____
_____
_____
_____
_____
_____
_____

Handout Master # 5.6: Culture and rewards

Exercise #5.6: Culture and the distribution of rewards

Instructions: Read the following scenario and then answer the questions at the end.

    Assume that you are a teaching assistant for a professor. Your job requires that you help students who are working together in activity groups for special independent study credits required by your university. The major part of students' grades for independent study comes from a group project. This semester students are to develop an intervention plan proposal by working closely with student organizations, the faculty, and the administration. The students' proposal is actually going to be implemented to reduce prejudice at their university. The following students are involved in the activity group:

    Student A: the hardest worker of the group and has clearly been responsible for at least 40% of the work on the project and proposal.

    Students B, C, & D: competent students but not particularly outstanding. Each has contributed about 15% of the work on the proposal.

    Student E: a well-known student leader who actually hasn't done any of the physical work on the proposal but has used her connections to interest students, faculty, and the administration in the project.

    Student F: like Students B, C, & D, has contributed about 15% of the work on the project. Unlike the other students, Student F needs to get a good grade in order to retain her student financial aid or she will no longer be able to attend school.

After completing their project, the students are to make recommendations to the independent study professor (i.e., your supervisor) concerning what grade they think each individual deserves. One week before the end of the semester, the group members come to you because they can't agree on what to recommend. They have agreed that, since you have supervised their work closely all semester, they will go along with the grades that YOU recommend should be given.

What grades would you give to each student and why?
Student A: A   B   C   D   F _____
Student B: A   B   C   D   F _____
Student C: A   B   C   D   F _____
Student D: A   B   C   D   F _____
Student E: A   B   C   D   F _____
Student F: A   B   C   D   F _____

To what extent do you think cultural expectations affects your decision and how?
_____
_____

What differences would you expect in the distribution of grades depending on whether you came from a collectivist culture? An individualistic culture?

Mind Matters CD-ROM Faculty Guide

•LEARNING TABLE OF CONTENTS

I. INTRODUCTION TO LEARNING

II. LEARNING THROUGH ASSOCIATION: CLASSICAL CONDITIONING
       II1. ★Pop-Up: A Profile of Ivan Pavlov
  A. What Is Conditioning?
  B. A Three-Step Process
  C. Later Work in Classical Conditioning
      C1. ★Pop-Up: The Classical Conditioning Matching Game
  D. Conditioned Phobias
      D1. ★Pop-Up: A Profile of John Watson
  E. The Case of Little Albert
      E1. ★Archival Footage of Little Albert
      E2. ★Pop-Up: Conditioning and Drug Addiction
  F. Watson and Behaviorism
  G. Instrumental Learning
      G1. ★Pop-Up: A Profile of E.L. Thorndike
Rapid Review 1

III. LEARNING FROM CONSEQUENCES: OPERANT CONDITIONING
      III1. ★Pop-Up: A Profile of B.F. Skinner
  A. Reinforcement
  B. Punishment
      B1. ★Pop-Up: Types of Reinforcement
      B2. ★Pop-Up: The Consequences Matching Game
      B3. ★Skinner Speaks
  C. How the Environment Shapes Behavior
  D. The Interaction Between Classical and Operant Conditioning
      D1. ★Little Albert, Hollywood Style
Rapid Review 2

IV. OPENING THE BLACK BOX: COGNITIVE LEARNING
      IV1. ★Pop-Up: A Demonstration of the Black Box vs. the Mind
  A. The Problem of Biological Preparedness
  B. The Problem of Language
  C. The Problem of Social Learning
      C1. ★Archival Footage of the Bandura Study
  D. The Problem of Representation
      D1. ★Pop-Up: An Experiment in Mental Rotation
Rapid Review 3

LEARNING
Annotated Outline

I. INTRODUCTION TO LEARNING

Learning is introduced and described as any change in behavior that is a result of experience. Any organism with a nervous system, from the simplest invertebrates to human beings, is capable of learning from experience.

II. LEARNING THROUGH ASSOCIATION: CLASSICAL CONDITIONING

Classical conditioning is discussed as a type of associative learning. The initial investigations of this form of learning were conducted by the Russian physiologist Ivan Pavlov at the turn of the century, using dogs as subjects.

•II1. ★Pop-Up: A Profile of Ivan Pavlov

A brief biographical sketch of Ivan Pavlov is provided, beginning with his early days as a student and continuing through his contributions to the description of classical conditioning.

•A Profile of Ivan Pavlov

Activity Type: Illustrated Essay

Learning Objective: Learn about Pavlov's early life and professional work in psychology.

Faculty Note: The intent of this biographical sketch is to personalize and perhaps humanize an historical figure in psychology that some students regard as distant and quaint.

Additional Resources:

The first account of Pavlov's work to appear in the United States was published by R. M. Yerkes and S. Morgulis in 1909. The text of that account can be found at http://www.yorku.ca/dept/psych/classics/Yerkes/pavlov.htm

---

A. What Is Conditioning?

Conditioning is said to occur when a previously neutral stimulus acquires the power to elicit simple reflexes in an organism.

B. A Three-Step Process

Conditioned responses are described as being acquired in a three-step process. In the first step, an unconditioned stimulus naturally evokes an unconditioned response. In the second step, a neutral stimulus is paired repeatedly with the unconditioned stimulus. In the third step, the previously neutral stimulus (now called the conditioned stimulus) now has the ability to evoke the conditioned response.

C. Later Work in Classical Conditioning

The process of extinction is described as the gradual breakdown of conditioned associations. Extinguished responses are rarely eliminated entirely, and may be relearned easily.

C1. ★Pop-Up: The Classical Conditioning Matching Game

Here we provide a drag-and-drop activity in which students classify the critical elements of five different learning situations.

The Classical Conditioning Matching Game

Type of Activity: Interactive Reinforcement

Learning Objective: Provide students with an opportunity to test their knowledge of the UCS, UCR, CS, and CR and to apply that knowledge to new situations.

Faculty Note: In this activity, students can test their knowledge of classical conditioning by reading scenarios and dragging the highlighted stimuli and responses to their appropriate labels (e.g., In Pavlov's studies, **meat powder** was the **UCS**).

This type of activity can be repeated in the classroom, once students get familiar with the one presented. New conditioning scenarios that are topical or tailored for the class can be introduced and students can identify the UCS, UCR, CS, and CR in the new descriptions.

Additional Resources:

A host of other conditioning examples can be found at
http://www.sfu.ca/~tbauslau/302/cc.html

D. Conditioned Phobias

Conditioning is argued to be an explanation of some phobias (intense, irrational fears). John B. Watson is credited with an early application of Pavlov's principles of classical conditioning to the learning of emotional reactions.

•D1. ★Pop-Up: A Profile of John Watson

A brief biographical sketch of John Watson is provided here, beginning with his early days as a student and describing some of the professional and personal controversies in which he was involved.

> **•A Profile of John Watson**
>
> **Activity Type:** Illustrated Essay
>
> Learning Objective: Learn about Watson's early life, his vision of behaviorism, and professional work in psychology.
>
> **Faculty Note:** Watson is one of the more colorful characters in the history of psychology. Not only did he create a paradigm (behaviorism) which dominated the field for decades, but the details of his life can provide the springboard for many discussions about professional ethics. The Little Albert study, for example, usually sparks debate about the appropriate use of children in research and the nature of informed consent. (e.g., Who volunteered Little Albert? What were the long-term consequences to Albert's emotional health or adjustment?) Watson's later career in advertising can be used to raise issues about persuasion, propaganda, and the commercial applications of psychology.

E. The Case of Little Albert

A brief account of the infamous "Little Albert" study is provided here. In this study John B. Watson and a research assistant named Rosalie Rayner attempted to condition a simple fear of rats in an 11-month-old infant. The conditioned fear was later found to have generalized to other similar stimuli. The study is noted to be ethically controversial.

•E1. ★Archival Footage of Little Albert

Here we see actual film footage of "Little Albert," John Watson, Rosalie Rayner and the rat.

> **•Archival Footage of Little Albert**
>
> **Activity Type:** Video
>
> **Learning Objective:** Observe Watson and Rayner's interactions with Little Albert.
>
> **Faculty Note:** Students frequently read about Watson and Rayner's study, but it's always more dramatic to see at least a part of the procedure. Students often critique the study on ethical grounds (that's the easy part) but it may prove informative to critique it on methodological grounds, as well. If you want to demonstrate the conditioning of emotional reactions, what other procedures might you employ? Although experimental methods may be the most desirable option, are there any other techniques that might allow you to collect information on this question (e.g., case studies of phobias, correlational evidence)?
>
> **Additional Resources:** Watson and Rayner's original report of their work with Albert can be found at http://www.yorku.ca/dept/psych/classics/Watson/emotion.htm

E2. ★Pop-Up: Conditioning and Drug Addiction

Classical conditioning of drug tolerance in rats and humans is described. Conditioning helps to explain an unusual finding: among heroin users who end up in emergency rooms with the symptoms of a heroin overdose, most (about 70 percent) have apparently not taken more than their usual dose.

•Conditioning and Drug Addiction

Activity Type: Illustrated Essay

Learning Objective: Help students see applications of learning theory to life outside the laboratory.

Faculty Note: This example uses the traditional pedagogical technique of presenting a puzzle or counter-intuitive finding that can be explained by the principle under consideration. In this case, it's the observation that 70% of heroin overdose cases seen in the ER don't actually involve a true "overdose" of the drug. Classical conditioning of tolerance or autonomic "opposition" to the drug in response to particular circumstances may help explain this effect.

It may be worth noting that it is possible to classically condition not only overt responses (observable behaviors), but also autonomic responses, such as drug tolerance and even immune system responses.

Additional Resources:

An electronic slide show of Seigel's 1975 study of conditioned drug tolerance can be found at http://www.personal.kent.edu/~dwallac1/Classic/ppframe.htm

---

F. Watson and Behaviorism

Watson was convinced that conditioning accounted for not only unusual emotional responses such as phobias and fetishes, but could provide an explanation of most human learning. Conditioning theory was also consistent with the goal of behaviorism, which was to explain behavior without referring to unseen mental processes.

G. Instrumental Learning

In this section, the more active process of instrumental learning is introduced. The pioneering psychologist E.L. Thorndike first articulated the notion that behaviors are shaped by their consequences, a principle known as the "law of effect."

•G1. ★Pop-Up: A Profile of E.L. Thorndike

A brief biographical sketch of E.L. Thorndike is provided here, including his early work with animal learning (the "puzzle box" studies) which led to his statement of the law of effect. His later work in educational psychology is also described.

> •A Profile of E.L. Thorndike
>
> **Activity Type:** Illustrated Essay
>
> **Learning Objective:** Learn about Thorndike's life and his progression from studies of animal learning to his more applied work with human learning and education.
>
> **Faculty Note:** Thorndike's life presents an interesting spectrum of interests and a fascinating career track in psychology.
>
> He began his career as a comparative psychologist studying learning in cats. It may be appropriate to note that a critical difference between a psychologist who studies animal behavior and researchers from other disciplines who study animal behavior (such as zoologists or ethologists) is that psychologists will, by definition, eventually attempt to apply their findings to human behavior. Such was the case with Thorndike.
>
> Skinner's more elaborate operant conditioning theory is the direct descendant of Thorndike's simple "Law of Effect."

•Rapid Review 1

•III. LEARNING FROM CONSEQUENCES: OPERANT CONDITIONING

B.F. Skinner described the role of positive reinforcement, negative reinforcement, and punishment in shaping behavior, a process that he called operant conditioning.

•III1. ★Pop-Up: A Profile of B.F. Skinner

A brief biographical sketch of B.F. Skinner is provided here, including his early days as a struggling writer, his chaotic graduate school program, and his development of the technology of behavior modification.

> •A Profile of B. F. Skinner
>
> **Activity Type:** Illustrated Essay
>
> **Learning Objective:** Learn about Skinner's life, work, and extensive advocacy of behaviorist principles.

> **Faculty Note:** Some of the more intriguing facets of Skinner's life are detailed here, such as his early interest in a literary career. (In a sense, he returned to that career with the publication of *Walden Two*.) The quirky "Project Pigeon," an attempt to employ shaping and discrimination training to produce pigeons capable of guiding explosive missiles, always seems to arouse student interest in those topics. The "baby-tender," an automated crib indirectly descended from the Skinner box, is also useful in stimulating discussion of the applications of operant conditioning technology to humans.
>
> We also note on the CD that Skinner was essentially the originator of what is now known as computer-aided instruction, and that this makes him partly responsible for the CD-ROM that the student is using.

A. Reinforcement

Positive reinforcement is described in this section as a rewarding consequence that encourages a behavior. Negative reinforcement is described as the process of encouraging a behavior that enables you to avoid or reduce an undesirable consequence.

B. Punishment

Punishment is described as any consequence that decreases the probability of a behavior being repeated.

- B1. ★Pop-Up: Types of Reinforcement in Humans

Here the distinction is made between primary reinforcers that are based on biological needs (such as food or water) and secondary reinforcers that are learned by association (such as money or praise).

> •Types of Reinforcement in Humans
>
> **Activity Type:** Illustrated Essay
>
> **Learning Objective:** Learn to distinguish between primary and secondary reinforcers.
>
> **Faculty Note:** The distinction between primary reinforcers and secondary reinforcers may seem an easy one, but to students it sometimes appears obscure.
>
> This essay might prove useful in making the point that not all reinforcers are the same; some are "naturally" capable of strengthening behaviors and some must be created by association and experience. Another point to make might be that many of the contingencies that shape our everyday social life (e.g., salaries, the respect and admiration of others) can be viewed in the context of secondary reinforcement.

> **Additional Resources:**
>
> The Animal Training at Sea World site contains lots of information about operant conditioning, types of reinforcement, and anecdotes of training travails. It can be accessed at http://www.seaworld.org/animal_training/atlearn.html

•B2. ★Pop-Up: The Consequences Matching Game

Illustrative examples of positive reinforcers, negative reinforcers, and punishments are provided, and the student is asked to correctly classify each example.

> •The Consequences Matching Game
>
> **Activity Type:** Interactive Reinforcement
>
> **Learning Objective:** Provide students with a chance to test their knowledge of reinforcers and their ability to apply that knowledge to new situations.
>
> **Faculty Note:** Many students find the distinctions among positive reinforcement, negative reinforcement, and punishment confusing. In this activity, their task is to identify and match examples of each of these concepts to the appropriate label by "dragging" it with the mouse. (So, the example, "A cookie for cleaning your room," would be correctly labeled as an instance of positive reinforcement.)
>
> While most of the examples are straightforward and easy to label, there may be some categorizations that will provoke discussion. It may also be useful to come up with additional examples for class that are more difficult to categorize. For example, when a convict gets "time off for good behavior," is the good behavior being positively reinforced by the prospect of freedom, or is the good behavior being negatively reinforced by the avoidance of unpleasant jail time?
>
> **Additional Resources:**
>
> Additional examples can be found at
> http://server.bmod.athabascau.ca/html/prtut/reinpair.htm
>
> http://www.sfu.ca/~tbauslau/302/rp.html

•B3. ★Skinner Speaks

A film clip of Skinner himself describing the basic elements of operant conditioning, using a pigeon and a Skinner box as part of the demonstration is included.

> **•Skinner Speaks**
>
> **Activity Type:** Movie
>
> **Learning Objective:** Provide an opportunity to see Skinner talking about his own work.
>
> **Faculty Note:** In addition to the dramatic value of actually seeing and hearing Skinner, several useful concepts are illustrated in the film clip, such as the actual use of a Skinner box and the reinforcement of turning behavior in a pigeon. Skinner's remarks on extinction are informative, as well.
>
> **Additional Resources:**
>
> A detailed description of the Skinner Box can be found at http://www.biozentrum.uni-wuerzburg.de/genetics/behavior/learning/SkinnerBox.html

C. How the Environment Shapes Behavior

Operant conditioning is said to shape behavior through a gradual process of trial and error. Even apparently complex behaviors can be built up over time from simpler ones.

D. The Interaction Between Classical and Operant Conditioning

Both classical and operant conditioning principles are sometimes necessary to account for complex behavior. In the case of a phobia, the initial fear may be classically conditioned but the later avoidance of the stimulus is a product of operant conditioning.

•D1. ★Little Albert, Hollywood Style

A "silent-film" style movie recounting of the classical conditioning of a simple phobia and the operant conditioning that helps perpetuate such fears.

> **•Little Albert, Hollywood Style**
>
> **Activity Type:** Movie
>
> **Learning Objective:** Help students to see the connections between classical conditioning and operant conditioning. Help them understand how phobias can become self-perpetuating.
>
> **Faculty Note:** Francis, the fictional character in this dramatization, is used to illustrate both the mechanism by which a phobia might be initially established (classical conditioning) and the mechanism by which it is maintained afterwards (negative reinforcement).
>
> One of the problems for a purely classical conditioning model of phobias was the

> difficulty in explaining why our fear doesn't simply extinguish itself over time as we encounter the conditioned stimulus on occasions where no unconditioned stimulus is present. However, our tendency to learn to avoid unpleasant stimuli (negative reinforcement) means that we never give ourselves the opportunity to unlearn these responses.
>
> The notion that a given behavior can be influenced by multiple factors, including more than one type of learning, is noteworthy.

Rapid Review 2

•IV. OPENING THE BLACK BOX: COGNITIVE LEARNING

Extreme or "radical" behaviorism is described as giving way to mounting evidence that other factors (e.g., cognition and mental representation) are important in the learning process.

•IV1. ★Pop-Up: A Demonstration of the Black Box vs. the Mind

Cognitive psychologists believe that behavior cannot be understood without taking into account internal mental processes. As students search for the solution to the puzzle in this activity, they should reflect on the mental processes and specific strategies used to solve the problem.

> •A Demonstration of the Black Box vs. the Mind
>
> **Activity Type:** Simulation
>
> **Learning Objective:** Help students subjectively understand the difference between behavioristic and cognitive accounts of behavior.
>
> **Faculty Note:** Radical behaviorists argued that psychology should try to explain behavior without making reference to any unseen mental process. In contrast, cognitive psychologists believe that behavior cannot be understood without taking into account internal mental processes such as plans, schemas, and mental images.
>
> The task for the student is to play a game in which they have to find a correct combination of settings that will solve a puzzle. After searching for the correct setting, students are asked about their attempts. Did they try different solutions at random (trial-and-error) or did they employ some sort of cognitive strategy?
>
> Is it possible to give a convincing account of the student's problem-solving behavior without exploring their mental representations of the problem?

A. The Problem of Biological Preparedness

The example of conditioned taste aversion in rats is used to illustrate the idea that some responses are more easily conditioned than others, perhaps because the organism is biologically "prepared" to learn them. Biological preparedness is presented as a challenge to radical behaviorism.

B. The Problem of Language

It is observed that the ease with which humans acquire language skills is a problem for behaviorism. It is particularly difficult to account for our learning of the syntax (rules) of language solely by trial-and-error learning.

•C. The Problem of Social Learning

Here it is noted that the ability to learn vicariously (through observation of others) is yet a third problem for radical behaviorism. In a powerful demonstration of social learning, Albert Bandura and his colleagues found that children imitate the aggressive behaviors of an adult model.

•C1. ★Archival Footage of the Bandura Study

In this footage from a classic study of the social learning of aggression, episodes of modeling are illustrated with clips of the adult model and the subsequent behavior of the children.

•Archival Footage of the Bandura Study

Activity Type: Movie

•Learning Objective: **Provide an opportunity for students to see footage from a classic study that demonstrated the power of social learning.**

Faculty Note: In this footage we see (and hear Bandura describing) the actions of an adult modeling aggressive behaviors, as well as the subsequent aggressive behaviors of a child in the study. The narration points out instances of direct imitation on the part of the child.

Not only does this illustrate actual subject behavior from an influential study of social learning, but it can be tied into a discussion of methodological choices, as well. Bandura's study was notable for being one of the earlier underlined experimental studies of the impact of observational learning on aggression, but there are other ways of addressing this question, such as looking for correlations between exposure to violent TV programming and aggressive behavior.

Additional Resources:

A brief biography of Albert Bandura's can be found at
http://www.ship.edu/~cgboeree/bandura.html

• D. The Problem of Representation

It is observed in this section that the final challenge to the views of radical behaviorists came in the form of an increasing interest in cognitive psychology. Studies of mental representation and imagery revealed that actions performed on mental images in many ways resemble those that we perform on objects in the real world. Roger Shepard's studies of mental rotation are cited as examples of this cognitive revolution.

• D1. ★Pop-Up: An Experiment in Mental Rotation

In this activity, students will get an opportunity to visualize and mentally rotate selected images in a simple simulation of an experiment in cognitive psychology. Roger Shepard's original study revealed that his subjects were constructing mental models of the objects that were similar to their real-world counterparts.

• An Experiment in Mental Rotation

Activity Type: Simulation

Learning Objective: Provide a concrete example of what it means to say that there is a mental representation of something and that that representation matters for behavior.

Faculty Note: In a simulated Shepard mental rotation task, students see two geometric figures in different rotations and are asked to decide whether the figures match. The time that it takes them to make these decisions and their subjective perceptions of how difficult each trial is will be recorded.

In the original study, Shepard found that the time it took subjects to decide whether the objects matched was predictable from the difference in their orientations. It was as if his subjects mentally rotated images of these objects just as they would have rotated real objects to determine if they matched. This illustrates a classic finding of the cognitive revolution, that although no one has ever "seen" a mental model of a physical object, their existence can be inferred from actual behaviors such as reaction times or judgments. Unseen mental events may be scientifically studied by inferences made from observable events.

• Rapid Review 3

CHAPTER 6

MEMORY

Chapter Overview
    Learning Objectives
    Chapter Outline

Additional Lecture Ideas
    Lecture Topics
    Additional Readings

In-Class Activities and Demonstrations
    Activities and Demonstrations
    Sources for Additional Activities
    Journey II Software

World Wide Web

Audio-Visual Support

Handout and Transparency Masters

Chapter Overview

Learning Objectives

After studying this chapter, you should be able to do the following:

1. Define the three memory processes.

2. Describe the functions of the three memory systems.

3. Explain how memories are constructed.

4. Describe how memories are forgotten and reconstructed.

5. Explain how culture and education affect memory.

6. Describe strategies for improving your own memory.

Chapter Outline

Memory

I. Introduction
    A. Memory: the active mental system that encodes, stores, and retrieves information
    B. Effects: our reaction to the environment, interpretation of events, expectations of others

II. The Information-Processing Model: Memory Processes and Systems
    A. Three Memory Processes
        1. <u>a basic assumption</u>: people are active processors of information
        2. three connected processes
            a. <u>encoding information</u>: transforming information into mental representations that the brain can process
            b. <u>storing information</u>: maintenance of encoded information in memory for immediate or future use
            c. <u>retrieving information</u>: locating information stored in memory and using it
    B. Three Memory Systems
        1. sensory memory
            a. memory system that momentarily stores immediate sensory experiences
            b. <u>examples</u>: iconic memory, eidetic memory, echoic memory
        2. short term memory
            a. memory system that temporarily holds a limited amount of information for current use
            b. <u>storage capacity</u>: 7 units of information
                i. increased using <u>chunking</u>
            c. <u>storage time</u>: 30 seconds without rehearsal
            d. <u>maintenance rehearsal</u>: repeatedly entering information into STM as to keep it past the usual time limit
        3. long term memory
            a. an unlimited storehouse of skills, vocabulary, experiences, and knowledge
            b. encoding according to meaningful groupings
            c. <u>tip-of-the-tongue phenomenon</u>: subjective sense of being on the verge of remembering a piece of information
            d. types of long-term memory
                i. explicit
                    1. <u>declarative memory</u>: episodic & semantic memories
                ii. implicit
                    1. procedural memory

4. short- vs. long-term memory
      a. separate but connected vs. parts of one memory arguments
         i. serial position effect
         ii. levels-of-processing hypothesis
            1. elaborative rehearsal

III. Constructing Memories
A. Different Types of Remembering
   1. conscious remembering
      a. <u>recall</u>: retrieving information into conscious awareness without any external assistance
      b. <u>recognition</u>: correctly identifying information as being previously encountered
   2. unconscious remembering
      a. <u>relearning experiments</u>: measuring how fast one can relearn information as a measure of unconscious memory
B. Mental Mechanisms in Remembering
   1. the role of clues
      a. <u>retrieval cues</u>: incidental information that is stored along with main information
      b. internal cues (state-dependent cues)
         i. emotional or biological states that influence memory performance
      c. external cues (context-dependent cues)
         i. features of the physical environment in which we encode information
   2. the role of personal significance
      a. <u>flashbulb memories</u>: vivid and detailed memories of personally significant events
      b. explanations for flashbulb memories
         i. neural activity
         ii. repetition of the memory
C. Biological Mechanisms in Remembering
   1. the role of neurons
      a. Penfield's neurosurgical approach
      b. <u>long-term potentiation explanation</u>: biological and biochemical changes in neurons as the result of repeated stimulation
   2. the role of brain structures
      a. <u>sources of evidence</u>: cases of amnesia
      b. cerebellum involvement in implicit memory
      c. hippocampus and frontal lobe involvement in explicit memory

IV. Forgetting and Reconstructing Information
A. Forgetting: the inability to access information stored in memory

1. the forgetting curve

B. Forgetting What's in Storage
1. <u>decay theory</u>: neural traces have decayed
   a. effects of decay and aging in STM and for different types of memory
2. <u>interference theory</u>: information still exists but isn't retrieved
   a. <u>retroactive interference</u>: newly learned informtion disrupts recall of previously learned information
   b. <u>proactive interference</u>: previously learned information disrupts recall of newly learned information
3. <u>deliberate forgetting theory</u>:
   a. <u>motivated forgetting</u>: consciously or unconsciously hiding certain memories from conscious awareness
      i. <u>suppression</u>: conscious efforts to rid oneself of certain memories
      ii. <u>repression</u>: unconscious efforts to hide information from conscious awareness

C. Reconstructing What We've Forgotten
1. <u>memory reconstruction</u>: the process of piecing together recalled information with inferences or assumptions to create a complete memory
2. <u>reconstruction is affected by</u>:
   a. the separation of information and its source
   b. the use of inferences
   c. the merging of misinformation

V. Culture, Education, and Memory
  A. Cultural Scripts
  1. guide interpretation and acts as a framework for understanding information
  2. affect memories of events through the inference process as reconstruction of memories occurs
  B. Memories about Ourselves
  1. affected by cultural values and experiences
  2. memories of ourselves help define who we were, are, and will become
  3. cross-cultural differences in RFT of memories recounted by children
  C. Cultural Differences in Memory Strategies and Activities
  1. cultural and education affect how we process info, situations in which we use different memory strategies, values placed on memories
  2. culture and STM
     a. cross-cultural differences in nature of language and/or emphasis on memorization
  3. culture and LTM
     a. examples of unique individuals with extensive LTM
     b. use of mnemonics

Additional Lecture Topics

Eyewitness testimony: The case of Ted Bundy.

Most students will undoubtedly have heard of Ted Bundy, the infamous perpetrator of the murders known as the "Ted Cases" to law enforcement agents in the Northwest during the 1970s. Few may know, however, that noted researcher Elizabeth Loftus played a pivotal role in the development of his defense on charges of aggravated kidnapping in 1975. In November, 1974, Carol DaRonch met Ted Bundy in a Utah mall. Bundy, who had introduced himself as a police officer to Ms. DaRonch, eventually left the mall with her ostensibly to go to the local police station. En route he handcuffed and attempted to hit her over the head with a crowbar before she was able to escape. Eleven months later she picked Bundy's picture out of a book of mug shots. Bundy's attorney in the case, John O'Connell, contacted Dr. Loftus to serve as an expert on eyewitness testimony. Her subsequent conversations with O'Connell serve as an intriguing example of the application current research to trial cases involving eyewitness testimony. Some of the points considered from memory research in Bundy's defense:

- Our memory does not function as a literal, passive tape-recording of events but rather pieces of information are gathered from the environment and enter the memory systems where it interacts with our previous experiences, knowledge, and expectations. Moreover, memory involves acquisition, retention, and retrieval of information. During her testimony, Ms. DaRonch had responded with "I don't know" or "I can't remember" concerning the events of her kidnapping, suggesting that some failures in the memory process had occurred.
- Memory, unless rehearsed, deteriorates over time. Loftus noted that the memory of a stranger's face is likely to deteriorate, particularly after the passage of 11 months.
- Memory is severely affected by conditions of high stress. Although the events of Ms. DaRonch's kidnapping were very likely to have provoked extreme distress, Loftus noted that the first part of DaRonch's encounter with Bundy probably only produced moderate stress and had occurred in a well-lit mall, conditions more optimal for good memory.
- Unconscious transfer, where separate or different visual images observed in different situations become confused or merged, can occur. Ms. DaRonch was shown two different photos of Bundy, a mug shot and a copy of his driver's license. As a result of these visual presentations, Loftus argues, police could have helped DaRonch create a memory of Bundy.
- Interviewer bias can influence an eyewitness' memory of an event via unintentional cueing and reinforcement. Increasing activity and excitement on the part of police officers, in addition to showing DaRonch several photos of Bundy, may have sent her the message that

police believed he was the appropriate suspect. This, coupled with her own desires to help police and end her ordeal, may have lead DaRonch to change her initially tentative identification to a more firm identification.

Despite these points, Bundy was convicted and sent to prison for kidnapping Carol DaRonch. He escaped and was later captured for the murders of two Florida coeds. His connection to the murders in the Pacific Northwest were subsequently uncovered. Although the eventual details of Ted Bundy's criminal activity horrified the nation, the details of the DaRonch kidnapping case and the emphasis on eyewitness testimony and memory research serve as an interesting courtroom application of the model of memory discussed in most General Psychology classes.

Source:
Loftus, E. & Ketcham, K. (1997). Witness for the defense: The all-American boy: Ted Bundy. In Sattler, D. & Shabatay, V. (eds.), Psychology in context: Voices and perspectives. Boston: Houghton Mifflin.

Remembering in a cultural context.

Two children, each from different cultural origins, recall a cultural myth told to them by an adult. When one's recall exceeds the other's, are we to assume that they have different memory capabilities? Mistry & Rogoff suggest that the appropriate answer to that question is no, based on their contention that memory or remembering skills are not "pure" skills but rather "develop for the purpose of solving practical problems and that they are tied to the familiar tasks and practices in which remembering takes place." (p. 140). In short, unlike traditional models that view memory skills as context-free, theirs is a contextual or "enmeshed process" perspective on memory. Two quotes from their work expand on their message:

"Memory does not involve context-free skills that may be applied indiscriminately across widely different problems or tasks, but rather involves skills tied to somewhat specific activities in context."

- "Remembering is an activity that is defined in terms of the meaning of a task and its materials to the people remembering, and in terms of its function in the social and cultural system."

Take, for example, typical free recall tasks performed during laboratory studies on memory. Participants hear lists of words and then are asked to recall them. In explaining the observation that Western participants tend to outperform non-Western participants in such tasks, Mistry & Rogoff argue that the former group's memory advantage stems from their use of chunking and/or rehearsal strategies. Strategies of this nature develop from the school experience of Western literate people, which demands that they learn such techniques in their efforts to learn and subsequently recall materials that include isolated or unrelated pieces of information. Simply put, they learn and use remembering skills in a *context* as a *means* to support the goals for using those processes. Thus, remembering skills and culture become enmeshed with one another.

- Culture interacts with remembering skills in several other important ways:
- Remembering skills serve as a means for satisfying important economic or social goals, as is the case for the Swazi herdsman who must develop vast memories for characteristics of cattle for their economic and social livelihood.
- Immediate social interactional contexts shape remembering skills. Culturally-significant status differences between adults and children in testing or story retelling situations need to be considered when analyzing performance differences in cross-cultural studies. For example, Mayan children would be reluctant to show lack of respect or impertinence toward the higher-status adult by demonstrating more knowledge than them (i.e., answering recall questions directly).
- To arrive at "socially appropriate solutions to problems", cultures also provide culturally-relevant tools and procedures such as story mnemonics for remembering the positions of stars or using an abacus for performing mathematical operations.

In summary, Mistry & Rogoff conclude that "culture is involved in the remembering process through the practical goals of activities which make it worthwhile to remember, through the meaningful context that provides a natural organization of the material to be remembered, through familiarity with the material to be remembered, and with the social interactional context of the activity, and through the cultural tools and practices related to the activity of remembering." Thus, culture does more than just amplify a context-free memory process. As noted by Bartlett (1932), "both the manner and the matter of recall are often predominantly determined by social influences."

Source:

Mistry, J., & Rogoff, B. (1995). Remembering in cultural context. In Looner, W., & Malpass, R. (eds.), <u>Psychology and culture</u>. Needham Heights, MA: Allyn and Bacon.

Hormones and memory.

Emotional memories, often rich, poignant, and powerful, may be based in the biochemistry of our brains. Wade & Tavris (1998) reviewed some of the psychophysiological phenomena underlying such memories. During stress and emotional arousal, hormones such as epinephrine and certain steroids released by the adrenal glands cause glucose to rise in the bloodstream and, eventually, in the brain. Once there, glucose may either directly enhance memory or may indirectly enhance it by altering neurotransmitter activity (Gold, 1987). From an evolutionary perspective, the linkage between arousal and enhanced memory makes sense: arousing events or information should probably be remembered for future survival.

Empirical evidence?

- People given drugs that suppress adrenal production of these hormones remember less information about emotional stories than do controls (Cahill et al., 1994).
- Animals given epinephrine after learning show memory improvements (McGaugh, 1990).
- Alzheimer's patients given glucose show enhanced ability to recognize words, prose passages, faces (Manning, Ragozzino, & Gold, 1993).

Although exact mechanisms underlying the connection between hormones and memory are not yet clear (and, as Wade & Tavris note, spark controversy), the topic is likely to intrigue students....could they be able to take a memory-enhancing pill someday?

Source:
Wade, C. & Tavris, C. (1998). Chapter 9: Memory. In *Psychology* (5th ed.), pg. 365. Pacific Grove, CA: Brooks/Cole.

Gender differences in memory?

Do men and women differ in their memory capabilities? Matlin (1993) argues that, generally speaking, "males and females probably have similar memory capacities." (pg. 118). However, she notes, some inconsistent differences have been reported in the sex differences literature. For example, in a review of memory studies contained in their book, *The psychology of sex differences*, Maccoby and Jacklin (1974) report that some memory studies on verbal content found that women remembered more material than did men whereas, in other studies, no gender differences have been found. Although women and men demonstrate similar memory performance for numbers and objects (Maccoby & Jacklin, 1974), some studies show that females outperform males when social content, such as memory for classmates' names and faces, is involved (Bahrick et al., 1975; Feldstein, 1976). In her explanation for such observed differences, Matlin contends that they are not based in literal differences in memory abilities but rather are more probably due to "females' slight superiority in these content areas" (i.e, verbal and social material; pg. 118). Combine discussion on these topics with exercise # 6 and **Activity Handout 6.2** in the Activity/Demonstrations section.

Source:
Matlin, M. (1993). The psychology of women. Fort Worth: Harcourt Brace Javanovich.

5. **The mind of a mnemonist**.

Soviet psychologist, A. R. Luria, presents his case study of the famous "S." The narrative provides students with insight into the unique memory experience and process of "S" as well as the methodology used during Luria's discovery. As has been historically the case in many memory experiments designed to test memory capacity and duration, Luria presented "S" with increasingly longer lists of numbers, letters, nonsense syllables, and meaningful words. Regardless of list length or type, "S" demonstrated nearly flawless recall...so long as the list was presented with a 3-4 sec. pause between each item on the list. Luria came to the astounding conclusion that "S" had a memory with no distinct limits regarding capacity. In an even more phenomenal discovery, "S" was able to reproduce lists even 15 or 16 years after having learned them. But what were the bases for his otherwise inexplicable capabilities?

Curiously, "S" reported that if some disturbance occurred in the room or the examiner said something during the experiment, the experience would be converted into a blur or "puff of steam" or "splash" that interfered with his memory process. Luria surmised that "S" experienced *synesthesia*, which occurs when "the stimulation of one sense evokes another sense, as in visualizing a color when hearing a particular sound" (pg. 108). When "S" heard voices, speech sounds, tones, they were converted into an experience of light, color, taste, or touch. Luria observed: "Every speech sound immediately summoned up for S. a striking visual image, for it had it own distinct form, color, and taste. Vowels appeared to him as simple figures, consonants as splashes, some of them solid configurations, others more scattered--but all of them retained some distinct form. When S. read through a series of words, each word would elicit a graphic image." (pg. 110). S's unique synesthesic experience formed the basis for his remarkable memory skills. In short, he demonstrated the ability of routinely converting word series into graphic image series. Additionally, once graphic images were created, he would take "mental walks" through familiar localities and "distribute" the graphic images he had created along the roadways or scenes. Thus, the case of "S" provides an intriguing example of the role of imagery and his unique "method of loci", mnemonic processes that all of us might use (albeit to a lesser extent than "S") to improve our memory capabilities.

Source:
Luria, A. (1997). The mind of a mnemonist. In Sattler, D., & Shabatay, V. (eds.), Psychology in context: Voices and perspectives. Boston: Houghton Mifflin.

Suggestions for Additional Readings

Allport, S. (1986). *Explorers of the black box: The search for the cellular basis of memory*. New York: Norton

Ashcraft, M. (1994). *Human memory and cognition*. Glenview, IL: Scott, Foresman.

Baddeley, A. (1982). *Your memory: A user's guide*. New York: Macmillan.

Baddeley, A. (1990). *Human memory*. Boston: Allyn and Bacon.

Brown, A. (1987). *Maximizing memory power: Using recall to your advantage in business*. New York: Wiley.

Campbell, R., & Conway, M. (1995). *Broken memories: Case studies in memory impairment*. Oxford: Blackwell.

Davies, G., & Thomson, D. (Eds.) (1988). *Memory in context: Context in memory*. New York: Wiley.

Goldman-Rakic, P. (1992). Working memory and the mind. *Scientific American, 267*(3), 110-117.

Hermann, D., McEvoy, C., Hertzog, C., Hertel, P., & Johnson, M. (Eds.) (1996). *Basic and applied memory research* (vols. I and II). Hillsdale, NJ: Erlbaum.

Higbee, K. (1988). *Your memory: How it works and how to improve it*. Englewood Cliffs, NJ: Prentice-Hall.

Loftus, E., & Ketcham, K. (1991). *Witness for the defense: The accused, the eyewitness, and the expert who puts memory on trial*. New York: St. Martin's Press.

Loftus, E., & Ketcham, K. (1994). *The myth of repressed memory: False memories and allegations of sexual abuse*. New York: St. Martin's Press.

Mace, N., & Rabins, P. (1981). *The 36-hour day*. Baltimore: Johns Hopkins University Press

Minninger, J. (1984). *Total recall*. New York: Pocket Books.

Mishkin, M. & Appenzeller, T. (1987). The anatomy of memory. *Scientific American, 256*(6), 80-89.

Rose, S. (1993). *The making of memory: From molecules to mind*. New York: Anchor Books.

Rubin, D. (Ed.) (1995). *Remembering our past*. New York: Cambridge.

Schacter, D. (1996). *Searching for memory: The brain, the mind, and the past*. New York: Basic Books.

Sporer, S., Malpass, R., & Koehnken, G. (Eds.) (1995). *Psychological factors in eyewitness identification*. Hillsdale, NJ: Erlbaum.

Terr, L. (1994). *Unchained memories: True stories of traumatic memories, lost and found*. New York: Basic Books.

Turkington, C. (1996). *12 steps to a better memory*. New York: Arco.

Wells, G., & Loftus, E. (Eds.) (1984). *Eyewitness testimony: Psychological perspectives*. Cambridge: Cambridge University Press.

In-Class Activities and Demonstrations

TRAIL blazing: Using Transparency Masters 6.1 - 6.4, review with students the "Checking Your TRAIL" sections in the chapter. Have students work in small groups to answer the questions and then review with the class as a whole to tie the text reading to activity in class.

Reaching critical mass: Using Transparency Masters 6.5 - 6.7, review with students the "Critical Thinking" sections in the chapter. Have students work in small groups to answer the questions and then review with the class as a whole to tie the text reading to activity in class.

Getting down to IT: Using Transparency Masters 6.8- 6.13, review the "Integrative Thinking" sections in the chapter with students. Have students work in small groups to answer the questions and then review with the class as a whole to tie the text reading to activity in class.

Crossword Puzzle: Using **Activity Handout # 6.1**, have students complete the crossword puzzle for terms contained within Chapter 6.

Memory for masculine vs. feminine words: Using a transparency copy of **Activity Handout # 6.2,** present students with the following list of 21 words as presented on that handout: 7 related to stereotypic masculine activities/objects, 7 related to stereotypic feminine activities/objects, 7 pertaining to neutral objects in the environments. After giving students several minutes to memorize the list, ask them to free recall (i.e., remember as many of the words as they possibly can) items from the list. If your data follow the trends from Brown et al. (1980) your male students should demonstrate higher recall for masculine terms, female students for feminine terms.

Source:
Brown, A., Larsen, M., Rankin, S., & Ballard, R. (1980). Sex differences in information processing. Sex Roles, 6, 663-673.

STM exercises: The following activities are fun demonstrations concerning short term memory measure its capacity, the effects of distraction on recall, and the process of chunking.

capacity: Read the following lists of digit strings to students, asking them to recall each list in order after you finished. When done with all the digit strings read over the list once again so students can check their lists for recall accuracy. Most students recall the early lists of fewer digits and generally only 1 or 2 are able to reproduce the longer digit lists.

2 5 4 8
7 8 2 1
6 9 2 4 5
8 1 4 2 7
8 4 6 1 4 2
7 6 3 9 2 5
8 1 5 2 6 9 7
2 5 4 3 7 5 6
1 5 2 8 3 7 9 3
8 2 9 3 7 3 5 8
4 7 5 6 8 2 9 1 0
5 7 6 8 9 7 2 4 3 5
1 3 2 4 7 5 8 6 9 1
5 6 4 7 3 8 2 9 2 3 4
9 6 4 3 2 6 7 3 5 7 3
4 9 6 7 3 7 4 6 3 6 7 4
1 7 2 9 5 4 0 7 8 3 2 8

chunking: To demonstrate the power of chunking, take the last two lines from the preceding list and chunk the items as follows:
    4 9 6 - 7 3 7 - 4 6 3 - 6 7 4
    1 7 2 - 9 5 4 - 0 7 8 - 3 2 8
After each line ask students to recall the items. Recall will probably increase dramatically, demonstrating the power of chunking on memory capacity.

effects of distraction on rehearsal: Read the following nonsense syllables to students allowing for differing amounts of time (from 3 to 15 seconds) before they are asked to recall the information. The tricky part of this exercise occurs for the students when they are told that after you give them the nonsense syllable, they are to begin counting out loud backwards from some number (say 75 or so) by 3s. At the end of the distraction period, students are to write down the nonsense syllable. If you vary the distraction time intervals, remembering to keep track of the distraction time interval order you've used (!), and then ask for a show of hands for students who recalled the syllable accurately, you'll generally find that most students have accurate recall for items with only short distraction-recall delays and increasingly poorer recall as the distraction-recall delays increase. In fact, if you plot your data a forgetting curve tends to emerge.

Time Interval	Nonsense Syllable
3 seconds	TMQ
6 seconds	CWD
9 seconds	QPZ
12 seconds	WKV
15 seconds	DXW
18 seconds	RPF

Imagery and memory: Colorful variations of the name game: Different versions of the name game abound but all allow students to learn the names of their classmates (which often seems to increase their levels of interaction with one another). I've used this technique in both large and small section classes with success and tie the activity into my discussion of memory mnemonics. Try some of the following variations after dividing students into relatively large groups or using the entire class if the enrollment isn't too prohibitive:

Going on a picnic: Each student is to think of some food or object that he or she would take on a picnic and that item must start with the first letter of his or her name. Students proceed around the group and introduce themselves by saying "Hi! My name is _____ and I'm going on a picnic with __person preceding them in the circle or group__ who is bringing ___food or object___ (and ___next person___ who is bringing __ their food or object___, and etc.) and I'm going to bring __food or object for their own name___."

Names and vivid objects: Bring a large group of students to the front of the class stating that you are going to demonstrate your amazing memory skills. Have students stand in line and then each tell you his or her name. As they tell you their names, silently associate their names with some highly memorable aspect of their appearance and some memorable object in the environment. For example, when doing this demonstration once I had a male student who shaved his head tell me his last name was Koehler. This reminded me of a plumbing manufacturer by the name of Koehler who made toilet bowls...I associated his shiny shaved head with the shiny bowl of a toilet and I've never forgotten this student's name (not to mention he got a huge laugh when I told him about my imagery association). To astound and amaze your students, first recall all the students name and then reveal your technique.

Peg words and names: Another variation involves using the peg word system described in most General Psychology textbooks. I use this one with smaller classes where chairs are arranged in rows. Again ask students their names and associate them with the Peg word system (one: bun; two: shoe; three: tree, etc.)

Would you make a good eyewitness?: Have 2 persons of differing races enter your classroom and take items from the classroom during the week or two weeks prior to discussing memory. Then ask students to describe the persons. When I do this demonstration I have the "target" posing as a research assistant take something from the front of class and then leave the room. A couple of days later I announce that I'm missing (whatever the articles were) and wonder if one of my research assistants may have come in and borrowed the items. I then ask students if they remember seeing anyone take the items and have them describe the supposed research assistants. A good deal of discussion and confusion tends to arise as students have different memories for clothing and features of the "research assistant". I also ask them if they have differing success remembering details about individuals based on their race. Another variation would be to show students pictures of various people (including the research assistants) to determine if they have variable degrees of accuracy for correctly identifying the "research assistants" and tend to make more accurate identifications for people of their own ethnic or racial group. Needless to say, it's important to reveal the contrived nature of the demonstration so students don't leave thinking something was actually taken but this demonstration is a relatively tamed down version of studies on eyewitness identification that involve staged crimes. This tends to be a fun activity that introduces eyewitness testimony literature and general memory processes to your class.

Sources:
    Platz, S. & Hosch, H. (1988). Cross-racial/ethnic eyewitness identification: A field study. Journal of Applied Social Psychology, 18, 972-984.

Sources for Additional Activities
Books:
Benjamin, L. & Lowman, K. (1981). Activities Handbook for the Teaching of Psychology. Washington DC: American Psychological Association.

Halonen, Jane 1995). Chapter 7: Memory. In The Critical Thinking Companion For Introductory Psychology (Worth Publ.).

Singelis, T. (1998). Teaching about culture, ethnicity, & diversity: Exercises and Planned Activities. Thousand Oaks, CA: Sage Publ.

Makosky, V. et al. (Eds.) (1995). Activities Handbook for the Teaching of Psychology (Vol. III). Washington DC: American Psychological Association.

Journey II Software: The Journey II software program contains 2 units related to memory:

Chunking: This unit provides students with the opportunity to learn about the use of chunking to increase the amount of information they can maintain in short term memory. Following a brief discussion of the typical limits of STM capacity (7 +/- 2 bits of information), students attempt to memorize two strings of letters (one 22 bits long, the other 26 bits). Students' answers are compared to the original lists and results compared to typical performance.

Deja Vu: Students are prompted to recall times when they have had the feeling of *deja vu*...the vague feeling that they've been somewhere or done something before but can't quite recall the full details of the memory. To illustrate the phenomenon, students are asked to view a list of sleep-related words and then attempt to recall as many words as they possibly can from the list. Many students will make the common error of adding the word "sleep" to the recalled list, even though it was not on the original list. The explanation given for the error involves the activation of "bins" of related information in the memory (i.e., because the words on the list were in the same "bin" as sleep, we assume sleep was too.) Although the introduction of deja vu is a bit confusing, this unit can be related to discussions of schema in memory.

World Wide Web: Check out the following WWW sites for information and activities relevant to this section of the text!

Addison Wesley Longman's Website -- **http://longman.awl.com/**
- PsychZone link -- **http://longman.awl.com/**
- Psych Web -- **http://www.gasou.edu/psychweb/psychweb.htm**

Self-Quizzes for Introductory Psychology --
http://www.gasou.edu/psychweb/selfquiz/selfquiz.htm

Psychology Jumping Stand --
http://www.indiana.edu:80/~iuepsyc/PsycJump.html

The Psychology Place --**http://www.psychplace.com**

Memory techniques and mnemonics --
   http://www.demon.co.uk/mindtool/memory.html
Memory skills, techniques and mnemonics--
   http://ww.gac.peachnet.edu/Student_Life/study_skills/effstudy.htm
   or
   http://iquest.com/~fitz/csicop/si/9503/memory.html
   or
   http://www.gasou.edu/psychweb/mtsite/memory.html
Experiments in memory -- **http://www.exploratorium.edu/memory/index.html**
Alzheimer's Disease -- **http://www.biostat/wustl.edu/alzheimer/**

Audio-Visual Support
Films/Videos:
Overview
Discovering Psychology: Remembering and Forgetting (Annenberg, 30 minutes)
Memory (CRM, 30 minutes)
Human Memory (Harcourt, 28 minutes)
Memory: Fabric of the Mind (FFHS, 28 minutes)
The Brain: Learning and Memory (PBS, 60 minutes)
The Nature of Memory (FFHS, 26 minutes)
The Study of Memory (FFHS, 74 minutes)
Memory: The past imperfect (Insight Media, 46 minutes)

Related Topic
Alzheimer's: The Tangled Mind (FFHS, 23 minutes)
Alzheimer's Disease: How Families Cope (FFHS, 28 minutes)

Psychology Encyclopedia Laserdisc IV:
Still Images

Sperling's partial recovery experiment [UN]	Frame 53536	Side	all
Pennies [UN]	53537		all
Rudolph's reindeer friends [1/2] [9.1]	53538		all
Rudolph's reindeer friends [2/2] [9.1]	53539		all
Memory systems [1/4] [9.2]	53540		all
Memory systems [2/4] [9.2]	53541		all
Memory systems [3/4] [9.2]	53542		all
Memory systems [4/4] [9.2]	53543		all
Conceptual grid in long-term memory [9.3]	53544		all
Serial-position effect [9.5]	53545		all
Retention in short-term memory [9.6]	53546		all
Elaborated encoding [1/3] [9.7]	53547		all
Elaborated encoding [2/3] [9.7]	53548		all
Elaborated encoding [3/3] [9.7]	53549		all
Brain areas critical for memory [9.8]	53550		all
Ebbinghaus's forgetting curve	53551		all
Interference in memory [1/2] [9.12]	53552		all
Interference in memory [2/2] [9.12]	53553		all

Transparency Master 6.1: Checking Your TRAIL 6.1

Memory includes three mental processes: _____, _____, and retrieving information.

According to the information-processing model of memory, what are the three distinct but interrelated memory systems?

Clive Wearing can only remember the beginning and the end of a song. This phenomenon is the _____ _____ effect.

Match the term with the correct statement(s):

implicit memory	1. memory for facts, such as
procedural memory	2. a type of implicit memory
semantic memory	3. memory for how to do things,
episodic memory	4. cannot be measured with
	5. a subtype of declarative
	6. memory for a specific

Transparency Master 6.2: Checking Your TRAIL 6.2

True or False: Memory performs best when the learning and testing contexts are the same, whether or not the test involves recall or recognition.

At one time, people thought that a memory of an event resided in a specific neuron. Do researchers still believe that specific neurons store specific memories? If not, how do researchers think memories are stored in the brain?

Procedural memories involve a brain structure known as the _____, which coordinates body movements, while declarative memories are processed in the part of the brain known as the _____.

After her motorcycle crash, Erikah could not recognize her parents or her own face. What type of memory loss is this?

Jason always crams for his exams. The night before a test, he memorizes as much material as he can by rehearsing it over and over. He does not have time to think about the meaning of what he reads, but he can remember it well enough to pass his tests. How long would you expect him to retain this information, compared to someone who understood its meaning? Use the forgetting curve to explain your answer.

Fernanda finished studying for her French final, then played in a soccer match before taking the exam. What type of interference might she experience? Why?

True or False: Flashbulb memories are exceptionally accurate memories.

Tyrone is convinced that he was lost in a shopping mall when he was about 5 years old. No one else remembers the incident, although his mother recalls that as a child he once got lost in the grocery store for two or three minutes. Assume that Tyrone has reconstructed a memory of being lost in the shopping mall. Give two different explanations for how Tyrone's reconstruction might have occurred.

Transparency Master 6.4: Checking Your TRAIL 6.4

After reading the story about John's date in Table 6.1, Amado, a Mexican-American student, remembered it better than did all of his non-Mexican classmates. How might Amado's cultural experiences have influenced his excellent recall of the story?

Zoe, who never attended school, can remember just as many items on the playground as her peers who attend school. However, Zoe has to struggle to remember a telephone number, whereas her educated peers do not. How might educational experience explain this weakness in Zoe's memory abilities?

When describing himself to his European-American friends, Jay, a Korean immigrant student, talks about how his career choices reflect his desires to please his parents and to fulfill his social obligations. His friends, in contrast, talk about their personal interests and how they will choose their own careers. How might cultural differences in autobiographical memories explain the difference in attitudes between Jay and his friends?

Griots **and other people who do not read are able to remember huge amounts of socially relevant information. From a cultural perspective, how would you explain their remarkable ability?**

Transparency Master 6.5: Critical Thinking 6.1

This book includes critical thinking questions and integrative thinking questions throughout its chapters. According to the levels-of-processing hypothesis, how might these questions facilitate your memory for what you have read?

Transparency Master 6.6: Critical Thinking 6.2

Not all students are able to study in environments similar to those in which they are tested. Students from crowded households may not have desks or other quiet places in which to work. Given what you've just learned about context cues, why might these students be at a disadvantage when taking an exam?

Transparency Master 6.7: Critical Thinking 6.3

Imagine that you remember your ancestral history because it is profoundly important to your culture. You remember the names of your relatives from several generations ago, their occupations, experiences, values, and beliefs. How would you judge the memory abilities of people who cannot even remember the names of their immediate cousins?

Transparency Master 6.8: Integrative Thinking 6.1

How is latent learning, discussed in the Learning Chapter, similar to procedural memory?

Transparency Master 6.9: Integrative Thinking 6.2

Consider for a moment the work of neurosurgeon, Wilder Penfield described on pg. 626-628 in your text. In the Introductory chapter, we discussed scientific investigation. What assumptions of the scientific method did Penfield (the surgeon) break when he drew his conclusions?

Transparency Master 6.10: Integrative Thinking 6.3

The hippocampus was described in the Biopsychology chapter. An injury to what part of the head would be most likely to damage it and cause loss of memory?

Transparency Master 6.11: Integrative Thinking 6.4

Sleep can aid memory by reducing interference. However, recall the Repair theory of sleep described in the Consciousness chapter. Use the Repair theory to explain why the students who slept recalled more than the students who stayed awake.

Transparency Master 6.12: Integrative Thinking 6.5

How might multiple levels of consciousness explain the misinformation effect that occurs during suggestive questioning?

Transparency Master 6.13: Integrative Thinking 6.6

Consider for a moment the study described on p. 246. This study was a field study, a type of research study described in the Introductory chapter. How might you design a survey and a case study of teenagers to examine cultural differences in autobiographical memories?

Crossword Puzzle: Using **Activity Handout # 6.1**, have students complete the word search puzzle using terms contained within Chapter 6 and other dictionary words (i.e., the word list with the puzzle). The solution for the puzzle is the term *hippocampus*.

Handout Master # 6.1: Memory

Chapter 6

```
N O I T I S O P L A I R E S N
F O R G E T T I N G H V P O O
N E V I T C A O R P I P I P I
S E M A N T I C R T M T O A S
E Y R E A L I O C A C T N H S
V R O B L N C A I U E O O B E
I O C A O E O N R N I R L L R
T M C C D R T T T T U A O P
A E I U T E S I I T B V S N P
R M R E N N A N E H E E R G U
A A R A O T G R S I N C A T S
L S N C I O M A R C I U E E L
C C E O C P L T O N D M H R I
E R N E S F E D E C A Y E M D
D A R E P R E S S I O N R I E
```

Instructions: Complete the word search puzzle above by finding the following list of words from Chapter 6 and dictionary words. To solve the puzzle, use the letters that remain in the puzzle to create a term used in Chapter 6.

ARCS	BREN	CINE	DECAY
DECLARATIVE	DINE	ENCODE	ETNA
FLASHBULB	FORGETTING	ICONIC	LONG TERM
MAINTENANCE	MEMORY	POTENTIATION	PROACTIVE
PROCEDURAL	RECALL	RECOGNITION	REHEARSAL
RECONSTRUCTION	REPRESSION	RETRIEVAL	SLIDE
SUPPRESSION	RETROACTIVE	SUPPRESSION	SEMANTIC
SERIAL POSITION	TELE		

Puzzle solution: (Hints--11 letters:zoo animal's university) __ __ __ __ __ __ __ __ __ __ __

Memory for masculine vs. feminine words: Using a transparency copy of **Activity Handout # 6.2,** present students with the following list of 21 words as presented on that handout: 7 related to stereotypic masculine activities/objects, 7 related to stereotypic feminine activities/objects, 7 pertaining to neutral objects in the environments. After giving students several minutes to memorize the list, ask them to free recall (i.e., remember as many of the words as they possibly can) items from the list. If your data follow the trends from Brown et al. (1980) your male students should demonstrate higher recall for masculine terms, female students for feminine terms.

Source:
    Brown, A., Larsen, M., Rankin, S., & Ballard, R. (1980). Sex differences in information processing. Sex Roles, 6, 663-673.

Activity Handout # 6.2

**Football
Tree
Lipstick
Wrench
Balloon
Salon
Engine
Milk
Baby
Screwdriver
Bread
Kiss
Fight
Apple
Heels
Spikes
Couch
Blender
Gun
Desk
Nails**

Mind Matters CD-ROM Faculty Guide

V. INTRODUCTION TO MEMORY
        V1. ★A Test of Memory I
  A. Ebbinghaus and the Process of Forgetting
  B. The Problem of Meaning
        B1. ★A Test of Memory II
  C. Information Processing and Memory

VI. THE PROCESS OF REMEMBERING
  A. Stage 1: Memory Encoding
        A1. ★A Test of Memory III
  B. Stage 2: Memory Storage
  C. Sensory Memory Storage
  D. Short-Term Memory Storage
        D1. ★Pop-Up: An Experiment in Short-Term Memory
  E. Short-Term Memory and Chunking
        E1. ★A Test of Memory IV
  F. Long-Term Memory Storage
  G. Long Term Memory and the Serial Position Effect
  H. Long Term Memory and Depth of Processing
  I. Stage 3: Memory Retrieval
        I1. ★Pop-Up: Types of Retrieval
  J. The Construction of Memory
        J1. ★Pop-Up: A Demonstration of Déjà Vu
        J2. ★Pop-Up: A Demonstration in Point of View and Memory
Rapid Review 4

Quick Quiz

V. INTRODUCTION TO MEMORY

It is pointed out that the processes involved in memory are much more active, interpretive, and open to bias than we would like to believe. Memory is not simply a straightforward "recording" of events.

V1. ★A Test of Memory I

Students often fail to recognize the image of a commonly seen object (a real penny) when presented with many slightly different distracters. This is used to dramatize the limitations of memory.

> **A Test of Memory I**
>
> **Activity Type:** Demonstration
>
> **Learning Objective:** Encourage students to reflect on the accuracy and reliability of memory.
>
> **Faculty Note:** In this demonstration, students are confronted with a series of drawings of U.S. pennies, only one of which is actually accurate in all details. Most students find it more difficult than expected to pick out the "real" coin from among the distracters.
>
> Despite seeing pennies often (probably daily), and with the added advantage of using recognition instead of free recall as the means of assessing memory, this task is difficult because the appearance of a penny is not extremely interesting or relevant for most of us. Little attention is paid to pennies, and so we fail to encode them at an extremely detailed level.
>
> This is a useful demonstration when trying to make the point that memory is not a simple passive recording of our environment, but involves the active selection, filtering, and processing of incoming information.

A. Ebbinghaus and the Process of Forgetting

Hermann Ebbinghaus was the first psychologist to systematically study memory. Based on tests of his own memory, he was able to quantify remembering and forgetting, and evolve a model of memory based on the principle of association.

B. The Problem of Meaning

Although Ebbinghaus intentionally studied memory for "meaningless" information (such as nonsense syllables), it is well established that memories for material that is meaningful to us are more easily created and retrieved. This departs from a simple association model of memory.

B1. ★A Test of Memory II

A narrated description of "Washing Clothes" is used to illustrate the importance of meaningfulness in the encoding of new memories.

> **A Test of Memory II**
>
> **Activity Type:** Audio Demonstration
>
> **Learning Objective:** Help students see the advantages that "meaning" confers on items that are to be remembered.

Faculty Note: Students hear an audio clip of a narrator describing what at first seems like a meaningless sequence of actions. Memory for an arbitrary set of actions such as these is contrasted with memory for the same passage once it is given new meaning by the label "Washing Clothes."

Early models of memory based only on the principle of association (such as that of Ebbinghaus) fail to explain the impact of meaning on memory.

Additional Resources:

Ebbinghaus' *Memory: A Contribution to Experimental Psychology* can be found at http://www.yorku.ca/dept/psych/classics/Ebbinghaus/index.htm

C. Information Processing and Memory

Examples like the Washing Clothes exercise described above demonstrate that there is more to memory than simple associations. Information is actively processed and infused with meaning.

VI. The Memory Process

In theories of memory that emphasize information processing, it is often found to be useful to look at memory as if it occurs in three stages: encoding, storage, and retrieval.

A. Stage 1: Memory Encoding

Information to be remembered first has to be brought into the system. Selective attention is the most important principle governing this encoding process.

A1. ★A Test of Memory III

A complex video clip first used by the cognitive psychologist Ulrich Neisser provides an illustration of the role of selective attention in the encoding of memories. Students "filter out" elements of the action in the video when they are attending to other stimuli.

A Test of Memory III

Activity Type: Demonstration

Learning Objective: Learn about the role that selective attention plays in memory.

Faculty Note: This is a demonstration of selective attention that is constructed from a presentation of Neisser's classic video. The video begins with 4 people bouncing a basketball back and forth. Several men play basketball in a confusing montage of overlapping images. At one point during the video, a woman with an umbrella strolls by in the midst of the activity. After watching the video, the students will be asked to recall details from the game and player characteristics. In addition, they will be asked about the presence of the woman. Neisser found that the majority of people, selectively intent on watching the game, fail to see the woman.

Attention is a central mechanism in the formation of memories. One reason why we might find ourselves unable to retrieve information is that it was never really stored in the first place. We selectively attend to and encode only a fraction of the "booming, buzzing" confusion of events in the world around us, and so our allocation of attention "filters out" a substantial number of events that are thus "lost."

B. Stage 2: Memory Storage

For memory to function, information must be retained or stored over time. Psychologists have identified three steps that are involved in storing memories: sensory memory, short-term memory, and long-term memory.

C. Sensory Memory Storage

Sensory memory is described as a memory register that briefly preserves a faithful copy of incoming sensory information. George Sperling's classic studies of the duration and capacity of sensory memory are described in this section.

D. Short-Term Memory Storage

Short-term memory is described here as "working" memory, in which information is consciously rehearsed, elaborated, and linked to existing knowledge. Short-term memory is said to have limited capacity and limited duration.

D1. ★Pop-Up: An Experiment in Short-Term Memory

In this activity, the goal is to examine the limits of short-term memory by testing the student's memory for repeating patterns of color.

An Experiment in Short-Term Memory

Activity Type: Simulation

Learning Objective: Learn about the limits of short-term memory.

Faculty Note: In this Simon-like activity, the goal is to examine the limits of short-term memory by testing memory for patterns of color. On each trial, the computer will present

> a series of lights and the student's task is to repeat the series by clicking on each color in the order that it appeared; the series gets longer as the activity progresses.
>
> Students should notice that as the number of items in the sequence increased, their memory probably became less reliable. It is harder to hold nine items in working memory than it is to remember two items. Research suggests that most people are only able to keep between five and nine items in short-term memory at any given time.
>
> It should be noted that this is only demonstrating the limitations of short-term (working) memory, not long-term memory.
>
> **Additional Resources:**
>
> George Miller's seminal paper on memory, *The Magical Number Seven, Plus or Minus Two: Some Limits on Our Capacity for Processing Information* can be found at http://www.well.com/user/smalin/miller.html

E. Short-Term Memory and Chunking

The amount of information that can be processed in short-term memory depends on our ability to organize the material. One way to increase our memory capacity is by "chunking" information into a smaller number of meaningful units.

E1. ★A Test of Memory IV

An exercise in organizing a string of digits into "dates" (meaningful chunks of four numbers, such as 1998) illustrates the role of organization in short-term memory.

> **A Test of Memory IV**
>
> **Activity Type:** Audio and Animated Demonstration
>
> **Learning Objective:** Learn about the role that organization (i.e., chunking) can play in short-term memory.
>
> **Faculty Note:** Students hear a series of numbers presented individually, and then the numbers are organized into meaningful "chunks" such as dates ("1998") to illustrate the advantages this offers in the encoding process.
>
> It should be easy to come up with additional "chunking" demonstrations that would facilitate recall, e.g., C F B I I I A R S = FBI, CIA, IRS.

F. Long-Term Memory Storage

Long-term memory is described as a practically limitless store of information and experience that persists over long durations.

G. Long Term Memory and the Serial Position Effect

The serial position effect refers to the finding that when people attempt to remember a long list of items, they tend to remember more items from early in the list, a few items from late in the list, and relatively fewer items from the middle of the list. The concepts of short-term and long-term memory are needed to account for this finding.

H. Long-Term Memory and Depth of Processing

It is noted here that a factor that determines whether items make it into long-term memory is the "depth" of processing that is involved. The example given is of the effects of structural vs. semantic judgments on eventual recall.

I. Stage 3: Memory Retrieval

In order to say that you've "remembered" something, you have to be able to retrieve it. Many failures of memory are problems with retrieval, not encoding or storage. The "tip of the tongue" phenomenon is given as an illustration.

I1. ★Pop-Up: Types of Retrieval

A memory exercise is used to distinguish between recall memory and recognition memory. Recognition memory tends to be significantly easier because the item itself provides a retrieval cue.

Types of Retrieval

Activity Type: Demonstration

Learning Objective: Learn to distinguish between recall and recognition memory.

Faculty Note: Recall refers to the ability to reproduce an item that you've previously been exposed to. In contrast, recognition memory refers to the ability to recognize an item that you've previously been exposed to. Recognition memory tends to be significantly easier because the item itself provides a retrieval cue. Students can demonstrate this for themselves by trying to retrieve items via both recall and recognition.

J. The Construction of Memory

Although memories feel as if they are "recordings", it is more likely that they are "reconstructions." The research of Elizabeth Loftus on the unreliability of eyewitness testimony provides many examples of the discrepancy between memory and reality. The misinformation effect and the construction of false memories are discussed.

J1. ★Pop-Up: A Demonstration of Déjà Vu

The experience of déjà vu is used as a starting point to discuss inaccuracies in retrieval. Psychologists who study memory would argue that these experiences can be explained simply as a natural consequence of the way in which the mind stores and retrieves information.

A Demonstration of Déjà Vu

Activity Type: Demonstration

Learning Objective: Encourage students to question the everyday assumption that memory is a passive recording and is almost always accurate.

Faculty Note: In this demonstration, students hear a list of eighteen words that are linked by a "medical" theme (i.e., hospital, nurse, etc.). Their task is to try to remember the words without writing them down or repeating them out loud. After completing the list, they are given a recognition memory test. Many students will falsely remember that the word "doctor" appeared on the list because of its similarity to other words that were on the list. In fact, the word does not appear on the list of words to be remembered.

False alarms such as this (sometimes referred to as feelings of "déjà vu") can be explained as the result of basic memory processes.

J2. ★Pop-Up: A Demonstration in Point of View and Memory

A simple recall exercise is used here to demonstrate the constructed nature of memories and how they can diverge significantly from actual events.

A Demonstration of Point of View and Memory

Activity Type: Demonstration

Learning Objective: Encourage students to question the everyday assumptions that memory is a passive recording and that simple episodic memories are almost always accurate.

Faculty Note: Students are simply asked to remember the last occasion on which they went swimming. Some will remember swimming from the same visual perspective they had at the time of the event (i.e., from a "first-person" perspective). Many people, however, "remember" the event as if they were spectators, outside their bodies watching themselves. In other words, they "remember" the event from a perspective they could not have had.

This may provide a vivid and personal example of the transformations which memories sometimes undergo, and of the sometimes automatic assumptions we make concerning the reliability of memories.

Additional Resources:

Both this demonstration and the déjà vu demonstration the precedes it attest to the constructed nature of many of our memories. Perhaps the hottest current debate in the memory literature is about the false memory syndrome and repression. Elizabeth Loftus' *Skeptical Inquirer* article entitled "Remembering Dangerously" can be found at http://www.csicop.org/si/9503/memory/html

Rapid Review 4

Quick Quiz

CHAPTER 7

COGNITION & INTELLIGENCE

- **Chapter Overview**
  Learning Objectives
  Chapter Outline

- **Additional Lecture Ideas**
  Lecture Topics
  Additional Readings

- **In-Class Activities and Demonstrations**
  Activities and Demonstrations
  Sources for Additional Activities

- **World Wide Web**

- **Audio-Visual Support**

- **Handout and Transparency Masters**

Chapter Overview

Learning Objectives

After studying this chapter, you should be able to do the following:

1. Describe how concepts relate to behavior.

2. Explain how concepts are formed.

3. Identify strategies for understanding information.

4. Describe how concepts are used in problem solving.

5. State how psychologists define and measure intelligence.

6. Discuss the interpretations and implications of cultural, racial, and gender differences in intelligence tests scores.

7. Describe how heredity and the environment affect intelligence.

8. Describe creative thinking from a psychological perspective.

Chapter Outline

Cognition & Intelligence

I. Cognition
    A. **Definition**: cognition is the gathering, storing, retrieving, and using of information

II. Concepts: The Building Blocks of Our Thoughts
    A. **Concepts:** the mental categories or underlying ideas we use to think about and remember situations, ideas, objects, and qualities
        1. help us interpret stimuli, think efficiently, form impressions, determine behavior options
    B. **Concept Formation**
        1. critical features model: a way of explaining the formation of concepts that states that a stimulus must have particular characteristics to fit the concept of an object, event, person, quality, or idea
        2. prototype model: concepts are based on an example that is most typical, has most of the characteristics of members of the concept, or is the most memorable member of the category
        3. resembles-an-instance model: a new stimulus is compared with various instances of a concept and if it is sufficiently similar to an instance it is regarded as part of the concept
    C. **Similar Concepts**
        1. across cultural, gender, SES, some concepts are similar: e.g., time, primary/secondary colors

III. Information-Processing Strategies: Using Concepts to Think
    A. **Assimilation vs. Accommodation**
        1. assimilation: interpreting new stimuli in terms of existing concepts; doggie/cow example
        2. accommodation: changing concepts to fit new stimuli; small dog/big dog example
        3. effect of situation, person's values, personality, & motives on assimilation v. accommodation
    B. **From the Bottom Up or the Top Down**
        1. bottom-up information processing: collecting bits of information and then forming an overarching concept
        2. top-down information processing: when concepts and expectations affect which stimuli (data) are noticed, how they are organized and interpreted

C. Differences in Thinking Processes
1. <u>basic idea</u>: people think differently because they use these processes differently (i.e., individual differences emerge).
2. <u>differences due to concept accessibility</u>: people differ in concepts accessible to them due to recency, frequency, vividness of previous experience, expectation (e.g., ***representativeness heuristic***), emotional defense, mood states. Accessibility may affect personal actions as well as impressions of others, judgments about likelihood of events (e.g., ***availability heuristic***).
3. <u>differences due to cognitive structure</u>: people differ in ways in which concepts are organized and connected to other concepts. As a result, affects what information is sought, noticed, assimilated, & remembered as well as the meaning attached to information.
    a. individuals' personality, ability to tolerate ambiguity, openness to complexity affects organization
4. <u>cultural perspectives on the concepts we form</u>: cross-cultural differences emerge with respect to which concepts/schemas formed, degree of accessibility and representativeness. May reflect cultural needs and values.
5. <u>racial perspectives on the concepts we form</u>: people in different racial groups may form and use different concepts/schemas regarding themselves and others from different groups. <u>Example</u>: in-group/out-group distinctions

D. Conceptual Barriers to Problem Solving
1. <u>basic ideas</u>:
    a. processes we use may act as barriers when over-used or used in inappropriate situations.
    b. concepts we use may be restrictive in problem solving attempts (e.g., functional fixedness).

E. Using Cognitive Strategies to Solve Problems
1. <u>mental imagery</u>: solving a problem by cognitive visualization of the problem and its possible solutions. Example: using a cognitive map to help find our way around some physical environment.
2. <u>algorithms</u>: cognitive strategy that considers all possible solutions to a problem in systematic, step-by-step manner; always produces a solution but may not be efficient. Example: long division steps.
3. <u>heuristics</u>: selective problem-solving strategies based on previous experience or knowledge that may or may not lead to a solution.
    a. <u>working backwards</u>: working back from the goal to determine steps to it.
    b. <u>analogies</u>: comparing a current situation/problem with a previous situation.
    c. <u>means-ends analysis</u>: breaking down a problem into small problems or subgoals.

IV. Intelligence: Finding Smart Solutions

A. Definitions of Intelligence: ability to adapt successfully to the environment by using cognitive processes to guide behavior.

1. good judgment: good sense, practical sense, initiative, the faculty of adapting one's self to circumstances.
    a. Binet's three processes: facing problems and identifying the correct solution; monitoring solution progress; modifying solution as needed.
2. general intelligence: Terman said intelligence = single, measurable capacity for abstract thinking; Spearman found evidence of high correlations between subscales of intelligence and coined the term *g-factor*, indicative of general intelligence
3. multiple intelligences: Gardner (1996) proposes 7 types of intelligence encouraged/discouraged by culture.
    a. linguistic: ability to write and speak
    b. logical-mathematical: ability to solve abstract problems
    c. spatial: ability to analyze spatial relationships
    d. interpersonal: ability to understand other people
    e. intrapersonal: ability to know one's self
    f. body-kinesthetic: ability to use one's body to solve problems
    g. musical: ability to understand, create, perform music
4. triarchic theory of intelligence: Robert Sternberg's theory that intelligence includes academic, experiential, and practical intelligences that develop and decline as people age.
5. critiques of multiple and triarchic intelligence theories:
    a. need further empirical study
    b. no standardized, commercially available tests for measurement

B. Measuring Intelligence

1. what psychologists do: generally operationally define intelligence in terms of individuals' performance on tests
2. group intelligence and aptitude tests: often are multiple-choice tests administered to large groups of people for efficiency and cost control
    a. issues noted: group testing may limit some students to certain career or academic opportunities; aptitude tests differ from intelligence tests in that the former are designed to predict ability to learn specific sets of occupational skills whereas the latter measure a broader range of skills and are less affected by training.
3. the Stanford-Binet intelligence scale: Terman's adaptation of Binet's original intelligence test that measures intelligence via performance on verbal and performance tasks appropriate to an age range.
    a. critique: because most tasks require verbal skills, the test tends to underestimate cognitive abilities of examinees who have limited English language skills.

4. <u>the Wechsler intelligence scales</u>: three versions (one for adults, two for children) of intelligence test with greater balance between performance and verbal skills.
5. <u>the I.Q.(Intelligence Quotient) score</u>: I.Q. = MA/CA x 100
    a. <u>MA or mental age</u>: the age level determined by individual's performance on test
    b. <u>CA or chronlogical age</u>: actual age
    c. <u>IQ of 100</u> = mental age is the same as chronological age
    d. score indicates a person's ability relative to others in age group.
    e. <u>deviation score</u>: score that reflects an examinee's performance in comparison to the average performance of people of same age.
6. <u>extreme I.Q. scores</u>: tests are designed so that most people score around 100.
    a. <u>intellectually gifted</u>: people whose I.Q. scores are in the top 2-3% of the population; effects of giftedness (e.g., social, educational, occupational success).
    b. <u>mentally retarded</u>: people whose I.Q. scores are in the bottom 2-3% of the population; effects of mental retardation (e.g., labeling)

C. Evaluating Intelligence Tests: when are results of intelligence tests meaningful?
1. <u>reliability</u>: predictable (consistent) results; <u>example</u>: retest reliability = similar results on multiple testing times.
2. <u>validity</u>: the test measures what it was intended to measure
    a. <u>criterion validity</u>: test score is related to a behavioral measure of the attribute.
    b. <u>content validity</u>: test items reflect the attribute
3. <u>standardization</u>: examinees receive same instructions, time limits, test conditions, and materials. Tests are scored according to the same criteria.
4. <u>cultural perspectives on intelligence tests</u>:
    a. tests contain material that is culturally specific, which places persons from different cultures at a disadvantage.
    b. culture influences tests because responses may reflect values of culture not ability to think.
    c. need to develop culturally fair tests

D. Differences in Intelligence
1. <u>racial differences</u>:
    a. <u>controversy</u>: Jensen's argument of racial differences in intelligence based on heritability estimates; counterargument = intelligence differences as measured by heritability estimates underestimate environmental differences between racial groups.
2. <u>gender differences</u>: three male/female differences noted = speech fluency, mathematics, visual-spatial tasks.
    a. <u>causes</u>: motivational differences, play experience, levels of sex hormones (testosterone/estrogen)

3. <u>hereditary differences</u>: limitations of genes (possible range of intelligence) vs. limitations of environment (determine how close people come to reaching full potential).

4. <u>environmental differences</u>: effects of environmental enrichment; school & playground environment; poverty

V. Creativity: Generating Novel Ideas
A. Definition
1. <u>creativity</u>: thinking that produces constructive, meaningful, and original ideas
2. <u>creative thought</u>: incorporates originality, fluency, flexibility
3. <u>Alternate Uses test</u>: ways to use a brick
   a. originality = unusual uses
   b. fluency = number of uses
   c. flexibility = variety of uses suggested

B. Creative Processes
1. <u>generating novel ideas</u>: the importance of knowledge and expertise in generating novel ideas (i.e., more knowledge, more concepts = more ideas).
   a. <u>divergent thinking</u>: a process that facilitates creativity via exploring apparently unrelated ideas and alternative solutions to problems; involves flexible organization of concepts
   b. "sudden" insights may be the result of years of incubation of ideas.
2. <u>evaluating ideas</u>: creative thinking involves analysis, questioning, examining assumptions
   a. positive correlation between creativity and intelligence **but** they are independent concepts.

B. Developing the Ability to Be Creative
1. <u>training in divergent thinking</u>: creativity can be learned/enhanced

Additional Lecture Topics

1. **Classic Studies: Born First, Born Smarter?:**

   Uba and Huang discuss genetic and environmental factors that contribute to intellectual development. Whereas they focus on enriched environmental factors, poverty, and inadequate schools/playgrounds in their presentation, other authors have contributed to the literature by suggesting that birth order within a family may also promote differential environmental influences on children's intellectual development. For example, in his book covering pivotal research conducted in psychology, Roger Hock provides a different perspective on intellectual development in his coverage of the intriguing work done by Zajonc and Markus (1975) that led to the formulation of their confluence theory on the relationships between birth order and intelligence.

   At the heart of their theory, Zajonc and Markus believed that (1) children develop greater intellectual capabilities if they grow up in an environment that provides more intellectual stimulation and (2) such stimulation is determined, in part, by the combined intellectual influences occurring between parents and children in the household. They proposed that the intellectual environment within a household can be calculated by averaging the intellectual contributions of all family members. For example, suppose a couple had one newborn child. Presumably, the parents would contribute more to the intellectual climate than would the infant. Using arbitrarily assigned point values reflecting those differential intellectual contributions, the intellectual environment for this family could be calculated using the following formula: mother (100) + father (100) + infant (0)/number in family (3) = 200/3 = 67.

   As the child ages and as additional children enter the family, the formula and resulting average intellectual climate changes. If the same family has another child in two years, for example, the formula is adjusted to reflect the increasing intellectual contribution of the first child by adding 5 points per year and includes the zero contribution of the second born infant (e.g., m (100) + f (100) + first child (10) + second child (0)/number in family (4) = 210/4 = 52.5). In short, the average intellectual climate actually declines with the addition of another child to the household. Generally speaking then, Zajonc and Markus offered that, as family size increased, the average intellect decreased, and that the effect was particularly pronounced in the case of families with children born at close intervals.

   Zajonc and Markus applied and supported their theoretical propositions in a reconsideration of research data collected in the 1960s and 1970s by Belmont and Marolla (1973). Their study was designed to investigate the effects of malnutrition on intellectual abilities of over 350,000 male 19-year-olds who had been born toward the close of World War II in the Netherlands. Part of their findings had revealed a significant relationship between intelligence scores on the Raven test and birth order such that as intelligence declined with family size and birth order. Zajonc and Markus explained those findings with their theoretical model concerning the intellectual climate within the family environment.

Two other findings from the Belmont and Marolla study received particular attention by Zajonc and Markus. First, based on the general premises of the confluence theory, one might expect that only children would have scored the highest on the Raven, but this was not consistent with the finding in Belmont and Marolla (1973). They had found that, in a family of four, only children scored at the same intelligence level as first-born children. Second, in large families (i.e., those with five or more children), intelligence scores tended to level off or increase slightly in latter born children, with the exception of the last born child, whose score tended to drop off significantly. Zajonc and Markus addressed the only-child and last-child effects within the context of the confluence theory by "looking for factors in the intellectual environment that might be similar for the only child and the last child" (pg. 148). They noted that, in both cases, these children never had the opportunity to act as "teachers" to siblings, and apparently this opportunity contributes to intellectual development.

Hock notes two implications discussed in Zajonc and Markus' research: one directed toward parents planning the birth interval between children, the other focused on understanding trends in intellectual abilities as measured by the Scholastic Aptitude Test (SAT). Regarding the first, Hock writes, "the authors themselves acknowledge that they have presented a parents' dilemma. Obviously it would be best for the first-born child if a second child arrived after only a short gap, since this would reduce the time that the first child would suffer from the lack of teaching opportunity (the "last-child effect"). However, the second child would then enter an inferior intellectual environment. It would be better for the second child to arrive after the longest possible gap, but this increases the "last-child" handicap for the first child. For larger families, the researchers draw the conclusion that longer gaps are generally beneficial. However (and there is always a "however"), as the gaps get larger, siblings end up spending less time together because they share fewer interests, and the older children leave home earlier in the lives of their younger siblings."

Regarding the latter, Zajonc and Markus link changes in national averages on SAT scores to their confluence concept. Again from Hock, "prior to 1980, this country saw a decline in high school students' average scores on the Scholastic Aptitude Test (SAT). After 1980 the scores began to rise. Zajonc, along with other researchers in the field, explained these trends based on the effects of birth order as follows: Prior to 1980, more later-born children were taking the test. During the 1980s the first-born children of the parents from the "baby-boom" generation reached high school age and began to take the SAT. The model developed by Zajonc and Markus predicts that SAT scores will continue to rise until approximately the year 2000, when they will level off and then begin to decline again as a greater number of later-borns are included in the average scores (Zajonc, 1986)."

Hock notes that Zajonc and Markus are not claiming that family size and birth order are the only determinants of intellectual capabilities, but rather that they are part of the larger scope of multiple factors (including genetic heritage, child-rearing practices, prenatal care, educational experience, etc.) that combine to affect intellectual development. It should be pointed out that critics of the confluence theory have argued that the Raven scores of first born children in 2-children families are only 5 points higher than those of last-born children from 9-children families. The practical, everyday significance of this difference may have little effect on people's lives. Nevertheless, Zajonc and Markus's confluence theory has influenced the literature and represents an environmental influence not discussed by Uba and Huang.

Sources:
Zajonc, R. & Markus, G. (1975). Birth order and intellectual development. Psychological Review, 82, 74-88.

Hock, R. (Ed.) (1992). Forty studies that changed psychology: Explorations into the history of psychological research (pg. 143-150). Englewood Cliffs, NJ: Prentice Hall.

2. **Stereotypes, Intellectual Identity, and Performance**:
When considering gender and ethnic differences in academic performance in general, or performance on standardized achievement tests in particular, what factors influence successful academic performance and shape one's intellectual identity within an academic setting? While Uba and Huang generally focus our attention on theory and research concerning the impact of biology, gender roles, inadequate schooling, and poverty, Claude Steele suggests that, in some individuals, *stereotype threat*, or "the social psychological threat that arises when one is in a situation or doing something for which a negative stereotype about one's group applies" (pg. 203) has a significant negative impact on educational outcome (such as performance on standardized tests) and achievement. His theory begins with the central assumption that sustained academic success in school occurs when an individual holds school achievement as an important part of his or her self-definition. Moreover, he notes that, to identify with academic achievement, "one must perceive good prospects in the domain, that is that one has the interests, skills, resources, and opportunities to prosper there, as well as that one belongs there, in the sense of being accepted and valued in the domain." (pg. 203). Historically, he argues, socioeconomic disadvantages, segregating social beliefs & practices, and pervading cultural beliefs (e.g., negative stereotypes concerning intellectual capability and appropriate role-related behaviors) have served to limit the development of identification with school achievement in some groups of people. Generally speaking, for example, he suggests that African Americans and women have had to contend with negative stereotypes regarding their intellectual abilities - broadly across scholastic domains for African Americans, and particularly in the math and physical science domains for women. Thus, these forces may act as general barriers in the development of a self-identity including scholastic and/or domain-specific achievement (e.g., "Doing well in school or doing well in math is an important part of who I am.").

While acknowledging the importance of scholastic identification as a foundation to academic achievement, the primary focus of Steele's work is centered on investigating the effects of negative stereotypes on individuals who are already self-identified with academic achievement. Some of the research conducted by Steele and his colleagues concerning this phenomenon may be of particular interest when discussing performance on achievement tests with your students. A brief overview on stereotype threat is necessary before covering the findings. As mentioned previously, Steele believes that negative stereotypes concerning the intellectual abilities of African Americans and women may influence the process of self-identifying with academic achievement. If an individual has overcome these stereotypes and become identified with academic achievement, however, negative stereotypes may still influence academic performance. For example, he notes that "if the threat is experienced in the midst of a domain performance--classroom presentation or test-taking, for example--the emotional reaction it causes could directly interfere with performance. My colleagues and I have tested this possibility with women taking standardized math tests and African Americans taking standardized verbal tests" (pg. 204).

In these studies, Steele and his colleagues argue that stereotype threat represents a situational threat "cued by the mere recognition that a negative group stereotype could apply to oneself in a given situation," and "the situational relevance of the stereotypes is threatening because it threatens diminishment in a domain that is self-definitional" (pg. 211). They propose, then, that situational stereotype threat affects only those students who identify with the academic domain. In short, activating a negative stereotype regarding performance interferes more with the performance of domain-identified students than it would for non-domain-identified students. In an empirical test of this hypothesis, Spencer, Steele, & Quinn (1997) matched male and female college sophomores with respect to high math skills and strong mathematics identification. In other words, good math performance was an important skill for both groups, and the participants were equally advanced in their skills. Spencer et al. then gave each group math problems from the advanced math General Records Examination (GRE) and found that, compared to the male participants, the female participants underperformed on these questions. In the same experiment, male and female participants matched on literature skills and tested with an advanced literature test produced equal performance outcomes. The researchers concluded that the negative stereotype pertaining to women's' math performance expectations affected their performance in the experiment. They provided an even more convincing demonstration of this interpretation in a later experiment in which they told some participants that the tests were known to produce gender differences (i.e., that women tended to not do as well as men on the test). Math-skilled female participants who had been given stereotype information underperformed significantly more than males who received the same information. Male and female participants who had not received this information performed equally well. Since all participants were equally skilled in mathematics, the researchers argued that the underperformance of the first group of females was related to pressure stemming from the activation of the negative stereotype regarding women's performance in mathematics.

Using a similar method and research design, the impact of stereotype threat on test performance in African Americans was demonstrated in a study conducted by Joshua Aronson and Steele (C. M. Steele & Aronson, 1995). Black and White participants from a highly selective university were administered questions from the verbal GRE exam. Some participants were told the test was ability diagnostic (i.e., indicative of intellectual ability), and some were not. As was the case in the study concerning women in mathematics, these researchers found that the Black participants in the ability diagnostic condition underperformed on the test relative to participants in the White ability-diagnostic and no information groups. In this study, they also demonstrated that stereotype threat had been activated by having participants engage in a word completion task that indicated the Blacks in the ability-diagnostic group were more likely to complete the task with negative, stereotype-related words than were Blacks in the no information group. Thus, they argued that stereotype threat had been activated in this group and that it negatively influenced GRE test responses.

In relating the impact of stereotype threat to group performance/differences on standardized tests, Steele states "inherent to the science of quantifying human intelligence is the unsavory possibility of ranking societal groups as to their aggregated intelligence. ...To the set of possible causes for these group differences, our findings add a new one: the differential impact of stereotype threat on groups in the testing situation itself. Thus, stereotype threat may be a possible source of bias in standardized tests, a bias that arises not from item content but from group differences in the threat that societal stereotypes attach to test performance" (pg. 222).

Source:
    Steele, C. (1998). A threat in the air: How stereotypes shape intellectual identity and performance. In J. Eberhardt & S. Fiske (Eds.), <u>Confronting racism: The problem and the response</u> (pgs. 202-233). Thousand Oaks, CA: Sage.

3. **Culture and the Cultural Construction of Intelligence**:

In his Introductory Psychology text, Robert Sternberg provides an excellent discussion and overview of anthropological models of intelligence, emphasizing definition and measurement issues concerning intelligence from the contextualistic perspective. Anthropological, contextualist theories of intelligence investigate intelligence, assuming that (1) one cannot understand this human phenomenon outside of the real-world context in which it occurs, (2) intelligence is "inextricably linked" to culture, and (3) intelligence is a phenomenon created by a culture to help define adaptive performance and explain differences in performance between different people on culturally-valued tasks.

Defining intelligence. Sternberg notes: "People in different cultures may have quite different ideas of what it means to be smart" (pg. 366). One intriguing study that exemplifies this point was conducted by Cole et al. (1971). Using a word sorting task similar to those used in intelligence tests, these authors noted that intelligence level predicts differences in word sorting strategies used by Western participants; participants with higher levels of intelligence sorted words in a hierarchy (e.g., grouping different types of fish together under the main heading of "fish"), whereas those participants with lower intelligence levels sorted words according to function (e.g., fish are to eat). When these researchers conducted a similar sorting task in a cross-cultural sample consisting of adults from the Kpelle tribe in Africa, they found that these participants sorted the words by function and not by hierarchy, even when encouraged to do so. One frustrated researcher asked a participant to sort the words as a foolish person might, and the participant demonstrated the "foolish" strategy of hierarchical sorting. These authors concluded that functional sorting relates more to everyday styles of thinking and problem solving, whereas hierarchical sorting, as tested in intelligence tests, results from demands in the testing situation learned in Western-style schooling. The Kpelle, though capable of hierarchical sorting, did not view it as relevant to everyday intelligent thinking styles and needs within their cultural context.

In his overview, Sternberg also points to the collected work of Robert Serpell, a psychologist whose work has focused on the sociocultural factors influencing cognitive development and intelligence. Sternberg notes, "According to Serpell (1994), the language, legacies, needs, and beliefs of a society combine to form a culturally appropriate conception of intelligence" (pg. 367). Whereas the traditional Western conception of intelligence focuses on cognitive skills, the Chi-Chewa community in Zambia conceptualize intelligence or *nzelu* as consisting of "wisdom, cleverness, and responsibility within the Zambian cultural context" (pg. 367). As a result of this view of intelligence, "Zambian schoolchildren learn to value a much broader notion of intelligence and may be expected to demonstrate a broader range of behaviors that would be deemed intelligent within their culture" (pg. 367). In addition to this example, which emphasizes cultural definitions of intelligence via the shared systems of meanings associated with the concept of intelligence, and thus, intelligent behavior, it is also important to note that Serpell, in a recent chapter in the text *Psychology and culture*, envisions that culture influences the construction of intelligence in two additional ways: by serving as the nurturing environment in which children learn and play according to the materials locally available to them, and thus develop their intellect; and as the forum through which "alternative approaches to the definition and measurement of intelligence are debated" (Serpell, 1994; pg. 158). In summarizing the importance of culture in the construction of intelligence, Serpell says, "Culture structures the effective opportunities for intellectual development, defines the goals of socialization, and constitutes the context within which the definition of goals and opportunities for attaining them is debated among the people who collectively own, belong to, and construct that culture" (pg. 163).

Measuring intelligence. Given that different cultures vary in their beliefs about what constitutes intelligence, and these differences result in different behavioral expressions of intelligence, these issues take on central importance when deciding how to measure intelligence. As do Uba and Huang, Sternberg points out that debates on the cultural validity of intelligence test questions have arisen in response to observations that people of various ethnic and immigrant groups have historically scored lower than Caucasian groups on standardized measures of intelligence, and that those differences have been attributed to the effects of heredity or other nonenvironmental factors (i.e., Goddard, 1917; Jensen, 1969). Such biologically-/evolutionary-based arguments fly in the face of observations by some researchers that IQ scores in such groups have increased with cultural assimilation, changes in educational opportunity/expectations, sociopolitical changes (c.f., Ceci, 1996).

As noted in Uba and Huang, one response by the measurement community has been to attempt the development of *culture-fair tests*. As Sternberg points out, however, creating a culture-fair test becomes complicated by differing cultural definitions and expressions of intelligent behaviors/responses. Moreover, the testing situations themselves may reflect a culture's underlying beliefs about intelligence. Case in point: "Consider, for example, the concept of mental quickness. In mainstream U.S. culture, quickness is usually associated with intelligence. To say someone is "quick" is to say that the person is intelligent, and indeed, most group tests of intelligence are quite strictly timed... In many cultures of the world, however, quickness is not at a premium. In these cultures, people may believe that more intelligent people do not rush into things....In other words, the smart person is someone who does not rush into action but thinks first. Even in our own culture, no one will view you as brilliant if you decide on a marital partner, a job, or a place to live in the 20 to 30 seconds you might normally have to solve an intelligence-test problem. So, is it culturally fair to include a speed or timing component in an intelligence test?....at present and for the foreseeable future, there are no perfectly culture-fair tests of intelligence. Even among the tests devised to date, performance on those tests that have been labeled as "culture-fair" seems to be influenced to some degree by cultural factors, such as years of schooling and academic achievement" (pg. 368). In light of such criticisms of even this attempt, another alternative might be to construct *culture-*

relevant tests that "employ skills and knowledge that relate to the cultural experiences of the test-takers" (pg. 368).

Source:
  Serpell, R. (1994). The cultural construction of intelligence. In W. Lonner & R. Malpass (Eds.), <u>Psychology and culture</u> (pg. 157-164). Boston: Allyn and Bacon.
  Sternberg, R. (1998). <u>In search of the human mind (2nd Ed.),</u> (pg. 366-370). Fort Worth, TX: Harcourt Brace.

4. **<u>Culture and Problem Solving:</u>**
  Uba and Huang present students with examples of how different methods of processing information can present barriers in problem-solving activities. In his text integrating the traditional perspectives typically studied in Introductory Psychology with relevant results obtained from cross-cultural psychology, David Matsumoto addresses the topic of problem solving. In a brief overview, problem solving is defined as those processes "by which we attempt to discover ways to achieve goals that do not seem readily attainable" (pg. 57). Moreover, people engage in different problem solving strategies depending on the nature of the problem with which they are confronted. For example, problems related to structure lead people to engage in attempts to "discover relationships among the various components or elements involved in the problem" (pg. 57). Problems concerning arrangement focus people on discovering how the components or elements of the problem are to be arranged to best address it. Finally, problems of transformation require people to uncover a sequence of steps necessary to solve the problem. Thus, research often attempts to discover how people select and use these different strategies and what factors influence problem solving skills. From the traditional perspective, problem solving difficulty may be linked to the presence of irrelevant information, misapplying mental sets or solutions from similar problems encountered in one's past, or functional fixedness. To demonstrate several ways in which cultural influences affect problem solving and cross-cultural research efforts, Matsumoto reviews examples of two commonly studied phenomena: sequential problem-solving tasks and verbal word problems using syllogisms.

  According to Matsumoto, cross-cultural studies of logic and problem-solving skills, esp. those conducted in naturalistic settings, are at greater risk for confounded explanations. Watching people in everyday problem solving tasks does not tell the researcher whether differences in outcomes are due to differences in logic use or differences in cultural backgrounds. In attempts to eliminate the problem of confounding, therefore, psychologists have moved problem-solving tasks into artificial settings (i.e., the laboratory). Such efforts have not been without their own sources of cultural bias, however. As an example, he reviews a study conducted by Cole and his colleagues in 1971. To obtain a prize, American and Liberian participants of various ages were to complete a 2-step problem-solving task involving pressing the correct button on a machine-like apparatus to obtain a marble, and then placing the marble in a slot in the apparatus to open a panel concealing the prize. Age differences in problem solving abilities were noted for American participants; Americans over 10 yrs. of age were able to complete the task, whereas those under 10 yrs. had difficulty. At the same time, Liberian participants of all ages found the task difficult to complete. Is one to conclude from these data that cross-cultural differences in advanced problem solving capabilities and the use of logic exist? Matsumoto writes: "this experiment may have been biased toward the Americans, despite its apparent objectivity. That is, the American subjects may have benefited from the hidden advantage of living in a technological society. As Americans, we are accustomed to mechanical devices; buttons, levers, dials, and slots on machines are common in our daily environment. But, in some non-Western cultures, people seldom operate machines, and the unfamiliarity of the apparatus may have influenced the outcome by intimidating or bewildering the Liberian subjects" (pg. 58). Indeed, in a second study using materials more familiar to Liberian participants, participants obtained the prize if they could remember which of several keys opened a lock on the box containing the prize and which of several matchboxes contained the correct key. More Liberian participants successfully solved this task. Results from a third study, which required participants to obtain the key from the original machine-like apparatus, mimicked the first study; again, Liberian participants had difficulty solving the problem. Cole et al. concluded that problem-solving skill (i.e., the ability to reason logically) is linked to context. To test for logic skills, then, researchers must ensure that problem-solving tasks used in their studies are presented in such a manner that concepts and materials used are already familiar to research participants. When confronted with strange, "wholly unfamiliar concepts and technology", participants respond with utter confusion and may, in fact, become "visibly frightened by the tests that employed the strange apparatus."

In exploring the use of verbal problems to assess logic and problem-solving skills, Matsumoto notes that some studies have used syllogisms as part of their methodology (e.g., "all children like candy; Mary is a child; does Mary like candy?"). For example, Luria (1976) found cross-cultural differences in responses to syllogisms such as these, and his interpretation was that such differences were influenced, not by cross-cultural differences in logic capabilities, but rather by number of years of Westernized schooling. Luria and others have hypothesized that illiterate peoples (i.e., those without education) actually think differently regarding logic questions because "logical reasoning is essentially artificial, because it is a skill that must be learned in a Westernized school setting" (pg. 59). In a study investigating factors related to why uneducated people have difficulty with logic-based, verbal problems, Scribner (1979) found that these individuals explained their seemingly illogical responses by citing evidence from personal experience. Apparently, it is not that these individuals lack forms of logical reasoning; instead, Matsumoto claims "they do not understand the hypothetical nature of verbal problems. People who have attended school have had the experience of answering questions posed by an authority who already knows the correct answers. Uneducated people, however, have difficulty understanding that questions need not be requests for information. Schooling seems to affect people's ability to solve verbal problems because in a school setting people become accustomed to answering questions that would be silly in most social settings. They also are trained to respond in a particular way to the authority figures--teachers--in the school setting. Students learn about matters beyond their own everyday experience and are coerced into remembering and using what they have learned in ways that are very similar to experimental tasks used by psychologists" (pg. 60).

Matsumoto's examples demonstrate the importance of cultural context, explain why schooling influences logic/problem-solving strategies, and sensitize students to these issues as they relate to research on problem solving.

Source:

Matsumoto, D. (1994). People: Psychology from a cultural perspective (pg. 57-61). Pacific Grove, CA: Brooks/Cole.

Suggestions for Additional Readings

Adams, J. (1991). Conceptual blockbusting. New York: Norton.

Anderson, J. (1990). Cognitive psychology and its implications. San Francisco: W. H. Freeman.

Ashcraft, M. (1993). Human memory and cognition. New York: HarperCollins.

Beirne-Smith, M., Patton, J., & Ittenbach, R. (1994). Mental Retardation. New York: Macmillan.

Bell, D., Raiffa, H., & Tversky, A. (Eds). Decision-making: Descriptive, normative, and prescriptive interactions. Cambridge: Cambridge University Press.

Berry, J., & Dasen, P. (Eds.) Culture and cognition. London: Methuen.

Best, J. (1992). Cognitive psychology. St. Paul, MN: West.

Bolton, N. (1977). Concept formation. Oxford: Pergamon Press.

Cole, M., Gay, J., Glick, J. A., & Sharp, D. (1971). The cultural contest of learning and thinking: An exploration of experimental anthropology. New York: Basic Books.

Cole, M., & Scribner, S. (1974). Culture and thought: A psychological introduction. New York: John Wiley.

Fraser, S. (Ed.) (1995). The bell curve wars: Race, intelligence, and the future of America. New York: Basic Books.

Gardner, H. (1993). Multiple intelligences: The theory in practice. New York: HarperCollins.

Gardner, H. (1994). Creating minds: An anatomy of creativity seen throughout the lives of Freud, Einstein, Picasso, Stravinsky, Eliot, Graham, and Gandhi. New York: Basic Books.

Gardner, H., & Hatch, T. (1989). Multiple intelligence go to school: Educational implications of the theory of multiple intelligences. Educational Researcher, 18, 4-10.

Goleman, D., Kaufman, P., & Ray, M. (1992). The creative spirit. New York: Dutton.

Halpern, D. (1996). Thought and knowledge: An introduction to critical thinking. Mahwah, NJ: Erlbaum

Herrnstein, R., & Murray, C. (1994). The bell curve: Intelligence and class structure in American life. New York: The Free Press.

Klahr, D. & Kotovsky, K. (Eds.) (1989). Complex information processing: The impact of Herbert A. Simon. Hillsdale, NJ: Erlbaum.

Luria, A. (1976). Cognitive development: Its cultural and social foundations. Cambridge, MA: Harvard University Press.

Piaget, J. (1973). The child and reality: Problems of genetic psychology. New York: Viking Press.

Rosenthal, R., & Jacobson, L. (1968). Pygmalion in the classroom: Teacher expectations and intellectual development. New York: Holt, Rinehart, & Winston

Scribner, S., & Cole, M. (1981). The psychology of literacy. Cambridge, MA: Harvard University Press.

Sternberg, R. & Davidson, J. (1982). The mind of the puzzler. Psychology Today, June.

Sternberg, R. (1988). The triarchic mind. New York: Viking.

Sternberg, R. (1996). Successful intelligence: How practical and creative intelligence determine success in life. New York: Simon & Schuster.

Stievater, S. (1985). Bibliography of recent books on creativity and problem solving. Supplement XXIII. The Journal of Creative Behavior, 4, 276-282.

Tversky, A., & Kahneman, D. (1980). Causal schemas in judgments under uncertainty. In M. Fishbein (Ed.), Progress in social psychology (Vol. 1). Hillsdale, NJ: Erlbaum.

Tversky, A., & Kahneman, D. (1973). Availability: A heuristic for judging frequency and probability. Cognitive Psychology, 5, 209-232.

In-Class Activities and Demonstrations

1. **TRAIL Blazing**: Using **Transparency Masters 7.1 - 7.6**, review with students the "Checking Your TRAIL" sections in the chapter. Have students work in small groups to answer the questions and then review with the class as a whole to tie the text reading to activity in class.

2. **Reaching Critical Mass**: Using **Transparency Masters 7.7 - 7.9**, review with students the "Critical Thinking" sections in the chapter. Have students work in small groups to answer the questions and then review with the class as a whole to tie the text reading to activity in class.

3. **Getting Down to IT**: Using **Transparency Masters 7.10 - 7.15**, review the "Integrative Thinking" sections in the chapter with students. Have students work in small groups to answer the questions and then review with the class as a whole to tie the text reading to activity in class.

4. **Emotional Intelligence**: Daniel Goleman describes emotional intelligence as a new concept that has emerged from a contemporary, multifaceted view of intelligence. Defined as "abilities such as being able to motivate oneself and persist in the face of frustrations; to control impulse and delay gratification; to regulate one's moods and keep distress from swamping the ability to think; to empathize and to hope, the concept of emotional intelligence reflects a theoretical expansion of Gardner's model of multiple intelligences and incorporates emotions as they relate to most closely to Gardner's interpersonal and intrapersonal intelligences. Emotional intelligence focuses on five basic domains: self-awareness or knowing one's emotions, managing one's emotions, motivating oneself by "marshaling emotions in the service of a goal", empathy or recognizing emotions in others, and handling relationships or social competence. According to Goleman, IQ and EQ are separate competencies. Men and women high in emotional intelligence are described as "socially poised, outgoing and cheerful, not prone to fearfulness or worried rumination, capacity for commitment to people or causes, for taking responsibility and for having an ethical outlook, they are sympathetic and caring in their relationships. Their emotional life is rich, but appropriate; they are comfortable with themselves, others, and the social universe they live in....Their social poise lets them easily reach out to new people; they are comfortable enough with themselves to be playful, spontaneous, and open to sexual experience" (pg.45). Use **Handout Master 7.1** to allow students to calculate their levels of emotional intelligence.

Answers:

1. Anything but D, which reflects a lack of self-awareness (A,B,C = 20)

2. B. Emotionally intelligent parents use such moments to help children understand what made them upset, what they are feeling, and what they can do about it. (B = 20)

3. A. Emotionally intelligent people can use their emotions to motivate themselves to face challenges and overcome obstacles. (A = 20)

4. C. Rather than giving up, blaming oneself or getting discouraged, seeing a setback as a challenge is a mark of emotional intelligence. (C = 20)

5. C. The manager of an organization plays an important role in defining the norms of the group. Publicly stating what is and is not tolerated in the group is the most effective way to encourage respect in the group. (C = 20)

6. D. Shifting the person's attention from the focus of the rage, empathizing, and suggesting an alternative way of seeing the situation are all effective strategies in calming rage. (B = 5; C = 5; D = 20)

7. A. Taking a time out allows for the physiological arousal of anger to subside. With increased calm, clearer thinking and better communication are possible. (A = 20)

8. B. Groups work most creatively when people feel a comfortable rapport with one another. This allows for a freer expression of ideas. (B = 20)

9. D. Manageable challenges for the child will encourage an increasing sense of social competence (D = 20)

10. B. Moderate challenges help keep frustration low and motivation high due to pleasures associated with accomplishment. (B = 20)

What the scores mean:
- 200 - Emotional Genius
- 150 - Highly empathic
- 100 - Average
- 50 - Emotionally challenged
- 0 - Neanderthal

Sources:
  Goleman, D. (1995). "What's Your Emotional Intelligence Quotient?" Utne Reader, 72, 74-76.
  Goleman, D. (1995). Emotional intelligence: Why it can matter more than IQ. New York: Bantam.

5. **Concept Learning**: This exercise was originally developed and presented by Ludy Benjamin in the *Activities handbook for the teaching of psychology,* and is outlined here with some minor modifications to his recommended procedures. The activity provides students with the opportunity to experience the processes involved in learning and applying a new concept. Students will be presented with overheads of 6 trials consisting of 12 Greek-letter trigrams. The concepts to be learned are that phi (Φ) equals false and theta (Θ) equals true. Begin the exercise by telling students that they are going to participate in a concept-learning task and that their task is to decide which trigrams are true and which are false. Using overheads made from **Transparency Masters 7.16-7.23** and **Handout Master 7.2**, proceed through each trial by pointing to the trigram at the beginning of the list, give the students approximately 5 seconds to decide T/F, and then place their answers on the handout. After students have marked their answer, tell them whether the trigram is true or false and then go on to the next trigram on the list for that trial. Benjamin suggests conducting 8 12-trigram trials, but points out that fewer trials may be conducted if less time is available. To complete the exercise, have students decide if the last trigram ($\Delta\Theta\Phi$) is true, false, or ambiguous and then ask, by show of hands, how many students answered T, F, or ambiguous. Benjamin notes that usually there will be students who raise their hands for each answer. In discussing the exercise, ask students what concepts they believe they learned. Benjamin predicts that you will have some students who learn only one concept (either that Φ is false or Θ is true). Those students will probably answer the last trigram as either true or false depending on the one concept they learned. Other students will have learned both concepts as evidenced by their answer that the last trigram was ambiguous (either T or F). Benjamin offers that the exercise is helpful in discussing the learning curve for concepts (i.e., more students will correct T/F responses across the 8 trials) as well as providing the opportunity to discuss different strategies or false hypotheses attempted by students in learning the concept. Some discussion of learning concepts from unfamiliar stimuli (such as people might when unfamiliar with a new culture) might link the exercise with the text discussion of cultural influences on concept learning.

Source:
>Benjamin, L. (1994). Concept learning. In L. Benjamin & K. Lowman (Eds.), <u>Activities handbook for the teaching of psychology</u>. Washington, DC: American Psychological Association.

6. **Problem solving: Groups vs. Individuals**: During everyday activities, problem solving may be attempted by individuals working alone or in collective, group efforts. The following exercise, developed by McKeachie

and his colleagues (McKeachie, Doyle, and Moffett, 1994), introduces students to the study of problem solving, and is designed "to help students explore some of the variables that affect the relative problem-solving capabilities of individuals and groups" (pg. 92). Begin the activity outlined on **Handout Master 7.3** by having students count off by 2s. All students who count 1 are to further split into groups up to 5-6 members; students who count 2 are to work on the exercise by themselves. Students earn 1 point each for the number of ball players correctly identified plus 1 point for each 30-second interval below the 20-minute time allotment. McKeachie et al. (1994) suggest that the exercise is effective when discussing why individuals vs. groups work more effectively on a problem. They note that groups are more effective at solving problems that require a "correct answer or clever contribution, because the probability is greater that a group will contain an expert than that an individual will be an expert." Groups are also helpful when estimates are part of the problem-solving efforts (i.e., some people may over-estimate whereas others underestimate, thus producing a group average more likely to be close to reality). Group *size* might also contribute to an effective outcome. If a task requires that members' contributions be added together, some loss of effort occurs, so that at some point the loss of contribution with added members equals the potential gain from those members. Efforts to counter the loss of contribution in large groups would be needed for effective problem solving. McKeachie et al. note that individuals are more likely to be effective at tasks that would be slowed down by the least able people in group efforts. Your students might also consider how familiarity with such tasks and cultural relevance could affect their problem-solving skills in this example.

Source:
   McKeachie, W., Doyle, C., and Moffett, M. (1994). Problem solving: Groups versus individuals. In L. Benjamin & K. Lowman (Eds.), Activities handbook for the teaching of psychology. Washington, DC: American Psychological Association.

7. **Cognitive Maps:** Renfro and Hardwick describe cognitive or mental maps as part of "a social constructivist theoretical approach to meaning making", and suggest that cognitive maps consist of a mind's eye picture of how a "human reads physical or spatial environment(s) based on individual experiences and cultural backgrounds" (pg. 200). Cognitive maps are defined as "an organized representation of part of the spatial environment which is filtered throughout the individual's experience-based values, biases, interests, and sense of self" (pg. 200). The following exercise is a variation of several they suggest for classroom use to help students learn how they perceive and understand their physical environment through their individual and cultural experiences. To conduct

this activity, have students draw a map of their college campus using **Handout Master 7.4**. After students have completed their maps, place an overhead transparency of the campus map (found in most college booklets) and discuss with them how their maps reflect cultural and gender influences and individual values/needs/experiences (i.e., what buildings stood out in the drawing? which were omitted? which buildings/structures remembered reflect cultural values?). Have students compare their maps to observe individual differences in their drawings and discuss some possible sources for those differences. Renfro and Hardwick also suggest that this exercise becomes more powerful by using overhead transparencies of maps taken from the following texts to illustrate some various forms of cultural and gender influences on mean-making in cognitive maps.

Suggested texts for maps:
- neighborhood maps drawn by a boy and a girl:
    Matthews, H. (1988). Gender and geography. The Geographical Magazine, 60, 47-49.
- a medieval conception of the universe:
    Spielvogel, J. (1994). Western civilization. St. Paul, MN: West Educational.
- cognitive sit maps of Los Angeles by different groups:
    Downs, R., & Stea, D. (1973). Image and environment. New York: Aldine.

Source:
   Renfro, E., & Hardwick, S. (1994). Cognitive site mapping: Placing yourself in (con)text. In T. Singelis (Ed.), Teaching about culture, ethnicity, & diversity: Exercises and planned activities. Thousand Oaks, CA: Sage.

Sources for Additional Activities
Books:
   Benjamin, L. & Lowman, K. (1981). Activities Handbook for the Teaching of Psychology. Washington DC: American Psychological Association.
   Halonen, Jane 1995). Chapter 8: Thinking, language, and intelligence. In The Critical Thinking Companion For Introductory Psychology (Worth Publ.).
   Singelis, T. (1998). Teaching about culture, ethnicity, & diversity: Exercises and Planned Activities. Thousand Oaks, CA: Sage Publ.
   Makosky, V. et al. (Eds.) (1987). Activities Handbook for the Teaching of Psychology (Vol. II). Washington DC: American Psychological Association
   Makosky, V. et al. (Eds.) (1995). Activities Handbook for the Teaching of Psychology (Vol. III). Washington DC: American Psychological Association.
   McCormick, T. (1994). Creating the Nonsexist Classroom: A multicultural Approach. New York: Teachers College Press.

- **World Wide Web**: Check out the following WWW sites for information and activities relevant to this section of the text!
    - Psych Web -- **http://www.gasou.edu/psychweb/psychweb.htm**
    - Self-Quizzes for Introductory Psychology -- **http://www.gasou.edu/psychweb/selfquiz/selfquiz.htm**
    - Psychology Jumping Stand -- **http://www.indiana.edu:80/~iuepsyc/PsycJump.html**
    - The Psychology Place -- **http://www.psychplace.com**
    - Reviews of *The Bell Curve* -- **http://www.apa.org/journals/bell.html**
    - Sternberg's theory of intelligence and response to *The Bell Curve* -- **http://www.skeptic.com/03.3fm-sternberg-interview.html**
    - Theories of intelligence -- **http://www.gettysburg.edu/~arterber/psy101/intelligence1.html**
    - Discussion of theories of intelligence -- **http://www.valdosta.peachnet.edu/~whuitt/psy702/cogsys/intell.html**
    - Cognitive information processing -- **http://education.indiana.edu/~cep/courses/p540/coginfo.html**
    - Intellectual handicap -- **http:/www.massey.ac.na/~rchweb/mencur.htm**
    - IQ test -- **http://www.voicenet.com/~dmileaf/iq.htm**
    - IQ test -- **http://www.iqtest.com/**
    - Metacognition -- **http://www.valdosta.peachnet.edu/~whuitt/psy702/cogsys/metacogn.html**
    - Artificial intelligence -- **http://ai.iit.nrc.ca/misc.html**
    - Braintainment Center -- **http://www.brain.com**
    - Creativity Web -- **http://www.ozemail.com.au/~caveman/Creative/**
    - Intelligence Page -- **http://www.netlink.co.uk/users/vess/mensal.html**

- **Audio-Visual Support**
    ### Films/Videos:

    #### Overview
    - *Discovering Psychology: Cognitive Processes* (Annenberg, 30 minutes)
    - *Discovering Psychology: Judgment and Decision Making* (Annenberg, 30 minutes)
    - *The Mind: Thinking* (PBS, 60 minutes)

    #### Intelligence:
    - *The IQ Myth* (CBS, 50 minutes)
    - *Intelligence: A Complex Concept* (CRM, 28 minutes)
    - *Discovering Psychology: Testing and Intelligence* (Annenberg, 30 minutes)
    - *May's Miracle: A Retarded Child With the Gift of Music* (Filmakers, 28 minutes)

- *David: A Portrait of a Retarded Youth* (Filmakers, 28 minutes)
- *Age of Intelligent Machines* (AIMS, 29 minutes)

Creativity:
- *Creative Problem Solving* (CRM, 27 minutes)
- *Why Man Creates* (Pyramid, 25 minutes)
- *Problem-solving Strategies: The Synthetics Approach* (MCGH, 27 minutes)
- *Productivity and the Self-fulfilling Prophecy: The Pygmalion Effect* (CRM, 28 minutes)

Related Topics:
- *Breaking the Silence Barrier: Inside the World of Cognitive Disabilities* (FFHS, 57 minutes)
- *Autism: The Child Who Couldn't Play* (FFHS, 47 minutes)
- *Special Needs Students in Regular Classrooms? Sean's Story* (FFHS, 45 minutes)
- *Dyslexia: A Different Kind of Mind* (FFHS, 29 minutes)
- *Learning Disabilities* (FFHS, 19 minutes)
- *Animals: How Smart Are They?* (FFHS, 26 minutes)

Psychology Encyclopedia Laserdisc IV:
Still Images

Sound bite length	Frame 53530	Side all
Wechsler test performance tasks [1/5] [8.2]	53531	all
Wechsler test performance tasks [2/5] [8.2]	53532	all
Wechsler test performance tasks [3/5] [8.2]	53533	all
Wechsler test performance tasks [4/5] [8.2]	53534	all
Wechsler test performance tasks [5/5] [8.2]	53535	all

Transparency Master 7.1: Checking Your TRAIL 7.1

I. A prototypical example of a concept is:
   A. the most unusual example.
   B. the most typical and memorable example.
   C. the most vague example.
   D. the most colorful example.

II. Once you have the concept "bird," how do you decide that a particular creature is or is not a bird from the perspective of the critical features, prototype, and resembles-an-instance concept-formation models?

III. Why would several individuals, all using the critical features method of concept formation, differ in their concepts of "bird"?

IV. Why would individuals using the prototype method differ in their concepts of "bird"?

V. Why would people using a resembles-an-instance concept-formation model differ in their concept of "bird"?

VI. Name three seemingly universal concepts.

Transparency Master 7.2: Checking Your TRAIL 7.2

I. **Are you assimilating or accommodating in the following situations?**
   A. The results of a study contradict your beliefs or experiences. You critically assess the study and don't find any flaws, so you alter your belief.
   B. You recognize that a problem you are having with your boyfriend (or girlfriend) is like a problem you had with your brother (or sister).

II. Suppose you are trying to assemble a child's toy. You read the assembly instructions rather than just diving in and experimenting to see which pieces fit. Are you using a top-down or a bottom-up approach to your cognitive task?

III. **Which one of the following statements is true?**
   A. The same concepts are equally accessible for everyone.
   B. A person's mood has no bearing on which concepts become accessible to that person.
   C. A schema can affect what information a person notices and remembers.
   D. People who see themselves and other people in simple, rigid ways are unlikely to use stereotypes when characterizing other people.

IV. **True or False:** An Asian American is likely to see more variability among Asian Americans than is a Latino/a American because of differences in the way in-group and out-group members are perceived. For the same reason, Latino/a Americans are more likely to perceive differences among Latino/a Americans than Asian Americans are.

Transparency Master 7.3: Checking Your TRAIL 7.3

I. You recently had an argument with a co-worker and are now ready to interpret that co-worker's behavior in unfavorable ways. Your orientation reflects
   A. a means-end analysis.
   B. set.
   C. working backward.
   D. mental imagery.

II. You realize that a problem you are trying to solve is similar to another problem you successfully dealt with, so you decide to take the same approach to the current problem. Which problem-solving method are you using?
   A. mental imagery
   B. analogy
   C. working backward
   D. means-end analysis

III. You want to learn how automobiles work so you take one apart. Which method are you using to form your concept of how automobiles work?
   A. algorithm
   B. functional fixedness
   C. set
   D. working backward

IV. <u>True</u> or <u>False</u>: Heuristics eventually lead to a useful solution.

Transparency Master 7.4: Checking Your TRAIL 7.4

I. **Explain the difference between general intelligence and Gardner's concept of multiple types of intelligence.**

II. <u>**True**</u> **or** <u>**False**</u>**: According to the triarchic theory of intelligence, a person's academic intelligence determines the path his or her life will take.**

III. **As people age, particularly after 50, their _____ intelligence tends to decline, whereas their _____ intelligence remains stable.**

IV. **The top _____% of the general population are intellectually gifted and the bottom _____% of the general population are mentally retarded.**

Transparency Master 7.5: Checking Your TRAIL 7.5

I. **Explain standardization and identify at least two factors that are difficult for an examiner to standardize during a test situation.**

II. **If you used intelligence test scores to identify students who could perform well in school, you would be using academic performance as the _____ variable for testing the _____ of intelligence test scores.**
   A. standardizing
   B. validity
   C. reliability
   D. criterion

III. **Explain two ways in which intelligence tests can be culturally biased.**

IV. **What are the main gender group differences on intelligence test performance, and how do psychologists interpret them?**

Transparency Master 7.6: Checking Your TRAIL 7.6

I. Using the Alternate Uses Test as an example, explain flexibility, originality, and fluency in thinking.

II. The creative process generally involves two phases: (1) _____, and (2) _____.

III. Give three reasons why incubation might help the creative process.

IV. Describe two methods for increasing creativity.

Transparency Master 7.7: Critical Thinking 7.1

Based on what you have learned about what determines concept accessibility and the availability heuristic, why might some African Americans regard someone's behavior as disrespectful even when it wasn't intended to be disrespectful? Why might some European Americans think that members of racial minorities who are innocently walking down a street want to rob them?

Transparency Master 7.8: Critical Thinking 7.2

Sometimes a schema can function as a stereotype. For example, some people have the schema that stupid people don't speak in a normal way. So when they hear a deaf person having difficulty enunciating, they mistakenly assume that he or she is stupid. In terms of assimilation, why do they do so and what implication does this schema have for attitudes toward people who speak English with an accent?

Transparency Master 7.9: Critical Thinking 7.3

What are three reasons unrelated to intelligence that could explain why an individual with limited English skills might perform poorly on the Stanford-Binet Intelligence Scale?

Transparency Master 7.10: Integrative Thinking 7.1

Consider the example of the little girl who mistakes a cow for a doggie (pg. 711). In light of what you read in the Learning chapter, in order for the girl to learn that a cow isn't a dog, does she need to generalize, discriminate, or be shaped?

Transparency Master 7.11: Integrative Thinking 7.2

Based on what you read in the Learning chapter, explain learned helplessness in terms of assimilation.

Transparency Master 7.12: Integrative Thinking 7.3

Different concepts help us to describe and explain behavior and mental activities from alternative perspectives. Recalling the Consciousness chapter's discussion of deja vu, explain deja vu in terms of schema.

Transparency Master 7.13: Integrative Thinking 7.4

Recall the limitations of interpreting correlations described in the Introductory chapter. Given these limitations, how should you interpret the modest correlation between intelligence test performance and occupational success?

Transparency Master 7.14: Integrative Thinking 7.5

As discussed in the Introductory chapter, psychological research tends to focus on group differences in order to identify principles of behavior. What are two important dangers in focusing on group differences in intelligence test performance?

Transparency Master 7.15: Integrative Thinking 7.6

Recall the memory strategies described in the Memory chapter. Describe three that you could use to remember creative ideas from a dream.

Transparency Master 7.16: Concept Learning

Trial 1

ΑΒΘ ___

ΔΕΦ ___

ΓΦΔ ___

ϑΘΒ ___

ΜΝΦ ___

ΠΘΡ ___

ΦΤΥ ___

ΘΩΞ ___

ΨΖΘ ___

ΔΟΦ ___

ΘΕΩ ___

ΚΧΦ ___

Transparency Master 7.17: Concept Learning

Trial 2

ΓΗΘ ___

ΚΟΦ ___

ΛΝΦ ___

ΣΩΘ ___

ΜΖΘ ___

ΩΕΦ ___

ΠΟΦ ___

ΡΠΦ ___

ΑΒΘ ___

ΨΙΦ ___

ΞΨΘ ___

ΚΞΘ ___

Transparency Master 7.18: Concept Learning

Trial 3

KNΦ ___

ΦΣΔ ___

PEΘ ___

IΦΔ ___

MΘB ___

YΘΨ ___

ΠΞΦ ___

KBΘ ___

ςΘZ ___

ΦXΔ ___

ΘBΞ ___

HΦΔ ___

Transparency Master 7.19: Concept Learning

Trial 4

ϑΨΘ ___

ΑΝΦ ___

ΘΒΑ ___

ΚΘΕ ___

ΦΛΑ ___

ΨΦΞ ___

ςΘΜ ___

ΣΣΦ ___

ΗΘΣ ___

ΠΡΘ ___

ΜΦΕ ___

ΦΦΦ ___

Transparency Master 7.20: Concept Learning

Trial 5

AΘA ___

ΔMΦ ___

ΦΔΩ ___

ϑΘB ___

MNΦ ___

EΘP ___

ΦNE ___

ΘΩΞ ___

ΨZΘ ___

ΔOΦ ___

ΘEΩ ___

ΦKΞ ___

Transparency Master 7.21: Concept Learning

Trial 6

ΘΝΘ ___

ΛΟΦ ___

ΖΝΦ ___

ΣΘΠ ___

ΝΘΠ ___

ΞΕΦ ___

ΠΟΦ ___

ΡΠΦ ___

ΑΒΘ ___

ΨΙΦ ___

ΞΨΘ ___

ΚΞΘ ___

Transparency Master 7.22: Concept Learning

Trial 7

ΞΦΦ ___

ΦΣΔ ___

ΡΕΘ ___

ΙΦΔ ___

ΜΘΒ ___

ΥΘΥ ___

ΤΞΦ ___

ΓΘΚ ___

ΜΘΖ ___

ΔΦΧ ___

ΘϑΞ ___

ΗΦΔ ___

Trial 8

ϑΨΘ ___

ΔNΦ ___

ΘΩA ___

ΘME ___

ΔΦΛ ___

ΩΦΞ ___

ΠΘM ___

ΣΦZ ___

KΘΣ ___

ΠPΦ ___

MΦE ___

ΘΘΘ ___

Handout Master 7.1: Emotional Intelligence

Emotional Intelligence

Instructions: While there is as yet no single well-validated test for emotional intelligence, the following questions will give you a rough sense of your EQ. Answer the following questions honestly, on the basis of what you really would be most likely to do.

1. You're on an airplane that suddenly hits extremely bad turbulence and begins rocking from side to side. What do you do?
   a. continue to read your book or magazine, or watch the movie, paying little attention to the turbulence.
   b. become vigilant for an emergency, carefully monitoring the flight attendants and reading the emergency instruction card.
   c. a little of both a and b.
   d. not sure; never noticed.

2. You've taken a group of 4-year-olds to the park, and one of them starts crying because the others won't play with her. What do you do?
   a. stay out of it; let the kids deal with it on their own.
   b. talk to him and help him figure out ways to get the other kids to play with him.
   c. tell him in a kind voice not to cry.
   d. try to distract the crying boy by showing him some other things he could play with.

3. Assume you had hoped to get an A in one of your courses, but you have just found out you got a C on the midterm. What do you do?
   a. sketch out a specific plan for ways to improve your grade and resolve to follow through on your plans.
   b. resolve to do better in the future.
   c. tell yourself it really doesn't matter much how you do in that particular course, and concentrate instead on other classes where your grades are higher.
   d. go to the professor and try to talk her into giving you a better grade.

4. Imagine you are an insurance sales representative calling prospective clients. Fifteen people in a row have hung up on you, and you are getting discouraged. What do you do?
   a. call it a day and hope you have better luck tomorrow.
   b. assess qualities in yourself that may be undermining your ability to make a sale.
   c. try something new on the next call, and keep plugging away.
   d. consider another line of work.

5. You are a manager in an organization that is trying to encourage respect for racial and ethnic diversity. You overhear someone telling a racist joke. What do you do?
   a. ignore it--it's only a joke.
   b. call the person into your office for a reprimand.
   c. speak up on the spot, saying that such jokes are inappropriate and will not be tolerated in your organization.
   d. suggest to the person telling the joke he go through a diversity training program.

6. You are trying to calm down a friend who has worked himself up into a fury at a driver in another car who has cut dangerously close in front of him. What do you do?
   a. tell him to forget it; he's okay now and it's no big deal.
   b. put on one of his favorite tapes and try to distract him.
   c. join him in putting down the other driver, but exaggerate your reaction.
   d. tell him about a time something like this happened to you and how you felt as mad as he does now, but then you saw the other driver was on the way to a hospital emergency room.

7. You and your boyfriend or girlfriend have gotten into an argument that has escalated into a shouting match; in the heat of anger, you are both making personal attacks you don't really mean. What's the best thing to do?
   a. take a 20-miute break and then continue the discussion.
   b. just stop the argument--go silent, no matter what your partner says.
   c. say you're sorry and ask your partner to apologize too.
   d. stop for a moment, collect your thoughts, then state your side of the argument as clearly as you can.

8. You have been assigned to lead a work group that is trying to come up with a creative solution to a nagging problem at work. What is the first thing you do?
   a. draw up an agenda and allot time for discussion of each item so you make best use of your time together.
   b. have people take the time to get to know each other better.
   c. begin by asking each person for ideas about how to solve the problem, while ideas are fresh.
   d. start with a brainstorming session, encouraging everyone to say whatever comes to mind, no matter how wild.

9. Imagine that you have a 5-year-old son who is extremely timid, and has been hypersensitive about--and a bit fearful of--new place and people since he was born. What do you do?
   a. accept that he has a shy temperament and think of ways to shelter him from situations that would upset him.
   b. take him a child psychiatrist for help.
   c. purposely expose him to lots of new people and places so he can get over his fear.
   d. engineer an ongoing series of challenging but manageable experiences that will teach him he can handle new people and places.

10. For some time now, you have been wanting to get back to playing the musical instrument you learned to play when you were younger. You have finally gotten around to practicing again, and want to make the best use of your time. What do you do?
    a. hold yourself to a strict practice time every day.
    b. choose pieces that stretch your abilities a bit.
    c. practice only when you are really in the mood.
    d. pick pieces that are far beyond your ability, but that you can master with diligent effort.

Handout Master 7.2: Concept Learning

Concept Learning

Instructions: Your task in the following exercise is to determine the concept or rule being used to determine that each of the Greek-letter trigrams listed is either true or false. At the beginning of each trial, your instructor will place a list of the trigrams on the overhead projector. Starting at the beginning of the list, decide if you think the trigram is **true** or **false**. Wait for your instructor to tell you the correct answer before moving to the next trigram for that trial. After completing all three trials, consider the last trigram at the bottom of the page and determine if it is true, false, or ambiguous.

Trial 1	Trial 2	Trial 3	Trial 4
ΑΒΘ __	ΓΗΘ __	ΚΝΦ __	ϑΨΘ __
ΔΕΦ __	ΚΟΦ __	ΦΣΔ __	ΑΝΦ __
ΓΦΔ __	ΛΝΦ __	ΡΕΘ __	ΘΒΑ __
ϑΘΒ __	ΣΩΘ __	ΙΦΔ __	ΚΘΕ __
ΜΝΦ __	ΜΖΘ __	ΜΘΒ __	ΦΛΑ __
ΠΘΡ __	ΩΕΦ __	ΥΘΨ __	ΨΦΞ __
ΦΤΥ __	ΠΟΦ __	ΠΞΦ __	ςΘΜ __
ΘΩΞ __	ΡΠΦ __	ΚΒΘ __	ΣΣΦ __
ΨΖΘ __	ΑΒΘ __	ςΘΖ __	ΗΘΣ __
ΔΟΦ __	ΨΙΦ __	ΦΧΔ __	ΠΡΘ __
ΘΕΩ __	ΞΨΘ __	ΘΒΞ __	ΜΦΕ __
ΚΧΦ __	ΚΞΘ __	ΗΦΔ __	ΦΦΦ __

Trial 5	**Trial 6**	**Trial 7**	**Trial 8**
ΑΘΑ ___	ΘΝΘ ___	ΞΦΦ ___	ϑΨΘ ___
ΔΜΦ ___	ΛΟΦ ___	ΦΣΔ ___	ΔΝΦ ___
ΦΔΩ ___	ΖΝΦ ___	ΡΕΘ ___	ΘΩΑ ___
ϑΘΒ ___	ΣΘΠ ___	ΙΦΔ ___	ΘΜΕ ___
ΜΝΦ ___	ΝΘΠ ___	ΜΘΒ ___	ΔΦΛ ___
ΕΘΡ ___	ΞΕΦ ___	ΥΘΥ ___	ΩΦΞ ___
ΦΝΕ ___	ΠΟΦ ___	ΤΞΦ ___	ΠΘΜ ___
ΘΩΞ ___	ΡΠΦ ___	ΓΘΚ ___	ΣΦΖ ___
ΨΖΘ ___	ΑΒΘ ___	ΜΘΖ ___	ΚΘΣ ___
ΔΟΦ ___	ΨΙΦ ___	ΔΦΧ ___	ΠΡΦ ___
ΘΕΩ ___	ΞΨΘ ___	ΘϑΞ ___	ΜΦΕ ___
ΦΚΞ ___	ΚΞΘ ___	ΗΦΔ ___	ΘΘΘ ___

What concept or rules are being used to determine whether a particular trigram is true or false? _____

Is this trigram true, false, or ambiguous?

ΔΘΦ ___

Handout Master 7.3: Group vs. Individual Problem Solving

Problem Solving

Instructions: Your task is to solve the following problem within a 20-minute time limit.

Nine men play the positions on a baseball team. Their names are Brown, White, Adams, Miller, Green, Hunter, Knight, Smith, and Jones. Determine from the following information the position played by each man.

a. Brown and Smith each won $10 playing poker with the pitcher.
b. Hunter is taller than Knight and shorter than White, but each weighs more that the first baseman.
c. The third baseman lives across the corridor from Jones in the same apartment house.
d. Miller and the outfielders play bridge in their spare time.
e. White, Miller, Brown, the right fielder, and the center fielder are bachelors, and the rest are married.
f. Of Adams and Knight, one plays an outfield position.
g. The right fielder is shorter than the center fielder.
h. The third baseman is a brother of the pitcher's wife.
i. Green is taller than the infielders and the battery (i.e., the pitcher and catcher), except for Jones, Smith, and Adams.
j. The second baseman beat Jones, Brown, Hunter, and the catcher at cards.
k. The third baseman, the shortstop, and Hunter made $150 each speculating in General Motors stock.
l. The second baseman is engaged to Miller's sister.
m. Adams lives in the same house as his sister but dislikes the catcher.
n. Adams, Brown, and the shortstop lost $200 each speculating in grain.
o. The catcher has three daughters, the third baseman has two sons, but Green is being sued for divorce.

Answers:

_____ : pitcher   _____ : catcher
_____ : first base   _____ : second base
_____ : third base   _____ : shortstop
_____ : left field   _____ : center field
_____ : right field

Handout Master 7.4: Cognitive Maps

Cognitive Maps

Instructions: From memory, draw a map of the college campus in the space below.

CHAPTER 8

DEVELOPMENT FROM BIRTH THROUGH CHILDHOOD

- **Chapter Overview**
    Learning Objectives
    Chapter Outline

- **Additional Lecture Ideas**
    Lecture Topics
    Additional Readings

- **In-Class Activities and Demonstrations**
    Activities and Demonstrations
    Sources for Additional Activities
    Journey II Software

- **World Wide Web**

- **Audio-Visual Support**

- **Handout and Transparency Masters**

Chapter Overview

Learning Objectives

After studying this chapter, you should be able to do the following:

1. Identify general similarities and differences in prenatal development.

2. Describe sensory and physical development in young children.

3. Identify reasons for infant-parent attachment.

4. Describe cognitive development in children.

5. Compare two models that describe the development of moral reasoning.

6. Explain the development of gender identity and sex-typed behaviors.

Chapter Outline

Development From Birth Through Childhood

I. **How We Develop: Similarities and Differences**
   A. **The Nature of Development**
      1. gradual and continuous: growth/development is a cumulative process.
      2. according to stages: development reflects a series of stages/periods that involve different developmental tasks or challenges that most people face.

II. **Prenatal Development: Similar Paths, Different Influences**
   A. **Definitions**
      1. prenatal period: stage of development from conception to birth
         a. conception: sperm fertilizes an egg.
         b. zygote: the fertilized egg
         c. dyzygotic vs. monozygotic twins: fraternal (2 eggs with different sperm) vs. identical (egg/sperm pair that splits) twins
   B. **Similarities in Prenatal Development**
      1. gestation: the term for prenatal development
      2. maturation: genetically determined timing of physical development
      3. germinal period: the first gestational period which lasts the first two weeks after conception, marked by multiplication of cells and the zygote attaching to the walls of the uterus
      4. embryonic period: the second gestational period from two to eight weeks after conception marked by the formation of the placenta and beginnings of spinal cord, head, blood vessels, face, organs, and limbs
      5. fetal period: the third gestational period from approximately two months after conception until birth marked by development of increasingly complex structures and movement; discussion of neuronal development
   C. **Differences in Prenatal Development**
      1. prematurity: birth occurring prior to 38 weeks gestation that puts baby at greater risk of illness
      2. hormones: sex hormones during embryonic period, esp. the presence of androgens, determine external sex characteristics and some sex differences in brain structure; discussion of effects of differential exposures to sex hormones (e.g., bisexuality & homosexuality)
      3. chemicals and infections: exposure to teratogens (such as aspirin, tetracycline, alcohol, cocaine) or infections (e.g., HIV, rubella, syphilis) may result in birth defects or miscarriage
         a. Fetal Alcohol syndrome: physical and mental defects caused by maternal alcohol abuse
      4. socioeconomic perspectives: poverty is associated with prenatal complications (often due to poor prenatal care) and affects physical and psychological development (e.g., malnutrition-related growth impairments)

III. Infants and Toddlers: New Contacts with the World
A. Definitions
1. <u>infancy</u>: period from birth to approximately one year (when child begins walking)
2. <u>toddler period</u>: period between one to five years

B. Similarities in Sensation and Perception
1. <u>vision</u>: neonates extremely near-sighted and depth perception doesn't emerge until around six months; use of visual cliff in research on depth perception
2. <u>hearing</u>: research demonstrates that fetuses may respond to sound prior to birth; newborns suck pacifiers harder to stories heard while in mother; also recognize familiar voices and can localize sounds
3. <u>taste and smell</u>: newborns react differently to sweet, salty, and bitter solutions; can recognize mother's smell

C. Similarities in Physical Development
1. <u>congenital reflexes</u>: automatic behavioral responses occurring naturally at birth and shared by all members of a species if development is normal; help infant survive until learn needed behaviors and may disappear later
    a. <u>examples</u>: grasping, moro, rooting, stepping, sucking
2. <u>physical development</u>:
    a. three "rules" of physical development include:
        i. development progress from inner organs to extremities
        ii. control over large muscle movement precedes that of small muscle movement
        iii. development proceeds most rapidly in the head and gradually moves down the body
    b. continued development of head/muscles/bones after birth related to size of birth canal
    c. motor milestones are discussed
3. <u>cultural perspectives on motor development</u>:
    a. cultural factors that affect motor development
        i. cross-cultural differences in introduction of developmental tasks by parents
        ii. cultural practice of parenting and child care (e.g., carrying children on parents' backs strengthens muscles needed to sit/walk)

D. Temperamental Differences
1. <u>temperament</u>: baby's typical emotional reactions, moods, and energy level reflect genetic tendency or predisposition to behave in characteristic ways
2. <u>temperament types</u>:
    a. <u>easy</u>: cheerful/agreeable moods, relaxed and adaptable responses, predictable patterns of eating, sleeping, and eliminating; 40% of children are of this type
    b. <u>slow-to-warm</u>: shy behaviors, guarded expressiveness, slow adaptation to new situations/people; 15% of children

        c. <u>difficult</u>: intense emotional reactions, quick frustration, anger, unpredictable eating, sleeping, and elimination; 10% of children
        d. <u>remainder</u>: no consistent patterns; 35% of children
    3. temperament types may be biological/genetic in origin but reinforced or modified by environment

E. Psychosocial Development
    1. <u>definition</u>: the ability to form interpersonal relationships and interact with other people
    2. <u>Erikson's psychosocial stage model</u>:
        a. <u>psychosocial developmental crises</u>: resolution of which determine personality
        b. problem of culturally biased assumptions in the model
    3. <u>forming attachments</u>:
        a. <u>definition</u>: emotional, affectionate bonds with other people or animals
        b. <u>need for contact comfort</u>: Harlow's research with monkeys revealed the need for contact comfort; hugging, holding, touching increases attachment, rate of development, well-being
        c. <u>fear of desertion</u>: distress is demonstrated when left by attached caregivers; e.g., stranger and separation anxieties
        d. <u>the two-way bond</u>: bond between parent-child result of baby's physical attributes & congenital reflexes, processes of positive and negative reinforcement
        e. <u>attachment types</u>: work of Ainsworth and observing parent-child attachment relationships
            i. <u>secure</u>: 65% of relationships demonstrated attentive caregiver with child who showed distress in caregiver's absence but comforted by caregiver's return; child sought out caregiver
            ii. <u>ambivalent</u>: 10-15% of relationships involved semi-attentive caregiver with child showing distress in strange situation but seeking/anger behavior upon caregiver's return
            iii. <u>avoidant</u>: in 20-25% of relationships, caregiver demonstrated little/no affection and child showed little distress or interest in caregiver upon return
        f. <u>critique of attachment types research</u>:
            i. labels represent value judgments, bias
            ii. parent-child interactions aren't universal, cross-cultural
            iii. individualist vs. collectivist cultures place different values on independence/dependence
    4. <u>play</u>:
        a. for young children: play promotes development of motor coordination as well as bonds with parents (i.e., greater attachment and higher self-esteem) but occurs within cultural context of meaning

  b. for toddlers: often engage in solitary or parallel play
  c. for older children: play develops hand-eye coordination, muscular control and balance; burns off excess energy; promotes psychosocial development (e.g., getting along with others, learning rules for interaction)

IV. Childhood: Developing Mind and Identity
A. Cognitive Development
1. <u>Piaget's stage theory of cognitive development</u>: focus on how children understand environment
  a. <u>sensorimotor</u>: from birth to 2 yrs.; children learn from what senses tell them and the motor activities they perform
    i. <u>object permanence</u>: understanding that objects/people exist even if not seen or heard
  b. <u>preoperational</u>: 2-7 yrs.; haven't learned operations (ability to transform objects and reorganize thoughts)
    i. <u>egocentrism</u>: perception of situations and people from only one's own perspective coupled with the assumption that other people share that perspective
    ii. <u>lack conservation capabilities</u>: don't understand that a quantity stays the same even though presented in different arrangements, shapes, forms
    iii. <u>animism</u>: thinking that inanimate objects have feelings and act intentionally
    iv. increasing ability to <u>think using symbols</u> emerging
  c. <u>concrete</u>: 7-11 yrs.; thinking based on actual experiences and simple concepts
    i. reverse operations: e.g., addition/subtraction
    ii. classification of objects
    iii. thinking logically
  d. <u>formal</u>: 11 yrs.-adulthood;
    i. thinking about logical possibilities and using analogies
    ii. using deductive and inductive reasoning
    iii. comparison using abstract qualities
    iv. knowledge involves interpretation

2. <u>evaluating Piaget's model</u>:
  a. general support for model and sequence of progression through stages
  b. cross-cultural differences: the role of societal social experiences and skills
  c. not all people attain formal operational thought; may occur more in scientific, industrialized societies due to nature of schooling

B. The Development of Moral Reasoning
1. <u>moral reasoning</u>: thinking about right/wrong; reflects psychosocial and cognitive development
2. <u>Piaget's ideas</u>: thinking about right/wrong dependent on good/bad results or outcomes

3. <u>Kohlberg - levels of moral reasoning</u>: concerned with underlying reasoning for moral judgments; studied through use of moral dilemmas
    a. <u>preconventional</u>: first level of moral reasoning in which morality is judged in terms of the practical consequences (punishment or rewards) of one's actions
    b. <u>conventional</u>: second level of moral reasoning in which behavior considered moral as long as it conforms to societal rules and other people's expectations
    c. <u>postconventional</u>: third level of moral reasoning in which behavior is judged in terms of one's own moral principles and conscience while considering the different needs and concerns of everyone involved in a moral dilemma
4. <u>Gilligan - weighing justice and care</u>: thought Kohlberg's model emphasized fairness, justice, rights but valued collectivist concerns about responsibilities for others to lesser extent (i.e., justice orientation); proposed care orientation as reflecting female socialization
5. <u>critically analyzing the two models</u>: empirical evidence lacking for male=justice, female=care differences; type of moral reasoning varies with nature of moral decision and social roles

C. Developing a Self-Concept
1. <u>self-concept</u>: a sense of own unique personality, behavior, appearance, abilities, and worth
2. <u>basis of self-concept</u>: one basis of self-concept is how other people view us (e.g., society/media representations of minorities)
3. <u>developing gender identity</u>: person's sense of being female or male
    a. <u>gender constancy</u>: learning that sex doesn't change; perception that is limited in preoperational thought children
    b. <u>sex-typed behaviors</u>: the behaviors, skills, and interests that a culture considers more appropriate for one sex than for the other (e.g., playing with trucks for males, dolls for females); affected by parental treatment, ethnic culture, physiological differences in genes/hormones
4. <u>developing sex-typed behaviors</u>: how are sex-typed behaviors learned
    a. <u>cognitive-developmental theory</u>: develop gender identity first, then conclude behaviors associated with own gender are good
    b. <u>social learning theory</u>: acquire sex-typed behaviors via observational learning and conditioning
    c. <u>gender-schema theory</u>: notice certain behaviors generally performed by one sex; develop a concept of sex-typed behaviors; compare self to concept; alter attitudes, appearance, behaviors, personality to conform to concept

D. Socioeconomic Perspectives on Childhood
1. <u>effects of poverty</u>: inadequate housing, increased vulnerability to crime related to feelings of isolation/low self-concept
    a. parenting styles may reflect need for greater obedience for protection sake; results in emotional/behavioral effects on children

Additional Lecture Topics

1. **Universality of Moral Development Across Cultures:**

    Lutz Eckensberger, a German psychologist who currently studies and writes on the Kohlbergian theory and methods concerning moral development, has been actively studying cross-cultural psychology since the mid 1960s. His focus in his work has been upon testing the cross-cultural universality of Kohlberg's stage model. In a recent article, Eckensberger discusses a number of issues concerning the cross-cultural application and tests of the theory that would be relevant for discussion in culturally-inclusive General Psychology courses.

    First, he notes that Kohlberg actually startled relativistic social sciences with the claim that moral reasoning was not culturally relativistic. The more common belief among relativists was that cultures were indeed different in behaviors that would be considered both appropriate or inappropriate, right or wrong and that socialization processes were the vehicles for learning appropriate modes of moral conduct. When Kohlberg argued that peoples from different cultures developed moral reasoning according to the same sequence of stages, the universal perspective, cross-cultural tests and criticisms of his assertions concerning both theory and method began. Indeed, Eckensberger suggests that cross-cultural investigation has been critical to addressing questions concerning the generality and differential development of the stages or moral reasoning (i.e., Is there universal invariance in the sequence of stages in moral reasoning? Do all stages occur in all cultures? Do stages development at different rates due to cultural factors?).

    In his overview and analysis of results from over fifty cross-cultural studies, (not exhaustive but have included cultures from around the globe), Eckensberger points out that Stages two, three and four are often present in many cultures and general consistency in stage sequencing tends to occur. Thus, Kohlberg's universality assumption receives basic support. However, the impact of culture appears to manifest itself with respect to the following observations.

    - Using moral dilemmas: In many cross-cultural studies, researchers have generally used Kohlberg's nine moral dilemmas with only minor adaptations (e.g., name changes for the actors involved.) Critics have offered that, because the dilemmas were developed and originally applied in research in the West, both cultural and gender bias may emerge. Eckensberger notes that the dilemmas, as they were originally developed, were never intended to prompt respondents to consider the situations within particular cultural contexts but rather were "intended to trigger general 'moral arguments' about what people should do *ideally*." (pg. 75). Moreover, attempts to make culturally-relevant adaptations have produced contradictory findings ranging from no differences to significant differences from typical findings. Thus, Eckensberger argues that a minimum requirement for using moral dilemmas is that the facts contained within the dilemmas be understood by and represent a genuine moral conflict for the respondents -- "one that is as equivalent as possible across cultures" (pg. 75).

- Scoring responses: Over the years, Kohlberg and his associates developed a scoring manual based on response types noted in research conducted in the United States. In cross-cultural research, Eckensberger notes, responses may not correspond to those listed in the scoring manual, and thus researchers find "it is often necessary to 'detect' the underlying moral structure of an argument which is not contained in the scoring manual's compendium of examples." Sensitivity to this potentially problematic aspect of assessment is necessary for the cross-cultural researcher.

- Developmental antecedents to moral reasoning: A number of environment/social factors appear to contribute to movement across the stages of moral reasoning. For example, socioeconomic status and education level have been found to affect movement across stages transculturally. Additionally, religiousness, living condition, experiences outside of the family, child-rearing practices, and orientation towards others may influence moral reasoning. Eckensberger concludes this discussion by noting that a cultural complexity distinction rather than a Western/nonWestern distinction most likely accounts for the cross-cultural differences in moral reasoning trends that have been found, and argues that this type of distinction is consistent with the central premises of Kohlberg's theory.

- Universality of moral themes: Kohlberg originally claimed not only universal similarity in moral reasoning structure but also that types of moral issues were universal. Recent studies have challenged this belief, finding cultural differences in moral themes or issues of concern (e.g., the moral perspective of nonviolence prevalent in India; filial piety and collective utility in traditional Chinese moral reasoning).

Source:
Eckensberger, L. H. (1994). Moral development and its measurement across cultures. In W. Lonner & Malpass, R. (eds.), Psychology and culture. (pg. 71-78). Boston: Allyn and Bacon.

2. **Values and Culture:**

To extend discussion/lecture on moral and self-concept development, introduce students to a consideration of values; their own and the role of culture in the development of their value system. Norman Feather (1994) suggests that, although the study of similarities and differences in cultural values has been a central topic to cross-cultural psychologists, special problems concerning definition and measurement require thoughtful consideration. Because of their subjective and abstract nature, values are often difficult to define...certainly they are more difficult to define than are simple, observable behaviors. Moreover, issues of reliability and validity are particularly significant in the development of values tests.

Definitions of values tend to include structural as well as functional components: what they are and what they do. Values, as described by Feathers, "involve general beliefs about desirable or undesirable ways of behaving and about desirable or undesirable goals or end-states" (pg. 184); they incorporate the dimension of *goodness, badness, oughtness* in evaluations of objects, actions, and events. They are assumed to be "core aspects of the self-concept and ...closely linked to our basic emotions" (pg. 184). They transcend our many specific attitudes, "but influence the form those attitudes take." Thus, like many of the cognitive structures discussed in the Cognition chapter, values focus our perception and interpretation of events and serve as behavioral guidelines. So central are values to our self-concept that when our values are affirmed, positive emotions emerge; when challenged or threatened, negative emotions emerge. In addition to the general influences of culture on value development and structure, the unique characteristics of one person's value system may vary developmentally with changes in age or as a function of gender, SES or individual personality.

To address measurement concerns, many researchers frequently rely on standard surveys developed to assess differences and similarities in value systems and types such as Rokeach's Value Survey (1973) and the Schwartz Value Survey (Schwartz, 1992). Aside from the survey approach, other researchers have attempted to measure the important values for a culture by content analysis of media presentations, literature & cultural myths; laws, rules & norms within a culture; language patterns. Feather cautions that, even if researchers are able to construct universal lists of values for use in their investigations, one must pay attention to the contextual meanings for values (i.e., does the same value mean something different from culture to culture perhaps because it coexists with or is intricately connected to other values within a particular culture). Thus, understanding a value system within a particular cultural context and determining functional equivalencies of a value across cultures are central tasks for the cross-cultural psychologist.

As seen thus far, cross-cultural studies have attempted to note similarities and differences across cultures in terms of the nature and importance of various value systems. Feather suggests that cross-cultural study of values should also consider the conditions under which some values are activated: what situational cues are likely to activate a value? Once activated, how will values reveal themselves in behavioral expression? Feather offers that strongly held values tend to be more easily accessible and may be cued by situational cues. Moreover, behavioral expressions of value systems may depend on situational constraints as well as expectations concerning the likelihood of positive or negative consequences of the behavior. According to Feather, continued cross-cultural research concerning differences and similarities in situational cues that activate values and affect their expression is needed.

Combine this lecture/discussion area with **Activity Handout # 8.2**, which requires students to assess media advertisements from men's and women's magazines to determine value systems being represented.

Source:
Feather, N. T. (1994). Values and culture. In W. Lonner & Malpass, R. (eds.), Psychology and culture. (pg. 183-190). Boston: Allyn and Bacon.

3. **Establishing the Developmental Niche:**
When scholars say that culture has a powerful effect on shaping an individual's behavior and thinking, it seems reasonable to ask the processes through which the influence process occurs. Super & Harkness (1994) have developed a framework for understanding human development within a cultural context, one that many students may find to be an effective organizational tool in their efforts to understand how individual personality, local customs, properties of the experienced environment, parental or caregiver beliefs, and larger societal influences all co-exist and interact in ways to affect development in an ongoing fashion.

The concept of the developmental niche stems from similar ideas in biological ecology concerning the interactive relationships between species of animals and their fit with their immediate living habitat. Different species and individual animals within a species, although living in the same area, utilize the environment differently, according to their own unique experiences and needs. In developing human beings, each child enters the world with his or her own unique temperaments and dispositions. The child is the central focus of the developmental niche framework. According to Super & Harkness, three major aspects of the child's culture surround him or her and will influence his or her development: the physical and social settings found in his or her everyday life, the customs observed pertaining to child care and child rearing, and the beliefs (or psychology) of his or her parents or caregivers. These three aspects comprise the developmental niche:

- *the physical/social setting*: Social setting refers to the people with whom the child is likely to interact; thus consideration of who those individuals are (i.e., parents, siblings, extended family members, community members) and the sheer number of social contacts should be considered. With respect to the physical setting, the living conditions, size and shape of the living space itself, proximity to others, placement of furnishings may serve as powerful influences on living patterns (such as eating and sleeping schedules).

- *customs of child care and child rearing*: Customs regarding appropriate, normative, or traditional ways to care for children may provide the framework for determining who expected to provide care. For example, child care may be provided by an older sibling or family members other than the parents (e.g., grandparents) in some cultures. Use of formal and informal daycare providers may be a prevalent practice. Customs concerning the methods involved in child care may involve, for example, using playpens to provide a safe environment or allowing the child to be a part of ongoing activities in the home or daycare. Super & Harkness note that not all customs regarding the care of children serve obviously discernable functions, but rather some customs are highly symbolic in their nature. One such example, they argue, is the practice of circumcision for male children for reasons other than hygiene. They note "to understand these customs of child care and child rearing, one needs to take into account cultural traditions related to spirituality and concepts of the person. Although these abstract dimensions of culture are difficult to describe, the study of customs which represent them can provide insights into the cultural ways of thinking that organize the lives of families and children."
- *caregiver beliefs or psychology*: Parental or caregiver beliefs and emotions about child care serve as the third component of the developmental niche. Super & Harkness state that these beliefs "underlie the customs of child rearing and validate the organization of physical and social settings of life for children." For example, in cultures where children sleep with or close to parents, parents may feel having a child sleep in a different room or not attending to a child who awakens in the night crying would constitute neglectful care giving. In other cultures, where children sleep in their own rooms or are taught to quiet themselves if waking in the night, these practices may be seen as fostering independence.

Super & Harkness believe that the three elements of the developmental niche surround the child and must interact flexibly with one another and the unique and changing characteristics of the child. For example, the nature of care for a particular child will require adaptations of child care customs, will need to meet the demands of a particular physical and social setting, and will need to fall within the range of acceptable beliefs for the caregivers. They note "the points of contact are somewhat flexible" and "the niche operates as a system, the semi-independent parts constantly influencing and adapting to each other." Moreover, as the child ages, the dynamics between the child and the developmental niche change owing to changes in his or her competencies and personality growth.

Lastly, these authors point out that the developmental niche is nestled within an even larger human ecology (society, cultural group), which also influences the nature of the child's development. Overarching traditional customs concerning conduct, societal economic conditions, and demographic variables may thus influence and change elements of the developmental niche. For example, changes in community or societal beliefs regarding children (such as the skills children may need to be competent adults in the future) may influence caregiver beliefs and customs of child rearing.

To return to the earlier question of how culture influences and has such a powerful effect on development, "it is clear that the cultural environment of the child is powerful not only because it is experienced during the formative years of life, but also because it constitutes an interactive system in which the same cultural messages are conveyed through a variety of modalities. Just as in language, where the same idea may be communicated through choice of words, grammatical structure and tone of voice, so in cultural environments the child may learn the same ways of thinking and acting through the physical and social settings of daily life, the customs in which he or she participates, and the expressions of parents' ideas that are conveyed in a variety of ways. Over the span of development, these messages become so internalized that they form the core of our understandings of the world and ourselves" (pg. 99).

Source:
Super, C. & Harkness, S. (1994). The developmental niche. In W. Lonner & Malpass, R. (eds.), Psychology and culture. (pg. 95-100). Boston: Allyn and Bacon.

4. **Culture and Cognitive Development:**
Pierre Dasen studied cognitive developmental psychology with Jean Piaget in Geneva and then spent a number of years testing Piaget's theory in Australia, Canada, Cote d'Ivoire, and Kenya. He considers Piaget to be nothing short of "a genius"..."at least we can say that without his many contributions, we would not have the same understanding of the cognitive development of humans" (pg. 145). Piaget considered his stage model of cognitive development to reflect universal trends in thinking processes. Testing this assumption has been a central task for cross-cultural psychologists. Are some aspects of the theory indeed universal? Are others culturally-dependent?

Dasen notes several points to bear in mind when considering cross-cultural tests of the theory: some relevant to the samples of children who were the basis for Piaget's original observations, others to the "clinical method" used to discern their cognitive processes. Concerning the first issue, Piaget developed his theoretical assumptions based on his observations of his own children and children in highly selective schools in Geneva (representing only roughly 5% of the population of children in that age range). Critics have questioned both the sample size involved as well as the combined effects of formal schooling and participant sampling biases. These biases produce problems in interpretation of results given that schooling, type of schooling, and age were confounded in these early studies. Cross-cultural studies were confronted with the task of unraveling the effects of schooling and cognitive development, a particularly challenging question when one considers that children are learning about testing procedures as well as new ways of conceptualizing the world via the educational process--all of which may affect results obtained in theory tests. Thus, cross-cultural research had to pay attention to questions such as how to test schooled and non-schooled children so as to be certain that sampling procedures were not biased and non-schooled children would be able to understand both the process and questions involved in the interview sessions.

In some of his own research, Dasen studied schooled 8-14-year-old children from nomadic Australian Aboriginal and Inuit groups, whose sustenance was based on hunting activities, and children from sedentary peoples in West Africa (the Ebri and the Baoule of Cote d'Ivoire), whose sustenance was supported by agricultural activity. Using Piagetian tasks involving conservation of liquid and spatial reasoning, Dasen found that nomadic children did grasp the concept of conservation in the same stages as did traditional samples of children from Geneva, albeit at later ages (between 10-13 years old vs. 5-7 years old). He also noted that "a fairly large proportion of adolescents and adults also gave non-conservation answers" (pg. 147). However, the Aboriginal children performed the spatial reasoning tasks more easily than did children from Geneva. From these observations, he concluded "for the Aboriginal children, concrete operational reasoning in the spatial domain develops more rapidly than it does in the area of quantification" and that this result stems from the cultural necessities of nomadic life in which counting or quantification skills is of less adaptive value than are spatial skills required for finding one's way about the environment. In his studies with sedentary peoples, reverse results were obtained. Children grasped quantification skills more readily than spatial reasoning, as compared to students from Geneva.

In explaining his observations, Dasem offers "the relative rate of cognitive development in different domains, such as space and quantification, reflects what is highly valued in the culture, and what is less valued, and also what is needed, what is adaptive...Cross-cultural research points to the importance of the *context* in which the developmental changes and adaptations take place. In other words the settings, child-rearing customs and parental ethnotheories that make up the developmental niche are central" (pg. 147).

Dasen summarizes important theoretical implications concerning the findings of cross-cultural research on Piagetian theory:
- Piaget's ideas concerning the types and sequences of stages have been supported.
- Cross-cultural differences emerge in rates of cognitive development that are dependent on ecocultural factors.

- Due to variability of skills within a particular stage, it does not make sense to categorize individuals or a group of peoples as "preoperational" or "concrete operational".
- Due to the ecocultural influences and necessities for different skills within different cultures, value judgments pertaining to level of cognitive functioning are unwarranted. For example, giving a conservation answer is not necessarily better than giving a non-conservation answer if those skills aren't considered adaptive within the ecocultural environment.
- Formal reasoning skills probably occur in some way in most cultures, but the form of that higher-level reasoning may not necessarily consist of hypothetico-deductive scientific reasoning. Dasen argues that formal reasoning, as Piaget describes it, is the result of formal schooling, but that does not mean that logic or abstract reasoning is any less valued in other cultures.

"Another way to express these findings is that the *deep* structures, the basic cognitive processes, are indeed universal, while at the *surface* level, the way these basic processes are brought to bear on specific individuals in specific contexts is influenced by culture" (pg. 149).

Source:
Dasen, P. (1994). Culture and cognitive development from a Piagetian perspective. In W. Lonner & Malpass, R. (eds.), <u>Psychology and culture</u>. (pg. 145-150). Boston: Allyn and Bacon

5. **<u>Issues Confronting Children</u>:**
The text covers the amazing ways in which children change physically, cognitively, and socially starting from birth. A brief discussion concerning the challenges confronting children in our current cultural environment seems warranted. In her text, *Psychology*, Margaret Matlin outlines but a few:
- **Health risks**: Children may experience exposure to <u>HIV</u> and nearly 8,000 pediatric AIDS cases were documented in 1997; prenatal <u>parental substance abuse</u> may result in premature birth, low birth weight, attention and cognitive impairments, physical defects, and mental retardation; <u>physical abuse</u> kills between 1,200-5,000 children annually.
- **Poverty**: It has been estimated that nearly 1/4 of all children under 6, half of whom are children of color, live in poverty, which reduces the likelihood that these children receive adequate housing, nutrition, caregiving, and education. Matlin also points out that 38% of the homeless are parents with children who experience health problems, starvation or inadequate nutrition, cognitive deficits and/or psychological problems.

Dick Gregory, in his poignant article entitled *Shame*, describes vividly his childhood experiences with poverty. In particular, he expressed his frustration with his teachers who couldn't understand why he wasn't learning up to their standards. He says, "Teachers were never interested in finding out that you couldn't concentrate because you were so hungry, because you hadn't had any breakfast. All you could think about was noontime...Maybe you could sneak into the cloakroom and steal a bite of some kid's lunch out of a coat pocket. A bit of something. Paste. You can't really make a meal of paste....but sometimes I'd scoop a few spoonfuls out of the paste jar in the back of the room." Aside from the intense hunger, Gregory recounts his humiliation in front his classmates when his teacher revealed "We know you don't have a Daddy." He says, "Now there was shame everywhere. It seemed like the whole world had been inside that classroom, everyone had heard what the teacher had said, everyone had turned around and felt sorry for me." Poverty and shame marked his experiences with the educational system.

- **Violence**: As has been noted in the Learning chapter, children watch media displays of violence on a daily basis. Moreover, children's daily living experiences may be marked by actual violence in their homes, in schools, or in their neighborhoods from adults and other children, with estimates of 1child dying from gunshot wounds every 2 hours. Over 1 million latchkey kids have access to guns within their homes.
- **Racism**: Children of color are exposed to societal prejudices in interpersonal interactions with other children, because of poverty, discrimination in housing, lack of occupational opportunities for their parents, or by the ways in which people of their ethnic or racial group are portrayed by the media.
- **Divorce**: Between 40-50% of all children will spend at least 5 years in a single-parent home due to divorce, some of whom may experience long-term negative effects.
- **The "hurried child problem"**: Well-intended efforts to enrich the lives of children may result in intense academic pressures on children at early ages, sometimes resulting in pressures for academic tutoring as early as the day-care age levels. Other manifestations of hurrying the developmental growth can be seen when children are encouraged to dress and adorn themselves as "miniature adults" with makeup and designer jeans. (I would also add activities such as competitive sports and beauty pageants beginning at very young ages in this category as well.)

These issues facing children can serve as an interesting starting point for class discussion on the lives of children.

Source:
>Gregory, D. (1997). Shame. In D. Sattler & Shabatay, V. (Eds.), <u>Psychology in context: Voices and perspectives.</u> (pg. 144-147). Boston: Houghton Mifflin.

>Matlin, M. (1999). <u>Psychology</u> (3rd ed.) (pg. 345-348). Fort Worth, TX: Harcourt Brace.

6. **Child's Play:**
>Uba and Huang describe play as an activity that promotes attachment and facilitates physical and psychosocial development. Piaget believed that cognitive development occurred through play and that forms of play are indicative of cognitive development. For example, during the **sensorimotor stage**, infants engage in exploration play in which they learn about their bodies and how movements of the body (such as kicking) influence or exert control over the environment. Play with toys such as rattles and the like also emerges as the young child learns control over the environment. The "pretend" play (i.e., pretending to engage in simple everyday behaviors) that emerges around 1 year of age reflects increasing understanding of symbolism, and becomes more complex in the 2nd year of life as a result of decentration and decontextualization (as evidenced by the child pretending to be other people or using objects to represent other objects...such as my daughter pretending the footstool was a pony).

>During the **preoperational stage** various forms of play emerge and becomes increasingly social over that period (Parten, 1932): unoccupied play (playing in a seemingly aimless fashion); solitary play (playing alone); onlooker play (watching others' play but not interacting with them); parallel play (playing in the company of other children but not interacting); associative play (playing with other children but without a common goal); cooperative play (engaging in coordinated, purposeful play with other children). Imaginary playmates may develop out of the child's growing ability to differentiate himself or herself from others.

>As the child enters school, **concrete operational** thinking emerges and play of a rule-based, organized nature begins to emerge. Children may be rule-oriented, and reactions to violations of rules reflect the limitations of this stage of cognitive development. As the **formal operational** stage develops, children become less rule-bound and may change or create new rules upon agreement with other players. Thus, the very nature of play varies with levels of cognitive development. Moreover, as Uba and Huang point out, the culturally contextualized, interactive nature of play affects childrens' growing sense of self-worth and teaches social competencies.

Sources:
>Parten, M. (1932). Social participation among preschool children. Journal of Abnormal and Social Psychology, 27, 243-269.

Shaffer, D. (1993). Developmental psychology: Childhood and adolescence (3rd ed.). Pacific Grove, CA: Brooks/Cole.

Sigelman, C. & Shaffer, D. (1991). Life-span human development. Pacific Grove, CA: Brooks/Cole.

7. **Gender Identities: The Nature vs. Nurture Debate:**

Discussing gender identity with General Psychology students provides a number of opportunities for introducing the interactive relationships between the biological and the social determinants of this aspect of the self. In his text, *Becoming a Sexual Person*, Robert Francoeur reviews and outlines Money's (1975; 1980) roadmap to psychosexual or gender development, which includes twelve gates or changes in humans from the point of fertilization to adulthood. I find that an overview of these "gates" refreshes some students' memories concerning relevant issues in human physiology and allows for some discussion on biological and sociocultural variations in factors that contribute to gender identity. In this model, Money suggests that human psychosexual development progresses through a series of gates, some of which close and thus lock "the individual in as male or female both anatomically and behaviorally" (pg. 75) and some of which remain open, influenced by culture and experience.

- *Gate 1--Chromosomal Gender*: At fertilization, the 46 chromosomes and genes of the egg and sperm unite and are arranged in 23 pairs. Twenty-two pairs (the autosomes or body chromosomes contribute to general body development). The twenty-third pair, the gender chromosomes, consist of either X or Y chromosomes in the sperm and an X chromosome from the egg. Thus, a genetic or chromosomal female has an XX pairing, whereas a genetic or chromosomal male has an XY pairing. If a zygote has no Y chromosome (i.e. XX pairing), development starts toward the female gender; if it does (XY pairing), development starts toward the male gender. Once the chromosomal pairing has been accomplished, this "gate" is locked (i.e., it can't be changed).
- *Gate 2--Gonadal Gender*: The embryo develops undifferentiated gonads (primitive reproductive glands) during the second month of pregnancy. Although genetically the embryo is determined as "male" or "female", anatomically neither distinction is made yet. If the embryo has the XX chromosomal pairing, the outer surface of the undifferentiated gonads develops into ovaries at about 12 weeks gestation; if XY, the inner core of the undifferentiated gonads develops into testes starting at 6 weeks. This gate locks at about 3 months.
- *Gate 3--Hormonal Gender*: With the beginning development of ovaries/testes, further sexual differentiation occurs due to the presence of hormones within the fetal environment. For the

XX fetus with ovaries, large amount of estrogens and smaller amounts of androgens and Mullerian Inhibiting Hormone are present; for the XY fetus with testes, the same kinds of hormones are present but in reverse quantities. The balance and amount of these hormones determines further sexual differentiation with the critical distinction that it is the presence of large quantities of androgens and MIH that contributes to further development of the male reproductive systems in either fetus.

- *Gate 4--Internal Sexual Anatomy*: In the XX fetus (due to the low levels of androgens & MIH), internal organs such as the vagina and fallopian tubes begin to develop and the Wolffian ducts (potential male organs) degenerate. In the XY fetus (due to the high level of androgens & MIH), the potential female reproductive organs (i.e., Mullerian ducts) are inhibited and degenerate and the vasa deferentia, prostate, seminal vesicles, and other male structures develop. Variations in hormonal balance brought on by chemicals or environment events or insensitivities to these hormones can produce variations in internal organ development, such as individuals with both sets of internal organs, genetic males with female internal organs, or genetic females with male internal organs.

- *Gate 5--External Sexual Anatomy*: For the male fetus, testosterone is converted into dihydrotestosterone (DHT), which results in production of the penis and scrotum. The absence of DHT results in production of the labia and clitoris in the female fetus. Again variations may occur.

- *Gate 6--Neural Encoding*: Hormones circulating in the bloodstream "may have a masculinizing or defeminizing effect on the cell's functioning" (pg. 88) in the brain, thus sensitizing areas of the brain (e.g., the hypothalamus) to the effects of hormones and establishing "templates" for reacting to environmental events. Franceour notes "Before birth, the development of neural cells and the functioning in the brain is controlled by genes and probably modified by hormones. There are some important and specific differences in the genes males and females carry on their X and Y chromosomes which can affect the development of the brain cells and their programming " (pg. 89). He does not, however, argue here for strict biological determinism.

- *Gate 7--Gender Assignment*: Occurring at birth, this gate involves the labeling of the newborn as male or female and represents the first major point in which social and cultural influences begin to shape gender identity development.

- *Gate 8--Gender Scripting*: Following the assignment of gender, persons within the newborn's environment (e.g., parents, siblings, etc.) begin to condition the child toward behaviors appropriate to the identified gender group.

- *Gate 9--Gender Role*: In response to gender scripting efforts, children learn to show preferences for objects and activities related to their gender group.
- *Gate 10--Core Gender Identity*: By 3 years of age, children have developed a core gender identity or "internalized conviction that allows us to say with absolute certainty "I'm a girl" or "I'm a boy". Franceour argues that this gate represents the combined effects of "the pathways and tendencies laid down in our brain before birth" and the postnatal influences of conditioning and learning.
- *Gate 11--Gender Orientation*: Different from the core gender identity (identifying oneself as male or female), gender orientation reflects our affectional, fantasy, and erotic orientations towards other people. Like the core gender identity, gender orientation reflects the interactive contributions of biological and social influences.
- *Gate 12--Pubertal Gender Development*: During puberty, the development of secondary sex characteristics (development of breasts, voice changes, etc.) are again related to biological events and interpreted within a socially meaningful context.

This model provides an opportunity for viewing gender identity development from an integrative perspective, incorporating both biological and sociocultural influences on this core aspect of children's development. I often introduce the problematic aspects of talking about gender identity theory and research by discussing the 1965 case of identical twin brothers. During circumcision, one of the twin's penis was accidentally severed. His parents authorized gender reassignment surgery: his testes were removed and surgery to create female external genitalia was performed. Estrogen replacement and vaginal surgery was done during her adolescent years to complete the reassignment. The parents treated and raised the reassigned girl as a girl and early reports indicated no problems. She looked and acted like any other young girl her age. However, during puberty, problems were noted with "masculinized" behaviors (e.g., unfeminine appearance and behavior). An excellent case study to introduce the nature vs. nurture debate regarding gender identity.

Source:
Francoeur, R. (1991). Becoming a sexual person (2nd ed.) (pgs. 74-95.) New York: Macmillan.

Suggestions for Additional Readings

Beal, C. (1994). Boys and girls: The development of gender roles. New York: McGraw-Hill.

Belle, D. (Ed.), (1989). Children's social networks and social supports. New York: Wiley.

Bjorklund, D. (1989). Children's thinking: Developmental function and individual differences. Pacific Grove, CA: Brooks/Cole.

Braithwaite, V., & Scott, W. (1991). Values. In J. Robinson, Shaver, P., & Wrightsman, L. (Eds.), Measures of personality and social psychological attitudes (Vol. 1, pp. 661-753). New York: Academic Press.

Children's Defense Fund. (1997). The state of American's children. Washington, DC: Author.

Clarke-Stewart, A., Perlmutter,. M., & Friedman, S. (1992). Lifelong human development (2nd ed.). New York: Wiley.

Eisenberg, N. (1992). The caring child. Cambridge, MA: Harvard University Press.

Gilligan, C. (1982). In a different voice: Psychological theory and women's development. Cambridge, MA: Harvard University Press.

Greenfield, P., & Cocking, R. (1994). Cross-cultural roots of minority children development. Hillsdale, NJ: Erlbaum.

Harkness, S., & Super, C. (1987). The uses of cross-cultural research in child development. In G. Whitehurst & Vasta, R. (Eds.), Annals of child development (Vol. 4) (pg. 209-244). Greenwich, CN: JAI Press.

Holmes, R. (1995). How young children perceive race. Thougsand Oaks, CA: Sage.

Hyde, J. (1991). Half the human experience. Lexington, MA: D.C. Heath.

Markus, H., & Kitayama, S. (1991). Culture and the self: Implications for cognition, emotion, and motivation. Psychological Review, 98-221-253.

Matsumoto, D. (1994). People: Psychology from a cultural perspective. Pacific Grove, CA: Brooks/Cole.

Maurer, D., & Maurer, C. (1988). The world of the newborn. New York: Basic Books.

Money, J., & Tucker, P. (1975). Sexual signatures: On being a man or woman. Boston: Little,Brown.

Mussen, P. (Ed.) (1983). Handbook of child psychology. New York: Wiley.

Osofsky, J. (Ed.) (1987). Handbook of infant development. New York: Wiley.

Schwartz, S. (1992). Universals in the content and structure of values: Theoretical advances and empirical tests in 20 countries. In M. Zanna (Ed.), Advances in experimental social psychology. New York: Academic Press.

Shaffer, D. (1993). Developmental psychology: Childhood and adolescence. Pacific Grove, CA: Brooks/Cole.

Watson-Gegeo, K., & Gegeo, D. (1989). The role of sibling interaction in child socialization. In P. Zukow (Ed.), Sibling interaction across cultures. New York: Springer-Verlag.

Whiting, B., & Edwards, C. (1988). <u>Children of different worlds: The formation of social behavior</u>. Cambridge, MA: Harvard University Press.

In-Class Activities and Demonstrations

1. **TRAIL Blazing:** Using **Transparency Masters 8.1 - 8.5**, review with students the "Checking Your TRAIL" sections in the chapter. Have students work in small groups to answer the questions and then review with the class as a whole to tie the text reading to activity in class.

2. **Reaching Critical Mass**: Using **Transparency Masters 8.6 - 8.8**, review with students the "Critical Thinking" sections in the chapter. Have students work in small groups to answer the questions and then review with the class as a whole to tie the text reading to activity in class.

3. **Getting Down to IT**: Using **Transparency Masters 8.9 - 8.14**, review the "Integrative Thinking" sections in the chapter with students. Have students work in small groups to answer the questions and then review with the class as a whole to tie the text reading to activity in class.

4. **Who am I?: Exploration of self-concept**: Uba and Huang introduce self-concept in this chapter. **Activity Handout # 8.1** involves a simple exercise for having students consider who they "are". I've done this exercise a number of times with students and find that often they are likely to list aspects of the self such as their names, roles they engage in (son, daughter, etc.), personality attributes, aspirations for the future. After allowing enough time for students to provide a fairly exhaustive listing of self items, I usually encourage them to look at what they've written from the standpoint of parts of the self that appear to stem more from social/culture factors & those aspects that might be inherited; which aspects can be changed, which not; are there any observable trends in self-description that appear to stand out as important themes? In other variations of this exercise, I have also asked students to consider gender and ethnicity themes present in the self-concept.

5. **American Values in the Media**: In the article "The great American values test" (Rokeach et. al., 1984) a national survey of American women and men found that the top 10 guiding principles (i.e., terminal or end-state values) at that time in our country were: family security, a world at peace, freedom, self-respect, happiness, wisdom, a sense of accomplishment, a comfortable life, true freedom, and salvation (in descending order). Feathers (1994) suggests that values can be measured by analyzing media presentations. Moreover, he says, that values may vary across gender, SES, and cultural boundaries. Using **Activity Handout # 8.2,** have students survey women's and men's magazines to determine if these value themes are indeed present in advertisements. After completing their surveys, have students discuss their results in class, providing examples of different advertisements they think demonstrate different value themes.

6. **What a dilemma!**: The classic Heinz dilemma is presented in the textbook. As noted in Additional Lecture topic #1, the use of Kohlberg's moral dilemmas in cross-cultural research has been the focus of claims concerning gender and cultural bias. Consider **Activity Handout # 8.3** as a variation of a Kohlbergian moral dilemma. Two versions of a moral dilemma are provided, both of which involve a sexual transgression within a relationship. Have half the class complete Version A, the other half complete Version B. In Version A, Jim "steps out on" his significant other, Jane; in Version B, Jane does so. As is the general case with moral dilemmas, you can ask the class if they think the behavior was appropriate and analyze it according to the preconventional, conventional, and postconventional perspectives. What makes for more interesting analysis (and lively discussion), however, is when students make different judgements on the extent of "wrongness" for the conduct based on the gender of the transgressor. What I find when I do this exercise with students is that they tend to be quite harsh on Jane and less so on Jim, despite the fact that they have done the same behavior. I ask students to consider if their judgments of rightness or wrongness concerning a behavior is affected by beliefs in appropriate gender role behavior. Different versions may also be created, inserting people from different ethnic backgrounds to assess similar trends in differences.

7. **The puzzle of childhood development**: Using **Activity Handout #8.4**, have students complete the crossword puzzle using terms and concepts from Chapter 8.

8. **Can I play with you?:** This exercise accompanies discussion/lecture on **Additional Lecture topic # 6: Child's Play**. Using **Activity Handout #8.5**, students observe 2-3 child from various age ranges to determine if they demonstrate various forms of play indicative of different levels of cognitive development.

9. **My childhood as I see it today**: This exercise accompanies discussion/lecture on **Additional Lecture topic # 2: Establishing the Developmental Niche**. Using **Activity Handout #8.6**, students are to consider the impact of the physical/social setting, child care and child rearing customs, caregiver psychology, and the larger human ecology on their childhood.

Sources for Additional Activities
Books:
Benjamin, L. & Lowman, K. (1981). Activities Handbook for the Teaching of Psychology. Washington DC: American Psychological Association.

Halonen, Jane 1995). Chapter 3: The developing person. In <u>The critical thinking companion for Introductory Psychology.</u> New York: Worth Publ.

Makosky, V. et al. (Eds.) (1995). <u>Activities Handbook for the Teaching of Psychology</u> (Vol. III). Washington DC: American Psychological Association.

Journey II Software: The Journey II program contains 3 units relevant to Chapter 8.

- Moral Development: The story of Heinz' dilemma over obtaining medications for his dying wife is used to illustrate Kohlberg's theory of moral development. After learning about 5 stages (the 6th stage is not reviewed) of moral reasoning, students consider examples and choose the appropriate stage being represented. They also complete an 8 question quiz concerning different moral judgements about Heinz' behavior and identify the stage reflected in that judgement. Carol Gilligan's critique and theory alternative to Kohlberg is discussed.

- Sex Role Development: Gender identity and the effects of sex typing are discussed. Students take a 56-item questionnaire, based on Sandra Bem's work, to determine masculine, feminine, or androgynous orientations.

- Cognitive Development: Some of Piaget's basic assumptions concerning cognitive development are reviewed. Particular attention is given to the phenomenon of object permanence during the Sensorimotor stage. Students observe 4 children of various ages between 6-24 months, determine if each child has achieved object permanence, and then answer several questions concerning all four children.

- **World Wide Web**: Check out the following WWW sites for information and activities relevant to this section of the text!
    - Addison Wesley Longman's Website -- **http://longman.awl.com/**
    - PsychZone link -- **http://longman.awl.com/**
    - Psych Web -- **http://www.gasou.edu/psychweb/psychweb.htm**
    - Self-Quizzes for Introductory Psychology -- **http://www.gasou.edu/psychweb/selfquiz/selfquiz.htm**
    - Psychology Jumping Stand -- **http://www.indiana.edu:80/~iuepsyc/PsycJump.html**
    - The Psychology Place -- **http://www.psychplace.com**
    - Theories of child development -- **http://www.idealist.com/children/cdw.html**
    - Cognitive development -- **www.valdosta.peachnet.edu/~whuitt/psy702/cogsys/piaget.html**
    - Constructivist theories -- **http://www.coe.uh.edu/~srmehall/theory/construct.html**
    - Vygotsky Centennial project -- **http://www.massey.ac.nz/~ALock/virtual/project2.html**

- Psychosocial development -- **www.valdosta.peachnet.edu/~whuitt/psy702/affsys/erikson.html**
- Kohlberg's Moral Reasoning theory -- **http://www.awa.com/w2/erotic_computing/kohlberg.stages.html**
- Families -- **http://www.personal.psu.edu/faculty/n/x/nxd10/family3.htm**
- Parenting -- **http://www.efn.org/~djz/birth/babylist.html**
- Child Behavior Checklist -- **gopher://moose.uvm.edu:70/11/Other%20UVM@20gophers%20and%20Information%20Resources/University%20Associates%20in%20Psychiatry/Child%20Behavior%20Checklist%20%28Achenbach%20CBCL%29**
- Attachment theory -- **http://galton.psych.nwu.edu/GreatIdeas/attachment.html**
- Piaget archives -- **http://www.uniage.ch/piaget/biog.html**
- Stand for Children homepage -- **http:// www.stand.org/**
- Child development -- **http://www.exnet.iastate.edu/Pages/nncc/Child.Dev./child.dev.page.html**
- Child abuse -- **http://idealist.com/cayp/**
- I Am Your Child homepage -- **http://www.iamyourchild.org/start.html**
- Sesame Street Parents (physical development) -- **http://ctw.org/parents/weekly/0496/04964t1.htm**
- Choosing Day Care -- **http://www.extnet.iastate.edu/Pages/nncc/Choose.Quality.Care/qual.care.page.html**
- Culture and education -- **http://www.nap.edu/readingroom/books/earlyed/contents.html**
- Temperament scales -- **http://www.temperament.com/**
- Middle Childhood Network homepage -- **http:/midchild.soe.umich.edu/**
- Prenatal Development -- **http://www.ptiweb.com/~cpc/9months.html** or **http://www.birthpsychology.com/lifebefore/fetalsense.html**
- Basic facts about babies -- **http://www.questionmark.com/qmwebquestions/babies.html**

- **Audio-Visual Support**
  <u>Films/Videos</u>:
  <u>Overview</u>
  - *Discovering Psychology: The Developing Child* (Annenberg, 30 minutes)
  - *Development* (CRM, 33 minutes)
  - *When Life Begins* (CRM, 14 minutes)
  - *Childhood: The Enchanted Years* (Films Incorporated, 52 minutes)
  - *Child Development* (FFHS, 60 minutes)
  - *Child Development* (Insight, 30 minutes)
  - *The Miracle of Life* (Time/Life, 57 minutes)
  - *Newborn* (Filmakers, 28 minutes)
  - *Human Development: The First 2 1/2 Years* (Concept Media, 25 minutes)

- *Seasons of Life: Infancy and Early Childhood* (Annenberg, 60 minutes)
- *Seasons of Life: Childhood and Adolescence* (Annenberg, 60 minutes)
- *The Amazing Newborn* (POLY, 26 minutes)
- *The Beginning of Life* (BENM, 30 minutes)
- *Conception to Neonate Series* (CM, 25-35 minutes)
    Program 1: *Pregnancy*
    Program 2: *Birth and the Newborn*
    Program 3: *Reducing Risk Factors*
- *The Developing Child: The Crucial Early Years* (FFHS, 26 minutes)
- *The First Signs of April: The Need for Early Stimulation* (CUAV, 22 minutes)
- *The Mind: Development* (HARR, 24 minutes)
- *The Miracle of Life* (Time/Life, 57 minutes)
- *The Psychological Development of the Child* Series (FFHS, 23 minutes each)
    Program 1: *Developmental Phases Before and After Birth*
    Program 2: *Psychological Development Before Birth*
    Program 3: *The Process of Birth*
    Program 4: *How Relationships are Formed*
    Program 5: *Mothers, Fathers, and Babies*
    Program 6: *Developing the Sense of Family*
    Program 7: *Discovering the Outside World*
    Program 8: *The Development of Self*

Cognitive Development
- *Cognitive Development* (Insight, 30 minutes)
- *Piaget's Developmental Theory: Classification* (POLY, 20 minutes)
- *Children, Science, and Common Sense* (FFHS, 23 minutes)

Social/Moral Development
- *Moral Development* (CRM, 28 minutes)
- *Right from the Start: Infant Bonding* (PBS, 58 minutes)
- *Child's Play: Window on Development* (HARBJ, 20 minutes)
- *Everybody Rides the Carousel, Parts 1, 2 and 3* (PYR, 73 minutes)
- *Feelings: Family* (PBS, 29 minutes)
- *Feelings: Schools* (PBS, 29 minutes)
- *Life's First Feelings* (CORT, 58 minutes)
- *Habits of the Heart: Early Relationships* (RMI, 60 minutes)
- *Moral Judgment and Reasoning* (CRM, 18 minutes)
- *Personality: Early Childhood* (CRM, 20 minutes)
- *Personality: Middle Childhood* (CRM, 19 minutes)
- *The Pinks and the Blues* (PSU, 57 minutes)
- *Socialization: Moral Development* (HARR, 22 minutes)
- *Emotional Intelligence: The Key to Social Skills* (FFHS, 28 minutes)
- *Men, Women, and the Sex Difference: Boys and Girls Are Different* (FFHS, 43 minutes)

Technology/Methodology
- *Infancy Research Methods* (IU, 18 minutes)
- *The Babymakers* (CRM, 43 minutes)
- *Body Doubles: The Twin Experience* (FFHS, 50 minutes)
- *Babywatching* (FFHS, 50 minutes)

Cross-cultural & Diversity Issues
- *China's Only Child* (PBS, 58 minutes)
- *Day Care for a Kibbutz Toddler* (PSUPCR, 23 minutes)
- *Development of the Child: A Cross-Cultural Approach to the Acquisition of Sex Roles and Social Standards* (PSUPCR, 23 minutes)
- *Feelings: Handicap* (PBS, 29 minutes)

Related Issues:
- *Childhood Sexual Abuse* (FFHS, 26 minutes)
- *Childhood Physical Abuse* (FFHS, 26 minutes)
- *No More Secrets* (FFHS, 24 minutes)
- *Child Molestation: Sorting Out the Truth* (FFHS, 20 minutes)
- *Society's Problems in Children's Lives* (FFHS, 28 minutes)
- *Fatherless in America* (FFHS, 26 minutes)
- *Children of Divorce* (FFHS, 28 minutes)
- *Children of Poverty* (FFHS, 26 minutes)
- *Foster Care* (FFHS, 24 minutes)
- *The Roots of Violence* Series (FFHS, 30 minutes each)
    - Program 1: *A Child's View of the World: Exhuming a Violent Past*
    - Program 2: *Children of Addiction*
    - Program 3: *Children of Violence*
    - Program 4: *Children of Neglect*
    - Program 5: *The Perfect Child: "Cold" Violence*
- *Children with OCD* (FFHS, 15 minutes)
- *Teen and Child Depression* (FFHS, 19 minutes)
- *Pressure-cooked Kids* (FFHS 28 minutes)
- *Unborn Addicts* (FFHS, 50 minutes)
- *Fetal Alcohol Syndrome and Other Drug Use During Pregnancy* (FFHS, 19 minutes)
- *Kids Under the Influence* (FFHS, 58 minutes)

Psychology Encyclopedia Laserdisc IV:
Movies
Changing times for gender roles	(3 mins. 30 sec.)	Side 2, Frames 13718-20014
Piaget: conservation of volume	(2 mins. 11 sec.)	Side 2, Frames 27976-31899
Kagan: infant response	(2 mins. 26 sec.)	Side 2, Frames 31900-36264

Still Images
Infant's understanding of events [13.3]	Frame 53562	Side	all
Sex typing internalization [13.5]	53563		all
Children's living conditions worldwide [1/3] [13.6]	53564		all
Children's living conditions worldwide [2/3] [13.6]	53565		all
Children's living conditions worldwide [3/3] [13.6]	53566		all

Transparency Master 8.1: Checking Your TRAIL 8.1

I. **<u>True</u> or <u>False</u>: Development is characterized by increasing complexity and is achieved through increasingly distinct and integrated behaviors.**

II. **Name the three broad areas of development that have been the primary concern of psychologists.**

III. **<u>True</u> or <u>False</u>: From a psychological point of view, development can be a gradual and continuous process or can occur in spurts.**

IV. **What do stage models assume about the developmental tasks or challenges people face?**

I. True or False: Most neural connections in the brain are established before birth.

II. Which one of the following statements is true?
   A. Miscarriages usually occur in the fetal period.
   B. Females have XY chromosomes.
   C. Androgens are masculinizing hormones.
   D. There is no evidence that hormones are related to the type of activities children prefer.

III. Name five substances a pregnant woman should avoid in order to protect her fetus.

IV. Name two ways in which individuals born into a poor family might be born at a developmental disadvantage.

Transparency Master 8.3: Checking Your TRAIL 8.3

I. In what ways are newborns perceptually prepared to respond to their parents?

II. Regarding the physical development of infants and toddlers, which one of the following statements is FALSE?
   A. Physical development begins in inner organs before the extremities.
   B. Physical development proceeds faster in the head and torso than in the lower parts of the body.
   C. Control is gained over small muscles before large muscles.
   D. A human's head grows most during the prenatal period and the first two years of life.

III. Temperament is probably primarily _____.
   A. genetically caused
   B. environmentally caused
   C. caused by teratogens
   D. caused by siblings (brothers and sisters)

IV. True or False: According to Erik Erikson, the way people respond to developmental crises determine how their personalities will develop.

Transparency Master 8.4: Checking Your TRAIL 8.4

I. **Name Piaget's four stages, in order.**

II. **By "operations", Piaget meant:**
   A. instructions.
   B. surgeries.
   C. the cognitive ability to transform and reorganize thoughts.
   D. math problems.

III. **A child who can think about an object or situation only from his or her own perspective is showing signs of:**
   A. egocentrism.
   B. object permanence.
   C. concrete operations.
   D. symbolic thought.

IV. <u>True</u> or <u>False</u>: **When looking at a moral dilemma with a care orientation, people think about morality in terms of rules and rights.**

Transparency Master 8.5: Checking Your TRAIL 8.5

I. Children's lack of gender constancy seems to be due to their:
   A. formal operational thinking.
   B. egocentrism.
   C. preoperational thinking.
   D. sex-typed behaviors.

II. The fact that research supports all three of the sex-typing theories suggests that:
   A. children don't have gender identities.
   B. sex-typed behaviors might not all develop in the same way.
   C. sex typing doesn't occur.
   D. gender constancy is a myth.

III. In what ways does socioeconomic status seem to distinguish the style of parenting children receive?

IV. With regard to the topics in this chapter, in what ways are most children similar? In what ways do they differ?

Transparency Master 8.6: Critical Thinking 8.1

How can fathers, who don't breast feed their babies, establish their babies' attachment to them?

Transparency Master 8.7: Critical Thinking 8.2

If "Heinz" in the Kohlberg scenario were an African American, do you think that people would interpret his behavior differently and, therefore, respond to the dilemma differently? Why?

In the United States, females are often considered to be more nurturing than males, who are not often described as having nurturing personalities (Bem, 1983). As a result, Americans might not notice much of the nurturing behaviors of boys or label these behaviors as nurturing. What are the implications for the personality characteristics we think people have and which behaviors are reinforced?

Transparency Master 8.9: Integrative Thinking 8.1

Given what you read in the Biopsychology chapter about identical twins' genes, can one identical twin be a different sex from the other?

Transparency Master 8.10: Integrative Thinking 8.2

Considering the "rules" for physical development in infants and toddlers described on p. 314 and in light of what you learned in the Biopsychology chapter, which part of the cortex develops to make such movement possible?

In light of what you learned in the Sensation & Perception chapter, which sense are toddlers developing that enables them to make coordinated movements?

Transparency Master 8.11: Integrative Thinking 8.3

What is considered important behavior to learn depends largely on culture. Based on what you learned in the Learning chapter, what differences do you expect in the social behaviors taught by parents from individualist and collectivist cultures?

Transparency Master 8.12: Integrative Thinking 8.4

In light of what you learned in the Biopsychology chapter about the functional divisions of the cerebral cortex, which part of the cortex is developing as children learn to bring together ideas and solve problems?

Transparency Master 8.13: Integrative Thinking 8.5

In terms of the scientific method described in the Introductory chapter, what was the main problem with the sample Piaget studied?

Transparency Master 8.14: Integrative Thinking 8.6

Kohlberg and Gilligan gathered data, like the statements quoted on pgs. 333-334 of the text. Given what you learned in the Introductory chapter, what type of studies did they conduct?

Activity Handout # 8.1

Who am I?: Exploration of self-concept

Instructions: On the lines below write as many descriptions of yourself as you can think of in the time allowed.

_____
_____
_____
_____
_____
_____
_____
_____
_____
_____
_____
_____
_____
_____
_____
_____
_____
_____
_____
_____
_____

To what extent and how has your self-concept been affected by:
- culture: _____
- media: _____
- people around you: _____
- your gender: _____

Activity Handout # 8.2

American Values in the Media

Instructions: In a national survey of American women and men, Rokeach et. al., (1984) found that the top 10 guiding principles (i.e., terminal or end-state values) at that time in our country were: family security, a world at peace, freedom, self-respect, happiness, wisdom, a sense of accomplishment, a comfortable life, true freedom, and salvation (in descending order). For this exercise, review 2 women's and 2 men's magazines and select 2 advertisements from each that you think represents these value systems. Note any differences in value themes between the two types of magazines.

Women's magazines:
Magazine 1: _____
    Value theme in Advertisement 1: _____
    Value theme in Advertisement 2: _____

Magazine 2: _____
    Value theme in Advertisement 1: _____
    Value theme in Advertisement 2: _____

Men's magazines:
Magazine 1: _____
    Value theme in Advertisement 1: _____
    Value theme in Advertisement 2: _____

Magazine 2: _____
    Value theme in Advertisement 1: _____
    Value theme in Advertisement 2: _____

Differences in value themes noted:
_____
_____
_____
_____
_____
_____

Activity Handout # 8.3: Version A

What a dilemma!:

Instructions: Read the following scenario and then answer the questions that follow.

Jim, a college Senior, has just become engaged to marry his long-time girlfriend, Jane. He feels under a lot of pressure to complete his undergraduate college education by the upcoming Spring graduation ceremony so he can begin graduate work next Fall. In his last required course he finds that he is getting a failing grade. He must pass the cumulative final exam to get a passing grade. A very attractive female classmate offers to tutor him and give him access to her notes...with a catch. He must sleep with her. After thinking about the situation, he agrees and eventually passes the course.

Was Jim's behavior appropriate? _____

Why? or Why not?: _____
_____
_____
_____

Rate Jim according to the following dimensions:

1	2	3	4	5	6	7
Likeable					**Unlikable**	

1	2	3	4	5	6	7
Irresponsible					**Responsible**	

1	2	3	4	5	6	7
Competent					**Incompetent**	

1	2	3	4	5	6	7
Unintelligent					**Intelligent**	

1	2	3	4	5	6	7
Appropriate					**Inappropriate**	

Activity Handout # 8.3: Version B

What a dilemma!:

Instructions: Read the following scenario and then answer the questions that follow.

Jane, a college Senior, has just become engaged to marry her long-time boyfriend, Jim. She feels under a lot of pressure to complete her undergraduate college education by the upcoming Spring graduation ceremony so she can begin graduate work next Fall. In her last required course she finds that she is getting a failing grade. She must pass the cumulative final exam to get a passing grade. A very attractive male classmate offers to tutor her and give her access to his notes...with a catch. She must sleep with him. After thinking about the situation, she agrees and eventually passes the course.

Was Jane's behavior appropriate? _____

Why? or Why not?: _____
_____
_____
_____

Rate Jane according to the following dimensions:

```
    1      2      3      4      5      6      7
Likeable                          Unlikable

    1      2      3      4      5      6      7
Irresponsible                     Responsible

    1      2      3      4      5      6      7
Competent                         Incompetent

    1      2      3      4      5      6      7
Unintelligent                     Intelligent

    1      2      3      4      5      6      7
Appropriate                       Inappropriate
```

The puzzle of childhood development: Using **Activity Handout #8.4**, have students complete the word search puzzle using terms from Chapter 8 and some dictionary terms (i.e., the word list below the puzzle). The solution for the puzzle is the concept, *gender constancy*.

Handout Master # 8.4: The puzzle of childhood development

Chapter 8

```
M T D C N G E L J U S T I C E
S G E Y T E R A T O G E N S T
I L P T Y S D N P I A G E T O
R A Y I N T R O S S S E P O G
T I T T O A O I T E A I D R Y
N C X N I T T T N L L N E N Z
E O E E T I O N E F E O V O P
C S S D A O M E M C M I E I R
O O N I V N I V H O B T L T E
G H O R R S R N C N R P O A N
E C S E E A O O A C Y E P R A
G Y K D S Y S C T E O C M U T
A S I N N R N E T P N N E T A
T P R E O P E R A T I O N A L
S S E G C A S P N C C C T M N
```

Instructions: Complete the word search puzzle above by finding the following list of words from Chapter 8 and dictionary words. To solve the puzzle, use the letters that remain in the puzzle to create a term used in Chapter 8.

ATTACHMENTS	CONCEPTION	CONSERVATION
DEVELOPMENT	EGOCENTRISM	EMBRYONIC
ERIKSON	FLIP	GENDER IDENTITY
GESTATION	JUSTICE	MATURATION
PIAGET	PRECONVENTIONAL	PSYCHOSOCIAL
RYAS	SALE	SELF-CONCEPT
SENSORIMOTOR	SEX-TYPED	STAGE
TERATOGENS	ZYGOTE	

Puzzle solution: (Hints--15 letters;not Tootsie) __ __ __ __ __ __   __ __ __ __ __ __ __ __ __

Activity Handout # 8.5

Can I play with you?:

Instructions: Observe 2-3 children from different age ranges as they play. Look for indications of any of forms of play listed below. Also note if gender roles or cultural influences appeared to affect play.

Sensorimotor stage play (ages 0-2):
- learn about their bodies and how movements of the body (such as kicking) influence or exert control over the environment.
- playing with toys such as rattles and thus learning control over the environment.
- simple "pretend" play (i.e., pretending to engage in simple everyday behaviors)
- complex "pretend" play (playing another person's role; using objects in place of non-present object; engaging in sequences of behaviors)

Preoperational stage play (ages 2-5):
- unoccupied play (playing in a seemingly aimless fashion)
- solitary play (playing alone)
- onlooker play (watching others' play but not interacting with them)
- parallel play (playing in the company of other children but not interacting)
- associative play (playing with other children but without a common goal)
- cooperative play (engaging in coordinated, purposive play with other children).

Concrete operational stage play (ages 6-11):
- organized, rule-oriented games (board games, organized sports)

Formal operational stage play (ages 11 on):
- organized games but with flexibility in rules and rule changes

Child 1: (age: _____); Form of play: _____
Description: _____
Gender/Culture influences?: _____

Child 2: (age: _____); Form of play: _____
Description: _____
Gender/Culture influences?: _____

Child 3: (age: _____); Form of play: _____
Description: _____
Gender/Culture influences?: _____

Activity Handout # 8.6

My childhood as I see it today:

Instructions: In the space below, describe relevant events and people in your childhood that have shaped you into the person you are today. Some possible areas to consider include interactions with parents & siblings or with other persons with whom you had significant relationships (the social setting); the physical environment in which you grew up (the physical setting); child rearing practices that were common (child care customs); your parent's or caregiver's beliefs about child rearing (caregiver psychology); any major events within your community, region, or the nation, or your family's SES or major demographic moves (the larger human ecology).

The social setting:

The physical setting:

Child care customs:

Caregiver psychology:

The larger human ecology:

CHAPTER 9

DEVELOPMENT FROM ADOLESCENCE THROUGH OLD AGE

- **Chapter Overview**
    Learning Objectives
    Chapter Outline

- **Additional Lecture Ideas**
    Lecture Topics
    Additional Readings

- **In-Class Activities and Demonstrations**
    Activities and Demonstrations
    Sources for Additional Activities

- **World Wide Web**

- **Audio-Visual Support**

- **Handout and Transparency Masters**

Chapter Overview

Learning Objectives

After studying this chapter, you should be able to do the following:

1. Identify physical changes that occur in adolescence.

2. Identify cognitive characteristics of adolescents.

3. Identify factors that influence the self-concepts of adolescents.

4. Describe four developmental models of ethnic or racial identity.

5. Describe new tasks and responsibilities associated with adulthood.

6. Describe social, physical, and cognitive changes that take place in old age.

Chapter Outline

Development From Adolescence Through Old Age

I. Adolescence: A period of transition
  A. Definition
      1. adolescence: the transitional period between the onset of physical and sexual maturity and the acknowledgment that one is an adult
  B. Physical development: Hormonal changes
      1. puberty: beginning of physical changes associated with adolescence marked by increase in hormones and leading to maturation of the skeleton and reproductive systems.
      2. role of hormones: increases of estrogens (females) and androgens (males) prompt development of secondary sex characteristics
          a. males: growth of facial/pubic hair; growth of testes, scrotum, penis; spermarche; deepening of voice
          b. females: growth of pubic hair and breasts; menarche
  C. Cognitive development: New ways of thinking in adolescence
      1. role of the *imaginary audience*: adolescent egocentricism centered on imagined that others are watching, judging them; results in self-conscious or inhibited behavior
      2. the personal fable: adolescents' belief that they are exceptional or unique; results in beliefs of being indestructible and is correlated with risk-taking behaviors
      3. idealism: unrealistically high expectations for self and others based on what is logically possible rather than realistic concepts or experiences; results in intolerance or disappointment in self and others
  D. Social development: An expanding social world and identity
      1. trends in social events:
          a. independence from parents; possibilities for conflict and negotiation
          b. importance of peer relationships & dating
          c. forming a social identity: related to hormonal changes, formal operational thinking and sensitivity to others' opinions of them
          d. Erikson: identity development key task during adolescence
      2. forming identity and goals: beginnings of center life questions (e.g., who am I?); concerns for future including occupational goals/choices
          a. career-related experiences in adolescents may be related to later career experiences and socioeconomic status
      3. influences on self-concept:
          a. self-esteem: the aspect of the self-concept that involves positive/negative evaluations of oneself; affects thinking processes, emotional reactions, willingness to try new experiences
          b. self-concept & self-esteem influenced by:
              i. culture: individualistic vs. collectivistic emphasize different attributes as favorable

  ii. <u>socioeconomic status</u>: poverty is related to inferiority/efforts to achieve or be successful
  iii. <u>unemployment</u>: influences self-esteem, sense of self-efficacy

E. Developing an ethnic and racial identity
 1. <u>developing racial and ethnic awareness</u>:
  a. racial identity: belonging to a group with socially significant physical characteristics
  b. ethnic identity: belonging to a cultural group
  c. development of ethnic and racial identities are separate, proceed simultaneously
  d. people of color are often made more aware of/reminded of their ethnicity and race by others via questions and actions of others
  e. adolescents of color become increasingly aware of social significance, social standing, patterns of discrimination against their ethnic/racial group
  f. ethnic/racial identity may be a source of positive self-esteem & increased group strength/cohesion
 2. <u>alternative perspectives on minority identity</u>:
  a. <u>Minority Identity Development model (MIDM)</u> by Atkinson et al., 1989: five stage model
   i. <u>Stage 1</u>: preference for European Americans' beliefs/values, patterns of behaviors
   ii. <u>Stage 2</u>: doubts concerning Stage 1 beliefs; growing sense of connection to other oppressed groups
   iii. <u>Stage 3</u>: reject dominant group; completely embrace own ethnic culture
   iv. <u>Stage 4</u>: secure with own ethnic identity; no longer reject dominant group
   v. <u>Stage 5</u>: accept own and other ethnic groups' positive attributes
  b. <u>Phinney's three-stage model</u>:
   ii. <u>Stage 1</u>: ethnic identity is unexamined (too young to consider; recent immigrant status)
   ii. <u>Stage 2</u>: ethnic identity explored, wrestled with; dominant culture may or may be rejected
   iii. <u>Stage 3</u>: resolution of racial/ethnic identity
  c. both models provide framework for understanding identity development
 3. <u>alternative perspectives on white racial identity</u>:
  a. <u>White Racial Identity Model (WRIM)</u> by Helms, 1990: five stage model
   i. <u>Stage 1</u>: don't see how being white is relevant to identity
   ii. <u>Stage 2</u>: increasing consciousness of their race; dislike and guilt concerning unequal treatment; may avoid

minority groups, change ideas about minority groups, or claim race unimportant to deal with conflicting feelings

iii. <u>Stage 3</u>: continue to avoid minority groups; may claim minority groups are inferior, different from whites

iv. <u>Stage 4</u>: confronted by evidence they can't ignore, may question/abandon racist notions; avoid racist people; feel they don't fit with either European Americans or minorities; still perceive differences from a European American perspective

v. <u>Stage 5</u>: realize how being white affects experience; aren't racist; don't evaluate others from European American perspective; attempt to eliminate oppression

II. Adulthood: New tasks and responsibilities
A. Adulthood
1. <u>time span</u>: lasts for decades
2. <u>tasks of adulthood (for European Americans)</u>: taking responsibility for actions, being financially self-sufficient, living apart from parents
3. <u>stages of adulthood</u>: young adulthood, middle age, old age
4. <u>timing-of-events model</u>: adults move through stages with significant events or milestones
5. adulthood brings more opportunities to pursue individual goals; some experiences in adulthood may effect changes in personality (e.g., widowhood may led to developing independence)

B. Social roles in adulthood
1. <u>activities of adulthood</u>: intimacy (forming close relationships) & marriage
    a. marriage: source of companionship, emotional support, financial security, children, competing demands on time & energy
2. <u>gender perspectives on family roles</u>:
    a. competing social roles (positions that carry expectations for behavior) may produce role strain (stress resulting from difficulty in fulfilling multiple roles); males and females may experience different role strains and sexist beliefs of others may exacerbate role strain
        i. <u>example</u>: division of labor in the home for working women may be complicated by husbands believing that the division of labor is fair
    b. beliefs concerning family roles may be influenced by ethnicity and socioeconomic status
3. <u>caring for elderly parents</u>:
    a. caring for parents may increase role strain
    b. gender and ethnic differences occur in who is most likely to care for the parent and how person reacts to having to provide care
4. <u>ethnic perspective on family structure and roles</u>:

        a. <u>family structure</u>: composition of family and the relationships among its members
        b. <u>nuclear family</u>: the married couple and their children
        c. <u>extended family</u>: includes grandparents, uncles, aunts, cousins
        d. <u>fictive kin</u>: close friends who are treated as family members
        e. people of different ethnicities may define family differently

C. Parenting styles, roles, and conflicts
    1. <u>differing ideas on parenting</u>: parenting styles influenced by temperament of parents and children, upbringing, socioeconomic background, age, personality, styles of interacting
    2. <u>parenting types</u>: classification of parenting styles
        a. <u>authoritarian</u>: involves firm uncompromising limits on children's behavior; demand for total obedience
        b. <u>permissive</u>: involves few standards for behavior, little control over childrens' behavior, emotional distance/little involvement
        c. <u>authoritative</u>: involves setting firm standards for childrens' behavior, encouragement of child, expressions of love and involvement
    3. <u>ethnic and socioeconomic perspectives on parenting</u>:
        a. culture affects parental views of valued skills to pass on to children, child-rearing practices considered to be effective/appropriate
    4. <u>gender perspectives on parenting</u>:
        a. males/females viewed as having different parenting styles (authoritarian vs. authoritative)
        b. nurturing more a function of being in housekeeping/nurturing roles than due to biological capabilities in men/women
    5. <u>effects of divorce</u>:
        a. <u>effects of divorce on divorcing couple</u>: guilt, loss of friends, financial difficulties; need to mourn loss of marriage, dreams for future as couple, resolve anger, reexamine assumptions about marriage
        b. <u>effects of divorce on children</u>: affected by quality of relationship between divorcing parents, age of children at time of divorce

D. Middle-age accomplishments and cognitive reassessments
    1. <u>time span</u>: between 40-65 years old
    2. <u>tasks of middle-age</u>: generativity (Erikson) - productivity and accomplishing life goals (e.g., work/occupation)
    3. <u>cognitive reassessments</u>: reflecting on personal and occupational development
        a. may be triggered by death of parents, "mid-life crisis"

E. Physical and cognitive changes in adulthood
    1. <u>physical changes</u>: declines start to occur in strength, skin elasticity, cardiovascular efficiency, coordination, sensory acuity, reaction times, organ functioning; in women - menopause occurs

2. <u>cognitive changes</u>: some cognitive skills may improve but cognitive abilities generally decline after middle age

III. Old age: Changing responsibilities and abilities
A. Gerontology
1. <u>definition</u>: the study of the elderly
B. Social change: A change of social status for the elderly
1. <u>reasons for loss of social status</u>:
   a. <u>ageism</u>: prejudice and discrimination against people because of their advanced age; stereotype is that elderly are mentally and physically deficient
   b. <u>view of elderly in media</u>: elderly rarely appear in advertisements and when they do are often stereotyped
   c. <u>shift of knowledge sources</u>: elderly no longer viewed as having most current or valuable information based on experience
   d. <u>loss of usefulness</u>: retirement viewed as indication that person is no longer useful
C. Physical changes in old age
1. <u>normal changes of primary aging</u>:
   a. <u>primary vs. secondary aging</u>: natural changes brought about by age vs. changes brought about because of disease or deterioration due to lack of use
   b. <u>wear-and-tear theory</u>: predominant theory of primary aging that assumes people physically and mentally deteriorate as their body parts wear down
       i. deterioration occurs due to environmental damage or genetic errors
   c. examples of declines in functioning: declines in olfactory functioning, visual acuity, range of hearing
       i. declines in deterioration may be slowed by regular exercise
2. <u>disease and deterioration of secondary aging</u>:
   a. <u>example</u>: Alzheimer's disease
   b. <u>issue</u>: secondary aging confused with primary aging; underlying diseases sometimes left untreated
D. Cognitive changes in old age
1. <u>sources of cognitive change</u>:
   a. <u>wear-and-tear perspective</u>: brain neurons/nerve pathways wear out as we age, causing cognitive difficulties
       i. persons with less education (i.e., fewer neural pathways and connections) lose more memory
       ii. lack of stimulation may cause neural pathways to deteriorate
   b. diseases, such as heart disease, stroke, Alzheimer's disease, are related to cognitive functioning
E. Alternative perspectives on old age

   1. <u>gender perspective on old age</u>:
    a.<u> double jeopardy</u>: discrimination toward elderly women due to age and gender
     i. reflected in differences between elderly men and women in financial status
   2.<u> racial perspectives on old age</u>: may experience double and triple jeopardy for discrimination due to age, gender, race/ethnicity; may severely affect financial status
   3. <u>ethnic perspectives on old age</u>: ethnic differences in family structure may result in more social, emotional, financial support from extended family/fictive kin; elders in minorities may be given more responsibility/valued more highly; report greater life satisfaction than do European Americans

F. Dying
   1. <u>thanatology</u>: study of death and dying that focuses on the dying individual and survivors
   2. <u>near-death experiences</u>: area of study by some thanatologists

    a. <u>reasons for phenomena reported during near-death experience</u>:
     i. fear responses
     ii. activation of a new part of the brain
     iii. access to some spiritual energy
     iv. effect of diminished oxygen to the brain
   3. <u>survivors' coping with bereavement</u>:
    a. unconscious rehearsals for life as widow/widower
    b. consciously planning for roles after death
    c. rituals: funerals and funerary practice
    d. social support from family/friends
    e. story telling of final illness
   4. <u>stage models for coping with bereavement</u>: include shock, confusion, temporary disbelief, depression, anger, acceptance
   5.<u> dying from the perspective of the dying person</u>: need for compassionate listening

Additional Lecture Topics

1. **<u>Gay and Lesbian Identities</u>:**
  Among the "identities" one develops as part of the self-concept, one's sexual identity is an integral part. A number of stage or phase theories on the development of gay or lesbian identities occur in the literature. For example, Vivian Cass (1992) proposed the following set of stages describing the gay/lesbian identity formation process:
- *Stage 1--Identity confusion*: The person begins to recognize and question thoughts, feelings, or behaviors that might indicate that he or

she is gay or lesbian. Conclusion of this stage might involve acknowledging or rejecting that one is gay or lesbian
- *Stage 2--Identity comparison*: In acknowledging that one is gay or lesbian, awareness of the differences between oneself and others may emerge and accompany underlying feelings of alienation, "differentness", and estrangement from a heterosexual model for identity.
- *Stage 3--Identity tolerance*: Based in a need for belongingness, persons in this stage may seek out others who are gay or lesbian to develop a reference group; coming out to selected others who are also gay/lesbian may occur. However, feelings toward the self-identity are based in tolerance of rather than a true acceptance of the identity, reflecting internalized homophobia.
- *Stage 4--Identity acceptance*: The gay/lesbian identity becomes valued equally compared to others with heterosexual identity. Consideration of the positive aspects of gay/lesbian lifestyle as it fits in with the rest of society occurs as well as coming out to non-gay/lesbian others.
- *Stage 5--Identity pride*: Increasingly positive values associated with being gay/lesbian occur along with a growing commitment to gay/lesbian identity and identifying gays and lesbians as a primary reference group.
- *Stage 6--Identity synthesis*: Reduced alienation from interaction with heterosexuals along with reduced defensiveness and more openness regarding one's identity. Gay/lesbian identity is integrated into a larger perspective on the self as a complex person.

Similar to the ethnic identity models described in the text, sexual identity models of this nature propose stages of identity formation. It is worth noting that some authors, notably Anthony D'Augelli, caution that models of sexual identity formation (particularly those focusing on gay and lesbian identities) should reflect changes in sexual identity across the life span, considering vitally important developmental concepts of behavioral and developmental plasticity and interactive influences of biological, sociocultural, and political factors.

Additionally, the text highlights the development of ethnic identity in the context of a Caucasian-dominant society. Savin-Williams (1999) notes additional complicating factors that occur during the identification processes for ethnic-/sexual-minority youth. Specifically, "three tasks that ethnic-minority lesbian, bisexual, and gay youth face are: developing and defining a sexual and an ethnic identity; resolving potential conflict in allegiance with both reference groups or communities; and negotiating homophobia and racism" (pg. 122). Over the course of identity development, these youth may feel pressures to choose a primary identification with one or the other primary reference group, either ethnicity or sexual orientation, thus resulting in a sense of estrangement from or demands for denial of the other. Particular problems have been noted due to experiences with racism within the gay, lesbian, and bisexual communities (sometimes manifested in assumptions that gay, lesbian and bisexual issues are uniformly experienced across all ethnicities without consideration for unique cultural or ethnic assumptions concerning same-sex orientations) and homophobia in ethnic communities which may stem from cultural or traditional beliefs concerning gender-role expectations regarding the expression of masculinity/femininity, the nature of intimate relationships, and obligations toward family. For many ethnic youth, Savin-Williams points out, the family provides the basis for ethnic identity and may be rooted in collectivitistic beliefs concerning family obligation and honor, such that one's behavior affects and reflects upon multiple generations (past, present, and future) of an extended family network. Moreover, many ethnic-/sexual-minority youth may find that "coming out" about their sexual orientation challenges cultural beliefs about the taboo nature of discussion about one's sexuality and directly confronts expectations about marriage and production of heirs. Traditional family interpretations for neglect of these obligations because of one's sexual orientation may include beliefs that the individual is being selfish, has been drawn in too deeply into or "seduced" by a decadent, urban Anglo-American culture, or is rebelling against his or her traditional cultural background. Coming out may be viewed as a direct affront to those values, and thus may not be likely to occur, resulting in greater likelihood of decreased or inhibited identity development. Two passages summarize Savin-Williams' conclusions nicely; one summarizes the problematic issues whereas the other focuses on strengths that may be fostered by such experiences:

> "It is important to understand the dual identities, multiple roles, emotional conflicts, and psychological adjustments that result from the complex situations in which lesbian, bisexual, and gay ethnic-minority youths find themselves. Such youths endure two stigmas: being an ethnic minority and being bisexual, gay, or lesbian. Consequently, they encounter racism in gay and lesbian communities and homophobia in their cultural communities. It is a risky venture with profound repercussions for a healthy integration of personal and group identities." (pg. 131-132).

> "Forming an integrated multiple self-identification that includes ethnic and sexual identities is a protracted developmental process. Learning the skills to integrate and manage one aspect of a dissonant group identity, such as an ethnic-minority status, may facilitate the subsequent integration and management of a second dissonant group identity, such as sexual-minority status." (pg. 132).

Sources:

Cass, V. (1992). Lesbian/gay identity formation and coming out. Paper presented at the Seminar on Lesbian and Gay Health Issues

D'Augelli, A. (1994). Lesbian and gay male development: Steps toward an analysis of lesbian's and gay men's lives. (pg. 118-132). In B. Greene, and Herek, G. (Eds.), Lesbian and gay psychology: Theory, research, and clinical applications. Thousand Oaks, CA: Sage.

Savin-Williams, R. (1999). Ethnic-minority and sexual-minority youths. In L. Peplau, DeBro, S., Veniegas, R., & Taylor, P. (eds.), <u>Gender, culture, and ethnicity: Current research about women and men.</u> (pg. 121-134). Mountain View, CA: Mayfield Publishing Co.

2. **Three Historical Perspectives For Developing the "American" Identity:**

Uba and Huang suggest that "forming an ethnic and racial identity can be an important aspect of adolescent social development," and certainly that statement makes sense within the context of their discussion of the psychological perspectives on the development of self-concept. It also be important to note, however, that these psychological (and to some extent internal and private) events occur within a larger socio-political environment that bring larger historical pressures to bear on people (esp. people of color) to make them indistinguishable from a dominant or core cultural group (i.e, how they might become assimilated into a dominant group). This perspective is consistent with the ideas concerning the developmental niche presented in the additional lecture/discussion suggestions in the previous chapter. Milton Gordon describes 3 models of assimilation historically seen in the United States: anglo-conformity, the melting pot thesis, and cultural pluralism, and it is these three ideologies that continue to be present in some manner in our contemporary "larger human ecology". Before turning to these conceptual models, however, a quick snapshot of the early peoples who immigrated to what became the United States sets the stage.

Gordon describes the "story of America's immigration": At the time of the American Revolution, the Caucasian population was largely Protestant English in origin and had already "absorbed" the smaller numbers of immigrants from other Western European nations via "considerable ethnic intermixture". Gordon notes that the basic cultural differences between these groups of peoples were not particularly great and, since Africans were relegated to non-existent slave status and Native Americans were driven away, the process of assimilation on the citizenry posed few problems. With the continued influx of immigrants, however, discussions of and trends concerning assimilation emerged.

- *Anglo-conformity*: This ideological concept really embraces a number of beliefs and practices that appear to be centered around the preservation of and continuation of English sociocultural practices and institutions (including the use of English language) as "dominant and standard". It influenced political practice regarding immigration in two extreme ways by alternately supporting strict exclusion demands from some political groups (such as the American and Know-Nothing parties in the 1850s) on the one hand, but also by promoting no exclusion laws so long immigrants stripped themselves of previous cultural entanglements. Gordon contends that this perspective was embodied in John Quincy Adams' 1818 statement that immigrants were to understand that "if they cannot accommodate themselves to the character, moral, political and physical, of this country........,the Atlantic is always open to them to return to the land of their nativity....They must cast off the European skin, never to resume it." (pg. 93). It was also demonstrated in the "Americanization" movement during WWI when government and private organizations alike required immigrants to sign naturalization papers, learn English, and essentially "forget his former origins and culture." The strict immigration quotas established in the late 1920s were rooted in the Anglo-conformity ideologies.

- *Melting pot thesis*: Running counter to the Anglo-conformity ideology, the melting pot thesis represents the idea that the United States citizen, an "American", was in fact a new creation, and that the coming together of different ethnic groups of peoples would result in "a new race, a new religion, a new state, a new literature." --a totally new, blended group both culturally and biologically arising from the fusion of various peoples from different origins. All ethnic groups were considered eligible for incorporation from this perspective. The "open-door" immigration policies of the early 1900s, when interpreted from this perspective, allowed for this new creation to emerge, and was encouraged.

- *Cultural pluralism*: Gordon notes two trends that preceded the formal discussion of cultural pluralism in the literature. First, some melting pot theory investigators had found in their research that, while there were forms of merger occurring across nationality and ethnic boundaries, people from different origins were still tending to mix and marry within religious boundaries. Thus, according to one theorist, the one melting pot theory was more accurately described as a three melting pot reality (owing for the three major religious orientations discussed in the research: Catholic, Protestant, and Jew). Second, the concept of cultural pluralism grew out of early suggestions by settlement house workers who had found that immigrants' psychological states and family structures were being adversely affected by relentless attacks against their immigrant nationality/ethnicity origins. As a remedy, some settlement house workers advocated cultivating and nurturing the rich diversity of unique cultural perspectives and skills via public displays of cultural heritage such as what was done by Jane Addams at Hull House in Chicago. Authors of the day (circa 1915) embraced this theme by saying that cultural pluralism was the true embodiment of democracy and that the United States "must serve as an example of the harmonious cooperation of various heritages to a world inflamed by nationalism and war.." (pg. 99) - and "a multiplicity in a unity" (pg. 100). As a result, then, the ideology of cultural pluralism was taken up by many as the appropriate manifestation of the democratic founding of the country.

Remnants, both weak and strong, of each of these ideological themes continue to persist in the United States and, as they have historically, continue to influence cultural messages and political practices within this country. They provide part of the cultural context in which individual processes of ethnic identity formation occur.

Source:
Gordon, M. (1995). Assimilation in America: Theory and reality. In Aguirre, A., & Baker, D. (eds.), Sources: Notable selections in race and ethnicity. Guilford, CN: Dushkin Publishing Group.

3. **Hearing a voice on midlife transition:**
In describing the tasks and responsibilities of adult life, Uba and Huang mention that adulthood is sometimes defined by the significant events which occur in that time period. Moving away from parents, marrying, having children, developing financial independence are among but a few of the major events expected to occur. Moreover, some theorists note that transitions that occur in adult life are evaluated according to whether they occur within a culturally-expected time line (i.e., according to the social clock), and may include feelings of pressure and satisfaction relating to one's life (c.f., Scholossberg & Robinson, 1996; Helson & McCabe, 1993). Not only must we face a series of *anticipated transition*s, those events expected to happen, but we must also adapt to *unanticipated transition*s, events we don't expect to happen such as getting fired from a job. Additionally, *nonevent transitions* may arise when events we thought would happen don't materialize (e.g., not being able to have children, not getting into graduate school, etc.). Negative emotional reactions may emerge as a result of not meeting these culturally-dependent, social expectations that may affect our perceptions of our social and behavioral competencies as well as others' perceptions of us.

The following case study, presented by H. Michael Zal, represents the clinical impact of disruptions in the social clock and efforts to readjust the distressed individual's perceptions regarding herself and life's demands upon her. Nora, a member of the "sandwich generation", finds herself caught between the demands of adult children, her spouse, an aging parent and father-in-law, her job and her own expectations for what her life should be like as a 49-year-old woman. Growing emotional turmoil and signs of physical distress result. To her therapist, Nora complains "At this point in my life, I expected that I would be growing old gracefully and that everything would be O.K. I always assumed that as I got older I would get wiser, mellow, and have the answers to some questions. I thought that I would know what to expect and what others expected of me. I felt that I would be a calm and cool person. Instead, I feel terrible inside. I'm not who I should be. I'm not in control" (pg. 151). Committed to her family, Nora was still heavily involved in the lives of her children, all legal adults by this point. She worried extensively about the problems experienced by her 19-year-old in college, her 23-year-old unemployed son who was separated from his wife and daughter, and her 25-

year-old daughter who was living again in the family home with her fiancé and baby son. Nora's aging mother was experiencing a decline in health and, for the first time, Nora was considering her own health and mortality. Similar problems were occurring for her father-in-law. Her husband's extensive work commitments with his business and a housing addition, in addition to his history of heart problems worried Nora, and resulted in feelings of estrangement. As a managing supervisor who valued her job and the security it provided, she was faced with administrative changes and work-related stress and pressure, which she handled by increasing her work efforts and taking on more responsibilities. In short, Nora's beliefs and expectations about what she thought life would be like at 49 and what reality presented to her were two very different scenarios. As part of therapy, Nora confronted her traditional values and belief systems, grew more assertive and expressive. "Most of all, she tried not to feel guilty if she could not be everything to everyone."

Nora's story reflects the impact of expectations regarding the social clock and is also consistent with discussion on Erikson's views on generativity. Students might find the topic of the social clock to be interesting from the standpoint of culturally-derived frameworks for assessing role-related achievements in their lives. Another potential area for discussion might include discussing potential gender and/or ethnic differences in expectations concerning the social clock.

Sources:
Helson, R., & McCabe, L. (1993). The social clock project in middle age. In B. Turner, & Troll, L. (Eds.), Women growing older. Newbury Park, CA: Sage.

Scholossberg, N., & Robinson, S. (1996). Going to plan B. New York: Simon & Schuster/Fireside.

Zal, H. M. (1995). The squeezed generation. In D. Sattler & Shabatay, V. (eds.), Psychology in context: Voices and perspectives. (pg. 150-154). Boston: Houghton Mifflin.

4. **Models of Childbirth:**
The text offers discussion concerning parenting once children have arrived. It does not, however, speak to issues concerning pregnancy and child birth--issues pertinent to many adults. A number of excellent, informative overviews of historical perspectives on childbirth are available, covering the enforced decline of midwifery and the medicalization of childbirth, evidence of racism, classism, and sexism in the medical control of birthing technologies, and contemporary feminist attempts to regain natural childbirthing techniques and restore birthing rights/choice to women (see Andersen,1993 and Matlin,1993). The following discussion reviews a very current article by Margaret Nelson on the relationship between social class (a topic not discussed in the text but which clearly affects the lives of women and people of color) and childbirth.

Although a number of models for childbirth have been discussed in the literature, Nelson (1999) notes that two common models have generally been discussed: a medical model in which the child-bearing woman is largely passive and follows orders from medical personnel and a "natural childbirth" model in which the woman is an active participant in an experience, with as little technological intervention as is necessary. Certainly, these models may be at odds with one another, especially if medical personnel and the child-bearing woman hold different views about what should happen. Moreover, Nelson argues that the "natural childbirth" approach, at least the contemporary version which stems from feminist critique of the traditional medical model, essentially assumes this to be the most common "client" model (i.e., the model that most women would prefer) and that this assumption overlooks potentially important differences among women due to social class (or other authors might add, due to ethnic backgrounds). This concern, as it turns out, is grounded in Nelson's observation that the "natural childbirth" model was largely developed, written about, and articulated by middle-class women who were motivated by a feminist consciousness. She speculated about whether this model would appropriately apply to working class women, however. Thus, as part of an outcome assessment of changes in an obstetrics and gynecology department in a hospital in the Northeast, Nelson began investigating the role of class differences in the pregnancy and childbirth experience.

Nelson began her study expecting that biases of medical personnel toward women of different social economic status would predict the nature and quality of medical care received by these different women. Moreover, she thought that class differences would predict whether a woman's preferences for procedures was followed during the birth process, and that women in higher SES classes would be more likely to have their requests respected, and those in lower SES (those of lower status) would be more likely to have their preferences disregarded or replaced by "medical" opinions of the medical personnel. She found, however, that her original assumptions concerning conflict between women of different classes and the medical community were incorrect. Rather, she found that women of different social classes (in this study classified by amount of education and/or type of job held) differed significantly in terms of their attitudes toward pregnancy, their experiences during childbirth, and their post-partum evaluations of the childbirth experience. For example, middle-class women were more likely to view pregnancy, labor, delivery, and the presence of the baby following birth as interrelated pleasures, whereas working-class women made clear pleasure distinctions between these stages, such that the pregnancy, labor and delivery were viewed as less pleasurable than the baby's presence. Moreover, working women were more likely to be concerned about the pain of delivery, experiencing less pain or shortening the length of labor and delivery, and potential medical complications and technological safety, while middle-class women focussed on personality conflicts with doctors, obstacles to the delivery being a pleasurable experience, personal participation, and a more cooperative relationship with their doctor. Working-class women experienced more medical intervention during their birthing experience and less participation in the event than did middle-class women. Unlike what Nelson suspected would happen, neither group of women had all their requests during the process met. Post-partum evaluations varied in that working-class women again made reference to pain issues whereas middle-class women were more likely to refer to the "experience" in a broader sense and describe pleasurable aspects.

In considering the potential sources for class differences in the childbirth experience, Nelson speculated that understanding the data requires that we understand the different contexts in which these the groups of women experience birth. Working-class women were likely to have children at a younger age, have more children at home, and to have not planned the pregnancy. Nelson notes "they also had fewer material resources with which to raise these children." (pg.265). She argues that "the movements that created the "middle-class" model of birth experience do not clearly address the working-class context of childbirth." (pg. 265). The middle-class model she observed arose from sociocultural-political factors such as the natural childbirth movement, feminism, consumerism, and a "back to nature" romanticism which combined to urge women to become active participants in birthing, rejecting the authority of men or male control over birthing processes and choices, to "shop around" for good and services. Nelson points out that these social forces "do not have immediate relevance for working-class women", many of whom do not have the time, money, or luxury of taking natural childbirth classes and shopping around for different service providers. She also cautions that many of the changes being made in hospitals' birthing centers appear to be centered around the middle-class model for childbirth and, as a result, moving from the medical model to the middle-class model again assumes only one model of childbirth relevant to women.

The points raised by Nelson are interesting from the standpoint of delineating problems that arise from developing models that over-generalize women and neglect to consider the diverse set of individual, social, cultural, economic, and political factors that affect lives and determine human experience. Although Nelson does not introduce ethnicity into the discussion, this article provides a basis for considering how ethnicity and social class might interact to lead to even more complicated models of childbirth. Again, these are issues many students are likely to encounter.

Source:
Andersen, M. (1993). Thinking about women: Sociological perspectives on sex and gender (3rd ed.). (pg. 200-208). New York: Macmillan.
Matlin, M. (1993). The psychology of women (2nd ed.). (pg. 378-383). Forth Worth, TX: Harcourt Brace Jovanovich.
Nelson, M. (1999). Working-class women, middle-class women, and models of childbirth. In L. Peplau, DeBro, S., Veniegas, R., & Taylor, P.

(eds.), Gender, culture, and ethnicity: Current research about women and men. (pg. 251-268). Mountain View, CA: Mayfield Publishing Co.

5. **Cross-cultural studies on parenting**:

Uba and Huang describe issues concerning parenting according to Baumrind's classifications of authoritarian, authoritative, and permissive parenting styles and discuss ethnic, sociocultural, and gender perspectives with regard to parenting. The work of the following author expands on that theme by discussing cross-cultural comparisons investigating gender differences in parenting behaviors toward children.

Phyllis Bronstein (1999) conducted a study of parent sex differences in child-rearing behaviors because, she noted, historically many studies have assessed parenting behaviors in mothers rather than both mothers and fathers. Moreover, those studies that have included fathers have often focused on either children's perceptions of their parents' roles and behaviors, or assessed fathers' relationships with infants and pre-school aged children. Finally, such studies tended not to be conducted in naturalistic settings. Therefore, Bronstein sought to investigate the parental child-rearing behaviors of both fathers and mothers in Mexico toward their older children (ages 7-12) in everyday settings. In keeping with the findings from previous studies, she predicted mothers and fathers would differ in the affective nature of their interactions, with mothers being more nurturing and fathers more aloof. When giving feedback to children, she expected mothers to use more subtle, psychological means of controlling children, whereas fathers were expected to use more directive and informative messages. Finally, she expected that fathers would behave differently toward the children based on their gender.

Using an in-home observational method, she found that, far from the traditional view of fathers as the "aloof Mexican patriarch", these fathers were no less affectionate toward their children than where the mothers. They did tend, however, to interact differently towards boys versus girls. With boys, fathers tended to show more attention and use more of a cognitive/achievement orientation, whereas with girls they tended to engage in more sociable, gentle interactions. Thus, Bronstein concluded that fathers were important socialization agents in teaching children about traditional sex roles: boys received messages that their activities and ideas were important and that they were capable of achievement, whereas girls received messages that they were docile, and that information that girls had to share was less important since fathers tended to interrupt or ignore them more frequently. Bronstein notes "very different messages were being transmitted to girls and boys--about their roles, their temperaments, their thinking, and their expected behaviors--and father were the main transmitters of those messages" (pg. 79).

Bronstein also found that mothers and fathers differed in the nature of the interactions, such that mothers tended to engage in more caretaking activities, whereas fathers were more likely to engage in playful, participatory activities. She concludes these differences occur due to the separation of parental work domains. In other words, mothers' primary responsibilities involve household work, and thus many interactions with children involved monitoring children's duties around the home. Fathers, on the other hand, had less household work involvement, as their primary work domain existed outside the home. Thus, fathers' interactions with children involved attention with playful activities. In her final summary and conclusions, Bronstein notes that trends in this study were remarkably very similar to those found in studies in the United States with younger children using different methodologies. Moreover, she notes that these findings stand in contradiction to stereotypical beliefs and perceptions that fathers are nonparticipatory or aloof in their interactions with children. Although mothers and fathers may interact differently with their children, nevertheless, they are both active.

Source:
Bronstein, P. (1999). Differences in mothers' and fathers' behaviors toward children: A cross-cultural comparison. In L. Peplau, DeBro, S., Veniegas, R., & Taylor, P. (eds.), Gender, culture, and ethnicity: Current research about women and men. Mountain View, CA: Mayfield Publishing Co.

6. **Work and Culture's Effects on the World of Work:**
One of the central tasks for adults in most cultures, occupying a good deal of time as well as being central to self-concept, is work. Richard Brislin (1993) notes that occupational settings are increasingly placing people in intercultural contact due to the growing gender and ethnic complexity of the work force, as well as expanding international markets and contacts. From this perspective, consideration of the effect culture, or more specifically, cultural values in the workplace seems appropriate for discussion with students who already are or will soon be entering the work force.

Brislin suggests that five culturally-based values are important to consider:
- *Individualism and collectivism*: In cultures emphasizing collectivism, group needs and cohesion are held above individual needs and goals. Goals of work are satisfied through group effort, and it is expected that individual members of a group contribute to the group effort and be cooperative with other group members toward achieving the group goal. Organizations and work efforts are based upon group endeavors, and individuals are characterized in relation to their position within a group. In individualistic cultures, individuals may choose to pursue goals either through group work or individually. Once goals have been accomplished, groups may disband. In the United States, tolerance is shown for individual work patterns and working individually on projects whereas, in Japan, workers are expected to

cooperate in joint activities and participate in group-enhancing activities.

- *Power distance*: Related to status differences within cultures, low power distance cultures emphasize little status separation between bosses and subordinates; thus employees feel more free to offer suggestions for changes or criticisms to their bosses. In high power distance cultures, workers accept the power differences inherent in the status difference between themselves and their bosses; to disagree with one's boss would produce a great deal of discomfort. Moreover, high power distance cultures tend to expect that persons occupying different status level are responsible for their own obligated duties, and it would be inappropriate for either status position to tell the other what to do (a form of a "hands off" orientation).

- *Uncertainty avoidance*: Brislin notes that people everywhere tend to have concerns about the future in some form and that "all cultures have guidelines that help in the avoidance of uncertainty" (pg. 257). In high uncertainty avoidance cultures, this theme is manifested in the work environment through practices such as an increasing number of rules, laws, norms, or informal guidelines for work-related organization. For example, Social Security benefits being linked to work efforts and being drawn from paychecks represent to some degree this concern in United States workers (although, in general, the United States is characterized as a low uncertainty avoidance culture). More risk-taking with few rules and regulations occurs in low uncertainty avoidance cultures because, although peoples holding these beliefs realize that the future can be uncertain, generating rules does not appear to fit as a solution. In business arenas, getting firms from high uncertainty avoidance cultures to make changes or even agree to a business venture may be difficult, due to many rules and assurances being required from the onset and difficulty finding someone in authority to support the proposed project if failure is a possibility.

- *Masculinity-femininity*: The terms *masculinity* and *femininity* in this discussion refer to traditionally-held beliefs about masculine and feminine attributes. "Masculine" work values embrace assertiveness, competitiveness, and decision-making with less regard for the people-factor of the decision; "feminine" work values emphasize working conditions, worker relationships, cooperation, and consideration of people's feeling in corporate decision-making. Brislin suggests that some cultures operate mainly from the masculine perspective (e.g., Japan), whereas others (e.g., Scandinavian countries) from the feminine perspective. These themes may be reflected in business policy regarding employee benefits and family leave arrangements, and differential emphasis on work achievement vs. working conditions.

- *Confucian dynamism*: This last cultural theme, occurring mainly in Asian cultures according to Brislin, reflects the influence of Confucius' "set of practical ethical guidelines [as they apply] to guide everyday behavior' (pg. 262). In this example, Brislin notes that key principles of Confucian thought are reflected in the differing role obligations for individuals in boss-employee relations (for example); in beliefs that maintaining harmony and allowing individuals to maintain face (self-respect) is vital; and in expectations that a virtuous life is centered around "working hard, acquiring useful skills and as much education as possible, not being a spendthrift, and persevering when faced with difficult tasks." Occupational beliefs and practices may be shaped by these fundamental cultural beliefs regarding conduct in everyday life within that culture. Other cultures, based in other religious/philosophical perspectives, may carry those beliefs into the work environment (for example, the Protestant work ethic spoken of in the United States).

This discussion highlights the need to consider a primary adult activity, work, within the cultural context in which it occurs.

Sources:
Brislin, R. (1993). Understanding culture's influence on behavior. (pg. 245-267). Fort Worth, TX: Harcourt Brace Jovanovich College Publishers.

Suggestions for Additional Readings
Balka, C. & Rose, A. (Eds.) (1989). Twice blessed: On being lesbian and Jewish. Boston: Beacon Press.

Birren, J., & Schaie, K. (Eds.) (1990). Handbook of the psychology of aging. San Diego: Academic Press.

Boston Lesbian Psychologies Collective (Eds.) (1987). Lesbian psychologies: Explorations and challenges. Urbana, IL: University of Illinois Press.

Brooks-Gunn., J., Learner, R., & Petersen, A. (1989). The encyclopedia of adolescence. New York: Garland.

Clarke-Stewart, A., Perlmutter,. M., & Friedman, S. (1992). Lifelong human development (2nd ed.). New York: Wiley.

Cross, W. (1991). Shades of Black: Diversity in African-American identity. Philadelphia: Temple University Press.

Helms, J. (1990). Black and white racial identity: Theory, research, and practice. New York: Greenwood Press.

Ramos, J. (1994). Companeras: Latina lesbians. New York: Routledge.

Ratti, R. (Ed.) (1993). A lotus of another color: An unfolding of the South Asian gay and lesbian experience. Boston: Alyson.

Tremble, B., Schneider, M., & Appathurai, C. (1989). Growing up gay or lesbian in a multicultural context. Journal of Homosexuality, 17, 253-267.

Troiden, R. (1988). <u>Gay and lesbian identity: A sociological analysis</u>. New York: General Hall.

Wallerstein, J., & Kelly, J. (1980). <u>Surviving the breakup: How children and parents cope with divorce</u>. New York: Basic Books.

Woodruff-Pak, D. (1988). <u>Psychology and aging</u>. Englewood Cliffs, NJ: Prentice-Hall.

In-Class Activities and Demonstrations

1. **TRAIL Blazing**: Using **Transparency Masters 9.1 - 9.5**, review with students the "Checking Your TRAIL" sections in the chapter. Have students work in small groups to answer the questions and then review with the class as a whole to tie the text reading to activity in class.

2. **Reaching Critical Mass**: Using **Transparency Masters 9.6 - 9.8**, review with students the "Critical Thinking" sections in the chapter. Have students work in small groups to answer the questions and then review with the class as a whole to tie the text reading to activity in class.

3. **Getting Down to IT**: Using **Transparency Masters 9.9 - 9.14**, review the "Integrative Thinking" sections in the chapter with students. Have students work in small groups to answer the questions and then review with the class as a whole to tie the text reading to activity in class.

4. **Reflections at 75**: Life expectancy in the United States hovers at around 75 (c.f., Hoffman, 1988). Thus, many students no doubt anticipate a long life ahead in which to accomplish many personal and occupational achievements. Using **Activity Handout 9.1**, students are to envision themselves at their 75th birthday party describing what they will look like physically, what they will have accomplished occupationally, and how their social aspirations will have been met. After completing the handout, have students compare with one another their visions of themselves as older adults and consider to what extent those visions are influenced by cultural and gender-related expectations.

5. **Ethnicity and You**: For this activity students will need to have their textbook handy and have read the sections pertaining to the Minority Identity Development and White Racial Identity models. Students are to identify which stage they believe they are in presently and provide examples that support their responses. Engage in class discussion on the various stages being represented in class and, more generally, discuss students' reaction to the stage approach to ethnic identity formation.

6. **Media Parents:** **Activity Handout 9.2** asks students to consider the parenting styles represented on television and describe their observations concerning the apparent impact of those styles on the children involved. Discuss the extent to which media parents reflect true-to-life parenting within our culture, noting gender and ethnic distinctions that may be observed.

7. **Your social clock is ticking**: The concept of the social clock was described in Additional Lecture topic # 3. In completing **Activity Handout 9.3**, students consider relevant transition periods expected in our

culture from the standpoint of when they achieved or plan to achieve those accomplishments, and their beliefs of what is a generally accepted timeline for doing so. Note differences that may occur across students that appear to be linked to gender or ethnic backgrounds.

Sources for Additional Activities
Books:

Benjamin, L. & Lowman, K. (1981). <u>Activities Handbook for the Teaching of Psychology</u>. Washington DC: American Psychological Association.

Halonen, Jane 1995). Chapter 3: The developing person. In <u>The critical thinking companion for Introductory Psychology.</u> New York: Worth Publ.

Makosky, V. et al. (Eds.) (1995). <u>Activities Handbook for the Teaching of Psychology</u> (Vol. III). Washington DC: American Psychological Association.

- **World Wide Web**: Check out the following WWW sites for information and activities relevant to this section of the text!
    - Addison Wesley Longman's Website -- **http://longman.awl.com/**
    - PsychZone link -- **http://longman.awl.com**
    - Psych Web -- **http://www.gasou.edu/psychweb/psychweb.htm**
    - Self-Quizzes for Introductory Psychology -- **http://www.gasou.edu/psychweb/selfquiz/selfquiz.htm**
    - Psychology Jumping Stand -- **http://www.indiana.edu:80/~iuepsyc/PsycJump.html**
    - The Psychology Place -- **http://www.psychplace.com**
    - PsychZone -- **http://www.longman.awl.com**
    - Generation X issues -- **http://www.iherald.com/**
    - Midlife Moments homepage -- **http://www.bestyears.com/indes.html**
    - AARP Webplace -- **http:/www.aarp.org/**
    - Successful Midlife Development's homepage -- **http://midmac.med.harvard.edu/midmac.html**
    - Sexuality and relationships -- **http://www.campuslife.utoronto.ca/services/sec/bc.html**
    - Divorce -- **http://www.divorcenet.com/ny/nyart09.html**
    - Mental health issues for adolescents -- **http://education.indiana.edu/cas/adol/mental.html**
    - Death and dying -- **http://longhorn.jjt.com/~tcf_national/**
      or
      http://www.katsden.com/death/index.html
    - Physical loss, chronic illness, bereavement -- **http://asa.ugl.lib.umich.edu/chdocs/support/emotion.html**
    - Parent's Page homepage -- **http://www.efn.org/~djz/birth/babylist.html**
    - Birthing issues -- **http://www.efn.org/~djz/birthindes.html/**
    - Adolescence -- **http://www.personal.psu.edu/faculty/n/x/nxd10/adolesce.html/**

- Administration on Aging homepage -- **http://www.aoa.dhhs.gov/**
- Adult development -- **http://www.iog.wayne.edu/apadiv20/newslet.html/** *or*
  http://www.iog.wayne.edu/apadiv20/lowidv20.html/
- Families -- **http://www.personal.psu.edu.faculty.n/x/nxd10/family3.html**

- **Audio-Visual Support**
  <u>Films/Videos</u>:

  <u>Adolescence/Teens</u>
  - *Adolescence: A Case Study* (CRM, 20 minutes)
  - *Adolescence: The Winds of Change* (MOTO, 30 minutes)
  - *Dear Lisa: A Letter to My Sister* (NDF, 45 minutes)
  - *Frontline: Guess Who's Pregnant?* (PBS, 59 minutes)
  - *Personality: Adolescence* (CRM, 21 minutes)
  - *Targets* (LCA, 19 minutes)
  - *Teen Mother: A Story of Coping* (CHUH, 28 minutes)
  - *The Unknown Generation X* (FFHS, 28 minutes)
  - *The Spiritual Quest of Generation X* (FFHS, 30 minutes)
  - *Stop It! Students Speak Out About Sexual Harassment* (FFHS, 17 minutes)
  - *Dealing With Peer Pressure: I Made My Choice* (FFHS, 30 minutes)
  - *Putting Your Self-Esteem in Focus* (FFHS, 30 minutes)
  - *Teenage Pregnancy* (FFHS, 26 minutes)
  - *Too Soon for Jeff: Coping with Teen Pregnancy* (FFHS, 44 minutes)
  - *Teenage Pregnancy Series* (FFHS, 35-40 minutes)
       Program 1: *Teen Dads' Point of View*
       Program 2: *Going It Alone: Preparing for Single Parenthood*
  - *Teenage Turn-On: Drinking and Drugs* (CRM, 38 minutes)
  - *What Guys Want* (POLY, 16 minutes)
  - *When Teens Get Pregnant* (POLY, 18 minutes)
  - *Teen and Child Depression* (FFHS, 19 minutes)

Adult Life/Aging
- *The Human Animal Series* (FFHS, 52 minutes each)
    Program 1: *Love & Sex*
    Program 2: *War & Violence*
    Program 3: *Nature & Nurture*
    Program 4: *Woman & Man*
    Program 5: *Family & Survival*
- *Aging* (FFHS, 26 minutes)
- *Factors in Healthy Aging* (FFHS, 28 minutes)
- *Aging Well* (FFHS, 16 minutes)
- *The Aging Process* (FFHS, 19 minutes)
- *Live Long and Prosper: Longevity and High-Tech Medicine* (FFHS, 57 minutes)
- *Never Say Die: The Pursuit of Eternal Youth* (FFHS, 60 minutes)
- *The Gift of Aging* (FFHS, 28 minutes)
- *Menopause: Passage to Paradise* (FFHS, 24 minutes)
- *Abandoning the Elderly* (FFHS, 16 minutes)
- *To Be Old, Black, and Poor* (FFHS, 52 minutes)

Families/Relationships
- *Gay Couples: The Nature of Relationships* (FFHS, 50 minutes)
- *Man Oh Man* (NDF, 18 minutes)

Loss/Death
- *Heaven Can Wait* (FFHS, 40 minutes)
- *Terminal Illness: When It Happens to You* (FFHS, 50 minutes)
- *Living Fully Until Death* (FFHS, 29 minutes)
- *Toward a Better Death* (FFHS, 28 minutes)
- *Letting Go: A Hospice Journey* (FFHS, 90 minutes)
- *Death: An Overview* (FFHS, 50 minutes)
- *Death* (FFHS, 23 minutes)
- *Saying Goodbye* (FFHS, 26 minutes)
- *Between Life and Death* (FFHS, 51 minutes)
- *Coma: The Silent Epidemic* (FFHS, 53 minutes)
- *Calling Dr. Kevorkian: A Date with Dr. Death* (FFHS, 55 minutes)
- *Grief: The Courageous Journey* series (FFHS, 24 minutes each)
    Understanding Grief
    Loss of a job
    Loss of a family
    Loss of a relationship
    Loss of a daughter
    Loss of a son
    Loss of a spouse
    Facing death
    Portraits of grief

- *Teen Suicide* (FFHS, 35 minutes)
- *Teenage Suicide* (FFHS, 19 minutes)
- *"Don't Kill Yourself": One Survivor's Message* (FFHS, 23 minutes)
- *Everything to Live For* (FFHS, 52 minutes)
- *Suicide: The Teenager's Perspective* (FFHS, 26 minutes)
- *Grieving: Suddenly Alone* (CF, 26 minutes)

Transparency Master 9.1: Checking Your TRAIL 9.1

I. Which of the following developments is NOT a secondary sex characteristic?
   A. enlarged breasts in females
   B. deepening of voice in males
   C. mood swings
   D. growth of pubic hair

II. Research has found that among the reasons adolescents sometimes don't use contraceptives are (a) they are self-conscious about using them (Holmbeck et al., 1994); (b) they believe that contraception is unnecessary because negative consequences can never result from a loving relationship; and (c) they think *they* are so unique that *they* would never get AIDS or unintentionally create a pregnancy (Farber, 1994). What characteristics of adolescent thought can contribute to each of these reasons for failing to use contraceptives?

III. Name three factors that influence the self-concept a person forms.

IV. Based on the models presented, what general parallels exist between the development of racial identity for both minority and white Americans?

Transparency Master 9.2: Checking Your TRAIL 9.2

I. **True** or **False**: Across cultures, a person is considered an adult when that person becomes 18 or 21 years old.

II. What causes role strain?

III. Which of the following statements is FALSE?
 A. "Family structure" refers to the composition of a family and the relationship among its members.
 B. Culture affects which skills parents think children need and the parents' choice of child-rearing practices.
 C. Males in North America have more role strain than females.
 D. The effects of divorce on children depend partly on the age of the children at the time of the divorce.

IV. How would cross-sectional and longitudinal studies of parenting differ?

Transparency Master 9.3: Checking Your TRAIL 9.3

I. Middle age is roughly the period
   A. between 25 and 50 years old.
   B. between 40 and 65 years old.
   C. when everyone experiences a midlife crisis.
   D. when males undergo a male menopause.

II. What two changes in the family can cause middle-aged adults to assess their satisfaction with their lives and future?

III. <u>True</u> or <u>False</u>: Most people reach their physical peak in their 30s.

IV. Menopause is characterized by a drop in the level of
   A. testosterone.
   B. estrogens.
   C. androgens.
   D. neurons.

Transparency Master 9.4: Checking Your TRAIL 9.4

I. The wear-and-tear theory holds that we physically and mentally deteriorate as we age for two reasons: _____ damage and _____ errors.

II. Which one of the following statements is true?
   A. The wear-and-tear theory attempts to explain secondary aging.
   B. Wrinkled skin is a sign of secondary aging.
   C. Most people over 65 years of age have mental deterioration due to Alzheimer's Disease.
   D. The ability to detect odors and identify them deteriorates noticeably starting in the mid fifties.

III. <u>True</u> or <u>False</u>: The elderly are more likely to have difficulty hearing female voices than male voices.

IV. Which of the following statements is true?
   A. Retired U.S. males are usually poorer than retired U.S. females.
   B. The difference in income between European Americans and African Americans or Latino/a Americans decreases in old age.
   C. Elderly European Americans are more likely than elderly African Americans to live in a household with extended family members.
   D. Elderly African-, Filipino/a-, and Latino/a-Americans often receive support from fictive kin.

Transparency Master 9.5: Checking Your TRAIL 9.5

I. People who have had a near-death experience frequently report seeing
   A. a hearse and a funeral.
   B. a party and a rainbow.
   C. a tunnel and a light.
   D. a star and a cloud.

II. Which of the following explanations has NOT been offered for near-death experiences?
   A. they are a fear response
   B. they represent a stage of sleep
   C. they result from the brain being deprived of oxygen
   D. they are caused by activation of a new part of the brain

III. <u>True</u> or <u>False</u>: In the United States, widowers are more likely than widows to have an established network of people who can provide emotional support.

IV. Identify six emotional experiences people go through in dealing with the death of a loved one.

Transparency Master 9.6: Critical Thinking 9.1

Given the information in Table 9.3, if Al is white, which type of white racial consciousness characterizes his attitudes about race?

Consider for a moment the descriptions of cross-sectional and longitudinal studies on the effects of divorce in children. Which type of study would be more difficult to conduct, a cross-sectional or longitudinal study? If you wanted to compare the emotional impact of divorce on children in the 1970s versus children in the present, would you conduct a cross-sectional or longitudinal study? Why?

Transparency Master 9.8: Critical Thinking 9.3

What alternative interpretation could explain the difference in memory loss between educated and uneducated people?

Transparency Master 9.9: Integrative Thinking 9.1

Based on your understanding of operant conditioning, as described in the Learning chapter, what effect might such unnerving and annoying police behavior (i.e., following the Asian- and African-Americans for no apparent reason) have on a minority person's tendency to drive through Beverly Hills?

Transparency Master 9.10: Integrative Thinking 9.2

Based on what you learned about the three models of concept formation and the concepts of assimilation and accommodation in the Cognition & Intelligence chapter, describe how the social worker probably formed her concept of a male gender role and her interpretation of the adolescent's behavior in the example on pg. 363.

Transparency Master 9.11: Integrative Thinking 9.3

In light of what you read in the Learning chapter about modeling and scripts, what reasons can you give for the high rate of divorce among those persons whose parents divorced?

Transparency Master 9.12: Integrative Thinking 9.4

How might concept accessibility, discussed in the Cognition and Intelligence chapter, contribute to the maintenance or reinforcement of stereotypes about the aged?

Transparency Master 9.13: Integrative Thinking 9.5

Suppose your grandmother has little appetite. Given what you just read about olfactory loss and what you learned in the Sensation & Perception chapter, what reason might there be for her lack of appetite?

Transparency Master 9.14: Integrative Thinking 9.6

Recall from the Consciousness chapter that, compared to younger people, the elderly spend less time in REM sleep. During the REM period, nerve connections in the brain are thought to be checked or expanded and newly learned information is integrated into existing concepts. What sleep-related, biological explanation might account for poor memory in the elderly?

Activity Handout 9.1

Reflections at 75

Instructions: Imagine that you are at your 75th birthday party. In the space below, describe what you will look like physically and what you will have accomplished in your life by that point. What will your outlook on life be at that point and what will have influenced it the most? Consider how your gender and/or your ethnic background will have influenced your life experiences.

Activity Handout 9.2

Media Parents

Instructions: View one television show that involves parents in interaction with a child or children and complete the following questions.

Show: _____
Parental figures: _____
Child(ren): _____

Did the parents use the following parenting styles (as described in your textbook)? If so, provide examples for evidence.

    Authoritarian: _____
_____

    Authoritative: _____
_____

    Permissive: _____
_____

What were the child's or children's reactions to parenting styles? _____
_____
_____
_____
_____

To what extent did themes relevant to gender, socioeconomic status, or ethnicity as described in the text appear in the parent-child interactions you observed? _____
_____
_____
_____
_____

Activity Handout 9.3

Your Social Clock is Ticking!

Instructions: Consider the following events that may occur during your lifetime. For each event, note the age at which the event occurred for you or age at which you expect that it will happen. Similarly, at what ages do you think these events happened/will happen for your parents and what are generally expected ages for these events in our culture.

Event	You	Parents	Culturally Expected
First stayed home alone			
First stay away from parents			
First drove car			
First date			
First kiss			
First job (part-time)			
First serious romantic relationship			
Graduation from high school			
Graduation from college			
Marriage			
First job related to career			
First significant promotion			
First child born			
First home purchase			
Achieving significant life goals			
Achieving financial security			
Making your "mark" in job			
Retirement			

Note any events in which there are significant differences between expectations for you vs. your parents and write down potential reasons for those differences. Also note any events in which there are differences between you vs. cultural expectations and again write down potential reasons for those differences.

CHAPTER 10

COMMUNICATION

Chapter Overview
    Learning Objectives
    Chapter Outline

Additional Lecture Ideas
    Lecture Topics
    Additional Readings

In-Class Activities and Demonstrations
    Activities and Demonstrations
    Sources for Additional Activities

World Wide Web

Audio-Visual Support

Handout and Transparency Masters

Chapter Overview

Learning Objectives

After studying this chapter, you should be able to do the following:

1. Describe the components of interpersonal communication.

2. Explain the characteristics of interpersonal communication.

3. Examine the nature of human language and its relationship to thoughts, feelings, and the brain.

4. Describe the process of language acquisition and theories that attempt to explain it..

5. Explain the role of nonverbal behavior in communication.

6. Describe how gender and culture influence communication.

Chapter Outline

Communication

I. Communication: An interpersonal activity
  A. Interpersonal communication
   1. definition: the process by which people exchange information and give it meaning
   2. produces agreement and arguments/conflicts
   3. important role in individual behavior and interpersonal relationships
   4. what psychologists study:
      a. process of communication (i.e., component parts, channels of communication)
      b. how people learn to communicate
      c. how culture/gender affect communication
  B. The components of communication
   1. verbal communication: any communication with words
   2. nonverbal communication: communication through means other than words, such as through gestures or facial expressions
   3. components of communication: aspects of communication essential to the process
      a. sender: source of message
      b. message: thought or feeling conveyed by sender
      c. physical channel: speech, writing, gesturing used to communicate the message
      d. encoding: translation of an idea into a symbol (word, body movement) that represents the idea
      e. receiver: person who gets the message
      f. decoding: receiver's interpretation of the message
      g. feedback: receiver's reaction to the message
   4. role of social rules/conventions: influence choice of message recipient, nature of message, nature of the communication interaction
   5. miscommunication: communication failures can occur at any point of the process; decoding failures are major source of miscommunication because receiver's perceptions might not match sender's intention
   6. active listening: an active, effortful process whereby a person receives and thinks about a message, eliminates distractors, considers the sender's perspective; asking questions of sender/paraphrasing message clarifies meaning

C. The characteristics of communication
1. <u>communication has consequences</u>: successful communication creates reaction in receiver
2. <u>communications can be conscious or unconscious</u>: sending messages may be intentional and unintentional
3. <u>communications can be self-reflective</u>: we judge the message and receiver's reaction during the communication process; modifications in communication occur as a result
4. <u>communications are not reversible</u>: once a message is sent, it can't be taken back
5. <u>communications have contexts</u>: message meaning varies with context in which it is delivered; context helps us decode meaning of a message

II. Verbal communication: Using language
A. Language
1. <u>definition</u>: a system of communication that allows people to encode meanings into words and combine words to express ideas and feelings
2. <u>advantages</u>:
   a. increases communication precision and efficiency
   b. allows us to share knowledge and experiences
B. Producing unique expressions
1. <u>productivity</u>: the ability to create an infinite number of new sentences using a finite number of words and rules; such flexibility allows expression of unique thought
2. <u>words represent things</u>: each word act as a symbol representing objects, experiences, ideas and has at least one meaning allowing people who speak the same language to decode each other's messages
   a. denotative meaning: meaning equivalent to definition
   b. connotative meaning: personal, subjective meaning
3. <u>grammar organizes the message</u>: to use words effectively, need to combine them in orderly, predictable way
   a. <u>grammar</u>: rules for ordering of words and phrases into sentences
C. What the voice communicates
1. <u>paralanguage</u>: nonword sounds that accompany speech
   a. <u>prosody</u>: speed & pitch of voice
   b. <u>vocal qualifiers</u>: vocal sounds such as crying, sighing, that accompany speech
   c. <u>vocal segregates</u>: vocal sounds that break up a sentence (e.g., "uh")

2. <u>paralanguage</u>:
    a. is given greater weight than actual message when the two conflict
    b. underlies judgements about speakers
    c. is understood from a listener's cultural perspective
    d. is more integral to communication in some cultures than in others
    e. influences our behavior towards the speaker

D. Language and thought
1. Sapir said language shapes our perception of reality by defining thoughts
2. <u>linguistic determinism</u>: the theory that language structures thought and organizes our view of the world; strict linguistic determinism has been largely rejected
3. <u>implications</u>:
    a. if language shapes/organizes view of world, people who speak different language understand world in fundamentally different ways
    b. if haven't learned language, unable to think
    c. language differences affect ability to express ideas, not ability to have them
4. <u>impact of gendered terms on thinking</u>:
    a. use of gender-biased terms evokes images of males/may influence judgements of gender appropriate behavior in readers/listeners
5. <u>studying bilingual peoples</u>:
    a. studies reveal that bilingual people may have:
        i. greater ability to form concepts
        ii. more cognitive flexibility
        iii. enhanced verbal creativity
        iv. more motivation to learn

E. Language and emotions
1. <u>language shapes emotions</u>:
    a. studies on bilingual people reveal that they:
        i. express negative emotions in native language
        ii. discuss embarrassing issues in second language
        iii. retrieve emotionally charged information in native language

F. Language and the brain
1. <u>aphasias</u>: disorders involving an inability to comprehend or express ideas using language as a result of brain damage
2. <u>Broca's aphasia</u>: a disorder that results from damage to the lower part of the left frontal lobe and is characterized by difficulty in producing, but not in understanding, grammatical speech
3. <u>Wernicke's aphasia</u>: a disorder associated with damage to the upper part

of the left temporal lobe and characterized by an inability to understand the precise meaning of words

4. recovery of language skills following brain injury depends on age at the time of injury

III. Language development
A. Learning to talk
1. <u>developmental patterns</u>: same basic steps of language acquisition at approximately the same rate occur across cultures
   a. begin language acquisition through interactions with parents/caretakers
   b. <u>motherese/parentese</u>: changing paralanguage shown by adults when talking to babies characterized by a lilting, high-pitched voice and exaggerated tone
2. <u>cooing and babbling</u>:
   a. <u>cooing</u>: nonword vowel sounds made by infants beginning around 2-3 months of age; done in response to adult speech or to express themselves and to simulate conversation
   b. <u>babbling</u>: infant sounds made by stringing vowel-consonant pairs into sequences of syllables such as "bababa" to helps babies learn specific mouth/throat movements needed to create distinct sounds
3. <u>phonemes and accents</u>:
   a. <u>phonemes</u>: the smallest unit of sound in any language; although thousands of phoneme combinations are possible, babies learn which are part of their native language
   b. <u>accents</u>: learning to recognize and produce phonemes from their own language
4. <u>morphemes and meanings</u>:
   a. <u>morphemes</u>: the smallest unit of sound in a language that has meaning (either whole words or word elements)
5. <u>early words and sentences</u>:
   a. <u>overextension</u>: using a single word to refer to many items
   b. by 18 months, produce names, action words, nouns and verbs; then combine simple words into two-word units and two-word sentences
   c. by 2 years, using sentences containing several words
   d. between 2-3 years, use telegraphic speech involving short, correctly ordered noun-verb phrases that do not contain unessential elements
   e. by 4 years, adept at forming full sentences

B. How is language acquired?
1. <u>learning language occurs if</u>:
   a. environment provides the sounds of a spoken language
   b. have opportunities to practice the language
   c. biologically ready to learn a language
2. <u>learning language</u>:
   a. <u>learning theory</u> : language is an operant behavior reinforced by experiences in a language-rich environment; may affect rate of language acquisition
   b. <u>criticisms of learning theory perspective</u>:
      ii. doesn't explain language acquisition after hearing word only once or without external reinforcement
      ii. doesn't explain why children create nongrammatical sentences they probably haven't heard
      iii. deaf children make same language errors as hearing children
      iv. children master grammar without reinforcement
3. <u>an innate language mechanism</u>:
   a. babies born with innate ability to acquire language
   b. <u>language acquisition device (LAD)</u>: as proposed by Chomsky, an innate device that acts as a "blueprint" or guideline for grammar that babies use to make sense of the voices around them
   c. LAD tells us
      i. to divide words into categories
      ii. distinguish individual words or meaningful phrases within a string of sounds
      iii. figure out correct sequence for nouns/verbs
      iv. notice how wards are changed to denote plurality, ongoing action, and past tense

IV. Nonverbal communication
A. Introduction
1. <u>nonverbal communication</u>:
   a. convey emotions, meanings
   b. is influenced by cognitive schemas of receiver
   c. betray unspoken true feelings
2. <u>important nonverbal cues</u>:
   a. <u>turn taking</u>: taking turns in speaking during conversation
      i. varies between cultures

B. Body movements
1. <u>body language</u>: influences our perceptions of others
2. <u>example</u>: walking
   a. cross-cultural differences

C. Gestures
1. used in place of or to amplify speech
2. cross-cultural differences in meaning

D. Facial Expressions
1. may be used by sender to convey meaning or decoded by receiver to indicate interest/boredom/emotion
2. <u>eye contact</u>: discourages/encourages communication; may convey respect, dishonesty, attention, power/status over another person
    a. cross-cultural differences in meaning
3. <u>smiling</u>: most readily recognized facial expression
    a. conveys happiness as well as other emotions; conceals socially unacceptable emotions
    b. cross-cultural differences in meaning

E. Personal space
1. differences reflect living environment (urban vs. rural), relationships between speakers, conversation topic, emotions, gender of speakers more than cross-cultural differences

F. Cultural perspectives on nonverbal communication
1. <u>high-context communication</u>: meanings from communications are implied rather than stated in straightforward manner; predominate in collectivist cultures
2. <u>low-context communication</u>: communication in which meaning is stated explicitly; predominate in individualistic cultures

V. Communication between men and women in European American culture

A. Nonverbal communication
1. <u>gender differences noted in</u>:
    a. expression of nonverbals
    b. use of nonverbals for revealing different emotions
    c. decoding nonverbals
    d. amount of attention paid to nonverbals
2. <u>explanations for gender differences in nonverbal communication</u>:
    a. socialization; power differentials; social influence
3. <u>eye contact</u>: gender differences in frequency, duration, reciprocation of eye contact
    a. <u>interpretations of gender differences</u>:
        i. relationship status
        ii. gender of conversation participants
        iii. social status
4. <u>smiling</u>: gender differences in frequency of smiling
    a. <u>explanations for gender difference</u>:
        i. control of expression
        ii. social meanings

B. Verbal communication
- 1. <u>gender and verbal skill</u>:
  - a. females acquire verbal skills earlier and have greater verbal fluency
  - b. females/males are more similar than different in verbal skills
- 2. <u>gender and verbal style</u>:
  - a. <u>stereotypes</u>: females talk more, speak softly, express ideas as insecure questions; males talk less, speak with authority, state opinions strongly
  - b. <u>explanation</u>: imbalance of power
  - c. <u>problems with this perspective</u>:
    - i. gender/power not synonymous
    - ii. oversimplifies view of communication differences

C. Gender and conversational expectations
- 1. <u>general finding</u>: men/women similar in verbal communication
  - a. <u>gender difference</u>: women focus on preserving harmonious relationships/men focus on establishing dominance
- 2. <u>showing interest versus indicating agreement</u>:
  - a. females ask more questions, show signs of listening; ask questions to keep conversation going, express interest
  - b. males ask questions to request information
- 3. <u>expressing desire</u>:
  - a. males/females express desires in similar ways but use different strategies
  - b. females talk in inclusive terms, give explanations for saying no, phrase requests as proposals
  - c. males make commands, use self-promoting statements, make statements without explanation
  - d. <u>possible explanations</u>: socialization and childhood play experiences

Additional Lecture Topics

1. **Speech acts: Purposes achieved by language**:
    In 1975, philosopher John Searle noted that the way we use language is largely dependent on the underlying purposes we hope to accomplish. Almost all acts of speech, he contends, can be categorized in one of five basic groups:

    representative speech acts: an act of speech that conveys a belief that a given proposition is true and which ultimately may or may not be verifiable. *Example*: "Bill Clinton is not a good president."

    directive/indirective speech acts: an act of speech that attempts to get a listener to do something. Asking questions may be indirect speech acts designed for the purpose of obtaining information. *Examples*: "Please quiet down." (directive); "What date is this?" (indirective).

    commissive speech acts: an act of speech that commits the speaker to some course of action in the future. *Example*: "I'll pick you up at 8:00 am."

    expressive speech acts: an act of speech that conveys information about the psychological state of the speaker. *Example*: "I'm sorry I was late picking you up this morning."

    declarative/performative speech acts: an act of speech that results in a new state of affairs. *Example*: when a professor draws a close to her lectures on language by stating, "With that, I'm done with my discussion of language."

    Searle's taxonomy illustrates the purposive nature of language within its social context and provides an additional perspective to Uba & Huang's discussion on using language.

Source:
    Searle, J. (1975). Indirect speech acts. In Cole, P. & Morgan, J. (eds.), Syntax and semanitcs: Speech acts (Vol. 3, pp. 58-92). New York: Seminar Press.

2. **Cooperative enterprise in conversation**:
    H. Grice (1967) has argued that successful conversation requires cooperation between the involved parties. Specifically, the two parties have to communicate in ways so that the listener can understand what the speaker is attempting to convey. To achieve this final result, Grice suggests involved parties must follow four conversational maxims or postulates:

    Maxim of quantity: Comments made in conversation need to be informative at a level required for the conversation. Avoid providing too little or more information than the conversation requires.

    Maxim of quality: Contributions to a conversation must be truthful

    Maxim of relation: Comments need to be relevant to the conversation (i.e., digressions

    Maxim of manner: Comments need to be clear and to the point (i.e., free from vague or obscuring terms/phrases)

These ideas underscore the participants' expectations for the nature of content during a meaningful conversation and expand upon Uba and Huang's discussion of conversational expectations.

Source:
Grice, H. (1967). William James Lectures, Harvard University, published in part as "Logic and conversation." In P. Cole & Morgan, J. (eds.), <u>Syntax and semanitcs: Speech acts</u> (Vol. 3, pp. 41-58). New York: Seminar Press.

3. **Conversational Ballgames**:

Nancy Sakamoto has written an entertaining personal account of her observations concerning English-Japanese cross-cultural conversational differences that I think many of your sports-minded students would enjoy. Ms. Sakamoto was married and lived in Japan where she gradually developed her skills with the Japanese language. As her confidence with her ability to understand and speak the language increased, she attempted to take part in conversations with her husband and others...only to have the conversation end abruptly. What was the problem? Ms Sakamoto notes: "Finally, after listening carefully to many Japanese conversations, I discovered what my problem was. Even though I was speaking Japanese, I was handling the conversation in a western way." Here she draws colorful comparisons between Western/Japanese conversational styles and sports. She likens Western conversational style to tennis: A speaker "serves" out a conversational tidbit to which the conversational partner responds, agrees or disagrees, sending the conversational "ball" back to a different point on the original speaker's side of the court. The ball goes back and forth, the more vigorous the action the better. When conversation involves more than 2 people, the rules of "doubles" tennis or even volleyball apply: whoever is nearest the ball or whoever is quickest grabs it and hurtles it back into play. If the ball is on your side, it's your responsibility to do something with it then and there, or someone else will jump in to do something with it. The ball isn't kept on one side for any great length of time.

Japanese-style conversation is not like tennis but rather is more like bowling, claims Sakamoto. Conversation participants wait for their turn to participate and turn taking is based on status, relationships to the speakers, etc. When it is a speaker's turn, he or she picks a ball and carefully rolls it down the alley as others watch. After a pause in which that person's points are tallied, the next person in line does the same, putting his or her conversational ball into action but starting at the same starting line using a different ball than the first player. There is no back and forth in conversational bowling..."all the balls run parallel. And there is always a suitable pause between turns."

Sakamoto's initial experiences with conversations in Japan were less influenced by her early skills in the Japanese language as they were by essentially attempting to play the wrong game. She notes her early frustrations with Japanese students learning English conversational skills. She would serve a "ball" to them and be frustrated when their pauses would let the ball drop. When someone did speak, they didn't refer to what others had said, giving the appearance that no one was paying attention to what was happening in the conversation....it lost the back and forth quality of Western-style conversation with which she was more familiar.

The game rules of conversation apply even in the everyday circumstance of dinnertime conversation. Whereas Western conversationalists often chat away during the meal, grabbing bites of food while someone else at the table is batting the ball around, Japanese conversationalists generally find it inappropriate to hold extended conversation at dinner where the conversational rules for turntaking could result in losing time to eat. Sakamoto's lively and humorous writing style contributes to this addition to the idea of turntaking and conversational style differences.

Source:
Sakamoto, N. (1998). Conversational ballgames. In Sattler, D., & Shabatay, V. (eds.), <u>Psychology in context: Voices and perspectives</u>. Boston: Houghton Mifflin.

4. <u>Aria: A memoir of a bilingual childhood</u>:

Richard Rodriguez describes his touching personal experience growing up as a bilingual child in California. As the third of four children, he spoke English at school yet lived in the Spanish-speaking section of Sacramento, and spoke Spanish at home. He describes his childhood reactions to the two languages: English was a "public language" where words were "directed to a general audience of listeners", "meaningfully ordered" and "used to make oneself understood by many others." Spanish, on the other hand, was the private language, the language of home and intimacy. Upon the request of Richard's school teachers, his parents agreed to emphasize using English at home. In Richard's words, "in an instant they agreed to give up the language (the sounds) which had revealed and accentuated our family's closeness." (pg. 124).

Using English became a family game, yet it was still foreign and distant, until one morning he noticed the change in his parents' voices when they switched from Spanish in their private conversation to English with him: "The gringo sounds they uttered startled me. Pushed me away. In that moment of trivial misunderstanding and profound insight, I felt my throat twisted by unsounded grief. I simply turned and left the room. But I had no place to escape to where I could grieve in Spanish." From that point on, more determined to learn English, he noticed fewer "troubling sounds" of the language of *los gringos*....he no longer heard eccentric pitches or sounds of speech, the American accent. "Now when I heard someone's tone of voice--angry or questioning or sarcastic or happy or sad--I didn't distinguish it from the words it expressed. Sound and word were thus tightly wedded." (pg. 125).

As the children in his household learned more English, a growing silence at home occurred between parents and children. For his part, Richard was at a loss for even what to call his parents: "My mother! My father! After English became my primary language, I no longer knew what words to use in addressing my parents. The old Spanish words (those tender accents of sound) I had earlier used--*mama* and *papa*--I couldn't use any more. They would have been all-too-painful reminders of how much had changed in my life." (pg. 126). Richard's mother (who learned English) became the public voice for the family, his father silent unless in conversation with relatives. "In Spanish he expressed ideas and feelings he rarely revealed when speaking English. With firm Spanish sounds he conveyed a confidence and authority that English would never allow him." (pg. 126).

Rodriguez' passage exposes the reader to some of the personal, indeed, emotional ramifications of bilingualism.

Sources:
  Rodriguez, R. (1998). Aria: A memoir of a bilingual childhood. In Sattler, D., & Shabatay, V. (eds.), Psychology in context: Voices and perspectives. Boston: Houghton Mifflin.
  Sternberg, R. (1998). In search of the human mind. (pgs. 307-309). Fort Worth, TX: Harcourt Brace.

5. Getting used to Netiquette:

With the expanding use of the Internet for quick communication in academia and for personal use, students may be familiar (or may need to become familiar) with the term "netiquette", the rules for appropriate communication on the 'Net. Various books are available discussing the Internet and the following are a few of the rules noted in them:

- using all upper case letters (LIKE THIS) implies that the speaker is shouting (considered very bad manners)
- using emoticons, such as variations of the smiley face :-), and acronyms (IMHO, in my humble opinion or <g> for grin) conveys feelings or facial expressions
- e-mail, newsgroup, and discussion group messages are expected to be kept short (or at least one should warn others of lengthy messages) -- this is considered especially important for others who have to pay for Internet use.
- avoid the use of flaming (being intentionally rude or insulting) or engaging in flame wars (an Internet shouting/insult match)
- "lurk" before you leap -- if you are a "newbie" to the Internet, follow newsgroups for a while before posting your own messages to discern what topics are typically discussed and types of messages that are typically exchanged.
- some authors of newsgroup messages aren't reliable or accurate with their "facts" -- don't believe everything you read
- given the diversity of users, many who may not use English as their native language, be tolerant or politely correct errors in spelling or grammar
- don't spam -- spam is the Internet equivalent to junk mail and is highly irritating to users who find their mailboxes loaded with irrelevant

material.

avoid cross-posting -- cross-posting is sending the same message to different newsgroups, the Internet equivalent to running from room to room at a party with the same message. Frequently the same users belong to different newsgroups and will be receiving duplicate messages. Repetition can annoy other discussants.

Combine a discussion of the conventions for Internet communication with **Activity Handout # 10.3**.

Sources:

Mahony, D. (1996). The Internet guide for psychology. Boston: Houghton Mifflin Company.

Reddick, R., & King, E. (1996). The online student: Making the grade on the Internet. Forth Worth, TX: Harcourt Brace.

Whitford, F. (1998). Quick guide to the Internet for psychology. Boston: Allyn and Bacon.

6. Representing diversity in language:

A number of resources are available if you wish to include some lively and informative discussion of the relationships between language and gender, or ethnicity, or "differentness" into your class. For example, in *The psychology of women*, Margaret Matlin raises the following issues concerning gender and language:

Using non-parallel terms for men and women: When describing some occupations, people may insert the terms "lady" or "female" or "woman" to describe an individual (such as a "female pilot") suggesting that there is *something exceptional* about a woman doing this type of work whereas men doing the same work are not referred to as a "male pilot".

Words referring to women may be negative or carry sexual connotations: Consider, for example, the comparable terms *bachelor-spinster*, *master-mistress*, and *dog-bitch*. Matlin contends that terms such as these may start out equally positive in the language, but the terms referring to women have drifted toward negative meanings. She also points out that dictionary studies (e.g., Henley, 1989) have found that analysis of masculine versus feminine terms indicates that the former are more frequently associated with prestige, and that more negative connotations surround the latter.

Using different titles to address men and women: Married women may be referred to as *Mrs. John Doe* rather than as *Jane Doe* or *Mrs. Jane Doe*. In a personal observation, Matlin notes that her students may tend to address her as *Ms*. Matlin rather than *Mrs*. Matlin, but she wonders if they are more likely to address male professors as *Dr*. Rubin (1981) reports that students are more likely to call women who are professors by their first names.

Using generic masculine nouns and pronouns: In their writings and conversation, some students and authors continue the practice of using "he" to generally refer to all of humanity (e.g., "When the first year student enters the college classroom, he is likely to find..."). Students are likely to report that they have been taught that this is acceptable and a gender inclusive or neutral writing style. But Matlin (and others) have challenged the idea that the generic "he" is, in fact, neutral...they believe generic masculine terms bias the reader's perceptions. For example, two reviews of literature indicate that when people read information containing generic masculine terms they are more likely to think about males than females (Henley, 1989; Matlin, 1985). Schneider & Hacker (1973) had study participants select illustrations for a textbook. Participants were more likely to choose all-male pictures when chapter titles were "Social Man" or "Industrial Man" than if they were "Society" or "Industrial Life".

Using generic masculine terms may also influence the reader's career choice beliefs. For example, Briere and Lanktree (1983) have students read different versions of a paragraph describing psychologists, one using generic masculine terms and the other, gender-neutral terms. Those who read the generic masculine version rated psychology as a less attractive career for women than did those who had read the gender-neutral version. Thus, it appears that using the generic "he" is far from being gender-neutral.

The American Psychological Association has established a series of guidelines for reducing bias in language and writing, outlining the guiding principles to be observed. Use Activity Handout # 10.4, which reviews some of those principles and demonstrates inappropriate writing styles, as part of your discussion.

Source:
Matlin, M. (1993). The psychology of women (2nd ed.) (pg. 239-245). Fort Worth, TX: Harcourt Brace.

7. Active listening: When Uba and Huang discuss the communication process, they describe the practice of active listening as part of the listener's attempt to decode the sender's message. Many students probably think they are active listeners but may be surprised that the process actually takes as much energy as it does. In expanding on the topic, consider incorporating information from Egan's classic text, *The skilled helper*, which has been used to teach countless numbers of clinicians and counselors the skills for being effective helpers. Chapter 4 of the book covers important points involved in the listening process.

Attending: Attending skills involve being "present" during a conversation, paying attention and letting the speaker know by your posture, eye contact, etc. that you are with them. The basic skills of attending are summarized in the acronym SOLER which stands for:

S: <u>facing the speaker squarely</u>. In North American culture, this is the "posture of involvement" indicating to the speaker that the listener is present and available. Turning away, not facing the speaker reduces involvement.

O: <u>adopting an open posture</u>. By having our arms to our sides (rather than crossed in front of us) and out legs uncrossed in a nondefensive posture, we communicate openness and availability to the speaker.

L: <u>leaning toward the speaker</u>. Inclining our bodies toward a speaker indicates we are interested what the speaker is saying, there is some closeness or intimacy between speaker and listener.

E: <u>maintaining eye contact</u>. Eye contact, glancing away occasionally, staring...all send messages of level of interest in the speaker and the conversation.

R: <u>being relaxed</u>. Relaxed, comfortable, or natural body movements help the sender feel comfortable with the conversation and send messages about our comfort level with the conversation.

Active listening: Effective attending sets the stage for listening carefully to what is being said both verbally and nonverbally. Active listening requires that the listener listen to and attempt to understand both. Egan stresses that when speakers talk, they provide information about their experiences, behaviors, and affect. The effective listener incorporates all these messages into their understanding of the situation. Moreover, effective listeners learn how to listen to and read bodily behaviors, facial expressions, voice-related behaviors (i.e., pitch, pauses, silences, fluency, etc.), observable autonomic physiological responses (e.g., paleness, blushing, pupil dilation), physical characteristics (e.g., fitness, height, weight) and general appearance (e.g., grooming, dress) with the understanding that these nonverbals may be used to confirm or repeat, deny or confuse, strengthen or emphasize, or control or regulate a conversation. To fully understand what is being conveyed, the effective listener must consider the context of the speaker's experiences; how what they are expressing fits into the broader scope of events and meaning in that person's life. Finally, active listening involves empathic listening, learning to understand correctly the speaker's emotional state and responding based on that knowledge.

Barriers to effective listening (the shadow side of listening): A number of barriers may interfere with the active listening process. They may include:

inadequate listening due to distractions or being preoccupied with something else.

evaluative listening by judging the speaker's comments as good-bad, acceptable-unacceptable.

filtered listening, which includes listening through our own series of experiences, values, labels.

fact-centered vs. person-centered listening involves over-emphasis on collecting facts and information instead of finding out about the person.

rehearsing or practicing or thinking about what we as listeners should say in response to the speaker.

sympathetic listening: agreeing with, feeling sorry for, taking emotional sides with the speaker as opposed to understanding the speaker and the situation.

Listening to oneself: Egan contends that, to be an effective helper (or in a larger context, an effective partner in the communication process), "you need to listen not only to the client but also to yourself." In short, some level of self-awareness is required to truly be a partner in the communication process. How are you as a listener feeling toward the speaker, where are your thoughts, where should the conversation go? This "shadow conversation", as Egan calls it, can either be a distraction or a useful tool for helping (and being an effective communicator).

Source:
Egan, G. (1998). The skilled helper: A problem-management approach to helping. (pgs. 61-79). Pacific Grove, CA: Brooks/Cole.

8. Language and medical care:

When students consider the importance of the communication process, one area where breakdowns in communication or miscommunication may have serious ramifications is in the area of personal health. Shelley Taylor, in her book *Health Psychology*, notes that "poor patient-practitioner communication has been tied to outcomes as problematic as patient noncompliance with treatment recommendations and the initiation of malpractice litigation." (pg. 342). Lacking the technical expertise for judging technical quality of care, patients do know if they liked or disliked the practitioner, and satisfaction with care is frequently based on satisfaction with the quality of the interaction or communication between client and practitioner.

Taylor suggests that factors that erode the communication process can include "aspects of the office setting itself, the changing nature of the health care delivery system, practitioner behaviors, patient behaviors, and qualities of their interaction." (pg. 343).

The office setting: The office setting works against effective communication. The patient is ill but nevertheless is expected to respond to specific and difficult questions from a relative stranger. The practitioner, perhaps working under a tight schedule, must obtain information from a patient who may not have the same ideas about what is an important symptom.

Structure of the health care delivery system: The development of HMOs has altered the historical relationship between practitioners and patients. When patients were receiving care from a physician under private, fee-for-service conditions, keeping patients satisfied with care and service was of importance. It fostered a patient orientation. Some HMOs function heavily on a referral system, where one practitioner refers the patient to another practitioner for services. Since practitioners are paid on the number of cases they see, referrals are desirable and a colleague orientation rather than patient orientation develops. The referral process may develop feelings in the patient of being shuffled from one practitioner to another without developing any personal relationship with any one practitioner. The pressures to see as many patients as possible may also mean that the patient waits for a long time and has a relatively short visit with the practitioner. The factors combine to create lower patient satisfaction with care.

Practitioner behaviors: Taylor notes the following behaviors/beliefs on the part of the practitioner may interfere with effective communication:

not listening: as noted in a number of studies, practitioners are likely to interrupt patients (sometimes in less than 20 seconds from the beginning of the patient's description of symptoms) and may direct their descriptions of symptoms toward a certain disorder

using jargon or technical language: Practitioners may use terminology that is far too technical for patients to comprehend. Some authors contend that practitioners may do so to keep patients from asking too many questions, that it may be a carryover from their training, or that they simply are unskilled at determining what patients will be able to understand.

using simplified explanations or infantilizing talk: The opposite extreme of overly technical language, simplified explanations also result in miscommunications when patients feel insulted by being talked down to or by not having their questions answered at the technical level they themselves have used. Some authors have suggested that this might particularly be the case if patients aren't native English speakers and themselves speak in broken English.

depersonalizing the patient: objectifying the patient, replacing reference to him or her with reference to the disorder, may distance, confuse, or alarm the patient who may feel their presence or their personhood is being ignored.

affect communicated to the patient: when practitioners' nonverbal communication suggests anxiety or concern, patients may focus less on content of messages.

perjorative stereotypes held concerning patients: According to Taylor, numerous studies indicate that practitioners may be more likely to provide less information, be less supportive, be less clinically proficient, be less likely to engage in active treatment protocols, or initiate resuscitation in emergency rooms when dealing with patients of color or lower SES.

Patient behaviors: Since communication is a two-person process, patients also bring aspects to the process that might result in miscommunication.

not remembering instructions: Taylor notes that many patients are unable to recall pertinent information regarding diagnosis and treatment within minutes after having heard the information. Some forgetting may be due to the setting and practitioner factors listed above, whereas some may be due to factors unique to each patient (such as those listed below).

patient anxiety: heightened anxiety tends to reduce the amount of information that people are able to recall. Certainly, hearing information concerning one's health that might be potentially threatening along with the often unfamiliar context of medical settings serves to increase anxiety in patients.

intelligence : Patient with low intelligence level may have impaired capabilities for understanding medical information. Taylor notes that this may interact with class-based, sociolinguistic factors to result in miscommunication.

prior experience with the disorder: Patients with prior experience with an illness are more likely to recall information concerning instructions for treatment.

responding to different cues about the illness: Patients and practitioners respond to different cues concerning the patient's illness. Patients tend to emphasize pain and symptoms that interfere with life activities whereas practitioners are more concerned with the underlying illness. As a result patients may not understand questions that they view to be less relevant and pay less attention to instructions concerning treatments that don't address what they perceive to be the relevant symptoms.

providing faculty cues about their true concerns: Patients may present the symptoms that are concerning them the most, that they perceive to be indicative of something serious, as if they were of little or incidental concern to them. When practitioners don't provide more information about that concern, patients may interpret this as secrecy on the part of the practitioner.

Interactive aspects of the communication process: The communication process may not provide practitioners with information concerning outcome or success of the communication. If the patient does not return following a diagnosis and/or treatment recommendation, they may not know if the treatment was successful or, if it was not, if the patient sought services from another practitioner. Due to the cautious nature of patients' reactions to a practitioner, he or she might not receive feedback concerning patient satisfaction with the communication process and/or the emotional aspects of their relationship. When feedback is received, it often tends to be negative rather than positive. Lack of feedback and negative feedback does not provide adequate opportunity for the practitioner to assess his or her communication skills.

To reduce the chance that miscommunication might result in decreased satisfaction, low patient adherence to medical regimen, and potential medical complications, Taylor offers the following remedies:

- including courses in verbal and nonverbal communication skills in medical school curriculum.
- designing interventions to increase patient involvement in the treatment process.
- teaching patients to ask questions of physicians.
- providing written treatment instructions so patients may have something to refer to when needing to clarify and increase their understanding of the treatment program.
- changing treatment programs so they are less complicated, fit the individual patient's life style and goals, breaking advice into manageable sub-goals.

This is one additional topic area that is usually highly relevant to many students and one that tends to generate many anecdotes and much discussion with the students. A meaningful and relevant extension of the basic issues of communication covered in Chapter 10.

Sources:

Seijo, R., Gomez, H., & Freidenberg, J. (1995). Language as a communication barrier in medical care for Hispanic patients. In A. M. Padilla (ed.), Hispanic Psychology: Critical Issues in Theory and Research. (pgs. 169-181). Thousand Oaks, CA: Sage.

Taylor, S. E. (1995). Health psychology (3rd. ed.). (pgs. 342-369). New York: McGraw-Hill.

Suggestions for Additional Readings

Adler, R., Rosenfeld, L., & Towne, N. (1983). Interplay: The process of interpersonal communication. (2nd. ed.). New York: Holt.

Bickerton, D.(1983). Creole languages. Scientific American, 249(1),116-122.

Carroll, D. (1986). Psychology of language. Pacific Grove, CA: Brooks/Cole.

Cavalli,Sforza, L. (1991). Genes, peoples, and languages. Scientific American, 265(5), 104-110.

Clark, H. (1985). Language use and language users. In G. Lindzey & E. Aronson (Eds.), Handbook of social psychology (2nd ed. Vol. 2, pp. 179-231). New York: Random House.

Damassio, A., & Damassio, H. (1992). Brain and language. Scientific American, 267(3), 88-95.

Gamkrelize, T., & Ivanov, V. (1990). The early history of Indo-European languages. Scientific American, 262(3), 110-116.

Gleason, J. (Ed.). (1985). The development of language. Columbus, OH: Charles E. Merrill.

Greenberg, J., & Ruhlen, M. (1992). Linguistic origins of native Americans. Scientific American, 267(5), 94-99.

Gudykunst, W. (1994). Bridging differences: Effective intergroup communication (2nd ed.). Thousand Oaks, CA: Sage.

Hickson, M., & Stacks, D. (1993). Nonverbal communication: Studies and applications (3rd ed.). Dubuque, IA: Brown & Benchmark.

Jackendorf, R. (1994). Patterns in the mind: Language and human behavior. New York: Basic Books.

Kolers, P. (1968). Bilingualism and information processing. Scientific American, 218(3), 78-86.

Krauss, R., & Glucksberg, S. (1977). Social and nonsocial speech. Scientific American, 236(2), 100-105.

Lutz, W. (1989). Doublespeak. New York: HarperCollins.

Mindell, P. (1994). A woman's guide to the language of success: Communicating with confidence and power. Englewood Cliffs, NJ: Prentice Hall.

Moskowitz, B. (1978). The acquisition of language. Scientific American, 239(5), 92-108.

Pinker, S. (1994) The language instinct. New York: HarperCollins.

Premack, A., & Premack, D. (1973). Teaching language to an ape. Scientific American, 227(4), 92-99.

Renfrew, C. (1994). World linguistic diversity. Scientific American, 270(1), 116-123.

Rubin, J. (1990, May/June). The smart-talk syndrome. In Health, pp.38-39.

Sidransky, R. (1990). In silence: Growing up hearing in a deaf world. New York: St. Martin's Press.

Tannen, D. (1994). Talking from 9 to 5. New York: William Morrow.

Taylor, I., & Taylor, M. (1990). Psycholinguistics: Learning and using

language. Englewood Cliffs, NJ: Prentice-Hall.
In-Class Activities and Demonstrations

TRAIL Blazing: Using Transparency Masters 10.1 - 10.5, review with students the "Checking Your TRAIL" sections in the chapter. Have students work in small groups to answer the questions and then review with the class as a whole to tie the text reading to activity in class.

Reaching Critical Mass: Using Transparency Masters 10.6 - 10.8, review with students the "Critical Thinking" sections in the chapter. Have students work in small groups to answer the questions and then review with the class as a whole to tie the text reading to activity in class.

Getting Down to IT: Using Transparency Masters 10.9 - 10.10, review the "Integrative Thinking" sections in the chapter with students. Have students work in small groups to answer the questions, and then review with the class as a whole to tie the text reading to activity in class.

Slanguage game: create your own language: The purpose of this exercise is to emphasize the importance of shared knowledge or common understanding in the meanings of terms in conversation. Using **Activity Handout # 10.1**, students are to create 3-4 slang terms and then use them in conversations with their friends for a few days. Students should note their friends' reactions to the terms and any misunderstandings that arise from their use. Discuss some of their examples in class. Another fun addition to this activity would include bringing several examples of rap tunes to class (with lyrics typed out for students) and discuss possible meanings for the slang terms used in the songs.

Communication exercise: The following exercises emphasize the interactive nature of successful communication and the importance of questions and feedback in that process. Using **Activity Handout # 10.2**, have students complete the activity and then discuss their experiences as a class. Students should work in pairs. Their task is for one student to describe the geometric figures accompanying the handout as the other attempts to draw it according to the description. This exercise works best if students stand back-to-back, with one student describing the figures and the other drawing them. The exercise is even more interesting if you instruct them that the drawer cannot ask any questions of the describer until after they think the figures have been completed. Describer and drawer alike should note their frustrations with the task on the handout.

Emoticons and acronyms on the Internet: Using **Activity Handout # 10.3** have students attempt to guess the meanings of the emoticons and acronyms listed on the handout. In the space provided on the handout, they should then write several messages using emoticons and acronyms to incorporate emotional aspects into their messages. Ask for examples of messages for class discussion. Try varying the emotional valiance of the messages by removing the emoticons and/or changing them.

Key for emoticons/acronyms listed:
- :-)   I am happy (or joking)
- :-@   I am screaming (or cursing)
- :-~) I have a cold
- :-o   I'm surprised/shocked/scared
- 8-)   I wear glasses
- I-O   I'm yawning
- :-{   I have a moustache
- %-)   I've watched too much TV
- :-D   I am laughing
- :-&   I am tongue-tied
- <g>   grin
- <eg> evil grin
- afk   away from keyboard
- rofl rolling on floor laughing
- imho in my humble opinion

Source for emoticons/acronyms:
http://www.anton-small.net/emoticon.htm/
http://www.anton-small.net/shortcut.htm/

Reducing biases in language: This activity provides students with the opportunity to see differences between biased and inclusive language as outlined by the American Psychological Association's *Publication Manual* (more details and topics for discussion could be included in this activity), based on your reading of pgs. 46-60 in that manual). Spend some time going over the transparency that accompanies the worksheet **Activity Handout # 10.4,** and then have students generate more appropriate versions or corrections for the sentences listed on the handout. Discuss with them the impact of biased language on readers as well as on those persons being described by it.

Source:
American Psychological Association (1995). Publication manual of the American Psychological Association (4th ed.) (pg. 46-60). Washington, DC: American Psychological Association.

Sources for Additional Activities
Books:

Benjamin, L. & Lowman, K. (1981). <u>Activities handbook for the teaching of psychology</u>. Washington DC: American Psychological Association.

Halonen, Jane 1995). Chapter 8: Thinking, language, and intelligence. In <u>The critical thinking companion for Introductory Psychology.</u> New York: Worth Publishers.

Singelis, T. (1998). <u>Teaching about culture, ethnicity, & diversity: Exercises and planned activities.</u> Thousand Oaks, CA: Sage.

Makosky, V., Sileo, C., Whattemore, L., & Skutley, M. (1995). <u>Activities handbook for the teaching of psychology</u> (Vol. 3). Washington DC: American Psychological Association.

McCormick, T. (1994). <u>Creating the nonsexist classroom: A multicultural approach.</u> (pgs. 78-82). New York: Teachers College Press.

Paludi, M. (1990). Nonsexist language usage. In V. Makosky, C. Sileo, L. Whittemore, C. Landry, & M. Skutley (Eds.), <u>Activities handbook for the teaching of psychology</u> (Vol. 3, pp. 318-319). Washington, DC: American Psychological Association.

World Wide Web: Check out the following WWW sites for information and activities relevant to this section of the text!

Addison Wesley Longman's Website -- **http://longman.awl.com/**
- . PsychZone link -- **http://longman.awl.com/**
- . Psych Web -- **http://www.gasou.edu/psychweb/psychweb.htm**

Self-Quizzes for Introductory Psychology --
   http://www.gasou.edu/psychweb/selfquiz/selfquiz.htm

Psychology Jumping Stand --
   http://www.indiana.edu:80/~iuepsyc/PsycJump.html

The Psychology Place -- **http://www.psychplace.com**

Audio-Visual Support
Films/Videos:

Discovering Psychology: Language Development (Annenberg, 30 minutes)
Language (Insight Media, 30 minutes)
Out of the Mouths of Babes (Filmakers Library, 28 minutes)
- . The Mind Series
    program 25: *Infant Speech Sound Discrimination*
    - . program 26: *Language Predisposition*
    - . program 27: *Human Language: Signed and Spoken*
    - . program 28: *Animal Language*
    - . program 29: *Language and Culture*

Animals: How Smart Are They? (FFHS, 26 minutes)
Ape Language: From Conditioned Responses to Symbol (PSU, 96 minutes)

Talk to the Animals (CRM, 14 minutes)
Language Development (Harper & Row, 24 minutes)
Can We Talk to Animals? (MTI, 38 minutes)
Developing Language Skills (Insight Media, 30 minutes)
The First Signs of Washoe (PSU, 59 minutes)
Language (PBS, 30 minutes)
Nonverbal Communication (PSU, 22 minutes)
Signs of the Ages, Songs of the Whales (Time/Life, 57 minutes)
**A Word in Edgewise* (Women Make Movies, Inc., 26 minutes)
Speech (FFHS, 30 minutes)
**You Must Have Been a Bilingual Baby* (Filmakers Library, 46 minutes)

* = films/videos with content on women or ethnicity

Transparency Master 10.1: Checking Your TRAIL 10.1

Webster silently mouthed the words "don't come in" to his friends. Was he using a form of verbal or nonverbal communication?

List the components of communication. What function does each component serve?

Listening is an active, effortful process. As we listen, we _____ a message, pay attention to its important aspects, compare its contents to _____ _____ _____, and translate it into _____ _____.

List and explain five characteristics of communication.

Transparency Master 10.2: Checking Your TRAIL 10.2

Explain why language is described as being "productive."

The theory of linguistic determinism argues that language structures thought. Describe two types of evidence that challenge this view.

You overhear Paulo's phone conversation with his brother. He is describing, in Spanish, a recent fight with his girlfriend. Afterwards, he tells you about the same fight in English. You can't help noticing that he sounds much less upset when speaking with you than he did on the phone. How might his bilingualism explain his behavior?

After surviving a stroke, Allison had trouble speaking. She spoke with great hesitancy, often slurred her words, and used ungrammatical short sentences consisting mainly of nouns and a few verbs. Allison appears to have a form of aphasia known as (circle one) Broca's aphasia or Wernicke's aphasia.

Transparency Master 10.3: Checking Your TRAIL 10.3

Initially, babies communicate by making all kinds of sounds, including gurgles, grunts, clicks, and cries. Then they begin cooing and babbling. Describe cooing and babbling.

True or False: Morphemes combine to create phonemes.

Researchers suspect that the first six months of language acquisition result from the physiological maturation of a baby's speech equipment rather than from listening and learning. What is one line of evidence that supports this view?

Learning theory argues that children acquire language through imitation and external reinforcement. However, two-year-olds say ungrammatical sentences that they have probably never heard, such as "Mommy comed home." How does the LAD explain their production of such sentences?

Transparency Master 10.4: Checking Your TRAIL 10.4

When we engage in a conversation, nonverbal communication serves several important functions. Identify at least three types of information provided through nonverbal channels.

People generally use eye contact to invite or discourage communication. Give an example of how cultural differences regarding eye contact might result in miscommunication.

The amount of space separating people partly reflects their environment, emotional closeness, and cultural background. Give an example of how the same amount of space can be perceived as "distant" in one culture and "close" in another culture.

What is high-context communication? What are the advantages of using it in collectivistic cultures?

Transparency Master 10.5: Checking Your TRAIL 10.5

<u>True</u> or <u>False</u>: Women are better than men at interpreting nonverbal communication.

Women tend to express some emotions nonverbally better than men, and vice versa. What emotion do men tend to express nonverbally better than women?

Explain how gender differences in language style are thought to reflect and reinforce the relative power difference between men and women.

Soo-Yi wanted to find out if the European American gender difference in eye contact during mixed-gender conversations applied to Asian Americans. After observing her sample, she found that Asian American women make less eye contact than Asian American men during conversations. How might you explain the opposite findings among Asian Americans?

Transparency Master 10.6: Critical Thinking 10.1

Some college students make unfavorable judgments of instructors who speak with a foreign-sounding accent (Gill, 1994). Suggest two possible reasons for their unfavorable judgments.

Transparency Master 10.7: Critical Thinking 10.2

How can people reduce the chances of miscommunication caused by cultural differences in communication behaviors?

Transparency Master 10.8: Critical Thinking 10.3

Consider the authors' third hypothesis concerning gender differences in eye contact that posits that lower status people make eye contact as a way of seeking approval (see pg. 419-420). How might this third hypothesis relate to the eye contact between people of color and European Americans in the United States?

Transparency Master 10.9: Integrative Thinking 10.1

How might being in a state of meditation, a state of focused attention (see the Consciousness chapter), affect a person's ability to listen actively to a speaker?

Transparency Master 10.10: Integrative Thinking 10.2

To express ourselves in words requires long-term memory. How might the mechanism of long-term potentiation (see Memory chapter) explain why people have an easier time expressing themselves with words that they frequently use than with those that they rarely use?

Transparency Master 10.11: Integrative Thinking 10.3

Based on the trichromatic theory described in the Sensation & Perception chapter, how would you explain the ability of native Dani speakers to tell the difference between various colors for which they have no words?

How does the concept of development and maturation, explained in the Child Development chapter, apply to the way that children's vocalizations progress toward language?

Transparency Master 10.13: Integrative Thinking 10.5

Two-year-old Damion fearfully swears at the sound of a flushing toilet. How might the principle of observational learning (see the Learning chapter) account for his behavior?

Transparency Master 10.14: Integrative Thinking 10.6

Schemas influence our expectations of people (see the Cognition & Intelligence chapter). What changes in schema would you recommend to men and women who want to accurately decode each other's requests?

Activity Handout #10.1

The Slanguage Game

Instructions: Your task for this exercise is to create 3-4 novel slang terms and then use them in conversations with your friends over the next few days. In the space below, note the term used and your friends' reactions to them. Also note any miscommunications that arose from using the terms.

Term: **Meaning**:
1. _____ _____
2. _____ _____
3. _____ _____

Observations:
Term: **Reaction/Miscommunication**:

Activity Handout #10.2

Communication Exercise

Instructions: You will need a partner to complete this exercise. Your task as a team is to reproduce a set of figures on the handout. While standing back-to-back, one of you will describe the set of figures as the other tries to draw the figures based on the description. To start off, the person doing the drawing is **NOT** to ask any questions of the person doing the description. When you think the drawing is complete, **THEN** you may start asking questions. When you are done with the task, write your reactions to the exercise in the space provided.

Drawing:

Reactions:_____

_____

What were some barriers to your communication?_____

What could have improved your ability to perform the task?_____

_____

Figures for Communication Exercise

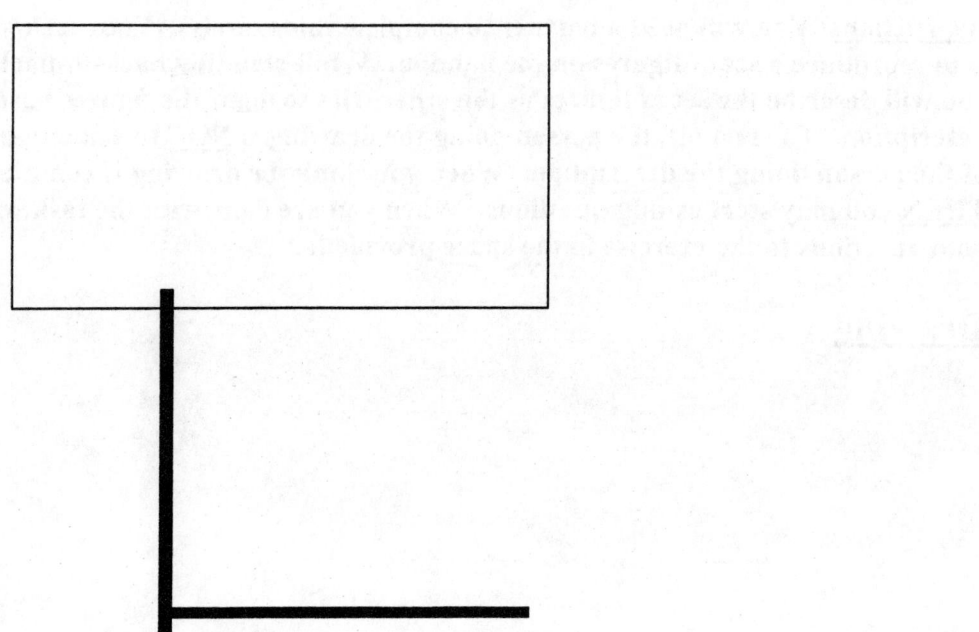

512

Activity Handout #10.3

Emoticons and acronyms on the Internet

A. Instructions: The following symbols are emoticons (icons used to express emotions or information about the message sender) and acronyms (abbreviations) used on the Internet. See if you can determine the meanings for each.

1. :-) _____
2. :-@ _____
3. :-~) _____
4. :-o _____
5. 8-) _____
6. I-O _____
7. :-{) _____
8. %-) _____
9. :-D _____
10. :-& _____
11. <g> _____
12. <eg> _____
13. afk _____
14. rofl _____
15. imho _____

B. In the space below write 2 Internet messages using emoticons/acronyms.

Activity Handout #10.4

APA guidelines for reducing biases in language

Guideline 1: Use an appropriate level of specificity.
   Avoid using terms that reflect stereotypes concerning behaviors; specifically describe behaviors.
   Example: "Girls in the sample engaged in typical school girl activities during recess periods." vs. "Girls in the sample played in small same-gender groups and spent a majority of their time engaged in jump-rope games."

Guideline 2: Be sensitive to labels.
   Avoid using terms that label people or broadly categorize them into groups; use adjectival forms or put the person first.
   Example: "Schizophrenics" vs. "People with schizophrenia"

Guideline 3: Acknowledge participation.
   Rather than referring to people as "subjects", write about them in ways that describe their participation.
   Example: "Subjects" vs. "Respondents" or "Participants"

Guidelines Concerning Gender

Avoid use of the generic "he", or using masculine or feminine pronouns to define roles by sex. One solution is to rewrite the passage so that pronouns are unnecessary or are replaced by an article.

Example: "The successful researcher publishes his work...." vs. "Publication of research is part of the definition of a successful researcher."

Example: "One problem arose when attempting to determine who should man the observation post." vs. "Difficulties in staffing the observation post occurred such that..."

Guidelines Concerning Sexual Orientation

Avoid using stereotyped labels to describe people and/or confusing sexual orientation with specific sexual behaviors. Be specific when describing gender of participants, marital status, and/or sexual behaviors.

Example: "Gays have historically experienced discrimination." vs. "Gay males and lesbians have..."; "The sample included 10 married and 10 single women." vs. "The sample included 10 married, 7 women living with domestic intimate partners, and 3 women not currently in intimate relationships."

Guidelines Concerning Racial and Ethnic Identity

Describe human samples fully with respect to gender, age, race/ethnicity. Note preferences of participants regarding racial/ethnic identities.

Example: "Fifty American Indian children were chosen as respondents.." vs. "Respondents included 25 Hopi and 25 Seminole children."

Guidelines Concerning Disabilities

Avoid labeling people by their disabilities, overextending severity or referring to disabilities with negative emotional overtones

Example: "We were interested in how depressives respond to negative cues...." vs. "We were interested in how people with clinical depression respond..."; "Previous research has found that people suffering from mental illness..." vs. "Previous research has found that people with a history of mental illness..."

Activity Handout #10.4

Reducing biases in language

Instructions: read each of the following sentences, note the guideline that has been violated and make a corrected version.

1. The conclusions drawn from these data will have a powerful impact on all mankind.

   violation: _____
   correction: _____
   _____

2. Participants in our study included 150 Hispanics.

   violation: _____
   correction: _____
   _____

3. Previous studies did not include homosexuals and thus.....

   violation: _____
   correction: _____
   _____

4. Participants in this study included 20 Whites and 20 Non-whites.

   violation: _____
   correction: _____
   _____

5. After being confined to a wheelchair for the past 20 years, ...

   violation: _____
   correction: _____
   _____

CHAPTER 11

MOTIVATION & EMOTION

- **Chapter Overview**
  Learning Objectives
  Chapter Outline

- **Additional Lecture Ideas**
  Lecture Topics
  Additional Readings

- **In-Class Activities and Demonstrations**
  Activities and Demonstrations
  Sources for Additional Activities
  Journey II Software

- **World Wide Web**

- **Audio-Visual Support**

- **Handout and Transparency Masters**

Chapter Overview

Learning Objectives

After studying this chapter, you should be able to do the following:

1. Describe several different perspectives on motivation.

2. Explain motivations for eating, aggression, sexual behavior, and achievement.

3. Explain how culture and gender roles influence motivation.

4. Describe the components of emotion.

5. Explain how culture influences the experience and expression of emotion.

6. Describe four theories of emotion.

Chapter Outline

Motivation & Emotion

I. Motivation: The Driving Force Behind Behavior
    A. Introductory concepts:
        1. definition:
            a. motivation = a process that initiates, directs, and maintains psychological and physical behavior toward a goal; influences choice of goals, reasons for pursuing them, persistence of goal pursuit.
            b. goal = mental representation of something we want; goal-oriented behavior contributes to well being.
        2. psychologists' study of motivation:
            a. taking individualistic vs. collectivistic perspectives
                i. individualistic: person motivated by individual needs
                ii. collectivistic: person motivated by group needs
    B. Biological motivations
        1. an instinct for action:
            a. instinct: an enduring, inherited, rigid pattern of behavior shown by all members of a species that motivates and directs behaviors.
            b. examples: maternal instinct; Freud's life and death instincts
            c. problems with concept:
                i. doesn't explain cause of behavior
                ii. fails to account for full complexity and unpredictability of human behavior
        2. a drive to fulfill needs:
            a. drive-reduction theory: theory that proposes that a drive-motivated behavior that will reduce the bodily deficiencies that cause the drive.
                i. drive: a temporary state of tension that motivates behavior intended to resolve the tension
                ii. homeostasis: a balanced and steady state of tension
            b. Maslow's hierarchy of needs:
                i. humans born with 5 needs
                ii. types of needs (in order of importance for survival):
- biological well-being
- safety and security
- belonging
- esteem
- self-actualization

                iii. application of Maslowian theory:
- blueprint for European American individualistic values concerning personal growth
- used in business, health, self-help

    iv. <u>problems with approach</u>:
     - lacks empirical support
     - theoretical/behavioral inconsistencies (i.e., sometimes higher need states satisfied before lower need states)
   3. <u>a search for stimulation</u>:
    a. <u>stimulus motivation</u>:
     i. unlearned curiosity and desire to explore and seek novelty
    b. <u>individual differences in sensation levels</u>:
     i. sensation-seekers: persons with high sensation needs
      - correlation with negative risk-taking
 C. Psychological motivations
  1. some motivations are learned
   a. consequences of behavior may serve as motivation
   b. beliefs and expectations may affect motivation
  2. <u>the power of incentives</u>:
   a. <u>incentives</u>: desirable consequences of behavior that may motivate goal-directed behavior
   b. <u>intrinsic vs. extrinsic motivations</u>:
    i. <u>intrinsic motivation</u>: the desire to engage in a behavior for its own sake; generally more enduring
    ii. <u>extrinsic motivation</u>: the desire to engage in a behavior for the sake of a reward
   c. perils of replacing intrinsic with extrinsic motivation:
    i. potential loss of interest in activity for own sake, esp. if use extrinsic motivation for specific aspect of behavior
    ii. extrinsic may be useful to encourage initial involvement
  3. <u>a response to beliefs and expectations</u>:
   a. <u>cognitive perspective</u>: people are active thinkers who make conscious decisions that affect motivation
   b. decide on value of a particular goal; evaluate likelihood of success; select path for pursuing/avoiding goal
   c. beliefs developed via direct/indirect experiences

II. Motivated Behaviors: Why People Eat, Aggress, Have Sex, and Achieve
 A. Eating
  1. <u>hunger</u>: a primary (unlearned) drive necessary for survival that may become influenced by social motivation (i.e., a force that drives behavior and is learned through socialization)
  2. <u>biological motivations for eating</u>:
   a. <u>role of biological homeostasis</u>: body balances use and replacement of energy; hunger occurs when energy needs replenishing

b. <u>role of stomach contractions</u>: early idea was that stomach contractions coincide with subjective reports of hunger (therefore cause hunger)
c. <u>role of lateral and ventromedial hypothalamus</u>:
    i. <u>lateral hypothalamus</u>: feeding center; if stimulated, even full animal will eat; if destroyed, animal won't eat.
    ii. <u>ventromedial hypothalamus</u>: satiety center; if stimulated, animal will stop eating; if destroyed, animal will eat until obese
d. <u>set point theory</u>: body has set point for weight (represents homeostasis) and is controlled by lateral and ventromedial regions of hypothalamus
  3. <u>psychological motivations for eating</u>:
    a. <u>role of intrinsic/extrinsic incentives</u>: eating may be encouraged by approval of others or pleasure
    b. <u>role of food cues</u>: eating may be influenced by appearance, flavor, aroma of food; may stimulate both thoughts and digestive processes

B. Aggression
  1. <u>aggression</u>: physical or psychological actions/behaviors with the intent of causing harm.
  2. <u>biological motivations for aggression</u>:
    a. <u>instinct theory</u>: aggression is a basic human instinct that aids survival (i.e., more food, sexual partners) and is passed on in genes; not supported empirically
    b. <u>drive-reduction theory</u>: aggression arise from innate need to reduce frustration; theory doesn't explain aggression not due to frustration or frustrated people who don't aggress
    c. <u>genetic theory</u>: aggression runs in families; significant correlations in aggression levels found in twin studies
    d. <u>CNS dysfunction</u>: higher levels of aggression in people with temporal lobe tumors or frontal lobe damage; role of septum & amygdala; impact of amygdalectomies in reducing aggression
    e. <u>testosterone</u>: may act as an amplifier for already existing aggressive thoughts/tendencies
  3. <u>psychological motivations for aggression</u>:
    a. aggression result of learning experiences and thoughts
    b. <u>role of threat/insult</u>: may increase likelihood of aggression
    c. <u>role of alcohol/being overheated</u>:
        i. <u>alcohol</u>: Ss who drink (or think they are had alcohol) behave more aggressively; effects may be due to reduction in fear of threats, reduction in accuracy of memory concerning others' actions, distortion of thoughts about others' intentions (i.e., alcohol myopia)

  ii. <u>overheating</u>: Ss who are in uncomfortably warmer temperatures more aggressive, perceive others' as threatening; findings inconsistent or effects may be linked to interaction with alcohol

 d. <u>role of personal experience and observational learning</u>:
  i. parents who use spanking model aggression for children
  ii. television shows: children may mimic aggression they see on television
   - identify with aggressive characters
   - mentally rehearse aggressive scripts

C. Sexual Behavior
 1. <u>theories/research</u>:
  a. <u>Kinsey's survey research</u>: interviewed convenience sample about their sexual behaviors
  b. <u>Masters and Johnson</u>: monitored sexual experiences of volunteers in laboratory
   i. <u>human sexual-response cycle</u>: a sequence of biological changes that characterize sexual response in both men and women
    - <u>desire</u>: urge to engage in sexual behavior brought on by thoughts, smells, visual stimuli
    - <u>excitement phase</u>: initial phase of the sexual response cycle during which increased blood flow to the genitals causes a partial erection in a man's penis and swelling of a woman's clitoris, labia and breasts, and vaginal lubrication
    - <u>plateau phase</u>: a phase of sexual arousal following the excitement phase during which breathing, heart rate, blood pressure and muscle tension increase
    - <u>orgasm</u>: a brief, intensely pleasurable phase of sexual arousal during which excitement peaks with rhythmic muscle contractions in the genitals
    - <u>resolution</u>: a reduction in sexual arousal following orgasm during which blood flows away from the genitals
   ii. <u>criticisms of model</u>:
    - extensive focus on orgasm
    - individual variability in satisfaction, progression through stages, desirability of potential partners
   iii. <u>contribution of theory</u>:
    - study of sexual dysfunctions (e.g., female sexual-arousal disorder; male erectile disorder)
 2. <u>biological motivations for sex</u>:
  a. <u>Masters & Johnson</u>: sexual-response cycle is an unlearned, inborn drive toward orgasm

b. <u>role of hormones</u>: decreases in testosterone and estrogen may dampen sexual desire

c. <u>role of hypothalamus</u>: hypothalamus monitors hormone levels and stimulates parasympathetic branch of ANS (necessary for penile erections); destruction of ventromedial hypothalamus affects sexual behaviors/responsivity

3. <u>psychological motivations for sex</u>:

    a. <u>gender perspectives on sexual scripts</u>:

        i. <u>sexual scripts</u>: knowledge of social relationships that influences the way we interpret and respond to sexual situations

        ii. <u>gender differences in sexual scripts</u>:

           - in United States, males learn more permissive sexual script; females learn mixed messages about sexual script

           - males/females vary on reactions to first coital experience

           - scripts may influence approach to sexual activity

    b. <u>cultural perspectives on sexual scripts</u>:

        i. socialization affects understanding of what sexual behaviors are desirable, acceptable (e.g., protection of virginity in women)

        ii. culturally different sexual scripts may result in confusion over which to adopt

        iii. individual variability in adopting sexual scripts may be due to personal history, characteristics, attitudes, values, and opportunities

    c. <u>sociocultural perspectives on sexual behavior</u>:

        i. research emphasizes individualistic perspective; however, sexual activity occurs within social context

        ii. <u>example</u>: social expectations on women in 1930s to only have sex with husband or fiancé

D. Achievement

1. <u>achievement motivation</u>: the desire to excel and accomplish a significant goal

    a. achievement rewarding because productive

    b. goals shaped by experience

    c. <u>example</u>: achievement by persons of color in class

2. <u>individualist motivations for achievement</u>:

    a. <u>achievement motivation</u>: individual's desire to dominate, control, gain mastery, surpass others

    b. <u>personal characteristics</u>: set challenging but realistic goals; prefer feedback on performance; pursue goals with disciplined effort

c. three competing factors: need to achieve, expectations for success, fear of failure
d. high achievement motivation associated with parental encouragement
3. collectivist motivations for achievement:
a. like individualist, collectivist motivated to achieve but may pursue different goals and for different reasons
b. motivated toward achievement goals that meet with social approval and satisfy best interests of group
c. disapprove of individuals whose success takes them above group
d. value goals that promote group harmony, personal loyalty, humility, interdependence; value goals set by group rather than individual goals
e. strive for success to bring honor to family, gain approval from peers/teachers

III. Emotion: An Excited State of Body and Mind
A. Definitions
1. emotion: a coordinated package of biological arousal, thoughts/mental evaluations, behavioral expressions
B. Experiencing emotion
1. primary and secondary emotions:
a. primary emotions: basic emotions thought to be universal (e.g., joy, surprise, disgust, anger, fear, shame, sadness)
b. secondary emotions: mixtures/blends of primary emotions (e.g., disappointment)
c. "color wheel" of emotion: represents relationships between primary/secondary emotions
2. emotional balance: emotions may counteract one another
a. opponent-process of emotion: brain naturally seeks emotional homeostasis
b. process: one strong emotion it is followed by an opposing emotion; net result = what we feel is first emotion minus second emotion
c. habituation: getting used to an initially intense emotion such that intensity decreases
C. Biological arousal
1. process: during emotional moments, body becomes physiologically aroused (i.e., sympathetic branch of ANS stimulates adrenal glands to release epinephrine and norepinephrine; promotes body to mobilize stored energy; calming process occurs when parasympathetic branch of ANS is activated

2. <u>arousal and performance</u>:
   a. <u>effects of arousal</u>: optimal levels may focus attention, sharpen perceptions; too much interferes with performance
   b. optimal levels dependent on familiarity with task
3. <u>patterns of arousal</u>:
   a. current research suggests each primary emotion has specific pattern of arousal
   b. emotion-specific arousal patterns occur across cultures

D. Cognitive appraisal
1. <u>cognitive appraisal</u>: a mental evaluation of a situation or stimulus that may occur so automatically that we are unaware of them
   a. <u>appraisal processes</u>:
      i. assess relevance of event to self
      ii. assess relationship of event to achieving goals
      iii. assess if event is threatening
2. <u>cultural perspectives on appraisal</u>:
   a. cultural differences may influence appraisal because people pay attention to different things (thus explaining why two people have very different reactions to same event)
3. <u>cognition and emotion</u>:
   a. <u>debate</u>: does cognition always precede emotion? can emotion occur without cognition beforehand?
      i. example study
      ii. debate centered around definition of "cognition"
         - <u>traditional</u>: cognition = conscious use of mental processes
         - <u>others</u>: cognition = any activity of the brain (e.g., the activity of the amygdala)

E. Expressing emotion
1. <u>facial expressions</u>:
   a. cross-cultural agreement on expressions corresponding to primary emotions (with exceptions of fear and surprise)
   b. <u>theory</u>: certain facial expressions of primary emotions fundamental to human nature
      i. <u>evidence</u>:
         - cross-cultural consistency
         - baby studies
2. <u>cultural perspectives on facial expressions</u>:
   a. cross-cultural differences in aspects of expression such as verbal vs. nonverbal, spontaneity vs. control
   b. <u>display rules</u>: socialized guidelines for when, how, and to what degree people should show emotion in a given situation
   c. emotion display also influenced by social context of situation, nature of the interpersonal relationships involved, expected consequences of expressing emotion

IV. Behavior and Emotion: The Motivating Force of Emotion
    A. Psychologists' interest in emotion
        1. assumption that emotions are associated with behavior
    B. Theories of emotion
        1. James-Lange and Cannon-Bard theories:
            a. James-Lange theory: emotions occur as the result of inferences we make based on changes in our body
            b. Cannon-Bard theory: emotional feelings and autonomic arousal occur at the same time because the hypothalamus simultaneously activates the physical and conscious experience of an emotion
        2. facial feedback hypothesis: facial muscle movements magnify or initiate emotion by sending information to the brain
            a. not known how facial feedback causes emotions
            b. culture may affect how facial feedback appraised
        3. Schacter-Singer two-factor theory: biological arousal occurs and then people give meaning to their physical sensations by appraising them in context
            a. classic studies: epinephrine study and men-on-swinging-bridge study
    C. Emotion as motivation
        1. emotion intensity may motivate behavior
        2. pleasant emotion may motivate behavior to maintain pleasant feelings
        3. cultural differences in what motivates
            a. individualistic: personal emotions motivate
            b. collectivistic: social/situational factors motivate

Additional Lecture Topics
1. **Gender, class, and race difference in weight:**

Bowen et al. (1999) describe gender, poverty, and race as three of the major risk factors--the "triple threat"--contributing to weight-related problems, including obesity, in the United States. An increasingly prevalent problem in this country, excess weight, or obesity, has been linked to a variety of physical as well as psychological hazards: diabetes, hypertension, arthritis, atherosclerosis, gall bladder disease, menstrual/reproductive problems, cardiac dysfunction, negative and distorted self-image, anxiety, and discrimination. However, despite these problematic potential health outcomes and findings from survey research that indicates that obesity is not evenly distributed over race, sex, and social class, little research has focused on the interactive effects of these factors as they relate to obesity and its opposite, excessive thinness.

- gender and weight: Substantial research indicates that women and men differ concerning a number of weight-related phenomenon. For example, women are more likely to be dissatisfied with their bodies, wish they weighed less, and report their current weight is heavier than what is attractive or ideal than are men. As a result, according to Bowen et al., chronic dieting and restrained eating patterns are more likely to become "normative aspects of women's lives"--presumably because of intense cultural emphasis on women's bodies as a primary source of their value and pressures to obtain thinness. Women who do not meet these standards (i.e., are less than ideal or even obese) experience intense stigma as a result of these sex-specific standards. Whereas a great deal has been written concerning these general culture-biased expectations for women, additional research suggests that social class and gender interact; women of lower socioeconomic status (SES) are more likely to be obese than are women from middle or upper SES levels .

- social class and weight: A number of studies have demonstrated that a negative correlation between weight and SES exists and, as mentioned above, this finding is particularly strong among women (c.f., the Midtown Manhattan study; Goldblatt et al., 1965). In discussing factors thought to mediate this finding, Bowen et al. note the recent review by Sobel & Stunkard (1989) in which those authors argued that class differences in weight levels may result from: genetic and social inheritance, differing physical activity levels, and differing levels of dietary restraint. Other factors discussed include lack of adequate economic resources (which may force low SES women to purchase less expensive, high calorie, high fat/sugar foods), advertisement efforts directed to low SES populations promoting cheap high-fat foods, greater commercial development of fast food restaurants in low income areas, lack of adequate nutritional knowledge, and women's' beliefs that external factors resulted in their weight levels (i.e., their weight was not within their control). Bowen et al. express frustration with the present state of literature concerning social class and weight, however, pointing out that much of the current research is descriptive and/or does not include an exploration of the specific aspects of SES that contribute to weight.

- <u>race/culture and weight</u>: Of the three factors considered in the Bowen et al. article, the contribution of race to weight has received the least empirical attention. Those studies that have been conducted (cf. the San Antonio Heart Study; Stern et al., 1982) suggest that obesity occurs at higher rates in ethnic minorities. Discussions on factors associated with this trend focus on: differences in cultural ideals concerning thinness, historically residual fear of hunger associated with previous experience with lack of food, viewing fatness as a sign of prosperity & well-being, ethnic preferences for heavier weights and greater body-image satisfaction, greater preferences for sweet foods and the consumption of more calories, and cultural meanings associated with food and eating. Interestingly, Bowen et al. note that, as women in ethnic minorities become more acculturated socially and economically within the dominant culture, they are more likely to adopt beliefs oriented towards thinness and restrained eating patterns. In summary they state that empirical data investigating specific causal assumptions between race and obesity are lacking. Moreover, they emphasize the need to develop weight-related intervention programs that are sensitive to and preserve cultural integrity in their attempts to modify a culturally meaningful activity (i.e., eating).

Although gender, SES, and race independently contribute to weight, the interactive or "triple threat" receives special attention from Bowen et al. They note that the growing population of poor within the United States is over-represented by women of color. The combined effects of race, gender, and poverty may be seen in eating patterns involving cheap but high fat/sugar foods, lack of access to diet centers and health clubs due to finances and living restrictions, and a lack of safe and adequate outdoor exercise areas in high crime living environments. Attempts to seek assistance for weight concerns may be limited by the general lack of access to medical care for the poor and the lack of intervention or prevention programs regarding weight and dietary concerns targeting minorities or the poor. Additionally, cultural stereotypes regarding minority women as "being nurturing, well-nurtured, and overweight", together with negative racist and classist attitudes may act as barriers to behavior changes and "promote and maintain damaging and unhealthy images of poor women of color which unfortunately feed back on their self-esteem and self-worth, and cause further problems" (pg. 300).

To rectify the current state of affairs as these authors see it, they suggest: increasing research concerning previously excluded groups, demythologizing the cultural emphasis on thinness, developing exercise programs designed to increase participation by low-income minority women, and establishing programs and policies designed "to empower and enable women to take control of their lives and of their health" (pg. 303).

Source:
   Bowen, D., Tamoyasu, N., and Cauce, A. (1999). The triple treat: A discussion of gender, class, and race differences in weight. In L. Peplau, S. Debro, R. Veniegas, & P. Taylor (Eds.), Gender, culture, and ethnicity: Current research about women and men. (pg. 291-306). Mountain View, CA: Mayfield.

2. **Emotion from a cross-cultural Perspective:**
   David Matsumoto, in a fascinating review of emotion in his text *People: Psychology from a Cultural Perspective*, places traditional studies and conceptualizations of emotion in juxtaposition with cross-cultural studies in the area. For educators in Introductory Psychology, this chapter qualifies as a "must read"! In his introductory analysis of the traditional perspectives in psychology, Matsumoto reviews the traditional theories of the experience of emotion (included in the Uba and Huang text): the James/Lange and Cannon/Bard, and Schacter/Singer two-factor theory of emotion. Matsumoto summarizes these theories as "attempts to explain the nature of that subjective, inner state we call emotion" (pg. 118) that share common assumptions regarding the central roles of the subjective, inner nature of emotion and labeling of those inner states. From Matsumoto's view, the traditional perspectives concerning the expression of emotion include the work of Ekman, Izard, Tomkins, and Plutchik--perspectives that emphasize the universality of emotions common to "all people of all cultures and ethnicities" (pg. 118). He notes that, although these approaches carry intuitive appeal to most theorists, "this way of understanding emotion may be a particularly Western--or even more specifically, an American--way of understanding emotions." Moreover, he contends, "not all cultures view emotions this way" (pg. 119). What is the basis for this contention? He begins his critique with data drawn from anthropological research.
   Defining emotions. A key point in his discussion focuses on whether there are cultural differences in defining and understanding emotions. One approach is to determine whether different cultures have a word for "emotion" in their language system. Whereas some authors have noted a shared term generally meaning "emotion" (e.g., as in the Indonesian, Japanese, Korean, Malaysian, Spanish, and Sinhalese languages as discussed by Brandt & Boucher, 1986), other cultures appear to lack a word that captures that essence. For example, it has been noted that neither Tahitians nor the Ifaluks of Micronesia have such a word (c.f., Levy, 1983; Lutz, 1983). Thus, the concept of "emotion" is not necessarily universal. More importantly, Matsumoto cautions that cross-cultural differences in meaning for the word "emotion" may exist even when cultures share a similar term; in other words, "not all concepts of emotion are equivalent" (pg. 120). For example, he claims some words referring to

emotions in the Japanese language might not be terms English speakers consider as emotion-related (e.g., considerate and lucky; Matsuyama et al., 1978). Moreover, cross-cultural differences may emerge when considering how specific types of emotions are labeled. Whereas the English terms for *anger, joy, sadness, liking,* and *loving* also appear in other cultures, there are instances where some emotion-related English words have no direct equivalents in other languages and emotion-related words from other languages are not present in English language (e.g., the word *frustration* doesn't appear in Arabic languages and the English terms *terror, horror, dread, apprehension,* and *timidity* are expressed with the single word *gurakadi* in the Australian aboriginal language of Gidjingali). In summary, Matsumoto suggests that different cultures "divide the world of emotion" differently within their languages.

The subjective, inner nature of emotion. In American psychology, the traditional perspectives on emotion emphasize the personal, inner, subjective nature of emotion and, once again, this viewpoint may reflect a culturally bound perspective. Matsumoto suggests that in other cultures emotion may be viewed as "originating or residing somewhere else." Take, for example, the (romanticized) Western notion that emotions arise from the heart. Not so in other cultures: in Japan, they are identified with the gut; in the Chewong of Maly, the liver; Tahitians believe in an intestinal origin; and the Ifaluk, more broadly, the "insides". Thus, the location or origin of emotions is even culturally bound. Moreover, the idea that emotions are related to inner states is not universally shared. Some cultures believe that emotions arise from relationships among people, between people and events, or due to situations; it is not a property within an individual. For example, "the Japanese concept of *amae*, which is typically considered a central emotion in the Japanese culture, specifies an interdependent relationship between two people" (pg. 121).

Psychological studies of emotion. Although the cross-cultural differences noted in anthropological research are significant, findings from psychological research also speak to telling differences in a number of areas of study concerning emotions. A brief summary of major findings and issues follows:

- emotional expression: Although the Ekman and Izard research speaks to universality in expression of the six major emotions (supporting a biological explanation for emotional expression), cultural differences emerge in *display rules* concerning situationally-appropriate settings for emotional expression, as noted by Uba and Huang. In some of his own work, Matsumoto found that display rules varied across ethnic groups within the United States such that Caucasian, African American, Asian, and Hispanic/Latino participants varied significantly in the extent to which they believed it was appropriate to display disgust, fear, contempt, and sadness, with whom those feelings could be expressed, and whether those emotions were appropriate for public vs. private expression.

- emotional perception: Cultural differences have emerged in terms of ratings of the intensity of emotions being displayed. For example, Matsumoto (1994) found that African Americans perceived expressions of anger, disgust, and fear as more intense and expressions by Caucasians and females as more intense than did some other ethnic groups in his study. Additionally, some studies report that people are more accurate in perceiving emotions in others from their own ethnic group than across ethnic lines. Matsumoto explains these cross-cultural differences in emotional perception as emerging from cultural differences in *decoding rules*, or culturally-based, learned rules governing the interpretation and perception of emotion that act as a filter for viewing and interpreting emotional expressions.
- emotional experiences: Studies of frequency of emotion find cross-cultural differences in such experiences. For example, Americans report feeling joy and anger more often than Europeans; Japanese report experiencing higher frequencies of all emotions when compared to either Americans or Europeans. Cultural differences in intensity and duration of feeling also emerge.
- emotion antecedents & the cognitive evaluation of emotion antecedents: At one point in the literature, the events that trigger emotional experiences were thought to be universal--just as emotions were thought to be universal in experience. More recent studies have found that cross-cultural differences exist in emotion-eliciting events and the degree or extent to which different events produce various emotions. For example, achievement-related situations evoke joy (and fear!) in Europeans and Americans; death of a family member or physical separation from loved ones elicit sadness for the same groups. Anger is often produced in situations involving strangers in Japanese people whereas it is likely to be elicited in situations involving relationships in Americans. In attributing the cause of emotions, Americans and Japanese individuals differ in their explanations of the causes of joy, fear, and shame (e.g., to other people for the former group and to chance or fate in the latter).
- the physiology of emotion: Although no cross-cultural studies have been conducted to directly test for cultural differences in physiological reactions to emotions, some studies indicate that people from different cultures *report* experiencing different changes in physiological reactions. For example, Americans and Europeans report more physiological changes such as stomach problems, cardiovascular changes (i.e., racing pulse), and body temperature (i.e., flushing) as compared to Japanese respondents.

In his chapter conclusion, Matsumoto argues that cross-cultural studies of emotion based on nationality or ethnicity will ultimately continue to uncover "facts" concerning emotion. A more fruitful approach, from his perspective, would be to engage in research that defines culture according to constructs such as individualism and collectivism that provide broader cultural explanations for influences on emotions.

Source:
Matsumoto, D. (1999). Emotion. In People: Psychology from a cultural perspective. (pg. 117-131). Pacific Grove, CA: Brooks/Cole.

3. **Stereotype threat and academic achievement:**
This additional lecture topic picks up where lecture topic 2 in Chapter 7 left off. You might like to take a few moments to refresh your memory of that reading if it's been a while. Recall that Claude Steele suggests that the phenomenon of stereotype threat has an immediate negative effect on standardized test performances for domain-identified African Americans and women in the sciences. For the current chapter, his remaining arguments regarding long-term achievement are particularly relevant.

Picking up where we left off, Steel offers: "Stereotype threat is assumed to have an abiding effect on school achievement--an effect beyond its impairment of immediate performance--by preventing or breaking a person's identification with school, in particular, those domains of schooling in which the stereotype applies" (pg. 222). In other words, the presence of stereotype threat serves to impede academic progress...in this case, not just for the domain-identified students.

Self-esteem and stigmatization. In an article by Crocker and Major findings were somewhat counter-intuitive. Whereas one might expect that stigmatized groups would experience lower self-esteem, these authors found that their self-esteem levels were as high as those not stigmatized. Their explanation was that stigmatized people don't attribute failure to themselves but rather associate it to the prejudice of out-groups. These individuals may also limit their social comparison of abilities to similarly stigmatized in-group members and devalue the domains in which they feel devalued. Thus, domain disidentification may serve as an esteem-saving adaptation and contributes to self-esteem resiliency.

Stigmatization and poor school achievement. Steele suggests that disidentification with and resulting underachievement may be a reaction to ability-stigmatization. If this is the case, one should expect to find the relationship between stereotype threat and underachievement wherever it occurs globally. He points to studies done on caste-like minorities around the world that demonstrate significant IQ differences, poorer school performance, higher dropout rates, and other behavioral problems. Steele contends that their caste status, which occurs due to cultural stereotypes, contributes to their school disidentification.

Dissociation of self-esteem and school achievement. One final premise is offered regarding the impact of stereotype threat: "If the poor school achievement of ability-stigmatized groups is mediated by disidentification, then it might be expected that among the ability stigmatized, there would be a disassociation between school outcomes and overall self-esteem" (pg. 224). Several lines of support can be found for this expectation. African American students tend to underperform on tests relative to Caucasian students, yet their self-esteem levels are as high or higher. Some studies indicated that African American youths' self-esteem was more linked to their relationships with peers rather than academic or home life. Repeated findings reinforce the disidentification theory premise that stereotype threat, then, may be associated with domain disidentification. Does it cause it, however? In a study done by Steele and Kirsten Stoutemeyer, stereotype threat feedback was varied such that women test-takers were told that typical gender differences in the math test they were about to take were due either to innate ability or social causes. Identification with math and math-related careers was measured. Overall results indicated that women in the stereotype threat condition disidentified more with math than did women in the social cause condition.

In summary, Steele has demonstrated that the presence of stereotype threat has the potential for immediate effects on domain-identified students and may contribute to domain disidentification in students to whom the stereotype is applied. Wise strategies for school administration and policy should include efforts at "affirming domain belongingness" from this evidence.

Source:
Steele, C. (1998). A threat in the air: How stereotypes shape intellectual identity and performance. In J. Eberhardt & S. Fiske (Eds.), Confronting racism: The problem and the response (pgs. 202-233). Thousand Oaks, CA: Sage.

4. Violence and U.S. regional culture:

Richard Nisbett has written a provocative paper involving an analysis of regional violence and develops the argument that cultural traditions underlie differences in the expression of aggression. At the heart of the paper: throughout history, Southerners have been and are more likely to engage in some particular forms of violence compared to Northerners, as can be supported by anecdotal evidence and homicide rates alike. Nisbett's effort is to determine what regional factors contribute to this trend:

Although, historically five explanations have been offered, Nisbett chooses to expand on the last in his presentation: temperature differences between the North and South: hotter temperatures have been associated with greater likelihood for aggressive actions (cf., Reifman et al., 1991); a theory that is not supported by evidence that violence rates varied in small vs. large towns in the South (and presumably temperature rates were not dramatically different). The warmest areas of the South had the lowest homicide rates...poverty: and association between the relative poverty in the South compared to that of other regions in the U.S. and crimes of all kind has been noted (Blau & Blau, 1982), an assumption that has been refuted by evidence that Southern towns that were wealthier than some Northern towns still had higher crime rates. The institution of slavery: the institution of slavery brought more idle time for Whites to engage in exciting, dangerous pastimes (Tocqueville, 1835/1969); a notion that has been discharged by evidence that areas with highest slave concentrations in the past have the lowest crime rates today ...mimicking of slave violence: violence in Southern Whites was unconscious mimicking of violence seen in African Americans (Cash, 1941); an illogical conclusion given that counties with small slave populations had the highest White homicide rates...the herding economy and the culture of honor: the final explanation discussed (and the one supported) by Nisbett, involves historical immigration patterns into the region. Nisbett notes that two major types of immigrants to the region tended to be of noble or landed gentry status (who brought with them a code for manly honor and virtue) and Celtic herding peoples whose economic livelihood was in part determined by their fierce protection from herd thefts. The latter group, to protect their flocks, cultivated a posture of extreme vigilance toward any act that might be perceived as threatening in any way, and responded with sufficient force to frighten the offender and the community into recognizing that they are not to be trifled with (pg. 340). Masculine courage was defined by swift and abrupt response to danger, threat, and insults in such an environment. Thus, cultural value systems emerged that favored the development of a pro-violence attitudinal system in the South. In his recent research in the contemporary South, Nisbett has found three attitudinal variables that distinguish North from South:

1. White Southern men are more likely to accept statements that violence is acceptable for protection of property and human life. They are also more likely to report owning a gun and to oppose gun control.
2. Violence is viewed as an appropriate response to insult, and failure to do so would make a man less than a man. In controlled studies, Nisbett and colleagues found that Southern men became angrier when insulted than did Northern men and seemed primed to future violent responses if confronted with an insult stimuli.
3. Socialization patterns include violence such as spankings or beatings. Expectations for fighting to defend or stand up for oneself may be especially socialized in young males. Nisbett's work is summarized in the following observations: The South has a culture of honor with historical roots that underlies its preferences for violence. Southerners do not endorse violence in the abstract more than do Northerners, nor do they endorse in all circumstances. Rather, they are more likely to endorse violence as an appropriate response to insults, as a means of self-protection, and as a socialization tool in training children. This is the characteristic cultural pattern of herding societies the world over. Consistent with the culture-of-honor interpretation, it is argument-related and felon-related homicide that is more common in the South (pg. 353). The emphasis on the sociocultural perspective in identifying connections between economic/historical factors, regional cultural values, and aggressive behavior makes this article an addition to Uba and Huang's discussion of aggression as a motivated behavior.

Source: Nisbett, R. (1997). Violence and U.S. regional culture. In L. Peplau & S. Taylor (Eds.), Sociocultural perspective in social psychology: Current readings (pg. 338-356). Upper Saddle River, NJ: Prentice-Hall.

Suggestions for Additional Readings

Ben-Zur, H., & Breznitz, S. (1991). What makes people angry: Dimensions of anger-evoking events. Journal of research in personality, 25, 1-22.

Carlson, J., & Hatfield, E. (1992). Psychology of emotion. Fort Worth, TX: Harcourt Brace Jovanovich.

Csikszentmihalyi, M. (1990). Flow: The psychology of optimal experience. New York: Harper & Row.

Clements, M. (1994, Aug. 7). Sex in America today. Parade Magazine, pg. 4-6.

Ekman, P., & Oster, H. (1979). Facial expressions of emotions. In M. Rosenzweig & L. Porter (Eds.), Annual review of psychology, 30, 316-354.

Fordyce, M. (1988). A review of research on the Happiness Measures: A sixty-second index of happiness and mental health. Social indicators research, 20, 355-381.

Frankl, V. (1959). Man's search for meaning. N.Y.: Washington Square Press.

Green, R., Beatty, W., Arkin, R. (1984). Human motivation. Boston: Allyn & Bacon.

Hatfield, E., Caccioppo, J., & Rapson, R. (1993). Emotional contagion. Current directions in psychological science, 2, 96-99.

Hyde, J. (1990). Understanding human sexuality. New York: McGraw-Hill.

Logue, A. (1986). The psychology of eating and drinking. New York: Freeman.

Maslow, A. (1987). Motivation and personality. New York: Harper & Row.

Masters, W., Johnson,V., & Kolodny, R. (1988). Human sexuality. Glenview, IL: Scott, Foresman.

McClelland, D. (1985). Human motivation. Glenview, IL: Scott, Foresman.

Mook, D. (1987). Motivation: The organization of action. New York: Norton.

Myers, D. (1992). The pursuit of happiness: Who is happy and why. New York: William Morrow.

Plutchik, R.(1980).Emotion: A psychoevolutionary synthesis.NY:Harper & Row.

Reinisch, J. (1990). The Kinsey Institute new report on sex: What you must know to be sexually literate. New York: St. Martin's Press.

Rodin, J. (1984, Dec.) A sense of control. Psychology today, pg. 38-45.

Russell, J. (1991). Culture and categorization of emotions. Psychological Bulletin, 110(3), 426-450.

Sharkin, B., & Gelso, C. (1991). The anger discomfort scale: Beginning reliability and validity data. Measurement and evaluation in counseling and development, 24, 61-68.

Siegel, J. (1986). The multidimensional anger inventory. Journal of Personality and Social Psychology, 51, 191-200.

Tavris, C. (1989). Anger: The misunderstood emotion. New York: Touchstone/Simon & Schuster.

Weiner, B. (Ed.) (1974). Achievement motivation and attribution theory. Morristown, NJ: General Learning Press.

Weiner, B. (1980). Human motivation. New York: Holt, Rinehart, & Winston.

Zuckerman, M. (1978). Sensation seeking. In H. London & J. Exner (Eds.), Dimensions of personality (pg. 487-560). New York: Wiley.

In-Class Activities and Demonstrations

1. **TRAIL Blazing**: Using **Transparency Masters 11.1 - 11.4**, review with students the "Checking Your TRAIL" sections in the chapter. Have students work in small groups to answer the questions and then review with the class as a whole to tie the text reading to activity in class.

2. **Reaching Critical Mass**: Using **Transparency Masters 11.5 - 11.7**, review with students the "Critical Thinking" sections in the chapter. Have students work in small groups to answer the questions and then review with the class as a whole to tie the text reading to activity in class.

3. **Getting Down to IT**: Using **Transparency Masters 11.8 - 11.13**, review the "Integrative Thinking" sections in the chapter with students. Have students work in small groups to answer the questions and then review with the class as a whole to tie the text reading to activity in class.

4. **Levels of aspiration exercise**: Fernald & Fernald (1981) developed an activity to test three hypotheses regarding level of aspiration: group standard affect level of aspiration; level of aspiration is linked to actual performance with the general tendency to aspire to levels slightly higher rather than lower than performance; and success leads to increases in aspiration whereas failure leads to decreases in aspiration. To conduct the exercise, select 4 students from the class with the explanation that they will be participants in a manual dexterity exercise. Ask them to leave the room until called. Place 2 containers, one empty and one with 60 marbles in it, on a table in front of the class. As you bring each volunteer into the room, instruct the student that he or she is to attempt to move as many marbles as they can, moving one marble at a time and using one hand, from the full container to the empty container, in 30 seconds. The first two volunteers are also to be told "Most students can generally move 15 marbles in 30 seconds."; the last two volunteers are told "Most students can generally move 35 marbles in 30 seconds." Before beginning each student's marble moving trial, ask him or her to estimate how many marbles he or she will be able to move. Then conduct the 30-second trial and count the actual number of marbles moved. After counting, tell the volunteer that you're going to conduct a second trial and ask if he or she would like to change their performance estimate for the next trial. Repeat the marble-moving task.

    To test Hypothesis 1, that group performance standards influence personal performance estimates, compare the Time 1 estimates of the low standard (15) vs. high standard (35) volunteers. Fernald & Fernald find that students' estimates tend to agree with the group standard they had heard. For Hypothesis 2, that level of aspiration remains close to but slightly above actual performance, compare Time 2 estimates with Time 1 performance. The authors report that typically Time 2 estimates will be close to but often a bit higher than Time 1 performance. To test Hypothesis 3, that success or failure results in increases/decreases in level of aspiration, you'll need to compare the Time 1 and Time 2 estimates for the low standard (15) volunteers and then the same scores for the high standard (35) volunteers. Presumably the former group would be more likely to experience success and thus increase their estimates, whereas the latter would be more likely to experience failure and thus decrease their estimates.

Fernald & Fernald suggest applying class results to other academic experiences. To add a gender & ethnicity emphasis, consider discussing how levels of aspiration may be affected by experiences related to gender or culture.

Source:
Fernald, P., & Fernald, L. (1981). Level of aspiration. In L. Benjamin, & K. Lowman (Eds.), Activities handbook for teaching of psychology, Vol. 1. pg 183-184.

5. **Psychological vs. physical violence towards women:** It has been argued that aggression toward women may take various forms ranging from psychological events (such as withholding affection as a form of coercion or punishment, name-calling, sulking, etc.) to physical events (such as punching, slapping, pinching, hair pulling, etc.). Some authors have argued that psychological as well as physical violence or aggression is damaging to psychological well being of women. Moreover, it has been suggested that psychological abuse may be a precursor to physical violence . Have students complete **Handout Master 11.1**, which includes various examples of psychological and physical events taken from Tolman's (1989) Psychological Maltreatment of Women Inventory and Tolman & Molidor's (1995)Teenage Dating Survey. As part of the exercise, students are to estimate the extent to which they believe this is a form of aggression. You are likely to find general agreement that the physical acts represent aggression whereas there will probably be more disagreement concerning the psychological acts. Begin a discussion of class results by asking students the basis for these differences and consider the connections between psychological vs. physical forms of aggression (i.e., does psychological violence lead to physical violence?).

Source:
Molidor, C. & Tolman, R. (1995). Adolescent dating violence: Frequency and contextual issues. Unpublished manuscript, University of Texas at Arlington.

Tolidor, R. (1989). The development of a measure of psychological maltreatment of women by their partners. Violence and victims, 4(3), 159-177.

6. **Identifying emotions in literature passages:** Carolyn Simmons has created an interesting exercise that is based on the debate around the universal nature of emotional expressions. She has combined a number of sentences drawn from English and Chinese literature that are descriptions of emotional expressions. Her fundamental assumption is that some expressions of emotions "have strong experiential physiological components and are therefore well recognized across cultures. However, other displays of the same emotions are elaborated with culture-specific expressions and gestures that result either in misinterpretation or bafflement in observers who are not members of the culture in which the expressions originated" (pg. 232). She suggests that most students start the exercise assuming that there will be no cultural differences in expression. However, she finds that confusions do arise. The key for the passages on **Handout Master 11.2** are as follows:

   1, 9 = fear
   2, 5 = surprise
   3 = shame
   4, 6, 8 = anger
   7, 12, 14 = joy
   10, 11 = sadness
   13 = disgust or contempt

   In her previous use of the quotes, Simmons has found that most students accurately identify description 1, 3, 4 (to a lesser extent), 6, 9, 11, 13, and 14. More errors are made on 8 (often that it is surprise) and 5 (that it is disgust or contempt). Descriptions 2, 7, 10, and 12 are rarely recognized by most U.S. students--they are derived from Chinese literature. A fun exercise linked to topics in the chapter.

Source:
Simmons, C. (1998). Are emotional expressions universal or culture specific? In T. Singelis (Ed.), Teaching about culture, ethnicity, & diversity: Exercises and planned activities (pg. 231-235). Thousand Oaks, CA: Sage.

7. **Gender and display rules:** In their section on Cultural perspectives on facial expressions, Uba and Huang discuss the use of display rules, learned expectations of when, where, and with whom emotions are to be

expressed. They use as an example that boys are discouraged from crying in this culture. Use **Handout Master 11.3** to offer students a chance to think about their own learning of display rules and their experiences when they violated such rules. Especially discuss gender (and cultural) differences that may emerge in their responses during discussion.

8. **The cultural meaning of food**: Uba and Huang discuss the psychological motivations for eating from the stimulus cue perspective. Other authors suggest that food and eating rituals also occur within a culturally meaningful context. Many of us can relate to "always" having turkey at Thanksgiving...certainly advertising equates the turkey with the season. Consider having students complete **Handout Master 11.4**, which asks them to relate different cultural meanings they have learned to associate with certain foods. You may find some interesting differences between local, regional, and national norms.

Sources for Additional Activities

Batson, C., & Johnson, A. (1976). Arousing intrinsic motivation as a goal for introductory classes: A case study. Teaching of psychology, 3, 155-159.

Benjamin, L. & Lowman, K. (1981). Activities handbook for the teaching of psychology. Washington DC: American Psychological Association.

Deffenbacher, H. (1990). Demonstrating the influence of cognition on emotion and behavior. Teaching of psychology, 17, 182-185.

Halonen, J. (1995). Chapter 9: Motivation. In The critical thinking companion for Introductory Psychology. New York: Worth Publishers.

Halonen, J. (1995). Chapter 10: Emotions, stress and health. In The critical thinking companion for Introductory Psychology. New York: Worth Publishers.

Hergenhahn, B. (1987). Influence of success and failure on level of aspiration. In V. Makosky, L. Whittemore, & A. Rogers (Eds.), Activities handbook for the teaching of psychology (Vol. 2) (pg. 231-234). Washington, DC: American Psychological Association.

Kasschau, R. (1981). Human emotions. In L. Benjamin, & K. Lowman (Eds.), Activities handbook for the teaching of psychology. (pg. 209-211). Washington, DC: American Psychological Association

Kite, M. (1990). Defining normal sexual behavior. Teaching of psychology, 17, 118-119.

McCary, J. (1975). Teaching the topic of human sexuality. Teaching of psychology, 2, 16-21.

Makosky, V., Whittemore, L., & Rogers, A. (1987). Activities handbook for the teaching of psychology (Vol. 2). Washington DC: American Psychological Association.

Makosky, V., Sileo, C., Whittemore, L., Landry, L., & Skutley, M. (1990). <u>Activities handbook for the teaching of psychology</u> (Vol. 3). Washington DC: American Psychological Association.

Rice, R., & Neider, L. (1979). A classroom motivation scale illustrating the VIE theory of motivation. Teaching of psychology, 6, 94-97.

Singelis, T. (1998). <u>Teaching about culture, ethnicity, & diversity: Exercises and planned activities.</u> Thousand Oaks, CA: Sage.

Smith, J. (1987). The Origami game. In V. Makosky, L. Whittemore, & A. Rogers (Eds.), <u>Activities handbook for the teaching of psychology (Vol. 2)</u> (pg. 235-238). Washington, DC: American Psychological Association.

Smith, J. (1987). Vicarious motivation. In V. Makosky, L. Whittemore, & A. Rogers (Eds.), <u>Activities handbook for the teaching of psychology (Vol. 2)</u> (pg. 239-240). Washington, DC: American Psychological Association.

Walls, J. (1981). Experiment on smiling. In L. Benjamin, & K. Lowman (Eds.), <u>Activities handbook for the teaching of psychology.</u> (pg. 162-163). Washington, DC: American Psychological Association.

Whitford, F. (1998). Motivation and emotion. In <u>Quick guide to the Internet for psychology</u> (pg.76-78). Boston: Allyn and Bacon.

Winchell, L. (1981). Flashing faces. In L. Benjamin, & K. Lowman (Eds.), <u>Activities handbook for the teaching of psychology</u>. (pg. 212-213). Washington, DC: American Psychological Association

World Wide Web: Check out the following WWW sites for information and activities relevant to this section of the text!

General
- Addison Wesley Longman's Website -- **http://longman.awl.com/**
- PsychZone link -- **http://longman.awl.com/**
- Psych Web -- **http://www.gasou.edu/psychweb/psychweb.htm**
- Self-Quizzes for Introductory Psychology -- **http://www.gasou.edu/psychweb/selfquiz/selfquiz.htm**
- Psychology Jumping Stand -- **http://www.indiana.edu:80/~iuepsyc/PsycJump.html**
- The Psychology Place -- **http://www.psychplace.com**

Emotions
- Affective/emotional system -- **http://www.valdosta.peachnet.edu/~whuitt/psy702/affsys/affsys.html**
- Emotion/facial expression--**http://mamb.ucsc.edu/psl/ekman.html**
- Theories of emotional experience--**http://www.gasou.edu/psychweb/selfquiz.htm**
  or
  http://psych.wisc.edu/faculty/pages/croberts/topic8.html
  or
  http://www.latimes.com/HOME/NEWS/SCIENCE/REPORTS/THEBRAIN
- Physiological aspects of emotion--**http://www.hib.gov/news/NIH-Record/06_03_97/story04.htm**
- Amygdala Home Page--**http://marlin.utmb.edu/~nkeele/**
- Theories of emotion-- **http://www.valdosta.peachnet.edu/~whuitt/psy702/motivation/motivate.html**
  or
  http://www.people.memphis.edu/~clong/emotiont.htm
- Classic writings on emotion-- **http://www.cns.nyu.edu/home/ledoux/authors.html**
- Emotion Home Page--**http://emotion.salk.edu/emotion.html**
  or
  http://emotion.ccs.brandeis.edu/emotion.html
- Emotional intelligence-- **http://trochim.human.cornell.edu/gallery/young/emotion.htm**
  or
  http://www.utne.com/lens/bms/9bmseq.html
- Human emotion research--**http://www-white.media.mit.edu/vismod/demos/affect/AC_research/emotions.html**

Motivation
- Motivation--**http://www.ed.ac.uk/~mlc/marble/psycho/topic2/topic2_c.htm**

- or
  http://www.cmhc.com/psyhelp/chapt4/chap4i.htm
  or
  http://choo.fis.utoronto.ca/FIS/Courses/LIS1230/LIS1230sharma/motive1.htm
- Motivation level--**http://www.und.nodak.edu/dept/ULC/rf-mot.htm**
- Maslow--**http://snycorva.cortland.edu/~ANDERSMD/MASLOW/THEORY.HTML**
  or
  http://www.coba.usf.edu/Marketing/Faculty/Kennedy/6-consum/sld011.htm
  or
  http://www.ping.be/jvwit/Maslovmotivation.html
  or
  http://sol.brunel.ac.uk/~jarvis/bola/motivation/masmodel.html
- Self quiz on motivation--**http://beowulf.simplynet.net/ejones/PsyTest/ch09mcq.htm**
- Motivation and business settings--**http://www.liraz.com/webquiz.htm**
- Motivation and performance--**http://www.apa.org/pubinfo/orient.html**

Weight/eating

- Nutrition guide/quiz--**http://arborcom.com/**
  or
  http://www.olen.com/food/
  or
  http://www.mayohealth.org/mayo/9411/htm/quiz_sb.htm
- Controlling hunger--**http://www.dinesystems.com/control.htm**
- Food-nutrition or pleasure?--**http://www.arise.org/Rozin.html**
- Being overweight--**http://www.newswise.com/articles/FATMMWR.CHS.html**
  or
  http://www.quantumhcp.com/obesity.htm
- Diet, weight loss, & fitness--**http://www1.mhv.net/~donn/diet.html**
  or
  http://www1.mhv.net/~donn/diet.html
- Eating disorders--**http://www.something-fishy.com/ed.htm**
  or
  http://www.fsci.umn.edu/~AFED/

Sexuality

- The Kinsey Institute--**http://www.indiana.edu/~kinsey**
- Journal of Sex Research--**http://www.ssc.wisc.edu/ssss/jsr.htm**
- Sex survey results--**http://www. rwjf.org.library/win95ar2.htm**
- Sexual orientation--**http://www.apa.org/pubin/orient.html**

Audio-Visual Support
Films/Videos:

General: Motivation and emotion
- *Discovering Psychology: Motivation and emotion* (Annenberg, 30 minutes)
- *Motivation* (Insight Media, 30 minutes)
- *Maslow's hierarchy of needs* (UM, 15 minutes)
- *A New Look at Motivation* (CRM, 32 minutes)

Emotions
- *Face Value* (PERED, 38 minutes)
- *Life's First Feelings* (IU, 58 minutes)
- *When You're Smiling* (IU, 6 minutes)
- *Anger* (IU, 15 minutes)
- *Emotional Intelligence: The Key to Social Skills* (FFHS, 28 minutes)
- *Emotion* (Insight Media, 30 minutes)

Aggression
- *Resolving Conflicts* (CRM, 22 minutes)
- *Aggression: The Explosive Emotion* (PSUPCR, 58 minutes)
- *Psychling* (CRM, 25 minutes)
- *The Roots of Violence Series* (FFHS, 30 minutes each)
    Program 1: A Child's View of the World: Exhuming a Violent Past
    Program 2: Children of Addiction
    Program 3: Children of Violence
    Program 4: Children of Neglect
    Program 5: The Perfect Child: "Cold" Violence
- *Recovery from Sexual Abuse* (FFHS, 47 minutes)
- *Juvenile Sex Offenders: Voices Unheard* (FFHS, 44 minutes)
- *Childhood Sexual Abuse* (FFHS, 26 minutes)
- *Childhood Physical Abuse* (FFHS, 26 minutes)
- *No More Secrets* (FFHS, 24 minutes)
- *Child Molestation: Sorting Out the Truth* (FFHS, 20 minutes)
- *Male Rape* (FFHS, 42 minutes)
- *Society's Problems in Children's Lives* (FFHS, 28 minutes)
- *Avoiding Conflict: Dispute Resolution Without Violence* (FFHS, 47 minutes)
- *Peace on the Playground* (FFHS, 27 minutes)
- *Violence: An American Tradition* (FFHS, 55 minutes)
- *Teen Violence: Wot U Lookin' At?* (FFHS, 60 minutes)
- *Reading, Writing, and Revolvers: Coping with Teenage Violence* (FFHS, 45 minutes)
- *What Can We Do About Violence? Series* (FFHS, 56 minutes)

Program 1: Juveniles Locked Up
Program 2: domestic Violence, Street Violence
Program 3: Crisis in Our Inner Cities
Program 4: Solutions for Children
- *Solutions to Violence with Bill Moyers Series* (FFHS, 30 minutes each)
Program 1: On Parenting
Program 2: Making Our Neighborhoods Safe
Program 3: Rebuilding Communities
Program 4: Early Intervention
Program 5: Understanding Violence
Program 6: Decoding the Rap: Gangs and Rap Music
- **Violence Against Women* (FFHS, 46 minutes)
- *Male Violence: A Room Full of Men* (FFHS, 49 minutes)
- *Family Violence: Breaking the Chain* (FFHS, 25 minutes)
- *Domestic Violence: Behind Closed Doors* (FFHS, 28 minutes)
- *You Can't Beat a Woman* (FFHS, 95 minutes)
- *Domestic Violence: 'Til Death Do Us Part* (FFHS, 20 minutes)
- *The Impact of Violence on Children* (FFHS, 28 minutes)
- *The Rape Drug: A New Menace* (FFHS, 26 minutes)
- *Date Violence: A Young Woman's Guide* (FFHS, 22 minutes)
- *Rape: An Act of Hate* (FFHS, 30 minutes)

Achievement
- **The Impossible Takes a Little Longer* (IN. Univ, 48 minutes)
- *Motivation: It's Not Just the Money* (DOCA, 26 minutes)
- *Productivity and the Self-fulfilling Prophecy: The Pygmalion Effect* (CRM, 30 minutes)
- *The Leadership Challenge* (CRM, 26 minutes)

Sexuality
- **And I still rise* (Women Make Movies, Inc., 30 minutes)
- *Embracing Our Sexuality* (New Day, 45 minutes)
- *Finding Our Way* (New Day, 38 minutes)

Eating
- *The Psychology of Eating* (HBJ, 29 minutes)
- *Anorexia and Bulimia* (FFHS, 19 minutes)
- *On Being Fat in a Thin World* (xxx, 50 minutes)

Psychology Encyclopedia Laserdisc IV:

Movies

Cool look at anger	3 minutes 28 sec.	Frames 07477-13714	Side 2
Changing times for gender roles	3 minutes 30 sec.	13718-22014	2
Productivity and the self-fulfilling prophecy	1 minute 30 sec.	20015-22722	2

Still images

Emotional expression drawing [1/4] [UN]	Frame 53554	Side all
Emotional expression drawing [2/4] [UN]	53555	all
Emotional expression drawing [3/4] [UN]	53556	all
Emotional expression drawing [4/4] [UN]	53557	all
Emotion and the brain [1/2] [UN]	53558	all
Emotional expression drawing [4/4] [UN]	53559	all

Transparency Master 11.1: Checking Your TRAIL 11.1

I. Instincts and drives are both thought to be innate. However, unlike drives, instincts
   A. motivate behavior toward satisfying needs.
   B. originate from deficiencies.
   C. are temporary.
   D. are rigid patterns of behavior.

II. Explain how replacing intrinsic motivation with extrinsic motivation often affects creative behavior, and how extrinsic motivation can be used to increase intrinsic motivation.

III. Describe Maslow's hierarchy of needs.

IV. Ralph does everything to the extreme. He has many sex partners, tries different drugs, drives over the speed limit, and travels to foreign places. Explain how this behavior could be motivated by instincts, drive reduction, sensation seeking, and incentives.

Transparency Master 11.2: Checking Your TRAIL 11.2

I. **<u>True</u> or <u>False</u>: Stimulation of the lateral hypothalamus stimulates eating.**

II. **Explain how cognition contributes to aggressive behavior. Give an example to illustrate your explanation.**

III. **Describe the sexual-response cycle and give examples of how sexual dysfunctions might disrupt the cycle.**

IV. **Lee Ann worked hard to graduate with honors from college in three years. Immediately after graduation, she entered medical school and finished at the top of her class. Explain her achievement goals and pursuit of them, first from a collectivistic perspective, then from an individualistic point of view.**

Transparency Master 11.3: Checking Your TRAIL 11.3

I. Identify and describe the three components of an emotion.

II. Explain the difference between primary and secondary emotions, and evidence in support of the idea that primary emotions are universal.

III. True or False: Cognitive appraisal is necessary for the experience of emotion.

IV. Some women smile when they are angry. Use the concept of display rules to explain their facial expression of emotion.

Transparency Master 11.4: Checking Your TRAIL 11.4

I. Name three of Cannon's criticisms of the James-Lange theory.

II. Shaquil, an airline steward, is required to smile constantly while on the job. According to the facial feedback hypothesis, how might smiling help him provide genuinely cheerful service to his flyers?

III. While waiting at a stoplight, Kendall, a stoic young man, is rear-ended. He gets out of his car to exchange information with the woman who hit his car. By the end of the conversation, he decides that he is attracted to her and asks her out to dinner. How might mistaken appraisal and the two-factor theory explain his attraction to her?

IV. Some psychologists hypothesize that specific emotions motivate behaviors that aid human survival. Give three or more examples of specific emotions and the behaviors they might motivate.

Transparency Master 11.5: Critical Thinking 11.1

Some teachers avoid using extrinsic rewards in the classroom because of the risk of replacing intrinsic motivation with extrinsic motivation. Yet, extrinsic rewards can sometimes increase intrinsic motivation. Give an example of how a teacher could use extrinsic motivation to enhance students' intrinsic motivation to cooperate on planning and painting a mural.

Transparency Master 11.6: Critical Thinking 11.2

Identify at least two ways that the laboratory arrangement that produced longer and more intense shocks from participants who had drank alcohol might have limited generalizability to real-life aggression.

Transparency Master 11.7: Critical Thinking 11.3

Masters and Johnson described a sexual-response cycle that implies a series of progressive steps. How would you expect people to feel if they were told that their sexual behavior was "normal" only if it was characterized by this series of steps?

Transparency Master 11.8: Integrative Thinking 11.1

Use the principles of classical conditioning described in the Learning chapter to explain why some people might become sensitive to food cues.

Transparency Master 11.9: Integrative Thinking 11.2

We discussed personal fables in the Adolescent & Adult Development chapter. How might a personal fable prevent adolescents who have a high fear of failure from accepting a teacher's encouragement?

Ian always feels a mixture of anger and sadness when he sees a BMW. His fiancée died in a car crash caused by a drunken driver in a BMW. Use the role of external cues in memory, as described in the Memory chapter, to explain Ian's reaction.

Transparency Master 11.11: Integrative Thinking 11.4

Recall the process of cognitive development during childhood described in the Child Development chapter. How might children at the preoperational stage be limited in their ability to appraise a threatening situation?

Transparency Master 11.12: Integrative Thinking 11.5

Recall the role of the conceptual frameworks known as schemas described in the Cognition & Intelligence chapter. Imagine that the researchers had a schema of Japanese people as emotionally expressive and polite. How might such a schema have influenced their tendency to interpret the Japanese participants' smiles as an attempt to hide their true feelings?

Transparency Master 11.13: Integrative Thinking 11.6

Recall the theory of linguistic determinism and criticisms of it as described in the Communication chapter. If a culture has no word for sadness, as in Tahiti, can people of that culture experience sadness?

Handout Master 11.1: Relationship Events

Relationship Events

Instructions: Below is a list of 25 different psychological and physical events that may occur within an intimate relationship. For each event, indicate the degree to which it reflects a form of aggression.

Event	Not at all aggressive						Extremely aggressive
1. "put downs" of physical appearance	1	2	3	4	5	6	7
2. kicking partner	1	2	3	4	5	6	7
3. insulting or shaming in front of others	1	2	3	4	5	6	7
4. intentionally scratching partner	1	2	3	4	5	6	7
5. insisting a partner steal money for him/her	1	2	3	4	5	6	7
6. pulling partner's hair	1	2	3	4	5	6	7
7. bringing up past events to hurt partner	1	2	3	4	5	6	7
8. preventing partner from doing things to help self	1	2	3	4	5	6	7
9. name calling or swearing	1	2	3	4	5	6	7
10. slapping partner	1	2	3	4	5	6	7
11. treating partner like an inferior	1	2	3	4	5	6	7
12. painfully pinching partner	1	2	3	4	5	6	7
13. sulking or refusing to talk about a problem	1	2	3	4	5	6	7
14. telling partner his/her feelings are crazy/irrational	1	2	3	4	5	6	7
15. giving the silent treatment	1	2	3	4	5	6	7
16. throwing objects at partner	1	2	3	4	5	6	7
17. withholding affection	1	2	3	4	5	6	7
18. punching partner	1	2	3	4	5	6	7
19. not allowing partner to talk about his/her feelings	1	2	3	4	5	6	7
20. being insensitive to partner's sexual feelings	1	2	3	4	5	6	7
21. intentionally choking partner	1	2	3	4	5	6	7
22. blaming partner for own problems	1	2	3	4	5	6	7
23. threatening partner with weapon	1	2	3	4	5	6	7
24. cheating on partner with another person	1	2	3	4	5	6	7
25. forcing partner to engage in sexual activity against his/her will	1	2	3	4	5	6	7

Handout Master 11.2: Culture and emotions in literature

Culture and Emotions in Literature

Identifying emotions in literature passages: Carolyn Simmons has created an interesting exercise that is based in the debate around the universal nature of emotional expressions. She has combined a number of sentences drawn from English and Chinese literature that are descriptions of emotional expressions. Her fundamental assumption is that some expressions of emotions have strong experiential physiological components and are therefore well recognized across cultures. However, other displays of the same emotions are elaborated with culture-specific expressions and gestures that result either in misinterpretation or bafflement in observers who are not members of the culture in which the expressions originated (pg. 232). She suggests that most students start the exercise assuming that there will be no cultural differences in expression. However, she finds that confusions do arise. A fun exercise linked to topics in the chapter.

Source:
Simmons, C. (1998). Are emotional expressions universal or culture specific? In T. Singelis (Ed.), Teaching about culture, ethnicity, & diversity: Exercises and planned activities (pg. 231-235). Thousand Oaks, CA: Sage.

Handout Master 11.3: Display rules

Display rules

Instructions: In the space below, list 5 display rules you remember having been toward either directly or indirectly over your lifetime. Describe the consequences of violating these rules and give some examples of situations you committed such a violation. To what extent did the display rule reflect cultural or gender expectations?

Display rule # 1:_____
Consequence:_____
Example: _____
Cultural/gender expectations: _____

Display rule # 2:_____
Consequence:_____
Example: _____
Cultural/gender expectations: _____

Display rule # 3:_____
Consequence:_____
Example: _____
Cultural/gender expectations: _____

Display rule # 4:_____
Consequence:_____
Example: _____
Cultural/gender expectations: _____

Display rule # 5:_____
Consequence:_____
Example: _____
Cultural/gender expectations: _____

Handout Master 11.4: Cultural meaning of food

Cultural meaning of food

Instructions: Consider 3 events in which food and the ritual of eating takes on a cultural meaning (e.g., turkey at Thanksgiving). What foods are present? What do they mean?

Event 1:
　　Food: _____
　　Meaning: _____
　　_____
　　_____
　　_____

Event 2:
　　Food: _____
　　Meaning: _____
　　_____
　　_____
　　_____

Event 3:
　　Food: _____
　　Meaning: _____
　　_____
　　_____
　　_____

CHAPTER 12

PERSONALITY & TESTING

- **Chapter Overview**
    Learning Objectives
    Chapter Outline

- **Additional Lecture Ideas**
    Lecture Topics
    Additional Readings

- **In-Class Activities and Demonstrations**
    Activities and Demonstrations
    Sources for Additional Activities
    Journey II Software

- **World Wide Web**

- **Audio-Visual Support**

- **Handout and Transparency Masters**

Chapter Overview

Learning Objectives

After studying this chapter, you should be able to do the following:

1. Describe the concept of personality and its cultural bias.

2. Discuss the primary perspectives on personality.

3. Identify the usefulness and limitations of each of these perspectives.

4. Describe the purposes, characteristics, usefulness, and limitations of three methods of personality assessment.

Chapter Outline

Personality & Testing

I. The Concept of Personality: Who We Are
   A. Definition
      1. <u>personality</u>: the relatively stable combination of beliefs, attitudes, values, motives, temperament, and behavior patterns arising from underlying, internal inclinations that an individual exhibits in many situations
   B. Assumptions
      1. personality is stable: people behave the same across situations; an individualistic assumption about thought/behavior
      2. personality affected by mix of flowing psychological processes including environment

II. Alternative Perspectives on Personality
   A. Six primary perspectives
      1. trait
      2. psychodynamic
      3. learning
      4. social cognition
      5. behavior genetic
      6. humanistic

III. Why We Are the Way We Are
   A. The trait perspective: Describing personalities
      1. <u>definition</u>: general characteristics and dispositions that are presumably the basis for an individual's particular behavior patterns
      2. <u>theory characteristics</u>:
         a. focus on describing people's traits (not why people have the traits they do)
         b. use of questionnaires
         c. interest in surface and source traits
            i. <u>surface</u>: readily evident, observable personality characteristics
            ii. <u>source</u>: basic personality characteristics that underlie surface traits
         d. use of factor analysis to identify clusters of traits
      3. <u>theorists</u>
         a. <u>Cattell</u>: found 16 source traits characteristic of all people
         b. <u>Hans & Sybil Eysenck</u>: 2 personality dimensions
            i. <u>introversion-extroversion</u>: quiet/withdrawn vs. sociability/outgoing

  ii. <u>stability-instability</u>: calm/even-tempered vs. easily aroused anxiety/distress
  iii. <u>four personality temperaments</u>:
   - melancholic
   - choleric
   - phlegmatic
   - sanguine
 c. <u>Costa & McCrae</u>: the "Big Five" dimensions of personality found cross-culturally/between sexes
  i. <u>extroversion</u>: adventurousness, outspokenness, spontaneity, gregariousness, assertiveness
  ii. <u>conscientiousness</u>: perseverance, efficiency, thriftiness, carefulness, punctuality, precision, diligence in work, dependability, politeness, flexibility, self-discipline, trustfulness, unselfishness
  iii. <u>openness to experience</u>: intelligence, curiosity, perceptiveness, originality, creativity, artistic inclination, wisdom, wittiness, resourcefulness
  iv. <u>emotional stability</u>: even-tempered, easy-going, careful, secure, self-controlled
  v. <u>agreeableness</u>: good-natured, warm, kind, trusting, lenient, generous, compassionate, gets along with others

5. <u>the consistency of traits</u>:
 a. issue of consistency/stability has plagued this approach
 b. assumption of consistency central to approach
 c. <u>Allport's work on stability differences in traits</u>: different people may have the same trait (e.g., shyness) but it may vary as a prominent/stable part of their personalities
  i. <u>cardinal traits</u>: those one or two dominant traits that, in some people, affect almost all aspects of their personality and behaviors
   - extremely stable but not all people have them
  ii. <u>central traits</u>: the few dominant traits that are thought to summarize an individual's personality
  iii. <u>secondary traits</u>: the many traits that are more subject to change over a lifetime and less important in defining a person than are cardinal or central traits
 d. <u>Mischel's situationist perspective</u>: personality better viewed a set of probable responses to a particular situation rather than as consistent, internal traits
 e. <u>the interactionist perspective</u>: the belief that people have relatively stable personality traits, but that their behaviors depend on the situation at hand
 f. <u>other issues in the consistency debate</u>:

i. trait consistency depends on how define traits and number of situations observed
ii. collectivist vs. individualist orientation may influence trait consistency measures
6. <u>the usefulness and limitations of the trait approach</u>:
    a. <u>useful aspects of perspective</u>:
        i. defines personality in terms of understandable everyday concepts
        ii. doesn't require theoretical assumptions be met
        iii. has led to great deal of research
    b. <u>limitations of perspective</u>:
        i. doesn't explain why people develop traits
        ii. cross theory differences in trait descriptions

B. Psychodynamic perspectives: Focusing on childhood and the unconscious
1. <u>theory characteristics</u>: a group of theories that explain personality and behavior in terms of past experiences and thoughts, feelings, memories, and intrapsychic conflicts at various levels of consciousness
    a. <u>levels of consciousness</u>:
        i. <u>conscious</u>: a level of consciousness defined by psychodynamic psychologists as containing feelings, thoughts, and memories we are aware of having
        ii. <u>preconscious</u>: a level of consciousness that psychodynamic psychologists believe contains memories we can recall with effort
        iii. <u>unconscious</u>: a level of consciousness that psychodynamic psychologists believe contains very disturbing or socially unacceptable fantasies, thoughts, impulses, memories, and psychological conflicts that play a major role in determining behavior and personality
    b. personalities reflect psychodynamic processes in which people deal with, transform, and express dynamic psychological urges and tensions
        i. <u>libido</u>: the psychosexual energy that fuels the transformation and expression psychological urges and tensions and, therefore, is a source of personality
2. <u>Sigmund Freud's psychoanalytic theory of personality</u>: theory of personality that focuses on the role of the unconscious and internal conflicts in determining personality
    a. <u>id, superego, ego</u>: three parts of the personality that are in conflict with one another; nature of conflicts, attempts to channel libido's energy, our attempts to deal with, express, transform, or resolve conflicts determines personality
        i. <u>id</u>: Freud's term for the part of personality consisting of biological drives and instincts; ruled by pleasure principle; no contact with reality

  ii. <u>superego</u>: Freud's term for a partially unconscious, internalized sense of morality and social constraints; sets unrealistically high/strict moral standards; demands we behave in ideal way
  iii. <u>ego</u>: Freud's term for the combination of mental abilities and self-concept that tries to balance the id's desire for pleasure and the superego's moral demands, within the limits of what is realistically possible; responsible for making rational decisions
 b. <u>psychosexual stages</u>:
  i. stages include oral, anal, phallic, latency, and genital (see table 12.2)
  ii. id's urges change/are expressed and satisfied in different ways as we age
  iii. changes in id's impulses during various stages create new imbalances between id/superego that ego must balance thus shaping personality
  iv. during various stages, pleasure sought from particular erogenous zone; source of gratification produces satisfaction and anxiety
  v. fixation: state of being stuck at a Freudian psychosexual stage if child was praised excessively, not given behavior standards, or became frustrated with task faced during that stage
  vi. personality develops from resolution of conflicts between desires to receive pleasure from erogenous zones and demands of reality

3. <u>Carl Jung</u>:
 a. unconscious composed of personal and collective components
  i. <u>personal unconscious</u>: unconscious thoughts based on an individual's personal experiences
  ii. <u>collective unconscious</u>: the content of the unconscious that is shared by all people, including memories, ideas, and ways of behaving; causes people to respond in generally similar ways to certain stimuli and to share some concepts, dream symbols, and religious beliefs
 b. <u>archetypes</u>: human's shared mental images or ways of perceiving and responding to situations and images (e.g., mothering)
 c. emphasis on opposing parts to our personality (e.g., animus and anima)
 d. <u>psychological health/psychic wholeness dependent on</u>:
  i. integrating opposing parts of personality including archetypes

  ii. resolving inconsistency between inner self (i.e., who one truly is) and persona (i.e., part of personality that is presented to others)
 e. differences in personality between people arise from difference in how opposing archetypes and tendencies balanced and integrated, degree of consistency between inner self and persona, and how well people know themselves

4. <u>Karen Horney</u>: personalities are the result of peoples' relationships with their parents and efforts to find protection from imagined/real threats
 a. children feel anxiety because of dependence on other people
  i. when parents unable to immediately meet child's needs, child feels frustrated, anxious, hostile toward parents
  ii. child uncomfortable with hostility, have limited means to express it, keep it within themselves by forcing hostility into unconscious and is only consciously aware of anxiety
  iii. personality reflects ways child has managed conflict between feelings of anxiety and hostility
 b. <u>dealing with anxiety</u>:
  i. may use one of 3 coping behaviors:
   - moving toward others
   - moving against others
   - moving award from others
  ii. coping behaviors become part of personality
  iii. well-adjusted people choose different coping style to situation; maladjusted people overuse one of them
 c. <u>maladjusted personality types</u>: based on use of one coping style
  i. <u>compliant type</u>: move toward people; insecure; excessive need for approval; overly compliant and anxious to please; give in to others and not express true feelings
  ii. <u>aggressive type</u>: move against people; relate to others in hostile and dominating way; lash out at others
  iii. <u>detached type</u>: moving away from others; socially withdraw to protect themselves from hurt
 d. potential for personality change throughout life

5. <u>Alfred Adler</u>: emphasis on vulnerability and birth order (i.e., ordinal position)
 a. people dependent/vulnerable when young; create inferiority
 b. birth order contributes to feelings of inferiority
 c. ordinal position and inferiority play major role in determining personality
 d. analyze personality by determining how person deals with feelings of inferiority
 e. desire to become superior/overcome life challenges are basic motivators

  f. <u>inferiority complex</u>: unshakable feelings of inferiority that underlie efforts to compensate
  g. goals, interests, values, perceptions, attitudes, behaviors, and personalities influenced by areas in which we feel inferior and way we cope with those feelings
  h. changes in personality can occur throughout life because real/imagined inferiority can arise at any time in life
 6. <u>the usefulness and limitations of psychodynamic theories</u>:
  a. <u>contributions</u>:
   i. identification of childhood experiences as a basis for personality
   ii. unconscious feelings/motives connected to everyday feelings, thoughts, behaviors
   iii. acknowledging that behavior sometimes represents a compromise among desires, fears, reality
   iv. aggressive/sexual urges and feelings have underlying role in determining personality
   v. opposing parts of personalities and feelings of anxiety/inferiority can affect personality
   vi. theories provide many hypothetical constructs
  b. <u>limitations/criticisms</u>:
   i. theory ideas haven't received a lot of empirical support
   ii. some psychodynamic concepts vague, untestable
   iii. view humans as victims of drives beyond their control (i.e., excuses people from responsibility for behavior)
   iv. doesn't account for development of healthy personalities
   v. overestimates permanency of personality characteristics

C. Learning perspectives: Emphasizing the environment
 1. <u>theory characteristics</u>:
  a. based on application of empirical learning principles
  b. psychologists using this perspective observe and describe patterns of behavior
 2. <u>the behaviorist perspective</u>:
  a. <u>personality</u>: an accumulation of behavior patterns learned through conditioning and observational learning
  b. focus on directly observable behaviors, not underlying, unobservable dispositions
  c. consistency in behaviors result of consistencies in reinforcement history and generalization of behaviors
 3. <u>the social learning perspective</u>:
  a. <u>personality</u>: the result of a combination of learning (including modeling) and cognitive processes (such as expectations and interpretations)
  b. Albert Bandura

          i. departed from behaviorist rejection of concept of personality as scientifically legitimate
          ii. emphasized reciprocal determinism or interaction between:
- person's thinking, perceptions, feelings
- person's behavior
- environmental factors
          iii. personality affect how person perceives self, interprets situations, environments sought, which in turn affect personality
          iv. example: impact of self-efficacy beliefs on self-beliefs and activities attempted
          v. analyzing personality, from social learning perspective, involves considering person's reinforcement history, knowledge, culturally based patterns of behavior, sense of self-efficacy, values, and learned ways of interpreting events
    4. the usefulness and limitations of learning perspectives:
        a. contributions:
          i. helps us see how environment affects personality
          ii. research has demonstrated that many behaviors associated with personality are learned
        b. limitations/criticisms:
          i. emphasis on behaviors hides richness underlying personality
          ii. ignores unconscious motives and genetic influences
          iii. behaviorist perspective ignores how people interpret situations; how personal beliefs affect behavior

D. Social-cognition perspectives: Identifying personality types
    1. theory characteristics:
        a. personality: defined by person's cognitive processes and ways of relating to other people
        b. theories usually lead to identification of personality types (i.e., identifiable sets of characteristic that tend to be found together)
        c. often examine family upbringing as source for personality type
    2. beliefs systems theory: a theory of personality that identifies four personality types, characterized by different beliefs and different degrees of abstract, differentiated, and integrated thinking and ways of relating to people
        a. Type 1: least differentiated/abstract in thinking; hold traditional beliefs/values; make black-and-white judgments; assume authority figures are right; obey authority figures without question
        b. Type 2: believe authority usually wrong; don't make many distinctions in thinking; often alienated from other people

c. Type 3: more differentiated/integrated thinking than previous types; swayed by outlooks of others; believe in doing whatever will result in social approval

d. Type 4: most differentiated/integrated thinking patterns; believe behavior should reflect what they think is appropriate rather than what others say/believe

3. the authoritarian personality: example of a major set of interrelated characteristics that plays a major role in personality

    a. characteristics of person with authoritarian personality:
        ii. high in ethnocentrism
        ii. tendency toward prejudice
        iii. obey/respect people of higher status; hostile toward people of lower status
        iv. don't precisely differentiate concepts so view events/people as all good/all bad
        v. disinterested in understanding themselves
        vi. come from families with harsh/arbitrary discipline in which relationships based on domination and challenging parental statements not accepted

4. the usefulness and limitations of social-cognition perspectives:

    a. contributions:
        i. have received considerable empirical support
        ii. focus attention on how values and family relationships affect personality

    b. limitations/criticisms:
        i. for personality syndromes - don't account for full range of personality characteristics
        ii. assume that socioeconomic class and ethnicity have little effect on personality
        iii. don't pay enough attention to unconscious processes or genetic influences

E. The behavior genetic perspective: Focusing on genes and environment

1. theory characteristics:

    a. personality: the product of genes, environment, and the interaction of genes with the environment

    b. emphasizes research findings more than theoretical perspective

    c. focus on how much genes influence personality characteristics rather than why they do

    d. attempt to estimate how heritable a group's (rather than individual's) trait is

2. searching for genetic effects:

    a. methods of study:
        i. animal studies: studying frequently reproducing animals allows examination of genetic transmission of traits across generations in a family in relatively short time period

        ii. <u>adoption studies</u>: compare personality traits of adopted children, adoptive parents, and biological parents; assumption = heritability measured by comparing degree to which adopted children and biological parents share trait minus degree to which adopted children and adoptive parents share trait
        iii. <u>twin studies</u>: compare identical twins reared apart for measure of shared genetic influences
    3. <u>genes and their impact on personality</u>:
        a. psychological characteristics that have genetic basis result of combination of numerous genes
        b. of personality traits known to have genetic basis, about 20 to 50% of variance explained by influence of genes; implies that environment accounts for 50% or more of the variance
        c. environmental factors influencing personality include birth order, gender, friends
        d. examples of traits influenced by genes include shyness, intelligence, sociability, aggressiveness, nervousness, sensation-seeking, recreational/vocational interests, activity levels, responses to stress, tastes in food, some psychological disorders, emotional reactivity
    4. <u>the usefulness and limitations of the behavior genetic approach</u>:
        a. <u>contributions</u>:
            i. logic of approach makes sense since genes influence hormone levels, the manufacture of proteins, and aging, which are likely form biological basis for personality
        b. <u>limitations/criticisms</u>:
            i. distinguishing between genetic and environmental effects is difficult
            ii. most behavior genetic studies done on European Americans and the environments in which they live
            iii. potential cultural biases of researchers in types of traits investigated

F. Humanistic perspectives: Choosing a personality
    1. <u>theory characteristics</u>:
        a. explanations of behavior and personality that regard people as basically good and naturally seeking to fulfill their potential
        b. assume people have existential freedom (i.e., freedom to choose personality, how to interpret what goes on around them, what kind of persons they are, and how to behave at any point during life)
        c. emphasizes the need to embrace freedom and responsibility, face true feelings, characteristics, vulnerabilities, fears
    2. <u>Abraham Maslow</u>:
        a. believed that desire to achieve self-actualization is the driving force in personality development

              b. other basic needs must be met before self-actualization needs
              c. self-actualization not a end-point but an on-going process
       3. Carl Rogers:
              a. why don't people self-actualize? deny their true feelings in order to gain social approval
              b. conditional positive regard: approval that occurs only when children mimic approved attitudes and values and behave in particular ways
              c. unconditional positive regard: constant expression of love and acknowledgement of a child even when disapproving of a child's behavior
                     i. increases likelihood child will embrace existential freedom, fulfill potential, be free of intrapsychic conflict, develop self-concept that reflects own abilities/interests
       4. the usefulness and limitations of humanistic perspectives:
              a. contributions/strengths:
                     i. positive view of people as thinking creatures who make choices
                     ii. encourages people to take personal responsibility
                     iii. helps people see behavior options and opportunities for personal growth
              b. limitations/criticisms:
                     i. overly optimistic about ability to move beyond past experiences
                     ii. lack of emphasis on unconscious
                     iii. cultural bias toward individual vs. group actualization
                     iv. theoretical concepts vague, untestable
G. Other perspectives: Identifying cultural, racial, gender, and power effects
       1. cultural perspectives on personality:
              a. socialization within a culture affects personality that people develop
              b. examples:
                     i. United States emphasis on freedom of behavior, pursuit of material prosperity, interest in practical knowledge
                     ii. Latino/a script of simpatico, machismo
                     iii. Asian American social assertiveness emphasizes getting along
              c. variations in personality due to individualistic/collectivistic cultural orientations
       2. racial perspectives on personality:
              a. social reactions to race may affect experiences and personality that develops
              b. example: "black personality" perspective to focuses on similarities in personalities of African Americans due to experiences with racism; includes African-based concepts of

spirituality and political identification, energy flows and bodily rhythms
3. <u>gender perspectives on personality</u>:
    a. gender differences in personality
        i. <u>males</u>: more dominant, autonomous, and aggressive than females
        ii. <u>females</u>: more affiliative, deferential, and nurturing than males
    b. effects of cultural influences on gender differences in personality
        i. different cultural standards for males/females
        ii. cultural influences may distort/override biological tendencies
    c. perspective suggests both biological predispositions and cultural socialization affect personality
    d. more variability within gender groups than between
4. <u>social power perspectives on personality</u>:
    a. access to resources/power influences personality
    b. higher- and lower-power groups reinforced for certain personality characteristics
    c. meaning of personality characteristics depends on social power person has
        i. example: locus of control
        ii. cultural and economic biases in values placed on construct of locus of control

IV. Methods of Assessing Personality: Comparing People
   A. Projective tests: Revealing the unconscious
      1. <u>general description</u>:
         a. instruments consisting of a set of ambiguous stimuli designed to elicit interpretations that reflect the respondents' needs, motivations, attitudes, and conflicts, as well as other unconscious aspects of their personalities
         b. interpretations of test results somewhat subjective
         c. well-known projective tests: Rorshach Inkblot Test and Thematic Apperception Test
      2. <u>Rorshach Inkblot test</u>:
         a. a projective measure consisting of a set of symmetrical abstract images that respondents describe
         b. interpretation of results based on respondent's description and themes underlying these responses
      3. <u>telling a tale in the T.A.T.</u>:
         a. <u>Thematic Apperception Test</u>: a projective measure in which a respondent tells a story about each of a series of illustrations
         b. responses evaluated in terms of how story and characters reflect respondent's own attitudes, motives, behaviors, conflicts, feelings, and needs
      4. <u>the usefulness and limitations of projective tests</u>:
         a. <u>contributions</u>:
            i. useful to gain a quick sense of client's attitudes, beliefs, conflicts
            ii. discussions about test stimuli help to establish therapist-client rapport
         b. <u>drawbacks</u>:
            i. responses compared to those of European Americans
            ii. tests have questionable reliability and validity

   B. Self-report tests: Consciously describing ourselves
      1. <u>general description</u>:
         a. questionnaires that ask people to characterize their customary behaviors, attitudes, and feelings
         b. questions often written so respondent reports how applicable statements are to them; responses scored objectively using answer key
      2. <u>Minnesota Multiphasic Personality Inventory</u>:
         a. an example of an objective test; is reliable, inexpensive, scored by computer
         b. designed to reveal range of personality characteristics and help psychologists diagnose variety of problems
         c. consists of 10 clinical scales used to indicate possibility of different psychological disorders and 4 scales to determine if respondents faking answers

3. <u>the usefulness and limitations of questionnaires</u>:
    a. <u>usefulness</u>:
        i. many people can be tested cheaply and simply; as a result, researchers can study larger groups of people
        ii. checking reliability is relatively easy to do
        iii. frequently used in research efforts
        iv. newest version has increased representativeness of norm sample
    b. <u>limitations</u>:
        i. less valid measure for use with some cultural groups
        ii. underestimates the degree to which personality characteristics vary across cultures/change during different time in history
        iii. don't provide sufficient frame of reference
        iv. don't know if respondents are answering accurately; respondents may misremember or fake good/bad
        v. wording of questions may bias responses

C. Observations and interviews
    1. <u>general description</u>:
        a. <u>observation</u>: identifying and recording instances of behaviors in experimental or natural settings
            i. use of multiple trained observers
            ii. <u>advantages</u>:
                - possibly more reliable than self-report, esp. with people with poor memory/low self-awareness
                - useful in field/child studies
            iii. <u>drawbacks</u>:
                - observers might not see all behaviors
                - not clear whether observed behaviors are typical
                - observers might misinterpret behaviors (e.g., cultural misunderstanding of meaning of behaviors)
        b. <u>interviews</u>: sometimes used to supplement observation/to diagnose problems and screen job applicants
            i. <u>structured interviews</u>: interviewer asks preplanned questions in particular order; responses from various respondents can be compared
            ii. <u>unstructured interviews</u>: interviewee and discussion guide nature of questions asked; may provide irrelevant, useless information but also lead to unexpected insights

Additional Lecture Topics
The self in culture and social psychology:

Other perspectives for construing the self or personality of an individual exist outside the domain of traditional personality psychology that interface nicely with a sociocultural orientation such as Uba & Huang have adopted for this textbook. Two current social psychology textbooks each devote considerable, extensive discussion to the self, particularly from the standpoint of how the self develops and is shaped through the interface with the sociocultural environment. A detailed overview of the topics presented in those chapters would be prohibitive for this manual; however, you might find them extremely helpful resource tools for expanding this section of the course. Below are listed some of the major topics covered in each text:

Moghaddam (a text heavily oriented in cross-cultural literature and perspectives)
- the role of self in social psychology
- concepts of the self -- independent and interdependent self
- features of the self -- singularity of location, continuity
- the self-confrontational model -- exploring the narratively structured self
- variations in the self across cultures -- the Japanese inner self; the Western self-schema
- social origins of the sense of self -- the looking-glass self
- boundaries of the self -- bounded vs. diffuse self
- self-referent behavior -- self-reference effect, self-generation effect, ego-involvement effect
- self-perception theory and the role of introspection in self-perceptions
- self-knowledge vs. self-enhancement motivations -- social comparison theory
- self-presentation -- the dramaturgical model; performance and social norms; self-presentational strategies
- self-complexity and culture
- objective self-awareness -- inner/outer focus of attention

Taylor, Peplau, & Sears (text covers major classic and contemporary theory with some aspects of culture included)
- defining the self
- sources of self-knowledge -- socialization, reflected appraisal, social feedback, self-perception. environmental distinctiveness, social comparisons, social identity
- aspects of self-knowledge -- self-schemas, self-discrepancies
- self-regulation -- the working self-concept, self-complexity, self-efficacy and personal control, self-awareness
- motivations and the self -- accuracy, consistency, self-improvement, self-enhancement
- social comparison theory -- goals, the comparison process
- self-presentation -- making good impressions, ineffective self-presentation, self-handicapping, self-monitoring
- culture and the self -- independent and interdependent self

Sources:

Moghaddam, F. (1998). The self in culture. In Social psychology: Exploring universals across cultures. (pg. 57-94). New York: Freeman.

Taylor, S., Peplau, L., & Sears, D. (1999). The self: Learning about the self. In Social Psychology (10th ed.), (pg. 110-137). Upper Saddle River, NJ: Prentice-Hall.

2. **Phases of feminist re-vision in the psychology of personality:**
In the suggestions for Chapter 1 lecture topics, it was noted that Jane Torrey has written a Teaching of Psychology article focused on a gender inclusion analysis of personality psychology within the overall discipline. Torrey adopts the five "interactive" phase model set out by McIntosh (1983) in describing the role of women in personality psychology.

- Phase 1--Womanless psychology: Torrey demonstrates how psychology in general and personality psychology has historically excluded or ignored consideration of women. Theories are criticized as based on research conducted almost entirely on male research participants. Topics of empirical study also tended to reflect the theoretical issues more of interest to men: aggression, achievement, the values of reason.
- Phase 2--Adding women to psychology: The addition of the work of women in psychology is considered a sign that psychology has begun adding women. Differences between the perspectives of Horney and Freud are used as an example in personality psychology.
- Phase 3--Women as inherently different and deviant: Torrey critiques the work of Freud and Jung as they place the psychological development of women against a male standard. She discusses the development of critical research and theory designed to "expose" assumptions that men and women were inherently different (e.g., Bem).
- Phase 4--Taking the psychology of women seriously: The contemporary work that has sought to explore a perspective where "the study of women, their viewpoint, and their world are the main focus" (pg. 156). As an example of this perspective, Torrey points to Miller (1976) who emphasized "problems that are peculiar to women's lives and motivations" (pg. 156). The work of Carol Gilligan is another illustrative example of personality theory in representing this stage of disciplinary development.
- Phase 5--All the human experience, Psychology redefined: Torrey calls for phase 5 development to reassess issues relevant to all people--a truly integrated personality psychology.

Source: Torrey, J. (1987) Phases of feminist re-vision in the Psychology of Personality. Teaching of Psychology, 14(3), 155-160.

3. **Teaching personality psychology:**
   The following is not so much an additional lecture suggestion as it is a personal suggestion to read how one of our colleagues has reoriented her personality psychology toward a perspective of greater diversity. Phyllis Bronstein describes her efforts by dividing her description of the personality course into general theoretical issues presented in the curriculum and how she has modified the presentation of otherwise traditional discussion.

   - Psychoanalytic theory: Bronstein describes supplementing traditional discussion of Freud by discussing feminist critiques of his views on women, new psychoanalytic perspectives on women, the contributions of Karen Horney, and the influence of sociocultural factors on his seduction theory.
   - The nature-nurture controversy: In discussing biological vs. social influences on personality, Bronstein discusses body-type theory as it would most likely be applied to fashion models, full-bodied Polynesian women, a sumo wrestler, and a tall, slim Black man. She presents relatively recent articles assessing perceptions of women's' personalities associated with their bust sizes and allows the class to determine the relevance of such comparisons.
   - Biological explanation of gender differences: Review articles critiquing biologically based gender and racial differences are introduced in this section of the course, as are critiques of the sociobiological perspective.
   - Environmental factors in personality development: Ethnographic data drawn from nonliterate societies are used to illustrate the impact of food production and household maintenance demands on socialization practices.
   - Gender and personality: Gender role literature describing socialization and child-rearing practices are introduced. Gould's imaginative tale of gender-free childrearing is discussed, and readings on adult development are included.
   - Sociocultural factors in personality development: Mead's (1935) classic, Sex and Temperament in Three Primitive societies provides information for discussion of values, customs, and child-rearing practices within cultures.
   - The measurement of personality: The role played by women in the development of testing instruments is highlighted and the Authoritarian Personality study is used to discuss a multi-instrument approach.
   - Assignments, projects, and exercises: Pedagogy consists of small group discussions, group sharing with the class as a whole, short paper assignments, an empirical research project requiring that students create their own personality inventory, and a course-related journal.

Source:
   Bronstein, P. (1988). Personality from a sociocultural perspective. In P. Bronstein, & K. Quina (Eds.), Teaching a psychology of people: Resources for gender and sociocultural awareness. (pg. 60-68). Washington, DC: American Psychological Association.

Suggestions for Additional Readings

Aiken, L. (1989). Assessment of personality. Boston: Allyn & Bacon.

Bandura, A. (1977). Social learning theory. Englewood Cliffs, NJ: Prentice-Hall.

Carver, C., & Scheier, M. (1992). Perspectives on personality. Boston: Allyn & Bacon.

Eaves, L., Eysenck, H., & Martin, N. (1989). Genes, culture and personality: An empirical approach. San Diego: Academic Press.

Freud, S. (1920/1977). Introductory lectures on psychoanalysis. New York: Norton & Company.

Hall, C., Lindzey, G., Loehlin, J., & Manosevitz, M. (1985). Introduction to theories of personality. New York: Wiley.

Hogan, R. (1986). What every student should know about personality. In V. Makosky (Ed.), The G. Stanley Hall lecture series, Vol 6. Washington DC: American Psychological Association.

Kleinmuntz, B. (1985). Personality and psychological assessment. Malabar, FL: Krieger.

Maslow, A. (1987). Motivation and personality. New York: HarperCollins.

Mindess, H. (1988). Makers of psychology: The personal factor. New York: Human Sciences Press.

Mischel, W. (1986). Introduction to personality: A new look. New York: Holt, Rinehart & Winston.

Pervin, L. (1990). Handbook of personality: Theory and research. New York: Pergamon Press.

Rogers, C. & Stevens, B. (1971). Person to person: The problem of being human--A new trend in psychology. New York: Pocket Books.

In-Class Activities and Demonstrations

1. **TRAIL Blazing**: Using **Transparency Masters 12.1 - 12.5**, review with students the "Checking Your TRAIL" sections in the chapter. Have students work in small groups to answer the questions and then review with the class as a whole to tie the text reading to activity in class.

2. **Reaching Critical Mass**: Using **Transparency Masters 12.6 - 12.8**, review with students the "Critical Thinking" sections in the chapter. Have students work in small groups to answer the questions and then review with the class as a whole to tie the text reading to activity in class.

3. **Getting Down to IT**: Using **Transparency Masters 12.9 - 12.14**, review the "Integrative Thinking" sections in the chapter with students. Have students work in small groups to answer the questions and then review with the class as a whole to tie the text reading to activity in class.

4. **Who am I and how did I get to be this way?:** For this activity, students are to write a brief paper concerning some aspect of their personality from the standpoint one of the personality theories discussed in the text or in class. In doing this exercise, guide students to select only one part of their personality first and describe that aspect in some detail--they really need to focus on one aspect or else the task becomes too complicated (although many students may still try to describe themselves expansively). In the second part of the paper, they are to briefly describe the central tenets of one of the theories covered in class. The third part of the paper consists of specific application of theoretical concepts to their personality aspect. A final part of the paper, if you choose, could focus on how they might attempt to change that aspect of personality according to the theory they've selected (if you've discussed change techniques or perspectives during this section of the course, as well as personality development). I have done this activity with large section classes and generally have highly favorable comments about really having to think about themselves. Most students find writing about themselves somewhat enjoyable. One note: I do urge students to consider the nature of the aspect they want to reveal to me very seriously and not tell me about problematic (or illegal) things. For those students who simply don't want to write about themselves, I've let them write the paper on a fictional character (e.g., Bart Simpson).

5. **Comparing personality theories**: Using Handout Master 12.1, have students distinguish among the three main theoretical approaches in personality theory.

   Answers:
1. Humanist	5. Psychoanalyst	9. Behaviorist
2. Psychoanalyst	6. Humanist	10. Humanist
3. Humanist	7. Behaviorist	11. Behaviorist
4. Behaviorist	8. Psychoanalyst	12. Psychoanalyst

6. **Personality tests**: The following exercise was developed by Nancy Felip Russo, and concerns the use of personal agreement as an often invalid method for verifying personality assessment. It also speaks to the need for writing assessment questions so they are not general statements most people can agree with. So the demonstration will take less time, rather than conduct it on the whole class, select 10-12 students several days before you plan to demonstrate the findings. To conduct the exercise, create a full sheet of positive and negative adjectives drawn from any dictionary or thesaurus. The day before the demonstration, give a copy to each of your volunteers and ask them to check or circle all adjectives that apply, and return the sheet to you so you can do a "personality analysis" on them. On the day of demonstration, call all volunteers to the front of the class and hand each a sheet that supposedly contains their individualized personality analysis. (This is more convincing if you have their name typed on the feedback sheet.) Of course, all volunteers are going to receive the same feedback from their so-called personality analysis. It should read as follows:

   - You want other people to like and admire you.
   - You have a tendency to be critical of yourself.
   - You have a great deal of unused capacity that you have turned to your advantage.
   - While you have some personality weaknesses, you are generally able to compensate for them.
   - Your adjustment to the opposite sex has presented problems to you.
   - More disciplined and self-controlled outside, you tend to be worrisome and insecure inside.
   - At times you have serious doubts as to whether you have made the right decision or done the right thing.
   - You prefer a certain amount of change and variety and become dissatisfied when hemmed in by restrictions and limitations.
   - You pride yourself on being an independent thinker and do not accept other's statements without satisfactory proof.

- You have found it unwise to be too frank in revealing yourself to others.

After students have read their personality analysis, have them rate how accurately the analysis describes them, and then rate each item on its accuracy (0 = not at all and 5 = extremely accurate). Russo indicates that most students will rate the analysis as accurate, and you can demonstrate your amazing skills as a clinician, since the volunteers generally rate their analysis 3 or greater. Of course, then you reveal that all the descriptions were the same and can open discussion for problems in test development involving self-verification and vaguely worded statements.

Source:
> Russo, N. (1981). Personality tests. In L. Benjamin, & K. Lowman (Eds.), Activities handbook for the teaching of psychology. Washington, DC: American Psychological Association.

7. **Puzzling Personality**: Using Handout Master 12.2, have students complete the crossword puzzle using terms from Chapter 12.

Sources for Additional Activities

Benjamin, L. & Lowman, K. (1981). Activities handbook for the teaching of psychology. Washington DC: American Psychological Association.

Embree, M. (1986). Implicit personality theory in the classroom: An integrative approach. Teaching of psychology, 13, 78-80.

Fernald, P., & Fernald, L. (1987). The sentence completion test. In V. Makosky, L. Whittemore, & A. Rogers (Eds). Activities handbook for the teaching of psychology (Vol. 2) (pg. 172-176). Washington DC: American Psychological Association.

Halonen, J. (1995). Chapter 11: Personality. In The critical thinking companion for Introductory Psychology. New York: Worth Publishers.

Hess, A. (1976). The "parts party" as a method of teaching personality theory and dynamics. Teaching of psychology, 3, 32-33.

Howard, G., & Konstanty, P. (1990). An exercise for personality courses on methodological issues of assessment. In V. Makosky, C. Sileo, L. Whittemore, L. Landry, & M. Skutley (Eds). Activities handbook for the teaching of psychology (Vol. 3). (pg. 154-157). Washington DC: American Psychological Association.

Kerber, K. (1987). What is personality? A personal appraisal. In V. Makosky, L. Whittemore, & A. Rogers (Eds). Activities handbook for the teaching of psychology (Vol. 2) (pg. 182-184). Washington DC: American Psychological Association.

Logan, R. (1988). Using a film as a personality case study. Teaching of psychology, 15, 103-104.

Mueller, S. (1985). Persons in the personality theory course: Student papers based on biographies. Teaching of psychology, 12, 74-78.

Polyson, J. (1983). Student essays about TV characters: A tool for understanding personality theories. Teaching of psychology, 10, 103-105.

Polyson, J. (1985). Students' peak experiences: A written exercise. Teaching of psychology, 12, 211-213.

Schick, C., & Arnold, J. (1987). Increasing students' self-awareness of their theoretical orientation toward personality. In V. Makosky, L. Whittemore, & A. Rogers (Eds). Activities handbook for the teaching of psychology (Vol. 2) (pg. 185-190). Washington DC: American Psychological Association.

Singelis, T. (1998). Teaching about culture, ethnicity, & diversity: Exercises and planned activities. Thousand Oaks, CA: Sage.

Makosky, V., Sileo, C., Whittemore, L., Landry, C., & Skutley, M. (1990). Activities handbook for the teaching of psychology (Vol. 2). Washington DC: American Psychological Association.

Makosky, V., Sileo, C., Whittemore, L., & Skutley, M. (1995). Activities handbook for the teaching of psychology (Vol. 3). Washington DC: American Psychological Association.

Whitford, F. (1998). Personality. In Quick guide to the Internet for psychology (pg.82-84). Boston: Allyn and Bacon.

- **Journey II Software:**

    Enter the Personality lab by clicking on the icon in the Main Menu. In the Personality Assessment segment, students complete several personality measures including a Type A survey, Sensation Seeking, and Locus of Control questionnaire. In each case student's scores are interpretation and related to the theory in question. There may be a program problem that causes questionnaires to repeat themselves however.

World Wide Web: Check out the following WWW sites for information and activities relevant to this section of the text!

General
- Addison Wesley Longman's Website -- **http://longman.awl.com/**
- PsychZone link -- **http://longman.awl.com/**
- Psych Web -- **http://www.gasou.edu/psychweb/psychweb.htm**
- Self-Quizzes for Introductory Psychology -- **http://www.gasou.edu/psychweb/selfquiz/selfquiz.htm**
- Psychology Jumping Stand -- **http://www.indiana.edu:80/~iuepsyc/PsycJump.html**
- The Psychology Place -- **http://www.psychplace.com**
- Personality theories--**http://magma.Mines.EDU/students/k/ksiggins/**
  or
  http://galton.psych.nwu.edu/GreatIdeas.html
  or
  http://www.wynja.com/personality/theorists.html
  or
  http://pmc.psych.nwu.edu/revelle/publications/AR.html
- The Personality Project--**http://pmc.psych.nmu.edu:80/personality.html**
  or
  http://fas.psych.nwu.edu/personality.html
  or
  http://pmc.psych.nwu.edu/personality

Psychodynamic
- The American Psychoanalytic Foundation-- **http://www.cyberpsych.org/apf.htm**
- FreudNet--**http://plaza.interport.net/nypsan/**
- The Freud Web-- **http://stg.brown.edu/projects/hypertext/landow/HTatBrown/freud/Freud_OV.html**
- Sigmund Freud Museum Vienna--**http://freud.t0.or.at/freud/e/navigate.htm**
- Freud Museum of London-- **http://www.dalton.org/students/DBS/freud/index.html**
- Freud's psychosexual stages--**http://idealist.com/children/freud.html**
- Defense mechanisms--**http://www.cmhc.com/psyhelp/chap5/chap5j.htm**
- That's my theory: **Freud--http://www.pbs.org/wgbh/aso/mytheory/freud**
- Psychoanalysis--**http://www.haverford.edu/psych109/freud.pas.html**
  or
  http://www.cmhc.com/guide/pro11.htm
  or
  http://galton.psych.nwu.edu/GreatIdeas/psychoanalysis.html
- Jung Home Page--**http://www.cgjung.com/cgjung/**
- Jung Index--**http://www.jungindex.net/**
- Jung's writings--**http://enteract.com/~jwalz/Jung/**

- JungWeb--**http://www.onlinepsych.com/jungweb**
- Adlerian psychology--**http://ourworld.compuserve.com/homepage/hstein**
- Horney--**http://www.1w.net/karen/**

Humanistic
- Association of Humanist Psychology--
  http://ahpweb.org/aboutahp/whatis.html
  or
  http://pmc.psych.nwu.edu:80/personality.html
- Rogers--**http://www.1rider.edu/~si;errpgers/html**
  or
  http://psy1.clarion.edu/jms/Rogers.html
  or
  http:/www.wisc.edu/depd/html/un2tab1.htm
- Maslow--**http://utoledo.edu/homepages/ddavis/maslow.htm**
  or
  http://ww.maslow.com/index.html

Biological/genetic/traits
- Humoral theory--**http://www.parlez.com/word-of-the-day/humors.html**
- Sheldon's somatotypes--
  http://www.fitnesszone.com/features/archives/body-types.html
- Eysenck-- **http://www.psych101.com/bio/eysenck.html**
  or
  http:152.52.2.152/newsroom/ntn/health/0908897/health8_29468_noframes.html
- Minnesota Twin study--**http://cla.umn.edu/psych/psylabs/mtfs/rfindex.htm**
- Sensation seeking--
  http://165.112.78.61/NIDA_Notes/NNVol10N4/MeasureSens.html
- **The Big Five--http://fujita.iusb.edu/big5.html**
  or
  http://galton.psych.nwu.edu/GreatIdeas/bigfive.html
  or
  http:www.psych-test.com/bigfive.htm
- Keirsey Temperament Sorter--**http://sunsite.unc.edu/jembin/mb.pl**

Audio-Visual Support
Films/Videos:

Overview
- *Discovering Psychology: Personality* (Annenberg, 30 minutes)
- *Individual Differences* (CRM, 18 minutes)
- *Personality: Early Childhood* (CRM, 20 minutes)
- *Personality: Middle Childhood* (CRM, 19 minutes)
- *Personality* (CRM, 30 minutes)
- *Personality* (Insight Media, 30 minutes)

Psychodynamic theory
- *67,000 Dreams* (TLF, 30 minutes)
- Freud Under Analysis (IU, 58 minutes)
- *Discovering Psychology: The Mind Hidden and Divided* (Annenberg, 30 minutes)
- *Freud--The Hidden Nature of Man* (LCA, 29 minutes)
- *The Story of Carl Gustav Jung Series* (FFHS, 31 minutes each)
    - Program 1: In Search of the Soul
    - Program 2: 67,000 Dreams
    - Program 3: Mystery That Heals
- *Carl Gustav Jung: An Introduction* (FFHS, 60 minutes)
- *Mind and Matter* (FFHS, 60 minutes)
- *Your Mythic Journey: Sam Keen* (FFHS, 57 minutes)
- *The Will to Win* (FFHS, 28 minutes)
- *Freud's Interpretation of Dreams* (FFHS, 23 minutes)
- *Psychological Defenses* (FFHS, 45 minutes)
- *Jung--The World Within* (FFHS, 60 minutes)
- *The Wisdom of the Dream* (FFHS, 3 videos of 60 minutes each)
- *C. G. Jung: A Matter of Heart* (FFHS, 107 minutes)
- *Boundaries of the Soul: Exploration in Jungian Analysis* (90 minutes)
- *Erik Erikson: A Life's Work* (FFHS, 38 minutes)
- *Erik Erikson (2 part interview)* (FFHS, 2 videos of 50 minutes each)
- *Everybody Rides the Carousel (Erikson)* (FFHS, 72 minutes)
- *Erich Fromm* (FFHS, 2 videos of 50 minutes each)

Behavioral theory
- *The Skinner Revolution* (REPR, 23 minutes)
- *A World of Difference: B.F. Skinner and the Good Life, Parts 1 and 2* (TLF, 53 minutes)
- *B. F. Skinner* (FFHS, 2 parts of 50 minutes each)
- *A Demonstration of Behavioral Processes by B. F. Skinner* (FFHS, 28 minutes)

Humanistic theory
- *Being Abraham Maslow* (Filmaker's Library, 30 minutes)
- *Discovering Psychology: The Self* (Annenberg, 30 minutes)
- *Carl Rogers* (FFHS, 2 parts of 50 minutes each)
- *Viktor Frankl*: The Search for Meaning in Life Today (FFHS, 90 minutes)
- *Conversation with Viktor Frankl* (FFHS, 43 minutes)
- *Reflections on Empathy: Heinz Kohut* (FFHS, 45 minutes)
- *Rollo May Series* (FFHS, 29 minutes each)
    Program 1: Anxiety, Love, Will, and Dying
    Program 2: Maturity and Creativity
    Program 3: Reactions to Psychoanalytic Concepts

Trait theory
- *Gordon Allport* (FFHS, 2 parts of 50 minutes each)

Psychology Encyclopedia Laserdisc IV:

Still Images
Rorschach test   Frame 53561   Side   all

Transparency Master 12.1: Checking Your TRAIL 12.1

I. **True or False:** To psychologists, the concept of personality includes beliefs, values, and temperament, among other characteristics.

II. Which one of the following statements is FALSE?
   A. The assumption that people have stable personality characteristics is based on Western ways of behaving and thinking about behavior.
   B. Individualist cultures emphasize situational determinants of behaviors more than they emphasize personality characteristics.
   C. Astrology was an early personality theory.
   D. Somatoform theory claimed that we can know about an individual's personality by looking at his or her body type.

III. Most research in psychology has been conducted in
   A. Japan.
   B. the United States.
   C. Great Britain.
   D. Russia.

IV. Today psychologists think personality is determined, in general terms, by a combination of _____ and _____.
   A. body type; the alignment of planets when one was born
   B. stability; temperament
   C. environment; genes
   D. individualist orientation; collectivist orientation

Transparency Master 12.2: Checking Your TRAIL 12.2

I. **Name the Big Five personality traits.**

II. **Name the part of the personality--the id, ego, or superego--that is responsible for each of the following:**
   A. guilt
   B. eating just a little of a delicious dessert
   C. sexual desire

III. **Which one of the following psychodynamic theorists discussed personality as a reaction to perceived inferiority?**
   A. Jung
   B. Freud
   C. Adler
   D. Horney

IV. **From a Freudian perspective, the unconscious**
   A. contains disturbing or socially unacceptable thoughts, impulses, and memories that reflect psychological conflicts.
   B. plays a minor role in determining personality.
   C. is another word for sexual energy.
   D. is the smallest part of consciousness.

Transparency Master 12.3: Checking Your TRAIL 12.3

I. The _____ perspective on personality stresses the importance of the unconscious and past experiences to explain why people have the personalities they do.
   A. learning
   B. trait
   C. behaviorist
   D. psychodynamic

II. A psychology professor doesn't accept the idea that "personality" can be studied. With which approach does the professor probably identify?
   A. behavior genetic
   B. social learning
   C. behaviorist
   D. social cognition

III. Which approach to personality tends to identify personality "types"?
   A. social learning
   B. social cognition
   C. behavior genetic
   D. behaviorist

IV. The behavior genetic approach
   A. has been more theoretical than empirical.
   B. focuses on *why* particular gene-environment combinations tend to produce particular types of personality.
   C. examines how much of a group's variability in a trait is due to genes.
   D. does NOT examine environmental influences on genes.

Transparency Master 12.4: Checking Your TRAIL 12.4

I. A father who expresses love for his children only when they achieve high grades is giving the children _____ positive regard.

II. Which one of the following statements is true?
   A. There is usually more variation in personality characteristics within gender than between genders.
   B. Females are more likely to be aggressive than are males.
   C. Females are more likely to behave in an autonomous way than are males.
   D. Males are more likely than females to acknowledge feelings of anxiety and guilt over any harm caused by their aggressive behavior.

III. True or False: People in lower-power groups are reinforced for developing certain personality characteristics, such as a tendency to be deferential, nonconfrontational, and aware of the desires, expectations, and behavior patterns of those in higher-power groups.

IV. Sarah is a jealous, possessive person. She demands that her boyfriend spend almost all his time with her, wants him to ignore everyone else except her, and insists that meeting her desires should take precedence over anything else he wants to do. Analyze Sarah's personality in terms of the behavior genetic, behaviorist, social learning, Freudian, Horneyian, Adlerian, and humanistic perspectives.

Transparency Master 12.5: Checking Your TRAIL 12.5

Match:
1. TAT   **A. the most widely used personality test**

2. Rorschach   **B. a projective test in which the test-taker looks at a picture and tells a story**

3. MMPI   **C. the inkblot test**

4. Suppose you have a vague feeling that you once had a traumatic experience, but don't remember the experience itself. You want to find out what happened to you, because you think it is affecting your behavior. Which type of test--a projective or self-report--is more likely to reveal that traumatic experience? Why?

Transparency Master 12.6: Critical Thinking 12.1

Consider Adler's concept of the inferiority complex and the text authors' discussion of male compensation via automobile modifications, boasting, hostility toward women, and marital infidelity. In what ways do some females compensate for their perceived inferiority?

Transparency Master 12.7: Critical Thinking 12.2

Freud interpreted gender differences in terms of females lacking qualities males have. Suppose you turned around Freud's interpretation of gender differences and instead considered males to be inadequate females. In what ways would males seem abnormal? (We aren't saying either perspective is valid, but we are asking, "What can you learn from purposefully taking alternative perspectives?")

Transparency Master 12.8: Critical Thinking 12.3

What behaviors promote interpersonal harmony? In terms of the power available to most women, explain why women might value behaviors that promote harmony more than men do.

Transparency Master 12.9: Integrative Thinking 12.1

Which of the Eysencks' temperaments, shown in Figure 12.2, is most similar to the temperament of "easy" babies, described in the Child Development chapter? Which is most similar to the temperament of "difficult" babies?

Transparency Master 12.10: Integrative Thinking 12.2

The Introductory chapter described different types of studies. What type of study provided the basis for Freud's theory, which was developed after analyzing individual patients?

Transparency Master 12.11: Integrative Thinking 12.3

In light of what you read in the Cognition & Intelligence chapter about similar concepts across cultures, identify a concept--other than one described in this chapter--that might be in the collective unconscious.

Transparency Master 12.12: Integrative Thinking 12.4

Based on the Adolescent & Adult Development chapter's discussion of ethnic and racial identity and in terms of the four belief systems types, explain why you think that some members of minorities, but not other members of the same minorities, think racism is at the root of almost every social problem? Why do some European Americans, but not other European Americans, refuse to see racism at the root of any problem?

Transparency Master 12.13: Integrative Thinking 12.5

Evidence supports the idea that biology contributes to some personality characteristics, such as aggressiveness. Based on what you learned in the Biopsychology chapter, if you were looking for biological reasons for a sex difference in aggression, which part of the brain and which neurotransmitters would you examine?

Transparency Master 12.14: Integrative Thinking 12.6

Based on what you learned in the Introductory chapter about different occupations in psychology, how might the following kinds of psychologists use personality tests:
    (1) an industrial/organizational psychologist
    (2) a clinical psychologist
    (3) a research-oriented psychologist?

Handout Master 12.1: Comparing Psychologists

Three Faces of Psychology

Instructions: Imagine that three psychologists are having lunch together, and that you are eavesdropping on their conversation. There is a psychoanalyst (P), a behaviorist (B), and a humanist (H). Which of the psychologists is most likely to have made each of the following statements?

_____ 1. I think people in our profession should put more effort into trying to understand mentally healthy people and prosocial behavior.

_____ 2. Aggression is a human instinct. Society can control it to some extent, but we will never eliminate aggressive behavior.

_____ 3. Your student may be under a lot of pressure from his parents, but that is no excuse for cheating. We are responsible for what we do.

_____ 4. If you want to understand why she did it, look to the environment for clues instead of at inferred internal forces like impulses and motives.

_____ 5. We humans are products of evolutionary forces that have preserved selfishness, pleasure-seeking, and a tendency to deceive ourselves.

_____ 6. It doesn't seem to me that you need to dig into a person's past in order to understand the person's current problems and concerns.

_____ 7. There aren't any values inherent in human nature. Values are acquired in the same way we learn to say "please" and "thank you".

_____ 8. If we wanted to improve the character of people in our society, we would need to start when they are very young. By the time a kid is five years old, it's probably too late.

_____ 9. You may think your choice of chili and ice cream for lunch was freely made, but your perception of free choice is an illusion. Choosing chili and ice cream is predictable from the consequences of past behavior.

_____ 10. General laws of behavior and experience that apply to all people are not very helpful if you want to understand a particular individual.

_____ 11. You say people are inherently good, and he say they are inherently pretty bad. I don't think people are inherently either good or bad.

_____ 12. The sex drive is with us at birth. People just don't want to believe that infants get sexual pleasure from sucking and exploring anything they get in their hands with their mouths.

Handout Master # 12.2: Personality Puzzle

Chapter 12

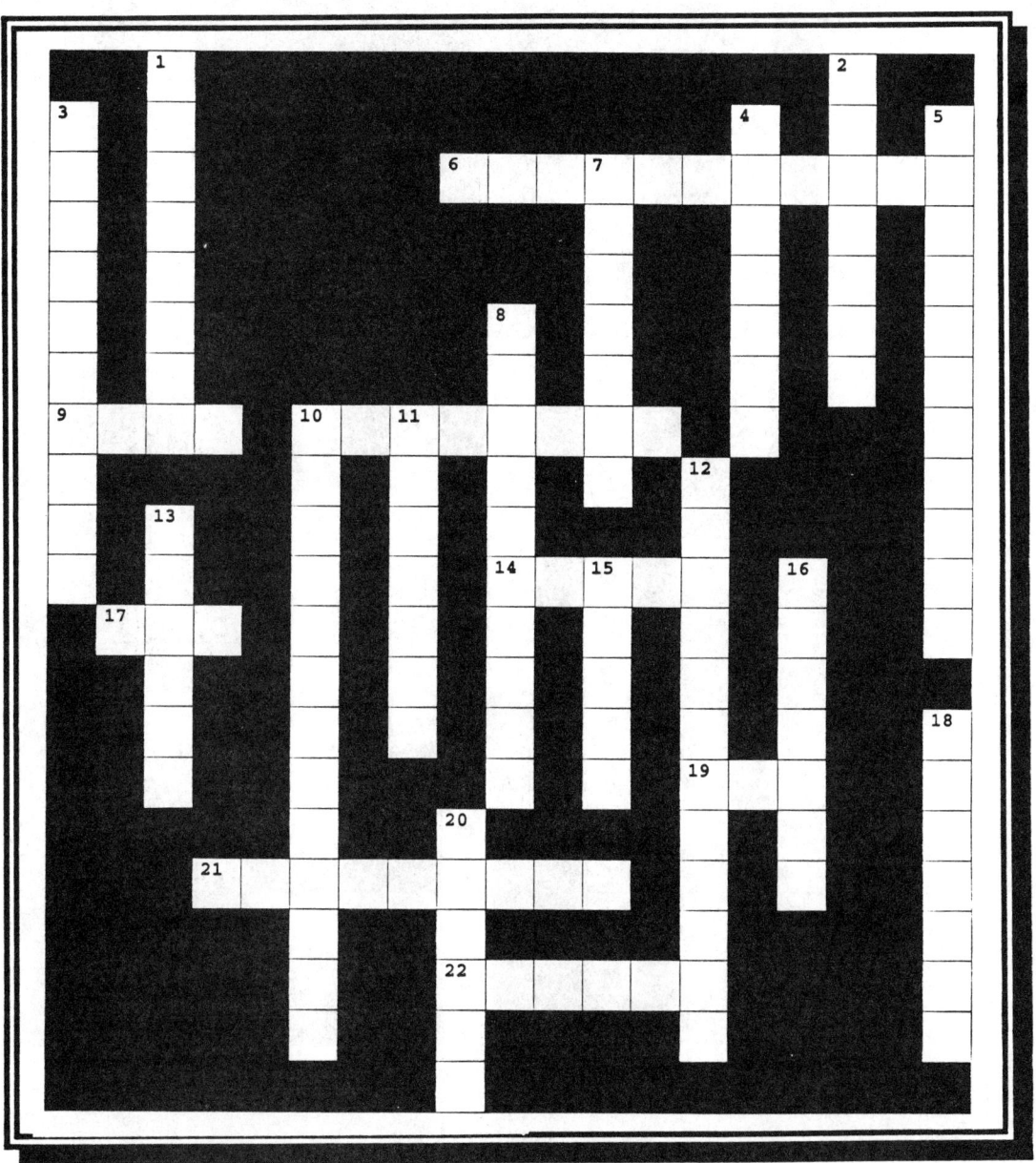

Across
6. watch
9. -efficacy
10. self-
14. surface
17. quite a picture
19. balancer
21. related to genes
22. sexual energy

Down
1. dominant trait
2. BF
3. people are good
4. wrote on reciprocal determinism
5. a complex thing
7. trait theorists
8. animus/anima
10. only own culture is valid
11. stuck
12. outgoing
13. stable characteristics
15. birth order author
16. you to others
18. inferiority
20. hierarchy

Solution for CrossWorld

CHAPTER 13

STRESS, COPING, & HEALTH

- **Chapter Overview**
    Learning Objectives
    Chapter Outline

- **Additional Lecture Ideas**
    Lecture Topics
    Additional Readings

- **In-Class Activities and Demonstrations**
    Activities and Demonstrations
    Sources for Additional Activities
    Journey II Software

- **World Wide Web**

- **Audio-Visual Support**

- **Handout and Transparency Masters**

Chapter Overview

Learning Objectives

After studying this chapter, you should be able to do the following:

1. Identify different types of stressors.

2. Describe reasons people face different stressors.

3. Describe the biological effects of stress.

4. Identify personality characteristics and behaviors associated with various levels of stress.

5. Compare approach and avoidance coping strategies.

6. Identify reasons for ethnic and gender differences in coping strategies.

7. Name and describe several types of defense mechanisms.

Chapter Outline
Stress, Coping, and Health

I. Introduction
    A. Introductory example
        1. "playing the dozens" or "signifying": African American coping strategy to hide emotional vulnerability, defense, think quickly under pressure derived from games developed during slavery period in United States; consists of attacks on mother
    B. Definitions
        1. stress: a person's response to stressors that stretch or exceed his or her ability to deal with them
        2. stressors: events, behaviors, or situations that threaten or put a strain on an individual
        3. eustress: a form of stress that can feel good; occurs when situations challenge rather than threaten
    C. Psychology and the study of stress
        1. psychologists study stress because it affects behavior, health, sense of psychological well-being
        2. What psychologists study:
            a. types of stressors
            b. body reaction to stress
            c. factors influencing perceptions of stressors
            d. strategies used to deal with stressors

II. Types of Stressors: From Everyone's Everyday Hassles to Unusual Disasters
    A. Types of stressors:
        1. hassles: seemingly minor, day-to-day difficulties
        2. pressure: the feeling that one's behavior must change or improve in quality to meet standards
        3. frustration: a feeling that arises from the inability to reach goals due to delays, failure, discrimination, or a lack of resources
        4. conflict: competition among desires, goals, demands, opportunities, needs, or behaviors
            a. approach-approach conflict: a situation in which a person is forced to choose between two desirable options
            b. approach-avoidance conflict: a situation in which a person is both attracted and repelled by one stimulus or circumstance
            c. avoidance-avoidance conflict: a situation in which a person must choose between two unattractive options
        5. disasters: psychological effects of major catastrophes
        6. other definitional issues in study of stress:
            a. temporary (short-term) vs. chronic (long-term, on-going) stressors:
            b. single, major stressor vs. multiple stressors

III. Alternative Perspectives on Stressors: Different Stressors for Different People

A. Multiple life changes
1. number of life changes associated with stress, depression/anxiety, illnesses & accidents
2. <u>measuring life changes</u>:
   a. <u>Social Readjustment Rating Scale (SRRS):</u> Holmes & Rahe's scale that assigns points to various life events that people assume to be stressful
      i. <u>problems with scale</u>:
         - assumes most people find same event stressful
         - doesn't consider differences in perception of events and coping skills
         - doesn't' include stress levels of significant others
         - stressors listed not representative of those experienced within different gender, socioeconomic, ethnic, and racial groups

B. Gender perspectives
1. gender differences in stress associated with differences in social status and roles; socioeconomic stressors as a result of sexism
2. <u>common stressors for men on the job</u>: stress due to physical danger, overwork; concerns about experienced sexual harassment due to inappropriate cultural expectations
3. <u>common stressors for women on the job</u>: stressors associated with lack of power, adequate income, fringe benefits, job security, opportunity for advancement, sexual harassment, discrimination

C. Socioeconomic perspectives
1. different stressors associated with socioeconomic status
   a. <u>example</u>: uneducated, poor experience more/different stressors than middle-class
      i. <u>chronic stressors</u>: low-paying jobs, low job security, living environment (crime, over-crowding); affect coping with short-term stressors
      ii. <u>effects on health</u>: depression, increased risk for health problems, high blood pressure, hostility
      iii. <u>effects on parenting</u>: more likely to punish children, offer less approval; children experience low self-esteem and own stress

D. Racial perspectives
1. <u>examples of racial differences in stress experiences</u>:
   a. pressure to become like middle-class European Americans
   b. racial discrimination, ethnic stereotyping, and cultural racism
   c. different racial groups experience different forms/levels of racism

IV. Biological Reactions to Stress: Similar Reactions Among Different People
A. The GAS response
1. <u>general adaptation syndrome (GAS)</u>: a general biological reaction to stress occurring in three stages
2. <u>stages</u>:
   a. <u>alarm</u>: autonomic nervous system is activated; heart rate/blood pressure increases, muscles contract, pupils enlarge, sugar released into bloodstream
   b. <u>resistance</u>: BP remains high, adrenal glands release hormones into bloodstream which suppress lymphocytes/immune system and increase buildup of fats/cholesterol on blood-vessel walls; sympathetic branch of ANS aroused above resting levels
   c. <u>exhaustion</u>: body can no longer maintain resistance, prolonged muscle tension produces fatigue/pain, liver runs out of sugar; vulnerability to disease increases

B. Hypertension, heart disease, and stroke
1. <u>hypertension</u>: chronic high blood pressure which leads to buildup of fat or cholesterol on blood vessel walls and clogging of blood vessels; heart must work harder to push blood along blood vessels resulting in eventual weakening of heart
2. <u>stroke</u>: blood vessels burst under pressure, loss of oxygen-carrying blood to brain; may result in death, permanent coma, severe disability (e.g., loss of speech/movement)

C. The immune system
1. <u>psychoneuroimmunologists</u>: individuals who study the relationships between health, psychological variables, and immune system
2. <u>functioning of the immune system</u>: defends body by detecting and destroying/neutralizing foreign substances (e.g., bacteria, viruses)
   a. <u>B- and T-lymphocytes</u>: white blood cells produced in bone marrow and the thymus gland
   b. under stress, adrenal gland produces hormones that suppress lymphocytes which increases vulnerability for disease
3. stress is moderately correlated with development of illnesses such as tuberculosis, cancer, arthritis, herpes, colds, digestive disorders
4. individual differences in reactions to stress, hormone production in response to stress, sensitivity of receptor sites to hormones
5. illness prevention requires understanding who is most vulnerable to disease including effects of stress, bodily characteristics of different people, roles of cognition and personality

V. Individual Characteristics Affecting Stress: Different Responses Among Different People

A. Interpretations of stressors

1. process: how stressor is interpreted affects amount of stress triggered, stressor's indirect effect on health; interpretation influenced by values, experiences, goals, ability to cope, beliefs about capabilities and response options, personality
   a. primary appraisal: assessing whether stressor is potentially harmful and how harmful, extent of demands stressor will make on oneself; combined with secondary appraisal, affects stress that results
   b. secondary appraisal: assessing one's ability to deal with stressor (i.e., capabilities and response options); combined with primary appraisal, affects stress that results
4. alternative perspectives on stressors:
   a. individual differences in response to same stressor: threatening vs. manageable difficulty vs. challenge and opportunity for growth
   b. lacking alternative views may create interpretation of stressor as catastrophic
5. can I affect the stressor?:
   a. feelings of control and stress: feeling we have control in a situation linked to less stress; more knowledge about situation and greater awareness of possible responses to it influences feelings of control
      i. correlational & experimental studies support linkage of perceptions of control with reduced stress

B. Personality

1. personality affects degree to which we are exposed to stressors, way we interpret them, stressfulness of experiences, how we deal with stressors
   a. examples: outgoing people, risk-takers expose themselves to more potential stressors; coping style affects stressor's consequences
   b. "Big Five" personality traits of agreeableness, openness, extroversion good predictors of coping with stress (i.e., less stress)
2. optimism: optimists tend to interpret situations hopefully; in primary appraisal, not as likely to view stressor as threatening as pessimists are; in secondary appraisal, more likely to emphasize ability to deal with stressors
   a. results of correlational studies suggest optimistic people more likely to be healthy, live longer than pessimists; results supported by longitudinal studies
3. a sense of humor: people who are humorous, value sense of humor typically use humor to deal with stress
   a. humor is an effective coping style & alleviates stress
   b. humor linked to interpretation of stressor (i.e., less as threat, more as challenge)

4. <u>Type A's anger</u>:
    a. <u>Type A personality</u>: a personality syndrome characterized by a high desire to achieve, restless body movements, and excessive competitiveness, aggression, impatience, anger; linked to health problems (i.e., cardiovascular disease, headaches, stomachaches, hypertension)
    b. <u>chronic anger/hostility</u>: component of Type A most strongly linked to health problems perhaps due to increased arousal of autonomic nervous system, which disrupts metabolism of fats, speeds development of cholesterol/cellular material in walls of arteries, increases blood pressure; sympathetic nervous system may be overly responsive, parasympathetic nervous system under-responsive in stressful situations
    c. <u>effects of unexpressed anger</u>: experimental study found that unexpressed anger more linked to mortality than was no anger or expressed anger
5. <u>a hardy personality</u>: a personality type characterized by a strong sense of commitment to work, values and goals, enjoyment of change as a challenge, and a sense of control over life
    a. support for relationship between hardy personality and less stress found in cross-sectional and longitudinal studies (regardless of levels of stress-buffering resources such as exercise)

VI. Coping Methods: Similar Ways People Deal with Stress
A. Relaxation and exercise
1. both relaxation and exercise calm sympathetic branch of ANS
2. <u>relaxation</u>: relaxation exercises such as deep breathing increase oxygen available to body (calming effect)
3. <u>exercise</u>: increases release of endorphins; aerobic exercise reduces stress and improves immune functioning; decreases chances of high blood pressure
4. <u>play</u>: combines relaxation, exercise, and companionship with friends

B. Social support
1. <u>social support</u>: the help people receive from others in dealing with a stressor
2. <u>types of social support</u>:
    a. <u>emotional</u>: when someone listens to problems and expresses concern, affection, sympathy, and understanding
    b. <u>material</u>: providing instrumental goods or tangible (e.g., money, transportation, food)
    c. <u>cognitive</u>: advice, information, alternative ways to interpret a problem
3. <u>effects of socializing</u>: simple social contact can lessen stress
4. <u>effects of level of support</u>:

            a. amount of support offered determines helpfulness of support (sometimes too much, sometimes too little)
        5. <u>source of help</u>: who gives support may be important
    C. Coping strategies
        1. <u>coping strategies</u>: plans on ways to deal with stressors; tailored to particular situations
        2. <u>approach and avoidance strategies</u>:
            a. <u>approach</u>: confronting a problem directly by gathering information, analyzing it, then taking active steps to deal with the problem
            b. <u>avoidance</u>: trying to minimize or escape from stressful situations, often by redefining a stressor as not stressful, distracting oneself, or ignoring the stressor; may result in denial of stressor or prevent formation of solutions
        3. <u>problem-focused and emotion-focused strategies</u>:
            a. <u>problem-focused coping</u>: dealing with stress by changing the stressor
            b. <u>emotion-focused coping</u>: dealing with stress by managing one's emotional reactions to the stressor; often used when people can't change the stressor
    D. Racial perspectives
        1. <u>key idea</u>: people from different racial groups may have different stressors, interpret them differently, and cope with them differently; again probably more variably within groups than between groups
        2. <u>example</u>: African-American woman who had been raped
    E. Ethnic and socioeconomic perspectives
        1. culturally based stressors may vary (e.g., emphasis on thinness)
        2. differences in access to support systems and types of support may be present
        3. coping strategies may be different
    F. Gender perspectives
        1. socialization differences may account for differences in coping strategies (women more likely to have social support & use avoidance strategies); linkage of coping strategy to power differential
    G. Defense mechanisms
        1. <u>defense mechanisms</u>: based in psychodynamic theory, a group of avoidance/palliative oriented protective coping methods designed to distort or hide from consciousness any thoughts that threaten self-esteem and cause anxiety
            a. usually unaware of using defense mechanisms, but can become conscious of them and learn what motivates our behaviors
            b. use of defense mechanisms protects us from stress but might not take advantage of opportunity to directly deal with stressors, prevents us from learning about ourselves

2. <u>types of defense mechanisms</u>:
    a. <u>regression</u>: reverting to childish or immature behavior; e.g., temper tantrums; cultural biases confuse interpretation of regression (e.g., man vs. woman of same age crying)
    b. <u>denial</u>: a defense mechanism in which people refuse to acknowledge that they have unacceptable feelings or personality characteristics or that threatening events occurred; e.g., denial of racism
    c. <u>displacement</u>: a defense mechanism in which people direct feelings toward a safe substitute target because directing the feelings toward the real target would be too upsetting; e.g., getting hostile with others around you when really mad at boss; acts as pressure valve to release built-up anger
    d. <u>identification</u>: a defense mechanism in which people adopt the behavior or role of another person; i.e., identifying with powerful others when feeling vulnerable such as identifying with a discriminating group when one has been the target of that group's discrimination (women wearing suits)
    e. <u>projection</u>: attributing one's own unacceptable feelings or faults to other people; e.g., low self-esteem person thinking others disrespect him/her
    f. <u>rationalization</u>: coming up with reasons for their behaviors and feelings that are not completely accurate, but plausible enough to protect their self-concepts and reduce anxiety; e.g., students saying too busy or prof gives too much homework rather than addressing own failure to be organized/responsible when homework not done
    g. <u>reaction formation</u>: making exaggerated claims about having certain feelings that are actually the opposite of one's true feelings; e.g., person who feels stupid acting like a know-it-all
    h. <u>sublimation</u>: a defense mechanism by which people reorient unacceptable impulses into socially valued and constructive activities; e.g., aggressive impulses transformed into piano playing
    i. others addressed in Table 13.4:
        i. <u>compensation</u>: attempting to make up for behaviors, feelings, or wishes that are regarded as bad or that lower self-esteem by behaving in ways that raise self-esteem so as to balance thoughts of self as good person
        ii. <u>intellectualization</u>: minimizing anxiety by emotionally detaching from the stressor and thinking of anxiety-provoking situations in abstract, intellectual terms
        iii. <u>repression</u>: unconsciously pushing upsetting or threatening thoughts and feelings into the unconscious
        iv. <u>suppression</u>: consciously and deliberately pushing thoughts or memories out of consciousness

Additional Lecture Topics

1. **Acculturative stress**

    "Acculturation", a concept first identified by anthropologists, has been defined as the changes that occur *both* to an immigrating groups and to the culture into which they enter. Although presumably both groups change, more frequently the dominant group experiences less change than does the nondominant group. Additionally, acculturation occurs at the individual level. John Berry, in his substantial writings on acculturation, has found that "there are vast differences in how people attempt to deal with acculturative change" (pg. 211) and reviews various factors involved in the production of acculturation stress.

    First, Berry notes that stress due to acculturation is not inevitable. In part, that experience is moderated by various orientations individuals have concerning acculturation (i.e., what are their beliefs regarding acculturation). Berry suggests four orientations toward acculturation exist and are derived from the consideration of two value-based questions: "Is it important to maintain one's cultural identity and characteristics?" and "It is important to maintain relationships with the other (dominant) group?"

    - When the answer to both questions is "yes", an individual adopts an *integration* orientation--the individual and his/her cultural group work to become an integral part of a larger, coordinated social group.
    - If one's cultural is of less importance but maintaining relationship with the dominant culture is important, *assimilation* or absorption into the dominant group occurs.
    - A *separation* orientation is adopted when one's cultural identity remains important but the dominant culture is not valued.
    - *Marginalization* occurs when neither one's cultural identity remains important nor is relating to the dominant group of importance.

    This framework has been used for understanding acculturation goals within acculturating groups and individuals as well as within the dominant groups and among members of that group. Berry (1994) describes the role of these acculturation orientations in addition to stage of acculturation, the nature of the larger society, and the characteristics of the acculturating groups and individuals as moderating variables in individual differences in experiences of acculturative stress--the stress that may arise as a result of moving into a different culture.

    The basic elements of Berry's model include some situations of acculturation in which an individual may participate to varying degrees. From the acculturation situation, any number of stressors may arise. Moderating factors influence how the individual experiences the situation and responds to stressors. It is the combination of these factors that results in the subjective experience call acculturative stress. Berry offers the following more specific proposals of how these factors produce stress:

    - Acculturation orientation may influence stress such that marginalized individuals experience the most stress, followed closely by those who maintain separation goals. Individuals with assimilation goals experience

moderate stress, whereas integration goals are thought to produce the least stress.
- The acculturative society influences individuals' felt stress by the pressures it exerts regarding acculturation. For example, societies that hold beliefs in pluralism are more likely to create supportive networks for acculturating individuals and demonstrate more tolerance of diversity. Monistic societies may attempt to enforce assimilation more stringently, and the acculturating individual may face overt and covert messages that his or her cultural identity is unacceptable. If admission into the dominant culture is allowed only under the dominant culture's rule, the potential for social conflict also emerges. If national and local policies are designed to exclude the acculturating individual or groups from full civic participation, and one's cultural group is relegated to low status, this denial may result in the marginalization that also contributes to acculturative stress levels.
- Certain psychological factors may moderate one's experience with acculturative stress. "Prior knowledge of the new language and culture, prior intercultural encounters of any kind, motives for the contact (voluntary vs. involuntary contact), and attitudes toward contact" all serve to lessen acculturative stress. The nature of initial contact experiences (i.e., whether they are positive or negative) influences perceptions and expectations towards subsequent contact and may also influence the stress experience.

Again, Berry notes that negative experiences due to acculturation are not inevitable but rather are a function of multiple factors working in combination. The negative consequences when they do occur, however, include "reduced health, lowered levels of motivation, a sense of alienation, and increased social deviance" at the individual level (pg. 214). The larger society is also affected by "increased health costs, lower educational and occupational attainment, increased social conflict, substance abuse, criminal activity, and a general societal malaise" (pg. 214). He argues that acculturative stress can be largely avoided or reduced "if both participation in the larger society and maintenance of one's heritage culture are welcomed by policy and practice of the larger society" (pg. 215).

Source:
Berry, J. (1994). Acculturative stress. In W. Lonner & R. Malpass (Eds.), Psychology and culture (pg. 211-215). Boston: Allyn and Bacon.

2. **Risk and culture**

Health psychologists have become increasingly interested in how individuals' perceptions of risk and risk-taking behaviors are related to adaptive and maladaptive health behaviors. Basically, the idea is that *beliefs* that a behavior is not risky, even when it may in fact be hazardous to our health, may support maladaptive health behaviors such as smoking, speeding, etc. In their research, George Cvetkovich and Timothy Earle consider how beliefs concerning risks are influenced by cultural differences in belief and value systems. A summary of their main findings follows.

At the onset it is important to note that risk estimates, the chances of something negative happening, derive from a combination of the physical properties of a thing that make it risky and the human judgments about that physical property. One might hear a sound but the perception of noise is based on judgment. One engages in the process of risk perception when one makes judgements and arrives at conclusions about some potentially hazardous venture on the basis of its likelihood of occurrence, possible severity, consequences, etc. Previous research has demonstrated that events that are judged to be "most risky" tend to be those that are considered "dreadful" (i.e., difficult to control and with catastrophic potential) and "unknown" (i.e., those events which are not fully understood, have unobservable effects, are new, and have delayed effects). Cross-cultural studies have found general agreement regarding the universal agreement on dreadful, unknown events being considered as resulting in the greatest risk--in other words, there seems to be a high level of cultural similarity in perceptions of risk.

In the process of understanding their risks of the occurrence of a negative event, people generally do not rely solely on objective estimators of risk (i.e., the statistical odds of something happening). Cvetkovich and Earle point out that, more frequently, people interpret a hazardous event as information regarding its likely (re)occurrence in the future. Thus, the incident at Three Mile Island, even though relatively unlikely to happen again according to statistical odds, was viewed by many as indicative of a risky situation--its "signal value" was high. These authors also point out that cultural beliefs concerning risk serve as sharing systems of understanding passed on from one person to another within a culture, and these cultural beliefs "tune in" the people of a culture "to be sensitive to particular risk signals." Cultural differences in perceptions concerning risk may underlie differences in seemingly "risky" behaviors. For example, noticeable differences in speed limits for driving exist between the United States and Germany; the French generate more of their electricity via nuclear generators than does the United States. One question for cross-cultural psychologists to address then would be how culture might account for these differences in risk perception or "risky: behavior.

Cvetkovich and Earle suggest that two functions of culture are important for consideration in this discussion: culture constructs reality (i.e., gives meaning to the world) and it "provides the means for coordinating our interactions with other individuals" (pg. 220). For an example of the first function, when a typhoon that struck the Pacific island of Yap, islanders believed it was due to ineffective performance of duties concerning supervision of food supplies by the village leader. Their understanding of the causes of physical events would then guide their conclusions concerning avoidance of the potential negative consequences of that event in the future--they worried over food supplies.

Cultural values also influence perceptions of risk. The authors note that, in cultures that place a high value on avoiding uncertainty, one might find more emphasis on the development of rules and regulations and fewer risky behaviors. Three other cultural value systems appear important to health risks as well. *Individualism* beliefs emphasize self-determinism and self-expression and are often reflected in self-regulation. Thus, health and safety issues focus on an individual's freedoms. The belief of *hierarchism* recognizes and values distinctions among people based on roles held in society. This belief system encourages following rules and regulations and discourages breaking those rules (these authors link their example to following regulations above concern for the environment....one could just as easily consider the role of hierarchism in the medical arena). Finally, *egalitarianism* reflects a cultural belief centered on equality among people. Distinctions among people, rules and roles are of little importance in determining interactions. The overuse of the earth's resources by a smaller segment of people at the exclusion of those who remain would run counter to this belief system. In summary, these authors contend that cultural beliefs shape the behavioral practices that influence health and safety.

As noted at the onset of this topic, perceptions of risk influence health relevant behavior. Cvetkovich and Earle have presented an interesting analysis of the interface between culture and health. This addition would work best with a broader discussion of other beliefs that influence health (or stress as emphasized in this chapter): locus of control, optimism...to name a few, and is connected to the idea that cognitive appraisals heavily influence health-related events.

Source:
Cvetkovich, G. & Earle, T. (1994). Risk and culture. In W. Lonner & R. Malpass (Eds.), Psychology and culture (pg. 217-224). Boston: Allyn and Bacon.

3. **Preparing to live and work elsewhere**
Some individuals, in anticipation of working and living in a culture other than their own, enter cross-cultural training programs designed to "give people information and introduce them to skills that will allow them to adjust to other cultures, to meet their goals, and to do work with the least amount of stress possible" (pg. 239). One commonly used technique used in such programs is

to introduce people to the new culture using short stories that will expose them to common experiences they may have in their new home. Brislin notes that "when cultural differences are discussed, they refer to visible distinctions in the guidance that a culture gives to behavior" (pg. 240). Although cultural expectations and messages form a guideline for conduct, it is important to remember that not all people behave according to those guidelines. Brislin offers that cross-cultural training programs should offer information concerning not only cross-cultural differences in guidelines for behavior but also information regarding exceptions for behavior. In illustrating the use of this principle, Brislin provides a brief short story of a Japanese graduate studying in the United States, who is concerned about not being called upon in classes and his lack of social invitations. In the scenario, a peer offers the student some understanding of differences in conduct in classroom and social settings as she understands them, based on the concepts of collectivism and individualism (e.g., volunteering responses in class and socializing at many different establishments as an individualistic pattern of behavior). The story continues with the Japanese student misinterpreting an enthusiastic "Thank you" for a small gift as the beginnings of romantic interest and his subsequent feelings of rejection when his friend turns down a dinner invitation. Brislin's analysis of this scenario centers on pointing out the importance of discussing the differences between collectivistic and individualistic beliefs and their influences on behaviors with the soon-to-be emigrant.

Guidelines for cross-cultural training programs recommend "that people's cognition, attitudes and emotions, and actual behaviors be addressed in training" (pg. 243)--helpful suggestions for preparing and helping the individual cope with a new environment.

- <u>Training aimed at cognition</u>: this aspect of the program emphasizes the delivery of information designed to familiarize the emigrant. Information on schooling, housing, transportation, availability of familiar foods, how they can pursue hobbies, engage in stress-reducing activities, and maintaining valued aspects of their job skills may be included.
- <u>Training aimed at attitudes and emotions</u>: the primary goal of this training component is to prepare the individual for the emotional challenges that come from "extensive intercultural interactions". Through role-playing activities, participants are exposed to various intercultural incidents and are given opportunity to discuss their feelings. Other related topics that may be addressed include: the development of friendships, reacting to misunderstandings and miscommunications, facing difficulties in achieving goals, assisting others in one's family during their adjustment to moving.
- <u>Training aimed at behaviors</u>: Behavioral modification may be required to successfully pursue personal goals in another culture. Some intensive programs literally establish a simulated culture setting to encourage participants to learn how to adapt their behaviors before

arriving in their new destination. For example, one program for individuals who were going to live in a remote island area in the Pacific lived in a simulated village setting in Hawaii. Here they learned to gather their own food, learned to do their job without the technological advantages they had been used to, and learned new living arrangements centered on less privacy (since the islands they were moving to were too small to allow for much privacy).

By the development of such cross-cultural training programs, Brislin suggests that psychologists may play a pivotal role in facilitating the process of adjustment and coping that is likely to be needed as more intercultural movement and contact occurs in the face of increased travel capabilities and a global marketplace. This article fits in nicely with discussion concerning coping with potentially stressful experiences.

Source:
Brislin, R. (1994). Preparing to live and work elsewhere. In W. Lonner & R. Malpass (Eds.), <u>Psychology and culture</u> (pg. 239-244). Boston: Allyn and Bacon.

4. **<u>Women and stress:</u>**
Pamela Mitchell observes that women tend to make more visits to health care professionals than do men. She asks: Is this a sign that women are under more stress than men? Does it indicate that women react to the stress of living by becoming ill more often than men? Or does it indicate that women are more willing to take on the sick role, to identify themselves as not well more frequently than men? (pg. 149). Noting gender differences in stress-related disorders (e.g., heart attacks and ulcers more common among men; neurosis and depression in women), Mitchell wonders if men and women manifest stress in different ways and if those manifestations are linked to biological or biological interacting with socialization processes.

After a thorough review of general physiologic responses to stress, Mitchell reviews more specific sex-related differences that appear in the literature (although she notes that very little actual research has been done regarding women's physiological responses to emotional and physical stimuli) …responses to exercise stressors: some studies report that following exercises (riding a stationary bike, running in place) women consistently had lower oxygen consumption, lower oxygen utilization, and higher pulse rate, but lower cardiac output compared to men (pg. 155). Additionally, women utilized glucose more efficiently than did men during such activity. …responses to temperature stressors: studies comparing men and women in hot temperature settings during exercise have found that men are likely to perspire sooner and have greater volume of sweat than are women, and women's bodies more quickly return to normal body temperature following exercise. No sex differences in response to maximal temperatures were noted. Reviews of cold temperature studies show no metabolic differences between men and women, although women have lower skin temperatures in cold due to greater subcutaneous fat layers. …emotional arousal and mental stressors: early stress research on the effects of psychological stressors involved in mental tasks have used physiological measures of corticosteriods as indicators of generalized stress and emotional arousal. Studies investigating men and women taking entrance examinations and laboratory cognitive-conflict tasks found that urinary cortisol (an indicator of emotional arousal) increased in both men and women but was

highest in the men. A similar study investigating both laboratory and real-world task stressors found similar differences in
epinephrine responses in men and women. Finally, in response to different emotionally-evocative films, men and women show similar differences in urinary epinephrine and norepinephrine as indications of differing levels of emotional response to exciting stimuli. Women were more likely than men to report psychic distress in these situations however.

... on the origins for differences in response: Mitchell offers that the data raise a number of old nature/nuture questions concerning the observed sex difference in response to stressors. Are differences in the stress experience linked to physiology or learned sex roles? She noted that, for women, the low correlation between epinephrine levels and
reported feelings of distress in some studies may suggest that epinephrine discomfort in animal studies have linked depleted catacholamine, gastric ulcers, increased corticosteroids, and altered immune function with being placed in uncontrollable, unpredictable fearful situations without opportunity for escape. Interestingly depressive illnesses (more frequently reported by women) have been linked to decreased brain and circulatory norepinephrine and ciurnal cycles of cortiocosteriods. Additionally, men's
higher incidence of cardiovascular disease may be linked to heightened chatecholamine response to stressors based on animals studies that find prolonged stimulation of the sympathetic nervous system results in hypertension, aeteriosclerosis, and heart disease. Mitchell suggests that women's decreased catecholamine responses to stress in interaction with estrogen may produce a buffering or protective effect regarding
cardiovascular disease. One author concludes that the effects of stressors carry higher physiologic cost for men but greater psychological cost in terms of subjective distress for women.

Source:
Mitchell, P. (1982). Physiologic response of women to stress. In G. Gladarom, R. McCorkle, & N. Fugate Woods, (Eds.), The complete book of womenís health (pg. 149-162). Inglewood Cliffs, NJ: Prentice-Hall.

Suggestions for Additional Readings

Allen, R., & Hyde, D. (1980). <u>Investigations in stress control</u>. Minneapolis, MN: Burgess Publishing Co.

Barnett, R., Biener, L., & Baruch, G. (1987). <u>Gender, stress, and health</u>. New York: Free Press.

Baum, A., & Singer, J. (Eds.) (1987). <u>Handbook of psychology and health: Vol. V. Stress</u>. Hillsdale: Erlbaum

Benson, H. (1975). <u>The relaxation response</u>. New York: William Morrow.

Berry, J., Kim, U., Minde, T., & Mok, D. (1987). Comparative studies of acculturative stress. <u>International migration review, 21</u>, 491-511.

Cohen, S., & Syme, S. (Eds.). (1985). Social support and health. New York: Academic Press.

DiMatteo, M. (1991). <u>The psychology of health, illness, and medical care</u>. Pacific Grove: BA: Brooks/Cole.

Elliott, G., & Eisdorfer, C. (Eds.) (1982). <u>Stress and human health: Analysis and implications of research</u>. New York: Springer.

Friedman, H. (Ed.). (1992). <u>Hostility, coping, and health</u>. Washington, DC: American Psychological Association.

Goldberger, L., & Breznitz, S. (Eds.) (1982). <u>Handbook of stress: Theoretical and clinical aspects</u>. New York: Free Press.

Goleman, D., & Gurin, J. (1993). <u>Mind/body medicine: How to use your mind for better health</u>. Yonkers, NY: Consumer Reports Books.

Greenberg, J. (1990). <u>Comprehensive stress management</u>. Bubuque, IA: William C. Brown.

Janis, I. (1958). <u>Psychological stress</u>. New York: Wiley.

Klein, A. (1989). <u>The healing power of humor: Techniques for getting through loss, setbacks, upsets, disappointments, difficulties, trials, tribulations, and all that not-so-funny stuff</u>. Los Angeles: Jeremy Tarcher.

Kleinke, C. (1991). <u>Coping with life challenges</u>. Belmont, CA: Brooks/Cole.

Lazarus, R., & Folkman, S. (1984). <u>Stress, appraisal, and coping</u>. New York: Springer.

Radner, G. (1989). <u>It's always something</u>. New York: Simon & Schuster.

Selye, H. (1974). <u>Stress without distress</u>. Philadelphia: Lippincott.

Selye, H. (1976). <u>The stress of life</u>. New York: McGraw-Hill.

Smith, J. (1993). <u>Understanding stress and coping</u>. New York: Macmillan.

Taylor, S. (1991). <u>Introduction to health psychology</u>. New York: Random House.

U.S. Department of Health and Human Services. <u>Plain talk about...handling stress</u>.

Williams, R. (1989). <u>The trusting heart</u>. New York: Random House.

Williams, R. & Williams, A. (1993). <u>Anger kills: 17 strategies for controlling the hostility that can harm your heart</u>. New York: Random House.

Woolfolk, R., & Richardson, F. (1978). <u>Stress, sanity, and survival</u>. New York: Sovereign.

In-Class Activities and Demonstrations

1. **<u>TRAIL Blazing</u>**: Using **Transparency Masters 13.1-13.6**, review with students the "Checking Your TRAIL" sections in the chapter. Have students work in small groups to answer the questions and then review with the class as a whole to tie the text reading to activity in class.

2. **<u>Reaching Critical Mass</u>**: Using **Transparency Masters 13.7-13.9**, review with students the "Critical Thinking" sections in the chapter. Have students work in small groups to answer the questions and then review with the class as a whole to tie the text reading to activity in class.

3. **<u>Getting Down to IT</u>**: Using **Transparency Masters 13.10-13.15**, review the "Integrative Thinking" sections in the chapter with students. Have

students work in small groups to answer the questions and then review with the class as a whole to tie the text reading to activity in class.

4. **Developing a local intervention strategy for coping with stress**: The text covers a number of ways in which people attempt to cope with the stress they encounter. For this exercise, divide students into groups of 5-6 and announce to them that they are to develop an intervention plan for reducing stress in students at your university. Part of their task with involve: assessing facilities available on campus that they might incorporate into their stress reduction plan (e.g., recreational programs, gym facilities, swimming pool, student health services, nutritional services, etc.), specifying participant selection criteria, and determining level of university's institutional involvement in their program (e.g., recommending a stress management class for all incoming freshmen, at-risk populations?). They will need to decide how to operationally define stress in their target, select coping methods to incorporate in their program (and why they think those might work), and outline some method(s) for assessing the success or failure of the intervention. When I have my students engage in this task, I also ask them to take into special consideration issues relating to gender and ethnicity in the development of their programs (e.g., diet plans that are culturally sensitive). Have students then give a brief in-class presentation of their proposal. I've done this exercise for the past 6 years in both General Psychology and Health Psychology classes, and students have had a great time exploring and uncovering the facilities available to them on campus. They have been able to demonstrate what they've learned about the stress/coping literature and research methodology/interventions at the same time.

5. **Creating a class survey of college student stressors:** The following is an exercise that you can begin on one day in class and conclude the following day. After covering the text material concerning types of stressors and, in particular, pointing out the authors' critique of biases in stressors listed on traditional stress surveys, tell students that they are going to develop their own class survey of stressors experienced by college students. To begin your survey development, ask each student to list the top 10 stressors he or she has experienced in the past 6 months. After collecting their responses, compile their answers into an overall survey of responses, keeping track of the frequency of each item listing. The next day in class, discuss and rank (by consensus votes of the students) the items that appear on the class inventory. Compare the stressors listed with those presented on the Holmes & Rahe SRRS and note items that were markedly different (absent on one, present on both). Discuss problematic assumption issues that occur with using stress inventories that do not fit the group upon which it is tested (i.e., underrepresenting their experiences with stress).

6. **Name that conflict**: Handout Master 13.1 includes 4 scenarios representing types of conflict as described in Chapter 13. Have students complete the handout and then personalize the exercise by having them write an example of 2 types of conflicts that they have experienced in their own lives. Discuss examples in class. Note any differences in students' examples that might be related to gendered experiences or cultural obligations/demands.

    Answers to handout master:
    1. multiple approach-avoidance
    2. avoidance-avoidance
    3. approach-avoidance
    4. approach-approach

7. **Keeping a stress log**: Using an easy to carry notebook, have students keep a record of stressful events that occur over the course of several days. To the extent that they can, they should attempt to record:
    (1) the antecedents leading up to their feeling of stress
    (2) the emotional, physical, & cognitive effects of the stressors
    (3) their efforts to cope with the stressor (using the various types of coping listed in the text as references).

    At the end of the stress log assignment, have students write a brief analysis of the trends they observed while doing the assignment. Have them offer one change they plan to make from observing their data.

Sources for Additional Activities

Benjamin, L. & Lowman, K. (1981). Activities handbook for the teaching of psychology. Washington DC: American Psychological Association.

Bracke, P. (1987). Progressive muscle relaxation: One component of effective stress management. In V. Makosky, L. Whittemore, & A. Rogers (Eds.), Activities handbook for the teaching of psychology (Vol. 2) (pg. 281-283). Washington, DC: American Psychological Association.

Calhoun, L., & Selby, J. (1977). A critical life problems approach to teaching psychology of adjustment. Teaching of psychology, 4, 151-152.

Eagleston, J. (1987). Understanding the Type A behavior pattern. In V. Makosky, L. Whittemore, & A. Rogers (Eds.), Activities handbook for the teaching of psychology (Vol. 2) (pg. 166-168). Washington, DC: American Psychological Association.

Halonen, J. (1995). Chapter 10: Emotions, Stress, & Health. In The critical thinking companion for Introductory Psychology. New York: Worth Publishers.

Martin, M. (1990). Biofeedback on a budget. In V. Makosky, C. Sileo, L. Whittemore, L. Landry, & M. Skutley (Eds). Activities handbook for the teaching of psychology (Vol. 3). (pg. 243). Washington DC: American Psychological Association

    Singelis, T. (1998). Teaching about culture, ethnicity, & diversity: Exercises and planned activities. Thousand Oaks, CA: Sage.

    Makosky, V., Sileo, C., Whittemore, L., Landry, C., & Skutley, M. (1990). Activities handbook for the teaching of psychology (Vol. 2). Washington DC: American Psychological Association.

    Makosky, V., Sileo, C., Whittemore, L., & Skutley, M. (1995). Activities handbook for the teaching of psychology (Vol. 3). Washington DC: American Psychological Association.

    Meck, D., & Ball, J. (1979). Teaching adjunctive coping skills in a personality adjustment course. Teaching of psychology, 6, 185-186.

    Puente, A. (1987). An introduction to meditation. In V. Makosky, L. Whittemore, & A. Rogers (Eds.), Activities handbook for the teaching of psychology (Vol. 2) (pg. 284-285). Washington, DC: American Psychological Association.

    Somerville, A., Allen, A., Noble, B., & Sedgwick, D. (1984). Effects of a stress management class: One year later. Teaching of psychology, 11, 82-85.

    Unger, B., & Palladino, J. (1978). The psychology of adjustment. Teaching of psychology, 5, 216-218.

    Whitford, F. (1998). Stress and health. In Quick guide to the Internet for psychology (pg.84-88). Boston: Allyn and Bacon.

Journey II Software:

Enter the Personality lab by clicking on the icon in the Main Menu and discover 2 exercises pertaining to the effects of stress.

- The effects of stress: In this exercise students complete several forms of stress tests: a student version of the Social Readjustment Rating Scale, and a hassles and uplifts diary. Discussions of the scales and interpretation/comparison of student's scores are given. The link between stress and health is discussed.

- Personality assessment: Part of this exercise is relevant to the Stress, Coping, and Health chapter. In this section, students complete a series of questions measuring Type A behavior pattern and receive feedback on their score. The rest of the exercise involves Zuckerman's Sensation Seeking scale and Rotter's Locus of Control scale. Be warned--there may be a glitch in this program...mine recycled through surveys several times and was confusing.

- **World Wide Web**: Check out the following WWW sites for information and activities relevant to this section of the text!
  - Addison Wesley Longman's Website -- **http://longman.awl.com/**
  - PsychZone link -- **http://longman.awl.com/**
  - Psych Web -- **http://www.gasou.edu/psychweb/psychweb.htm**

- Self-Quizzes for Introductory Psychology -- **http://www.gasou.edu/psychweb/selfquiz/selfquiz.htm**
- Psychology Jumping Stand -- **http://www.indiana.edu:80/~iuepsyc/PsycJump.html**
- The Psychology Place -- **http://www.psychplace.com**
- Virtual library on stress--**http://www.w3.org/vl/Stress**
- Stress--**http://www.cardinalpoints.com/stress/00stress.html**
  or
  http://helping.apa.org/stress4.html
  or
  http://healthguide.com/stress/default.htm
  or
  http://www.rtc-carlow.ie/SUHome/stress.html
  or
  http://www.cmhc.com/psyhelp/chap5/chap5d.htm
  or
  http://www.prcn.org/next/stress.html
  or
  http://www.unl.edu/stress/mgmt/
- Stress IQ--**http://cybertowers.com/selfhelp/articles/sports/spstress.html**
- Type A--**http://www.msnbc.com/onair/nbc/nightlynews/stress/default.asp**
  or
  http://www.msnbc.com/onair/nbc/nightlynews/stress/stresstypea.asp
  or
  http://www.workhealth.org/risk/rfbtypea.htm
- PTSD--**http://www.long-beach.va.gov/ptsd/stress.html**

- **Audio-Visual Support**

  <u>**Films/Videos**</u>:
  - *Discovering Psychology: Health, Mind, and Behavior* (Annenberg, 30 minutes)
  - *The Mind Series*
    --<u>Module 37</u>: Stress and Health
  - *The Brain Series*
    --<u>Module 29</u>: Emotions, Stress, and Health
  - *The Brain: Stress and Emotion* (PBS, 60 minutes)
  - *Stress* (FFHS, 26 minutes)
  - *Managing Stress* (CRM, 26 minutes)
  - *The AIDS Movie* (New Day Films, 26 minutes)
  - *The Art of Healing* (Ambrose, 58 minutes)
  - *Healing from Within* (Ambrose, 58 minutes)
  - *Learning to Cope: A Film About How to Deal With Your Tensions* (MOTO, 26 minutes)

- *Learning to Live with Stress: Programming the Body for Health* (DOCA, 20 minutes)
- *Managing Stress* (PSUPCR, 34 minutes)
- *Mind-Body Connection* (Ambrose, 58 minutes)
- *Mind Over Medicine* (IU, 55 minutes)
- *The Mystery of Chi* (Ambrose, 58 minutes)
- *One Nation Under Stress* (FFHS, 52 minutes)
- *Stress and Immune Function* (FFHS, 26 minutes)
- *Stress, Health, and You* (AEF, 16 minutes)
- *Those People: AIDS in the Public Mind* (PBS, 30 minutes)
- *Transitions: Letting Go and Taking Hold* (CRM, 29 minutes)
- *Your Own Worst Enemy* (SP, 26 minutes)
- *Youth Stress* (IU, 24 minutes)
- *Coping with Stress* (FFHS, 23 minutes)
- *Stress: Keeping Your Cool* (FFHS, 36 minutes)
- *Managing Stress* (FFHS, 19 minutes)
- *Getting a Handle on Stress* (FFHS, 26 minutes)
- *Running Out of Time: Time Pressure, Overtime, and Overwork* (FFHS, 57 minutes)
- *Reducing Stress* (FFHS, 19 minutes)
- *Emotion and Illness* (FFHS, 30 minutes)
- *Pressure-cooked* Kids (FFHS, 28 minutes)
- *Kids and Stress* (FFHS, 17 minutes)
- *Can't Slow Down* (FFHS, 28 minutes)
- *The Beyond Stress Series* (FFHS, 30 minutes each)
    - Program 1: Breathing away stress
    - Program 2: Relaxing muscle tension
    - Program 3: The relaxation response
    - Program 4: Focusing the mind
    - Program 5: Maximizing performance
    - Program 6: The session

Psychology Encyclopedia Laserdisc IV:

Movies
Sapolsky: research on stress   Frames 22723-27974   Side 2
    2 mins. 55 sec.

Still Images
Hostility and health [14.1]	Frame 53567 Side	all
Fitness and health [14.2]	53568	all
Stress and illness model [14.3]	53569	all

Transparency Master 13.1: Checking Your TRAIL 13.1

I. Situations that cause stress are s_____.

II. <u>True</u> or <u>False</u>: Whether an event is stressful depends only on the objective nature of the event.

III. You need to get a good grade on a final exam in order to graduate. What type of stressor are you facing?
    A. a hassle
    B. an avoidance-avoidance conflict
    C. pressure
    D. cumulative problems

IV. You want to sell your textbook at the end of the semester, but you don't want to stand in the long lines. What type of conflict are you facing?
    A. approach-approach
    B. approach-avoidance
    C. avoidance-avoidance
    D. hassle pressure

Transparency Master 13.2: Checking Your TRAIL 13.2

I. <u>True</u> or <u>False</u>: As long as the changes are desirable, multiple changes in a person's life don't cause stress.

II. In the United States, males are more likely than females to experience which of the following work-related stressors?
   A. inadequate income
   B. physical danger
   C. little job security
   D. limited opportunities for career development

III. Name four bases for differences in the stress experienced by different people.

IV. <u>True</u> or <u>False</u>: Some people have schemata that enable them to recognize racism against African Americans, but they don't perceive racism when it is directed against other groups.

Transparency Master 13.3: Checking Your TRAIL 13.3

I. The _____ branch of the _____ nervous system is switched on during times of stress.

II. Explain how chronic stress leads to high blood pressure and fatigue.

III. How does chronic stress weaken the immune system?

IV. <u>True</u> or <u>False</u>: Most cigarette smokers start smoking in adolescence, often through observational learning and positive reinforcement from friends, or because they believe in the personal fable.

Transparency Master 13.4: Checking Your TRAIL 13.4

I. **Which one of the following statements is true?**
   A. The results of an experimental study in which subjects looked at a film on Native Australians indicated that the way people interpret an event can affect how much stress they feel.
   B. When people make primary appraisals of an event, they evaluate their ability to deal with the stressor.
   C. When people make secondary appraisals of an event, they judge whether an event is potentially harmful.
   D. The feeling that one has no control over a stressful situation lessens the stress produced by the situation.

II. **Which one of the following traits is NOT a personality trait that helps people deal effectively with stress?**
   A. Agreeableness
   B. Stubbornness
   C. Openness
   D. Extroversion

III. **Growing evidence suggests that it is the _____ component of Type A personality that is associated with high risk for heart disease.**
   A. achievement
   B. hardiness
   C. anger
   D. competitive

IV. **Which one of the following personality characteristics does NOT characterize people with a hardy personality?**
   A. They tend to view change as a challenge and not as a threat.
   B. They feel they have control over their lives.
   C. They tend to be less susceptible to stress-related health problems than other people.
   D. They are usually angry.

Transparency Master 13.5: Checking Your TRAIL 13.5

I. Name four forms of social support.

II. A student who is doing poorly in class goes to his or her professor's office for help in understanding the class material. The student is using a(n) _____ strategy to cope with the difficulty.
   A. avoidance
   B. approach
   C. emotion-focused
   D. blunting

III. If the student described in question 2 tries not to think about her or his difficulties in class, the student is using a(n) _____ strategy to cope.
   A. monitoring
   B. approach
   C. avoidance
   D. instrumental

IV. Which one of the following statements is true?
   A. In general, avoidance strategies are helpful in dealing with chronic and unavoidable stressors.
   B. Heavy alcohol drinking is usually a sign of an approach coping strategy.
   C. Emotion-focused coping is the same as using an avoidance strategy.
   D. Effective coping usually involves choosing either an approach or avoidance strategy rather than use both.

Transparency Master 13.6: Checking Your TRAIL 13.6

I. Which one of the following statements is FALSE?
   A. Females are more likely than males to cope by seeking social support.
   B. Males tend to use more problem-focused strategies than females do.
   C. Females are more likely than males to use emotion-focused strategies.
   D. Males more often than females perceive stressful situations as unchangeable.

Identify the defense mechanism being used in the following:

II. Due to his own feelings of inadequacy and self-hate, a boy thinks that other children at his school are either stupid or stuck up.

III. Your mother had a fight with a co-worker today. Now she becomes angry at you over nothing.

IV. A man regularly speeds when driving, but believes he couldn't possibly get into a traffic accident.

Transparency Master 13.7: Critical Thinking 13.1

Stress scales often measure stress in terms of behaviors--such as admitted sadness and crying--that are more culturally acceptable in females than in males in the United States (Tavris, 1991). How might this bias affect findings regarding the incidence of stress among females and males?

Transparency Master 13.8: Critical Thinking 13.2

Women who had been diagnosed as having cancer were recruited for a correlational study. The women who reported feeling happiest at the start of the study tended to live longer than those who were not as happy (Levy et al., 1988). Based on these results, can we conclude that happiness protects people against cancer? Why?

Transparency Master 13.9: Critical Thinking 13.3

The attitude of many heterosexuals toward homosexuals is, "I don't care [if they are homosexual] as long as they don't bother me." But how might some cases of rapidly anti-homosexual attitudes be explained in terms of reaction formation?

Transparency Master 13.10: Integrative Thinking 13.1

Recalling the Introductory chapter's discussion of research ethics and the typical design of psychological experiments, what ethical problems can arise if researchers manipulate stress?

Transparency Master 13.11: Integrative Thinking 13.2

Recalling what you read in the Biopsychology chapter, what will be the stress responses of the endocrine system, the sympathetic branch of the autonomic nervous system, and the central nervous system?

Transparency Master 13.12: Integrative Thinking 13.3

Consider the study conducted by Geer & Maisel (1972) in which participants could or could not stop the presentation of gruesome pictures. In light of what you learned in the Biopsychology chapter, why was the arousal of the autonomic nervous system used to measure anxiety? If this study lasted for a long time, which group of subjects would have been more likely to develop "learned helplessness," discussed in the Learning chapter?

Transparency Master 13.13: Integrative Thinking 13.4

The Cognition & Intelligence chapter's discussion of problem-solving methods described means-ends analysis. Is means-ends analysis an approach or avoidance strategy?

Transparency Master 13.14: Integrative Thinking 13.5

Consider the statement that "African American churches offer support ... by providing a view of African Americans that counters the negative media images of African Americans and acknowledges their actual experiences" (Eugene, 1995). In light of what you read in the Cognition & Intelligence chapter, explain the usefulness of such counter images work in terms of concept accessibility.

Transparency Master 13.15: Integrative Thinking 13.6

Based on the Introductory chapter's discussion of different schools of thought in psychology, identify the school of thought that is least likely to believe that the concept of defense mechanisms is useful.

Handout Master 13.1: Name That Conflict

Name That Conflict!

Instructions: For each scenario described below, identify the conflict being described. At the bottom of the page, write 2 examples of conflicts you have experienced.

1. Mary couldn't decide whether to purchase the van or the sports car. Each had desirable qualities, but neither provided everything she wanted. Moreover, the costs were staggering. The choice was so frustrating that Mary decided to stick it out with her motorcycle until the next models became available.

   Type of conflict:

2. Curt, a young gay man who is a devout Catholic, experiences a great deal of emotional turmoil about his sexual orientation and his religion's views concerning it. As a result, he avoids the open members of the Gay/Lesbian/Bisexual student group on his campus and has stopped going to church.

   Type of conflict:

3. Miguel lives in Mexico but is so poor there he decides to sneak into the United States even though he can not obtain a work visa. He has been caught 3 times and taken back to Mexico by authorities. Each time he returns within days.

   Type of conflict:

4. Maggie has been offered two graduate school positions at equally prestigious universities upon completion of her undergraduate work. Both institutions offer exciting opportunities for study and will pay her a scholarship.

   Type of conflict:

Personal conflicts:

Example 1: _____
_____

Example 2: _____
_____

CHAPTER 14

PSYCHOLOGICAL DISORDERS

- **Chapter Overview**
    Learning Objectives
    Chapter Outline

- **Additional Lecture Ideas**
    Lecture Topics
    Additional Readings

- **In-Class Activities and Demonstrations**
    Activities and Demonstrations
    Sources for Additional Activities

- **World Wide Web**

- **Audio-Visual Support**

- **Handout and Transparency Masters**

Chapter Overview

Learning Objectives

After studying this chapter, you should be able to do the following:

1. Define abnormality.

2. Describe how psychological disorders are classified and identified.

3. Explain several perspectives on psychological disorders.

4. Identify core features of several psychological disorders and provide alternative explanations for their occurrence.

5. Describe gender and cultural differences associated with specific psychological disorders.

Chapter Outline

Psychological Disorders

I. Abnormality: The Key Feature of Psychological Disorders
   A. Defining abnormality
        1. definition: abnormality may describe a behavior that is statistically infrequent, socially unacceptable, biologically maladaptive, injurious, or that causes distress
        2. rare behaviors: behavior is defined as statistically abnormal if it occurs infrequently; a statistical definition of abnormality depends on sample of comparison
        3. socially disagreeable behaviors: abnormality is defined according to social norms--standards for acceptable behavior within a particular social group
        4. maladaptive behaviors: engaging in behaviors that may cause social or physical harm to oneself; need to consider context of behavior
        5. distressing behaviors: presence of physical or emotional pain; this definition overlooks persons engaging in maladaptive behavior who don't report distress; social context may alter feelings of distress
        6. behaviors that injure: definition includes attempts to commit suicide, homicide, self-mutilation as examples
   B. Classifying psychological disorders
        1. psychological disorder: a pattern of behavioral, emotional, and mental dysfunction that causes distress, abnormal behavior, or an important loss of freedom.
        2. the DSM-IV: guidebook of psychological disorders: an encyclopedic book by American Psychiatric Association that identifies over 300 psychological disorders
            a. provides common language for mental health professionals
            b. contains widely accepted definitions of psychological conditions
            c. describes characteristic patterns of symptoms (subjective thoughts or feelings) and signs (observable behaviors)
            d. organizes disorders according to key features
        3. limitations of the DSM-IV:
            a. "checklist" of sign/symptoms doesn't provide appropriate description
            b. medical model approach assumes underlying disease; doesn't account for why two people with similar signs/symptoms may have different psychological causes
            c. problems with labeling producing undesirable social consequences
                i. example: Rosenhan study

4. <u>recognizing cultural differences</u>:
   a. DSM-IV developed largely from research on European Americans; diagnoses based on it may not be appropriate in other cultural contexts
   b. some psychological disorders not universally recognized
      i. signs/symptoms of a psychological disorder may not have functional equivalence
   c. people from different cultures may focus on different symptoms
   d. <u>culture-bound syndromes</u>: psychological disorders that only occur in certain cultures (e.g., *mali-mali* in the Philippines)

C. Perspectives on psychological disorders
  1. <u>biological perspectives</u>:
     a. genetic and biological explanations
     b. <u>limitation</u>: can't tell if biological event produced psychological disorder or visa versa.
  2. <u>psychological perspectives</u>:
     a. <u>learning theory</u>: abnormal behaviors are shaped and reinforced
     b. <u>cognitive theory</u>: disorders due to maladaptive thoughts
     c. <u>psychodynamic theory</u>: disorders due to unconscious conflicts, use of defense mechanisms
  3. <u>biopsychosocial perspective</u>: disorders result of interactive effects of biological, psychological, and social factors
  4. <u>spiritual perspectives</u>: emphasizes the supernatural
     a. <u>example</u>: Native American cultural belief in soul wound or soul loss as basis for illness

II. Anxiety Disorders: Excessive Worries
  A. Disorders featuring anxiety
   1. <u>anxiety disorders</u>: a type of psychological disorder characterized by intense, maladaptive anxiety; most common of all psychological disorders in U.S.
   2. <u>panic disorder</u>: an anxiety disorder characterized by repeated, sudden panic attacks; after having experienced a panic attack, apprehension and dread of reoccurrence, avoidance of situations may occur; substance use may be one coping strategy
      a. <u>panic attack</u>: a sudden episode of intense apprehension, usually accompanied by physical symptoms, such as a pounding heart, dizziness, chest pain, excessive sweating, and fear of dying or losing control
   3. <u>phobia</u>: persistent irrational fears of a person, place, or situation that results in a maladaptive avoidance of the feared stimulus
      a. <u>social phobia</u>: fear of being humiliated in social situations thus avoid social contact
      b. <u>agoraphobia</u>: avoiding public places in which might not be able to get help

c. <u>simple phobia</u>: fear of a specific stimulus such as fire or germs
4. <u>obsessive-compulsive disorder</u>: anxiety disorder involving obsessions that cause anxiety and compulsions that reduce anxiety
    a. <u>obsession</u>: irrational thoughts that are intrusive, repeated, and anxiety producing; may recognize that thoughts are irrational but can't stop them
    b. <u>compulsions</u>: purposeful repetitive behaviors done to deal with obsession
    c. <u>examples</u>: fears of contamination, sinfulness, disorganization
5. <u>posttraumatic stress disorder</u>: an anxiety disorder that occurs following a life-threatening trauma, and is characterized by autonomic hypersensitivity or numbing, and intrusion or avoidance of trauma-related stimuli
    a. disorder added to legitimize experiences of war veterans
    b. <u>psychic numbing</u>: a form of dissociation that occurs in trauma victims who then feel as though the event did not actually occur or that it was not genuinely traumatic; may help people avoid pain of event but may prolong recovery
6. <u>generalized anxiety disorder</u>: an anxiety disorder characterized by general and excessive continued anxiety; a poorly understood disorder argued by some to be a catch-all diagnosis

B. Understanding anxiety disorders
1. <u>biological perspectives</u>: neurological conditions may contribute
    a. <u>examples</u>:
        i. <u>obsessive-compulsive disorder</u>: abnormalities in cerebral cortex and basal ganglia
        ii. <u>phobias or panic disorder</u>: may occur in persons with heightened startle response who have hypersensitivity to neurochemicals that alert sympathetic nervous system; may be due to genetics
        iii. <u>PTSD</u>: initial trauma may produce long-term change in noradrenergic system, making it hypersensitive
2. <u>psychological perspectives</u>:
    a. <u>learning theory</u>: learn phobias and anxiety through imitation, observation, or reinforcement
    b. <u>cognitive theory</u>: perceptions and interpretations fuel anxiety (e.g., misinterpreting minor sensations as signs of physical/psychological problem)
    c. <u>psychodynamic theory</u>: anxiety disorders result from maladaptive defense mechanisms against anxiety (i.e., overuse defenses to avoid acknowledging unacceptable, unconscious thoughts, thus triggering symptoms of anxiety disorders)
        i. <u>examples</u>: reaction formation and generalized anxiety disorder; undoing and obsessive-compulsive disorder; projection and phobias

C. **Cultural and gender perspectives on anxiety disorders**
    1. culture and panic disorders: cross-cultural studies indicate similar occurrence rates (~ 1.5%) and symptoms
        a. example of cultural difference: kayak-angst in Greenland and Alaska; Koro in Asia
        b. conclusion: panic disorder might be universal phenomenon but culture shapes person's interpretation and experience of panic attacks
    2. gender and anxiety disorders:
        a. trends:
            i. women more likely than men to experience generalized anxiety disorder, panic disorder, and phobias; perhaps due to genetic differences or combination of psychological and social factors that make women more susceptible
            ii. women's responses to traumatic events: more likely to develop PTSD; cope with trauma by denial and avoidance; face more emotional and socioeconomic hardships after trauma than do men

III. Mood Disorders: Excessive Emotional Lows and Highs
  A. **Types of mood disorders**
    1. mood disorder: a pattern of extreme emotions that interfere with functioning and cause significant distress
        a. depressive disorders: characterized by "down" mood
        b. bipolar disorders: alternating between "up" and "down" moods
    2. major depression: a mood disorder characterized by intense and painful "down" feelings, accompanied by a lack of interest in life, sleep disturbances, loss of energy, and negative thoughts
        a. anhedonia: inability to feel joy
        b. major depression differs from typical "blues" in intensity and persistence
    3. dysthmia: a long-lasting pattern of moderately "down" moods that still permit normal functioning
    4. seasonal affective disorder: depression that tends to occur as daylight hours shorten, as during short winter days in the Northern Hemisphere, and lifts with increasing daylight, as during the long spring days
    4. bipolar disorder: also known as manic depression; a mood disorder characterized by alternating extreme up and down moods, both of which interfere with general functioning
        a. mania: elevated mood and exaggerated interest in life activities; not simply excited; may not think clearly, remember what just said or maintain grasp of reality
        b. psychotic: seriously out of touch with reality
        c. cyclothymia: milder form of bipolar disorder characterized by mood swings that are not as severe as those in bipolar disorder

B. Understanding mood disorders

1. <u>biological perspective</u>:

    a. <u>evidence for biological explanation</u>: cross-cultural similarities in incidence rates; twin study data indicate identical twin of person with bipolar 3xs more likely to develop disorder

    b. <u>neurochemical explanations</u>: decreased dopamine associated with anhedonia; decreased serotonin linked to depressed mood; medications that block reuptake of serotonin alleviate mood symptoms

    c. <u>neurobiological explanations</u>: disruptions in basal ganglia; weakened connections between basal ganglia and other parts of brain; decreased activity in portion of frontal cortex

2. <u>learning perspective</u>: depression due to receiving too little reinforcement, or do not notice or respond to adequate levels of reinforcement; may behave in ways to elicit punishment

3. <u>cognitive perspective</u>: irrational, self-defeating beliefs, learned helplessness result in lower self-esteem and depression

4. <u>psychodynamic perspective</u>: depression results from psychological conflicts following loss; "holding on" to lost person, goal, self-perception through identification, making lost entity seem more valuable; feel anger at lost entity for leaving; person unable to express anger/grief, thus direct feelings inward and become depressed

5. <u>biopsychosocial perspective</u>: some people are biologically predisposed to depression and become depressed when encounter stressor; physical health, coping style, personality traits, social environment contribute to development of depression

C. Gender and major depression

1. <u>trends</u>: adult men/women equal in incidence of bipolar (1%); children equally likely to experience depression (2-3%); at midpuberty and on, males/females show differences in incidence of depression (2xs as many women as men)

2. <u>differences in detection</u>: major depression goes undetected in men due to nature of symptoms listed on depression scales (men either not likely to exhibit symptoms or report them); males more likely to act out depression; biased depression scales probably not sufficient explanation for gender differences in incidence

3. <u>differences in hormones</u>: hypothesis that women's' hormones contribute to depression; evidence = changes in depression trends beginning at puberty and ending after menopause, changes in mood during reproductive cycle; criticism = relationship very weak, probably insignificant; doesn't account for depression at times other than premenstrual period; some research indicates depression rates of menopausal women same as men

4. <u>differences in negative beliefs</u>: proposal that women have more negative beliefs than do men, perhaps due to more social and psychological stress; women more likely to be harassed, physically abused, experience dislike

for own body, receive insensitive treatment at work, discrimination, sexism, employment and economic disadvantage, conflicting social roles, poverty

5. a combination of differences--a biopsychosocial perspective: although specific biological vulnerability factors that might explain gender differences unknown, women's coping styles more oriented toward dwelling on problems in negative, self-focused way, believing can't do anything about them; thought focused on stressors rather than overcoming or avoiding them

IV. Schizophrenia: Detached From Reality
   A. Definitions
      1. schizophrenia: "split mind"; a split between thoughts and emotions and between perceptions and reality; a psychological disorder characterized by disturbances in thought, perception, emotion, and behavior resulting in loss of touch with reality
      2. psychosis: a loss of contact with reality that affects all areas of one's life
      3. course of disorder: approximately 1/4 experience sudden and dramatic symptoms; in most cases, symptoms obvious after weeks or months of worsening behavior
   B. Symptoms of schizophrenia
      1. disturbed thinking: usually among first symptoms observed; typically appear in adolescents/young adults
         a. word salad: senseless jumble of unrelated, seemingly random thoughts
         b. neologisms: meaningless, made-up words
         c. clang associations: strings of similar-sounding words that interrupt sentences
         d. delusions: a firmly held belief that has no basis in reality, is not shared by others, and that interferes with general functioning
            i. delusion of grandeur: belief that one is a very powerful or important person
            ii. delusion of persecution: belief that others seek to do one harm
            iii. delusion of reference: false belief that one is being talked about by others
      2. disturbed perceptions: perceptions not based on present sensory stimuli
         a. hallucination: a false sensory perception that is not based on sensory stimulus, such as hearing voices when none are present; seeing, smelling, or feeling things that do not actually exist
      3. disturbed emotions and actions: being "split off" from emotions and social environment
         a. examples: inappropriate affect to a situation; odd mannerisms or bizarre behaviors

C. Understanding schizophrenia

1. <u>general information</u>: incidence rate = 1% of population; approx. 2/3 of mental health costs spent on treating this disorder; considered most severe form of psychological disorder

2. <u>types of schizophrenia</u>: different characteristics experienced more predominantly in different types of schizophrenia
    a. <u>catatonic</u>: remaining unresponsive to environment, motionless for hours
    b. <u>paranoid</u>: characterized by nervousness, suspicion
    c. <u>hebephrenic</u>: marked by inappropriate affect

3. <u>types of symptoms</u>: clustering of symptom patterns into 3 groups; changes of symptoms in one group may not be correlated with changes in other groups
    a. <u>negative</u>: loss of ordinary functions such as thought/speech fluency, lack of emotion; associated with activity in one area of frontal cortex
    b. <u>disorganized</u>: inappropriate behavior and disorganized thought/speech; associated with activity in different area of frontal cortex
    c. <u>positive</u>: presence of disturbed perceptions, delusions, hallucinations; associated with activity in hippocampus

4. <u>the biological perspective on cause</u>:
    a. <u>dopamine hypothesis</u>: an oversensitivity to dopamine accounts for some of the symptoms of schizophrenia
        i. <u>evidence</u>: some persons with schizophrenia have 2xs the dopamine receptors as general population; symptoms of schizophrenia lessen with age as loss of dopamine receptors occurs in aging brain
        ii. <u>criticism</u>: no causal relationship proven; negative symptoms of schizophrenia associated with low levels of dopamine; dopamine sensitivity associated also with mania
    b. <u>reduction of brain tissue in limbic region/frontal cortex</u>: brain tissue is lost in regions controlling emotions, memory, attention, and problem solving; evidence of brain tissue loss = enlarged ventricles in the brain
    c. <u>prenatal exposure to viral infection</u>: during second trimester, maternal exposure to flu produced immune response or medication (aspirin) she took affected fetal brain development
    d. <u>genetic explanation</u>: twin and familial studies indicate higher concordance rates (50% for identical twin whose twin sibling has schizophrenia; 10-14% for fraternal twin)

5. <u>the biopsychosocial perspective on cause</u>: hypothesizes that people with underlying biological vulnerability to disorder developed into the disease after exposed to stressful psychosocial conditions

a. correlation of disorder with low socioeconomic status--3xs more likely in lowest socioeconomic groups; perhaps due to deprivations, stressors, stigmatization experienced in those groups
6. <u>cultural perspectives</u>: disorder exists throughout the world
   a. need to assess meaning and social appropriateness of behavior in sociocultural context; example: *amok*
   b. cultural differences in response to person with schizophrenia
      i. in developing countries, persons with schizophrenia tend to function at higher levels then do similar others in developed countries
      ii. cultural factors that influence functioning may include amount of support by community and family

V. Body-Focused Disorders: Maladaptive Bodily Concerns
A. Eating disorders
1. <u>eating disorders</u>: a type of psychological disorder characterized by maladaptive eating behavior, distorted body image, and dislike of one's body
2. <u>anorexia nervosa</u>: an eating disorder defined by efforts to minimize calorie intake, being driven by an intense irrational fear of weight gain
   a. <u>long-term consequences</u>: amenorrhea, loss of calcium from bones, heart attacks
3. <u>bulimia nervosa</u>: an eating disorder characterized by episodes of binge eating followed by purging of the food through vomiting, laxatives, diuretics, or exercise
   a. <u>physical consequences</u>: throat soreness, tooth decay, puffy checks, dehydration, life-threatening heart conditions
4. <u>understanding eating disorders</u>:
   a. <u>biological perspective</u>: eating disorders related to neurotransmitter imbalances associated with depression (low serotonin)
   b. <u>cognitive perspective</u>: cultural ideals of thinness combine with belief that one can and should use willpower to control the body; guilt and anxiety around small weight gains related to dieting cycles
   c. <u>psychodynamic perspective</u>: attempts to control the body reflect unconscious conflicts or disturbed interpersonal relationships (e.g., restrictive eating may be unconscious attempt to regress to earlier stage of development)
   d. <u>biopsychosocial perspective</u>: recent study of 116 teenage girls indicates that those who developed eating disorder had a biological predisposition toward higher-than-average body fat levels, psychological disorder at start of study, poor body image and poor family relations

5. <u>ethnic and gender perspectives on eating disorders</u>:
    a. disorders 10xs more likely to occur in women than men but still relatively rare (.5% of women have anorexia; 1-5 in 100 have bulimia)
    b. described as a culture-bound disorders that afflict affluent European American but occurs in women from all socioeconomic and ethnic backgrounds
    c. disorders influenced by level of identification with mainstream European American culture

B. Somatoform disorders
1. <u>somatoform disorders</u>: a psychological disorder characterized by physical symptoms that have no medical cause; medical disorders not well understood, yet can be mistakenly misdiagnosed as this psychological disorder
2. <u>hypochondriasis</u>: somatoform disorder characterized by the belief that insignificant physical sensations represent symptoms of serious illness; beliefs lead to persistent medical help seeking behaviors
3. <u>conversion reactions</u>: a somatoform disorder characterized by the sudden loss of function in a body part without medical reason; usually triggered by stressful conflict
4. <u>understanding somatoform disorders</u>:
    a. <u>biological explanation</u>: excess dopamine activity or other brain dysfunctions disturb attention/thinking that leads to misinterpretation of bodily sensations
    b. <u>learning theory</u>: receive positive reinforcement for behavior
    c. <u>cognitive theory</u>: tendency to think about and exaggerate physical symptoms; disorders represent a means of emotional expression; way of masking reactions to stress
    d. <u>psychodynamic theory</u>: symptoms serve as defense mechanisms against stressful, unconscious psychological conflicts, repressing painful emotions and symbolizing them with symptoms
5. <u>cultural perspectives on somatoform disorders</u>: expression and rate of occurrence differ cross-culturally although disorders occur in many cultures; some cultures value expression of emotions through physical symptoms

VI. Dissociative disorders: Detached From Oneself
  A. Definitions
    1. <u>dissociation</u>: a division of consciousness into multiple levels of awareness
    2. <u>dissociative disorders</u>: disorders characterized by divided consciousness that interferes with the normal integration of memory or identity
  B. Types of dissociative disorders
    1. <u>depersonalization</u>: feeling as though one's body is detached from oneself or not human

2. <u>psychogenic amnesia and psychogenic fugue</u>:
    a. <u>psychogenic amnesia</u>: an inability to recall important personal information following psychological trauma; memories suddenly dissociated from consciousness for psychological reasons
    b. <u>psychogenic fugue</u>: a state of dissociation from one's identity during travels away from one's usual surroundings, followed by psychogenic amnesia for the experience
3. <u>dissociative identity disorder</u>: multiple personality disorder; a splitting of the personality into two or more distinct personalities of which only one is dominant at a time

C. Understanding dissociative disorders
1. disorder linked to trauma; most research focuses on psychological explanations
2. <u>learning theory</u>: learn to dissociate by observing others or by random experience; may be guided by questions from psychotherapist to create alters
3. <u>psychodynamic theory</u>: dissociative disorder involves repression; alters may provide an emotional escape from the past, an unconscious expression of feelings associated with abuse

VII. Personality disorders: Rigid and maladaptive traits
A. Definition
1. <u>personality disorder</u>: an enduring, rigid socially maladaptive personality that causes distress or limits effective functioning and that violates social norms
2. <u>three categories of personality disorder</u>:
    a. PD marked by odd/peculiar behavior--<u>example</u>: paranoid personality disorder
    b. PD marked by high anxiety--<u>example</u>: obsessive-compulsive personality disorder
    c. PD marked by dramatic, erratic, impulsive, emotionally unpredictable behavior-- <u>example</u>: borderline personality disorder or antisocial personality disorder

B. Antisocial personality disorders
1. <u>definition</u>: manipulative or psychopathic personality disorders; a personality disorder that describes a person who consistently disregards and violates the rights of others without feeling guilty; deceive and use others to satisfy their selfish impulses; seek immediate gratification; don't care if they break the law
2. <u>demographics</u>: more men than women have antisocial PD; associated with behaviors that may appear in childhood

C. Understanding antisocial personality disorders
1. specific causes unknown

2. <u>neurological dysfunction</u>: evidence for neurological basis include less responsiveness to pain, less sensitivity to feelings of fear and arousal, less likely to fear punishment or learn from it

3. <u>learning perspective</u>: reinforcement for antisocial behavior includes excitement and pleasure from "beating the system"; direct positive reinforcement for antisocial behavior

4. <u>cognitive perspective</u>: dysfunctional beliefs that, unless they are overpowering, they will be controlled by others

5. <u>psychodynamic perspective</u>: a deficient superego resulting from childhood abuse and emotional neglect that reduced child's desire to internalize social ideals for behavior

Additional Lecture Topics

1. **Defining and expressing abnormality across cultures:**

    In their chapter review of issues in the study of abnormal behaviors, David Matsumoto and Dawn Terrell discuss three major themes of interest to cross-cultural psychologists: the definition of abnormality, the expression of and assessment of psychological disorders, and the treatment of psychological disorders. Their comments on the first two issues add to the coverage provided in Chapter 14; the remaining issue will be addressed in Chapter 15.

    Traditional viewpoints typically used in discussions of the definition of abnormality tend to highlight statistical rarity, violation of societal norms, and experiences of subjective distress as bases for defining experiences as "abnormal." Each perspective has some inherent problems associated with it. For example, although a behavior may be relatively common in the statistical sense, (drinking to the point of drunkenness for example), that behavior may still be considered as indicative of underlying pathology. Of perhaps greater interest to cross-cultural psychologists, criteria addressing the violation of societal norms speak to one way in which culture and psychopathology are related. The basic idea that one's behavior is compared to cultural standards for appropriate behavior and that different cultures have different standards has been talked about extensively in introductory psychology books. What these authors add is a reminder that this criteria is hardly absolute or static, since standards change within a culture over time, and that such standards are subjective rather than objective. Finally, the criteria of subjective distress is also considered problematic, because distress may be influenced by how others treat us. Peoples from different cultures vary in the extent to which they report experiencing distress associated with psychological disorders, display rules for showing distress, are subject to cultural influences, and some cultural values favor or prohibit reporting/focusing on subjective distress. Thus, as a result of dissatisfaction with traditional definitional views, cross-cultural psychologists argue that a full understanding of (abnormal) behavior can only occur within a cultural context--the principle of cultural relativism must be applied.

    Adopting an etic-approach to the expression of abnormality across cultures, a number of cross-cultural studies of disorder prevalence have been conducted, with schizophrenia and depression being the most widely studied. Let's take a look at some of those studies and their findings as examples of the etic-approach and address a few additional ways in which culture is thought to influence psychopathy.

    Schizophrenia. Matsumoto and Terrell discuss a series of studies sponsored by the World Health Organization that sought to determine the prevalence and course of schizophrenia in several countries around the world. These studies determined that a recognized set of symptoms regarded as defining schizophrenia occurred across all studied cultures, suggesting a basic universality to this disorder, a finding that is frequently noted in the literature. However, cross-cultural differences in the progress of the disorder and symptom expression were found as well. For example, persons with the disorder who were from developing (as opposed to industrialized) countries were more likely to demonstrate productive progress while living with the disorder, presumably because of the influence of supportive extended kin networks in those cultures and the tendency to return to work. Moreover, symptom expression varied such that patients from the United States were less likely to report lack of insight or hallucinations than were patients from some other countries. Matsumoto and Terrell note that this difference may occur, in part, because of the high regard for insight and self-awareness that underlies value systems in this country. Finally, they suggest that cultural differences in the tolerance for different symptom profiles may occur such that some of the symptoms (such as hearing voices) are more accepted in cultural experience.

Depression. Cross-cultural studies of depression have found significant variability in symptomology: some cultural groups are more likely to report somatic complaints whereas others report "extreme feelings of hopelessness." In a theme from the Emotion chapter in this book, Matsumoto and Terrell remind us that language constructs for emotions tend to vary across cultures--some cultures have few or no words that capture the emotions of sadness or anger. Moreover, other cultures express or locate feeling states through different parts of the body. Observations such as these help explain, to some extent, cross-cultural differences in symptom variability. In another interesting point, Matsumoto and Terrell review the perspective that distinguishes between depressive disease, the biological based disorder, and depressive illness, that reflects a personal and social experience of depression. Some authors argue that while depressive disease may be thought of as universal, depressive illness is culturally determined. Finally, Matsumoto and Terrell point to research by Marsella (1979 & 1980), who has found that depression may be influenced by the objective or subjective orientations of a culture. For example, in cultures that emphasize individualism, symptoms of loneliness or isolation may predominate the symptom presentation; cultures that emphasize communal structures (a subjective culture) may be related to more expressions of somatic complaints.

In summary, Matsumoto and Terrell provide a broader understanding of the issues relating culture and abnormal psychology. The studies and issues they review provide interesting examples of how culture may influence what we interpret, express, or experience as depression. In Chapter 15, we'll see how those issues are related to assessment and treatment of psychological disorders as well.

Source:
   Matsumoto, D. & Terrell, D. (1994). Abnormal psychology. In People: Psychology from a cultural perspective. (pg. 136-144). Pacific Grove, CA: Brooks/Cole.

2. **Culture and depression--Discovering variations in the experience of illness:**
   As a medical anthologist, Spero Manson has spent the bulk of his career interested in how "people talk about the nature of their distress and illness" (pg.

285). In an interesting chapter in *Psychology and culture*, Manson provides a glimpse into his efforts to understand the experience of depression and, in so doing, introduces interesting insights into yet another way of arriving at definitions for abnormal experience. Soon after his departure from graduate school in the late '70s, Manson began a faculty appointment at the Department of Psychiatry at the Oregon Health Sciences University. To more fully understand the relationship between culture and mental health, he undertook a clinical fellowship that took him into a psychiatric emergency room on a weekly basis. There he began observing diagnostic techniques and the institutional culture that influenced the practice of psychiatry in that setting. In particular, he took note of what he refers to as "the logic and language" through which his psychiatrist colleagues "brought coherence to the illnesses presented by their patients" (pg. 285). He says "I was amazed at the extent to which fellow trainees and supervising clinicians gleaned similar insight from the stories that they elicited from their patients: the words that they found important, the themes that they attempted to articulate, the consistencies or inconsistencies that they found therein" (pg. 286). In short, he found that their framework, their logic for understanding was guided by the DSM, and over the course of his own training he was acquiring the same framework for understanding.

However, he also spent a great deal of time observing patients in the reception room, with some startling results: "I noticed they tended to speak differently about their problems, using not only other words and phrases, but emphasizing different aspects of their experiences than did my colleagues" (pg. 286). With that, he decided to perform a more systematic investigation of the cognitive maps patients and psychiatrists were using to order the phenomena of depression and anxiety in their everyday worlds. Manson used a Q-sort technique based on 100 cards containing words used to describe anxiety and depression. He administered the cards to three groups of people in the clinic environment: middle class U.S. patients, American Indian patients at an outpatient clinic, and psychiatric residents in training. Participants were to sort the cards into as many piles as they deemed "belonged together", and then were queried about the piles' common features (both within and between) and distinctions between piles. He found significant differences in numbers of piles or distinguishing categories and explanations for category development across his three groups. The psychiatric residents created 5 piles and reported the DSM as the basis for their categorizations. American Indians created 8 piles with a noticeable lack of distinction between psyche and soma (which Manson argues reflected differences in beliefs about mind-body dualism). The middle-class U.S. patients created 15 categories with fine discriminations among the experiences being represented.

In his conclusions, Manson felt that this simple example represented in a powerful way how "subtle, but profound socialization processes deeply affect our perceptions, behavior, and attributions of meaning" (pg. 288). Lessons of socialization influence these events. The psychiatric residents, socialized by the profession, viewed the world through the DSM just as the other participants viewed the world of depression and anxiety through their own cultural frameworks. He suggested that these same cultural frameworks for understanding and interpreting the experience of depression and anxiety also influence beliefs about appropriate treatment and seeking help. Whereas the psychiatrist may view psychotherapeutic techniques as appropriate intervention based on his or her socialized worldview of depression or anxiety, the patient may try homeopathic or naturopathic medicines, visits to faith healers, acupuncture or herbal treatments-- again methods that validate symptom expression. In his final commentary, Manson suggests that the widely discussed cross-cultural deficiencies of the DSM will not be addressed by "tinkering with the kind, number, clustering, or duration of symptoms" (pg. 290). He urges that the understanding of mental illness needs to focus on the process of inquiry--how the clinician elicits the client's story of illness. He concludes, "A better understanding of the phenomenology of mood disorders across these settings will have to encompass much more than simply the symptoms expressed by a patient. It must take into account the social contexts and cultural forces that shape one's everyday world and that give meaning to interpersonal relationships and life events" (pg. 290).

Source:
Manson, S. (1994). Culture and depression: Discovering variations in the experience of illness. In W. Lonner, & R. Malpass (Eds.), Psychology and culture. (pg. 285-290). Boston: Allyn & Bacon.

3. **Revising the Framework of Abnormal Psychology:**
Hope Landrine states that the traditional teaching of abnormal psychology has been guided by a framework that determines what should and should not be taught in the course--a framework that is reflected by the topics and studies covered in abnormal psychology textbooks. In her chapter in *Teaching a psychology of people: Psychology from a cultural perspective*, she claims that traditional study of abnormal psychology has viewed ethnicity, gender, and social class as peripheral issues to the concepts of psychopathology explored in an abnormal psychology course and "has virtually ignored the historical and contemporary context of power relations in which such constructs are constructed" (pg. 37). Her effort in the *Teaching* chapter, therefore, is designed to "provide information and resources to compensate for two significant deficiencies in our texts: the role of misogyny and racism in the development of concepts of psychopathology and the relevance of social and cultural variables to contemporary concepts of normalcy and abnormalcy" (pg. 37). I'll review only her perspectives on the first deficiency in this writing, but you might find some her points on contemporary perspectives regarding normalcy and abnormalcy interesting reading.
Historical perspectives. Landrine contends that two important historical events have provided the historical bases for current clinical frameworks regarding women and Blacks: the persecution of witches and slavery.
- on witches and women: Landrine notes that most abnormal psychology textbooks include some discussion of witches in their historical

overviews of psychopathology that ultimately describes these few women as, not possessed by the Devil, but rather "possessed by psychopathology." The statements and actions of these severely disturbed women were products of hysterical or psychotic conditions to be addressed by treatment, not torture. The actual facts, as Landrine presents them, were that these women were part of a matriarchal religion that acted as midwives and practiced medicine and, because of their advocacy and medical practice, undermined the Catholic Church authority in those domains. Thus, efforts to control these women were based in issues related to power, woman hating, and economics issues. Landrine's concern about psychological interpretations of these historical events is that some text presentations describe these women from a perspective of hysteria, psychosis, and (psychodynamic) sexuality. She urges instructors to include readings from Szaz (1970), who gives detailed accounting of their persecution and the clinical construction of their "madness" in addition to the psychiatric persecution of gays, racist theories of Benjamin Rush, and social consequences of labeling.

- on slavery: Landrine offers that abnormal psychology textbooks tend to offer few, if any, theories on Blacks or on slavery. Clinical research in the 1800s did posit that slaves frequently demonstrated *drapetomania* (i.e., attempting to run away) and *dysthesia aethiopica* or "rascality" (characterized by "destroying plantation property, talking back, fighting with or attacking masters, and procrastinating or refusing to work.) In this era, mental health for slaves was centered on submission, and desires for freedom represented pathology. Later, based on data from the U.S. census that indicated that Blacks in the North had more psychopathology--data that were, by the way, fabricated--clinicians were discussing the relative mental health benefits of slavery as providing for the good of Blacks. During the early 1900s, theories were advanced designed to justify segregation on the grounds of mental health, speaking to clinicians' assumptions that the psychosocial levels of Blacks made them prone to schizophrenia; their emotionally simple, happy-go-lucky natures made them less prone to depression; and that their sexualized nature endangered White Americans' mental health. Similar racist concepts were applied from the 1950s up to as late as the 1970s, as evidenced by clinical writings that suggested increased civil rights would lend to "madness" in groups via a loss of their previously "well-defined status" within our culture. One 1967 article concerning the relationships between brain disease and urban rioting linked it to a neurological disorder in Blacks that necessitated psychosurgery. Landrine urges that discussion of these historical trends concerning the treatment of Blacks by the clinical establishment provides "a more complete picture of the sociopolitical context, particularly the role of racism, in concepts of psychopathology" (pg. 40).

Landrine's writings offer some fertile topics for discussion around the cultural, sociopolitical contexts in which the definition, assessment, and treatment of psychopathology have historically been influenced. The topics, though potentially upsetting to some students, introduce thought-provoking perspectives on the impact of mental health diagnosis on the lives of women and people of color.

Source:
Landrine, H. (1988). Revising the framework of abnormal psychology. In P. Bronstein, & K. Quina (Eds.), Teaching a psychology of people: Psychology from a cultural perspective. (pg. 37-44). Pacific Grove, CA: Brooks/Cole.

4. Reconstructing the impact of trauma on personality:

In considering the factors that have an impact on personality, traditional theories concerning the impact of trauma focused on patterns of psychological disorganization that altered the lives of (almost exclusively) white men as a result of war time experiences. With the social upheaval and civil unrest of the 60s and 70s in addition to the Vietnam War, new conceptualizations of the impact of trauma on personality began to develop. Recently Maria Root has offered a feminist conceptualization of trauma founded on greater inclusion of experiences from other individuals based on issues of gender, race, class, sexual orientation, and ability that have placed them in a position of target for hatred and oppression.

Root notes that the criteria used in diagnosing trauma was limited to symptoms based on trauma of war, and it was not until feminist critiques and influence that definitional issues began to be addressed. She criticizes the historical understanding of trauma as resting in definitions of experiences as traumatic from the clinician's perspective, not from the viewpoint of the experiencing individual. Additionally, conceptualizations of trauma have historically been constrained by emphasis on individual distress, disregarding events affecting larger groups of peoples such as the Holocaust, internment of Japanese Americans, dislocation and decimation of Native American peoples, etc.--thus providing a minimal understanding of the role of trauma in the lives of women, children, and minority groups.

The feminist reconstruction of theory on trauma and its impact on personality begins with an emphasis on an individual's subjective experience of event(s). Moreover, the feminist approach "depathologizes" what should be thought of as normal responses to horrible experiences and considers behaviors that follow trauma as specialized coping behaviors for survival. It also includes an analysis of the contribution of the social environment, and considers sociopolitical, systematic frameworks--trauma that has affected groups or communities of people.

In expanding the theoretical and diagnostic framework, the feminist conceptualization of trauma also includes various forms of experience: *direct traumas*-- maliciously perpetrated violence, war, accidents, disasters; *indirect traumas*--being traumatized by the trauma sustained by another, witnessing trauma (e.g., battering), receiving information about devastation (e.g., continual news reports of violence); *insidious traumas*--social status being devalued by racism, sexism, ageism, poverty, heterosexism, anti-Semitism, the results of direct trauma on an ancestor, the effects of significantly declining health due to AIDS, diabetes, multiple sclerosis, etc. In short, a broader range of traumatic events are considered from this perspective. Additionally, each case of trauma shatters in some manner the *dimensions of security* one holds about the world--through experiences of stimulus deprivation, pain, injury, starvation, being confronted with mortality, loss of significant others, perceived malicious intent, isolation, loss of control, witnessing death or destruction, crushing of one's spirit via emotional abuse, dislocation, betrayal, abuses of power, violations of personal space, rejection, and "invisibility". Moreover, experience with this broadened set of traumas "affects a person in a permanent way." Survival behaviors, described as understandably normative responses to horrible conditions, consist of self-referencing behavior (processing/assessing environment for presence of threat), egocentrism, perseveration, anger, withdrawal and shutting down, and splitting (dichotomizing people as good and bad).

Root's analysis provides a thought-provoking consideration and pushes beyond a traditional consideration of trauma as considered in PTSD, and is highly applicable to discussion of the impact of racism and sexism on mental health.

Source:
Root, M. (1992). Reconstructing the impact of trauma on personality. In L. Brown, & M. Ballou (Eds.), Personality and psychopathology (pg. 229-265). New York: Guilford.

Suggestions for Additional Readings

Adams, H., & Sutker, P. (Eds.) (1984). Comprehensive handbook of psychopathology. New York: Plenum Press.

Aldridge-Morris, R. (1989). Multiple personality: An exercise in deception. Hillsdale, NJ: Erlbaum

Andreasen, N. (1984). The broken brain: The biological revolution in psychiatry. New York: Harper & Row.

Bayh, B. (1983). Myths and realities: A report of the national commission on the insanity defense. Arlington, VA: National Mental Health Association.

Beck, A. (1967). Depression: Clinical, experimental and theoretical aspects. New York: Hoeber.

Beck, A., & Emery, G. (1985). Anxiety disorders and phobias: A cognitive perspective. New York: Basic Books.

Beers, S. (1981). A mind that found itself. Pittsburgh: University of Pittsburgh Press.

Bootzin, R., & Acocella, J. (1988). Abnormal psychology: Current perspectives (5th ed.). New York: Random House.

Braun, B. (1988). Treatment of multiple personality disorder. Washington, DC: American Psychiatric Association.

Burns, D. (1980). Feeling good. New York: Avon.

Burrow, T. (1979). A search for man's sanity: The selected letters of Trigant Burrow with biographical notes. Salem, NH: Ayer.

Carson, R., Butcher, J., & Coleman, J. (1988). Abnormal psychology and modern life. Glenview, IL: Scott, Foresman.

Dain, N. (1980). Clifford Beers: Advocate for the insane. Pittsburgh: University of Pittsburgh Press.

Davison, G., & Neale, J. (1990). Abnormal psychology. New York: Wiley.

Gaw, A. (Ed.) (1993). Culture, ethnicity, and mental illness. Washington, DC: American Psychiatric Press.

Gottesnman, I. (1991). Schizophrenia genesis: The origins of madness. New York: Freeman.

Holmes, D. (1991). Abnormal psychology. New York: HarperCollins.

Karno, M., Golding, J., Burnam, M., Hough, R., Escobar, J., Wells, K., & Boyer, R. (1989). Anxiety disorders among Mexican Americans and non-Hispanic Whites in Los Angeles. The journal of nervous and mental disease, 177, 202-209.

Laing, R. (1985). Wisdom, madness, and folly: The making of a psychiatrist. New York: McGraw-Hill.

Lilienfeld, S. (1995). Seeing both sides: Controversies in abnormal psychology. Pacific Grove, CA: Brooks/Cole.

Masling, J., & Bornstein, R. (1993). Psychoanalytic perspectives in psychopathology. Washington, DC: American Psychological Association.

Neal, A., & Turner, S. (1991). Anxiety disorders research with African Americans: Current status. Psychological Bulletin, 109, 400-410.

Rapport, J. (1989). The boy who couldn't stop washing: The experience and treatment of obsessive-compulsive disorder. New York: Dutton.

Robins, L., & Regier, D. (1991). Psychiatric disorders in America: The epidemiologic catchment area survey. New York: Free Press.

Rosenhan, D. (1973). On being sane in insane places. Science, 179, 250-258.

Seligman, M. (1975). Helplessness: On depression, development, and death. San Francisco: Freeman.

Spanos, N., Weekes, J., & Bertrand, L. (1985). Multiple personality: A social psychological perspective. Journal of Abnormal Psychology, 94, 362-376.

Styron, W. (1990). Darkness visible: A memoir of madness. New York: Random House.

Torrey, E. (1988). Surviving schizophrenia: A family manual. New York: Harper & Row.

Travis, C. (1988). Overview of eating disorders. In Women and health psychology: Mental health issues (pg. 133-156). Hillsdale, NJ: Erlbaum.

Travis, C. (1988). Eating disorders: Etiology and treatment. In Women and health psychology: Mental health issues (pg. 157-176). Hillsdale, NJ: Erlbaum

Wilson, R. (1986). Don't panic. New York: HarperPerennial.

Wurtzel, E. (1995). Prozac nation: Young and depressed in America. New York: Riverhead Books.

In-Class Activities and Demonstrations

1. **TRAIL Blazing:** Using **Transparency Masters 14.1-14.6**, review with students the "Checking Your TRAIL" sections in the chapter. Have students work in small groups to answer the questions and then review with the class as a whole to tie the text reading to activity in class.

2. **Reaching Critical Mass:** Using **Transparency Masters 14.7-14.9**, review with students the "Critical Thinking" sections in the chapter. Have students work in small groups to answer the questions and then review with the class as a whole to tie the text reading to activity in class.

3. **Getting Down to IT:** Using **Transparency Masters 14.10-14.15**, review the "Integrative Thinking" sections in the chapter with students. Have students work in small groups to answer the questions and then review with the class as a whole to tie the text reading to activity in class.

4. **What is your diagnosis?**: Using **Handout 14.1** students are to read 10 scenarios and then identify both specific diagnoses and the general class of disorders.

   Source:
   Brown, B. (1998). In Instructor's resource manual to accompany Wade/Tavris' Psychology (5th ed.) (pg.568-569). New York: Longman.

5. **Identifying the "mentally ill"**: For this exercise, 6 student volunteers will be needed to act out different roles that they are assigned. Pick 6 different roles and write them on a 3x5 card. Gardner (1981) suggests coordinating the roles in a skit where the 6 people are at a bus stop waiting for the bus and the sixth person is trying to determine if s/he is at the right bus, when it will come, etc. The 5 remaining volunteers are to act out their roles in relation to the sixth person's catalyst questions. The students in the audience are to observe the 6 volunteers and then attempt to assign roles to each of the six people. The kicker here is that the sixth person role is entitled "mentally ill person". After the skit is concluded and students make their role assignments for skit volunteers, discussion about role assignments and, in particular, who was judged to be mentally ill (and why) follows. General discussion of interpreting mental illness on the basis of behavioral cues can add to your presentation of defining mental illness.

   Source:
   Gardner, J. (1981). Mental illness. In L. Benjamin, & K. Lowman (Eds.), Activities handbook for the teaching of psychology (pg. 199-200). Washington, DC: American Psychological Association.

6. **Sex role stereotypes and mental health**: Students may find the following exercise to be informative combined with a discussion on their perceptions of "mentally healthy" people. Based on the Broverman et al. (1970) findings that perceptions of mentally healthy men showed more overlap with perceptions of a mentally healthy person than did perceptions of mentally healthy women. In short, what was considered healthy for a woman was not the same as what was considered mentally healthy for a man or person in general. Use the three versions of **Handout 14.2** to see if your students replicate that finding. Discussion around the social construction of mental and sociocultural influences on mental health can be tied to this activity.

   Source:
   Broverman, I., Broverman, D., Clarkson, F. Rosenkrantz, P., & Vogel, S. (1970). Sex role stereotypes and clinical judgments of mental health. Journal of Consulting and Clinical Psychology, 34, 1-7.

7. **DSM in the classroom**: David Young has developed a fairly extensive class activity for using the DSM in the classroom. This suggestion represents a modification of his exercise. After presenting an overview of the multiaxial nature of the DSM-IV, provide students with access to the DSM-IV for use in the project. You may also wish to provide students with a summary of the different diagnoses possible under Axes I-III and the rating levels for Axes IV-V. Then, using **Handout 14.3**, have students watch a contemporary popular film in which at least one character has a psychological disorder. Some examples include *As Good As It Gets, Rainman, One Flew Over the Cuckoo's Nest, 12 Monkeys, Seven, Silence of the Lambs, The Net, Copycat, Mister Jones, Single White Female, Leaving Las Vegas, Sybil, When Rabbit Howls, or The Fisher King*, but there may be many others with which you are familiar. (Note: students may need to be warned of graphic/explicit content of some films). After watching the film, students are to use Handout Master 14.3 to make their "diagnosis" of the character they've selected. The exercise allows for discussion of the use of the DSM-IV in diagnosis, potential misapplications of unskilled diagnosticians. Larger discussions concerning the gender and racial biases discussed in Uba and Huang are also a possibility.

   Source:
   Young, D. (1990). Bringing the clinic into the undergraduate classroom. In V. Makosky, C. Sileo, L. Whittemore, C. Landry, & M. Skutley (Eds.), Activities handbook for the teaching of psychology (pg. 163-169). Washington, DC: American Psychological Association

Sources for Additional Activities

Arnold, J. (1990). The psychosocial family tree. In V. Makosky, C. Sileo, L. Whittemore, L. Landry, & M. Skutley (Eds). Activities handbook for the teaching of psychology (Vol. 3). (pg. 151-153). Washington DC: American Psychological Association.

Benjamin, L. & Lowman, K. (1981). Activities handbook for the teaching of psychology. Washington DC: American Psychological Association.

Domino, G. (1980). Altering attitudes toward suicide in an abnormal psychology course. Teaching of Psychology, 7, 239-240.

Fernald, C. (1987). Feeling abnormal: A simulation of deviancy. In V. Makosky, L. Whittemore, & A. Rogers (Eds.), Activities handbook for the teaching of psychology (Vol. 2) (pg. 179-181). Washington, DC: American Psychological Association.

Fleming, M, Piedmont, R., & Hiam, C. (1990). Images of madness: Features films in teaching psychology. Teaching of Psychology, 17, 185-187.

Gardner, R. (1980). Exercises for general psychology. Minneapolis: Burgess.

Gilliland, K. (1982). Use of drama students as "clients" in teaching abnormal psychology. Teaching of Psychology, 9, 120-121.

Gorman, M. (1984). Using the *Eden Express* to teach introductory psychology. Teaching of Psychology, 11, 39-40.

Halonen, J. 1995). Chapter 12: Psychological disorders. In The critical thinking companion for Introductory Psychology. New York: Worth Publishers.

Hubbard, R., & McIntosh, J. (1992). Integrating suicidology into abnormal psychology classes: The revised facts on suicide quiz. Teaching of Psychology, 19, 163-165.

LeUnes, A. (1984). The institutional tour: Some reflections. Teaching of Psychology, 11, 42-43.

Lyons, M., Bradley, C., & White, J. (1984). Video taping and abnormal psychology: Dramatized clinical interviews. Teaching of Psychology, 11, 41-42.

Osberg, T. (1992). The disordered monologue: A classroom demonstration of the symptoms of schizophrenia. Teaching of Psychology, 19, 47-48.

Perkins, D. (1991). A case-study assignment to teach theoretical perspectives in abnormal psychology. Teaching of Psychology, 18, 97-99.

Puente, A. (1990). Understanding abnormal behavior: Wearing the other shoe. In V. Makosky, C. Sileo, L. Whittemore, L. Landry, & M. Skutley (Eds). Activities handbook for the teaching of psychology (Vol. 3). (pg. 174-175). Washington DC: American Psychological Association.

Rabinowitz, F. (1989). Creating the multiple personality: An experiential demonstration for an undergraduate abnormal psychology class. Teaching of Psychology, 16, 69-71.

Ragland, R. (1990). Doing deviant behavior. In V. Makosky, L. Whittemore, & A. Rogers (Eds.), Activities handbook for the teaching of psychology (Vol. 2) (pg. 177-178). Washington, DC: American Psychological Association.

Scogin, F. & Rickard, H. (1987). A volunteer program for abnormal psychology students: Eighteen years and still going strong. Teaching of Psychology, 14, 95-97.

Singelis, T. (1998). Teaching about culture, ethnicity, & diversity: Exercises and planned activities. Thousand Oaks, CA: Sage.

White, G. (1977). An abnormal psychology community-based interview assignment. Teaching of Psychology, 4, 200-202.

Whitford, F. (1998). Who is crazy? In Quick guide to the Internet for psychology (pg. 93-94). Boston: Allyn and Bacon.

Young, D. (1990). Bringing the clinic into the undergraduate classroom. In V. Makosky, C. Sileo, L. Whittemore, L. Landry, & M. Skutley (Eds). Activities handbook for the teaching of psychology (Vol. 3). (pg. 163-169). Washington DC: American Psychological Association.

World Wide Web: Check out the following WWW sites for information and activities relevant to this section of the text!
- Addison Wesley Longman's Website -- **http://longman.awl.com/**
- PsychZone link -- **http://longman.awl.com/**
- Psych Web -- **http://www.gasou.edu/psychweb/psychweb.htm**
- Self-Quizzes for Introductory Psychology -- **http://www.gasou.edu/psychweb/selfquiz/selfquiz.htm**
- Psychology Jumping Stand -- **http://www.indiana.edu:80/~iuepsyc/PsycJump.html**
- The Psychology Place -- **http://www.psychplace.com**
- Mental health/psychological disorders--**http://mentalhealth.com/**
  or
  http://www.grohol.com/
  or
  http://www.psychlink.com/
  or
  http://http://www.nimh.nih.gov/
  or
  http:/www1.rider.edu/~suler/tcp.html
  or
  http://www.mental-health.com/PsychScapes/home.html
  or
  http://www.shef.ac.uk/~psyc/InterPsych/inter.html
  or
  http://http://www.webweaver.net/psych/
  or
  http://www.cmhc.com/
  or
  http://www.mhsource.com/
  or
  http://netra01.colchsfc.ac.uk/~psycholgy/rosenhan.htm
  or
  http://library.scar.utoronto.ca/ClassicsC42/Fecteau/WEBPAGE/PSYCH.HTM
  or
  http://www.nimh.nih.gov/research/amer.htm
  or
  http://www.mentalhealth.com/p.html
- Depression--**http://sandbox.xerox.com/pair/cw/testing.html**
  or
  http://www.cmhc.com/disorders/sx22.htm
  or
  http://www.ndmda.org/ID.HTM
  or
  http://www.psycom.net/depression.central.html
  or

http://www.apa.org/pubinfo/depress.html
or
http://www.psych/helsinki.fi/~janne/asdfaq/
- Bipolar--http://www.cmhc.com/disorders/sx20.htm
or
http://www.pendulum.org/info.htm
- Anxiety disorders--http://www.adaa.org.1a_doors/1a_01.htm
- Phobia--http://www.sonic.net/~fredd/phobia1.html
- OCD--http://www.fairlite.com/ocd/
- Panic disorder--http://www.medaccess.com/panic/panic_01.html
or
http://heirisc.cs.binghamton.edu/~slands/ajp/panic.htm
or
http://www.algy.com/anxiety
- Somatoform disorders--
http://housecall.orbisnews.com/sponsors/aafp/topics/common/somato/page0.html
or
http://www.cmhc.com/disorders/sx94.htm
or
http://housecall.orbisnews.com/databases/ami/convert/000955.html
- Eating disorders--http://www.stud.unit.no/studorg/ikstrh/ed/
- Dissociative disorders--http://www.cmhc.com/disorders/sx46.htm
or
http://www.cmhc.com/disordrs/sx87.htm
or
http://www.dhearts.org/libraries/read/treatmpd.html
or
http://www.auburn.edu/~mcquedr/psyinfo/mpd.htm
or
http://www.tezcat.com/~tina/dissoc.shtml
- Schizophrenia--http://www.cmhc.com/disorders/sx31.htm
or
http://www.healthanswers.com/database/ami/converted/000928.html
or
http://www.mentalhealth.com/dis/p20-ps01.html
or
http://www.mentalhealth.com/book/p40-sc02.html
or
http://www.psyweb.com/Mdisord/schid.html
or
http://www.schizophrenia.com/
or
http://www.mhsource.com/advocacy/narsad/schiz.html

- Personality disorders--
  http://www.healthguide.com/Personality/default.htm
  or
  http://personality disorders.cmhc.com/
- Antisocial PD--**http://www.mentalhealth.com/dis/p20-pe05.html**
- The DSM-IV--**http://www.psych.org.clin_res/q_a.html**
  or
  http://www.apa.org/science/lib.html

Audio-Visual Support
Films/Videos:

Overview
- *Discovering Psychology: Psychopathology* (Annenberg, 30 minutes)
- *Back From Madness: The Struggle for Sanity* (FFHS, 53 minutes)
- *Mental Illness* (FFHS, 23 minutes)
- *Mysteries of the Mind* (FFHS, 58 minutes)
- **Mistreating the Mentally Ill* (FFHS, 56 minutes)
- *Diverting the Mentally Ill from Jail* (FFHS, 25 minutes)
- *Madness* (Brooks, 58 minutes)
- *The World of Abnormal Psychology* (PBS, 60 minutes each)
  Relevant program titles: Looking at Abnormal Behavior
  The Anxiety Disorders
  Personality Disorders
  Mood Disorders
  The Schizophrenias
- **Abnormal Behavior** (CRM, 26 minutes)

DSM/Diagnostic vignettes
- *Diagnosis according to the DSM-IV* (FFHS, 58-69 minutes)
  Program 1: Interviews with Major Depressive Disorder, Dipolar, Male hypoactive disorder and male erectile disorder.
  Program 2: Interviews with panic disorder, obsessive-compulsive disorder, schizophrenia, amnesic disorder.
  Program 3: Interviews with antisocial personality disorder, alcohol dependence and alcohol abuse, anorexia nervosa; series conclusion
- *Psychopathology-Diagnostic Vignettes* (IU, 35 minutes each)
  Relevant programs: Dysthymic Disorder and Major Affective Disorders
  Bipolar Affective Disorders
  Schizophrenic Disorders

Anxiety disorders
- *Panic Attack: Causes and Treatments* (FFHS, 29 minutes)
- *Coping with Phobias* (FFHS, 28 minutes)
- *When Panic Strikes* (FFHS, 19 minutes)
- *Obsessive-Compulsive Disorder* (FFHS, 24 minutes)
- *The Compulsive Mind* (FFHS, 28 minutes)
- *Obsessive-Compulsive Disorder: An Alternative Treatment* (FFHS, 15 minutes)
- *Children with OCD* (FFHS, 15 minutes)
- *Anxiety: The Endless Crisis* (IU, 59 minutes)
- *Phobias* (FFHS, 28 minutes)

- *Attacking Anxiety* (Veritas, 28 minutes)
- *Panic Prison* (MTP, 28 minutes)
- *When Panic Strikes* (FFHS, 19 minutes)
- *Why Am I Doing This?* (AIMS, 15 minutes)

Mood disorders
- *Schizophrenia and Depression* (FFHS, 23 minutes)
- *Depression and Manic Depression* (FFHS, 28 minutes)
- *Prozac Diary* (FFHS, 40 minutes)
- *Nature's Antidepressant* (FFHS, 13 minutes)
- *Unmasking Depression* (FFHS, 28 minutes)
- *Depression: Beating the Blues* (IU, 28 minutes)
- *Depression: Biology of the Blues* (FFHS, 26 minutes)
- *Depression: The Dark Side of the Blues* (BARR, 25 minutes)
- *The Mind: Depression* (HARR, 24 minutes)
- *Depression: Back From the Bottom* (FFHS, 17 minutes)
- *Understanding Depression: Through the Darkness* (FFHS, 24 minutes)
- *Serious Depression* (FFHS, 28 minutes)
- *Portrait of Manic Depression* (FANL, 60 minutes)
- **Women and Depression: When the Blue Won't Go Away* (FFHS, 28 minutes)
- *Teen and Child Depression* (FFHS, 19 minutes)
- *Teen Depression* (FFHS, 16 minutes)
- *The Mind Series* (Worth, varies)
    - Module 30: Mood Disorders--Mania and Depression (approx. 7 minutes)
    - Module 31: Mood Disorders--Hereditary Factors (approx. 5 minutes)
    - Module 32: Mood Disorders--Medication and Talk Therapy (approx. 6 minutes)
    - Module 34: Treating Depression: Electroconvulsive Therapy (approx. 6 minutes)

Suicide
- *Teen Suicide* (FFHS, 35 minutes)
- *Teenage Suicide* (FFHS, 19 minutes)
- *Teenage Suicide: The Ultimate Dropout* (PBS, 29 minutes)
- *"Don't Kill Yourself": One Survivor's Message* (FFHS, 23 minutes)
- *Everything to Live For* (FFHS, 52 minutes)
- *Suicide: The Teenager's Perspective* (FFHS, 26 minutes)
- *Suicide* (FI, 25 minutes)

Somatoform/eating disorders
- *The Silent Hunger: Anorexia and Bulimia* (FFHS 46 minutes)
- *Eating Disorders* (FFHS, 26 minutes)
- *Eating Disorders: The Hunger Within* (FFHS, 42 minutes)
- *An Anorexic's Tale: The Brief Life of Catherine* (FFHS, 80 minutes)

- *Dying to Be Thin* (FFHS, 28 minutes)
- *Self-Image and Eating Disorders: A Mirror for the Heart* (FFHS, 24 minutes)
- *Diet Unto Death: Anorexia Nervosa* (MOTO, 16 minutes)
- *Dieting: The Danger Point* (CRM, 20 minutes)
- *You, Your Body, and Your Self-Image* (FFHS, 28 minutes)

Schizophrenic disorders
- *Schizophrenia and Depression* (FFHS, 23 minutes)
- *Preventing Relapse in Schizophrenia* (FFHS, 18 minutes)
- *Unlocking the Secrets of Schizophrenia* (FFHS, 21 minutes)
- *Schizophrenia* (FFHS, 28 minutes)
- *Schizophrenia: Out of Mind* (FFHS, 52 minutes)
- *Abnormal Behavior: The Psychoses* (HARR, 22 minutes)
- *Full of Sound and Fury: A Film About Schizophrenia* (IU, 54 minutes)
- *The Brain, Mind, and Behavior Series* (IU, 60 minutes)
    Program 7--Madness
- *The Brain: Schizophrenia* (PBS, 60 minutes)
- *The Brain Series* (Annenberg, varies)
    Module 25: Schizophrenia (approx. 6 minutes)
    Module 26: Schizophrenia--Etiology (6 minutes)
    Module 27: Schizophrenia--Treatment and Research (approx. 6 minutes)
- *Schizophrenia: Surviving in the World of Normals* (Wellness, 58 minutes)
- *Through Madness: The Subjective Experience of Psychotic Experience* (Filmakers, 28 minutes)

Dissociative disorders
- *Multiple Personality Disorder: In the Shadows* (FFHS, 24 minutes)
- *The Brain Series* (Annenberg, varies)
    Module 24: Multiple Personality (9 minutes)

Psychology Encyclopedia Laserdisc IV:

Movies
Holmes: Betty; person
   with schizophrenia   2 minutes, 54 sec.   Frames 48040-53266 Side 1

Still Images

Anxiety and the antisocial personality [15.2]	Frame 53570	Side all
Drugs and Vietnam veterans [15.3]	53571	all

Transparency Master 14.1: Checking Your TRAIL 14.1

I. Name and explain five different ways the psychologists have defined abnormality.

II. The DSM-IV describes psychological disorders according to a descriptive medical model. Explain why this "checklist" approach has been criticized by some psychologists.

III. Give one example of a case in which the signs and symptoms of a psychological disorder lack functional equivalence among different cultures.

IV. What general explanation do biopsychosocial psychologists give for the existence of psychological disorders?

Transparency Master 14.2: Checking Your TRAIL 14.2

I. **Name four types of anxiety disorders.**

II. **Obsessive-compulsive disorder is characterized by obsessions that _____ anxiety, and compulsions that _____ anxiety.**
   A. increase, further increase
   B. increase, decrease
   C. decrease, decrease
   D. decrease, increase

III. **State one hypothesis regarding the biological basis of anxiety disorders, such as panic disorder and phobias.**

IV. **The psychodynamic explanation of anxiety disorders suggests that symptoms are defense mechanisms against anxiety. Give an example to illustrate how a defense mechanism could underlie an anxiety disorder.**

Transparency Master 14.3: Checking Your TRAIL 14.3

I. **True or False: A profound indifference to life activities is one of the two hallmark features of major depression.**

II. **Eshita complains to her doctor during her annual checkup that she is very tired and feels depressed. She cannot concentrate well, although she is keeping up with her schoolwork. Yet, during the previous week, she felt energetic and excited all the time, and found herself talking on the phone late into the night, and sleeping very little. What type of mood disorder might Eshita be experiencing?**

III. **Ever since Leroy failed his midterm, he cuts classes, stays in his room all day, does not bother to bathe, avoids his friends, and complains that he is a loser. How might a cognitive psychologist explain his depression?**

IV. **Which of the following factors was not mentioned as a significant contributor to the gender difference in depressive disorders?**
   A. **exposure to social stressors**
   B. **coping style**
   C. **biological vulnerability**
   D. **physical size**

Transparency Master 14.4: Checking Your TRAIL 14.4

I. Schizophrenia features disturbances in ____, ____, ____, and ____.

II. Jackson, a college student, begins to believe that his neighbors are trying to kill him by sending electricity into his body when he is asleep. He is probably experiencing ____.
   A. a delusion of grandeur
   B. a delusion of persecution
   C. hallucination
   D. delusion of reference

III. The signs and symptoms of schizophrenia cluster into three factors. Describe each factor.

IV. Which of the following biological conditions were not mentioned as being associated with schizophrenia?
   A. fetal exposure to influenza virus
   B. enlarged brain ventricles
   C. dopamine sensitivity
   D. serotonin sensitivity

Transparency Master 14.5: Checking Your TRAIL 14.5

I. Shoshana is 10% below her normal body weight, yet she menstruates regularly. She carefully restricts her diet because she is terrified of becoming fat. About every three or four days, she binges on peanut butter sandwiches then makes herself throw up. Shoshana shows signs and symptoms of _____.
   A. eating problems
   B. bulimia nervosa
   C. anorexia nervosa
   D. no problem

II. What is the biopsychosocial view on possible causes of eating disorders?

III. Ernesto cannot feel anything in his left hand. A medical exam shows that his symptom has no medical cause. He may have _____.

IV. After screaming hateful words at her father, Salma left the house. That evening, her father died of a sudden heart attack. Since then, Salma has lost her voice. How would the learning approach explain her conversion symptom?

Transparency Master 14.6: Checking Your TRAIL 14.6

I. Psychogenic amnesia involves the loss of _____, whereas psychogenic fugue involves the loss of one's _____, along with travel away from familiar surroundings.

II. Professor Arnold acts very friendly and encouraging some days. He jokes with students and invites them out to lunch. On other days, he is mean and sarcastic, humiliating students in class and raising his voice. He seems to have two different personalities. Does Professor Arnold have a dissociative identity disorder?

III. What are the three categories of personality disorders described in the DSM-IV?

IV. Describe the characteristic behaviors of a person with antisocial personality disorder.

Transparency Master 14.7: Critical Thinking 14.1

In most situations, deliberately cutting oneself or others is considered to be abnormal. Suggest two situations in which such behavior might be considered normal.

Transparency Master 14.8: Critical Thinking 14.2

Some researchers have suggested that the definition of PTSD should be modified to include the experience of being treated inferior or subhuman as the result of racial and gender discrimination (Fullilove et al., 1992). What arguments could you make in support of and against this suggestion?

Transparency Master 14.9: Critical Thinking 14.3

Consider for a moment Thomas Huskey's plea of innocence for the murders committed by his alternate personality, Kyle. If you were Huskey's lawyer, what would you argue in his defense? If you were the prosecuting attorney, what would you argue?

Transparency Master 14.10: Integrative Thinking 14.1

Regression was described in the Stress, Coping & Health chapter. What is regression and how is it supposedly related to unconscious conflicts?

Transparency Master 14.11: Integrative Thinking 14.2

Recall the discussion of serotonin in the Biopsychology chapter. What is serotonin's general role? Explain how reduced serotonin levels could lead to symptoms of obsessive-compulsive disorder.

Transparency Master 14.12: Integrative Thinking 14.3

Based on your understanding of social learning, operant conditioning, and classical conditioning in the Learning chapter, which learning theory is illustrated by a child who develops a fear of flying after becoming nauseated on a bumpy airplane flight?

Transparency Master 14.13: Integrative Thinking 14.4

Validity and reliability of test items was discussed in the Introductory and the Cognition & Intelligence chapters. Explain what it means for a depression scale to have validity and reliability when used with men.

Transparency Master 14.14: Integrative Thinking 14.5

Researchers believe that people with schizophrenia have garbled thoughts because they are unable to focus their attention. What role might dopamine, discussed in the Biopsychology chapter, play in their disturbed thinking?

Transparency Master 14.15: Integrative Thinking 14.6

Consider the example of Charles, the chemistry graduate student who seduces his female students and who was charged with sexual harassment. The defense mechanism of rationalization was described in the Stress, Coping, & Health chapter. Explain how Charles rationalized the behavior that caused his student to sue him.

Handout Master 14.1: What is your diagnosis?

What is your diagnosis?

Instructions: For each case listed below, state the general class of disorders to which that disorder belongs (anxiety disorders, mood disorders, personality disorders, dissociative disorders, somatoform disorders, or schizophrenia) and give a specific diagnosis.

1. Tony sometimes seems very "wound up." At those times he seems full of energy, talks very rapidly and makes very grandiose plans. One time he gave away all of his belongings and was planning to move to Washington, DC so he could advise the President. At these times he also seems to need almost no sleep. During other periods of time Tony seems very "down." During these times he doesn't take care of himself. He seems to want to sleep all the time, and he often makes thinly veiled references to wanting to commit suicide.
    General class of disorder _____ **Specific diagnosis** _____

2. Brad is a college wrestler who desperately wants to wrestle at a weight class 2 levels below what he currently weighs next year. To this, he has not eaten more than minimal amounts of food and finds that he thinks even water is likely to add calories to his diet so he's severely limited that too. He's begun using laxatives to hasten his weight loss.
    General class of disorder _____ **Specific diagnosis** _____

3. Judith has not left her house for several months. When she tries to go out, she experiences great anxiety. She says she is afraid that if she leaves her house to go somewhere, she will not be able to get back. Before all this started Judith seemed fairly normal except for having several episodes where, for no apparent reason, her heart started pounding, she started to sweat profusely, and she experienced all the symptoms of fear and terror. One of the reasons she is afraid to leave the house is because she is afraid she will have one of these episodes again. (Hint: there are two specific diagnoses here.)
    General class of disorder _____ **Specific diagnosis** _____
    Specific diagnosis _____

4. Miwha sleeps a lot, has great difficulty getting out of bed in the morning, and generally does not want to do anything. She has stopped seeing friends whom she used to see often, and declines all invitations to do things socially. Her most common response is "I just don't feel like it." She looks sad all the time and does not seem to take pleasure in everyday activities. This has been going on for the past two months.
    General class of disorder _____ **Specific diagnosis** _____

5. Patricia is a 44-year-old female who reports that she has periods of time where she cannot remember what she has done. She reports that after one such period she received a telephone call from a man who claimed to have met her in a bar where she was "the life of the party." She had also told the man her name was Priscilla. Patricia thinks that this is odd because she does not drink, and she is a rather shy and retiring person. However, the man had her correct telephone number and was able to give a good physical description of her.
       General class of disorder _____ **Specific diagnosis** _____

6. Jaunita is a 34-year-old female showing signs of disorganized thought and flat affect. She says that she hears voices telling her to do things. She believes that her behavior is being controlled by other people and she thinks that all her former friends have formed a conspiracy and are out to get her. She also tends toward repetitive, highly ritualized behavior.
       General class of disorder _____ **Specific diagnosis** _____

7. Zachary is a 17-year-old male who appears to be quite charming. He uses that charm in a very manipulative way, however, and has recently been arrested for frauding several people in his neighborhood out of thousands of dollars on a phony investment scheme. His parents were continually frustrated with him as a child by his frequent lies and skipping out of school so frequently that the principal threatened to prevent him from moving into high school due to absences.
       General class of disorder _____ **Specific diagnosis** _____

8. Samual feels dirty unless he bathes and changes clothes at least four times a day, and he is fastidious about the house as well. Every room is scrubbed at least twice a week and the bathroom is fully cleaned several times every day. In fact, he cannot leave the house in the morning unless he has cleaned it twice with strong disinfectants.
       General class of disorder _____ **Specific diagnosis** _____

9. Although he was not personally injured, Jose has had problems since the earthquake two years ago. He is listless and quarrelsome and sleeps fitfully, reliving the quake in nightmarish dreams.
       General class of disorder _____ **Specific diagnosis** _____

10. Frank was attending college in San Francisco during the recent earthquake. He lived in the area that was hardest hit by the quake. Frank was not home when the earthquake hit and was not injured in any way, but when he returned home he found his building demolished and his two roommates had been crushed to death. Frank immediately drove himself to the airport, bought a ticket to Boston, and got on the plane. His parents found him on their doorstep in Boston the next morning. Frank remembers nothing about the earthquake and nothing about going to college in San Francisco. The last thing he remembers is being a high school student and living with his parents in Boston.
       General class of disorder _____ **Specific diagnosis** _____

Handout Master 14.2: Perceptions of Mental Health

Perceptions of Mental Health

Instructions: Using the list below, check each item that describes a mature, healthy, socially competent adult person.

_____	aggressive	_____	easily influenced by others
_____	concerned about appearance	_____	objective
_____	ambitious	_____	self-confident
_____	acts as a leader	_____	dependent
_____	hides emotions	_____	likes numbers and the sciences
_____	sneaky	_____	direct
_____	emotional	_____	passive
_____	active	_____	gets excited during crises
_____	logical	_____	adventurous
_____	competitive	_____	submissive
_____	gets feelings hurt easily	_____	avoids aggression
_____	cries easily	_____	is indecisive
_____	has strong needs for security		

Handout Master 14.2: Perceptions of Mental Health

Perceptions of Mental Health

Instructions: Using the list below, check each item that describes a mature, healthy, socially competent adult male.

_____	aggressive	_____	easily influenced by others
_____	concerned about appearance	_____	objective
_____	ambitious	_____	self-confident
_____	acts as a leader	_____	dependent
_____	hides emotions	_____	likes numbers and the sciences
_____	sneaky	_____	direct
_____	emotional	_____	passive
_____	active	_____	gets excited during crises
_____	logical	_____	adventurous
_____	competitive	_____	submissive
_____	gets feelings hurt easily	_____	avoids aggression
_____	cries easily	_____	is indecisive
_____	has strong needs for security		

Handout Master 14.2: Perceptions of Mental Health

Perceptions of Mental Health

Instructions: Using the list below, check each item that describes a mature, healthy, socially competent adult female.

_____ aggressive	_____ easily influenced by others
_____ concerned about appearance	_____ objective
_____ ambitious	_____ self-confident
_____ acts as a leader	_____ dependent
_____ hides emotions	_____ likes numbers and the sciences
_____ sneaky	_____ direct
_____ emotional	_____ passive
_____ active	_____ gets excited during crises
_____ logical	_____ adventurous
_____ competitive	_____ submissive
_____ gets feelings hurt easily	_____ avoids aggression
_____ cries easily	_____ is indecisive
_____ has strong needs for security	

Handout Master 14.3: What is your diagnosis?

What is your diagnosis?

Instructions: After watching a film that portrays a person with a psychological disorder, complete the following diagnosis based on class discussions of the DSM-IV.

Historical antecedents to the problem:

Current observations of the person:

Axis I: Major Clinical Conditions
Data observed:

Disorders noted:

Axis II: Personality Disorders
Data observed:

Disorders noted:

Axis III: Physical Disorders and Conditions
Data observed:

Disorders noted:

Axis IV: Severity of Psychosocial Stressors
Rating: _____
Data:

Axis V: Highest Level of Adaptive Functioning
Rating: _____
Data:

CHAPTER 15

THERAPY

- **Chapter Overview**
  Learning Objectives
  Chapter Outline

- **Additional Lecture Ideas**
  Lecture Topics
  Additional Readings

- **In-Class Activities and Demonstrations**
  Activities and Demonstrations
  Sources for Additional Activities

- **World Wide Web**

- **Audio-Visual Support**

- **Handout and Transparency Masters**

Chapter Overview

Learning Objectives

After studying this chapter, you should be able to do the following:

1. Identify the similarities and differences between spiritual and scientific treatments.

2. Explain the benefits and risks of the three principal biomedical therapies.

3. Describe the goals and techniques of the four traditional psychological therapies.

4. Evaluate the effectiveness of psychotherapy.

5. Explain why the healing relationship is essential to success in all forms of psychotherapy.

Chapter Outline

Therapy

I. Psychological Treatment: Using Spirits and Science
    A. Healing relationships
        1. healers: people who provide treatments meant to reduce another person's abnormal behavior or emotional distress through spiritual, physical, or psychological means
        2. cultural similarities: across cultures, a socially sanctioned healer provides some sort of help to a client/patient who seeks it usually through some kind of structured meeting; sessions may include family members or several clients at once
        3. cultural differences: different cultures view the healing process differently, thus beliefs about cause and type of treatment vary
    B. Spiritual healing
        1. the religio-magical approach: belief that supernatural agents cause abnormal behavior/distress; become troubled by living in disharmony with the spiritual world
        2. variety in therapeutic methods:
            a. examples: *mudang* in Korea and healing traditions of Ndembu culture in Zambia
    C. Scientific healing
        1. the empirical-scientific approach: approach to healing based on rational theories supported by empirical studies
        2. main perspectives:
            a. biological: rely on biomedical therapies such as drugs and medical procedures; used in combination with nonmedical treatments
            b. psychological: a relationship in which clients talk with a psychotherapist in order to reduce, remove, or alter their troubling emotions, attitudes, or thoughts; attribute emotional distress/mental disorders to psychological dysfunction
        3. issues in psychotherapy:
            a. psychotherapists' theoretical perspective
            b. psychotherapists' own cultural values/beliefs
        4. principal types of psychotherapy:
            a. psychodynamic
            b. humanistic
            c. behavioral
            d. cognitive
        5. life as a psychotherapist
            a. expectation that one remains detached regarding outcome of treatment
            b. need for specialized training: focus on development of empathy

    c. adhering to professional standards and following guidelines for professional conduct
    d. licensure requirements
    e. autonomy as a professional
    f. working through managed care organizations
    g. may use combination of biological and psychological interventions esp. if disorder has biological basis; may need psychotherapy for coping

II. Biomedical Approaches: Restoring Normal Biological Functions
   ### A. Electroconvulsive therapy
   1. <u>description</u>: a biomedical treatment primarily used as a last resort for severe depression, in which brief electrical pulses are delivered to the brain
   2. <u>effects</u>: actual effect on brain unknown but thought to change neurotransmitters such as GABA, norepinephrine, serotonin, and dopamine and/or alter brain waves in frontal cortex; alleviates depression in ~ 50% of cases; however, rigorously designed studies on effectiveness have not been done; patient may exhibit confusion/problems with attention after session and some memory loss for up to 6 months afterwards
   3. <u>use as an intervention</u>: public fears, advocacy against use, and negative media portrayals may contribute to less use of ECT as intervention
   ### B. Psychosurgery
   1. <u>description</u>: last resort treatments or procedures designed to destroy or remove abnormal parts of the brain and thus alleviate sever emotional or behavioral problems
        a. example: lobotomy--a psychosurgical procedure in which surgeons cut through several inches of neurons that connect the frontal lobe to the rest of the brain;
   2. <u>effects</u>: 1/3 patients showed improvements after procedure
   3. <u>use as an intervention</u>: original forms of psychosurgery (e.g., lobotomy) no longer done because of questionable benefits; also risks of procedure included excessive bleeding, seizures, infection, undesirable personality changes, death
        a. <u>contemporary version</u>: localized destruction of areas of the limbic system for disorders such as severe depression, OCD, chronic anxiety; still only last resort measure
   ### C. Medications
   1. <u>description</u>: drugs used to treat psychological disorders; began to rise in use in 1950s
   2. <u>types of psychotropics</u>:
        a. antipsychotic
        b. antidepressant
        c. antimanic
        d. antianxiety

3. <u>effects</u>: unlike other mind-altering drugs, tend to not affect persons who do not suffer from psychological disorder; drugs produce biological changes but act of taking drug also produces effects (e.g., placebo effect)
    a. placebo effect: an improvement in symptoms that occurs because the patient expects to feel better, and not as a result of the physical effects of a drug
4. <u>use as an intervention</u>: prescribed by psychiatrists; used in combination with psychotherapy; used with disorders suspected of having biological basis
5. <u>antipsychotic medications</u>: drugs that reduce psychotic symptoms, particularly the positive symptoms of schizophrenia (i.e., hallucinations & delusions); effects due to blocking excessive dopamine activity in brain
    a. proper medication could improve lives of 1/3 to 1/2 people with schizophrenia; not a cure
    b. side effects could include involuntary muscular twitches, rigidity, irregular heart beats, increased blood pressure, increased body temperature; also don't work on negative symptoms of schizophrenia
    c. <u>atypical antipsychotics</u>: new class of antipsychotic medications, thought to work on both positive and negative symptoms; however, are costly and require weekly tests of white blood cell count
6. <u>antidepressant and antimanic medications</u>: psychotropic drugs that alleviate symptoms of depression, reduce mania
    a. effects produced by blocking reuptake of norepinephrine or serotonin
    b. <u>three categories of antidepressants</u>:
        i. <u>selective serotonin reuptake inhibitors</u>: Prozac
        ii. <u>monamine oxidase inhibitors</u>: Nardil
        iii. <u>tricyclics</u>: Elavil
    c. drug of choice depends on patient's level of depression, medical history, body chemistry, eating habits, personality, tolerance for side effects
    d. <u>treatment of bipolar disorder</u>:
        i. <u>lithium carbonate</u>: reduces symptoms of mania perhaps by enhancing serotonin and norepinephrine
        ii. <u>valproate</u>: used in treating epilepsy; an alternative for patients who don't respond to lithium alone
7. <u>antianxiety medications</u>: drugs that reduce symptoms of anxiety
    a. benzodiazepines: control symptoms in 75% of people with panic disorder, phobia, generalized anxiety disorder
        i. <u>side effects</u>: drowsiness, reduced motor coordination (esp. with alcohol); abrupt cessation of drug may produce *rebound anxiety*

ii. not effective with all anxiety disorders such as PTSD or OCD; tricyclics, MAO inhibitors, or SSRIs used in those cases

III. Psychodynamic Approaches: Resolving Unconscious Conflicts
  A. Theoretical basis
     1. psychological disorders result from unconscious conflicts, which usually arise during childhood; insight into nature of conflicts helps person gain mastery over emotions
        a. <u>insight</u>: an understanding of the psychological processes that cause one's own behavior and emotions
        b. <u>principal components of unconscious conflicts</u>:
           i. unacceptable impulses and feelings
           ii. anxiety that these impulses and feelings will enter conscious awareness
           iii. unconscious behaviors that serve as defenses against anxiety or against unacceptable impulses and feelings
        c. behaviors are viewed as symbolic communications of unconscious desires and conflicts; discussions with therapist concerning behaviors uncover unconscious feelings and drives that underlie distress
  B. Psychoanalysis
     1. <u>definition</u>: the original psychodynamic psychotherapy, developed by Sigmund Freud; uses free association, dream analysis, and interpretation of transference to bring clients' unconscious thoughts and feelings into their conscious awareness; believe that people use psychological defenses to repress traumatic memories or unacceptable impulses
     2. <u>description</u>: originally, therapist sat behind client who would lie on couch to encourage client to focus on self and avoid unintentionally influencing client with body language or facial expressions; technique no longer mandatory part of psychoanalysis
     3. <u>techniques & processes</u>:
        a. <u>free association</u>: a psychoanalytic technique in which clients mention any feelings, fantasies, or wishes that come into their mind regardless of how embarrassing, silly, or offensive these thoughts might be
        b. <u>dream analysis</u>: a method of examining clients' dreams and their symbolic meanings as a way to reveal unconscious thoughts and desires
        c. <u>transference relationship</u>: in response to psychoanalysts' passivity and neutrality, emotional reactions arise when client in psychoanalysis attributes another person's feelings and ideas to the therapist; usually the source of the attributed feelings has an important relationship with the client

d. <u>interpretation</u>: when the therapist points out the meaningful, unconscious significance of a client's thoughts, feelings, and actions
    i. <u>resistance</u>: in response to therapists' interpretations, reflects avoidance or rejection of unconscious feelings that are becoming conscious

e. <u>catharsis</u>: the client's experience of emotional release as he or she becomes conscious of emotions, thoughts, or memories for the first time; moments of full insight facilitated by neutral role of therapist who avoids saying/doing anything that reinforces defenses or influences material discussed
    i. <u>corrective emotional experience involved in catharsis</u>: reliving an unresolved conflict and giving it a new outcome

B. Psychodynamic psychotherapies

1. <u>definition</u>: brief forms of psychoanalysis that aim to resolve unconscious conflicts

2. <u>description</u>: few face-to-face sessions with less free association, dream analysis and more active role on part of therapist; focus on resolution of specific conflicts; agree with traditional psychoanalysts on power of corrective emotional experience of catharsis

IV. Humanistic Approaches: Reducing the Barriers to Growth

A. Theoretical basis

1. approaches are designed to help constructive, positive, rational human beings increase maturity and autonomy
    a. assume capacity for actualization
    b. believe people become emotionally distressed, engage in maladaptive behavior when natural desire for personal growth is thwarted
    c. goal of therapy is to help people overcome barriers that interfere with personal growth

B. Client-centered psychotherapy

1. <u>definition</u>: a form of humanistic psychotherapy that uses unconditional positive regard and empathy to restore a consistent relationship between a client's behavior and self-concept; founder = Carl Rogers

2. <u>premises</u>: believe empathy is the key to therapeutic change
    a. <u>active listening</u>: restating the client's feelings in an empathic manner; way in which therapist shows empathy and unconditional positive regard;

C. Gestalt psychotherapy

1. <u>definition</u>: a form of psychotherapy designed to overcome barriers that prevent clients from becoming fully engaged in their emotions, sensations, and thoughts, and that encourages clients to take responsibility for their experiences and feelings; founder = Fritz Perls

  2. <u>premises</u>: self-awareness completes person's total experience and automatically restores one's potential for growth; therapist engages in active encouragement of client
  3. <u>therapeutic techniques</u>: designed to push clients toward full recognition of immediate thoughts and feelings
    a. pointing out when words & behaviors don't match
    b. exaggerating or experimenting with behaviors
    c. <u>two-chair technique</u>: using two chairs, client adopts different perspectives exposing different, opposing parts to personality
    d. comparing wants with actual behaviors
 D. Cultural perspectives on humanistic psychotherapy
  1. <u>cultural differences in therapist assumptions</u>:
    a. individualistic perspectives on self-awareness, self-fulfillment, self-discovery
    b. collectivistic perspectives view personal needs as fundamentally selfish; need to overcome selfishness to live in harmony with others
    c. differing notions between therapist and client on what constitutes personal growth

V. Active Approaches: Consciously Changing Behaviors and Ideas
 A. Behavioral therapy
  1. <u>definition</u>: psychotherapy that uses learning principles to reduce unwanted behaviors; follows basic behaviorist belief that all behaviors are learned
  2. <u>premises</u>: therapy provides clients with new learning experiences designed to alter behavior
  3. <u>basic process</u>:
    a. analyze target behavior
    b. examine trigger situations
    c. identify possible reinforcements
    d. use behavior modification techniques such as systematic desensitization, flooding, behavioral contracts
  3. <u>reinforcement</u>: used to increase desirable behaviors
  4. <u>punishment</u>: used to reduce maladaptive behaviors
    a. <u>aversion therapy</u>: a behavioral therapy technique intended to reduce undesirable behavior by systematically associating it with punishment
    b. <u>example</u>: Antabuse
 B. Cognitive therapies
  1. <u>definition</u>: therapies focusing on distorted thoughts that lead to negative emotional consequences
  2. <u>premises</u>: people actively construct their views of the world through thoughts; biases in thoughts, maladaptive thoughts result in anxiety, depression
    a. <u>examples of biased/distorted thoughts</u>:

                    ii. overgeneralizing
                    ii. polarized thinking
            b. therapy is time-limited and structured; uses instructions & homework
            c. <u>cognitive restructuring</u>: a technique used by cognitive psychotherapies to replace irrational or maladaptive thoughts with rational, adaptive ones
        3. <u>Rational-emotive psychotherapy</u>: a form of cognitive psychotherapy in which therapists use logic, authority, humor, and persuasion to convince clients to give up irrational ideas; founder = Albert Ellis
            a. <u>ABCs of RET</u>:
                    ii. a = activating event
                    ii. b = beliefs following triggering event
                    iii. c = (emotive) consequences of the belief
        4. <u>Cognitive-behavioral psychotherapy</u>: a form of cognitive psychotherapy in which clients discover evidence that can be used to challenge their irrational or distorted ideas; founder = Aaron Beck
            a. <u>premise</u>: uses evidence collected by client as basis for cognitive restructuring
            b. focus on changing automatic thoughts--repetitive, unintentional, conscious thought
            c. <u>process</u>:
                    i. identify/keep diary of automatic thoughts
                    ii. examine assumptions underlying automatic thoughts
                    iii. identify false assumptions
                    iv. conclude evidence either support/contradicts automatic thoughts
            d. <u>effects of therapy</u>:
                    i. PET scan studies

VI. Evaluating Psychotherapy: Overall Outcomes, the Client, and the Therapist
   A. How effective is psychotherapy?
        1. <u>general trends in outcome</u>:
            a. individuals who receive therapy show significant improvement compared to no treatment controls
            b. effects both immediate and long-lasting; on average, dramatic improvement occur throughout first 8-26 sessions; effects of even 12 session can last as long as a year
            c. studies on effectiveness of therapy on severe depression found 1/2 showed reduced symptoms at end of 8 or 16 sessions; 29% still symptom free at end of 1 year; booster sessions may be indicated
            d. <u>cautions</u>: studies assess specific treatment procedures, include carefully selected participants & therapists; results may not reflect experience on many clients and therapists

B. Consumer satisfaction
1. <u>general trends in satisfaction outcomes</u>:
   a. Consumer Reports study: majority of respondents felt psychotherapy helped ease problems, improved ability to function, gave sense of mastery, enhanced personal growth
   b. <u>criticisms</u>:
      i. only 4% of pool answered questions
      ii. lack of control group
      iii. lack of random assignment
      iv. potential inaccuracy of retrospective design (i.e., might have remembered original problem as being worse that it actually was)

C. The therapeutic alliance: A key to psychotherapy
1. <u>definition</u>: the collaborative bond between therapist and client that is essential for success in all types of psychotherapy
   a. key predictor of psychotherapy effectiveness
   b. qualities of successful therapist: positive regard, accurate empathy, warmth, acceptance, honesty, humor, reassurance, affirmation, understanding, help, respect for clients expresses through words and behaviors
2. <u>cultural perspectives on the therapeutic alliance</u>:
   a. different cultural backgrounds of therapist & client may:
      i. complicate definitions of central problem
      ii. result in different ideas about causes of emotional distress and psychological disorders
      iii. may affect client's perception of therapist empathy
   b. therapist flexibility in modifying course of psychotherapy in response to clients' cultural expectation needed; build cultural/social bridges in cultural communities and with clients
3. <u>racial perspectives on the therapeutic alliance</u>:
   a. racism and discrimination may produce sense of cultural mistrust in clients
   b. clients may not talk honestly/openly about experiences of racism/discrimination
   c. successful therapist talks in straightforward manner about race, pays attention to clients' expectations, reflects on own beliefs & feelings about racial issues, recognizes how ethnic/racial identity applies to client and self

4. <u>gender perspectives on the therapeutic alliance</u>:
    a. results of studies provide conflicting evidence about effects of gender of therapist on effectiveness with female clients
    b. <u>problems with studies</u>:
        i. correlational designs
        ii. designs didn't ensure equivalent experience and skill; gender differences found might be due to differences in ability

Additional Lecture Topics
1. <u>**Assessment and treatment of abnormal behavior across cultures**</u>:

Continuing with the theme established in Chapter 14, Matsumoto and Terrell describes assessment as a process that "involves identifying and describing an individual's symptoms within the context of his or her overall level of functioning and environment" (pg. 144). Thus the tools of assessment should, for all intents and purposes, be sensitive to culture and environmental influences on functioning and behavior. In keeping with Uba and Huang's discussion, however, assessment tools have a history of being criticized due to problems of bias and insensitivity to culture, particularly when those tools are transported across cultures without adjustment. Matsumoto and Terrell note that "traditional tools of clinical assessment are primarily based on a standard definition of abnormality and use a standard set of classification criteria for evaluating problematic behavior". When used in cultures that don't share that standard meaning, these measures provide little understanding or misunderstandings regarding the nature of psychopathology and "may mask or fail to capture culturally specific expressions of disorder" (pg. 144). Guidelines for developing measures for cross-cultural assessment emphasize examining cultural definitions of both mental health and mental illness. Additionally some authors suggest that exploring how people use "culturally sanctioned systems of healing" such as folk healers will reveal a more comprehensive view of expression of mental illness, as well as expand on considerations of appropriate treatment options.

It has been observed that traditional treatment methodologies underserve or inappropriately serve a culturally diverse clientele. Moreover, high drop rates and poor treatment outcomes when exposed to traditional therapy has been noted in all non-European American groups, perhaps due to the cultural insensitivity (cf. Sue, 1977; Sue & Zane, 1987; also note the issues raised specifically concerning women of color in the presentation of Margaret Matlin's review noted below). This insensitivity may be manifested in the treatment modalities' assumption of causality not matching that of the client's cultural worldview about abnormality. Matsumoto and Terrell note that people of various cultural orientations may prefer different therapeutic orientations based on how active vs. non-directive the interventions are. Client responses to intervention may also be affected by the match between client and clinician worldviews and attitudes toward treatment, in addition to the client's level of acculturation. A growing area of discussion in the literature centers on the use of culture-specific interventions, such as Naikan and Mortia therapy in Japan, designed to "address the unique definitions and expressions of abnormal behavior in a given culture" (pg. 147). Successful culturally sensitive therapists will have acquired the following skills and awarenesses:

- knowledge of diverse cultures and lifestyles
- skills and comfort with administering innovative treatment interventions
- personal experience in working with a culturally-diverse clientele

- insights concerning his or her own cultural background
- an understanding of how culture influences treatment

Source:
Matsumoto, D. and Terrell, D. (1994). Abnormal psychology: Assessment and treatment of abnormal behavior across cultures. In People: Psychology from a cultural perspective. (pg. 144-148). Pacific Grove, CA: Brooks/Cole

2. **A culture-centered approach to counseling:**

Paul Pedersen describes counseling as "a broadly defined aspect of communication focused on giving help toward the solving or management of personal problems by skilled providers" (pg. 291) that occurs across settings ranging from the formal, structured arrangement in an office to less structured spontaneous settings. He contends that counseling has served a variety of goals historically: psychotherapy, guidance, or psychoeducational. One motive underlying all these goals, however, has been the emphasis on "values based in a Euro-American, dominant culture perspective" that has resulted in counseling that serves only to "support the status quo and protect the interests of a majority culture without regard to the interests of minorities" (pg. 291).

To address this narrow, and ultimately discriminatory focus, Pedersen proposes the use of a culture-centered approach to counseling that emphasizes "*both* the person *and* the cultural context in which that person lives" (pg. 291). Moreover, he notes that the term "culture" should more accurately reflect the multiple cultures that shape an individual's identity. Counseling, from this perspective is best described as occurring "not just with the individual client or counselee but with the many different culture teachers who have taught the individual the values and expectations which shape that person's behavior" (pg. 293). The individual person represents in internal "committee" and the counseling process involves hearing "the internal dialogue among those culture teachers that is taking place inside the person" (pg. 293).

Counselors adopting a culture-centered approach are trained via triadic counseling role playing sessions involving 3 people: a coached "client" and two culturally similar "counselors" voicing the positive and negative aspects of the client's internal dialogue which he or she is speaking but not saying. Via this process, "listening to the client's culture teachers will help counselors understand and translate the values and expectations behind behaviors to find their common ground" (pg. 293). Moreover, culture-centered counseling involves developing "awareness of culturally-learned assumptions, knowledge of culturally relevant facts, and skill for culturally appropriate action" (pg. 293).

Pedersen claims the culture-centered approach carries several advantages to traditional approaches with culturally diverse groups. First, the emphasis on culture will increase counselor's matching of client's cultural values/expectations with an understanding of behaviors. Second, as a result of involvement in the culture-centered approach, counselors will become more aware of how their own culture influences behaviors. Third, the broader definition of culture allows the counselor to uncover common ground with the client. Fourth, the central focus on culture keeps the counselor focused even when the client may be pulled in different directions by his or her internal dialogue. The end result, according to Pedersen, is more accurate diagnosis.

Source:
Pedersen, P. (1994). A culture-centered approach to counseling. In W. Lonner & R. Malpass (Eds.), Psychology and culture (pg. 291-295). Boston: Allyn and Bacon.

3. Reaching the underserved--Mental health services systems and special populations:

Social programs or, in this case, mental health programs are created by governments when the private sector has not provided for the needs of all people. Regarding mental health services, the Community Mental Health Center Act of 1963 authorized the development of a national network of community mental health centers. Highest priority is directed toward provision of services to the elderly, children and adolescents, cultural and ethnic minority groups, and residents in rural regions. Each group has a unique set of problems that require specialized attention.

- the elderly: older persons experience a combination of both biological and social problems that may create mental health issues. The effects of ageism and lack of information/knowledge concerning health issues in the elderly affect their psychological well being.
- children & adolescents: for adequate development, children require both psychological and physical nurturance. Cultural expectations that child care practices are the sole or primary obligations of the child's parents means that some children's needs are not being met due to indifference, abuse, or neglect. Appropriate mental health services for children and adolescents has been found to be lacking.
- cultural & ethnic groups: as discussed in Uba and Huang and other authors in this manual, culture affects understandings for meanings and expression of symptoms and influences assessment and treatment alternatives.
- residents in rural regions: delivery of mental health services in rural regions may be hampered by concerns of the stigma involved with mental illness (esp. in having the diagnosis made known in a small, close-knit community network) and reluctance in mental health professionals to reside in rural regions.

Mental health service delivery is also affected by the fact that many people label problems in terms of physical illness and may first go to a physician before considering psychotherapy. Moreover, people may be more likely to confer with a supportive lay network of healers (i.e., family members) or cultural healers rather than or prior to seeking psychotherapy. To encourage appropriate use of the mental health services systems, the system itself must consider how to design programs so as to encourage their use. This may be done by involving community leaders in running programs, consulting with the folk or native healers used by some cultural groups, and ensuring that programs incorporate cultural practices and traditions. Locating services in the communities would also encourage greater use of those services. Additionally, financing of mental health services, esp. when clients suffer from poverty, remains a significant barrier to service utilization. Finally, service delivery to under-served people must consider the issue of modification of treatment protocols and/or availability of alternative forms of assistance.

Source:
   Snowden, L. & Hines, A. (1994). Reaching the underserved: Mental health services systems and special populations. In W. Lonner & R. Malpass (Eds.), Psychology and culture (pg. 297-302). Boston: Allyn and Bacon.

4. **Treating psychological disorders in women:**
   In her text, *The psychology of women*, Margaret Matlin addresses four topics concerning women and experiences with psychotherapy: sexism in psychotherapy, psychotherapy and women of color, traditional approaches to psychotherapy as they affect women, and alternative therapies that address women's needs.
   - sexism in psychotherapy: According to Matlin's presentation, in 1975, the American Psychological Association surveyed a sample of women and men psychotherapists to determine some ways in which psychotherapy incorporates biased treatment of women. Findings included observations that therapists: might foster traditional gender roles; have low expectations for women's' value as demonstrated by sexist jokes or ignoring violence toward women; may employ sexist psychoanalytic concepts; may regard women as sex objects (i.e., having inappropriate sexual relationships with women clients). More current studies have found that some therapists may lack adequate knowledge about the psychology of women or life issues relevant to women or may have lower expectations for their women clients (as demonstrated by evaluations of women functioning "better" than men who had similar psychological symptoms). Other studies have found therapists to have better recall for the problems of male clients than for those of female clients. Biases exist in differential types of questions asked of clients, with women being asked more about family issues. Matlin notes that little systematic research has been conducted in this area and calls for additional attention to be paid to these issues.
   - psychotherapy and women of color: Compared to White American women, women of color are less likely to use mental-health services for a number of reasons, including lack of awareness of mental health services, shame in talking about personal problems to nonfamily

members, distrust of (especially White) therapists, reluctance to recognize that help is needed, a culturally-based preference for nontherapy interventions, and language barriers. In discussing potential problems for Black, Latina, and Asian-American women, Matlin notes that these women may be disadvantaged in therapy that incorporates at some level cultural stereotypes regarding Black matriarchy and the need for submissiveness in Latinas and Asian-American women. Matlin lists 7 general strategies for therapists who work with women of color, including increasing their knowledge about the culture of minority-group women, developing interventions that respect the client's cultural values, and not making assumptions that client's values are the same as her culture.

- <u>traditional approaches to psychotherapy as they affect women</u>: This is a very interesting section in Matlin's chapter. She reviews ways in which psychodynamic, cognitive-behavioral, and humanistic therapies as well as biomedical interventions may be biased against women. Freud's ideas on women are discussed as the most biased and problematic. Points raised include ideas that the masculine is the human norm within the theory; women are portrayed as narcissistic and masochistic in the theory; women's moral development is less advanced due to never fully resolving the Oedipal complex; penis envy as the basis for women's shame and envy and need to bear (male) children. One critique has offered that, despite contemporary modifications of Freud's original ideas, psychodynamic theory can never really be modified enough to redress these issues. The basic principles of cognitive-behavioral and humanistic therapies are reviewed with the primary criticisms being that neither theory group tends to address the problems of women as having to do with societal limits and gender biases. Noting that psychotropic medications have historically been overly prescribed to women, Matlin presents a "middle-of-the-road" perspective, urging that clinicians remember that medications may not help all people, should be monitored frequently for side effects, and should only be given in combination with psychotherapy (especially assuming that medications will only be given when the situation is serious enough to warrant their use).

- <u>alternative therapies that address women's needs</u>: Four alternative forms of psychotherapy with women are presented. *Nonsexist therapy* involves the fundamental belief that women and men are to be treated equally. Nine guiding steps for engaging in nonsexist therapy are included in her overview, including acknowledging the pervasiveness of sexism in our society, viewing clients as individuals with rights, and avoiding gender-biased tests and language. *Feminist therapy* incorporates the essential qualities of nonsexist therapy but adds to its perspectives the beliefs that "society has been responsible for shaping women's behavior" and power differentials between client and clinician are to be avoided. *Conscious-raising groups* are discussed from the perspectives of the benefits women derive by exploring experiences of and forming bonds with other women. Finally, *assertiveness training* focusing more on "helping groups of women to organize themselves to change the injustices of society" rather than on "fixing" nonassertive women is reviewed.

Source:

Matlin, M. (1993). Treating psychological disorders in women. In The psychology of women (pg. 464-480). Fort Worth, TX: Harcourt Brace Jovanovich.

Suggestions for Additional Readings

Amada, G. (1995). A guide to psychotherapy. New York: Ballantine.

American Association for Counseling and Development (1991). Multiculturalism as a fourth force in counseling (Special issue). Journal of Counseling and Development, 70(1), entire issue.

American Psychiatric Association. (1989). Treatments of psychiatric disorders (Vols. 1-3). Washington, DC: Author.

Atkinson, D., Morten, G., and Sue. D. (1993). Counseling American minorities. Dubuque, IA: Brown & Benchmark.

Baruth, L., & Manning, M. (1999). Multicultural counseling and psychotherapy: A lifespan perspective (2nd ed.). Upper Saddle River, NJ: Merrill.

Beck, J. (1995). Cognitive therapy: Basic and beyond. New York: Guilford.

Berger, P., & Brodie, H. (Eds.) (1986). American handbook of psychiatry: Vol. 8. Biological psychiatry. New York: Basic Books.

Bloom, B. (1984). Community mental health: A general introduction. Pacific Grove, CA: Brooks/Cole.

Brown, L. (1994). Subversive dialogues: Theory in feminist therapy. New York: Basic Books.

Burns, D. (1989). The feeling good handbook. New York: William Morrow.

Christensen, A., & Jacobson, N. (1994). Who (or what) can do psychotherapy: The status and challenge of nonprofessional therapies. Psychological Science, 5, 8-14.

Corey, G. (1996). Case approach to counseling and psychotherapy. Pacific Grove, CA: Brooks/Cole.

Corsini, R. & Wedding, D. (Eds.) (1989). Current psychotherapies. Itasca, IL: Peacock.

Ehrenberg, O., & Ehrenberg, M. (1986). The psychotherapy maze. Northvale, NH: Aronson.

Ellis, A. (1973). Humanistic psychotherapy: The rational-emotive approach. New York: Julian Press.

Engler, J., & Goleman, D. (1992). The consumer's guide to psychotherapy. New York: Simon & Schuster.

Epstein, M. (1995). Thoughts without a thinker: Psychotherapy from a Buddhist perspective. New York: Basic Books.

Eysenck, H. (1952). The effects of psychotherapy: An evaluation. Journal of Consulting Psychology, 16, 319-324.

Fancher, R. (1995). Cultures of healing: Correcting the image of American mental health care. New York: Freeman.

Garfield, S., & Bergin, A. (Eds.) (1986). Handbook of psychotherapy and behavior change. New York: Wiley.

Gonzalez, R., Biever, J., & Gardner, G. (1994). The multicultural perspective in therapy: A social constructionist approach. Psychotherapy, 31, 515-523.

Grasha, A. (1995). Practical applications of psychology (4th ed.). New York: HarperCollins.

Havens, L. (1986). Making contact: Uses of language in psychotherapy. Cambridge, MA: Harvard University Press.

Jackson, M. (1995). Multicultural counseling: Historical perspectives. In J. Ponterotto, J. Casas, L. Suzuki, & C. Alexander (Eds.), Handbook of multicultural counseling (pg. 3-33). Thousand Oaks, CA: Sage.

Kakar, S. (1983). Shamans, mystics, and doctors: A psychological inquiry into India and its healing traditions. Chicago: University of Chicago Press.

Korchin, S. (1976). Modern clinical psychology: Principles of intervention in the clinic and community. New York: Basic Books.

Kottler, J. (1991). The complete therapist. New York: Jossey-Bass.

Kramer, P. (1993). Listening to Prozac: A psychiatrist explores antidepressant drugs and the remaking of the self. New York: Viking.

Krause, I. (1998). Therapy across culture. Thousand Oaks, CA: Sage.

Kutash, I., & Wolf, A. (Eds.) (1993). Psychotherapist's casebook: Theory and technique in the practice of modern therapies. Northvale, NJ: Jason Aronson.

Lee, C. (1995). Counseling for diversity: A guide for school counselors and related professionals. Boston: Allyn and Bacon.

Loeng, F. (1986). Counseling and psychotherapy with Asian-Americans: Review of the literature. Journal of Counseling Psychology, 33, 196-206.

Luborsky, L., Crits-Christoph, P., Mintz, J., & Auerbach, A. (1988). Who will benefit from psychotherapy? New York: Basic Books.

Martin, G., & Pear, J. (1978). Behavior modification: What it is and how to do it. Englewood Cliffs, NJ: Prentice-Hall.

Nevid, J., Rathus, S., & Greene, B. (1994). Abnormal psychology in a changing world (2nd ed.). Englewood Cliffs, NJ: Prentice-Hall.

Phares, E. (1988). Clinical psychology: Concepts, methods, and profession. Pacific Grove, CA: Brooks/Cole.

Price, R., Cowen, E., Lorian, R., & Ramos-McKay, J. (Eds.) (1988). 14 ounces of prevention: A casebook for practitioners. Washington, DC: American Psychological Association.

Rogers, C. (1951). Client-centered therapy. Boston: Houghton.

Sabbagh, K. (1986). The psychology of fringe medicine. The Skeptical Inquirer, 10, 154-158.

Sackeim, H. (1985, June). The case for ECT. Psychology Today, pp. 36-40.

Smith, M., Glass, G., & Miller, R. (1980). The benefits of psychotherapy. Baltimore, MD: Johns Hopkins University Press.

Stern, R., Drummond, L, & Assin, M. (1992). The practice of behavioral and cognitive therapy. New York: Cambridge University Press.

Strauss, J. (1979). Social and cultural influences on psychopathology. In M. Rosenzweig and L. Porter (Eds.). Annual review of psychology, Vol. 29. Palo Alto, CA: Annual Reviews Inc.

Sue, D. (Ed.) (1996). Theory of multicultural counseling and therapy. Pacific Grove, CA: Brooks/Cole.

Sue, D., & Sue, D. (1990). Counseling the culturally different: Theory & practice (2nd ed.). New York: Wiley.

Travis, C. (1988). Women and health psychology: Mental health issues. Hillsdale, NJ: Erlbaum.

Valenstein, E. (Ed.) (1980). The psychosurgery debate. San Francisco: Freeman.

Valenstein, E. (1986). Great and desperate cures: The rise and decline of psychosurgery and other radical treatments for mental illness. New York: Basic Books.

Walker, C. (1991). The history of clinical psychology in autobiography, Vol 1. Pacific Grove, CA: Brooks/Cole.

Walker, C. (1992). The history of clinical psychology in autobiography, Vol 2. Pacific Grove, CA: Brooks/Cole.

Wedding, D., & Corsini, R. (Eds.) (1979). Great cases in psychotherapy. Itasca, IL: Peacock.

Welwood, J. (1983). Awakening the heart: East/West approaches to psychotherapy and the healing relationship. New York: Random House.

Yalom, I. (1989). Love's executioner and other tales of psychotherapy. New York: Basic Books.

Yates, B. (1985). Self-management. Belmont, CA: Wadsworth.

Zeig, J. (Ed.) (1987). The evolution of psychotherapy. New York: Brunner/Mazel.

In-Class Activities and Demonstrations

1. **TRAIL Blazing**: Using **Transparency Masters 15.1-15.4,** review with students the "Checking Your TRAIL" sections in the chapter. Have students work in small groups to answer the questions and then review with the class as a whole to tie the text reading to activity in class.

2. **Reaching Critical Mass**: Using **Transparency Masters 15.5-15.7**, review with students the "Critical Thinking" sections in the chapter. Have students work in small groups to answer the questions and then review with the class as a whole to tie the text reading to activity in class.

3. **Getting Down to IT**: Using **Transparency Masters 15.8-15.13**, review the "Integrative Thinking" sections in the chapter with students. Have students work in small groups to answer the questions and then review with the class as a whole to tie the text reading to activity in class.

4. **Evaluating a self-help program:** With the growing trend for do-it-yourself programs found conveniently on grocery store book shelves, no doubt many of your students will have heard about or read some of these popular forms of "psychotherapy" and may be wondering why some psychologists are skeptical of the whole business. In his book containing critical thinking exercises for psychology, Randolph Smith explores criteria for examining whether self-help programs are effective. **Handout Master 15.1** has been developed to provide guidelines for students in evaluating a self-help program of their choosing. Instruct students to select a self-help program from a local library or bookstore and evaluate it using the criteria on the handout. Students should bring their evaluations to class for discussion. Review some of the following points/issues as part of that discussion:
    - over 6 million American adults were involved in self-help groups in 1987 (Jacobs & Goodman, 1989)
    - benefits of self-help therapy:
        - expanded range of services: more people may receive help & therapists can spend time with others who require help
        - educating consumers about psychotherapy: books may contain pretherapy information that adds to success of conventional therapy if they enter it
        - maintaining treatment effects: may help prevent relapse
        - prevention: may act as an "inoculation" measure
    - potential risks of self-help therapy:

- claims of programs not tested in empirical studies: compared to the numbers of programs available, relatively few have been evaluated
- claims may actually exaggerate or misrepresent study findings
- improper assessment may occur: people may try a self-help program for a problem that is too severe for such an approach or may try to apply a psychological approach for a problem with a physical basis
- choosing appropriate treatment is problematic: a wide variety of treatment programs for similar problems exist; which one is appropriate to select?
- risk of failure: if person fails in the self-help attempt, there isn't a therapist to suggest alternatives or refer him or her to other services (Berrera et al., 1981)

Source:
  Rosen, G. (1981). Guidelines for the review of do-it-yourself treatment books. Contemporary Psychology, 26, 189-191.
  Smith, R. (1995). Is bibliotherapy helpful? In Challenging your preconceptions: Thinking critically about psychology (pg.103-112). Pacific Grove, CA: Brooks/Cole.

5. **Puzzle**: Using **Handout Master 15.2**, have students complete the crossword puzzle using terms from Chapter 15.

6. **Identifying types of psychotherapy**: Using **Handout Master 15.3**, have students identify the 5 general types of psychotherapy approaches (biomedical, psychodynamic, cognitive, behavioral, and humanistic) discussed in Chapter 15. They are also prompted to provide the specific therapy type or process as well.
    Answers:
    1. biomedical (ECT)
    2. biomedical (antipsychotic medication)
    3. psychodynamic (dream analysis)
    4. humanistic (Gestalt therapy)
    5. cognitive (RET)
    6. behavioral (adding reinforcement)
    7. cognitive (Beck's cognitive-behavioral homework assignments)
    8. humanistic (Roger's client-centered therapy)

7. **Developing a self-directed behavior change program**: Janet Morahan-Martin describes a semester-long activity that can be modified for use during your coverage of therapy interventions. Using **Handout Master 15.4** students are to select a target behavior for change, engage in baseline

procedures, develop and implement a behavior modification plan, chart their progress, and analyze the effectiveness of their change attempt. This activity provides a number of opportunities for discussion focusing on issues of assessment, program delivery, the use of behavioral techniques, relapse prevention, and program outcome assessment.

Source:
   Morahan-Martin, J. (1990). A module for a self-directed behavior change project. In V. Makosky, C. Sileo, L. Whittemore, C. Landry, & M. Skutley (Eds.), Activities handbook for the teaching of psychology (pg. 219-221). Washington, DC: American Psychological Association.

Suggested reading:
   Watson, L., & Tharp, R. (1989). Self-directed behavior: Self-modification for personal adjustment (5th ed.). Monterey, CA: Brooks/Cole.

8. **Exploring wheels of influence**: Clemons et al. (1998) discuss the importance of incorporating both "self-awareness and understanding of the worldview of the culturally different client" in counselor training programs. As part of that focus, these authors suggest that the follow areas should be explored by counselors as part of a self-discovery process designed to understand how these factors influence the clinician-client interaction:
   - racial identity: to what extent has your race influenced your life?
   - ethnicity: to what extent have cultural traditions and rituals influenced your life?
   - socioeconomic status: has your socioeconomic status influence your life? do you view yourself as economically deprived or privileged?
   - gender: does your gender influence your life? is your gender the basis for feelings of deprivation or privilege?
   - sexual orientation: to what extent does your heterosexual, gay, lesbian, bisexual orientation influence your life? how has it affected how you relate to others? them to you?
   - education: are there links between your educational status and that of your parents? between educational status and socioeconomic status? what is the influence of your educational achievements?
   - age: does your age influence opportunity? how others treat you? are there generational issues tied to your experiences due to the era in which you were born?
   - religion: are you acculturated into a religion? agnostic or atheist? very religious or nonreligious?

One exercise using this approach is to have students develop a pie graph divided into 8 sections, with each section representing one factor and sized to represent the extent to which that factor has influenced the person's life and worldview. The instructor might complete his or her own pie graph and make an overhead copy of it to demonstrate those influences on his/her own ways of interacting with people (or clients). Small group and large groups discussions in which students compare their findings can tie this exercise into Uba and Huang's discussion of factors that facilitate/inhibit the therapeutic alliance. A blank format of the pie graph with the 8 factors is provided on **Handout Master 15.5**.

Source:
Clemons, D., Coleman Heckman, J., & Lamb, S. (1998). The wheel of influence: A training exercise in client-centered multiculturalism. In T. Singelis (Ed.), Teaching about culture, ethnicity, & diversity: Exercises and planned activities (pg. 187-190). Thousand Oaks, CA: Sage.

Sources for Additional Activities

Balch, W. (1983). The use of role-playing in a classroom demonstration of client-centered therapy. Teaching of Psychology, 10(3), 173-174.

Benjamin, L. (1990). Clinical psychology in the introductory course. Teaching of Psychology, 17, 201-202.

Benjamin, L. & Lowman, K. (1981). Activities handbook for the teaching of psychology. Washington DC: American Psychological Association.

Claiborn, W., & Lemberg, R. (1974). A simulated mental hospital as an undergraduate teaching device. Teaching of Psychology, 1, 38-40.

Eison, J. (1987). Using systematic desensitization and rational emotive therapy to treat test anxiety. In V. Makosky, L. Whittemore, & A. Rogers (Eds.), Activities handbook for the teaching of psychology (Vol. 2) (pg. 159-163). Washington, DC: American Psychological Association.

Halonen, J. (1995). Chapter 13: Therapy. In The critical thinking companion for Introductory Psychology. New York: Worth Publishers.

Karten, S. (1987). Assertiveness: A simulation in social skills training. In V. Makosky, L. Whittemore, & A. Rogers (Eds.), Activities handbook for the teaching of psychology (Vol. 2) (pg. 299-300). Washington, DC: American Psychological Association.

Klos, D. (1976). Students as case writers. Teaching of Psychology, 3, 63-66.

Kuppersmith, J., Blair, R., & Slotnick, R. (1977). Training undergraduates as co-leaders of multifamily counseling groups. Teaching of Psychology, 4, 3-6.

Lestina, T. (1990). Using student community service as part of a high school psychology course. In V. Makosky, C. Sileo, L. Whittemore, L. Landry, & M. Skutley (Eds). Activities handbook for the teaching of psychology (Vol. 3). (pg. 235-236). Washington DC: American Psychological Association.

Matthews, J. (1980). Adjuncts to the textbook for an undergraduate clinical psychology course. Teaching of Psychology, 7, 47-50.

Morahan-Martin, J. (1990). Paradigms on the etiology and treatment of abnormal behavior. In V. Makosky, C. Sileo, L. Whittemore, L. Landry, & M. Skutley (Eds). Activities handbook for the teaching of psychology (Vol. 3). (pg. 176-177). Washington DC: American Psychological Association.

Puente, A., Matthews, J., Williams, J., & Matthews, L. (1991). Integrating clinical neuropsychology into the undergraduate curriculum. Teaching of Psychology, 18, 17-21.

Schofield, L., & Klein, M. (1975). Simulation of the mental hospital experience. Teaching of Psychology, 2, 132-134.

Singelis, T. (1998). Teaching about culture, ethnicity, & diversity: Exercises and planned activities. Thousand Oaks, CA: Sage.

Smith, G. (1982). Introducing psychology majors to clinical bias through the adjective generation technique. Teaching of Psychology, 9, 238-239.

Ulman, J. (1980). Synthesizing the elements of behavior modification: A classroom simulation game. Teaching of Psychology, 7, 182-183.

Weiss, A. (1986). Teaching counseling and psychotherapy skills without access to a clinical population: The short interview method. Teaching of Psychology, 13, 145-147.

World Wide Web: Check out the following WWW sites for information and activities relevant to this section of the text!

General issues
- Addison Wesley Longman's Website -- **http://longman.awl.com/**
- PsychZone link -- **http://longman.awl.com/**
- Psych Web -- **http://www.gasou.edu/psychweb/psychweb.htm**
- Self-Quizzes for Introductory Psychology -- **http://www.gasou.edu/psychweb/selfquiz/selfquiz.htm**
- Psychology Jumping Stand -- **http://www.indiana.edu:80/~iuepsyc/PsycJump.html**
- The Psychology Place -- **http://www.psychplace.com**
- Self-improvement ideas -- **http://www.mindtools.com/**
- Choosing a therapist -- **http://www.apa.org/pubinfor/howto.html**
- General on psychotherapies -- **http://www.gallaudet.edu/~11mgourn/**
  or
  http://www.grohol.com/therapy.htm
  or
  http://abulafia.st.hmc.edu/~mmiles/faq.html
  or

http://www.cmhc.com/disorders/
- Historical issues -- **http://www.hist.unt.edu/witch01a.htm**
or
http://www.klammeragge.org/~brandy/hexen/MalleusMalificarum/
or
http://www.alaska.net/~enigma/psychsoc/landmark.htm

Psychoanalysis
- Psychoanalysis -- **http://www.apa.org/monitor/sep96/modern.html**
or
http://uslink.net/ddavis/jundgrued.html
or
http://www.umdnj.edu/psyevnts/psa.html
or
http://www.harvard-magazine.com/jf97/freud.html
- Techniques -- **http://www.utoledo.edu/homepages/ddavis/freudfre.htm**
or
http://www.stg.brown.edu/projects/hypertext/landow/HTatBrown/freud/Hypnosis_Catharsis.html
or
http://www.stg.brown.edu/projects/hypertext/landow/HTatBrown/freud/Free_Association.html

Humanistic Therapies
- Rogers -- **http://www.gallaudet.edu/~11mgourn/client.html**
or
http://www.apa.org/journals/patterso.html
- Gestalt therapy -- http://www.gestalt.org/index.htm

Cognitive Therapies
- Cognitive therapy -- **http://mindstreet.com/cbt.html**
or
http://www.pacificcoast.net/~aegis/prin_cb1.htm
- RET -- **http://www.IRET.org/**
or
http://www.apa.org/monitor/oct95/ellis.html
or
http://www.apa.org/joutnals/wiener.html

Behavior Therapies
- Behavior therapy (general) --
http://www.gallaudet.edu/~11mgourn/bt.html
or
http://www.primenet.com/~dannell/andy/psych/personality/kcbehave.html
- Counterconditioning -- **http://psy1.clarion.edu/jms/Wolpe.html**

- Biofeedback --
    http://pages.nyu.edu/~1qh6007/BehavioralAssociates/biofeedback.html
        or
        http://www.aapb.org/

Biomedical Therapies

- Psychotropic medication -- **http://www.onlinepsych.com/treat/drugs.htm**
    or
    http://panicdisorder.minigco.com/msub5d.htm
    or
    http://www.dentaldigest.com/prescrip/anxiety.html
    or
    http://www.schizophrenia.com/ami/meds/benzo.html
    or
    http://www.avm.com/au/agtm/drugprofiles/chlorpromazine.html
- ECT -- **http://www.psyh.org/public_info/ECT~1.HTM**
    or
    http://www.nmha.org/info/factsheets/62.html
    or
    http://www.noah.cuny.edu/illness/mentalhealth/cornell/tests/ect.html

Multicultural Therapies

- Multicultural counseling --
    http://www.yorku.ca/faculty/academic/pwaxer/multi.htm

Audio-Visual Support

Films/Videos:
- *Discovering Psychology:Psychotherapy* (Annenberg, 30 minutes)
- *A Feminist Perspective: Implications for Therapists* (Menninger, 33 minutes)
- *The Talking Cure: A Portrait of Psychoanalysis* (AIMS, 56 minutes)
- *Anyplace But Here* (IU, 50 minutes, 2 parts)
- *Behavior Therapy: An Introduction* (MOTO, 29 minutes)
- *Carl Rogers Conducts an Encounter Group* (EMC, 70 minutes)
- *Madness and Medicine* (IU, 51 minutes, 2 parts)
- *The Otto Series* (IU, 25-27 minutes)
    - Otto: The Behavioral Perspective
    - Otto: The Phenomenological Perspective
    - Otto: The Psychoanalytic Perspective
    - Otto: The Social Perspective
- *Peer-Conducted Behavior Modification* (REPR, 24 minutes)
- *Psychotherapy* (IU, 26 minutes)
- *Rational-Emotive Therapy* (REPR, 30 minutes)
- *Understanding Group Psychotherapy* (Brooks Cole, 111 minutes, 2 parts)
- *The World of Abnormal Psychology Series* (PBS, 60 minutes each)
    - Program 12: Psychotherapies
    - Program 13: An Ounce of Prevention
- *Approaches to Therapy* (Insight Media, 30 minutes)
- *Freud--The Hidden Nature of Man* (LCA, 29 minutes)
- *The Mind Series*
    - Module 32: Mood Disorders: Medication and Talk Therapy
    - Module 34: Treating Depression: Electroconvulsive Therapy (ECT)
- *Mental Health--New Frontiers of Sanity* (Document, 18 minutes)
- *Treating Tourette's and Other Mental Illnesses* (FFHS, 24 minutes)
- *Preventing Relapse in Schizophrenia* (FFHS, 18 minutes)
- **Mistreating the Mentally Ill* (FFHS, 56 minutes)
- *Three Approaches to Psychotherapy* (Psychological Films, 32-48 minutes)
- *Phobias: Overcoming the Fear* (Filmakers, 60 minutes)

Psychology Encyclopedia Laserdisc IV:

Still Images
Mental illness treatment - historical approach [UN]   Frame 53530   Side all
Therapy duration and benefit [16.3]   53573   all

Transparency Master 15.1: Checking Your TRAIL 15.1

I. **Some healers take a religio-magical approach, and others base their treatments on empirical-scientific ideas. Identify two similarities and two differences between these contrasting therapeutic approaches.**

II. **Lobotomy, once a popular biomedical treatment of psychological disorders, involved**
   A. delivering electric shock to the brain.
   B. cutting nerve fibers that connect the frontal lobe to the rest of the brain.
   C. restoring neurochemical imbalances in the brain.
   D. removing brain structures that control emotion.

III. **Although a year of psychotherapy has lessened Running Wind's symptoms, he still suffers from severe depression. Now he will try to get relief by taking antidepressant medication. Name two or more important issues that Running Wind's psychiatrist must consider when deciding which medication she will prescribe for Running Wind.**

IV. **May-Lee has generalized anxiety disorder. The benzodiazepine she has been taking for over a year has been so effective that she has not had a single anxiety attack. Thinking that she is "cured," May-Lee decides to stop taking the medication. Within days, she suffers an intense attack. Why did this happen? How might May-Lee have prevented it?**

Transparency Master 15.2: Checking Your TRAIL 15.2

I. **Which of these techniques are employed by psychodynamic psychotherapists and psychoanalysts?**
   A. examining a client's ego strengths
   B. facilitating a client's insight into the unconscious conflicts that underlie her or his mental distress
   C. convincing the client to change
   D. a and b

II. **Psychodynamic therapists attempt to bring their clients' unconscious conflicts into conscious awareness. What three components of unconscious conflict do psychodynamic therapists examine?**

III. **The client-centered approach to psychotherapy aims to**
   A. accurately interpret clients' psychological distress.
   B. increase clients' self-centeredness.
   C. restore the balance between a client's behavior and self-concept by providing unconditional positive regard, empathy, and acceptance.
   D. offer empathic advice to a client.

IV. **Alejandra has bulimia, a type of eating disorder. Whenever her parents pressure her to achieve, she feels angry and ashamed. Instead of sharing her feelings, she binges on junk food, then vomits. During a session, Alejandra's therapist notices that she is frowning while describing her parents in glowing terms. How would a Gestalt therapist and psychodynamic psychotherapist deal with Alejandra's inconsistent words and behavior?**

Transparency Master 15.3: Checking Your TRAIL 15.3

I. How might aversion therapy be used to treat alcoholism?

II. Describe a sample homework assignment for a client of cognitive-behavioral therapy. What is the primary purpose of such assignments?

III. Match each of the following theoretical orientations with its primary assumption regarding the source of psychological problems:

Theoretical Orientation	Assumption of Source
1. Psychodynamic	a. unconscious conflicts
2. Behavioral	b. maladaptive learning experiences
3. Cognitive	c. barriers to natural drive toward growth and actualization
4. Humanistic	d. maladaptive beliefs

IV. Rational-emotive therapy is a form of
A. humanistic   B. cognitive   C. psychodynamic
therapy that uses
A. cognitive restructuring   B. emotional expression
C. rationalizations
to alter clients' emotions.

Transparency Master 15.4: Checking Your TRAIL 15.4

I. **The therapeutic alliance is a key ingredient in successful psychotherapies of all kinds. Describe two or more characteristics of psychotherapists who consistently establish strong alliances with their clients.**

II. <u>True</u> or <u>False</u>: **Research indicates that psychotherapy positively affects most clients, who tend to be satisfied with their psychotherapy experiences.**

III. **Explain the concept of cultural mistrust and how it might hinder the establishment of a therapeutic alliance.**

IV. **Give an example of how a cultural mismatch between a client and a therapist might weaken the therapeutic alliance.**

Transparency Master 15.5: Critical Thinking 15.1

The placebo effect causes some people to feel better simply because they have taken a pill. Is a treatment that works primarily through the placebo effect less valuable than one that works mainly through chemical action?

Transparency Master 15.6: Critical Thinking 15.2

If a therapist and client have led very different lives, do you think the therapist can truly empathize with the client's experience?

Transparency Master 15.7: Critical Thinking 15.3

Many medical treatments, such as open-heart surgery, don't lead to improvement in most patients. In comparison, psychotherapy appears to benefit half or more of the people who receive it--yet, most people feel much more willing to pay for medical treatments. Why do you think this is so? Give as many reasons as you can.

Transparency Master 15.8: Integrative Thinking 15.1

Obsessive-compulsive disorder is associated with insufficient serotonin in the brain (see the Psychological Disorders chapter). If antidepressants work by blocking the reuptake of serotonin, why does it make sense that they improve the symptoms of obsessive-compulsive disorder?

Since people influence one another with facial expressions during conversation (see the Communication chapter), do you think you would speak more openly if you faced toward or away from a therapist during psychotherapy?

Transparency Master 15.10: Integrative Thinking 15.3

Given the discussion of operant conditioning in the Learning chapter, describe how punishment, negative reinforcement, and positive reinforcement might be used to change a shy person's behavior.

Transparency Master 15.11: Integrative Thinking 15.4

Recall the description of experimental design from the Introductory chapter. How might you use an experiment to test the relative effectiveness of cognitive and humanistic psychotherapy in the treatment of panic disorder?

Transparency Master 15.12: Integrative Thinking 15.5

Social scripts can influence behavior, as explained in the Learning chapter. What kinds of difficulties would have to be overcome in order to establish a therapeutic alliance between a client and therapist who have different social scripts regarding their roles as client and healer?

Transparency Master 15.13: Integrative Thinking 15.6

Considering the gender differences in nonverbal communication described in the Communication chapter, why might both men and women clients prefer to see a female psychotherapist?

Handout Master 15.1: Evaluating a self-help program

Evaluating a self-help program

Instructions: Select a self-help program from a local library or bookstore and evaluate it using the following questions as a guideline.

Program: _____ Author(s): _____

Stated purpose of program:

- Is there information concerning empirical tests or support for the program?:

- Is there adequate information and guidelines for self-diagnosis or assessment? Does the author say if those guidelines have received empirical support?

- Have the techniques that are suggested received empirical support? How does the author inform the reader about those studies? What have their outcomes been?

- Are issues of relapse considered by the author? What about other potential explanations for the person's problems (i.e., medical conditions)?

- Has the entire program been tested for its effectiveness? Is there stated evidence for whom it tends to work?

- Is this self-help program compared to other types of therapy? If so, what were the outcomes?

- In light of the above questions, do the claims of the program sound accurate?

Handout Master 15.2: Chapter 15 puzzle

Chapter 15

Instructions: Complete the crossword puzzle above by using terms from Chapter 15.

Across
4. brings down mania
9. meds
15. that's a thought
17. rare treatment
18. tell me about your childhood
19. turned off
20. not Mr.
22. overcomes barriers
23. from dad to therapist

Down
1. therapeutic
2. identify, understand
3. a real inhibitor
5. won
6. Freud's aha!
7. not passive
8. a cutting experience
10. replacing the irrational
11. based on expectations
12. release
13. tou
14. active
16. perspective
21. Ellis approach

Solution for CrossWorld

Handout Master 15.3: Identifying psychotherapy approaches

Identifying psychotherapy approaches

Instructions: Identify the general type of psychotherapy represented in each statement below, choosing from the list below. Underneath the blank write the specific type of therapy or technique based on information from your book.

<u>Biomedical</u>   <u>Psychodynamic</u>   <u>Behavioral</u>
     <u>Cognitive</u>   <u>Humanistic</u>

_____ 1. Imagine! After years of severe depression and all those medication changes...a few moments of electricity and I'm feeling so much better.

_____ 2. Since Clozapine came into my life, those voices have gone away.

_____ 3. What do you suppose your dream about flying the Space Shuttle means?

_____ 4. Juanita, I hear you say you *want* to change your major. What is it you're *doing* about that?

_____ 5. In therapy today, I found out that all my "shoulds" and "musts" are causing me to be pretty upset.

_____ 6. According to my therapist, I need to get a bit more fun into my life. Then I wouldn't feel quite so miserable.

_____ 7. Criminy! Homework at school...now I have to do more homework by keeping track of what I'm thinking in this diary too!?

_____ 8. I think my therapist has a lot of empathy for my situation...she really seems to accept me unconditionally!

Handout Master 15.4: Developing a self-directed behavior change program

Developing a self-directed behavior change program

Instructions: Your basic task for this exercise is to select one behavior about yourself that you'd like to change or a goal you'd like to accomplish and develop an behaviorally-oriented change program. Use the following suggestions as you work on this exercise.

1. Identify a specific goal you'd like to accomplish (e.g., I want to get my psychology paper done early or I'd like to exercise 3-4 times a week). Consider subgoals that would also need to be accomplished to achieve your overall goal.

2. Evaluate the pros and cons for change -- in other words, what are the advantages and disadvantages of what you'd like to do.

3. Think about your self-efficacy beliefs - what beliefs about your skills and resources to do this program will effect its outcome? Do you need to change some negative beliefs? Add positive beliefs?

4. Develop and conduct a baseline of behaviors you want to change - use a structured diary or some kind of charting method to determine how frequently you currently in engage in behaviors relevant to your goal.

5. Based on your baseline data, establish a behavioral contract that outlines what you plan to accomplish by the end of your program. Write it out and make a public commitment.

6. Develop a plan with specific techniques for achieving your goal. Include shaping principles and reinforcement/punishment contingencies. Develop alternatives in case relapse occurs.

7. Implement your plan making sure to chart when behaviors have occurred and the contingencies you've self-administered.

8. Evaluate your progress throughout the program. Do some techniques or contingencies need to be modified to make them work for effectively?

9. Evaluate your overall progress at the end of the program. Did you achieve your goal?

Handout Master 15.4: Wheels of influence

Exploring wheels of influence in the therapeutic alliance

Instructions: Complete the following pie graph by dividing it into 8 segments, one for each of the influence factors listed below. Each segment should represent the extent of influence that factor has had in your life and interactions with others.

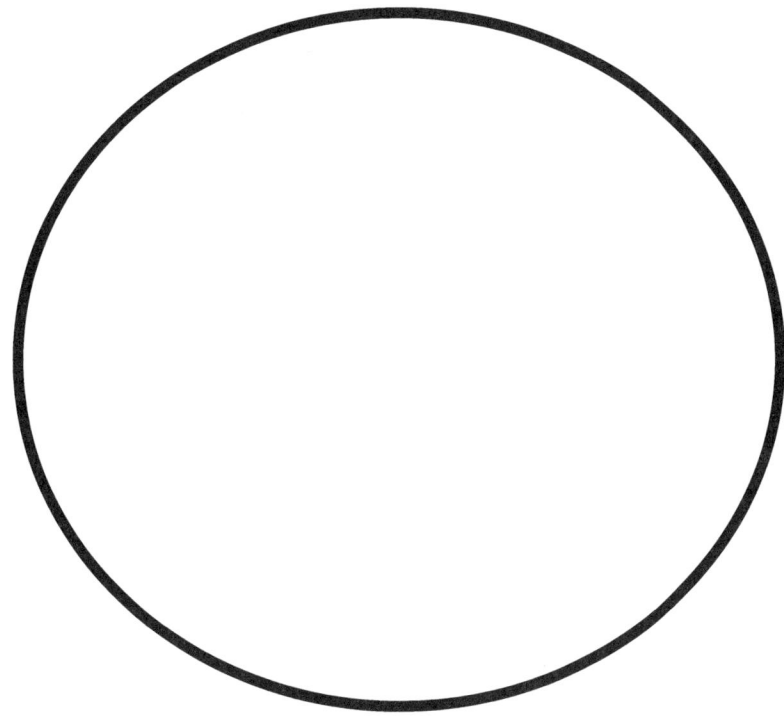

- racial identity: to what extent has your race influenced your life
- ethnicity: to what extent have cultural traditions and rituals influenced your life
- socioeconomic status: has your socioeconomic status influence your life? do you view yourself as economically deprived or privileged?
- gender: does your gender influence your life? is your gender the basis for feelings of deprivation or privilege?
- sexual orientation: to what extent does your heterosexual, gay, lesbian, bisexual orientation influence your life? how has it affected how you relate to others? them to you?
- education: are there links between your educational status and that of your parents? between educational status and socioeconomic status? what is the influence of your educational achievements?
- age: does your age influence opportunity? how others treat you? are there generational issues tied to your experiences due to the era in which you were born?
- religion: are you acculturated into a religion? agnostic or atheist? very religious or nonreligious?

CHAPTER 16

SOCIAL PSYCHOLOGY

- **Chapter Overview**
    Learning Objectives
    Chapter Outline

- **Additional Lecture Ideas**
    Lecture Topics
    Additional Readings

- **In-Class Activities and Demonstrations**
    Activities and Demonstrations
    Sources for Additional Activities
    Journey II Software

- **World Wide Web**

- **Audio-Visual Support**

- **Handout and Transparency Masters**

Chapter Overview

Learning Objectives

After studying this chapter, you should be able to do the following:

1. Discuss how attitudes affect social behavior.

2. Explain why we form impressions of people the way we do.

3. Identify factors that influence feelings of attraction and love.

4. Discuss criteria that make people more or less likely to help others, conform to their expectations, or obey them.

5. Explain how the presence of others can affect individual performance.

6. Describe how individuals influence groups, and, conversely, how a group can affect its members' behavior.

Chapter Outline

Social Psychology

I. Definition
  A. Social psychology: the study of how we relate to other people, and how they influence our behaviors, feelings, and thoughts

II. Social Cognition: Attitudes and Impressions
  A. Definition
    1. social cognition: cognitive processes that influence social behavior
  B. Attitudes
    1. definition: a learned predisposition to respond to certain people or situations in a particular way; based on enduring thoughts, feelings, and behavioral tendencies that influence social interactions
    2. attitudes and behaviors: study attitude-behavior relationship because of assumption that attitudes predict behavior
        a. strongly held attitudes may be better predictors of behavior
        b. conflicting attitudes may affect prediction of behavior
            i. example: LaPierre study concerning attitudes toward Chinese and service to Chinese couple
    3. attitude formation: attitudes may be learned via behaviorist principles of learning and experiences
        a. classical conditioning: may associate pleasant/unpleasant arousal due to an unconditioned response with object/person/situation in the environment
        b. operant conditioning: may be reinforced/punished for stated attitudes/behaviors associated with attitudes
        c. social learning: may observe others being reinforced/punished for their attitudes/behaviors associated with attitudes
    4. persuasion: a deliberate attempt to influence another person's ideas and beliefs by using a message
        a. direct persuasion: when a listener accepts idea after deliberately analyzing evidence for and against; favorable analysis may change attitude
        b. indirect persuasion: when attitude is changed without conscious, effortful thinking via use of heuristics, length of message, or impact of messenger attributes
        c. persuasion usually occurs via combination of characteristics of speaker, listener, and message
            i. speaker variables: credibility, likability, honesty, expertise
            ii. message variables:
                - contains numerous strong, logical arguments
                - addresses both sides of an argument

                        - targets issues listeners care about
                        - appeal to peoples' emotions--especially fear
                        - make points directly and have clear conclusion
                iii. <u>listener variables</u>: relevance of message to self-concept, mood, recognizing and resisting persuasive attempt
        5. <u>attitudes and behavioral changes</u>: behaviors can change attitudes
            a. <u>cognitive dissonance</u>: tension that results from the awareness that one's behavior contradicts one's attitudes
                i. tension can be relieved by changing one's attitudes
                ii. <u>evidence</u>: counterattitudinal studies
                iii. <u>cultural differences</u>: individualistic cultures more likely to evidence cognitive dissonance (due to stronger needs for consistency) than collectivistic cultures (more likely to shape behavior to social situation); differences may be due to relative emphasis on importance of attitude-behavior consistency
                iv. <u>new explanation</u>: not all people experience dissonance; suggestion that only inconsistencies that make person feel incompetent, foolish, or immoral motivate attitude change

C. Forming impressions of people
    1. <u>social perception</u>: the process of forming impression of people or social situations
    2. <u>attributions</u>: the identification of characteristics of people or social situations; determining causes for behaviors
        a. <u>dispositional attributions</u>: an explanation of behavior in terms of a person's personality, desires, or needs
        b. <u>situational attributions</u>: an explanation of behavior in terms of circumstances
        c. <u>differences in perceptions & attributions stem from differences in</u>:
            i. values
            ii. perspectives
            iii. attitudes
            iv. defenses
            v. schemata about people
            vi. accessible concepts
            vii. ways of thinking
            viii. relationship to the person we are perceiving

d. <u>biases in attributional judgments common in individualist cultures</u>:
    i. <u>fundamental attribution error</u>: tendency to attribute other people's behaviors to stable personality characteristics rather than to situational factors; leads to assumption that people caused events they didn't
    ii. <u>temporal extension</u>: assuming that the way a person behaves on limited occasions reflects a constant personality characteristic
    iii. <u>egocentric bias</u>: when a person overestimates the extent to which others feel, think, and behave as he or she does

e. <u>collectivist cultures</u>: less likely to make dispositional attributions see they see themselves as tailoring behaviors to situation and assume others do too

f. cross-cultural misunderstandings due to differences in understandings of causes for behavior, assuming people in other cultures think as they do, seeing their cultural perspective as correct

4. protecting ourselves
   a. impressions we form may be affected by defensive elements in our schemata that protect us from knowledge or events that could lower self-esteem or heighten anxiety
      i. <u>just world hypothesis</u>: the idea that bad events happen to bad people whereas good circumstances arise and desirable events happen to good people;
         - decreases our sense of vulnerability to bad events
         - can lead to incorrect attributions

5. personal theories of personality
   a. <u>implicit personality theory</u>: a usually unarticulated schema that contains one's personal ideas about what traits generally occur in which people, why the traits develop, and why they appear to occur together
      i. based on person's unique combination of defenses, personal experiences, ways of thinking, culture
      ii. any gaps in information about others unconsciously filled by information from our implicit personality theory
      iii. interpret ambiguous behavior in terms consistent with expectations of implicit personality theory
      iv. use concepts of implicit personality theory to categorize people

6. categorizing people
    a. <u>categorization</u>: a process by which one uses available information to place someone in a cognitive category and assumes that a person in that category has particular characteristics
        i. affected by need to know about people, flexibility of schemata, conceptual structure
        ii. <u>transference</u>: the usually unconscious attribution of characteristics to someone we meet because that person reminds us of someone else with those characteristics
        iii. <u>functional inference</u>: when conclusions are drawn about someone's personality based on physical characteristics
        iv. <u>halo effect</u>: a result of categorization, in which a person who has one positive characteristic is assumed to have other favorable characteristics; <u>example</u>: physical attractiveness and competence
7. stereotypes
    a. <u>stereotype</u>: assuming that everyone in a particular social group shares certain characteristics; simplifying perceptions of people and underestimating the variability within groups
        i. ingroup heterogeneity vs. outgroup homogeneity
    b. <u>factors contributing to formation of stereotypes</u>:
        i. <u>ignorance</u>: less education associated with holding more stereotypes
        ii. <u>socialization</u>: learning stereotypes via parents, peers, media
        iii. <u>competition over limited resources</u>: when threatened by potential loss of limited resources, displace aggression on targeted, vulnerable groups who compete for those resources
        iv. <u>rationalization of inequalities</u>: justifying existing inequities as natural and right or explaining own poor situation as due to inequality
8. why prejudice and stereotypes persist
    a. regarding individuals who don't match stereotype as unusual (rather than thinking stereotype is inaccurate)
    b. <u>confirmation bias</u>: a tendency to seek information that fits a preexisting schema rather than a range of information, resulting in "finding" evidence for the schema
    c. <u>stereotypes affect types of attributions made for behaviors</u>:
        i. if behavior consistent with stereotype, dispositional attribution made
        ii. if behavior inconsistent with stereotype, situational attribution made
        iii. example: Steele and Aronson (1995) study on African Americans and test performance

III. Social Relations: Attraction, Affections, and Love
A. Liking another person
1. <u>interpersonal attraction</u>: the feeling of affection that draws one person to another
2. <u>factors that influence interpersonal attraction</u>:
    a. <u>proximity</u>: geographic closeness
        i. increases opportunity for interaction
        ii. <u>mere exposure effect</u>: increased liking for things familiar
        iii. <u>endogamy</u>: marrying within one's own racial, ethnic, cultural, and socioeconomic group; probably more likely to live nearby and be similar, in addition to social pressures to marry within group
    b. <u>similarity</u>: similar age, gender, socioeconomic status, ethnicity, personality characteristics, attitudes/preferences influence attraction
        i. <u>explanation</u>:
            - increases sense of ease/comfort around another
            - positively reinforce one another
            - extrinsic reinforcement (social approval)
        ii. complementarity theories (i.e., "opposites attract" notions) haven't been supported
    c. <u>physical attraction</u>: what is considered attractive is subjective
        i. <u>common physical features considered attractive</u>:
            - bodies with symmetrical features
            - in females: curvy figure, high cheekbones, thin jaws, large, wide-set eyes, small noses
            - in males: larger-than-average jaws
        ii. <u>explanations for cross-cultural similarities</u>: international prominence of European American cultural norms; impact of media messages of attractiveness cross-culturally
        iii. <u>halo effect</u>: attractive people also thought to have other positive attributes (e.g., intelligence, out-going, competent)
3. gender perspectives on interpersonal attraction
    a. women use beauty to attract men; men use socioeconomic security to attract women
    b. <u>survey research on mate preference attributes</u>: men rated physical attractiveness higher than did women; women rated financial prospects higher than did men

c. <u>explanations</u>:
                    i. learned preference through repeated exposure to cultural messages
                    ii. <u>social exchange theory</u>: seek relationships in order to achieve items/experiences we value and offer attributes we think others will value
     B. Loving another person
          1. <u>defining love</u>: difficult to do; psychologists identify factors that combine to produce feelings we call love
               a. <u>passionate love</u>: being absorbed in thought about, intensely attracted to, physically attracted toward, seek to merge with, and idealize (i.e., magnify desirable traits and minimize undesirable) another person
                    i. behave in ways to demonstrate this
                    ii. a type of love that tends to be short-lived
                    iii. rejection may actually intensify passion/longing for lost loved one
               b. <u>companionate love</u>: a less arousing, but more secure form of love characterized by feelings of care, commitment to the relationship, and the sharing of life experiences
                    i. may tend to move from passionate love to companionate love
                    ii. rejection/negative experiences may damage levels of emotional closeness
          3. <u>the triangular theory of love</u>: a model of love based on three components of love--passion, intimacy, and commitment--in various combinations
               a. <u>liking</u> = intimacy only
               b. <u>empty love</u> = commitment only
               c. <u>infatuation</u> = passion only
               d. <u>romantic love</u> = intimacy + passion
               e. <u>companionate love</u> = intimacy + commitment
               f. <u>fatuous love</u> = passion + commitment
               g. <u>consummate love</u> = intimacy + passion + commitment; most likely to endure

IV. Social Influence: Helping, Conforming, Obeying, and Complying
     A. Influences in groups
          1. <u>social roles</u>: positions that carry the expectation that a person perform particular behaviors
          2. <u>social norms</u>: standards of accepted and expected behaviors in a group of people

B. Altruism: Helping others
   1. altruism: helpful, unselfish, prosocial behavior
   2. explanations for altruism:
      a. social norms call for it
      b. people are genetically predisposed to being altruistic
   3. characteristics associated with altruistic behavior:
      a. perceived, clear need for help
      b. empathy for persons needing help
      c. personality
      d. see relationships as interdependent rather than independent
      e. competent to help
      f. being a lone witness to situation calling for help
         i. bystander effect: if others present, may experience diffusion of responsibility (i.e., thinking someone else will help)
   4. gender perspectives on helping:
      a. findings: men help more than women
         i. explanation: operational definition for helping and situation manipulated tapped in to cultural expectations for male role; studies required helping in a short-term, potentially dangerous encounter with a stranger
      b. helping in women: more likely to provide emotional nurturance in long-term relationships; research supports
      c. gender differences in helping occur if persons are traditionally sex-typed
      d. if situation doesn't involve risk or nurturance, gender differences in helping reduced
   5. a biased frame of mind
      a. frame of mind at the moment influences helping
         i. Good Samaritan study: helping least likely to occur if student was in a hurry; most likely if had plenty of time
            - social role of student may have influenced helping

C. Conforming to group norms and social roles
   1. conformity: the adoption or mimicry of other people's attitudes or behaviors due to rewards, requests, or pressure
   2. going along with the group
      a. Asch study: 1/3 of participants in study conformed (agreed) with confederates' wrong answers on line-matching task
         i. study criticized as artificial
      b. gender differences in conformity: women conform more than men
         i. more pressure to conform to social norms
         ii. less power than men in society
   3. basing behaviors on social position

    a. <u>simulated prison study</u>: students randomly assigned roles as "guards" or "prisoners" adopted role-related behaviors(i.e., behaviors reflected the way they interpreted their social role)
    b. <u>everyday examples</u>: people who don't conform to social, gender, racial roles may experience punishment
  D. Obeying authority
    1. <u>obedience</u>: following orders from a person in authority
    2. obeying orders to harm
      a. <u>Milgram study</u>: 62% of "teachers" delivered maximum shock levels to "learner"
    3. when and why people obey
      a. cross-cultural studies have found obedience rates similar to Milgram study
      b. nonexperimental examples also given such as 1930s incidents between Japanese/Chinese and My Lai incident
      c. <u>factors that influence obedience</u>:
        i. being removed from the process of harming another
        ii. physical closeness to victim
        iii. status of person giving orders to harm
        iv. others also involved in harming person
        v. no social support for disobeying orders to harm
      d. <u>role of personality</u>:
        i. <u>authoritarian personality</u>: authoritarians believe those who follow orders are less responsible for the harm done
        ii. some may obey due to fear of arousing anger, embarrassing themselves, appearing rude
  E. Complying with requests
    1. <u>compliance</u>: fulfilling requests without expectation of reward or threat of punishment; influence attempts that rely on merely making a request
      a. person may not comply & we may have no way of influencing them
      b. sequence in which requests made influences likelihood of compliance
    2. <u>the foot-in-the-door approach</u>: making small request first, then larger request
      a. <u>example study</u>: 75% of respondents who had agreed to a smaller sign later agreed to larger sign in yard
      b. <u>explanations</u>:
        i. <u>availability heuristic</u>: compliance with small request increases cognitive accessibility of related attitude of helpfulness
        ii. compliance leads to increased involvement
        iii. need to maintain a consistent perception of self
    3. <u>the door-in-the-face approach</u>: making large request first, then smaller request

  a. <u>example study</u>: more than 1/2 of people who had turned down a large request to distribute 100 flyers later agreed to hand out 10
  b. <u>explanations</u>:
    i. <u>compromise principle</u>: in negotiations, if perceive other person has compromised, we do too so as to not appear unfriendly
    ii. simply easier to agree with slightly unreasonable (smaller) request than to say to person it was unreasonable

V. Group Processes: Individual Effort and Group Decisions
 A. Social facilitation: Working hard
  1. <u>social facilitation</u>: enhancement of individual performance due to the presence of others
   a. <u>examples of early studies</u>: winding fishing reels alone or with others
   b. examples of everyday behaviors
   c. <u>relationship between arousal & performance</u>: presence of others leads to arousal; arousal facilitates performance of well-learned behaviors but decreases performance on new, unfamiliar, complex behaviors
 B. Social loafing: Hardly working
  1. <u>social loafing</u>: decreased individual effort in a group in which unique efforts go unnoticed
   a. <u>may contribute to less output</u>:
    i. some people notice others are loafing & cut their own input
    ii. <u>diffusion of responsibility</u>: some loaf since don't feel individual responsibility for group behavior
  2. <u>deindividuation</u>: loss of individual identity and individual responsibility by members of a group
   a. may result in letting groups make decisions
    i. <u>example given</u>: riots after Rodney King verdict
 C. Decision making as a group
  1. making extreme decisions
   a. <u>group polarization</u>: the tendency for a group to shift toward a position more extreme than that originally taken by any individual member; the shift is usually in the direction of the initial consensus
    i. <u>risky shift</u>: tendency for a group to take larger gambles than individuals would make alone
    ii. <u>cautious shift</u>: tendency for a group to take less risk than individuals would take alone
   b. <u>processes that contribute to polarization</u>:
    i. <u>validation</u>: hearing own arguments repeated by others in group

    ii. <u>additional arguments</u>: hearing more arguments that strengthen position
    iii. <u>comparison of arguments</u>: comparing opinions with those expressed by other group members may lead to modification of original opinion to join group's consensus
 2. false consensus
  a. <u>groupthink</u>: a type of polarization in which the group seeks consensus at the expense of careful decision making
  b. <u>processes involved</u>:
    ii. equating consensus with being right
    ii. discussing only a few options
    iii. not asking for outside advice
    iv. not fully considering information that challenges groups' view
    v. not questioning decision once made
    vi. not reviewing objectives or weighing pros/cons of decision due to overconfidence
  c. groupthink allows members to preserve self-esteem, offers false sense of security; results may be disastrous however
 3. the influential few
  a. can a minority group member influence rest of group?
    ii. depends of majority's willingness to consider minority member's ideas; may overlook or automatically disqualify minority opinion
  b. <u>minority member can influence majority by</u>:
    i. making convincing arguments
    ii. giving impression of power, status, expertise
    iii. consistently/confidently repeating opinion
 4. cross-cultural perspectives on group decisions
  a. <u>collectivist culture</u>:
    ii. prizes group harmony and consensus
    ii. try to shift positions in ways that require all members to make the smallest total accommodation
    iii. minority members may act as though have high status to influence majority (e.g., speaking first, sitting in high status seat)
  b. role of knowledge of cross-cultural values in influencing international negotiations

Additional Lecture Topics
1. <u>**Social psychology across cultures:**</u>

   The challenge of social psychology:
   Fathali Moghaddam, in his recent textbook covering the interface between social psychology and culture, expands on some of the traditional lines of study in the discipline. He makes several points in his first chapter that may provide a helpful framework for introducing the topics of social psychology to your students. First, he writes about the historical development of social psychology as a discipline. Next he reviews several universals (or etics) and culturally-specific (or emics) social behaviors commonly discussed in the discipline.

   A note on historical development: Despite the fact that much of the early theory and research was based in scholarship originating in Europe, Moghaddam and others describe the United States as the first world of psychology and the major producer of social psychological knowledge. He notes that the vast majority of social psychological studies have addressed questions generated by U.S. researchers, have involved U.S. participants (typically undergraduate students), and have used research methods developed in the United States (pg. 7). Moreover, the journals through which professional discussions occur are written and edited predominantly by Americans. Similarly, the tests and measures used in research have been developed in this country. Theory, methodology, and practice regarding social psychology have been exported from the United States to other second and third world countries. In his subsequent chapter on research methods (and in writings elsewhere) Moghaddam cautions that research methods may be sensitive to shared cultural meanings. In the laboratory, for example, a white lab coat may have meaning in one culture quite different from that understood in another culture. Moreover, the methods traditionally used in social psychological studies tend to require literate groups of participants who are familiar with the idea and culture of research.

   Topics of interest may also carry different cultural definitions or expression (e.g., aggression, helping). It has been a relatively recent phenomenon that social psychology has begun to more fully incorporate issues of culture as relevant topics for discussion in theory, research, and classroom textbooks.

   The etics and emics in social psychology: The search for understanding of human social behavior requires that social psychologists seek cross-cultural similarities as well as dissimilarities. Moghaddam notes three general norms for conduct that appear to shape social life across cultures: the norms of trust, truth, and turn-taking in dialogue. These norms affect social interactions in that people interact with one another under the assumptions that they can generally trust one's words and actions, that conduct is centered around honesty, and that some minimal amount of respect is conveyed by taking turns in speaking and listening during social discourse. Moreover, these norms are so basic to social interaction that Moghaddam claims that social life breaks down without them. Additional cross-cultural similarities in human social functioning, driven by similar environmental conditions, include:

   ...   some belief in a roughly unified self within each person
   ...   the tendency to evaluate the world in terms of positives and negatives

- the tendency to search for understanding of causes of experienced events
- the universal presence of inequalities in status and resources between social groups
- common tendencies for conformity and obedience to some kind of authority figures
- similarity and physical proximity as factors that influence attraction to others
- some form of helping or altruism appears to exist across cultures (although culture may influence how and when help is sought and/or given)
- us/them categorization principles occur in all cultures with the general observations of ingroup favoritism/outgroup derogation also a prevailing consequence of that process
- aggression is expressed in some fashion in all societies (although the form and extent is influenced by culture and may be expressed differently by women vs. men)
- social groups governed by some form of leadership exist in all societies
- the interpersonal theme of fairness and justice influences social interactions and perceptions of injustice, are frequently linked to between-group conflict

Although part of his emphasis focuses on cultural universals, Moghaddum suggests that studying culturally distinctive behaviors (emics) rounds out our understanding of human social behavior. As we have seen in many previous chapters in Uba and Huang, cultural variables are often discussed in terms of individualism and collectivism. Moghaddum notes that "many of the differences across cultures are associated with individualism...rather than collectivism...". This is an interesting analysis of the impact of these dimensions and one that is somewhat different from what we have seen up to this point. Some of the cross-cultural differences in social behavior he summarizes include:

- in collectivistic cultures, the boundaries for the self are described as being more fluid, whereas in individualistic cultures they tend to be more rigidly bounded.
- consistency in (and between) attitudes and behaviors is more of a Western phenomenon whereas tolerance for inconsistencies (or contradictions) is emphasized in other cultures
- some ethnic groups in the U.S. that have historically experienced a greater number of external limitations maintain their self-esteem via self-protective attributions
- the research emphasis on how persuasive messages influence individuals are argued as being less appropriate for collectivistic cultures
- conformity (or nonconformity) has been found to be dependent on whether one is relating to family vs. strangers in some cultures
- the institution of marriage may reflect the joining of families rather than of individuals in some cultures
- underlying motives for prosocial behaviors in some cultures may include creating obligations and debts and thus serve to extend social networks
- wide variations in physical aggression across cultures are argued to result from differing socialization practices
- social behaviors of men and women vary widely from the egalitarian to

significantly unequal
... responses to inequalities and injustice experienced by disadvantaged groups varies widely depending on a cultural emphasis on individual mobility and status achievement or passive acceptance and collective action.

Moghaddam's introduction, in combination with the review of Sear's analysis of narrow subject samples and Matsumoto's review of cross-cultural findings for major areas of study in social psychology, provides an excellent basis for discussion of the cultural variables and the nature of study in social psychology.

Source:
Moghaddam, F. (1998). The challenge of social psychology. In Social psychology: Exploring universals across cultures (pg. 1-24). New York: Freeman.

2. **Social psychology across cultures:**

David Matsumoto challenges some of the traditional findings reported in most texts on social psychology. In particular, he provides discussion of cross-cultural differences noted in the literature on attribution, interpersonal attraction and love, social influence (i.e., conformity, compliance, and obedience), group behaviors (e.g., social productivity or loafing) and person perception.

... attribution: traditional discussions of the literature pertaining to attribution tend to highlight Kelley's covariation model, which explores the processes whereby individuals arrive at internal or external attributions for cause of another's behaviors, and Weiner's theory, which incorporates stability as a relevant dimension for analysis and arrives at 4 types of attributions for success and failure. Common biases in the attribution process include the fundamental attribution error, self-serving bias, and defensive attributions (i.e., blaming the victim). In his summary, Matsumoto notes that the fundamental attribution error and self-serving biases are not particularly common in more collectivistic cultures. Moreover, understanding how people make attributions for success and failure depends on how success or failure is defined in a particular culture. Likewise, cultural variations in definitions of effort, luck, and work may exist across cultures. Lastly, he points out that cultural motives underlying negative attributions need be considered for understanding of attributional processes. For example, racial, class, and gender stereotypes and discrimination present in a culture may underlie beliefs about causes for behaviors in stigmatized groups within that culture.

... interpersonal attraction and love: traditional studies of interpersonal attraction commonly report physical attractiveness, similarity, and reciprocity as factors that facilitate interpersonal closeness. Although the cross-cultural literature does not contain abundant discussion of these topics, according to Matsumoto, some studies do provide evidence for cross-cultural differences in the importance of love commitment, disclosure maintenance, relational ambivalence (i.e., confusion or uncertainty about one's partner), and conflict expression in close relationships. Moreover, romantic love is more highly valued in some cultures than in others.

... social influence: the phenomena of conformity, compliance, and obedience are traditionally discussed in reference to the findings of the classic Asch and Milgram studies. Cross-cultural studies report significant differences in the extent of conforming, compliant, and obedient behaviors as well as differences in cultural values for accepting such conduct. For example, collectivistic cultures are more encouraging of these behaviors as they relate to group cohesion, whereas individualistic cultures tend to view these forms of conduct negatively. These culture values are also reflected in child socialization practices that encourage or discourage these values.

...   group productivity: traditional reviews of group productivity incorporate some discussion of the phenomenon of social loafing--when group output falls below what one would expect based on individual capabilities and prior output. Again, distinctions in the extent to which people engage in social loafing vary across the individualistic/ collectivistic dimensions. Whereas people from individualistic cultures are more likely to engage in social loafing in group settings, people from collectivistic cultures are more likely to engage in social striving (i.e., their performance is enhanced in group settings). Apparently, this cultural phenomenon is rooted in cultural expectations for fostering coordination and collaboration with group members.

...   person perception: elements affecting person perception, including appearance and behavioral cues and the shared meanings for physical attributes, in addition to discussion of social and person schemas occupy most discussions of person perception in social psychology. Matsumoto notes that nonverbal behaviors are particularly affected by cultural guidelines for communication, and that misunderstanding of the culture-specific meanings of nonverbal behaviors may lend itself to misperceptions of people. Cultural differences in recognizing and interpreting facial expressions are a similar example. Moreover, it is relatively unsurprising to note that culture definitions of physical attractiveness or beauty exist and surely affect our perceptions of others as a result.

Source:
   Matsumoto, D. (1994). Social psychology. In People: Psychology from a cultural perspective. (pg. 153-174). Pacific Grove, CA: Brooks/Cole

3. College sophomores in the laboratory:
Influences of a narrow data base on social psychology's view of human nature:

In a thought-provoking article concerning the effect of participant selection biases prevalent between the 1960s and 1986, David Sears contends that social psychologists have engaged in biased theory development and testing due to "its heavy dependence during the past 25 years on a very narrow data base: college student subjects tested in the academic laboratory with academiclike materials" (pg. 515). Concerned that the overdependence on this data base in such settings "unwittingly led us to a portrait of human nature that describes rather accurately the behavior of American college students in an academic context but distorts human social behavior more generally" (pg. 515) led him to consider ways in which the social psychological view of humanity has been distorted by this methodological bias.

Sears begins his critique by noting that, by the 1960s, the dominant methodology in social psychology involve the "conjunction of college student subject, laboratory site, and experimental method, usually mixed with some deception" (pg. 516) and confirms that these are the nature of studies reported in social psychological textbooks and books of readings used in classes, and in most prestigious mainstream journals of the discipline. Does such a bias erode the validity of the research? Does it mean that it doesn't describe human social behavior accurately? Sears contends that social psychologists have long argued that the phenomenon being studied by researches were thought to be so universal as to cause the concern to be unwarranted. In other words, what they were measuring in this sample was thought to be generally reflective of people in general. Sears is not convinced and lists 13 ways in which the college student in the laboratory is unusual.

College students in Introductory Psychology, one of the most commonly accessed classes for the development of subject pools, take the course fairly early in their undergraduate experience. Thus the typically ages of research participants range between 17-19 years of age. Moreover, the students already represent the upper end of persons with educational background by virtue of their presence in the university setting. These two factors constitute the most obvious differences between typical research participants and the population at large. However, their psychological qualities make their overuse in social psychological studies even more problematic. Sears argues that, generally peaking, college sophomores tend:

... to have "a less fully formulated sense of self, manifested variously in mercurical self-esteem, identity confusion and diffusion, inadequate integration of past, present, and future selves, feelings of insecurity, and depression" (pg. 521)
... possess less crystallized social and political attitudes
... to be more egocentric compared with older adults
... "have a stronger need for peer approval, manifested in dependency, conformity, and overidentification with peers"
... to have highly unstable peer (group) relationships

Moreover, when compared to their same-aged noncollege students peers, college sophomore participants:

... have usually been selected for participation in studies due to "having unusually adept cognitive skills"
... have been selected for some level of compliance to authority as can be attested to by their years of navigating the educational system
... are more likely than their peers to have unstable relationships due to greater geographical and social mobility in addition to entering the work force and family life arenas later than their peers.

By placing college students in laboratory settings that use academiclike tasks and measures, the context of experiments are likely to:

... induce a more cognitive set in participants
... induce a set to comply with authority
... deliberately sever naturally occuring relationships to avoid the contamination associated with prior acquaintance

In providing support for each of these contentions, Sears provides convincing evidence drawn broadly from the most common observations in the discipline (and I'd strongly urge you to obtain a full copy of his article to pull out these explanations as they are numerous, well-written, and thoughtfully presented). Still, Sears' primary concern is how the use of this data base has shaped the view of human nature that we have seen in social psychology. In his words:

"First, modern social psychology tends, in a variety of respects, to view people in general as having a weak sense of their own preferences, emotions, and abilties: They have easily damaged self-esteem; they are quite compliant behaviorally; their attitudes and judgments are easily changed; their attitudes have a minor effect on their behavior; they are ignorant of or insensitive to their own true attitudes; and their long-standing personality predispositions are not important determinants of their sociopolitical attitudes. Second, material self-interest, group norms, reference group identification, and social support play little role in current research on attitudes and social cognition. Nor do stage-specific theories of attitudes, which assert that the individual's particular life stage may powerfully affect attitude formation and change. Third, contemporary social psychology views humans as dominated by cognitive rather than affective processes, especially emotionally based irrationalities. And, finally, sociopsychological theories tend to treat people as highly egocentric. In all these respects, the idiosyncrasies of social psychology's rather narrow data base parallel the portrait of human nature with which it emerges" (pg. 527).

To correct for its history of overuse of the college student sample and the biased view of human social behavior that has arisen as a result, Sears urges that social psychologists should be more tentative in their discussions of human activity based on that sample. Moreover, future research should be done including very different types of people (i.e., across age ranges) in very different settings (i.e., other than academic-like settings or tasks). Finally, some classic findings should be subjected to replication attempts with specific efforts to expand both the participant pool and research setting involved.

Source:

Sears, D. (1986). College sophomores in the laboratory: Influences of a narrow data base on social psychology's view of human nature. Journal of Personality and Social Psychology, 51, 515-530.

4. Individualistic and collectivistic perspectives on gender and the cultural context of love and intimacy:

Uba and Huang review several theoretical approaches regarding the definition of love. In a recent article, Karen and Kenneth Dion extend that discussion in their consideration of how "the differences between individualistic and collectivistic cultures may affect the experience of romantic love and emotional intimacy" (pg. 314). These cultural differences, also reflected in construals of self and expectations regarding gender, underlie one of our most significant human experiences. If you ask many of your students to tell you the ideal "story" of romantic love and marriage in the U.S., many might offer that most couples meet, fall in love, and marry or live together with an expectation of living "happily ever after." The underlying assumptions that form the bases for this idealized scenario are culturally based, according to Dion & Dion. More generally, if social psychologists wish to understand the factors that contribute to the development of intimate relationships, they contend, cultural perspectives regarding the self, gender, and relationships must be studied. As has been reviewed a number of times at this point, an individualistic culture tends to result in the promotion of self interests and rights, personal autonomy and independence, self-actualization and the realization of personal goals, individual achievement and initiative, and self-expression. Definitions of the "self" emphasize individual attributes and personal uniqueness. In interpersonal relationships, less emphasis is placed on the needs of others so much as the needs of the individual. The collectivistic perspective stresses the importance of relationship to one's group membership, group loyalty and needs override those of the individual, and concerns for interconnectedness. The self is defined in terms of interdependence rather than indepedence from others, and relationships are marked by greater awareness of and responsiveness to the needs of others. Such differences have been the bases for general discussions regarding cross-cultural differences in intergroup relations and personal identity. It is also important to note that, in the United States, it has been suggested that men and women have historically been socialized along individualistic vs. collectivistic orientations, respectively. Pointing these analyses toward love and intimate relationships, Dion & Dion contend "that in some individualistic societies there are gender differences in self-construal that in turn may be related to the experience of romantic love and the capacity for intimacy in close relationships" (pg. 318). In short, given that women and men from cultures that generally adopt an individualistic perspective are socialized toward different orientations, these differing tendencies are likely to affect the experience of intimacy within relationships. In collectivistic cultures, where the emphasis is on self-construals based interdependence, one might assume that the general cultural orientation facilitates intimacy for both sexes--an assumption that does not take into consideration gender experiences interacting with cultural orientation, however.

Dion & Dion discuss three propositions regarding the relationships between culture, love and intimacy:

...   "Romantic love is more likely to be an important basis for marriage in societies where individualism as contrasted with collectivism is a dominant cultural value" (pg. 318): The link between societal individualism and romantic love may occur because intimate relationships and romantic love are avenues through which an individual explores and reveals dimensions of the self to another (i.e., share oneself with another). Indeed romantic love has been described by some authors as allowing for self-expression and personal fulfillment through sharing of personal values and ideas and experiencing personal growth in the context of the relationship. In societal collectivism, love and intimacy between a man and woman are of less consideration than are fulfilling the wishes of parents and extended family members. As increasing trends towards individualism occur within some collectivistic cultures, greater sentiment toward marrying for love has appeared in cross-cultural survey literature. Indeed, in an interesting query, Dion & Dion consider the impact of the "one child per family" policy in the People's Republic of China on future trends toward individualism in that traditionally collectivistic country. This government-imposed child-bearing policy may ultimately move the orientation toward individualism as the needs of single children are placed in special favor within family households.

...   "Psychological intimacy in a marital relationship is more important for marital satisfaction and personal well-being for adults in individualistic societies than for those in collectivistic societies" (pg. 320): Dion & Dion note that cultures vary in the extent to which marriages or committed relationships are viewed "as an important source of personal well-being" (pg. 320). Indeed, in this country, reported linkages between psychological and physical health and social support via one's spouse have been found. Moreover, societal expectations for emotional support and intimacy in marriage are often linked to gender expectations, with women often given the responsibility for "maintaining the emotional tenor of the relationship" (pg. 320). The value of emotional intimacy with one's spouse as the primary basis for personl well-being does not present itself in collectivistic cultures, however. "The primary ties of intimacy in which the individual's psychological well-being was rooted were the family relationships with parents, siblings, and other relatives" (pg. 320) with particular emphasis for women on relating well with the husband's family and/or, in some cultures, deriving emotional intimacy from one's children and one's relationships with other married women. Men's primary relationship responsibilities were oriented around thier parents. Thus, the valuing of emotional intimacy and expected sources of emotional fulfillment vary across the individualistic/ collectivistic dimension and may be influenced by gender roles within the society. Moreover, the linkages between amounts of self-disclosure and perceptions of intimacy in a marriage may be a function of individualism and collectivism, such that self-disclosure is valued more in cultures where relationships are in an on-going state of negotiation and less so in cultures where commitment and tradition, mutual dependence and regard are assumed.

...   "Although individualism fosters the valuing of romantic love as a basis for marriage, certain aspects (or types of) individualism at the psychological level make developing intimacy problematic" (pg. 323): Dion & Dion offer that "within an individualistic society, there are differences in the degree to which people endorse the prevailing orientation" (pg. 323). For example, some individuals may adopt a form of individualism, self-contained individualism, that is characterized by strong values of autonomy and personal control and significant dislike for any kind of dependency. As a result of ambivalence about emotional dependence, obtaining intimacy in such a relationship is difficult, and is potentially one key factor contributing to high divorce rates in individualistic countries. Moreover, reports of marital dissatisfaction tend to indicate that married women are more likely to be unhappy, and the central issue is often reported to involve psychological intimacy. According to the authors: "In an individualistic society, both women and men may expect psychological intimacy in marriage. However, gender-related differences in how self is viewed in relation to others may in turn be related to the capacity for providing psychological intimacy to one's spouse" (pg. 325).

In closing their article, Dion & Dion make a number of interesting conclusions: although the cultural ideal for marriage and love emphasizes romantic love and personal fulfillment in marriage, some features of the individualistic orientation work counter to that ideal. On the other hand, collectivism generally fosters interdependence but intimacy is likely to be diffused across a variety of interpersonal relationships. As a result, marriages in individualistic cultures are subjected to a great deal of pressure due to high expectations for personal fulfillment within the context of the relationship. According to the authors, divorce rates may continue to increase as individualism rises. Similarly, the nature of marriage and love may be altered as collectivistic cultures move toward individualism. Moreover, as construals of self are altered by changes in societal individualism and collectivism, additional changes in experiences of love and intimacy may occur.

Source:

Dion, K., & Dion, K. (1997). Individualistic and collectivistic perspectives on gender and the cultural context of love and intimacy. In L. Peplau, & S. Taylor (Eds.), Sociocultural perspectives in social psychology: Current readings (pg. 314-329). Upper Saddle River, NJ: Prentice Hall.

Suggestions for Additional Readings

Ackerman, D. (1994). A natural history of love. New York: Random House.

Aronson, E. (1999). The social animal. New York: Freeman.

Baron, R., & Byrne, D. (1994). Social psychology: Understanding human interaction. Boston: Allyn & Bacon.

Berscheid, E., & Walster, E. (1978). Interpersonal attraction. Reading, MA: Addison-Wesley.

Bond, M. (1988). The cross-cultural challenge to social psychology. Newbury Park: Sage.

Bond, M., & Forgas, J. (1984). Linking person perception to behavior intention across cultures: The role of cultural collectivism. Journal of Cross-Cultural Psychology, 15, 337-352.

Brehm. S. (1985). Intimate relationships. New York: Random House.

Burns, D. (1985). Intimate connections. New York: William Morrow.

Cialdini, R. (1993). Influence: Science and practice. Glenview, IL: Scott, Foresman.

Cialdini, R. (1994). Influence: The new psychology of modern persuasion. New York: William Morrow.

Cook, M., &Wilson, G. (Eds.) (1979). Love and attraction. New York: Pergamon Press.

Devine, P. (1989). Stereotypes and prejudice: Their automatic and controlled components. Journal of Personality and Social Psychology, 56, 5-18.

Fiske, S., & Taylor, S. (1991). Social cognition. Reading, MA: Addison-Wesley.

Fletcher, G. & Fitness, J. (Eds.) (1995). Knowledge structures in close relationships. Hillsdale, NJ: Erlbaum.

Forsyth, D. (1990). Group dynamics. Pacific Grove, CA: Brooks/Cole.

Graham, S., & Long, A. (1986). Race, class, and the attributional process. Journal of Educational Psychology, 78, 4-13.

Hastie, R., Ostrom, T., Ebbesen, E., Wyer, R., Hamilton, D., & Carlston, D. (Eds.) (1980). Person memory: The cognitive basis of social perception. Hillsdale, NJ: Erlbaum.

Hatfield, E., & Rapson, R. (1993). Love, sex, and intimacy: Their psychology, biology, and history. New York: HarperCollins.

Hendrick, C., & Hendrick, S. (1983). Liking, loving, and relating. Pacific Grove, CA: Brooks/Cole.

Hendrix, H. (1988). Getting the love you want. New York: Holt.

Lerner, M. (1980). The belief in a just world. New York: Plenum.

Lindzey, G., & Aronson, E. (Eds.) (1985). Handbook of social psychology (Vols. 1-2). New York: Random House.

Macaulay, J., & Berkowitz, L. (Eds.) (1970). Altruism and helping behavior. Orlando, FL: Academic Press.

Marsh, P. (Ed.) (1988). Eye to eye: How people interact. Topsfield, MA: Salem House Publishers.

Matsumoto, D. (1996). Culture and psychology. Pacific Grove, CA: Brooks/Cole.

Milgram, S. (1974). Obedience to authority. New York: Harper & Row.

Miller, A. (1986). The obedience experiments: A case study of controversy in social science. New York: Praeger.

Moghaddam, F., Taylor, D., & Wright, S. (1993). Social psychology in cross-cultural perspective. New York: Freeman.

Nisbett, R., & Ross, L. (1980). Human inference: Strategies and shortcomings of social judgment. Englewood Cliffs, NJ: Prentice-Hall.

Oliner, S., & Oliner, P. (1988). The altruistic personality: Rescuers of Jews in Nazi Europe. New York: Macmillan.

Patzer, G. (1985). The physical attractiveness phenomena. New York: Plenum Press.

Pratkanis, A., & Aronson, E. (1992). Age of propaganda: The everyday use and abuse of persuasion. New York: Freeman.

Robinson, J., Shaver, P., & Wrightsman, L. (1990). Measures of social psychological attitudes. San Diego: Academic Press.

Smith, P., & Bond, M. (1993). Social psychology across cultures: Analysis and perspectives. Boston: Allyn and Bacon.

Sternberg, R., & Barnes, M. (Eds.) (1988). The psychology of love. New Haven, CT: Yale University Press.

Taylor, S., Peplau, L., & Sears, D. (1998). Social psychology (10th ed.). Englewood Cliffs, NJ: Prentice-Hall.

Triandis, H. (1994). Culture and social behavior. New York: McGraw Hill.

Vanzetti, N., & Duck, S. (1996). A lifetime of relationships. Pacific Grove, CA: Brooks/Cole.

Witte, E., & Davis, J. (1996). Understanding group behavior, Vols. I and II. Hillsdale, NJ: Erlbaum.

Zimbardo, P., & Leippe, M. (1991). The psychology of attitude change and social influence. New York: McGraw-Hill.

In-Class Activities and Demonstrations

1. **TRAIL Blazing**: Using **Transparency Masters 16.1-16.5**, review with students the "Checking Your TRAIL" sections in the chapter. Have students work in small groups to answer the questions and then review with the class as a whole to tie the text reading to activity in class.

2. **Reaching Critical Mass**: Using **Transparency Masters 16.6-16.8**, review with students the "Critical Thinking" sections in the chapter. Have students work in small groups to answer the questions and then review with the class as a whole to tie the text reading to activity in class.

3. **Getting Down to IT**: Using **Transparency Masters 16.9-16.14**, review the "Integrative Thinking" sections in the chapter with students. Have students work in small groups to answer the questions and then review with the class as a whole to tie the text reading to activity in class.

4. **Stereotypes and children's books:** In demonstrating the impact of media presentations in the development and perpetuation of stereotypes, one of my favorite activities has been to show students a children's book written in the mid 1970s (*I'm glad I'm a boy! I'm glad I'm a girl!*). The book demonstrates many traditional sex-typed behaviors and we have spirited discussion about what those pages may have taught girls and boys of that era. Invariably, someone in class says, "but things are different now!" So, for an assignment, I challenge them to obtain several old and new children's' books from the library to determine that for themselves. Schwartz (1990) describes a similar activity and suggests a series of questions (modified and expanded on Handout Master # 16.1) to structure students' analysis. Have students bring their analyses to class for small group and whole class discussion of their findings.

    Source:
    Schwartz, L. (1990). Sex role stereotyping in children's books. In V. Makosky, C. Sileo, L. Whittemore, L. Landry, & M. Skutley (Eds). Activities handbook for the teaching of psychology (Vol. 3). (pg. 310-311). Washington DC: American Psychological Association.

5. **Music videos and portrayal of men and women**: Michele Paludi and Bradley Waite outline an exercise designed to "acquaint students with the media's antiwoman message, especially as it is expressed in music videos" (pg. 315). They suggest that students watch 4-5 rock music videos and complete the Bem Sex-Role Inventory for the main male and female characters in each video. Students are also asked complete the short form of the Attitudes Toward Women Scale as they think the director of the video would respond (based on what they can infer from the video). Based on their observations, students are then led in class discussions on their findings and the question of whether videos of this type perpetuate gender-role stereotypes. I've found that this discussion works most effectively following the presentation of one of the following videos in class:

DreamWorlds or, the newer revision incorporating the rock music video images of women of color, *DreamWorlds II*. Related topics are discussed in the videos *Killing Us Softly*, *Still Killing Us Softly*, or *Stale Roles, Tight Buns*.

Addresses for obtaining the BSRI and AWS, respectively:

Consulting Psychologists Press, Inc.
College Avenue
Box 11636
Palo Alto, CA 94306

Janet T. Spence
Department of Psychology
University of Texas
Austin, TX 78712

Source:
Paludi, M., & Waite, B. (1990). Music videos and the portrayal of men and women. In V. Makosky, C. Sileo, L. Whittemore, L. Landry, & M. Skutley (Eds). Activities handbook for the teaching of psychology (Vol. 3). (pg. 315-317). Washington DC: American Psychological Association.

6. **Conformity in the classroom**: This demonstration is one of the quickest ways I've found for demonstrating social influence. Prior to the demonstration, cover the classroom clock if possible. Tell students that you are going to ask them to estimate the passage of time for a brief interval. Prompt students to not look at their watches during the exercise. You'll probably also need to urge them not to try counting to aid in their estimation. Start the timed interval by saying "start" or "begin" and at the end of 45 seconds, say "stop". Ask them to write down their estimates without talking to one another. Rerun the timed interval, again using 45 seconds, but this time rather than having students write down their estimates, have them state their estimate out loud one at a time as you record their results on the chalkboard or overhead. Then ask students to tell you their original time estimates. You'll probably notice several trends: more variability in the "written" time estimates compared to the "oral" time estimates and more movement toward a consensus in the "oral" time estimates toward the end of the list of times (as latter students have heard previous students report their estimates out loud and perhaps established a new estimate). You may also observe noticeable differences in students' changes of estimates (again, especially in the latter half of the scores). This is a fun exercise to use to begin discussion of informational and normative influences and allows you to introduce conformity in situations of ambiguity.

Source:
Montgomery, R., & Enzie, R. (1971). Social influence and the estimation of time. Psychonomic Science, 22, 77-78.

7. **Group dynamics--choosing a color**: James Johnson describes an exercise exploring how roles and hidden agendas influence the functioning of groups. In his activity, students are divided into groups of no less than 7 participants. Their task as a group is to decide on a color. Each student receives an envelope that outlines his or her role in the group and what position in the discussion his or she is to adopt--with the caution that they are not to let the other group members know their personal instructions. For example, one student is told to adopt an information-seeking role and advocate of the selection of the color blue. The seven assignments are as follows:

   Student 1: Role - Information seeking; Position - support blue
   Student 2: Role - Tension relieving; Position - suggest compromise alternate (orange)
   Student 3: Role - Clarifying; Position - support red
   Student 4: Role - Gate-keeping; Position - against red
   Student 5: Role - Initiating; Position - support green
   Students 6 & 7: Role - act in such a way so as to be selected chairperson in Phase II of activity

   After students have discussed their color choice for 10-15 minutes, have them select a chairperson who is then to lead them in an analysis discussion of the preceding task. This activity can tie in to several topics in Chapter 16, including the impact of roles as presented in the Stanford Prison study and the discussion of group decision-making.

   Source:
   Johnson, J. (1981). Group dynamics: Choosing a color. In L. Benjamin & K. Lowman (Eds.), Activities handbook for the teaching of psychology (pg. 168-169). Washington, DC: American Psychological Association.

8. **Attitude change and advertisements**: Having students consider magazine and television advertisements from the perspective of the attitude literature discussed in the text is a fun activity. Richard Kasschau suggests that doing such an activity is one way to demonstrate the cognitive, emotional, and behavioral components of attitudes as well as source, message, channel, and recipient variables discussed in the persuasive communication literature. Assign students to bring a number of magazine advertisements or copies of television advertisements to class. Divide the advertisements into groups corresponding to the 3 components of attitudes: those that appeal to cognitions (i.e., appeals to facts or knowledge), emotions (those that arouse pleasure or fear), and action (those that encourage some kind of activity such as getting money back if you try the product). Then lead students in discussion of the source, message, channel, and recipient aspects of the advertisements:

   source: credibility, expertise, likeability, etc.
   message: one-sided vs. two-sided appeals, multiple arguments, strength of arguments, etc.
   channel: compare TV vs. magazine ads of the same product if you get them
   recipient: who is the ad being directed toward? what are likely characteristics of that audience?

Discuss how the ads may function as attitude change techniques and the extent to which students feel they are influenced by advertisements in their everyday purchasing behaviors.

Source:

Kasschau, R. (1981). Attitude change and advertisements. In L. Benjamin, & K. Lowman (Eds.), <u>Activities handbook for the teaching of psychology</u>. (pg. 158-159). Washington, DC: American Psychological Association.

Sources for Additional Activities

Berrenber, J. (1987). A classroom exercise in impression formation. <u>Teaching of Psychology, 14</u>, 169-170.

Carducci, B. (1987). Looking for love: Demonstrating interpersonal attraction. In V. Makosky, L. Whittemore, & A. Rogers (Eds.), <u>Activities handbook for the teaching of psychology (Vol. 2)</u> (pg. 138-145). Washington, DC: American Psychological Association.

Carkenord, D., & Bullington, J. (1993). Bringing cognitive dissonance to the classroom. <u>Teaching of Psychology, 20</u>, 41-43.

Cole. D. (1981). Sexism in the classroom. In L. Benjamin, & K. Lowman (Eds.), <u>Activities handbook for the teaching of psychology</u>. (pg. 156-157). Washington, DC: American Psychological Association.

Dollinger, S. (1990). The aggression machine: A simulation. In V. Makosky, C. Sileo, L. Whittemore, L. Landry, & M. Skutley (Eds). <u>Activities handbook for the teaching of psychology</u> (Vol. 3). (pg. 147-148). Washington DC: American Psychological Association.

Dunn, D. (1989). Demonstrating a self-serving bias. <u>Teaching of Psychology, 16</u>, 21-22.

Engle, T. & Snellgrove, L. (1981). Stereotypes. In L. Benjamin, & K. Lowman (Eds.), <u>Activities handbook for the teaching of psychology</u>. (pg. 147-148). Washington, DC: American Psychological Association.

Fernald, P., & Fernald, L. (1987). Techniques of persuasion. In V. Makosky, L. Whittemore, & A. Rogers (Eds.), <u>Activities handbook for the teaching of psychology (Vol. 2)</u> (pg. 146-147). Washington, DC: American Psychological Association.

Fiebert. M. (1990). Teaching men's roles: Five classroom exercises. In V. Makosky, C. Sileo, L. Whittemore, L. Landry, & M. Skutley (Eds). <u>Activities handbook for the teaching of psychology</u> (Vol. 3). (pg. 303-307). Washington DC: American Psychological Association.

Gibson, B., Harris, P., & Werner, C. (1993). Intimacy and personal space: A classroom demonstration. <u>Teaching of Psychology, 20</u>, 180-181.

Goethals, G., & Demorest, A. (1979). The risky shift is a sure bet. <u>Teaching of Psychology, 6</u>, 177-179.

Goldstein, M., Hopkins, J., & Strube, M. (1994). "The eye of the beholder": A classroom demonstration of observer bias. Teaching of Psychology, 21, 154-157.

Goodman, J. (1981). Group decisions and stereotypes. In L. Benjamin, & K. Lowman (Eds.), Activities handbook for the teaching of psychology. (pg. 143-144). Washington, DC: American Psychological Association.

Gordon, R. (1989). Stereotype measurement and the "kernel of truth" hypothesis. Teaching of Psychology, 16, 209-211.

Halonen, J. (1995). Chapter 14: Social psychology. In The critical thinking companion for Introductory Psychology. New York: Worth Publishers.

Hollingsworth, F. (1990). Competitive versus cooperative behavior. In V. Makosky, C. Sileo, L. Whittemore, L. Landry, & M. Skutley (Eds). Activities handbook for the teaching of psychology (Vol. 3). (pg. 145-146). Washington DC: American Psychological Association.

Hom, H. (1994). Can you predict the overjustification effect? Teaching of Psychology, 21, 36-37.

Hunter, W. (1981). Obedience to authority. In L. Benjamin, & K. Lowman (Eds.), Activities handbook for the teaching of psychology. (pg. 149-150). Washington, DC: American Psychological Association.

Jegerski, J. (1990). Human judgment versus empirical evidence. In V. Makosky, C. Sileo, L. Whittemore, L. Landry, & M. Skutley (Eds). Activities handbook for the teaching of psychology (Vol. 3). (pg. 131-132). Washington DC: American Psychological Association.

Jessen, B. (1990). *Tootsie* and gender roles. In V. Makosky, C. Sileo, L. Whittemore, L. Landry, & M. Skutley (Eds). Activities handbook for the teaching of psychology (Vol. 3). (pg. 301-302). Washington DC: American Psychological Association.

Jones, M. (1991). Gender stereotyping in advertisements. Teaching of Psychology, 18, 231-233.

Jones, M. (1994). Linking dispositions and social behavior: Self-monitoring and advertising preferences. Teaching of Psychology, 21, 160-161.

Kite, M. (1991). Observer biases in the classroom. Teaching of Psychology, 18, 161-164.

Lashley, R. (1987). Using students' perceptions of their instructor to illustrate principles of person perception. Teaching of Psychology, 14, 179-180.

Lloyd, M. (1987). Advertising and attitude change. In V. Makosky, L. Whittemore, & A. Rogers (Eds.), Activities handbook for the teaching of psychology (Vol. 2) (pg. 148-149). Washington, DC: American Psychological Association.

Lloyd, M. (1990). Gender-role stereotyping in toys: An out-of-class project. In V. Makosky, C. Sileo, L. Whittemore, L. Landry, & M. Skutley (Eds). Activities handbook for the teaching of psychology (Vol. 3). (pg. 1293-294). Washington DC: American Psychological Association.

Lutsky, N. (1987). Inducing academic suicide: A demonstration of social influence. In V. Makosky, L. Whittemore, & A. Rogers (Eds.), Activities handbook for the teaching of psychology (Vol. 2) (pg. 123-126). Washington, DC: American Psychological Association.

Lyons, A. (1981). Introducing students to social psychology through student-generated first impressions of the professor. Teaching of Psychology, 8, 173-174.

Makosky, V. (1985). Identifying major techniques of persuasion. Teaching of Psychology, 12, 42-43

Makosky, V. (1987). Intergroup conflict. In V. Makosky, L. Whittemore, & A. Rogers (Eds.), Activities handbook for the teaching of psychology (Vol. 2) (pg. 153-155). Washington, DC: American Psychological Association.

McAndrew, F. (1985). A classroom demonstration of the primacy effect in attribution of ability. Teaching of Psychology, 12, 209-211.

Miserandino, M. (1992). Studying a social norm. Teaching of Psychology, 19, 103-106.

Olm, K., & Carsrud, A. (1990). Federated Services, Inc. In V. Makosky, C. Sileo, L. Whittemore, L. Landry, & M. Skutley (Eds). Activities handbook for the teaching of psychology (Vol. 3). (pg. 140-144). Washington DC: American Psychological Association.

Rhodes, N. (1987). Gender stereotypes in everyday life. In V. Makosky, L. Whittemore, & A. Rogers (Eds.), Activities handbook for the teaching of psychology (Vol. 2) (pg. 150-152). Washington, DC: American Psychological Association.

Scoville, W. (1990). The secretary game. In V. Makosky, C. Sileo, L. Whittemore, L. Landry, & M. Skutley (Eds). Activities handbook for the teaching of psychology (Vol. 3). (pg. 308-310). Washington DC: American Psychological Association.

Simpson, J. (1988). Self-monitoring and commitment to dating relationships: A classroom demonstration. Teaching of Psychology, 15, 31-33.

Snellgrove, L. (1981). Public opinion polls and cooperation with authority. In L. Benjamin, & K. Lowman (Eds.), Activities handbook for the teaching of psychology. (pg. 151-152). Washington, DC: American Psychological Association.

Snellgrove, L. (1981). Cooperation and competition. In L. Benjamin, & K. Lowman (Eds.), Activities handbook for the teaching of psychology. (pg. 160-162). Washington, DC: American Psychological Association.

Watson, D. (1987). The primacy effect in social judgments. In V. Makosky, L. Whittemore, & A. Rogers (Eds.), Activities handbook for the teaching of psychology (Vol. 2) (pg. 132-134). Washington, DC: American Psychological Association.

Wertheimer, M. (1990). Sex differences and the variability hypothesis. In V. Makosky, C. Sileo, L. Whittemore, L. Landry, & M. Skutley (Eds). Activities handbook for the teaching of psychology (Vol. 3). (pg. 298-300). Washington DC: American Psychological Association.

White, M., & Lilly, D. (1989). Teaching attribution theory with a videotaped illustration. Teaching of Psychology, 16, 218-219.

Journey II Software:
The Social Psychology lab in Journey II contains 3 activity modules relevant to this chapter.
- Attribution theory: The underlying assumptions for attribution theory are reviewed, including the distinctions between dispositional and situational attributions. Students are asked to determine the extent to which a variety of personality traits or situations characterize typical conduct for their best friend and for themselves, demonstrating the actor-observer bias.
- Conformity: Asch's classic conformity study is reviewed in this module. Students become the actual participant in a panel of computer confederates and see their results on accurate line selection compared to results found in the original study. Factors influencing conformity are discussed.
- Obedience: Students get a taste of the Milgram study when they punish Harry the rat for making wrong turns in the maze (and ultimately Harry expires from the whole ordeal). Milgram's obedience study is reviewed and students are asked to predict the shock level they would administer vs. what the typical student would be willing to do. Those predictions are compared to Milgram's psychiatrists' predictions. A review of 18 experiment variations and the conditions that fostered obedience is given and cautions on drawing inappropriate conclusions as inherent evil in human beings who shock at the command of an authority are given.

- **World Wide Web**: Check out the following WWW sites for information and activities relevant to this section of the text!
  - Addison Wesley Longman's Website -- **http://longman.awl.com/**
  - PsychZone link -- **http://longman.awl.com/**
  - Psych Web -- **http://www.gasou.edu/psychweb/psychweb.htm**
  - Self-Quizzes for Introductory Psychology -- **http://www.gasou.edu/psychweb/selfquiz/selfquiz.htm**
  - Psychology Jumping Stand -- **http://www.indiana.edu:80/~iuepsyc/PsycJump.html**
  - The Psychology Place -- **http://www.psychplace.com**
  - Social Psychology Network-- **http://www.wesleyan.edu/psyc/psyc260/social.htm**
  - Social psychology (general) -- **http://cac.psu/edu/~arm3/social.html**
  or
  http://swix.ch/clan/ks/CPSP1.htm#b_b
  or

http://www.richmond.edu/~allison/glossary.html
or
http://miavx1.muohio.edu/~shermarc/p324tuta.html
or
http://clem.mscd.edu/~psych/into/cncpsoci.htm
or
http://miavx1.muohio.edu/~shermarc/p324cart.html

Attitudes

- Attitude and attitude change -- http://www.gwu.edu/~tip/festinge.html
or
http:///www.carleton.ca/~rthibode/chapter4.html

Social Influence

- Persuasion --
  http://www.glam.ac.uk/schools/humanities/psychology/ps214/elm.htm
  or
  http://www.as.wvu.edu/~sbb/comm211/primer.htm
  or
  http://www.public.asu.edu/~kelton/
  or
  http://www.lafayett.edu/mcglonem/prog.html
- Compliance --
  http://cap.otago.ac.nz:801/grant/PSYC/COMPLIANCE.HTML
- Helping -- http://psychstan.stmarytx.edu/psysight/stuarts/stuart8-1.htm

Person Perception

- Attribution theories --
  http://www.sci.monash.edu.au/psych/courses/1022_97/social/social5.htm
- Social schemas --
  http://www.glam.ac.uk/schools/humanities/psychology/ps214/lecutres/wk5.htm
- Physical attractiveness -- http://www.cops.uni-sb.de/ronald/home.html
  or
  http://www.sp.uconn.edu/~marshall/html/afigure5.html
- Media and person perception --
  http://www.libertynet.org/~balch/comic/comic.html
  or
  http://www.csbs.utsa.edu/users/jreynolds/popcul.txt
- Prejudice -- http://miavx1.muohio.edu/~shermarc/p324bias.html

Interpersonal Attraction

- Attraction & love --
  http://www.cmhcsys.com/psyhelp/chap10/chap10c.htm
  or

http://world.topchoice.com/~psyche/love/
or
http://serendip.brynmawr.edu/bb/pd.html

Groups
- Social facilitation/loafing --
http://samiam.colorado.edu/~mcclella/expersim/introsocial.html
or
http://chip.eng.clemson.edu/htdocs/psych499/decision/main_decision.html
- Groupthink --
http://www.fis.utoronto.ca/people/faculty/choo/FIS/Courses/LIS2149/PreventGT1.html

- **Audio-Visual Support**

  ### Films/Videos:
  ### Overview/Series
  - *Discovering Psychology: Power of the Situation* (Annenberg, 30 minutes)
  - *Discovering Psychology: Constructing Social Reality* (Annenberg, 30 minutes)
  - *Social Psychology Series* (PSU, 30 minutes each)
    - Program 1: Communication--Social and Attribution
    - Program 2: Communication--Negotiation and Persuasion
    - Program 3: Friendship
    - Program 4: Prejudice
    - Program 5: Conformity
    - Program 6: Group Decision Making and Leadership
    - Program 7: Aggression
    - Program 8: Helping and Prosocial Behavior
  - *Invitation to Social Psychology* (MOTO, 25 minutes)
  - *Candid Camera Classics in Social Psychology* (McGraw-Hill, 60 minutes)

  ### Prejudice/Aggression
  - *A Class Divided* (PSU, 54 minutes)
  - *Crimes of Hate* (ADL, 30 minutes)
  - *Eye of the Storm* (XEROXFIL, 29 minutes)
  - *Sexual Harassment* (FFHS, 19 minutes)
  - *Stereotyping and Prejudice* (United Films, 25 minutes)
  - *War and Violence* (IU, 52 minutes)
  - *Faces of the Enemy* (Quest, 58 minutes)
  - *True Colors* (ABC, 15 minutes)

Gender/Ethnicity
- *Happy to Be Me* (Arthur Mokin, 25 minutes)
- *Men and Masculinity* (FIN, 30 minutes)
- *Women: The New Poor* (WMM, 28 minutes)
- *Voices* (CSU, 35 minutes)
- *Are We Different?* (Filmakers, 27 minutes)
- *Black by Popular Demand* (Redshoes)
- *Black Mother, Black Daughter* (National Film Board)
- *Ethic Notions* (California Newsreel, 56 minutes)
- *Killing Us Softly* (Cambridge, 30 minutes)
- *Still Killing Us Softly* (Cambridge, 32 minutes)
- *Myths That Maim* (Encinitas, 46 minutes)
- *Stale Roles and Tight Buns: Images of Men in Advertising* (OASIS, 29 minutes)
- *Mitsuye and Nellie: Asian American Poets* (Light-Saraf, 58 minutes)

Group Dynamics/Social Roles
- *Abilene Paradox* (CRM, 27 minutes)
- *Group Dynamic: Groupthink* (CRM, 23 minutes)
- *Leadership: Style or Circumstance* (CRM, 27 minutes)
- *Quiet Rage: The Stanford Prison Experiment* (Zimbardo, 52 minutes)

Social Influence
- *Captive Minds* (FML, 55 minutes)
- *Conformity and Independence* (IU, 23 minutes)
- *How's Your New Friend* (CRM, 12 minutes)
- *Moonchild* (PSU, 49 minutes)
- *The Wave* (IU, 44 minutes)

Interpersonal Attraction
- *Looks--How They Affect Your Life* (IU, 51 minutes)
- *Friendship* (PSU, 30 minutes)

Psychology Encyclopedia Laserdisc IV:

Movies
Japanese-American internment in WW II	2 minutes 48 sec.	Frame 44739-49780	Side 2
Los Angeles riot 1992	2 minutes 17 sec.	36266-40363	2
Milgram: obedience study	2 minutes 26 sec.	40364-44738	2

Still Images
Conceptions of self [1/2] [18.2]		Frame 53574	Side all
Conceptions of self [2/2] [18.2]		53575	all

Transparency Master 16.1: Checking Your TRAIL 16.1

I. Give an example of how someone might develop a favorable attitude toward water conservation.

II. Explain two routes by which someone could be persuaded to change an attitude.

III. Imagine trying to persuade a drunken friend to take a cab rather than drive. What four characteristics should your message have?

IV. Attitudes are the enduring thoughts, feelings, and behavioral tendencies that guide our behavior. Describe how cognitive dissonance can produce a change in someone's attitude.

Transparency Master 16.2: Checking Your TRAIL 16.2

I. **Situational** or **dispositional**? The fundamental attribution error is characterized by a tendency to make _____ attributions about other people's behaviors.

II. **Which one of the following is true?**
 A. People from individualist cultures are more likely to make situational attributions than people from collectivist cultures.
 B. The just world hypothesis implies that life is unfair.
 C. The implicit personality theory is one's ideas about which traits occur in which people; why people have the traits they do; and what traits occur together in people.
 D. Most people's impressions of other people are objective.

III. **Match the statement on the right to the attribution characteristic on the left:**

 1. halo effect   a. "If I were in the same situation as that person, I would feel lost. So that person must feel lost."

 2. transference   b. "She is kind. She must have lots of other good qualities."

 3. egocentric bias   c. "He became angry Wednesday. He must be a hot-headed person."

 4. fundamental attribution error   d. "He wears shirts like the one my old boyfriend --whom I can't stand--used to wear. I just met him. But for some reason, I already don't like him."

IV. **How does the confirmation bias contribute to the persistence of stereotypes?**

Transparency Master 16.3: Checking Your TRAIL 16.3

I. Interpersonal attraction is associated with _____ _____, _____, and similarity.

II. <u>True</u> or <u>False</u>: Judgments of facial attractiveness are more different than similar between people of different cultures.

III. How do evolutionary biologists explain gender differences in mate preference?

IV. Passionate love is characterized by physical arousal, intense feelings, and _____.

Transparency Master 16.4: Checking Your TRAIL 16.4

I. Name five characteristics of situations or people that are associated with altruistic behavior.

II. <u>True</u> or <u>False</u>: Social norms to provide help are more compelling in some situations than in others.

III. Which of the following statements is FALSE?
   A. U.S. females are more likely to conform than U.S. males.
   B. Large gender differences in conformity are usually found.
   C. Sometimes behaviors can be explained in terms of conformity to social roles.
   D. Minority members are sometimes put into the role of audience; if they don't conform to that role, they are seen as being pushy.

IV. In the Milgram studies, which one of the following variables lessened the likelihood that people would obey orders to harm someone?
   A. the authority figure was nearby
   B. the recipient of the harm was nice to them
   C. another person refused to obey orders to inflict harm
   D. the victims pleaded not to be hurt

V. Describe how you might use the foot-in-the-door sequence to solicit a charitable donation. Explain why this approach is likely to succeed.

Transparency Master 16.5: Checking Your TRAIL 16.5

I. Match the terms on the left with the correct definition(s).

    A. social loafing   1. the enhancement of individual efforts in the presence of others

    B. risky shift   2. the diminishment of individual effort in a group effort owing to the diffusion of responsibility

    C. social facilitation   3. a tendency to take larger gambles as a group than one might take alone

    D. groupthink   4. a group process in which members emphasize consensus at the expense of careful decision-making

Transparency Master 16.6: Critical Thinking 16.1

In a negative version of the halo effect, a negative impression leads to the attribution of other negative characteristics. Popular American culture generally portrays physically attractive people as having European American features. What are the implications of this portrayal and the halo effect for people of color looking for work?

Transparency Master 16.7: Critical Thinking 16.2

According to the triangular theory, what type of love did Shakespeare's characters Romeo and Juliet probably share?

Transparency Master 16.8: Critical Thinking 16.3

Does the fact that scientists have hypotheses to explain behavior excuse the behavior? That is, are reasons the same as excuses?

Transparency Master 16.9: Integrative Thinking 16.1

Imagine trying to design a message to persuade women to do monthly breast self-exams. Given the primacy effect and the recency effect described in the Memory chapter, where would you place key information in your message?

Transparency Master 16.10: Integrative Thinking 16.2

In terms of what you learned in the Sensation & Perception chapter, how does selective perception promote stereotypes?

Transparency Master 16.11: Integrative Thinking 16.3

Recall the White Racial Identity Model described in the Adolescent & Adult Development chapter. Imagine that a European American woman at the third stage of racial identity has a Latina roommate who shares many of her interests. Would racial differences be likely to stand in the way of their friendship? Why or why not?

Transparency Master 16.12: Integrative Thinking 16.4

When some people hear others making racists statements, they may privately disagree, but not voice their disagreement. Why do you think they don't publicly disagree with the racist statements? In terms of conformity and operant conditioning, what effect does this silence have on the racist?

Transparency Master 16.13: Integrative Thinking 16.5

For the peace of mind of the subjects, participants in the Milgram study had a friendly talk with the "learner" after the experiment. They were assured that the learner was unhurt. Nevertheless, the Milgram study raised ethical concerns about how research should be conducted. In light of the ethical guidelines discussed in the Introductory chapter, what is the key ethical concern raised by Milgram's study?

Transparency Master 16.14: Integrative Thinking 16.6

A speaker's paralanguage influences a listener's reaction to the speaker's message (see the Communication chapter). How should a person try to sound in order to increase his or her influence over other group members?

Handout Master 16.1: Stereotypes and Children's Books

Stereotypes and Children's Books

Instructions: Select 2 children's books from a local library; one from the 1970s and a current book. Consider the following questions for each.

Book 1: _____   Year of publication: _____
Author(s): _____

1. Who are the leading characters in the book and how do you know that?

2. Describe one of the activities in which these characters are engaged. Are these activities stereotypically sex-typed? How?

3. If adults are shown in the book, are they shown in stereotypical sex-typed roles? Explain.

4. Are there any themes in the book that reflect cultural messages?

5. Is diversity represented in the book? How?

Book 2: _____   Year of publication: _____
Author(s): _____

1. Who are the leading characters in the book and how do you know that?

2. Describe one of the activities in which these characters are engaged. Are these activities stereotypically sex-typed? How?

3. If adults are shown in the book, are they shown in stereotypical sex-typed roles? Explain.

4. Are there any themes in the book that reflect cultural messages?

5. Is diversity represented in the book? How?

STATISTICS APPENDIX

Appendix Overview
Learning Objectives
Appendix Outline

Additional Lecture Ideas
Lecture Topic

World Wide Web

Audio-Visual Support

Transparency Masters

Appendix Overview

Learning Objectives

After studying this appendix, you should be able to do the following:

1. Distinguish between descriptive and inferential statistics.

2. Describe two ways to present data in a graph.

3. Calculate three different types of average.

4. Describe two measures of variance.

5. Explain the difference between positive and negative correlations.

Appendix Outline

Statistics Appendix

I. Descriptive Statistics: Summarizing Data
   A. Definition
      1. descriptive statistics: a way of organizing, portraying, and summarizing data by revealing mathematical relationships among variables a. showing patterns in data helps to describe and remember findings in an efficient way
         a. example: percentages vs. total numbers of persons in different groups experiencing some event
   B. Frequency distributions
      1. definition: a simple descriptive statistic indicating the number of times a behavior or event of interest occurs
         a. arranging numerical scores on a graph so that they can be compared visually
         b. examples:
            i. bar graph (histogram):
            - how to read the bar graph
            - paying attention to scaling
            - combining different sets of data
            - graphing qualitative variables
            ii. frequency polygons:
            - useful in displaying quantitative variables
            - how to read the frequency polygon
            - combining different sets of data
   C. Averages
      1. definition: measures of central tendency that summarize data in a single number
      2. types of central tendency
         a. mean: arithmetic average calculated by dividing the total of all scores by the number of scores
            i. avoids distorting effects of differences in sample sizes
            ii. can be misleading due to extreme scores
         b. median: middle score when all scores are arranged from highest to lowest
         c. mode: the score that occurs most often
            i. can be misleading due to frequently occurring extreme scores
   D. Bell-shaped distributions
      1. definition: the normal distribution--a symmetrical distribution of scores that is in the shape of a bell; more frequent scores cluster around the mean and less frequent scores occur away from the mean
   E. Variance: How much scores differ
      1. definition: the degree to which scores differ from each other
         a. range: the distance between the lowest and highest scores, which is a crude measure of variability
         b. standard deviation: measures how closely scores cluster around the mean
            i. percentage of scores falling within different standard deviations from the mean on the bell-curve
            ii. calculating the standard deviation
   F. Correlations: Relationships between variables
      1. correlation coefficient: a number that indicates the degree to which

two variables are related to each other
- a. range of the correlation coefficient
- b. interpreting the correlation coefficient
- c. positive correlations: as score on one variable increase so does the score on other variable
- d. negative correlations: high scores on one variable are associated with low scores on the other variable
- e. perfect correlations
- f. scattergram: graphical representation of scores on variables

2. limitation of correlation
- a. correlation does not imply causation

3. situations that call for correlational studies
- a. ethics of the study
- b. when independent variables cannot be experimentally manipulated

II. Inferential Statistics: A Basis for Drawing Conclusions
A. Definition
1. inferential statistics: mathematical methods used as a basis for drawing conclusions about data
2. what inferential statistics tell us:
   - a. the probability that the differences between two groups are due to chance
   - b. statistically significant results: when probability that a finding is due to chance is low (less than 5 out of 100 or $p \leq .05$)

Additional Lecture Topic

1. Cultural influences on data analysis and the interpretation of findings:
Many researchers have discussed the concerns for cross-cultural use of methodology, as though appropriate selection of measurement devices were the primary issues for concern in cross-cultural research. Matsumoto notes that differences in use of scales can and do have implications for the way we analyze data from cross-cultural studies (pg. 33). Central to his concern and discussion is the phenomenon of cultural response sets, a cultural tendency to respond a certain way on tests or response scales (pg. 33). You may wish to incorporate some of his discussion in your coverage of statistical analyses in class.

Matsumoto contends that making responses on a measurement device are no less immune to cultural influences than are any other forms of behaviors. As a result the data obtained on a measure may reflect cultural response sets as well as the phenomenon the device is intended to measure. Moreover, cultural influences may affect response patterns on certain types of measures. For example, one influence of collectivistic cultures may be to discourage the use of the ends of bipolar response scales. A person from a collectivistic culture may hesitate to respond at either extreme of the scale, preferring instead to use more of the middle range. A person from an individualistic culture may not be so hesitant to respond at the extremes (pg. 34). In fact, response patterns on just about any scale may reflect cultural differences in response sets. In interpreting data, then, the research must be aware that differences in data between cultural groups may mean actual or true differences and cultural response sets. However, Matsumoto offers that there are statistical manipulations that researchers can use to deal with the possible influences of cultural response sets (pg. 35), and reviews those possible for use with quantitative (continuous) data and nominal data in some detail. His discussions rely on several data set examples, too detailed to adequately cover here, that you may wish to read about personally.

Source:
Matsumoto, D. (1994). Cultural influences on research methods and statistics (pg. 33-53). Pacific Grove, CA: Brooks/Cole.

Additional Readings
Berry, J. (1979). Research in multicultural societies: Implications of cross-cultural methods. Journal of Cross-Cultural Psychology, 10, 415.

Brislin, R. (1983). Cross-cultural research in psychology. Annual Review of Psychology, 34, 363-400.

Brislin, R., Lonner, W., & Thorndike, R. (1973). Cross-cultural research methods. New York: Wiley.

Buss, A., & Royce, J. (1975). Detecting cross-cultural commonalities and differences: Intergroup factor analysis. Psychological Bulletin, 82, 128-136.

Chon, K., Campbell, J., & Yoo, J. (1974). Extreme response style in cross-cultural research. Journal of Cross-Cultural Psychology, 5, 464.

Drenth, P., & Van der Flier, H. (1976). Cultural differences and comparability of test scores. International Review of Applied Psychology, 25, 137-144.

Gilovich, T. (1991). How we know what isn't so. New York: The Free Press.

Howell, D. (1987). Statistical methods for psychology (2nd ed.). Boston: Duxbury.

Huff, D. (1954). How to lie with statistics. New York: Norton.

Hui, C., & Triandis, H. (1985). Measurement in cross-cultural psychology:

A review and comparison of strategies. Journal of Cross-Cultural Psychology, 16, 131-152.

Kleiner, R., & Barnallas, I. (1991). Advances in field theory: New approaches and methods in cross-cultural research. Journal of Cross-Cultural Psychology, 22, 509-524.

Krause, M., & Howard, K. (1983). Design and analysis issues in the cross-cultural evaluation of psychotherapies. Culture, Medicine and Psychiatry, 7, 301-311.

Leigh, M. (1983). Ethnocentrism in cross-cultural research, and what to do about it. Behavior Science Research, 18, 213-227.

Rosenthal, R., & Rosnow, R. (1991). Essentials of behavioral research: Methods and data analysis. New York: McGraw Hill.

Sprinthall, R. (1994). Basic statistical analysis (4th ed.). Needham Heights, MA: Allyn and Bacon.

Stole-Heiskanen, V. (1972). Contextual analysis and theory construction in cross-cultural family research. Journal of Comparative Family Studies, 3, 33-49.

Triandis, H., & Berry, J. (1980). Handbook of cross-cultural psychology, vol. 2: Methodology. Boston: Allyn & Bacon.

In-Class Activities and Demonstrations

1. TRAIL Blazing: Using Transparency Masters A.1-A.2, review with students the Checking Your Trail sections in the chapter. Have students work in small groups to answer the questions and then review with the class as a whole to tie the text reading to activity in class.

2. Reaching Critical Mass: Using Transparency Masters A.3-A.4, review with students the Critical Thinking sections in the chapter. Have students work in small groups to answer the questions and then review with the class as a whole to tie the text reading to activity in class.

3. Getting Down to IT: Using Transparency Masters A.5-A.7, review the Integrative Thinking sections in the chapter with students. Have students work in small groups to answer the questions and then review with the class as a whole to tie the text reading to activity in class.

Sources for Additional Activities

Bates, J. (1991). Teaching hypothesis testing by debunking a demonstration of telepathy. Teaching of Psychology, 18, 94-97.

Beers, S. (1987). Descriptive statistics. In V. Makosky, L. Whittemore, & A. Rogers (Eds.), Activities handbook for the teaching of psychology: Vol. 2 (pg. 193-194). Washington, DC: American Psychological Association.

Beins, B. (1985). Teaching the relevance of statistics through consumer-oriented research. Teaching of Psychology, 12, 168-169.

Fernald, P., & Fernald, L. (199). Normal probability curve. In V. Makosky, C. Sileo, L. Whittemore, L. Landry, & M. Skutley (Eds). Activities handbook for the teaching of psychology (Vol. 3). (pg. 181-182). Washington DC: American Psychological Association.

Hettich, P. (1974). The student as data generator. Teaching of

Psychology, 1, 35-36.

    Hunter, W. (1981). Hypothesis testing--To coin a term. In L. Benjamin, & K. Lowman (Eds.), Activities handbook for the teaching of psychology. (pg. 16-17). Washington, DC: American Psychological Association.

    Jacobs, K. (1980). Instructional techniques in the introductory statistics course: The first class meeting. Teaching of Psychology, 7, 241,242.

    Jegerski, J. (1990). Probability and chance variation. In V. Makosky, C. Sileo, L. Whittemore, L. Landry, & M. Skutley (Eds). Activities handbook for the teaching of psychology (Vol. 3). (pg. 183-184). Washington DC: American Psychological Association.

    Salzinger, K. (1990). On the average. In V. Makosky, C. Sileo, L. Whittemore, L. Landry, & M. Skutley (Eds). Activities handbook for the teaching of psychology (Vol. 3). (pg. 185-186). Washington DC: American Psychological Association.

    Schwartz, L. (1990). Measures of central tendency in daily life. In V. Makosky, C. Sileo, L. Whittemore, L. Landry, & M. Skutley (Eds). Activities handbook for the teaching of psychology (Vol. 3). (pg. 187-188). Washington DC: American Psychological Association.

    Shatz, M. (1985). The Greyhound strike: Using a labor dispute to teach descriptive statistics. Teaching of Psychology, 12, 85-86

    Snellgrove, L. (1981). Sampling and probability. In L. Benjamin, & K. Lowman (Eds.), Activities handbook for the teaching of psychology. (pg. 12-13). Washington, DC: American Psychological Association.

    Stang, D. (1981). Randomization. In L. Benjamin, & K. Lowman (Eds.), Activities handbook for the teaching of psychology. (pg. 18-19). Washington, DC: American Psychological Association.

    Trice, A., Trice, O., & Ogden, E. (1990). Teaching the concept of statistical variability. In V. Makosky, C. Sileo, L. Whittemore, L. Landry, & M. Skutley (Eds). Activities handbook for the teaching of psychology (Vol. 3). (pg. 189-191). Washington DC: American Psychological Association.

    Wallace, J. (1987). A demonstration of correlation and prediction. In V. Makosky, L. Whittemore, & A. Rogers (Eds.), Activities handbook for the teaching of psychology (Vol. 2) (pg. 207). Washington, DC: American Psychological Association.

    Wertheimer, M. (1987). ESP, central tendency, and probability. In V. Makosky, L. Whittemore, & A. Rogers (Eds.), Activities handbook for the teaching of psychology (Vol. 2) (pg. 199-200). Washington, DC: American Psychological Association.

    World Wide Web: Check out the following WWW sites for information and activities relevant to this section of the text!

    Psych Web -- http://www.gasou.edu/psychweb/psychweb.htm

    Self-Quizzes for Introductory Psychology -- http://www.gasou.edu/psychweb/selfquiz/selfquiz.htm

    Psychology Jumping Stand -- http://www.indiana.edu:80/~iuepsyc/PsycJump.html

    The Psychology Place -- http://www.psychplace.com

    Statistics on the Web -- http://www.execpc.com/~helberg/statistics/html

    Research designs/methods -- http://gateway1.gmcc.ab.ca/!digdonn/psych104/think.htm

Statistics glossary -- http://www.stats.gla.ac.uk/steps/glossary/index.html

Audio-Visual Support
Films/Videos:

    Statistics at a glance (Wiley, 28 minutes)
    Statistics: Decisions through data series (Comap, 5 at 60 minutes)
    Against all odds: Inside statistics series (Annenberg, 26 at 30 minutes)
    Inferential Statistics series (Wiley, 2 at 20-25 minutes)

Psychology Encyclopedia Laserdisc IV:
    Still Images

Histogram [A.1]	Frame 53576	Side	all
Frequency polygon [A.2]	53577		all
Scale effects [A.3]	53578		all
Normal curve diagram [A.4]	53579		all
Skewed curves diagram [A.5]	53580		all
Statistical significance diagram [A.6]	53581		all

Transparency Master A.1: Checking Your TRAIL A.1

I. On a graph, the independent variable is usually located
A. at the mean.
B. along the horizontal axis.
C. along the vertical axis.
D. on the left.

II. True or False: On a bar graph, the vertical axis usually indicates
 the frequency of the scores.

III. The method psychologists most often use to calculate an average score
 is the
A. mode.
B. frequency polygon.
C. mean.
D. median.

IV. The most commonly occurring score is the
A. histogram.
B. frequency polygon.
C. mean.
D. mode.

I. **True or False: In a negative correlation, people who have a low score on one variable tend to have a low score on the other variable.**

II. **Identify which of the following results show a positive correlation and which show a negative correlation**
A. The taller individuals are, the more they weigh.
B. The more television a child watches, the worse the child's grades.
C. The younger individuals are, the smaller their vocabulary.

III. **A correlation of 0.30**
A. accounts for 30% of the variance in scores.
B. accounts for 90% of the variance in scores.
C. accounts for 9% of the variance in scores.
D. is an inferential statistic.

IV. **Suppose a study finds that males and females differ in their average number of school suspensions at a 0.04 level of statistical significance. That finding means**
A. there is a 96% chance that the difference is due to chance.
B. the odds are less than 4 in 100 that the difference is due to chance.
C. the odds are less than 4 in 100 that the difference is not due to chance.
D. gender accounts for 16% of suspensions from school.

Studies often report the differences in the means of an experimental and a control group. What, if anything, do mean differences between groups tell us about how a particular individual behaved or responded? Explain your answer.

Besides ethical considerations, what other two reasons might psychologists have for conducting correlational studies rather than studies that involve massive intervention into the lives of subjects?

Transparency Master A.5: Integrative Thinking A.1

Based on what you read in the Introductory chapter about surveys and case studies, which type of study is more likely to call for a calculation of a frequency distribution?

Transparency Master A.6: Integrative Thinking A.2

Based on what you read about averages and range, explain the Introductory chapter's statement that the type of statistic chosen by a researcher can affect interpretations of data.

Transparency Master A.7: Integrative Thinking A.3

The Introductory chapter stated that, contrary to myth, a person can't make statistics say anything she or he wants. Explain that statement in terms of mean, range, and correlation.